Mastering Constitutional Law

Carolina Academic Press Mastering Series
Russell L. Weaver, Series Editor

Mastering Bankruptcy
George W. Kuney

Mastering Civil Procedure
David Charles Hricik

Mastering Constitutional Law
John C. Knechtle, Christopher Roederer

Mastering Corporate Tax
Reginald Mombrun, Gail Levin Richmond, Felicia Branch

Mastering Corporations and Other Business Entities
Lee Harris

Mastering Criminal Law
Ellen S. Podgor, Peter J. Henning, Neil P. Cohen

Mastering Evidence
Ronald W. Eades

Mastering Family Law
Janet Leach Richards

Mastering Intellectual Property
George W. Kuney, Donna C. Looper

Mastering Legal Analysis and Communication
David T. Ritchie

Mastering Legal Analysis and Drafting
George W. Kuney, Donna C. Looper

Mastering Negotiable Instruments (UCC Articles 3 and 4) and Other Payment Systems
Michael D. Floyd

Mastering Products Liability
Ronald W. Eades

Mastering Professional Responsibility
Grace M. Giesel

Mastering Secured Transactions
Richard H. Nowka

Mastering Statutory Interpretation
Linda D. Jellum

Mastering Tort Law
Russell L. Weaver, Edward C. Martin, Andrew R. Klein,
Paul J. Zwier II, Ronald W. Eades, John H. Bauman

Mastering Constitutional Law

John C. Knechtle
Florida Coastal School of Law

Christopher J. Roederer
Florida Coastal School of Law

Carolina Academic Press
Durham, North Carolina

Library of Congress Cataloging in Publication Data

Knechtle, John C.
  Mastering constitutional law / John C. Knechtle, Christopher J. Roederer.
    p. cm.
  ISBN 978-1-59460-479-9 (alk. paper)
  1. Constitutional law--United States. I. Roederer, Christopher J. II. Title.
  KF4550.K542 2009
  342.73--dc22

                              2009028975

Carolina Academic Press
700 Kent Street
Durham, NC 27701
Telephone (919) 489-7486
Fax (919) 493-5668
www.cap-press.com

Printed in the United States of America

We dedicate this book to our students.
They encourage and inspire us in the teaching of constitutional law.
In particular this book is dedicated to all of those students
who ask us for the "black letter" Constitutional Law
as they prepare for course and bar exams.

Contents

Table of Cases

Series Editor's Foreword

The Carolina Academic Press Mastering Series is designed to provide you with a tool that will enable you to easily and efficiently "master" the substance and content of law school courses. Throughout the series, the focus is on quality writing that makes legal concepts understandable. As a result, the series is designed to be easy to read and is not unduly cluttered with footnotes or cites to secondary sources.

In order to facilitate student mastery of topics, the Mastering Series includes a number of pedagogical features designed to improve learning and retention. At the beginning of each chapter, you will find a "Roadmap" that tells you about the chapter and provides you with a sense of the material that you will cover. A "Checkpoint" at the end of each chapter encourages you to stop and review the key concepts, reiterating what you have learned. Throughout the book, key terms are explained and emphasized. Finally, a "Master Checklist" at the end of each book reinforces what you have learned and helps you identify any areas that need review or further study.

We hope that you will enjoy studying with, and learning from, the Mastering Series.

Russell L. Weaver
Professor of Law & Distinguished University Scholar
University of Louisville, Louis D. Brandeis School of Law

Preface

Professor Knechtle and Professor Roederer would like to thank Dean Peter Goplerud and Florida Coastal School of Law for their support through summer research grants and research assistants. We thank Professor Paul F. Rothstein of Georgetown University Law School and our colleagues Professors Jeff McFarland and John Stinneford, for reviewing draft chapters. We also thank the numerous talented research assistants who have assisted with this project over the last couple of years, including: Jason Pfeil, Marcus Colicelli, Laura Stevens, Brian Hart, Kevin W. Moore, W. Jeremy Salter, Melanie C. Schneider, Jessica R. Rieffel, Nina L. Banaie, and Heather L. Gurgiolo.

Mastering Constitutional Law

Introduction to Constitutional Law ·

Constitutional law encompasses far more than the Constitution itself. In fact, if one simply read the document, he or she would have only a glimpse of the body of constitutional law. Constitutional law includes not only the Constitution but also the many volumes of Supreme Court decisions representing how the Constitution has been interpreted and applied for over 200 years. Some phrases of the Constitution have been developed substantially, while others have been relegated to the dustbin. Over the years, the interpretation and application of phrases have changed showing the fluidity and change in circumstances and logic to interpreting. Although a sincere and thoughtful justice may interpret the Constitution one way, other sincere and thoughtful justices may interpret the same language differently, revealing, among other things, that a certain interpretation is not always self-evident. Underlying these different interpretations are myriad approaches to interpretation and theories of constitutional adjudication. This interpretation, application, and theory of the Constitution constitute the body of constitutional law.

A. The Articles of Association, Declaration of Independence, Articles of Confederation and Perpetual Union, and the Constitution

The U.S. experiment in democracy began long before the American Revolution and the adoption of a constitution. For example, democratic practice and institutions evolved in New England through town hall meetings, where the residents of a town regularly met to discuss and vote on budgets, laws, and other important political issues. It was largely due to these practices and the increasingly accepted democratic notions that the revolutionary phrase "no taxation without representation" held any sway.

Efforts by the kingdom of Great Britain in the 1760s and early 1770s to increase tax revenue from the North American colonies to pay for war debt and maintenance of the British Empire met with resistance in the colonies in part because they were not represented in Parliament and in part because British mercantile policies limited colonial merchants' earning potential. Between 1772 and 1774 patriot committees created Provincial Congresses, or something similar, that effectively replaced the British ruling apparatus in the colonies.

In Boston a group called the Sons of Liberty dumped tons of taxed tea into Boston Harbor, an act of protest against the Tea Act of 1773 that became known at the Boston Tea Party. The British Parliament responded by adopting a series of acts called the Coercive Acts, which were designed to punish Boston for this destruction of private property and rein in rebellious colonial governments.

The First Continental Congress met in Philadelphia on September 5, 1774 to discuss how to respond to the British Parliament's adoption of the Coercive Acts (referred to as the Intolerable Acts in the American colonies). The fifty-six delegates from the legislatures of twelve of the thirteen colonies created the Continental Association to serve as the vehicle to impose economic sanctions against Great Britain. The Continental Association's Articles of Association imposed an immediate ban on British tea and on the importation or consumption of any goods (including slaves) from Britain, Ireland, and the British West Indies. It took effect on December 1, 1774. The Articles of Association also threatened an export ban to Britain if the Coercive Acts were not repealed by September 10, 1775.

During this time the colonies formed militias, which the British perceived as a threat. When the British sent 1,000 troops on April 19, 1775, to confiscate weapons and arrest revolutionaries in Concord, Massachusetts, they clashed with the local militia, marking the beginning of the American Revolution.

The Second Continental Congress met in May 1775 in Philadelphia with representatives from all thirteen colonies. This Congress managed the war effort and on July 4, 1776, adopted the Declaration of Independence, which became the nation's most cherished symbol of liberty and Thomas Jefferson's most enduring monument. In exalted and unforgettable phrases, Jefferson articulated the American people's convictions. He summarized John Locke's and the Continental philosophers' ideals of individual liberty in "self-evident truths" and set forth a list of grievances against the King to justify before the world the breaking of ties between the colonies and Britain.

During this time most states adopted their own constitutions, sometimes just updating their colonial charters and local political compacts. Replacing parliamentary sovereignty with popular sovereignty, these constitutions typically outlined three branches of government and a list of individual rights. Of the twenty-six rights later contained in the U.S. Bill of Rights, all were found in colonial codes of law and in the bill of rights of these pre-1789 state constitutions. They also contained restrictions that later influenced the drafters of the Constitution (for example, all but two had a religious test for holding public office; some had property requirements to vote; some allowed free blacks to vote; and New Jersey momentarily allowed women to vote).

In this environment, the Second Continental Congress turned its attention to creating a federal constitutional order. In 1777 the Second Continental Congress adopted and sent out for ratification the first U.S. constitution, which was called the Articles of Confederation and Perpetual Union (commonly known as the Articles of Confederation but whose full name indicated the drafters' intent for the Confederation's longevity). The document could not become effective until it was ratified by all thirteen colonies, which did not occur until 1781.

The Articles of Confederation created "The United States of America" as a new nation, a sovereign union of sovereign states, and, while giving states open-ended power, limited federal power to those expressly delegated. Congress was a unicameral legislature that had the power to conduct foreign affairs, control the military, and set weights and measures (including coins and postage). It did not have the power to levy taxes or institute a military draft, which meant it could only submit such requests to the states. At times this left the military under George Washington's leadership in a precarious position. In the national legislature, each state was allocated one representative, appointed by the state legislature, ending the power struggle between the large and small states regarding representation in Congress.

Article II of the Articles of Confederation provided that "Each state retains its sovereignty, freedom, and independence." With most authority reserved to the states, states developed semiautonomous status, printing their own paper money and repudiating debts. The federal government had no power to tax or regulate commerce, so states erected trade barriers and local uprisings like the Whiskey Rebellion disrupted public order.

Although there was a Committee of the States that could act when Congress was not in session, and although the president presided over Congress and this Committee, there was no executive branch. The president's terms were short and he performed duties assigned by Congress. In the eight years of this Congress's existence, it was led by ten different presidents.

The only judicial body was a national appellate tribunal for maritime cases. Congress was to settle any disputes between states. The Articles contained no bill of rights but did provide for individual freedom of movement between states and granted extradition rights to states. Canada was preapproved for membership if it desired, but all other decisions to admit new states required the support of nine states. Any amendment to the Articles required ratification by all state legislatures.

Recognizing the weakness of the Articles of Confederation, some put forward proposals to amend them starting in 1786. However, they all failed because they could not garner a unanimous vote. In 1786, state representatives met in Annapolis, Maryland, to discuss problems of the Articles. They adopted a resolution to meet in Philadelphia in May 1787 in a "Grand Convention" to "devise such further provisions as shall appear to them necessary to render the Constitution of the federal government adequate to the exigencies of the union."

Although the representatives to the Constitutional Convention were only authorized to amend the Articles, they held secret, closed-door sessions and wrote a new constitution. Instead of following the Articles of Confederation amendment requirement of ratification by all (100 percent) states, the new constitution required the ratification by only nine states (69 percent) to replace the Articles of Confederation.

The Constitutional Convention met in Philadelphia from May 25 to September 17, 1787. Competing plans for a new government were introduced and many compromises were struck. Large and small states compromised on the issue of representation by agreeing to a bicameral legislature—a senate where states were represented equally and a house with proportional representation based on population. Another compromise was to only create a supreme court and leave it up to Congress to decide whether to create lower federal courts.

The ratification debates were extensive and fierce, with several states initially opposed to ratification. Those opposed to ratification were called Antifederalists, and they centered their criticism on the threat of a more powerful federal government and the weakening of state power, as well as the absence of a bill of rights. Those who supported ratification were called Federalists, and they pointed to the weaknesses of the Articles of Confederation and espoused the benefits of federalism, checks and balances, separated powers, pluralism, and representative government. Alexander Hamilton, James Madison, and John Jay wrote eighty-five essays in support of the draft constitution in an effort to persuade the New York Convention to ratify the Constitution. These became known as the *Federalist Papers* and have been often cited by the Supreme Court as an authoritative contemporary interpretation of the meaning of its provisions and as evidence of the Framers' intent.

When the Continental Congress met in September 1788, eleven states had ratified the Constitution, so it passed a resolution to put the new Constitution into effect. On April 30, 1789 George Washington was inaugurated as the first president of the United States under the new Constitution. New York, Virginia, Massachusetts, and New Hampshire ratified the Constitution with a recommendation that a bill of rights be appended, so James Madison, as a member of the House of Representatives, gathered the various amendment proposals.

Seventeen amendments were passed by the House, twelve by the Senate, and ten by the states. These ten amendments became known as the Bill of Rights.

B. A Brief History of Interpreting the Constitution

Different theories of law have been used to interpret the Constitution. During the eighteenth century, natural law and natural rights were the dominant theories of law in this country (they were the dominant theory of law since the time of Aristotle and Greek civilization). Natural law theory states that there are objective moral principles embedded in the nature of the universe. Judges, legal theorists or others use reason, instinct, and the natural moral sense implanted in all humans to discover these basic principles of the natural law. Natural law can flow from God or from nature itself, but in either case, it is the preeminent source of law from which all other law flows. Because positive law may ignore, misunderstand, abuse or defy these natural law principles, natural law offers an outside critique of positive law.

Natural law birthed the natural rights philosophy, which emphasized the restraint which ought to be imposed on government vis-à-vis individuals. John Locke, the political theorist who had a strong influence on the country's founders, subscribed to natural law and natural rights. Statements from the Declaration of Independence such as "We hold these truths to be self-evident, that all men are created equal, that they are endowed by their Creator with certain unalienable Rights," use natural law and natural rights language.

One reason the Federalists and their opponents, the Jefferson-Republicans, did not debate over competing theories of constitutional interpretation was because both groups accepted the English declaratory theory of law. The declaratory theory of law states that judges do not create law; they just discover and declare the law that already exists within the immutable legal principles of the common law. This theory parallels natural law in many ways and holds that the law never changes, so judges simply need to discover and declare the law. Alexander Hamilton and Supreme Court Chief Justice John Marshall followed the thinking of Sir William Blackstone, another natural law theorist who wrote in his *Commentaries on the Laws of England* (1765–1768) that judges were "depositories of the laws; the living oracles" of law. This view imbued a reverence for the law because it viewed law as based on enduring natural principles, not on personal preferences.

During the nineteenth century, respect for natural law gradually diminished with the ascendancy of legal positivism. Positivist theory is defined by two characteristics: the separation of laws and morals, and the disentanglement of human law from natural law. Under positivism, law was definable without any presuppositions and could be identified exclusively from factual sources such as law and court decisions. People like Oliver Wendell Holmes (1841–1934) sought to debunk the idea that law is "a brooding omnipresence in the sky." As far as Holmes was concerned, judges made law, so he encouraged the empirical study of law. He said, "I hate justice, which means that I know that if a man begins to talk about that, for one reason or another he is shirking thinking in legal terms."

Positivism birthed formalism, which asserts that judges can examine laws and court decisions and render decisions in a logical process not influenced by a judge's own values and preferences. Holmes rebelled against legal formalism. In his words,

> The life of the law has not been logic; it has been experience. The felt necessities of the time, the prevalent moral and political theories, intuitions of public policy, avowed or unconscious, even the prejudices which judges share with their fellow men, have had a good deal more to do than the syllogism in determining the rules by which men should be governed.

Holmes was a legal realist, which like positivism, shares the belief that law is purely a human construct. However positivists are strict textualists, replacing metaphysics with an internally defined system and meaning, whereas realists are contextualists and thus believe that the meaning of a law consists of the meaning the interpreter brings to the text. The 1920s and 1930s saw the advent of American legal realism. Led by Karl Llewellyn (1893–1962), legal realism further questioned the determinacy of legal rules and argued that the Supreme Court "shaped the living Constitution to the needs of the day as it felt them."

As another reaction to formalism, Roscoe Pound (1870–1964) founded the approach of sociological jurisprudence, which encourages the study of law in relation to changing social forces. Pound encouraged judges to be social engineers, molding law to the changing needs of society. Louis Brandeis, before he became a justice, filed a brief in *Muller v. Oregon* (1908) that contained only two pages of legal argument but ninety-seven pages of statistics and social science data documenting the health risks for women working long hours. Brandeis considered social science essential to court decisions if the law was to keep pace with the developments in other fields.

Liberalism focuses on individual rights and demands freedom from state interference except to protect others from harm. These individual rights include freedom of religion, conscience, speech, association, and, more recently, sexuality. Liberalism's roots lie in the religious wars of Europe and the religious discrimination in the colonies, which proved to liberals that the only stable ground for government was to separate church and state. Liberals extend this principle of toleration to other areas where citizens have conflicting ideas of what is right. The role of the state is not to resolve these differences but to create a neutral framework that allows its citizens to pursue their ideals of the good life. For liberals, this is the only healthy response to the demands of modern pluralistic societies. Although its roots go back a few centuries, liberalism experienced a period of growth after World War II.

One critique of liberalism questions why individual freedom should take priority over the community and the state's interest in preserving traditional customs. Liberalism's response is that state coercion and paternalism produce worse results in the long run than does individual autonomy. Critics of liberalism argue that by encouraging individual pursuit of self-interest, liberalism was used to promote capitalism. Although that may be true, most liberals today agree that justice requires some regulation of the market to ensure equal opportunity.

Although conservatism's roots also go back a couple of hundred years, the past thirty years or so have seen the revival of conservatism. Conservatism seeks to preserve the status quo and favors limited government, autonomous institutions, and individual freedom. Conservatism's sense of the darker side of humanity and the corrupting influence of power causes it to prefer a limited government focused on security and a legal framework to facilitate transactions. Conservatism is hostile to regulation and government planning.

When freedom and equality compete, conservatives pursue freedom, preferring the right of individuals to succeed or fail on their own. Conservatives emphasize property rights and traditional views of social units such as the family, organized religion, and local government.

C. Challenges to Interpreting the Constitution

The Constitution is simultaneously the supreme law of the country and the fundamental political document. It turned the political choices of the founders into law. This combination of supreme law and politics has, particularly in recent times, produced controversy over who interprets the Constitution and how it is interpreted.

The first question is: Who interprets the Constitution, and is there a final interpreter of the Constitution? All branches of the federal government are sworn to uphold the Constitution and to carry out their duties, and this requires interpreting the Constitution. A lawyer filing and a judge hearing a constitutional claim, as well as a professor or student discussing constitutional law in-

terpret the Constitution. Thus a wide range of public officials and private individuals interpret the Constitution, which leads to the question: Who is the
final interpreter? As a practical matter, when there is a constitutional dispute,
it tends to be filed in court, giving the judiciary jurisdiction to rule. This un-
derscores Chief Justice John Marshall's conclusion that "it is emphatically the
province and duty of the judicial department to say what the law is." One hundred fifty years later, a unanimous Supreme Court declared "the basic principle that the federal judiciary is supreme in the exposition of the law of the
Constitution, and that principle has ever since been respected by this Court
and the Country as a permanent and indispensable feature of our constitutional system."

Certainty, efficiency, and stability are served by having one clear final interpreter.
However, even the Supreme Court has developed the political question doctrine to avoid interpreting certain constitutional provisions, which lends cre-
dence to the claim either that there is no authoritative interpreter or that a
different branch of government is the authoritative interpreter, depending on
the provisions. Nonetheless, despite the notable dissenters, the Supreme Court
is the final interpreter of the Constitution unless it gives that authority to the
president or Congress.

Constitutional interpretation is critical because no matter how detailed and
specifically legal drafters write, their words must be interpreted, and differences in interpretation can be substantial. This task of interpreting is not limited to law. Religions that have Holy Scriptures (e.g., Christianity, Judaism,
Islam) have major divisions within them based on different interpretations of
the same language. In theology, this is referred to as hermeneutics (Hermes
was the interpreter of the messages from the Greek gods); in law, this is called
constitutional interpretation.

Constitutional interpretation in the United States presents a number of challenges. First, much of the text is written in general terms (e.g. "liberty," "necessary and proper," "commerce among the states," "due process of law," and
"probable cause") that require substantial interpreting. A benefit of open tex-
tured language is the flexibility it allows over time to adapt to situations that
could not have been contemplated when written. However, the more general
the language, the more it calls on interpretive skills.

A second challenge is that many constitutional questions are not addressed,
and many principles underlying the Constitution are not mentioned in the text
(e.g., separation of powers, checks and balances, federalism, limited government, protection of liberty). This raises questions of how to address such issues, and the extent to which principles should be employed as opposed to just
the language of the text. This is particularly a challenge in the United States be-

cause the U.S. Constitution is short—a fraction of the length of the vast majority of the constitutions in the world today—and therefore does not expressly address numerous constitutional questions. One response to this challenge is to interpret the Constitution to the crisis of the times. Another response is to do nothing until the Constitution is amended to address the particular question. However, this leads to the third challenge in constitutional interpretation.

The third challenge is that the Constitution is difficult to amend; it is rigid. Article V requires proposal of amendments from either a two-thirds majority in each chamber of Congress or by a constitutional convention called by two-thirds of the states, followed by ratification by three-quarters of the state legislatures or by constitutional conventions in three-quarters of the states. Since the adoption of the Constitution, because of the difficulty and expense of creating constitutional conventions and the lack of interest in delegating them this authority, all amendments have followed the congressional and state legislature path. Because forty-nine of the fifty states have bicameral legislatures and ratification in bicameral states requires a majority of both houses, a negative vote by as few as thirteen of the country's ninety-nine state legislatures is sufficient to defeat a proposed amendment. Not only is this process lengthy and costly, but a small minority can block the adoption of a constitutional amendment, which helps explain why only seventeen amendments have been adopted since 1791. This makes the U.S. Constitution one of the most difficult to amend in the democratic world; most Western democracies have a more flexible amendment process, typically requiring only a supermajority in the national legislative body and/or national referendum.

How does a rigid constitution impact constitutional interpretation? It puts substantially more pressure on judges to interpret and apply the Constitution to constitutional questions that the Constitution has not expressly addressed. All societies need an outlet for change, and when the amendment process makes change extraordinarily difficult, pressure builds on other avenues for change, including constitutional interpretation. The opposing argument leads to the next challenge—namely, that flexible constitutional interpretation can replace constitutional amendment, and in some instances, lawmaking, clearly an overstepping of boundaries by an unelected judiciary.

The fourth challenge to constitutional interpretation in the United States is wrapped in the now well-established practice of judicial review. Under judicial review, an unelected, life-tenured federal judiciary can declare a federal or state law (adopted by a majority in a representative democracy) unconstitutional. When a court so acts, it inevitably incurs the wrath of the political majority. Courts survive on political capital, and if they go too far afield of the majority, they risk losing this political support. Courts are mindful of the political nature of judicial review, which in turn impacts their interpretation. Rarely do the courts stray far ahead or behind the majority because when they do, they risk that their decisions will be ignored. Arguably, the Court was about ten years ahead of its time when it handed down its famous decision in *Brown v. Board of Education* (1954). For the next ten years, many states ignored or found ways to get around the decision to integrate public schools. Not until Congress adopted the Civil Rights Act of 1964, which reflected the will of the majority, did the concept of integration receive more widespread support. Today the *Brown* decision has broad support and is considered one of the Supreme Court's most important decisions; however, it also reveals the tenuous nature of interpreting the Constitution in a way that challenges the status quo. A decision to avoid or minimize this countermajoritarian difficulty often motivates the many approaches to constitutional interpretation.

D. Interpreting the Constitution

Although there are innumerable ways to interpret the Constitution, evidenced by the unique jurisprudence of each Supreme Court justice, there are basic categories of constitutional interpretation. Some of the categories overlap, and although justices may claim to adhere exclusively to a particular approach, they often employ a combination of approaches in their jurisprudence. It is important to remember that typically one approach to constitutional interpretation is not determinative of outcome. So, for example, two justices using the textualist approach may well reach different conclusions in a particular case.

Although the divisions in constitutional interpretation sometimes run deep, there is widespread agreement on the following aspects: The text, history, structure, and precedent are valid sources of constitutional interpretation. The differences focus on how to use these sources and whether the court can look to additional factors.

1. Textualism

Textualism is an approach to finding the meaning of the Constitution by examining the words of the text. After a detailed examination of the words, the resulting reasoning is applied to resolve the legal problem at hand.

Pure textualists believe that judicial decisions must be based only on the text of the Constitution. This raises the question of what rules of construction should be employed in interpreting the Constitution. Should only the literal and natural meaning of words be employed? Dictionaries often provide multiple meanings of words, and choosing which meaning applies may be a subjective process.

The "original meaning" approach looks at how the words would have been commonly understood at the time they were written and adopted. Such interpreters would examine dictionaries in use at the time of the drafting.

What if the plain meaning leads to an unintended or absurd result? For example, the Court has never adopted the literal meaning of the First Amendment, which begins (significantly) "Congress shall make no law" establishing religion, prohibiting free exercise, or abridging freedom of speech, press, or association. The Court has allowed Congress, as well as states, to adopt laws limiting each of these First Amendment freedoms for various reasons, including the intent of the drafters.

Should words be examined in their context? A flaw of the literal approach is the assumption that words have plain meaning apart from their context. The contextual approach focuses on words surrounding the text in question, as well as from other parts of the Constitution, to shed light on the clause under consideration.

Often the principle or concept behind a word is more important than the wording itself, or two constitutional values compete with little help from the wording. When the text is inconclusive, as is often the case, the judiciary has developed other forms of constitutional interpretation to give meaning to the general language of the Constitution.

Other textualists, sometimes called strict constructionists, interpretivists, or legal formalists, would allow judges to examine the historical record to discern what the Framers and ratifiers intended the constitutional provisions to mean.

2. Structuralism

The structural approach involves drawing inferences from relevant parts of the Constitution as a whole and in relationship to one another. This approach argues that the structure of the Constitution and the government and institutional relationships it creates constitute an important interpretive tool. Chief Justice Marshall used a structural argument in *McCulloch v. Maryland* (1819) when addressing why a state could not tax the Bank of the United States. Looking at how the union was formed as well as the relationship between the national government and states, he argued for a kind of structural supremacy clause.

3. Stare Decisis

The common law doctrine of *stare decisis* ("let the decision stand") exerts significant influence in constitutional interpretation. Adherence to precedent constrains future courts by requiring past constitutional articulations to bind them. Of course, the greater the body of cases in an area, the less flexibility a court has to depart from the prior line of decisions.

Although *stare decisis* is part of our common law tradition, the judicial philosophy of each justice determines when to overturn or otherwise weaken precedents through explicit overrulings or to narrow or distinguish precedents, sometimes to the point of nullification.

4. History

There are a variety of ways history can be used to interpret the Constitution. History as a tradition can be used to resist change and, for example, maintain a 200-year-old understanding of a constitutional phrase such as "liberty" or "equality." Historical argument could also trace the arc of history and recognize the unfolding progress of liberty and equality through constitutional amendment and court decisions.

a. Original Intent

This approach says that the Constitution should be interpreted in accordance with the specific intent of the Framers and ratifiers. This inquiry focuses on what the framers intended the language at issue to mean. The Framers of the Constitution are usually considered the members of the Constitutional Convention; the framers of a constitutional amendment are the members of Congress who proposed it. Original intent could also refer to the ratifiers in the states because their intent may reveal why the provision was adopted. Establishing original intent is difficult; because few Framers or ratifiers spoke to the issue, it is unclear what the intent was for the others, and a public statement of a public official may reveal multiple intents or a smokescreen for his or her true intent. Often the best that historical research can produce is the view of "leading proponents."

b. Historical Context: Problem, Remedy, and Purpose

This approach seeks to understand a constitutional provision by examining the larger historical context that gave rise to its drafting. By understanding the social, economic, or political problem the provision was designed to address, the interpreter seeks to suppress the problem and advance the remedy, thereby achieving the purpose underlying the provision. This approach allows the interpreter to go beyond the mere language and specific intent of the Framers and take a more holistic perspective, examining the problem, remedy, and general intent of the Framers. James Madison listed this approach first on his "obvious and just guides applicable to the Constitution" ("the evils & defects for curing which the Constitution was called for & introduced"). Similar to the British Mischief Rule of statutory interpretation, this inquiry focuses on what was the "mischief and defect" for which this language was drafted, what was the remedy the Framers sought, and what was the true reason of the remedy.

5. *Prudential Reasoning*

Prudential reasoning is premised on the argument that the court should consider the outcomes of its decision — it should be pragmatic. Prudential reasoning is also called consequentialism because the consequences of a particular ruling should form the basis for any valid evaluation of that ruling. Chief Justice Marshall argued that for the Constitution to succeed, the court must interpret it in a way that "the exigencies of the nation may require." Utilitarianism — "that action is best which procures the greatest happiness for the greatest numbers" — is also a form of prudential reasoning. At its best, prudential reasoning preserves constitutional principles by moderating or delaying the pursuit of ideals when the costs are too high. At its worst, it turns constitutional interpretation into expediency, abandoning fundamental principles of the Constitution.

6. *Ethical or Moral Reasoning*

Under the ethical or moral reasoning approach, in addition to text, history, structure, and precedent, the judge employs the ethics or moral principles of the Constitution when interpreting its provisions. This reasoning seeks to vindicate what is moral, just, or desirable. This includes the natural or higher law approach and is exemplified by the following statement in Martin Luther King, Jr.'s Letter From a Birmingham Jail: "An unjust law is no law at all." Judge Learned Hand reportedly told Justice Oliver Wendell Holmes to "do justice" (moral reasoning approach), to which Holmes replied, "That is not my job. It is my job to apply the law" (positivist approach).

As Ronald Dworkin, a legal philosopher, says, "moral reading" asks an interpreter "to find the best conception of constitutional moral principles ... that fits the broad story of America's historical record. It does not ask them to follow the whisperings of their own consciences or the traditions of their own class or sect if these cannot be seen as embedded in that record."

Proponents of this position argue that moral reasoning provides grounds for challenging existing law and will always influence judicial decision making (which explains the battles over Supreme Court nominees), so it is better to make it explicit rather than force judges to hide those moral choices behind mechanisms that pretend to avoid those choices. Critics will argue that this approach is too subjective and antidemocratic and tends to entrench prejudicial beliefs.

7. Comparative Constitutional Theory

Comparative constitutional theory posits that the ideas, practices, and experiences of other countries can inform the Supreme Court's understanding, not as binding precedent but as persuasive authority. Although the federal courts have considered foreign sources of law since the founding of the country, this theory has recently become controversial because of the sensitivity of the cases involved (death penalty, homosexuality, affirmative action, and assisted suicide).

This approach brings up some methodological concerns, such as which countries should the Court survey, and whether there is sufficient expertise about the national legal context where the case originates. However, in an increasingly interconnected world, communication and sharing of ideas among justices and courts appears inevitable and perhaps as in other disciplines, beneficial.

8. Clustering of Approaches: Originalism versus Nonoriginalism

Two broad categories (also called clusterings) of approaches to interpreting the Constitution that have formed much of the recent debate are originalism and nonoriginalism, also called interpretivism and noninterpretivism. Originalism considers the text and the original intent of the drafters and ratifiers of the Constitution at the time of its adoption as authoritative for purposes of constitutional interpretation in the present. Originalists see the amendment process as the only way to change or develop the Constitution and therefore do not want the Supreme Court to recognize rights that are not expressly enumerated in the Constitution.

Nonoriginalists also examine text and original intent, but in addition, interpret constitutional principles in light of contemporary understandings. Nonoriginalists see the Constitution as a living document evolving over time, which makes room for unenumerated rights, such as the right to privacy. Nonoriginalists would interpret the equal protection clause to prohibit sex discrimination even though that was not the original intent of its drafters. This example also raises the question of the level of generality (as opposed to specificity) at which the Court finds a constitutional norm. Arguably, if the original intent was the principle that no person should be denied the equal protection of the laws, than even originalists could accept its application to women despite the absence of that specific intent at the time of adoption.

E. Recent External Critiques of Constitutional Interpretation

1. Critical Legal Studies

Critical legal studies is more of a critique of current constitutional theory, revealing its limitations and biases, than a proposal for how justices should analyze the Constitution. Growing out of the radical political culture of the 1960s, it asserts the inescapability of commitment and rejects any search for a value-neutral jurisprudence. It is concerned with the politics of law, particularly how legal reasoning has attempted to make a particular social order appear inevitable. It sees law as merely the assertion of power by those with power. It seeks to show that the social order is less structured and impartial and more complex and irrational than the law suggests. It hopes to overturn this legal consciousness and emancipate the individual.

Critical legal studies is a diverse group united by a concern for outgroups (i.e., the poor, racial, ethnic, sexual, and other minorities) and a commitment to a more egalitarian society. Its greatest legacy may be the many off-shoots it has spawned, such as critical race theory, feminist legal theory, the LatCrit movement (examines how law treats Latina/o communities), queer jurisprudence (challenges categories of gender and sexual orientation), and other outgroup jurisprudence.

2. Feminist Legal Theory

Feminist legal theory seeks for women the same social, economic, and political choices that men possess. It favors the elimination of legal barriers to equality of opportunity. To accomplish this goal, it emphasizes the ways men and women are the same, rather than ways they are different, in the hope that these will break down gender-based distinctions that limit equal opportunities for women. Feminist legal theory is reluctant to accept special treatment for women out of fear it will reinforce limiting views of women. Similar to liberal constitutional theory, it is committed to individual autonomy and therefore tends to focus on legal rights as the avenue to secure nondiscriminatory treatment.

3. Critical Race Theory

Critical race theory includes a variety of legal theories premised on the belief that the legal system or its white-dominated social institutions do not treat racial minorities equally or fairly. Following in the footsteps of the critical legal studies movement, it has developed various analytical techniques to demonstrate the racial bias built into the legal system. Critical race theorists continually ask the "race question" to reveal the ways in which seemingly neutral rules adversely affect racial minorities. For example, critical race theorists ask how federalism, privacy, traditional values, and established property interests serve as vessels of racial subordination. This theory values experiential knowledge of people of color and critical reflection on the lived experience of racism.

4. Postmodernism

Postmodernism, as its name suggests, implies a contrast with modernism and its commitment to Enlightenment ideas, such as reason, science, ethics, and the conviction that these prove an independent reality. Instead, postmodernism turns reason on its head, asserting that reason is nothing more than social practices. Therefore, ideas about what the Constitution means are really just social constructions, not an objective reality that exists independently of the speaker. Postmodernists doubt the possibility of objective truth and reject sharp dichotomies and hierarchy.

5. Law and Economics

The law and economics movement seeks economic efficiency in the law. It argues that the free-market economy functions best when the legal system defines entitlements so as to minimize information and transaction costs. This approach ranges from changing regulatory practice to allow for efficient markets, to returning to the unregulated pre-welfare state of the early 1900s, better known as the Lochner era. Economist Vilfredo Pareto came up with one definition of efficiency. Given a set of alternative allocations of goods or services, a change from one allocation to another that can make at least one individual better off without making any other individual worse off is called a Pareto improvement. An allocation is defined as Pareto efficient or Pareto optimal when no further Pareto improvements can be made. Nicholas Kaldor and John Hicks took this one step further. Under the Kaldor-Hicks efficiency, an outcome is considered more efficient if a Pareto optimal outcome can be reached by arranging some compensation from those that are made better off to those that are made worse off. Critics of this approach argue that it oversimplifies assumptions about human nature, and undervalues human rights, distributive justice, and the suffering of those who are inefficient.

Chapter 1

Judicial decides is what is law

The Federal Judicial Power

Roadmap

- The landmark decision of *Marbury v. Madison*, in which the Court established the authority of judicial review

- The judiciary has the authority and the duty to declare what the law is, including executive actions, legislative actions, and state actions

- However, there are limits on federal judicial power, including the doctrine of separation of powers, jurisdiction, and congressional limits

- Further, there are limits on whether a case or controversy is appropriate for the Court to decide, including advisory opinions, standing, ripeness, mootness, and political questions

- The judicial power of the federal courts and of the individual states is also limited by the Eleventh Amendment, which provides the states immunity from suit. There are exceptions, such as when a state waives its immunity or consents to suit; suits against municipalities, counties, or state officials; and suits instituted under the Civil War amendments

---

I. Judicial Review: The Beginning

Judicial can invalidate laws & conduct that violate constitution

Most constitutional law textbooks begin with *Marbury v. Madison* (1803), one of the earliest and most important cases in constitutional law. Understanding this rather odd case will help one understand not only judicial review but constitutional law in general.

Judicial review is one of the cornerstones of the checks and balances of the U.S. Constitution, as this doctrine provides the judicial branch with the power to invalidate government laws and conduct that conflict with the Constitution. It is hard to imagine American constitutional law without judicial review. We study constitutional law almost entirely through the lens of Supreme Court cases in which the Court is exercising the power of judicial review.

As is true with the bulk of the Constitution, there is no explicit textual provision in Article III or anywhere else that provides for judicial review. For this reason, and perhaps due to the fact that some authors are unaware that some of the colonies accepted the idea of judicial review, many textbooks treat judicial review as an invention of Chief Justice John Marshall.

Although the British system was one of parliamentary supremacy and did not allow for judicial review, there were influential English lawyers such as Lord Edward Coke, who suggested that it was the judiciary's task to enforce society's fundamental law against the other branches. This idea was adopted by the colonies; during the 1780s, a number of state courts had reviewed various state laws for conformity with their constitutions.

In *Marbury v. Madison*, Chief Justice Marshall drew on that idea to strike down Section 13 of the Judiciary Act of 1789, which he held conflicted with the provisions of Article III of the Constitution, which set out the original jurisdiction of the Court. Chief Justice Marshall rested his argument for judicial review in the rather straightforward idea that "It is emphatically the province and duty of the judicial department to say what the law is." Because Article VI establishes that the "Constitution and the Laws of the United States which shall be made in Pursuance thereof ... shall be the supreme Law of the Land," for Chief Justice Marshall it followed that it was the duty of the Court to resolve the conflict between the two laws (namely, the Judiciary Act and the Constitution) in favor of the Constitution. Arguably, this is no more controversial than deciding that a law passed later in time would trump an earlier law (under the last-in-time rule) or that a properly enacted federal law would trump conflicting state law (under the Supremacy Clause).

Although the argument makes perfect sense from today's perspective, nothing compels this result. The mere fact that the Constitution is the supreme law does not necessitate the view that it is the Court's job to enforce the Constitution. It could just as easily be the role of each branch of government to decide for itself how to interpret and resolve apparent conflicts between its conduct or its laws and the Constitution. For instance, it could be left to the legislature to determine if the laws it passed conflicted with the Constitution. The historical materials are inconclusive on the point of original intent of the Framers, and no other country at the time of the founding followed the doctrine. In fact, many countries still do not have full judicial review.

Marbury v. Madison is a nearly perfect case for the beginning of constitutional law for a number of reasons. First, the decision is set in the context of heightened political controversy that included Justice Marshall, acting in dual roles as Chief Justice of the Supreme Court and Secretary of State. Second, the case is rich with fundamental questions about the rule of law, the relation between rights and remedies, and the role of courts vis-à-vis the other branches of government. The case deals with not only the issue of the original jurisdiction of the federal courts but also judicial review over legislation, as well as the power of judicial review over executive conduct. Finally, Chief Justice Marshall was able to address and establish the Supreme Court's role, with respect to the executive and legislative branches' roles, without actually deciding any substantive issue. Although all of these issues were addressed, the upshot of the opinion is that the Court did not have jurisdiction to hear the case. This case is about the journey, not the destination.

A. *Marbury v. Madison*

1. *The Political Context*

Marbury v. Madison makes much more sense if one knows something of its background. The case followed one of the most unusual elections of all time (at least until the 2000 election). The election resulted in a tie in the Electoral College between Thomas Jefferson and Aaron Burr, which meant that the House of Representatives selected the new President. The House chose Jefferson, and thereby, President John Adams and his Federalists were on their way out of office. As they were leaving, President Adams appointed his Secretary of State, John Marshall, to be the Chief Justice of the Supreme Court (February 4, 1801). Adams then nominated forty-two new Justices of the Peace, who were confirmed the day before he left office (March 3). Marshall, who was still acting as Secretary of State, only had until the end of the day to deliver the sealed commissions. He delivered all but a few, and when President Jefferson took office, his new Secretary of State, James Madison, refused to deliver the remaining commissions. William Marbury, one of the unlucky ones who did not receive his commission, sued James Madison in the Supreme Court for a writ of *mandamus* to compel him to deliver the commission. The claim was brought under the Judiciary Act of 1789, which Justice Marshall interpreted to provide original jurisdiction before the Supreme Court for this issue.

2. *The Apparent Issue in the Case*

Thus, the apparent issue in the case was whether Marbury could get a writ of *mandamus*, which is a writ to compel a state official to do something, that is, to compel Madison to give him his commission. The case turned on whether the new Chief Justice Marshall would compel Madison to deliver what Marshall failed to deliver as Secretary of State.

3. The Other Issues in the Case

If the fact that Marshall was to decide the case was not odd enough, Congress suspended the Court for a full year, and Marbury had to wait even longer. When Marshall finally delivered his opinion, he decided, with a cruel twist, that although Marbury had a right to the commission and the violation of that right required a remedy, Marshall and the Supreme Court could not provide it because it lacked original jurisdiction. On the road to deciding this issue, Justice Marshall addressed the following issues:

1. Did Marbury have a *right* to the commission?
2. Did a violation of a right of this nature require a *remedy*?
3. Was *the judicial review of executive conduct* appropriate, and could the Court issue a writ of *mandamus* against the executive?
4. Was there a conflict between the Constitution and the Judiciary Act?
5. Was *judicial review of legislation* appropriate?
6. Did the court have original jurisdiction to hear this case?

In addressing these issues, Chief Justice Marshall established the following.

1. The right to the commission vested when it was signed by the President and sealed by the Secretary of State.
2. The *rule of law, rather than of men, establishes that the violation of rights requires a remedy* (even though Chief Justice Marshall avoided providing a remedy in this case; see point 8).
3. *Judicial review of executive conduct* is appropriate when the conduct in question is *ministerial* (i.e., involves nondiscretionary, nonpolitical functions), and thus, the judiciary can issue writs of *mandamus* against executive officials when they are to carry out clear nondiscretionary duties, like delivering the signed and sealed commissions (the Court would not have the power to review acts that were political or involved setting policy, as these are at the discretion of the executive).
4. Article III of the Constitution divides the Court's jurisdiction between original and appellate and sets out in detail the original jurisdiction of the Supreme Court.
5. Article III does not include original jurisdiction for this type of case, and thus, based on the maxim that when there is a list of what is included, the rest is excluded (*expressio unius, exclusion alterius*), original jurisdiction was excluded for this case (note that the Court held that Congress could expand the appellate jurisdiction of the Court).

6. As noted, the Judiciary Act included original jurisdiction for this type of case, and thus, there was a direct conflict between the act and the Constitution.

7. Allowing Congress to add to the original jurisdiction of the Court would, in effect, amount to an amendment of Article III, without going through the detailed amendment process set out in the Constitution.

8. Because:
   a. "It is emphatically the province and duty of the judicial department to say what the law is";
   b. the Constitution extended the judicial power to "all cases arising under the Constitution";
   c. judges take an oath to support the Constitution;
   d. the Constitution created a federal government of limited powers; and
   e. Article VI establishes that the "Constitution and the Laws of the United States which shall be made in Pursuance thereof ... shall be the supreme Law of the Land"; then
   f. it followed for Justice Marshall that it was the duty of the Court to strike down laws that conflicted with the Constitution because they were not "in pursuance thereof."

9. Thus, the Court did not have jurisdiction to hear the case.

Arguably, Chief Justice Marshall should have recused himself because of the obvious conflicts of interest, and he could have avoided the constitutional issue by simply deciding that there was no right to the commission until it was delivered. Alternatively, he could have decided that there was a right to the commission and the Court did not have original jurisdiction without reaching the constitutional question. In other words, he could have reached the same result by interpreting the Judiciary Act as providing for a cause of action to bring *mandamus* actions *only if* there was proper jurisdiction. The result would have been the same, but there would have been no need to address whether the Court had the power to strike down the legislation, as it would have been interpreted to be consistent with the Constitution. He also could have avoided the issue of whether there was a right to the remedy of a *mandamus* by deciding the jurisdiction issue first. In fact, it could be argued that Court's discussion of the right to a remedy and judicial review of the executive is all dicta, because the Court did not have jurisdiction to reach the merits of the case.

However, as noted, Chief Justice Marshall was not interested in the result, and this is not what makes this case both interesting and important. What makes it interesting and important is that Marshall chastised the Jefferson administration for denying Marbury his commission, and he asserted the power of the fledgling Court to review not only the acts of Congress but also the executive's conduct, while simultaneously appearing to limit its own constitutional power. The case establishes the notion of rule by and under law, and this means that neither the Supreme Court nor the legislative or executive branches are above the law. The executive is not immune from judicial review of its actions when the law imposes a clear duty on its officials; the Supreme Court cannot hear a case if the Constitution excludes it from the Court's jurisdiction; and the legislative branch cannot expand the Court's jurisdiction beyond what the Constitution allows.

4. Lessons from Marbury

The five principal lessons from *Marbury* are as follows.

1. The Constitution is not in the text alone (it is silent about judicial review).
2. The Constitution is regulatory (it can be judicially enforced), not just aspirational (not merely a set of goals or ideals).
3. Congress cannot restrict or increase the Court's original jurisdiction.
4. The Court may review executive action that is ministerial (nondiscretionary).
5. The Court may review legislation for constitutionality.

Although the Supreme Court did not strike down another federal statute as unconstitutional until *Dred Scott v. Sandford* (1857), Marshall was able to solidify the position he took in *Marbury*. In *McCulloch v. Maryland* (1819) (the foundational case for federal legislative power), Marshall held that Congress had the power to establish a national bank under the Constitution and that the state of Maryland did not have the power to tax the bank under the Constitution (see Chapter 2). Marshall held that the Constitution devolves the duty on the Supreme Court to be the ultimate arbiter of what the Constitution requires and to bind the federal government, as well as the states, with its interpretation of the Constitution. Later Supreme Courts have attributed the origin of this power to *Marbury* itself. For example, in *Cooper v. Aaron* (1958) the Court stated: "[*Marbury*] declared the basic principle that the federal judiciary is supreme in the exposition of the law of the Constitution, and that principle has been respected by this Court and the Country as an indispensable feature of our constitutional system."

Although some doctrines in constitutional law ebb and flow, the Court's statement in 1958 is as true today as it was then.

B. Judicial Review of State Conduct

McCulloch was not the first case in which the Court extended federal judicial review of the federal government to federal judicial review of the states.

For instance, the Court struck down a state statute in *Fletcher v. Peck* (1810) for violating the Contract Clause of Article I, Section 10. Six years later, the Court overruled a Virginia Supreme Court decision in *Martin v. Hunter's Lessee* (1816). In that case, the Virginia Supreme Court had asserted that because the several states and the federal government were coequal sovereigns, Article III should be read to only give the Supreme Court appellate review authority over the federal courts and not the state courts. Justice Joseph Story wrote the opinion, in which the Chief Justice Marshall did not participate (because he had a conflicting interest in the case). Justice Story held that the Article IV Supremacy Clause required state judges to follow federal law, and thus, any decision a state judge rendered that implicated the Constitution could trigger the Supreme Court's jurisdiction under Article III to hear cases. The people had chosen a constitution that limited state power, and it was imperative that the Constitution have a single final interpreter, so that there would be uniform federal law throughout the country. While each state has its own laws, there should not be fifty different versions of the federal laws, treaties, and the Constitution. Federal law should not be subject to "state attachments, state prejudices, state jealousies, and state interests," which might be perceived to "obstruct the regular administration of justice."

Justice Marshall used *Cohens v. Virginia* (1821) as an opportunity to reiterate some of these themes. In *Cohens,* he reaffirmed the Supreme Court's power to review state court criminal convictions when the defendants claimed that their federal rights had been infringed on. He took this opportunity to argue that "the people" created the Constitution, which was not only separate from but also superior to the notion of state sovereignty. Because the states could not always be trusted to adequately protect federal rights, it was the duty of the Supreme Court to review state court decisions when federal rights were at issue. Further, while the Eleventh Amendment does give states immunity from suit, when the state itself instituted the criminal suit, it cannot claim that immunity (see section E in part V).

II. Protection of Judicial Power and Discretionary Review

Article III of the Constitution sets out the judicial power of the United States. It is a short section, and the only court firmly established in it is the Supreme Court of the United States. The first sentence of the Article vests the judicial power in the Supreme Court "and in such inferior courts as Congress may from time to time ordain and establish." Although it is virtually impossible to imagine the United States without a full-blown district and circuit court system, these courts exist because Congress created them under this enumerated power. The first Congress, in fact, established federal district or trial courts almost immediately in the Judiciary Act of 1789. These "inferior" courts are generally referred to as Article III courts. (*Inferior* is in quotes because although they are inferior to the Supreme Court, Congress can also create courts under its Article I powers. These are generally referred to as administrative tribunals.) Article I administrative judges have less power and protection under the Constitution than Article III courts. Whereas Article III spells out the powers and protection provided to Article III judges and tribunals, Article I has no such provisions.

A. Constitutional Protections for the Federal Courts

The power given to Congress to create federal courts does not mean that Congress can do whatever it wishes with those courts. The doctrine of separation of powers, which is one of the organizing principles of the Constitution, limits congressional interference with the courts. The idea of separation of powers is that the Constitution created different branches with different sets of powers and responsibilities; although there are checks and balances of those powers by the different branches, no branch should overstep the limits of its own power and interfere with the powers that are properly given to the other branches. The text of Article III also protects the independence of the Supreme Court as well as Article III courts (the "inferior" courts). Article III provides that judges of both the Supreme Court and the inferior courts shall hold their offices under "good Behaviour" and that Congress cannot reduce their salaries once set. This means that the judges have tenure for life, unless they are impeached. These provisions protect the independence of the individual members of the federal judiciary.

It should be noted that nothing in the text of the Constitution stops Congress from expanding the size of the Supreme Court or reducing the size of the Court when vacancies occur (when a federal judge retires or is impeached). In fact, the Court was reduced by one in 1801 (from six to five), restored to its original number of five in 1802, increased again by one in 1807, by two more in 1837, and one more in 1864, to give the Court its current number of nine. The "Court-packing plan" of President Franklin Roosevelt in 1937, during the New Deal era, was controversial and remains so today, not because the Constitution directly forbids it but because it appears to interfere with the separation of powers doctrine and the independence of the judiciary.

B. The Powers of the Court

As noted in the discussion of *Marbury v. Madison*, Article III does not explicitly give the Court the power of judicial review, and it does not provide much guidance on how the Court should exercise its power in deciding the cases and controversies that come before it. It does provide that the judiciary is to share its responsibility of trying criminal cases with a jury, except in cases of impeachment and mandates that crimes be tried in the state that they are committed. It also stipulates the parameters of the crime of treason, and requires that there be at least two witnesses or a confession in open court before one can be convicted of the offense. Otherwise, the Article is silent on the sources of law, court procedures, and the methods by which the court is to decide the law (issues that other modern constitutions often address).

III. Limits on the Power of the Court

A. Interpretation as a Limit

Some textbooks treat the issue of interpretation as one type of limitation on the power of the Court. This issue is addressed in the Introduction because interpretation is relevant not only to the judiciary's role but to everyone's role in interpreting the Constitution. There is no question that different approaches to interpreting the Constitution more or less constrain the judiciary in the exercise of its power to decide cases and controversies, but it should also affect how the executive, the legislature, the states, the people, and especially lawyers and law students exercise their power vis-à-vis the Constitution.

B. Jurisdiction as a Limit

The bulk of Article III sets out the judicial power in terms of the types of cases and controversies that courts can hear. In other words, the bulk of Article III concerns the jurisdiction of Article III courts. As Marshall established in *Marbury*, the Constitution is a document that limits federal power. The Court is thus limited to hearing the types of cases and controversies that are enumerated therein. The Article starts with a list of a dozen or so categories of cases and controversies (Section 2, Clause 1); then, in the next subsection, there is a subset of these cases and controversies over which the Supreme Court has original jurisdiction (Section 2, Clause 2). As Chief Justice Marshall noted in *Marbury*, the cases involving the United States or its officials are not on the list of cases or controversies for which it has original jurisdiction, and Congress cannot expand the list, unless it amends the Constitution.

The full list is composed of matters based on the *subject matter* of the case or controversy and based on the parties before the court. This is often referred to as *subject matter jurisdiction*. Thus, the list includes *subject matter cases in law and equity* that arise under

1. the Constitution;
2. the laws of the United States;
3. treaties; and
4. maritime and admiralty law.

It also includes *party-based* matters known as diversity jurisdiction, including:

1. cases that affect ambassadors or other public ministers and consuls, and controversies between states in the union and other states (foreign or domestic);
2. cases between citizens of other/different states (foreign or domestic);
3. controversies between citizens from different states;
4. controversies between citizens from the same state that base a claim to land under the grant of different states; and
5. cases or controversies involving the United States.

This is often referred to as *diversity jurisdiction* because the parties are not from the same state but instead are diverse.

Although the text of Article III, Section 2, Clause 1 uses the term *cases* in granting jurisdiction over matters concerning some parties and the term *controversy* to cover other matters, the Section has been read to require either a *case or a controversy* in which there are adversarial parties.

The list makes functional sense, as it includes both cases and controversies that are of national concern, for which it is logical that there should be national uniformity, or where there is a risk that "state attachments, state prejudices, state jealousies, and state interests" might (or at least may be perceived to) "obstruct the regular administration of justice" (*Martin v. Hunter's Lessee*, 1816).

As noted, Article III, Section 2, Clause 2 creates a subset of this list, for which the Supreme Court has original jurisdiction. These cases are those in which it is most important to avoid subjecting another state (foreign or domestic) and its ambassadors, public ministers, and consuls to delay, harassment, or a multiplicity of suits. In cases involving these actors, the Supreme Court has original jurisdiction. It would also make sense that the Court should have *exclusive jurisdiction* in these cases, but the constitutional text does not require this. While Congress gave the Court exclusive jurisdiction over cases between two or more states, there is concurrent jurisdiction between the Supreme Court and the district courts in cases involving ambassadors or other public ministers or consuls, as well as other cases that involve states under 28 U.S.C. § 1251.

C. Congressional Regulation of Judicial Power: Discretionary and Nondiscretionary Appellate Jurisdiction

1. The Exceptions and Regulations Clause

The appellate jurisdiction of the Court, which is grounded in the remainder of the list of cases and controversies in Article III, Section 2, Clause 1 (as just discussed in section B, part 2), is not limited in the same way that original jurisdiction is limited because Section 2, Clause 2 states, "In all other Cases before mentioned, the Supreme Court shall have appellate Jurisdiction, both as to Law and Fact, with such Exceptions, and under such Regulations as the Congress shall make." The last clause has been interpreted to give Congress the power to control the content of the Supreme Court's appellate jurisdiction. In other words, not only can Congress add to this list, it can also subtract from the list in Article III.

The classic case in this area is *Ex parte McCardle* (1868). The case is extraordinary because it involved Congress stripping the Supreme Court of jurisdiction to hear a case on appeal while the case was still pending before the Court. William McCardle, a newspaper editor, was being held on charges of publishing a libelous and incendiary article by the U.S. military, which was occupying the state of Mississippi after the Civil War. He petitioned the Supreme Court on appeal from the circuit court, which had denied him a writ of *habeas corpus*. After arguments and before judgment, Congress passed a law that repealed an earlier congressional act, which had provided the Supreme Court with appellate review in the matter. Chief Justice Salmon Chase held the removal of jurisdiction to be within Congress's power under the Exceptions and Regulations Clause already quoted. As this case illustrates, Congress was able to create the grant of jurisdiction and remove the grant of jurisdiction.

A broad reading of this case is problematic, for it appears that it grants Congress extraordinary power to pull cases from the Court's docket if it fears that the Court may not decide the case the way that Congress wants. The case appears to be a blatant interference with the independence of the federal judiciary and the separation of powers. It also seems to undermine the principle enunciated by Marshall in *Marbury*—that the violation of rights requires that a remedy be provided. A broad reading of *McCardle* has led to numerous efforts to limit the jurisdiction of the Court in controversial areas ranging from reproductive rights, school busing, school prayer, voter reapportionment, and most recently, the so-called war on terror. Such efforts have not been successful because the Court has not followed an expansive reading of *McCardle*.

a. *McCardle* Narrowed, Based on the Principle of Separation of Powers

McCardle allows for a more narrow reading. As the Court noted, the repeal of the Act providing for appellate review of *habeas corpus* claims from the federal circuit courts only removed one source of Supreme Court review of *habeas corpus* petitions. There remained other avenues for *habeas corpus* review. In fact, in *Ex parte Yerger* (1868) (another case of a newspaper editor being held by the military during the post-Civil War Reconstruction era), the Court held that the removal of appellate review did not affect the Court's ability to hear *habeas corpus* petitions under its certiorari (or discretionary) review powers (see next subsection). However, before the Court could decide the case, the military dismissed the charges.

In fact, just a few years later, in *United States v. Klein* (1871), Chief Justice Chase revisited the issue of congressional interference with cases before the Court and held that Congress could not manipulate the jurisdiction of the Court to affect the outcome of cases. In *Klein*, Congress passed a statute that, although claiming to be a jurisdictional statute, spoke to how the Court should decide Klein's case, which was pending before it. Klein had recovered his property, which was taken during the Civil War, under a statute that allowed for such recovery on proof that the person had not aided the rebellion. The Supreme Court had already decided that under this statute, a presidential pardon was sufficient proof that the person had not aided the rebellion. Klein had won his case in the lower court on this basis. Congress, which was at odds with President Andrew Jackson (the Southern former Vice President, who took over after Lincoln's assassination, and who was later impeached), was not happy with this result because of the perception that Jackson was being too generous with his pardons. Thus, Congress passed a second statute expressly stating that presidential pardons would be proof of guilt in aiding the rebellion unless the pardon also contained an express disclaimer of guilt. The statute further provided that once it was determined that there was a pardon without the express disclaimer, the federal courts lacked jurisdiction to hear the claim. In other words, the statute gave the court jurisdiction up to the point that proof of a pardon without the disclaimer was established and at that point, the statute then ousted the jurisdiction of the court.

Chief Justice Chase held that this was not an exercise of Congress's power under the Exceptions and Regulations Clause but a decisional rule, or a rule dictating how the court was to decide the case before it. This violated the separation of powers doctrine; it had "passed the limit which separates the legislative from the judicial power."

It should be noted that if Congress changes the law prospectively, rather than changing the law that existed up to that point, then the Court will not invalidate the law based on *Klein* (*Robertson v. Seattle Audubon Society,* 1992).

2. Discretionary Review: Certiorari

Congressional enactments providing Article III courts appellate review have been interpreted as providing a right to appeal. In 1988, Congress narrowed this right to appeal to the Supreme Court in these cases by providing that the right to appeal was limited to appeals from the decisions of three-judge federal courts (and this is rare). This may sound like a large reduction in the Court's appellate jurisdiction, and in one sense, it is. It severely limits the rights of claimants to review of their case by the Supreme Court, because very few cases are heard by three-judge courts. Nonetheless, at the same time that Congress reduced individual rights to appellate review by the Court, it shifted power to the Court to decide which cases it would take, based on its *sound judicial discretion*. Most cases now come to the Court on what is called a writ of certiorari, which means that the Court decides to hear the appeal based on its discretion.

D. Justiciability: Constitutional and Prudential Limitations on the Cases and Controversies That Are Proper for the Court to Hear

Justiciability is a somewhat peculiar term that means that a matter is appropriate for a court to decide. Courts are not meant to resolve every problem in society. Courts decide legal problems, but not *all* legal problems (for example, one cannot petition a court to answer hypothetical constitutional law exam questions, even if they are very interesting and important). Although the courts in some other countries and some of the states within the United States give advisory opinions regarding legal matters, Article III federal courts do not give advisory opinions. One should go to a lawyer, rather than to the courts, if one wants legal advice. The courts hear cases or controversies between adversaries that are ripe or fully developed and are not moot or already resolved. Furthermore, the federal courts will generally only hear cases if the "right" people are bringing the case, namely, the real parties to the dispute (those with standing). Finally, the federal courts do not want to attempt to resolve disputes that are more political than legal.

All of these limitations arguably have some basis in the Article III requirement that the courts hear cases and controversies. "Cases and controversies" refers to the requirement that there be adverse parties to a suit with a genuine legal dispute between them. If all a party wishes for is advice, then it is not a real case or controversy under Article III. Furthermore, if the parties merely anticipate a legal dispute, but one does not exist yet, then there is not a fully ripe case or controversy for the court to hear. If the law has changed or the facts have changed so that the legal issue is moot, there is no longer a case or controversy to hear. Standing requires that only real parties to the case or controversy bring the case, not other intermeddlers, and the political question doctrine attempts to separate legal cases and controversies from political controversies.

Whereas Article III can form a basis for all of these areas of justiciability, the Court does not always rely on it in determining if a case is justiciable. Sometimes the Court is clear that it is relying on Article III, and sometimes it is not. Article III will often provide a minimal baseline, which the court expands for *prudential* reasons, such as judicial economy and respect for other branches of government, a fear of opening the court up for too many suits, or simply to decline issues that are not ready or are not absolutely necessary to decide. In some of these areas, it is unclear whether the court is acting consistently out of principle or is merely avoiding difficult or controversial work.

In some cases, the Court can avoid the constitutional issue without determining that it is nonjusticiable. If there are both constitutional and nonconstitutional grounds (e.g., federal statutory grounds) and the case can be resolved without reaching the constitutional grounds, then the Court often takes this path. The main reason for this form of avoidance is based on the idea that when the Supreme Court decides an issue based on the Constitution, its decision is generally the last word on the matter; it is final. Conversely, a decision based on statutory interpretation can be overturned by the legislature through the normal legislative process.

This last point is also relevant to the consequences of a decision by the court that a matter is nonjusticiable. If the ground for that decision is based in Article III, then the legislature cannot overturn the decision through the normal legislative process. As *Marbury* established, the legislature cannot give the courts jurisdiction to hear claims if the grant conflicts with the Constitution. However, if the grant is based on prudential reasons, the legislature should have the ability override the determination through the normal legislative process.

1. Advisory Opinions

The fact that Article III courts do not give advisory opinions is what the English sometimes call a trite point of law. It is common knowledge that people do not go to court for advice. Courts decide legal cases or disputes, which means that (1) there needs to be a genuine dispute between two or more adverse parties, and (2) the court's opinion must decide or settle the dispute and be given full faith and credit. This underlies the rule against advisory opinions, as well as the requirements for standing, ripeness, and mootness.

Although this is the rule for Article III courts, it is common practice for a number of state courts and courts abroad to give limited legal advice, in the form of advisory opinions, to other branches of government. There is also no bar on Article I courts providing advisory opinions. Although no one advocates opening up the courts to give advice to everyone, it does make sense for the branches of government to seek advice from the judiciary regarding the constitutionality of pieces of legislation or administrative action. One could imagine a President, who had concerns about the constitutionality of a piece of legislation, wanting the advice of the highest court before signing the legislation into law. This could save a good deal of time, resources, and contentious litigation. It would add credibility to both the government and the law.

One can also imagine the Secretary of State of a new nation, unsure about a difficult point of law in a tricky situation, requesting advice from the Court so that she or he could best advise the President. Thomas Jefferson was in this situation while acting as George Washington's Secretary of State during the war between the French and English (otherwise known as the French and Indian War). The United States was a neutral party, and the President did not want to jeopardize this neutrality, as it could mean dragging the country into war, but he wanted to be able to sell things, like ships, to both sides. Getting an opinion from the Court would, no doubt, let the President off the hook, so to speak, but the Court, in a very flattering letter, declined to give its advice. The Court considered such advice to be "extrajudicial" and a violation of the separation of powers and the checks and balances between the branches. The Court's role is not one of legal advisor to the President. Thus, it was not for the Court to give advice that the President could choose whether to follow.

a. Why No Advisory Opinions? Poor Process for Reaching the Truth

Advisory opinions of this nature are abstract and very distant from ripe disputes. Without a real case or controversy, one can only hypothesize about the application of the law to any given set of facts. Not only is the Court unaided by a fully developed set of facts, it is also unaided by opposing parties. U.S. courts are used to having the aid of engaged argument from advocates on both sides of a given legal issue. When the government seeks advice, there are no sides and no advocates for the sides, much less opposing advocates. It is much easier for the court to think through an issue if it has both concrete facts and vigorous arguments from both sides.

The classic case in this area is *Muskrat v. United States* (1911). In that case, Congress passed a law changing the number of Cherokees that could enroll in a program that transferred ownership of Cherokee Nation property to individual Cherokees and also increased restrictions on the ability to alienate or sell the property. This raised issues regarding Cherokee property rights. If an actual case arose where someone violated the law—for instance, by selling land that was restricted—then the federal courts could hear the claim. However, Congress passed a subsequent law that authorized suits in the Court of Claims with a right of appeal to the Supreme Court to determine the validity of this prior law. The legislation did not require an actual case or controversy between adverse parties. One could bring a claim to challenge the legislation before anyone had violated its provisions. Therefore, it was a grant of jurisdiction to hear and give advisory opinions on the matter. While this may have been acceptable for the Court of Claims (because it was an Article I court that regularly gave advisory opinions), it was not acceptable for the Supreme Court. As a result, the Court determined that the case was not justiciable.

A similar (although distinct) requirement is that if the Court is going to hear the case, its decision must actually decide the case or resolve the dispute. It is not enough that there are two adversaries to an actual dispute; the Court's determination must be final. Thus, Congress cannot pass a law that makes an Article III court's decision merely advisory or nonbinding. This was established in *Hayburn's Case* in 1792. In that case, Congress passed a law allowing Revolutionary War veterans to file pension claims in circuit courts, which were to make nonbinding determinations as to those claims and to inform the Secretary of War of their determinations. The fact that the Secretary of War could disregard the courts' determinations made them advisory.

There have been a number of other cases where the executive branch has retained the power to disregard or modify a decision by the Court, thereby denying the Court's decision full faith and credit and rendering any decision advisory. For instance, the Court declined to hear cases based on treaty violations in *United State v. Ferreira* (1852) because the Secretary of the Treasury had discretion to refuse to pay the claims. Similarly, the Court declined to review decisions by the Civil Aeronautics Board in *C & A Airlines v. Waterman Corp* (1948) because the President retained the discretion to ignore or modify the Court's decision.

b. Declaratory Judgments Distinguished

Although it is often difficult to distinguish declaratory judgments from advisory opinions, the Court will issue declaratory judgments. A *declaratory judgment* is simply a judgment that announces what the law is, which sounds very much like giving advice. Although the court does not award damages in declaratory judgment cases, it is guided by the foregoing requirements any time it contemplates providing a declaratory judgment. Namely, it asks: Is there a live legal dispute between two parties (is it ripe and not moot), and will the Court's decision resolve the dispute? If either of these is missing, then the opinion would be considered advisory, and the Court would decline to hear it. Declaratory judgments are common in property disputes because the declaratory judgment will usually resolve the matter. In other words, a simple declaration by a court that certain property belongs to person B, usually will resolve a property dispute between persons A and B.

2. Standing

Standing is the notion that only those with a stake in a matter should bring a claim before the Court. It might be argued that in a constitutional democracy like the United States, everyone is harmed when the Constitution is violated, and thus, everyone has a stake in having the Constitution enforced. In the words of Dr. Martin Luther King Jr.: "Injustice anywhere is a threat to justice everywhere." A similar view is taken in a number of constitutional systems. For instance, in Canada, India, Pakistan, and South Africa, people can bring constitutional claims if the claims are "in the public interest." India, in fact, requires that the person bringing the claim not have a personal stake in the outcome, thereby ensuring that the claim is for "the public interest" and not personal gain.

In contrast, the rule in the United States is that only those with a personal stake in the matter have standing to bring the claim. *Baker v. Carr* (1962) provides the classic formulation of the requirement, namely, that for a party to have standing, she or he must allege "such a personal stake in the outcome of the controversy as to assure the concrete adverseness, which sharpens the presentation of issues upon which the court so largely depends for illumination of difficult constitutional questions." Thirty years later, in *Lujan v. Defenders of Wildlife* (1992), the Court set out three *constitutional requirements* for standing:

1. an actual or imminent invasion of a legally protected interest of the plaintiff that is concrete and particularized (injury);
2. that is caused by the conduct of the defendant (causation); and

3. that can be redressed by a decision of the Court (redressability).

In addition to these three constitutional requirements, which have their roots in Article III, the Court has also articulated a number of *prudential requirements*. The prudential requirements include the grievance should be one's own and not that of a third party, and the grievance should be one within the zone of interest protected by the given statute. Although the three constitutional requirements must always be met first, the Court may also refuse to hear a case or a particular claim within a case if one or more of these prudential requirements is not met.

a. The Justifications for Standing Requirements: Best Process, Separation of Powers, Due Process

In much the same ways that advisory opinions are problematic from the standpoint of process, and perhaps even the separation of powers, cases that violate the standing requirements are also problematic.

i. Best Process

One justification for the standing requirements is rooted in our adversarial system and in what one might call "best process." The system is premised on having two adversarial parties advocating for their side of the case to their best ability. The idea is that the best advocates have something to gain and something to lose. If the person bringing the claim does not have a sufficient interest in the case, there is no real loss if that person does not vigorously pursue the claim and loses the case. Likewise, if the defendant is not the cause of the purported violation, then the defendant has nothing to lose if she or he fails to win the case. Finally, if the Court cannot redress the issue through its decision, again, the gains or loses in bringing the suit are unrelated to the legal point of the suit. When all three criteria are met, it is in everyone's interest to win, and thus, the hope and presumption is that this will generate the best arguments on each side, making it easier for the Court to come to the best solution.

There are a number of scenarios under which this reasoning is less than completely persuasive. One can imagine a law school clinical program or a human rights nonprofit group bringing constitutional claims with full passion and very competent skills, even if they lack a client with the required stake in the issue. In fact, some organizations look for the right party to fit the case, so they can vindicate the Constitution. In some cases, the resolution of the legal issue does not rely heavily on any given factual scenario, for example, when legislation regulating speech is substantially overbroad and chills a large amount of protected speech (see exceptions to third party standing).

ii. Separation of Powers

The best process justification also overlaps with and supports the idea of separation of powers. The judicial branch has its own niche, based on the structure of the Constitution, and its own competence. Its power and legitimate authority are strongest when it acts within its niche. When these criteria are not met, the Court moves out of its niche and risks venturing into the territory of the other branches.

iii. Due Process or Fairness

Another justification for these requirements is based on what one might call due process considerations. The U.S. judicial system has both the doctrines of *res judicata* (the issue has already been decided) and *stare decisis* (a court is bound by previous decisions or precedents). Because of these doctrines, it is important not only that the system employs the best process to arrive at decisions but also that those most affected by those decisions be the ones who bring the claim. This is because they will be bound by those decisions. Simple justice tells us that there is something unfair about a system that would allow an intermeddler with no stake in a case to champion others' claims when those others or the purported beneficiaries might not want the claim brought. It is particularly unfair if the champion loses the case, and the so-called beneficiaries are then bound by the decision. The champion is not really bound or does not lose anything, but the people with the real stake potentially do. Thus, even in systems that allow others to bring claims in the public interest or on behalf of others, there is often a requirement that there is not a party in interest who is able to bring the claim.

b. The Constitutional Requirements: Injury, Causation, Redressability

i. Injury: Personal and Particular, Not General

The claimant must have suffered an actual or threatened imminent personal injury in order to have standing. The Court has held that injuries to legal rights, along with aesthetic enjoyment, environmental injuries, reduced wildlife and water, and economic injuries, suffice (*Friends of the Earth, Inc. v. Laidlaw Environmental Services, Inc.*, 2000). It is sometimes difficult to understand what principle separates these recognized injuries from those that are unrecognized. A recurring theme is that the injury needs to be one that invades a personal right, liberty, or privilege. It is not enough that the Constitution or a federal statute is violated. Congress cannot simply provide for a right to sue under a federal statute; it must create a particular interest, right, or entitlement that one can sue to vindicate, and the plaintiff needs to allege an infringement or threatened infringement of that interest.

Until *Lujan v. Defenders of Wildlife* (1992) (already cited for the three constitutional requirements and addressed further shortly), the requirement that the injury must be particularized and not merely one shared by all citizens was considered prudential and not constitutional. This left open the question as to whether the general prohibition against taxpayer standing was also constitutional or was still prudential (because taxpayer standing refers to harm suffered by all taxpayers, it approximates a general harm). *Hein v. Freedom from Religion Foundation* (2007) (addressed shortly) settled the issue, and it is now a constitutional requirement that applies to citizen and taxpayer-standing suits. Thus, materials regarding citizenship and taxpayer standing that are often treated under sections on "the prudential requirements" for standing are addressed in a following section. After discussing the injury requirement generally, citizen and taxpayer standing suits are covered.

The distinction between particular and generalized grievances is not based on how many people have the grievance but whether each person would have suffered a specific or particular harm. If the government invaded everyone's home without a warrant or required everyone to obtain a license before talking to a neighbor about politics, these grievances would not be considered general because each and every person would have suffered (or would have been threatened with suffering) a harm that was particular to her or him. In contrast, generalized grievances are based on the government failing to abide by the separation of powers or the rule of law or simply failing to carry out their duties properly. Thus, individuals do not have standing to enforce such things as the separation of powers or the constitutional clauses related to the structure of government. A generalized grievance is a general harm that in a vague way hurts every citizen or taxpayer because the government fails to follow the Constitution or use tax funds properly. Arguably, these grievances are best dealt with through the ballot box and by the other branches exercising their checks and balances on one another.

In *Sierra Club v. Morton* (1972), the Supreme Court initially denied standing to the Sierra Club, who sued to stop the development of a ski resort in Mineral King Valley in the Sequoia National Park, California. The plaintiffs simply failed to allege that any of their members had ever used the valley, and thus the Court concluded that they could not show that their members would be affected by the development. The Sierra Club amended its complaint to allege that its members had used the park and that they would be adversely affected by the development. This gave the club standing.

In the case of *Lujan*, the plaintiffs sued because of a perceived gap in the regulations issued by the Secretary of the Interior on the enforcement of the

Endangered Species Act. The Act had a provision that allowed any person to sue for a court order to stop a violation of the Act. The regulation required consultation with the Secretary of the Interior on all projects within the United States and on the high seas to ensure that the project would not further endanger species on the endanger species list. However, it did not require any consultation on U.S. projects in foreign countries, and the plaintiffs sued to enjoin this alleged violation of the Act.

The plaintiffs argued that the regulations could result in harm to endangered species, which would harm their enjoyment of the wildlife in the countries that they had identified as having U.S. projects (Egypt and Sri Lanka). In this case, the plaintiffs, perhaps relying on *Sierra Club*, thought it was sufficient to allege that they had visited the countries in question. The Court was willing to accept the loss of enjoyment of wildlife as a cognizable harm; however, the plaintiffs were not able to show that they had concrete plans to visit those countries in the future. Thus, the Court concluded there was no actual or imminent harm to the plaintiffs. It was not enough that the Act granted the right to sue, the plaintiff had to demonstrate individualized harm.

Although these requirements are not overly onerous, they are somewhat petty. A person from Defenders of Wildlife may visit Egypt or Sri Lanka in the future, but the harm to any given person in this case is not the point. The harm is really to the system of government if the executive is not properly carrying out its functions according to the legislation. The harm is to endangered species, the environment, and everyone who hopes to enjoy wildlife in the future. The requirement of a particular harm to a particular person simply requires a plaintiff to jump through one more hoop.

In other types of cases, the claimant or plaintiff may not be able to jump through the next hoop. For instance, in *City of Los Angeles v. Lyons* (1983), after the police stopped Adolph Lyons for a minor traffic violation, they placed him in a chokehold until he passed out, coughed up blood, and soiled his pants. Lyons, an African American, sued for an injunction against the Los Angeles Police Department to stop them from using chokeholds in the future, unless the police are faced with the threat of death or serious bodily injury. The Court held that Lyons had standing to sue for damages that occurred from the chokehold (e.g., pain and suffering and medical costs), but the Court denied him standing to sue for an injunction to stop the police from doing it to anyone else. Lyons failed to demonstrate a substantial likelihood that he would be choked again by the L.A. Police. This was so even though he was stopped for a burned-out tail light and given a traffic citation, and even though the use of chokeholds by the police had caused over a dozen fatalities (the majority of which were black men) in Los Angeles by May 1982.

Nonetheless, the Court held there was not a substantial likelihood of Lyons being choked again, even if he was pulled over by the police. Of course, part of the ongoing harm to Lyons was the need to live in fear that the next time the police pulled him over for a routine traffic stop, they might place him in a chokehold, and he would again experience the humiliation of passing out, coughing up blood, and soiling his pants. For the Court, Lyons was no different than any other citizen who wants to stop the police from unconstitutional practices. He, like everyone else, has no standing. Perhaps if he and other young African American males in the city formed a club and provided evidence of the psychological trauma and the chances of being pulled over and put in a chokehold, then there would be standing for such a claim.

1. Citizen Suits and Taxpayer Suits

As noted above, until *Lujan* (the Endangered Species Act case), the requirement that the harm be particularized and not general was considered prudential and not constitutional. Before *Lujan*, the Court accepted that the Constitution itself did not bar standing for people alleging harm that was based on citizenship or taxpayer standing. Rather, the bar to these claims was based on a fear of a flood of claims by people with only an indefinite injury. Thus, in *Frothingham v. Mellon* (1923), the Court denied standing to a taxpayer who challenged the provision of federal tax revenues to states to reduce the mortality rates of mothers and infants. The taxpayer argued that this violated the Tenth Amendment, because issues relating to the health and welfare of mothers and children are issues reserved for the states to address. An unconstitutional use of tax revenues harms everyone that pays taxes. Presumably, one would either pay less taxes if the revenues were not used for the given purpose, or one would benefit from a better use of the taxes on something else. While it is hard to deny that some harm occurs, it is also hard to determine how much harm is caused and how much harm might be avoided for any given taxpayer if the Court intervened. Thus, for prudential reasons, the Court denied standing.

Note that the same prohibition would not exist if a particular subset of the population was being unconstitutionally taxed. This would result in a specific harm, rather than a generalized one. For instance, the Court, in *Follett v. Town of McCormick* (1944), invalidated a tax as applied to preaching, on grounds that it violated the First Amendment.

The same result as *Frothingham* occurred in the case of *Ex parte Levitt* (1937), in which a citizen sued, claiming that Justice Hugo Black's appointment to the Supreme Court was unconstitutional because Justice Black had voted to increase the salaries of the Justices on the Court when he was a Senator. The

Court held that even if this did violate Article I, Section 6, the grievance was a general one, suffered equally by all.

In *Flast v. Cohen* (1968), the Supreme Court relaxed these standing requirements and allowed taxpayer standing for plaintiffs who challenged the use of federal funds to subsidize parochial schools, in violation of the First Amendment Establishment Clause. The Court allowed the claim because (1) it was a taxpayer challenge to the taxing and spending power of Congress and not to the incidental spending that might occur with any administrative action, and (2) the claim was based on the violation of a specific provision of the Constitution and not a general grievance that Congress was exceeding its power under a separation of powers or federalism claim. The claim in *Frothingham* was distinguished from the claim in *Flast* because, while *Frothingham* invoked the Tenth Amendment, which was a general claim about the relative power of the state and federal governments, *Flast* concerned a specific limitation on the taxing and spending power of Congress under the First Amendment.

If you are having trouble understanding the principle behind the distinction between *Flast* and *Frothingham*, do not feel lost. *Flast* is probably best understood as an anomalous decision that allowed standing because of the importance of the First Amendment. Although *Flast* is still good law (*Bowen v. Kendricks*, 1988), it has been limited to cases involving the First Amendment Establishment Clause as a specific limit on the taxing and spending power of Congress. Thus, the Court declined to extend *Flast* in a case challenging the decision of the Secretary of Health, Education and Welfare to give federal property to a Christian college that trained people for "the Christian service as either ministers or laymen" (*Valley Forge Christian College v. Americans United for Separation of Church and State*, 1982). The claim in *Valley Forge* was also based on the Establishment Clause. However, since the claim was using that clause to limit the executive's conduct in the disposal of federal property and not the taxing and spending power of Congress directly, the nexus between taxpayer standing and taxing and spending did not exist. It also seemed to matter that this case was brought to challenge the conduct of the executive branch and not the power of Congress.

In *Hein v. Freedom from Religion Foundation* (2007), the Court refused to apply or extend *Flast* to cases involving spending by the executive that allegedly violated the Establishment Clause. *Hein* also settled the question as to whether the general prohibition on taxpayer standing was prudential or constitutional (based on Article III). The Court held that it was constitutional, stating: "As a general matter, the interest of a federal taxpayer in seeing that Treasury funds are spent in accordance with the Constitution does not give rise to the kind of redressable personal injury required for Article III standing."

In *Hein*, atheists challenged the executive's use of funds to support faith-based initiatives, to the exclusion of nonreligious groups. Only three Justices (Justice Samuel Alito, joined by Justices John Roberts and Anthony Kennedy), writing for the plurality (an opinion with no clear majority), believed that *Hein* could be distinguished from *Flast*. The plurality held that it would not extend *Flast* to cases involving the executive because of the separation of powers. The Court was concerned that if it allowed taxpayer standing for suits against the executive for use of general funds, then every executive action, including speeches, could be subject to suit. It concluded by citing *Valley Forge Christian Academy* and noting that "a necessary concomitant of the doctrine of *stare decisis* is that a precedent is not always expanded to the limits of its logic. That ... is the approach we take here. We do not extend *Flast*, but we also do not overrule it. We leave *Flast* as we found it."

A majority of the Court did not think that *Hein* could be distinguished from *Flast*. Nonetheless, they completely disagreed on the conclusion that should be drawn from this. Justices Antonin Scalia and Clarence Thomas, in their concurring opinion, did not think the cases could be distinguished and opined that *Flast* should be overruled. For the concurrence, there should be no standing for the psychological disapproval of the use of taxpayer funds. If *Flast* was good law, then there should be standing for all challenges to government expenditures that allegedly violate constitutional provisions limiting expenditures. In other words, the concurrence would abolish the *Flast* anomaly, since they did not believe there was a principled way to distinguish it from all the other cases, in which the Court found that there was not an injury in fact.

Justice David Souter, joined by Justices John Stevens, Ruth Bader Ginsburg, and Stephen Breyer, dissented and argued that the cases could not be distinguished. They held that the rule in *Flast* applied in this case and the applicant should be given standing. The dissent did not accept the federalism argument, as it did not see any difference between the respect owed to the executive branch and that owed to the legislative branch. Both branches were bound by the Establishment Clause, and judicial review over either raised the same federalism concerns.

Outside of the *Flast* exception, no other case has allowed standing merely on the basis of being a taxpayer or a citizen. In *Lujan*, the Court held that this bar was constitutional when it denied standing to the Defenders of Wildlife. If the requirement was merely prudential, then Congress could authorize suits by such plaintiff, as it purportedly did in the Endangered Species Act. Due to *Lujan* and *Hein*, Congress cannot authorize suits for general grievances based merely on taxpayer or citizen standing. As note, for such a grant of standing to be successful, Congress must create a right or a specific interest that individuals can sue under (*Federal Election Commission v. Adkins,* 1998; the Federal Election Campaign Act of 1971 expressly provided both standing to sue and a right to information about campaign-related activities, and thus, the Court held that the plaintiffs had standing).

ii. Causation

In most cases, causation and redressability go hand in hand. If the defendant's unlawful conduct caused the harm to the plaintiff, then in many cases, the court is in a position to redress the harm. Likewise, it is rare for the Court to be able to redress a harm if the defendant did not cause it. Nonetheless, there are cases in which the court has determined that one is satisfied, either causation or redressability, but not the other.

In *Warth v. Seldin* (1975), low-income and minority residents challenged a zoning ordinance that excluded low-income and multifamily housing, claiming that the ordinance prevented them from being able to live in the suburbs. The Court ruled that the plaintiffs lacked standing because they failed to show that the ordinance prevented a developer from building affordable housing—they failed to show that if the ordinance was removed, the housing would be built and the plaintiffs could actually afford to live there. The Court did not seem to appreciate that it would be rare for a developer to consider it worth the time and money to build low-income housing if it first had to litigate a zoning ordinance that excluded its development. It surely was a causal factor, if not the sine qua non (indispensable factor). Without a willing developer, it is unclear if it was the ordinance, the market, or simply the claimants' poor economic condition that caused their predicament. This case provides a good illustration of how intertwined causation and redressability are. Because it was unclear what the cause of the problem was, it was unclear if the requested remedy would redress the harm.

Warth was distinguished in *Northeastern Florida Chapter of Associated General Contractors of America v. Jacksonville* (1993). In this case, the contractors sued the city of Jacksonville, challenging a 10 percent set-aside of city contracts for minority businesses. Following *Warth,* the court of appeals held that the association did not have standing because it could not be shown that but for the set-aside, any of the association's members would have been successful in bidding for the given contracts. The Supreme Court distinguished *Warth,* holding that the harm caused was not the harm of an unsuccessful bid but that of the denial of an equal opportunity to compete. Therefore, the Court held that they had standing. Perhaps if low-income builders had challenged the ordinance in *Warth* on this basis (denial of an equal opportunity to build), they would have had standing.

In two separate cases involving the Internal Revenue Service (IRS) and the provision of tax-exempt status, the Court defied logic when it held that it could not be shown that either the provision or the withdrawal of tax-exempt status was the cause of the harm to the plaintiffs. In the first case, *Simon v. Kentucky Welfare Rights Organization* (1976), indigent plaintiffs claimed that they were denied medical care because the IRS changed the policy regarding tax-exempt status for hospitals. Before, a hospital had to provide all necessary health care to indigent people to obtain the tax exempt status; due to the policy change, hospitals were only required to provide emergency care to have tax-exempt status. The plaintiffs argued that this resulted in hospitals reducing services for the indigent to emergency care only. Even though the entire point of providing or withdrawing tax-exempt status was to influence the behavior of institutions, the Court concluded that it was "purely speculative" as to whether the change in policy was the cause of the denial of medical care services.

Similarly, in *Allen v. Wright* (1984), the Court considered the plaintiffs' causal claim "attenuated" and, therefore, denied them standing. The plaintiffs argued that segregated schools should not be tax-exempt; thus, the IRS's failure to deny the schools tax-exempt status diminished the ability of their children to receive a desegregated education. While Justice Sandra Day O'Connor, writing for the majority, was correct that the IRS was not the initial cause of segregation, and perhaps schools still might not desegregate if they were denied tax-exempt status, this surely has things upside down. Tax-exempt status is a benefit, and just as giving benefits to terrorists furthers the cause of terrorism, giving benefits to segregationist, private schools furthers segregation. The government was aiding and abetting segregation by providing the benefit of tax-exempt status.

In a footnote, the Court in *Allen* came close to conceding that denying tax-exempt status might have, in some way, redressed the alleged wrong to the plaintiffs. Yet because the Court found the causal claim to be attenuated, it was not enough that the IRS could solve the problem (i.e., force schools to desegregate to maintain their tax-exempt status); one would only have standing to bring a claim to force the agency to solve problems that it, in fact, caused.

In *Allen*, Justice O'Connor explicitly based her decision regarding causation in the separation of powers doctrine, noting that the Court was not the proper forum for cases involving how the executive (the IRS) should carry out its functions. It is not completely clear why the courts are not a proper forum for requiring the executive to abide by the Constitution. Perhaps the cases from *Warth* (1975) (zoning ordinance case) to *Allen* (1984) might best be explained by a shift in the Court's composition and in its attitude during the late 1970s and early 1980s. By this time, the Court had become weary from its long battle against desegregation, in which the federal courts not only told the executive when it was acting unconstitutionally but ended up taking over executive functions in running school districts. The Court of the mid- to late 1970s believed that the Court of the 1960s and early 1970s had ventured too far outside its constitutional niche, and thus, these cases might represent something of a recoil from what it considered to be a more activist Court (a Court that acted outside of its niche in trying to vindicate the Constitution). This was a more conservative Court.

Duke Power Co. v. Carolina Environmental Study Group (1978) was decided in the period between *Simon* (tax-exempt status for hospitals) and *Allen* (tax-exempt status for schools). In *Duke Power*, the environmental group challenged a federal law that limited the liability of nuclear power plants in the event of an accident. Although an accident was speculative, there were many nonspeculative harms that resulted from the construction of Duke Power Company's nuclear plants, ranging from radiation and pollution to the fear of an actual accident. In this case, there was ample evidence that Duke Power would not have started and would not finish building its plants without the protections afforded by the Act (although the evidence really pointed to smaller suppliers, architects, and engineers that needed the protection of the Act). Unlike *Simon* and *Allen*, the executive (i.e., the IRS) was not involved, and unlike *Warth* (zoning ordinance case), there was concrete evidence, in the form of testimony before the Joint Committee on Atomic Energy and Congress, that satisfied the Court that there was a substantial likelihood that, but for the Act, the nuclear reactors would not have been built.

iii. Redressability: Standing Only to Bring Claims That Will Redress Claimant's Injury, Not Another's Injury

As already noted, in most cases where the defendant is the cause of the problem, the harm can be redressed. Sometimes the two requirements of harm and redressability come apart because of the way the harm is captured or described. In the case of *Linda R.S. v. Richard D.* (1973), the Court denied standing to an unwed mother who challenged the state of Texas's policy of only enforcing child support claims against fathers of "legitimate" children. Here, similar to the injury claimed in *Jacksonville* (10 percent set-aside for minority contracts), the claim was based in equal protection. Rather than depicting the harm as the loss of an equal opportunity to receive child support due to unequal enforcement, the Court depicted the harm as simply the loss of support. It then reasoned that because the plaintiff's relief would result in the father going to jail, he would be less able to pay and thus less likely to make the support payments. Therefore, the remedy would likely not redress her harm. Similar to

the IRS cases cited, the Court appears to put on blinders to the connection between the executive's enforcement of the law and failure to enforce it. Rather
than look to the causal effect of deadbeat dads failing to provide support in
general, the Court limited its focus to the plaintiff before it.

This reasoning is in line with the reasoning in *Lyons*, already discussed (the
police brutality case). Although Lyons had standing to sue the L.A. police for
damages from the chokehold, he did not have standing to sue for an injunction. The Court reasoned that even if the injunction would help others, it
would not redress his injury because he lacked the high likelihood of being
choked in the future.

The Court came to the same conclusion in *Steel Co. v. Citizens for a Better
Environment* (1998). In *Steel Co.*, the Citizens for a Better Environment sued
under an act that required Steel Co. to file forms regarding its toxic chemical
inventory in a timely manner. Steel Co. admitted that it had failed to make
timely filings in the past, but that by the time of suit, the filings were up to
date. Although the act provided for suits and the recovery of attorney's fees, it
did not provide for damages for past violations. Rather, it provided for civil fines,
to be paid to the government. Although it appears that Congress wanted to
provide the right to sue and to receive attorney's fees as a way of enforcing the
act, the Court denied standing on the basis that there was no harm that it could
redress. It held that this was a request to vindicate "the rule of law—the "undifferentiated public interest" in faithful execution of [the act]" (*Steel Co.* quoting *Lujan*). Declaratory relief (a declaration of the existing law) was made
moot by the defendant's admission that it had violated the act in the past. This
meant that a declaration of the law would not remedy the harm. Furthermore,
attorney's fees do not remedy harms, and prospective injunctive relief (ordering the defendant to make timely filings in the future) will not remedy the past
harm. The plaintiffs did not allege future harm or the threat of future harm,
so prospective injunctive relief would only vindicate general deterrence in the
interest of the public and not any particular harm to the plaintiff.

c. The Prudential Requirements

As noted, it is necessary for a plaintiff to meet all three of the constitutional
requirements for standing, but in some cases, this will be insufficient because
prudential considerations may result in the Court denying standing. In addition
to the constitutional requirements, the prudential requirements require that the
grievance be one's own, not that of a third party, and that the grievance should
be one within the zone of interest protected by the given statute. The following
section discusses each of these general requirements and the exceptions to them.

i. Third-Party Standing

Initially, the bar against third-party standing would seem to be encompassed by the constitutional requirements that one must suffer a personal injury that is fairly traceable to the defendant's conduct and that it can be redressed by the courts. If one brings a claim on behalf of a third party, it appears to follow that it is not the claimant's injury.

However, the third-party standing issue only arises in cases where a party already has standing to bring his or her own claims and wishes to also raise the claims of others (often to bolster his or her own case). Although this is generally not allowed, there are a number of exceptions to the rule, namely:

1. when the second party cannot sue or it would be very difficult and unlikely that the second party will sue;
2. where there is a special relationship between the claimant and the third party (including associations); and
3. in First Amendment cases, where a statute is so overly broad that it chills the expression of third parties.

1. Exceptions

a. Hindrance for the Third Party to Sue

The court will allow one to raise a claim on behalf of a third party if the Court believes that the claimant will effectively represent the claim (well suited) and that it would be difficult for the third party to raise the claim (hindrance).

Thus, in *Barrows v. Jackson* (1953), the Court allowed the respondent to raise the rights of African Americans to buy and occupy property as a defense to a breach of contract claim between her and other Caucasians. The respondent breached a racially restrictive covenant when she allowed non-Caucasians to occupy her property and when she conveyed her property without including the restrictive covenant in the deed. She was not raising the claim merely as a person advocating for the rights of minorities, because she depended on their rights to defend herself from the breach of contract claim. Thus, there was little worry that she was not motivated or well suited to raise the claim. Perhaps more important, since the covenant was between white property owners, it would have been difficult (if not impossible) for African Americans to join the breach of contract claim.

Similarly, in *Eisenstadt v. Baird* (1972), the Court allowed a physician to raise the rights of his patients when he was prosecuted for violating a state statute that made it unlawful for physicians to distribute contraceptives to unmarried couples. Again, this was not a hypothetical case for the defendant. He, like Barrows, relied on the rights of third parties for his own defense. His patients were hindered from raising the claim themselves because they were not being prosecuted under the act and could not be prosecuted under the act. Similar to *Barrows*, the existing "law" restrained him, not the person who held the right to use contraceptives.

b. From Hindrance to Sue to Special Relationships: Hybrid Cases

There have been a few cases involving the exclusion of jurors on the basis of race, which straddle the hindrance to sue exception and the special relationship exception. In *Powers v. Ohio* (1991), the Court allowed standing for an African American defendant to raise the equal protection claims of jurors who were excluded from jury duty on the basis of their race. The Court articulated the test for the exception in these cases as:

1. the defendant suffered an "injury in fact";
2. he had a "close relationship" to the excluded jurors; and
3. there was some hindrance to the excluded jurors asserting their own rights.

The Court applied the same test in *Campbell v. Louisiana* (1998), when it held that a white defendant had standing to challenge the exclusion of African Americans from the grand jury in his case. The Court held that the first prong of the test was satisfied by the fact that discrimination brought the integrity and fairness of the entire process into doubt. It is hard to challenge the fact that a defendant suffers a particular harm when this is the case. Furthermore, the third prong was met. In cases involving the exclusion of jurors, jurors are unlikely to know why they have been struck from duty, and there is little incentive for any juror to bring his or her own claim. There would likely not be any money damages and few, if any, would seek the remedy of being placed back on a jury. In fact, if they were simply put back into the jury pool and selected for some other case, they would not be able to bring their own claims because there would be no injury. Thus, the third prong of the test is satisfied.

The real question, however, is how the Court reasoned that there was a special relationship between a white defendant and the excluded black jurors. Why not simply base standing on the exception of hindrance to sue? In fact, the Court satisfied the special relationship test with the "effective advocate" prong of the hindrance test. The Court held that the second prong had been satisfied by the fact that "the excluded juror and criminal defendant have a close relationship: They share a common interest in eliminating discrimination, and the criminal defendant has an incentive to serve as an effective advocate because a victory may result in overturning his conviction."

Hamdi v. Rumsfeld (2004) represents a nice example of the overlap of the hindrance and special relationship factors. In that case, a father was allowed standing to seek a writ of *habeas corpus* on behalf of his son, who was being detained in as an enemy combatant without access to an attorney. Thus, the son was hindered from bringing the claim himself, and it made sense that his father bring the claim on his behalf.

The requirement of a special or close relationship has been found in cases involving parochial schools and parents (*Pierce v. Society of Sisters*, 1925), doctors and patients, (*Singleton v. Wolf*, 1976), sellers of beer and potential (yet excluded) buyers of beer (*Craig v. Boren*, 1976), and organizations bringing claims on behalf of their members (e.g., cases such as *Sierra Club, Defenders of Wildlife*, and *Northeastern Florida Contractors*). This exception is based not merely on the closeness of the relationship but also on the relevance of the relationship to the suit. Thus, a mother was denied standing to challenge the death penalty sentence of her son in *Gilmore v. Utah* (1976). The son could have challenged the sentence if he had wanted (as distinguished from *Hamdi*, who was denied an attorney), and the mother, although having a special relationship with her son, had no real interest in the case, except for her moral and emotional interest in seeing her son live and justice being done. Similarly, in an even more controversial case, the Court held that a father lacked standing to bring a claim on behalf of his daughter to challenge the use of the word *God* in the Pledge of Allegiance (*Elk Grove Unified School District v. Newdow*, 2004). Generally, parents have standing to sue on behalf of their minor children under the doctrine of "best friend." However, the fact that the father did not have custody or the right to sue under California law as his daughter's "best friend" led the Court to decide that it would not be prudent to grant him standing. Also, there may have been some concern that the father was bringing the claim in his own interest, which did not necessarily serve his daughter's interest.

In the other cases, the interests of the claimant and the third party went hand in hand. Just as in the hybrid cases, many of these cases also satisfy the twin requirements under the hindrance exception—namely, there is some hindrance to the primary party bringing the claim, and the Court believes that the claimant is well suited to bring the claim. Notice that *Gilmore* (death penalty case) did not satisfy this first requirement and it was questionable whether *Newdow* (Pledge of Allegiance case) satisfied the second requirement.

In *Society of Sisters*, the legislation required that children attend public school. Although it is unclear if there was, in fact, a hindrance to parents bringing a claim, there was little question that the legislation drastically affected the private religious school. Even though the parents had the right to challenge the legislation, the school had the most to lose from the law. Given that the fate of the right and the school were inextricably entwined, the Court granted the school standing to raise the claim. This is analogous to the criminal defendant raising the rights of jurors (*Powers v. Ohio*, 1991), or the civil defendant raising the rights of African American to rent *Barrows v. Jackson* (1953).

In the case of *Singleton*, the Court allowed doctors to raise the rights of female patients to challenge the denial of Medicaid benefits for abortion. The effect of the denial harmed both the doctors, because they would not be paid by Medicaid for those services, and the female patients, who might not be able to afford to pay for the procedures themselves. While the special relationship between a doctor and a patient was important, the fact that the law impacted both the doctor and the patient in the same way made the doctor well suited to raise the claim. The Court also noted that the negative publicity and stigma surrounding the issue of abortion was a hindrance to women pursuing the claims themselves.

In *Craig v. Boren*, similar interests of the claimant and the third party in the outcome of the case was certainly the Court's primary justification for finding a special relationship between a bartender and his customers between the ages of eighteen and twenty-one in Oklahoma. Unless the Court omitted certain facts, the relationship between a bartender and every male customer in this age group is not the same as that between a school and parents or doctors and patients. What made their relationship close was that the bartender wanted to sell them beer, the males in this age group wanted to buy it, and the Oklahoma law changing the drinking age from eighteen to twenty-one would end that relationship.

As mentioned, organizations can bring claims on behalf of their members without instituting a class action if they satisfy the requirements laid out in *Hunt v. Washington Apple Advertising Commission* (1977). *Hunt* set out a three-part test for standing in these instances:

1. the members need to otherwise have standing to raise the claims in their own right;
2. the organization's claims must be germane to the organization's purpose; and
3. participation by the organization's members themselves is not required.

The first prong is the Article III requirement of a particular injury, and the other two prongs are prudential. Together, they ensure that organizations only bring claims where the interests of the organization and its members fairly coincide and the proceedings will not be prejudiced by the member's lack of direct participation. If the claims are limited to the organization's purpose, then there is little risk their interests will not coincide. These requirements are either explicitly or implicitly satisfied in the other third-party standing cases already mentioned, wherein the interests coincide and the lack of participation by the third parties do not jeopardize the proceedings.

Because the last two requirements are prudential, not constitutional, the Court in *United Food and Commercial Workers v. Brown Group* (1996) held that Congress could grant unions the right to sue on behalf of their members, even if the third requirement was not otherwise satisfied.

c. Substantial Overbreadth in Cases Involving Freedom of Expression

In much the same way that the Court carved out an exception for taxpayer standing in cases involving the First Amendment Establishment Clause (*Flast v. Cohen*, 1968), the Court has carved out an exception to the bar on third-party standing. This exception applies to cases where legislation substantially restricts protected expression under the First Amendment Freedom of Speech Clause. Overbreadth, which has been likened to using a sledgehammer to kill a fly, will be addressed in detail in Chapter 9, dealing with the First Amendment. Overbreadth occurs when legislation, designed to take care of a particular problem, includes provisions that not only address this problem but also capture protected expression. The problem of overbreadth is not limited to the First Amendment, as overly broad statutes can impact any of a number of rights. Nonetheless, the Court has only allowed for the exception to third-party standing based on overbreadth in cases involving freedom of expression. This may reflect something of a hierarchy of rights (valuing this freedom over others), but it also reflects the idea that the freedom of expression is vulnerable to the chilling effects of overly broad statutes.

For example, a piece of legislation designed to target incitement to cause imminent harm may make it a crime to say anything that might anger another or hurt another's feelings. This law may capture the person who is inciting imminent violence, but it will also capture many people who are not. Further, a person may not engage in otherwise protected speech because of fear of prosecution for hurting another's feelings. One may take note at the outset that the exception does not apply to commercial speech (i.e., advertising), because the Court believes that the benefits caused by the economic incentives to advertise counterbalance any negative effects that an overly broad statute might have (*Village of Hoffman Estates v. Flipside*, 1982). Further, advertisers have every incentive to litigate on their own.

The way the doctrine works is that if a statute is substantially overbroad in its regulation of expression, a claimant who has satisfied the other constitutional requirements for standing may raise the claims of third parties who are or may be engaged in expression that is constitutionally protected but who may be affected by the overly broad statute. If the law is substantially overbroad, then the claimant may raise these claims, even if the statute would rightly regulate her or his own expression. Thus, a person may challenge the statute in the example by raising the First Amendment rights of others, even she or he was engaged in conduct that was not protected by the First Amendment (e.g., if he or she was prosecuted for inciting others to commit imminent physical harm to people of a certain race under conditions that made it likely that the harm would occur). The defendant in such a case would not be engaging in constitutionally protected speech but would be able to bring what is called a facial challenge to the statute, which, if successful, would result in the entire statute being struck down.

Thus, in *Schad v. Borough of Mount Ephraim* (1981), the owner of an adult establishment that had live nude dancing was able to challenge a city ordinance that banned all live entertainment (and thus banned countless forms of protected expression, such as theater, concerts, and art), even though it was questionable as to whether the dancing at his establishment would be protected.

The Court does not take this lightly, and thus, it requires that the statute be substantially overbroad (versus some overbreadth) and not capable of an interpretation that makes it compatible with the Constitution. In fact, if the Court can sever the offending part of the statute, so that the remainder is constitutional, it will do so, rather than strike the entire provision.

These requirements ensure both that the Court is using the exception only in cases where there is a threat of serious harm to First Amendment rights and when the case is relatively easy. The more overbreadth, the less it matters whether the third parties could or would raise the claims themselves. The more overbreadth, the easier it is for the Court to simply strike down the entire statute, not just the unconstitutional provision.

ii. Zone of Interest Requirement

The zone of interest requirement is perhaps just another way of saying that claimants need to champion their own rights and are barred from raising the rights of others. The requirement arises in statutory and administrative law cases and simply mandates that a claimant be within the zone of interest that the statute was designed to protect. If a claimant is not within the zone of interest, then she or he would be attempting to bring a claim that should be brought by someone within the zone.

In *Clarke v. Securities Industries Association* (1987), the Court stated that the test "was not meant to be especially demanding: in particular, there need be no indication of congressional purpose to benefit the would-be plaintiff." Thus, in *National Credit Union Administration v. First National Bank & Trust Co.* (1998), the Court allowed banks to challenge federal regulations made by the National Credit Union Administration, pursuant to the Administration's interpretation of the Federal Credit Union Act. The banks argued that the Administration's regulations allowed for the creation of credit unions, in violation of the restrictions in the Act. The Administration's regulations would result in more competition for the traditional banks. Even though there was no showing that Congress intended to benefit the banks, and it was questionable whether the banks were really within the zone of interest that Congress wished to protect with the Act, this was not the test. Rather, the Court's job in these cases was to "discern the interests 'arguably ... to be protected' by the statutory provision and inquire whether the plaintiff's interests affected by the agency action in question are among them."

When deciding *National Credit Union*, Justice Thomas distinguished the case of *Air Courier Conference v. Postal Workers* (1991). In *Postal Workers*, the postal workers union was denied standing to challenge the U.S. Postal Service's decision to suspend a monopoly over "extremely urgent" letters under the Postal Express Statutes. The Court in *Postal Workers* appeared to rest its decision on the argument that the postal workers were not within the zone of interest of the Act because there was nothing in the statutes or legislative history indicating that the Act was meant to benefit the workers. Justice Thomas distinguished the cases by stating: "Unlike the plaintiffs there who were denied standing, respondents here [*in National Credit Union*] have 'competitive and direct injury,' as well as an interest 'arguably ... to be protected' by the statute in question." One could say the same of the postal workers. Thus, it appears that the Court has more sympathy for the bank's potential loss of business than the postal workers' loss of jobs.

3. Ripeness

Just as an apple is not ready to eat until it is ripe, a case is not ready for the courts until it has ripened into a full-blown controversy.

There is considerable overlap between the notion of ripeness and standing (already addressed in detail). A person generally does not have standing unless he or she has suffered a harm. This can be either because there is no standing or because the issue is not ripe. If the harm is uncertain or speculative (i.e., it has not occurred yet, and it is uncertain if it will occur), then this is a ripeness issue. If and when the harm does occur to the plaintiff, she or he will have standing. Once the apple is ripe, she or he can eat it. In other cases, the harm has already occurred, but it was not and will not be a harm to the plaintiff.

This is the standing issue. The issue is already ripe, but it is not ripe and never will be ripe for this plaintiff. It is not her or his apple to eat.

The Court does not wish to entertain unripe issues for many of the same reasons that it does not give advisory opinions. If the case is not ripe now, it may never be ripe. If there is a chance that a law could be enforced in a constitutional way or not enforced at all, then the Court may be wasting its time or rendering something close to an advisory opinion. If there has been no purported unconstitutional application of the law to particular facts, then it is speculative both as to how and to what extent there would be an infringement of the Constitution.

One does not always need to wait until harm has occurred for a case to be ripe. The chilling effect on constitutional rights is itself a harm, if there is a real threat of unconstitutional enforcement. Nonetheless, the harm cannot be speculative; there must be a significant threat of imminent harm.

As one can imagine, to determine what is certain versus what is too speculative requires a judgment call, and the Court's decisions on this point have not been entirely consistent. The Court not only considers the likelihood of harm, but as may be expected, it also considers how serious the harm may be, if and when it occurs.

The Court will usually not require that one violate a criminal statute to challenge it, because the harm of a criminal sanction is severe, and there is a presumption that the criminal law will be enforced. If compliance with the law or the avoidance of a sanction also has costs, then it causes harm, and the argument for ripeness is increased (e.g., if one needs to abstain from constitutionally protective activity or if compliance requires expenditures then both of these are harms). These cases are examples of being caught between the proverbial rock and a hard place.

For example, in *Steffel v. Thompson* (1974), when a plaintiff sued for a declaratory judgment that he had the right to distribute leaflets (handbills) in protest of the Vietnam War in a shopping mall, the Court determined that the case was ripe, even though he had never been arrested for passing out handbills. No doubt, it helped his case that he had narrowly avoided arrest previously, whereas his companions had not, thereby leaving little room for speculating that the law would be enforced. The Court reasoned that there was substantial hardship on the plaintiff, since his choice was either to give up what he believed to be his right to freedom of expression or to risk criminal sanctions. Similar results occurred in *United States Civil Service Commission v. National Association of Letter Carriers, AFL-CIO* (1973), when civil servants wishing to engage in specific political activities challenged the Hatch Act of 1940, which prevents federal employees from taking "an active part in political management or in political campaigns." Although no action had been taken against the employees, they were caught between either losing their jobs or forgoing what they believed was constitutionally protected conduct. Similarly, in *Abbott Laboratories v. Gardner* (1967), the U.S. Food and Drug Administration issued a regulation that required drug companies to list the generic name for the drug on all of their labels, under threat of both civil and criminal sanctions. The Court found the case to be ripe, even though the drug companies had not been prosecuted under the regulations. Like the Vietnam War protestors in *Steffel* and the federal employees in *Civil Service Commission*, the drug companies were caught between the choice of risking prosecution or incurring considerable expense to relabel all their products and change their literature.

One case that is often used as the counterexample is *International Longshoremen's and Warehousemen's Union Local 37 v. Boyd* (1954). As the law stood at the time, resident aliens who left the country were often not allowed to return to the United States. There was great demand for workers in Alaska, and during the summer, a number of alien residents wished to go to Alaska and come back to the continental United States. The problem was that Alaska was not yet a state, so it was unclear whether the immigration services would count this as remaining within the United States. Not wishing to jeopardize their resident status, they sought a court order to prevent immigration officials from denying them entry. Even though the hardship of choosing between employment and possible denial of reentry into the country is arguably as bad as or worse than a misdemeanor trespass charge in *Steffel* or relabeling medicines in *Abbott*, the Court considered the case to be merely hypothetical. However, because *Boyd* was decided before *Steffel* and *Abbott*, it is unclear if the Court would rule the same way today.

It is important to note that the mere existence of criminal statutes or other regulations that one believes to be unconstitutional is not sufficient. If the statute has remained on the books, yet is not enforced for a considerable period of time, it is truly speculative that there will be an actual case or controversy. Thus, in *Poe v. Ullman* (1961) the Court would not rule on whether an 1879 Connecticut law prohibiting the use of contraceptives was unconstitutional because the law had never been enforced. However, as the dissent pointed out, the plaintiffs had not been able to secure much-needed medical advice because they feared that the law might be enforced. Further, even if the law is likely to be enforced, this is not enough if the plaintiffs cannot convince the Court that they actually intend to violate the law or regulation. If the plaintiffs are not going to violate the given law or regulation, then there is no controversy (i.e., they will not be between a rock and a hard place). Thus, an earlier challenge to the Hatch Act of 1940, *United Public Workers v. Mitchell* (1947), failed because the Court could only speculate about whether the plaintiffs were going to engage in the prohibited political activities, and if so, what those activities might be.

This need for factual specificity leads to the other requirement for a case to be ripe. As addressed in the section on advisory opinions, an undeveloped factual record makes it difficult for the Court to determine whether there will be a constitutional violation and what the exact parameters or the extent of the violation might be. Facts make a difference. For instance, the Court will likely treat a constitutional challenge to the Hatch Act of 1940 differently if it involves employees wishing to arrive at work naked as part of their political expression or to participate in and advocate for sit-ins and hunger strikes at their place of work, than if the case involves employees who wish to volunteer after work in a get-out-the-vote campaign. Without the facts, it is difficult to know how to balance the state's interests with the rights and interests of the individual.

4. Mootness

Just as a case may not be ripe for adjudication, a case can also be moot. It is not so much that the apple is rotten, but rather, it has been eaten; there is no longer a case or controversy. The case may become moot either because of a change in the law or a change in the factual circumstances. The parties might decide to settle, or an offending party might stop violating the law. The parties might even pass away or outlive the reach of the law or conduct (e.g., might grow up and no longer be covered by the statute, regulation, or conduct).

If for any of these reasons the case becomes moot before the Court has ruled on the matter (and one of the following exceptions does not apply), the Court will generally vacate the circuit court judgment and remand to the district court to dismiss the complaint. If a state court decided the case first, then the Supreme Court does not have authority to order it to vacate its order or dismiss the complaint.

Exceptions to the rule of mootness include:

1   voluntary cessation — when a party stops the purported unconstitutional conduct but may start again;
2   matters capable of repetition, yet evading review — when a matter could cycle through being a moot and a live controversy so that review would be continually avoided; and
3   collateral consequences — when there are collateral matters that remain alive after the main legal question is moot.

a. Voluntary Cessation

Mootness will not attach merely because someone voluntarily stops unconstitutional conduct, if there is a chance that he or she will start the conduct again once the case is dismissed. Thus, the Court in *Friends of the Earth v. Laidlaw Environmental Services, Inc.* (2000) found that the case was not moot. The alleged polluter stopped polluting but could start polluting again at any time. In these cases, there is a heavy burden on the defendant to convince the Court that it will not resume its prior unconstitutional conduct.

The same heavy burden does not necessarily apply to the legislature when it acts to change the law after a suit is brought. Nonetheless, if the Court is not convinced that the legislature has changed its ways, and it fears that the legislature will reenact the legislation after the case is dismissed, then the Court will not declare the case moot (*City of Mesquite v. Aladdin's Castle Inc.*, 1982).

b. Matters Capable of Repetition Yet Evading Review Because They Repeatedly Become Moot

A classic example of matters capable of repetition yet evading review is illustrated by *Roe v. Wade* (1973). By the time a pregnant woman can have her case heard, it will often be the case that she will no longer be pregnant, either because she decided to have the child, miscarried, or opted for an abortion. In the case of *Roe*, the plaintiff had carried the child to term. It certainly would be cruel to not hear such a case, only to have the situation repeat itself. Another category is election cases, which are good examples, because the election will often be over before the case gets through the court system. Nonetheless, if the same issue is likely to arise in the next election, then the court will hear the case and not consider it moot (*Moore v. Ogilvie*, 1969). A third category of cases that often fit under this exception are court-ordered prior restraints on the media for a limited duration (e.g., gag orders or restraints on speech before one speaks). If a court places a prior restraint in the form of a gag order on the media with regard to a trial or a hearing, the restraint often expires or is lifted before the challenge to the restraint can be decided. This type of wrong is repeatable but would often evade review (e.g., *Nebraska Press Association v. Stuart*, 1976, (limited the pretrial reporting of a murder case; *Globe Newspaper Co. v. Superior Court*, 1982, excluded the press from a trial involving a rape victim who was a minor).

It is not enough that the alleged unconstitutional conduct be repeatable; it must be repeatable to the given plaintiff or at least to the class of plaintiffs in a class action suit. In *De Funis v. Odegaard* (1974), De Funis claimed that the University of Washington Law School's admission policy violated the Equal Protection Clause. The Court considered his claim moot, even though the university continued the policy with other applicants. De Funis was already admitted to the school, and the school indicated that they would still allow him to graduate, even if he lost his suit. The fact that the university did not change its ways was irrelevant, because whatever its course, it would not harm De

Funis again. Thus, if one grows up and out from beneath a piece of legislation, or if one graduates out from under certain restrictions on one's right, then the issue is moot. If De Funis wanted to avoid this form of mootness, he would have needed to form a class. If the issue remained live or was capable of repetition for at least some members of the class, then the case would not be moot.

c. Collateral Consequences

The collateral damage done by a wrongful conviction remains even after one has served his or her time. There are numerous legal consequences (not to mention social consequences) that result from a conviction. Thus, a criminal case is not moot simply because one is released from prison (*Sibron v. New York,* 1968). The same is true of a determination that one is insane. In other cases, one must demonstrate to the court that there is still a harm that remains that the court can remedy. For instance, in *Powell v. McCormack* (1969), Representative Adam Clayton Powell Jr., who was duly elected to Congress, was denied his seat by the House because of an allegation of the misuse of travel funds. Between this and the time his case reached the Supreme Court, he was reelected to Congress and, this time, was allowed to take his seat. Although the primary issue was moot, the case was deemed not to be moot because of the collateral consequences, namely, he had been denied pay while not seated. Thus, his claim for back pay kept the case alive.

5. *Political Questions*

It is not entirely clear whether the political question doctrine is a constitutional or a prudential justiciability doctrine. To the extent that it is constitutional, it is based more on the separation of powers than on the Article III case or controversy requirement. The doctrine is premised on the idea that some matters are political and not legal and are thereby best left to the political branches (and not the judiciary) for resolutions.

The political question doctrine was addressed in the beginning of this chapter, in *Marbury v. Madison.* The Court in *Marbury* held that *judicial review of executive conduct* is appropriate when the conduct in question is *ministerial* (i.e., involves nondiscretionary, nonpolitical functions), but the Court would not have the power to review acts that were political or about setting policy, as these are at the discretion of the executive (e.g., how to prosecute a war). While the executive may have discretion as to whom it chooses for the commission, it did not have discretion as to whether to deliver the commission because this was ministerial. Thus, the Court held that the judiciary could issue writs of *mandamus* against executive officials when they are to carry out clear nondiscretionary duties, like delivering the signed and sealed commissions (of course, the Court held that it did not have jurisdiction to hear the case on other grounds). *Marbury* also stood for the proposition that cases involving the infringement of a right required a remedy and were not political questions. Unfortunately, at least for some, this aspect of the doctrine has not survived, and the court may decline to hear a case even when a right has been violated or is under threat.

Under the modern doctrine, there are three different standards or paths that may lead a Court to the conclusion that the issue is a political question. These standards were articulated in *Baker v. Carr* (1962), and they appear to range from principled legal standards to political policy standards. In other words, some of the standards are based on the law or a principled distinction between what is legal and what is political, and some of them are based on prudential political considerations, such as the court's struggle with the possibility of causing tension with or embarrassment to the other branches (in other words, the worry that a legal decision will cause political problems).

First, the Court will consider an issue political and not legal if there is "a textually demonstrable constitutional commitment of the issue to a coordinate political department." In other words, if the text of the Constitution indicates that either the legislative or executive branch is responsible for the issue, then it is a political question and not for the Court to decide. Given that this test or standard is based on the constitutional text, it is likely fair to say that it is constitutional. Second, even if there is no "textual commitment" of the issue to the political branches, the Court will find an issue political if there is "a lack of judicially discoverable and manageable standards for resolving it." This test is based on a principled distinction between legal issues, for which the court can apply legal standards, and political or policy issues that the law cannot resolve but need a political resolution. This standard is also arguably constitutional, as it is based in the idea that some matters are legal "cases and controversies" under Article III and some are simply political controversies. Third, the court will consider an issue political based on

> the impossibility of a court undertaking independent resolution without expressing lack of respect due coordinate branches of government or an unusual need for unquestioning adherence to a political decision already made; or the potentiality of embarrassment from multifarious pronouncements by various departments on one question.

Thus, even if there is nothing in the text of the Constitution or in the nature of the issue that makes it inherently political, the Court may still decline to hear the case for these other policy reasons, namely, lack of respect, need for unquestioning adherence, or embarrassment. Sometimes this last set of standards is broken down into the three separate factors, but they all relate to the political thicket that may result from a conflict between the Court and one or more branches of government. These reasons sound more like the Court failing to carry out its duties out of fear, rather than principle, and as one might imagine, they are exceptionally malleable. This is not to say that the other standards provide clear litmus tests, given that the text of the Constitution is often open to multiple interpretations, and what may count as a "judicially discoverable and manageable standard" depends both on the will to find or create such standards and on deeper values about how rule-like the law needs to be. The result is an area of the law that often appears to lack consistency and coherence.

a. The Easy Case of Impeachment Procedures and Cases under the Origination Clause

In *Nixon v. United States* (1993), former Judge Walter Nixon challenged the process by which the Senate chose to impeach him. He had been impeached because he was convicted of lying before a grand jury during an investigation into his acceptance of donations in exchange for asking a district attorney to end a prosecution. Rather than have the full process in front of the entire Senate, the main hearing was before a Senate committee that reported to the full Senate. Unfortunately for Nixon, the Constitution provided a demonstrable textual commitment to a separate political department. Article I, Section 3, Clause 6 provides that the Senate has the "sole Power to try all Impeachments." Thus, the Court declined to hear the case, as the decision regarding the process for impeachment was committed to the Senate.

Another, rather easy case arose in the context of Article I, Section 7, Clause 1, which requires that bills raising revenues "shall originate" in the House of Representatives. In *United States v. Munoz-Flores* (1990), defendants argued that a law requiring them to pay a special assessment based on their conviction was unconstitutional because it did not originate in the House but in the Senate. Unlike in *Nixon*, there was no provision relegating this to the political branches, and there was no problem of discerning a judicially manageable standard. The questions as to whether the law raised revenues and which house it originated in was not a political question. Finally, the invalidation of a law on this ground is no more an affront to Congress than the invalidation of any other law on constitutional grounds.

b. Representation: Guarantee of a Republican Form of Government versus Equal Protection

A more difficult area for consideration involves political representation and clauses in the Constitution that guarantee a Republican form of government and equal protection. Is the "guarantee" of a "Republican form of government" for every state in the Union in Article IV, Section 4 something that the Court can decide or is it a political question? The Section reads:

> The United States shall guarantee to every State in this Union a Republican Form of Government, and shall protect each of them against Invasion; and on Application of the Legislature, or of the Executive (when the Legislature cannot be convened) against domestic Violence.

As late as 1841, Rhode Island did not have a "modern" constitution and was operating under a British royal charter since 1663. The charter was undemocratic by anyone's standards, and the apportionment of districts for representatives was particularly problematic because it resulted in rural populations being grossly overrepresented and urban populations being underrepresented. A dissident group of citizens protested and held a popular convention to draft a new constitution and elect a governor. The process was declared illegal by the existing charter government, but the election went through and a fleeting government was elected. The old charter government declared martial law, and Sheriff Luther Borden and the military broke into one of the organizers' homes to gain evidence about the organizers of the election. Martin Luther, whose house was invaded, sued for trespass; Borden defended the search and seizure as valid under the martial law.

To decide if this was an unlawful trespass or a lawful search and seizure, the Court, in *Luther v. Borden* (1849), was called on to decide which was the lawful "republican form of government" (the charter government or the newly elected government). The Court declined, holding that this was a political issue. Although Article IV, Section 4 does not explicitly state that it is the role of Congress to give effect to this "guarantee," the Court reasoned that since Section 3 placed the power of recognizing new states in the hands of Congress, it was also for Congress to affect the guarantee.

The Court reasoned that because it had the awesome power of reviewing and ensuring that states, as well and the other branches of the federal government, did not violate the separation of powers by going beyond the limits set by the Constitution, then the Court

> should be the last to overstep the boundaries which limit its own jurisdiction. And while it should always be ready to meet any question

confided to it by the Constitution, it is equally its duty not to pass beyond its appropriate sphere of action, and to take care not to involve itself in discussions which properly belong to other forums.

Although the case squarely fits into *Carr*'s first category, there are also supporting justifications for the outcome based on the other standards or tests. The Court is probably ill equipped to determine what constitutes "a republican form of government" and even less equipped to make decisions on such matters in the heat of political turmoil. Throughout the judgment, the Court is cognizant of the political mess it would be entering if it passed judgment on the matter. The executive had already taken some action, arguably under Article IV, Section 4 ("and on application ... of the Executive (when the Legislature cannot be convened)"). Thus, it would be dangerous for the Court to intervene.

i. Fourteenth Amendment Apportionment and Gerrymandering

Luther remains good law today when it comes to the Guarantee Clause and voter apportionment; however, challenges to apportionment that are based on the Fourteenth Amendment, Equal Protection Clause are a different story. *Baker v. Carr*, in fact, was the groundbreaking decision that held that equal protection claims challenging a given district or districts as being malapportioned are justiciable. The Court in *Baker* held that unlike under the Guarantee Clause, equal protection claims have "well-developed" standards. One may challenge this view, but it is hard to argue against the well-settled tradition of the Court hearing Fourteenth Amendment claims, and there is virtually no support for the view that the constitutional text has left these claims to the political branches of government.

It is also important to note that in these cases, like the cases of political gerrymandering discussed next, if the Court does not step in to correct these failures in the democratic process, it is unlikely that anyone will. Malapportionment and gerrymandering result in the entrenchment of one party over the other (Democrats or Republicans), and thus, it is highly unlikely that an entrenched political party would change the voting districts to give the other party a more fair chance in the next election.

ii. Political Gerrymandering

Although cases challenging gerrymandering districts based on race are justiciable, it is questionable whether challenges to political gerrymandering are justiciable. The Court has held that they are justiciable in theory under *Davis v. Bandemer* (1986). However, in the recent case of *Vieth v. Jubelirer* (2004), the

Court dismissed a claim that political gerrymandering in Pennsylvania violated the Fourteenth Amendment. While five Justices held that there was no judicially manageable standard to decide the case, Justice Kennedy, who was the swing vote for the majority, held out the possibility of a judicially manageable standard in the future. Three Justices from the majority joined Justice Scalia in the view that political gerrymandering cases are never justiciable because they fail the second test under *Baker*, namely, that there was no judicially manageable standard for deciding political gerrymandering cases. Although equal protection claims have justiciable standards when it comes to racial inequality, it is admittedly more difficult to parse out what is and what is not a proper standard for reviewing the creation of districts, based in part on the desire to capture more votes for one or another party. These Justices did not believe that there was a standard that could parse out legitimate political considerations from illegitimate considerations.

Members of the dissent could not rally the court behind a single judicially manageable standard, but this was not due to a lack of having standards to propose. For instance, according to Justice Stevens:

> The racial gerrymandering cases … supply a judicially manageable standard for determining when partisanship, like race, has played too great of a role in the districting process. Just as race can be a factor in, but cannot dictate the outcome of, the districting process, so too can partisanship be a permissible consideration in drawing district lines, so long as it does not predominate.

He would simply ask "whether the legislature allowed partisan considerations to dominate and control the lines drawn, forsaking all neutral principles."

It is therefore fair to ask whether there are really no judicially discoverable or manageable standards or whether the Court simply cannot agree on what those standards should be.

c. Foreign Affairs

Although not every area of foreign affairs is deemed a political question, the Court is generally quite hesitant to interfere with Congress or the executive in his (perhaps someday her) decisions in the arena of foreign affairs. Here, the Court is particularly sensitive to the fact that it is important that the country speak with one voice. Thus, questions regarding war, the recognition of foreign governments and diplomats, and treaties are often treated as nonjusticiable political questions.

For instance, in *Goldwater v. Carter* (1979), the Court declined Senator Barry Goldwater's invitation to decide if President Jimmy Carter's unilateral termination of a treaty with Taiwan was constitutional. The Court refused to consider Goldwater's argument that since the Constitution requires Congress to be involved in ratifying treaties, Congress also should be involved in terminating them. While Justice William Rehnquist held that this was a political question to be worked out between Congress and the executive, Justice Lewis Powell, in a concurring opinion, argued that the case simply was not ripe, because Congress had not voted on a resolution condemning the President's actions. Justice Rehnquist's strongest point was that given there was no clear textual answer to the question regarding the President's authority to terminate treaties, and since "different termination procedures may be appropriate for different treaties," there was no judicially manageable standard to resolve the issue. Although the Constitution is silent on the question of termination, Justice William Brennan, in his dissent, believed that the normal tools of constitutional interpretation could be used to decide the issue.

d. Congressional Self-Regulation

In *Powell v. McCormack* (1969), Representative Powell, who was duly elected to Congress, was denied his seat by the House because of an allegation of the misuse of travel funds. Between this time and the time his case had reached the Supreme Court, he was reelected to Congress and, this time, was allowed to take his seat. The case was deemed not to be moot because of the collateral consequences (he was suing for back pay), but the issue remained as to whether this was a political question to be decided by the House of Representative, not the Court.

The Court held that Article I, Section 5 did not give the House the authority to exclude someone who met all of the requirements under the Constitution and was duly elected. It did have authority to expel a member, but it would require a two-thirds vote. Further, the House's authority to "Judge the Qualification of its Members" under Article I, Section 5 was limited to the requirements listed there, including age, citizenship, and residence. Thus, if the case involved the House's judgment as to the satisfaction of one of these listed requirements, it would have been a nonjusticiable political question.

e. Constitutional Amendments

The issue of constitutional amendments is one in which the seemingly clear legal rules pull in one direction when policy pulls in the other. For the most part, Article V, which sets out the procedures for amending the Constitution, provides the basis for judicially manageable standards. Nonetheless, there may be something unsettling about the Court reviewing amendments, given that they are the one way in which judicial decisions can be overturned or trumped by Congress. Given the rarity of successful amendments, this concern seldom arises. Perhaps the real reason that some commentators are uneasy about judicial review in this area is because the Fourteenth Amendment was passed with such flagrant disregard for "the law" on the amending process. Southern states were denied entry back into the Union until they ratified it, and Ohio and New Jersey's ratifications were counted even though they rescinded them. Congress dealt with these issues, and the Court stayed out.

Coleman v. Miller (1939) provides a nice example of a case that includes both justiciable and nonjusticiable issues concerning the amendment process. *Coleman* was brought by a group of Kansas senators who were challenging the process by which their state purportedly ratified the Child Labor Amendment to the state constitution. After previously voting down the Amendment, a second vote took place, and the Kansas Senate was equally split. The Lieutenant Governor cast the deciding vote in favor of the Amendment. This occurred thirteen years after the Amendment had been proposed.

The petitioners challenged the Amendment on grounds that ranged from arguably legal to what the Court considered political. Those grounds included the following claims:

1. the Lieutenant Governor was not part of the legislature, could not cast the deciding vote, and thus, the Amendment was not passed;
2. the rejection of the Amendment could not be changed and thus could not be put to a second vote; and
3. the Amendment was no longer viable, as too much time had passed since ratification.

The Court held that the senators had standing to sue, but it was equally divided as to whether it was a political question to determine whether the Lieutenant Governor could cast the deciding vote. Turning to the second argument, the Court noted that the history of the ratification of the Fourteenth Amendment included the same issue regarding ratifications and rejections and that the issue had been addressed by Congress. Further, the fact that Congress addressed the issue was accepted by history. The Fourteenth Amendment case was considerably more problematic than the current case, given that Congress counted ratifications that had been rescinded, whereas in this case, a rejection was put to a new vote and was ratified. Nonetheless, the Court stated:

> We think that in accordance with this historic precedent the question of the efficacy of ratifications by state legislatures, in the light of previous rejection or attempted withdrawal, should be regarded as a po-

litical question pertaining to the political departments, with the ultimate authority in the Congress in the exercise of its control over the promulgation of the adoption of the amendment. (*Coleman*)

As to the third issue, the Court noted that it had previously held that Congress had the power to place time limitations on ratification. In the absence of such a limitation, the question as to whether an amendment was still viable was not one for the Court. The question of viability, given shifting political, economic, and social changes, was a political question for Congress. It is not for the Court to address if and when there has been sufficient ratifications for amendment. Given the longevity of most provisions of the Constitution, it would in fact be problematic for the Court to take it on itself to make such a determination, particularly when it had already decided that the power was within Congress's hands.

V. The Eleventh Amendment: State Immunity from Suit

The Eleventh Amendment provides that: "The Judicial power of the United States shall not be construed to extend to any suit in law or equity, commenced or prosecuted against one of the United States by Citizens of another State, or by Citizens or Subjects of any Foreign State."

Justice Brennan proposed one plausible, yet narrow reading of the Amendment in his dissenting opinion in *Atascadero State Hospital v. Scanlon* (1985). Justice Brennan held the view that it limits federal jurisdiction only in *diversity suits*, that is, suits brought against a state by "Citizens of another State, or Citizens or Subjects of any Foreign State" when there is no separate federal subject matter jurisdiction (no separate federal law questions). With this reading, cases that involve *federal questions*, even those brought by diverse citizens or subjects, would still fall under the "Judicial power of the United States" (federal court jurisdiction).

This reading has not prevailed. Over time, the Court has both expanded and contracted the meaning of the Amendment. The Eleventh Amendment is also limited by the Thirteenth, Fourteenth, and Fifteenth Amendments to the Constitution. With these changes in mind, the text could be read to provide:

> The judicial power of the United States shall not be construed to extend to any suit in law or equity [or admiralty], commenced or prosecuted against one of the United States [unless the state consents/waives] by [its own Citizens], Citizens of another State, or by Citizens or Sub-

jects of any Foreign State. [But it may extend to suits against counties and municipalities as well as to state officials (unless the state official is being sued in her or his official capacity for money damages to be taken from the state treasury) and to suits authorized by Congress under Section 2 of the Thirteenth, Section 5 of the Fourteenth, or Section 2 of the Fifteenth Amendments.]

If the amended reading is unclear, it means the following.

1. Not only is the judicial power of the United States limited by the Eleventh Amendment, but the judicial power of individual states is also limited, and thus, under *Alden v. Maine* (1999), Congress cannot authorize suits against states within their own courts.
2. Nonetheless, states can waive their own immunity to this power.
3. The Eleventh Amendment applies to not only cases of law and equity but also admiralty (with exceptions) (*Ex parte New York,* 1921).
4. The Amendment bars suits not only by citizens of other states but also by citizens of the state in question (*Hans v. Louisiana,* 1890).
5. The Amendment does not extend to municipalities or counties but only to states and arms of the state (*Workman v. New York City,* 1900; *Lake Country Estates, Inc. v. Tahoe Regional Planning Agency,* 1979; *Northern Insurance Company of New York v. Chatham County, Georgia,* 2006).
6. It does not apply to state officials (*Ex parte Young,* 1908; *Scheuer v. Rhodes,* 1974, suit against state officials involved in the death of students at Kent State), unless they are being sued in their official capacity for money damages that will be paid out of the state treasury.
7. It does not extend to suits instituted under Section 2 of the Thirteenth Amendment, Section 5 of the Fourteenth Amendment, or Section 2 of the Fifteenth Amendment.

It is arguable that this is an unfair reading of the Constitution, for in recent years, the Court has stated that the notion of "'Eleventh Amendment immunity'... is convenient shorthand but something of a misnomer, for the sovereign immunity of the States neither derives from, nor is limited by, the terms of the Eleventh Amendment" (*Alden v Maine,* 1999, quoted in *Northern Insurance Company of NY,* 2006). Rather, the majority of the present Court believes that state sovereign immunity predates the Constitution and that the states retain sovereign immunity, unless that immunity has been changed by the Constitution or constitutional amendments (e.g., the Thirteenth, Fourteenth, or Fifteenth Amendments).

Thus, after a brief look at the history of the Eleventh Amendment, the foregoing limitations on state immunity, including limitations sought under subsequent constitutional amendments, are addressed.

A. History

The Eleventh Amendment was not passed at the time of the first ten Amendments, but it did come early in U.S. constitutional history. The Amendment was passed in reaction to the Supreme Court's decision in *Chisholm v. Georgia* (1793), in which the Court found that it had jurisdiction over the state of Georgia to hear a debt action based on breach of contract for failure to pay for supplies provided by a citizen of South Carolina. Georgia refused to appear, contesting the jurisdiction of the Court. Thus, a default judgment was entered against the state.

The decision caused considerable uproar among the states, based in part on fears of a flood of suits by British and American Tory creditors wanting to collect on debts from before and during the American Revolution. Congress passed the Amendment almost immediately, and within five years, the states ratified it.

The few early cases involving the Eleventh Amendment limited it to debt actions (*Cohens v. Virginia,* 1821) and to cases where the state was a party of record (*Osborn v. Bank of the United States,* 1824), but these cases do not reflect the modern view of the law.

B. From What Judicial Power Does the State Have "Immunity?"

The first edit to the text of the Eleventh Amendment was the crossing out of "the United States." This edit occurred recently, in *Alden v. Maine* (1999), when the Court held that despite the language of the Amendment, state immunity from suit had a preconstitutional basis and a basis in the structure of the Constitution. The Court held that Congress could not authorize suits against a state in its own courts, unless the state consents, even if the suit was one by the state's own citizens for the violation of valid federal laws (here, the suit was by state employees concerning overtime under the Fair Labor Standards Act).

Although the gesture appears somewhat empty, the majority in *Alden* took pains to emphasize that immunity from suit against the state in its own courts did not mean that the state had a right to ignore or violate federal law or the

Constitution. Both the federal government and the claimants have other possible avenues for holding states accountable. These avenues, listed in points 5–7 above, are detailed next.

C. States Can Waive Immunity from Suit

As of 1999, a waiver of state immunity must be express. In other words, the Court will not base state immunity on an implied waiver (*College Savings Bank v. Florida Pre-Paid Postsecondary Education Expense Board,* 1999). Of course, this still leaves open the question as to what constitutes an express waiver, as opposed to an implied waiver. The Court, in *Lapides v. Board of Regents of the University System of Georgia* (2005), found that removal by the state, from state court to federal court, constituted an express waiver. Nonetheless, the Court held that the mere receipt of federal funds under federal law did not to constitute a waiver (*Atascadero State Hospital v. Scanlon,* 1985). The federal government can condition the provision of funds to the states based on consent to suit in the federal courts, but the condition must be explicit and "unmistakably clear" (*Atascadero State Hospital v. Scanlon,* 1985).

D. The Eleventh Amendment Extends to Cases in Admiralty (But Not to All *in rem* Cases in Admiralty and Bankruptcy)

The second edit to the text is a rather minor but clear extension of the scope of the Amendment. It reflects the fact that the Eleventh Amendment has been extended beyond *cases in law and equity* to cases of admiralty (with exceptions) (*Ex parte New York,* 1921).

It should also be noted that while sovereign immunity has been extended to admiralty actions, the Court has held that *in rem* admiralty actions (actions to get title to things) are not covered by state immunity, if the state is not in possession of the *res* (the thing). For instance, in *California v. Deep Sea Research Inc.* (1998), Deep Sea Research discovered a shipwreck in California's territorial waters, and it approached the federal courts in the *in rem* action to establish rights to the wreck. California intervened, claiming that it had title and that the federal courts did not have jurisdiction, based on sovereign immunity. The Court held that the matter was not covered by sovereign immunity, because it concerned *res* (a thing) that was not in the state's possession; thus, the case was fundamentally about establishing whether the company could claim title to the *res*. The plaintiff was not seeking damages or affirmative relief from the state. The Court could decide the case with Deep Sea alone. In fact, the state joined the action to claim property in the possession of the plaintiff. Thus, the state could not join and then claim sovereign immunity.

A similar result occurred in *Tennessee Student Assistance Corp. v. Hood* (2004) in an *in rem* bankruptcy action brought by a student seeking to include her student loans in the bankruptcy, under the doctrine of undue burden. As most law students know, one cannot avoid student loans simply by declaring bankruptcy at the end of one's education. The only exception is if the loans would constitute an undue burden on the student. Again, the Court reasoned that *in rem* bankruptcy proceedings are about the debtor and the *res*, not about the creditors, even when the state is a creditor. Bankruptcy jurisdiction is premised on jurisdiction over the debtor and the debtor's property, owed to the creditors. In these cases, plaintiffs are not seeking damages or coercive remedies against the state or against other creditors and are not subjecting the state to coercive judicial process. *In rem* proceedings are not adversarial but are matters between the court and the plaintiff to determine what is to happen with the debtor's property. For instance, the Court can proceed without the participation of all the creditors. The Court distinguished this case from adversarial proceedings, for example, one in which a bankruptcy trustee was trying to obtain property that was in the hands of the state. In that case, the state would need to be a party.

The Court emphasized that this was not a case of an *in rem* bankruptcy case trumping state sovereignty; rather, the action was not against the state and thus, did not affront state sovereignty.

E. Plaintiffs for Whom the Immunity Bars the Jurisdiction of the Court

The text of the Eleventh Amendment speaks to categories of potential claimants against whom the immunity runs. It explicitly states that the immunity extends to "any suit ... commenced or prosecuted against one of the United States a by Citizens of another State, or by Citizens or Subjects of any Foreign State." Nowhere does it say that that there is immunity from claims of citizens of a given state against their own state. Nonetheless, the Court, in *Hans v. Louisiana* (1890), extended immunity to claims by the states' own citizens.

It is important to note that this does not cover the entire field; both states and the federal government may sue states, even if they are bringing claims on behalf of individual citizens. Further, this immunity does not extend to cases in which the state institutes the cause of action.

F. Defendants: State Action for State Sovereign Immunity, but Municipalities, Counties, and State Officials Are Not Included

One of the striking features of the doctrine of *state sovereign immunity* is that it is narrower than the *state action* doctrine (see Chapter 5). While the actions of state officials, counties, and municipalities constitute state action for the purposes of the application of the Constitution, state officials, counties, and municipalities do not receive sovereign immunity. As the reader will learn in Chapter 5, under the state action doctrine, as a general rule the Constitution only applies to the states and federal government and not to private persons. Nonetheless, the "state" is read broadly to include officials, counties, and municipalities under that doctrine. Under the state immunity doctrine, the "state" is read narrowly and does not include officials, counties, municipalities, or other entities that have political independence.

This is subject to the caveat that the Court will consider a suit against a state official, county, or municipality as a suit against the state if the proceeds are to come out of the state treasury based on past violations of federal law. The Court does not wish to allow plaintiffs to avoid the core purpose of the Eleventh Amendment, which was to bar the federal courts from deciding cases that may result in judgments requiring that funds be paid out of the state treasury. If the state will have to pay, then the state is the party in interest.

The Eleventh Amendment does not apply to state officials (*Scheuer v. Rhodes,* 1974, state officials involved in the death of students at Kent State University) unless they are being sued in their official capacity for money damages that will be paid out of the treasury.

The Court held in *Ex parte Young* (1908) that although a state is immune, state officials do not have immunity under the Eleventh Amendment if they violate federal law when carrying out their state duties. If it is not possible for them to carry out their duties without violating federal law, then the court may enjoin them from enforcing the state law. The Court, in *Young,* used what is called a "legal fiction" to come to this conclusion. The idea is that given the Supremacy Clause, which provides that federal and constitutional law are supreme over state law, a state official does not have authority to violate federal law.

Actions against state officials must be prospective in nature—namely, actions to require or forbid them from violating federal law in the future. They cannot be actions that require damages to be paid out of the state treasury for past or present violations of federal law (*Edelman v. Jordan,* 1974). Nonetheless, a court can require that payments be made in the future to comply with a court order regarding federal law. The Court in *Edelman*, in fact, held that the state official involved could not be compelled to pay out past due welfare checks, but the official could be compelled to pay out future welfare checks, in conformity with federal law. The Court came to the same result in *Kimel v. Florida Board of Regents* (2000) when it held that persons fired in violation of the Age Discrimination in Employment Act could sue for prospective relief (i.e., injunctive relief), but could not sue for money damages.

However, the Court found that the Eleventh Amendment did not apply to the award of attorney's fees for bad-faith unconstitutional conduct on the part of prison officials (*Hutto v. Finney*, 1978) or court-ordered state expenditures to implement desegregation (*Milliken v. Bradley*, 1977) even though the funds for the attorney's fees and the desegregation efforts would need to be paid from state funds. In both cases, the funds were considered ancillary to the underlying action.

It should also be noted that this exception to sovereign immunity does *not* extend to requiring *state officials to comply with their own state law* (e.g., in a diversity suit). In such a case, no federal right is invoked, the Supremacy Clause does not come into play, and the state is considered the real party in interest (*Pennhurst State School & Hospital v. Halderman*, 1984).

G. The Civil War Amendments

The Civil War Amendments, the Thirteenth, Fourteenth, and Fifteenth Amendments, were passed after the Eleventh Amendment, and thus their provisions trump contrary provisions in the prior Amendment. Each of these Amendments limit state conduct, and each has sections empowering Congress to pass legislation to give the Amendments effect. It would be peculiar to go to all the trouble of amending the Constitution to allow Congress to pass legislation to give effect to these provisions if they could be undone by the then-existing Eleventh Amendment (for the full treatment of what suits are properly authorized under these Amendments see Chapter 2).

The same goes for the expanded view of "state sovereign immunity" (the view that sovereign immunity predates the Constitution and the Eleventh Amendment and is part of the Constitution's structure). Even if it is true that the doctrine predates the Eleventh Amendment and that the doctrine expands the reach of the Amendment, this, too, is subject to limits imposed by the subsequent Civil War Amendments.

There was a brief moment in time when the Court, in a plurality opinion (an opinion with no clear majority) held that Congress could authorize suits against the states based on the Commerce Clause in Article I, Section 8, Clause 3 (*Pennsylvania v. Union Gas Co.,* 1989). This provision reads: "The Congress shall have Power ... To regulate Commerce with foreign nations, and among the several States, and with the Indian Tribes." Though it makes sense that this provision could limit preconstitutional state sovereign immunity, Article I is still subject to the subsequent provisions in the Eleventh Amendment.

Thus, in *Seminole Tribe of Florida v. Florida* (1996), the Court, in a five-to-four decision, held that Congress could not authorize suits for money damages by Indian tribes against states in federal court under the Commerce Clause. The Court did, however, reaffirm that Congress could authorize suits for money damages under the Fourteenth Amendment.

There are two requirements that must be met for the Court to find that the authorization of suits for money damages under the Civil War Amendments is constitutional. First, Congress's intent to authorize such suits must be clear; second, the authorization must be justified as falling within the powers given to Congress under the Civil War Amendments. As already noted, the somewhat complicated rules for determining if this second requirement is met are covered in Chapter 2.

Checkpoints

- **Authority for judicial review**

  - Authority for judicial review is not in the text of the Constitution; it was established by the Supreme Court in *Marbury v. Madison.*

  - The Constitution is the supreme law of the land.

  - The judiciary has the authority and the duty to declare what the law is. It is appropriate for the judiciary to review:

    - executive actions, if they are nondiscretionary (i.e., there is a remedy and a right),

    - legislative actions,

    - state actions (*Martin v. Hunter's Lessee* and *Cohens v. Virginia*).

- **Congressional limits on federal judicial power**

  - Congress cannot restrict or enlarge the Court's original jurisdiction.

  - The appellate jurisdiction of the Supreme Court comes from the Constitution, not Congress. But Congress has the power to make "exceptions and regulations" (i.e., Congress has full power to regulate and limit the Court's appellate jurisdiction) (*Ex parte McCardle*).

Checkpoints *continued*

- Congress's power to regulate the Court's appellate jurisdiction is limited by the separation of powers doctrine and by the Court's holding in *Klein*. Congress can change the law itself by adopting a new law, but it cannot direct the judiciary's decisions under existing law (*Klein*), nor apply a new law retroactively to cases pending before the Court (*Robertson*).
- **Justiciability limits on federal judicial power**
  - Congress cannot override constitutional limits; Congress can change pragmatic/prudential limits.
  - *Prohibition against advisory opinions*
    - an actual dispute must exist between the parties; and
    - there must be a substantial likelihood that a federal court decision will bring about some change or have some effect.
      - Exceptions:
        - Some foreign courts, some state courts, and Article I courts can give advisory opinions.
        - Declaratory judgments and injunctions are not advisory and are therefore permissible if they meet the other requirements.
  - *Standing — whether it's the proper person to bring the case*
    - Constitutional requirements
      - an actual or imminent invasion of a legally protected interest of the plaintiff that is concrete and particularized;
      - that is caused by the conduct of the defendant; and
      - that can be redressed by a decision of the Court (*Lujan v. Defenders of Wildlife*).
    - Citizen Suits and taxpayer Standing
      - The requirement of a concrete and particularized harm, now generally bars citizen suits and taxpayer standing.
        - The plaintiff cannot sue as a citizen.
        - The plaintiff cannot sue as a taxpayer who has a grievance in common with all other taxpayers.
          - Exception: a taxpayer has standing to challenge a federal appropriation if
            - it was established under the taxing and spending power, and
            - it exceeds a specific limitation on the power (so far, only the Establishment Clause, per *Flast*)

Checkpoints *continued*

- Prudential requirements
  - Court may also deny standing on prudential grounds. Prudential considerations generally bar actions by third parties and claims by those whose grievances do not fall within the zone of interest protected by the statute she or he is suing under.
    - There is a general prudential prohibition against third party standing
      - Exceptions:
        - Obstacles prevent the third party from being able to sue (hindrance) and the plaintiff can effectively represent the third party's interests (well suited).
        - There is a close relationship between the plaintiff and the third party.
        - There is also an exception for third parties to raise the interests of others in cases where a statute regulating freedom of expression is substantially overbroad and thereby risks chilling the free speech of others.
    - Zone of interest: If one brings a claim under a given Act, she or he will only have standing if the Act can be fairly construed to protect the interest of the plaintiff and not merely others.
- *Ripeness bars consideration of claims before they have developed*
  - Constitutional requirement: In order for a case to be ripe, there must be either a substantial hardship, injury or significant threat of imminent harm to the plaintiff.
    - Choice between forgoing constitutionally protected behavior and risking likely prosecution with substantial consequences (*Abbott Laboratories*).
    - Inevitable that the law will apply, even though there may be a delay.
    - Prudential requirement: Fitness of the issues for judicial decision; quality of the record.
- *Mootness bars consideration of claims after they have been resolved*
  - Exceptions:
    - Voluntary cessation — when a party stops the purported unconstitutional conduct but may start again (*Friends of the Earth*).
    - Matters capable of repetition, yet evading review — when a matter could cycle through being a moot and a live controversy so that review would be continually avoided (*Roe*).

Checkpoints *continued*

- Collateral consequences — when there are secondary or collateral matters that remain alive after the main legal question is moot.
- Certified class action suits are one way to avoid having a claim go moot for a given plaintiff.

- *Political question doctrine (Baker)*

- issues that the Constitution gives to another branch of government ("a textually demonstrable constitutional commitment of the issue to a co-ordinate political department").
- issues that cannot be resolved or enforced by the judicial process ("lack of judicially discoverable and manageable standards").
- policy reasons: lack of respect, need for unquestioning adherence, or potential embarrassment

- **The Eleventh Amendment and State Immunity**

- The federal judicial power and the judicial power of individual states are limited by the Eleventh Amendment. Congress cannot authorize suits against states in federal court or within their own state courts (*Alden v. Maine*).
- States can expressly waive Eleventh Amendment immunity.
- The Eleventh Amendment applies to cases of law and equity and to cases of admiralty (*Ex parte New York*), but not *in rem* cases in admiralty and bank-ruptcy.
- The Amendment bars suits not only by citizens of other states but also by citizens of the state in question (*Hans v. Louisiana*).
- The Amendment only applies to states and arms of the state, not to mu-nicipalities or counties.
- It does not apply to state officials (*Ex parte Young*), unless they are being sued in their official capacity for money damages that will be paid out of the state treasury.
- It does not extend to suits properly instituted under the Civil War Amend-ments (Thirteenth, Fourteenth, and Fifteenth Amendments).

Chapter 2

The Federal Legislative Power

Roadmap

- The limited sources of legislative power: Congress is limited to powers enumerated in the Constitution and that which is necessary and proper to carry out enumerated powers.
- The four historical periods of the Commerce Clause: early expansion, the *Lochner* era, return to expansion of power, modern retrenchment.
- The modern test for the Commerce Clause: channels, instrumentalities, and substantial effects.
- Taxing and spending powers.
- Foreign affairs powers, which includes the treaty power, immigration and naturalization, and war powers.
- Civil War amendments and congressional power under the Enforcement Clauses of the Thirteenth, Fourteenth, and Fifteenth Amendments.
- Congress's power to authorize suits against state governments and state sovereign immunity under the Eleventh Amendment.

I. Sources of Legislative Power

Article I of the Constitution begins by providing that "All legislative Powers herein granted shall be vested in a Congress of the United States which shall consist of a Senate and House of Representatives." Thus, Congress has separate and exclusive powers to legislate, which are not available to the executive or judicial branches. Nonetheless, this power is checked by constitutional limits, the executive's power of veto, and by the judiciary's power to review congressional acts.

Although this may be surprising at first, it is important to know that while the states in the Union can legislate on any matter not prohibited by the Constitution (with some exceptions of course), Congress can only legislate on matters allowed by, or enumerated in, the Constitution. The Tenth Amendment provides the textual basis for this limitation. It reads: "The powers not delegated to the United States by the Constitution, nor prohibited by it to the States, are reserved to the States respectively, or to the people."

The bulk of this chapter addresses cases wherein the Court is exercising its power of review to decide if Congress is acting within or exceeding its powers. It exceeds its powers either by legislating outside of its enumerated powers or by infringing on some other constitutional provision or doctrine. For example, even if Congress has the authority to regulate the interstate sale of books and literature, it cannot do so in a matter that violates the First Amendment freedom of expression. Congress's powers are also limited by the powers of the other branches and the states through the doctrines of federalism and separation of powers.

As the Roadmap suggests, Congress has powers to regulate interstate commerce under the Commerce Clause, has powers to tax and spend under the Taxing and Spending Powers Clause, has certain powers in the area of foreign affairs (e.g., to declare war and to ratify treaties), and has some powers to enforce civil rights under the Civil War amendments (Thirteenth, Fourteenth, and Fifteenth Amendments).

By far, the most expansive use of congressional power has been under the Commerce Clause. Some of this can be attributed to the fact that unlike at the time of the framing of the Constitution, today almost everything is connected with interstate commerce. Nonetheless, as we will see, it is questionable whether everything that has come under this enumerated clause really belongs there. The history of the Court's review of congressional power under this clause has been a roller coaster of extreme highs and lows. Although there is little debate on the existence of the ups and downs, there is a great deal of argument over which points count as the high points and which the low points. There is also considerable debate over whether the Court is presently heading up, heading down, or simply leveling out this area of the law onto some reasonable steady plateau.

This chapter begins with the case of *McCulloch v. Maryland* (1819), which involved the question of the legitimacy of the federal bank and the power of states to regulate it within their borders. It is an interesting and important case to begin with, as it brings into question much of what was said above about Congress's powers being limited to those enumerated in the Constitution. The chapter then turns to the Commerce Clause and addresses the early expansion of powers under that doctrine, the contraction of that doctrine during the *Lochner* era from the late 1800s to 1937 that led to a type of constitutional crisis, the postcrisis return to expanding congressional power under the Commerce Clause from 1937 until 1995, and then the modern contraction or retrenchment of those powers since 1995. Finally, the chapter discusses, in relatively shorter sections, the taxing and spending powers, foreign affairs, intergovernmental immunities, and the congressional enforcement of civil rights.

A. *McCulloch v. Maryland* (1819)

There had been a debate among the Founders from the beginning over the legitimacy of a national bank, largely because there appeared to be a need for one, yet there was no mention of one in the Constitution. Nonetheless, a bank was established in 1790 and operated until 1811, when its charter expired. The Bank of the United States was then revived in 1816, in response to the country's economic woes, and it immediately started calling in loans from the states. Maryland reacted to the loan recall by taxing the bank for operating within its state. Under Maryland law, the bank could either issue notes on state paper for a fee or pay a sizable annual tax. It did neither; thus, the state of Maryland sued the Bank of the United States.

The case of *McCulloch* raised two issues:

1. Does Congress have the authority to incorporate a bank?
2. Do the states have authority to tax the bank?

Chief Justice John Marshall, who wrote the opinion of the Court, acknowledged that the federal government was one of enumerated powers and that the power to create a bank was not expressly enumerated. However, this did not settle the issue.

The case is often quoted for the idea that the Constitution is different from a mere statute. The Constitution is a living document that is meant to endure, and thus, it needs to be interpreted in light of history and changing times. Although this may sound like an invitation to unbounded judicial activism (i.e., the Court gets to rewrite the Constitution to make it current with the times), Marshall's opinion was not ungrounded. It is, in fact, a very good example of the Court using a number of standard tools of interpretation outlined in the Introduction. Marshall drew on the idea of a living Constitution, but he also drew on other parts of the constitutional text and history, already mentioned, to rule on an issue that at first blush appears to be an easy question under the first clause of Article I ("All legislative Powers herein granted shall be vested in a Congress").

Marshall emphasized that the issue had been debated by the Framers from the beginning, and that within a year of the founding, they had created the Bank of the United States, which had existed for the next twenty years. Maryland attempted to argue that this was a power that was reserved to the states and that the Bank undermined state sovereignty over this area of the law. Although it is true that the states ratified the Constitution, Marshall's response was that it was really "the people" who ratified the Constitution through their state representatives and not the states themselves. The final Constitution was for "we the people," and thus, the states could not invoke "state sovereignty" as a justification for effectively vetoing legitimate federal legislation creating a bank.

Marshall also relied on the text of the Constitution for his argument. Although creating a bank is not an expressly enumerated power, it was implied through the Necessary and Proper Clause. Article I, Section 8, Clause 18 gives Congress the power to make "all laws which shall be necessary and proper for carrying into Execution" its enumerated powers. The argument was that since Congress has the power to tax and to spend, it needed a bank to carry out its other functions under those powers.

Arguably, a bank was not absolutely necessary, since the government had been operating without one for approximately five years after the charter expired. Marshall's response was partially based on the nature and the structure of the Constitution. He noted that the Necessary and Proper Clause is part of Section 8, which expands the legislative powers, rather than Section 9, which generally limits legislative powers. The other part of his argument was that the Constitution is "meant to endure" and to "adapt to the various crises of human affairs." He used this idea of a living document to argue that the word *necessary* was modified by the word *proper* in such a way that the word *necessary* did not mean indispensable but rather "useful" or "desirable." One might argue that he reduced the meaning of the word *necessary* to that of the word *proper*.

Although Marshall did not abandon judicial review, which he established in *Marbury*, he articulated a very deferential test (which is very similar to the modern rational basis test for reviewing legislation and government conduct). He stated: "Let the end be legitimate, let it be within the scope of the constitution, and all means which are appropriate, which are plainly adapted to that end, which are not prohibited, but consist with the letter and spirit of the constitution, are constitutional." This test can be broken down as requiring:

1. legitimate federal ends within the scope of Constitution;
2. by appropriate means clearly adapted to that end;
3. not expressly prohibited; and
4. in the spirit of the Constitution.

If these criteria are present, the Court will defer to the legislature's judgment. Nonetheless, if the legislature invokes this power merely as a pretext, it would be necessary for the Court to check such an abuse of power by declaring the law unconstitutional.

As to the second issue, the Court held that Maryland could not tax the national bank. Drawing on the foregoing analysis, as well as the Supremacy Clause of the Constitution, it followed that Maryland law could not trump federal law. The federal government had a right to ensure that what it created was preserved and not destroyed. The Court reasoned that the power to tax is the power to destroy, and thus, Maryland could not tax the bank.

II. The Commerce Clause

Article I, Section 8 includes, among the powers granted to Congress, the Commerce Clause, which reads: "Congress shall have power ... to regulate Commerce with foreign nations, and among the several States, and with the Indian Tribes." As noted, Congress's power to pass laws under the Commerce Clause has changed considerably over time. As Marshall's decision in *McCulloch* suggests, the Court was deferential to Congress exerting its power in the early period of the republic. The relative dearth of cases during the first 100 years or so is also due to the fact that it took some time for the Industrial Revolution to take hold, and even longer for Congress and the law to respond to it. Congress was somewhat slow to spread its wings in this area.

When it began to spread its wings during the late nineteenth and early twentieth centuries, the Court was there to clip them. This began what is often referred to as the *Lochner* era or the laissez-faire era, in which the Court was active in ensuring that Congress as well as the various states were not active in regulating the market. It is called the *Lochner* era because of the famous case *Lochner v. New York* (1905), in which the Court struck down state legislation that was designed to protect the health of bakers. The Court struck down federal laws as exceeding the Commerce Clause power and state laws for infringing the "freedom of contract" (see Chapter 6, which addresses economic liberties). The *Lochner* era is generally seen as a low point in the Court's history because the Court struck down so many federal and state laws that were designed to help the people survive the excesses of capitalism during that period (e.g., by providing for better health conditions, minimum wages, and maximum hours). With the onslaught of the Depression in the early 1930s, the Court's laissez-faire approach led to a crisis. President Franklin Roosevelt threatened to pack the court with younger, more progressive judges so that some of this legislation would survive. This prompted Justice Owen Roberts to swing his vote, in *National Labor Relations Board v. Jones & Laughlin Steel Corp.* (1937), which ended the *Lochner* era. From 1937 until 1995, this area of the law became a dead letter or an unfettered letter, depending on your view. Not once was the Commerce Clause successfully invoked during this period. Congress was free to spread its wings as wide as it chose, and the Court did not interfere.

Not until relatively recently has the Court, once again, held that Congress's authority under the Commerce Clause has limits. The case marking the entry into the modern law in this area is *United States v. Lopez* (1995). The modern rule, articulated in *Lopez*, is that there are three areas that Congress can regulate under the Commerce Clause.

1. The channels: Congress can regulate the use of the "channels" of interstate commerce and anything that is reasonably related to such channels. For example, Congress can regulate highways, waterways, and air traffic, and it can regulate the use of these channels within the states.
2. The instrumentalities: Congress can regulate the "instrumentalities" of interstate commerce, which means that Congress can regulate trucks, ships, and boats, which travel through the channels to carry out commerce.
3. Activities that have a substantial effect on interstate commerce: Congress can regulate those activities that while local (e.g., local farm production) have a substantial impact on interstate commerce (e.g., impact on the supply, price and viability of the nation's agricultural products).

The Court also does not merely accept congressional findings that there is a substantial effect on interstate commerce. It will scrutinize those findings to ensure that the impact is in indeed substantial. The Court now looks to distinguish what is truly of national concern from what is merely a local issue.

A. Early Cases: The Founding to the 1890s

The case of *Gibbons v. Ogden* (1824) involved a straightforward conflict between two ship operators. Ogden was operating his ships between New York City and New Jersey, based on a monopoly right granted by the state of New York. Gibbons had been given a right to operate his ships in the same waters by the U.S. government. Ogden sought to enjoin Gibbons from operating his ships in competition with him. Ogden claimed that the federal government did not have exclusive authority over commerce, and since this was a matter of intrastate commerce rather than interstate commerce, it was New York's right to grant the monopoly. Gibbons argued that the matter was one of interstate commerce (i.e., commerce among the states), and thus, because the two regulations conflicted, New York's would need to yield to the federal regulation, and Ogden's injunction should be denied.

To decide the matter, Chief Justice Marshall had to address what Article I, Section 8 meant by both "commerce" and "among the states." He began his decision by drawing, once again, on the Necessary and Proper Clause and rejecting the notion that the clauses should be interpreted strictly.

When he turned to the definition of "commerce," he entertained the idea that its meaning should be limited to "traffic" (i.e., buying and selling), but he thought this was too narrow and would exclude "navigation." Perhaps more important, if the word was held not to include such things as navigation, the very means of carrying on so much of commerce, then this would undo the practice of the U.S. government regulating navigation from the time of the founding. He could not see how the Framers could have meant to exclude navigation from the meaning of the term. Thus, shipping was part of commerce.

Turning to the phrase "among the states," he defined it as "intermingled with." Things that are interstate (across states) clearly can be regulated. Matters that are completely internal to a state (intrastate) are not included. However, matters that are carried out entirely within a state but affect interstate commerce are included (note that he did not require *substantial effects* on interstate commerce). Thus, he concluded that the Commerce Clause authorized the federal government to license ships, and the New York law, granting a monopoly license, was invalid, at least to the extent that it conflicted with the federal law.

Although there were a few other cases during this period, most adopted Marshall's expansive view of what counted as "commerce among the states."

B. 1890s to 1937: The *Lochner* Era up to the Constitutional Crisis

1. "Commerce" Revisited

In 1895, the Court revisited the issue of what constituted commerce within the definition of the term. Congress passed the Sherman Antitrust Act of 1890 to regulate trade and stop the formation of monopolies and other practices that inhibited competition. The American Sugar Refining Company had acquired a number of sugar refineries, which led to an almost complete monopoly of the industry. The government brought an antitrust case against the company under the Act, which was dismissed, and it came up to the Supreme Court on appeal in *United States v. E.C. Knight Co.* (1895).

The question in this case was whether Congress had any power to regulate the manufacturing of sugar under the Commerce Clause. Even if Marshall was correct that commerce included navigation, does the term also include manufacturing? Chief Justice Melville Fuller held that at best, manufacturing was incidental or secondary to commerce but was not included in the definition of the term. The regulation of manufacturing, which is an intrastate activity (within one or more states), rather than an interstate activity (between states), could not be regulated under the Commerce Clause. The actual manufacturing only occurs within a given state, even though the final product is sold across states. Regulating manufacturing was held to be within the police power, which is the power of the states to regulate for the safety, health, welfare, and morals of the people (a power to be exercised by the states).

Justice John Marshall Harlan wrote a strong dissent, noting the impact that monopolies in manufacturing would have on interstate commerce. Restraints on trade directly impact commerce; they "crush out competition." Far from interfering with the police powers of the states, the law in question here would remove unlawful obstructions to free trade between and within the states. For Justice Harlan, this fell within the commerce power.

Harlan's view did not win out for some time. Thus, over forty years later, in *Carter v. Carter Coal Co.* (1936), the Court struck down the Bituminous Coal Conservation Act of 1935 because it dealt with matters that were within the states' police power and not Congress's commerce power. Congress passed the Act to stabilize the industry because coal was central to the national economy, and the nation was in the grips of the Great Depression. The legislation set up local coal boards that would set prices for the coal, as well as wages and hours for the workers.

The Court focused on the Act's provisions that set hours and wages and argued that these were related to production of coal and not trade or commerce in coal. Regulating labor was one step toward a "forbidden end." Regulating production and everything leading up to the mining of coal, such as wages and working hours, was within the states' police power. It was not for the federal government to regulate under the commerce power.

The Court here, as well as in *Knight*, was unwilling to accept that production and wages were intimately bound up with commerce. Although the Court in *Carter Coal Co.* recognized that the setting of wages and hours was concerned with "intercourse" (i.e., trade or commerce in labor), it was intercourse in labor for production and not intercourse in labor for trade or commerce. In other words, although this would impact the labor market, the labor market was for the production of coal (intrastate) and not for commerce, or the selling of coal (interstate). Of course, changes in the labor market, such as the cost or availability of labor, impact production and the availability of the product that ends up in interstate commerce. If there was no commerce in labor, there would be no production and thus no commerce in the thing produced.

The cases can be distinguished from *Stafford v. Wallace* (1922), in which the Court upheld the regulation of hours and wages for workers in the Chicago stockyards. The distinction is that while *Carter Coal* was about commerce in labor for production (producing coal), the commerce in labor here was for commerce or at the threshold of commerce (holding and selling cattle, a temporary stop). Although one could see the case going either way on this reasoning, the Court held that that the stockyards were at the "throat" of interstate commerce. The stockyards were the throat, if not the mouth, of what is often referred to as "the stream of commerce." Cattle was gathered and then sold for shipment into interstate commerce. Thus, this was held to fall within the Commerce Clause power, rather than the police power.

2. Police Power, State Sovereignty, and Commerce Power

All of these cases invoke the police power, which is the power of the states to regulate for the safety, health, welfare, and morals of the people. As noted at the outset, the federal government does not have this general power. Implicit in many of these decisions is the idea of state sovereignty over the police powers. Just as there is a separation and balance of powers between the federal branches, there is a separation and balance of powers between the federal government and the states. In the cases cited, the issue was whether the Constitution gave Congress the power to act under the Commerce Clause. In the few cases discussed next, the question is: Even if the Constitution provides authority for Congress to act under the Commerce Clause, does the Tenth Amendment, which reserves other powers to the states and the people, act as a positive check on the Commerce Clause powers?

Two cases during this era are often used because they represent conflicting answers to this question and are based on facts that are hard to distinguish or reconcile. The general conclusion is that the Court was not acting based on a legal principle in these cases but on its own view of right and wrong. The cases are *Champion v. Ames* (1903) and *Hammer v. Dagenhart* (1918), otherwise known as the *Lottery Case* and the *Child Labor Case*. Both cases involved issues generally thought to be within the police power, namely, the power to regulate for the health, welfare, and morals of the people. In both cases, the laws prohibited interstate commerce in an evil or immoral product (lottery tickets or the products of child labor).

The law in *Ames* prohibited the importing, mailing, or transporting from one state to another any lottery ticket. The Court in *Ames* held that this was within Congress's commerce power. The law did not prohibit or regulate commerce that was carried on exclusively within a state. Activities within a state are left to the states under their police powers. The Court reasoned that just as the states could legislate for the purpose of protecting or guarding the morals of its people, the federal government could also legislate to guard public morals within the realm of interstate commerce. The Tenth Amendment did not bar the exercise of Congress's power in this case. With respect to lottery tickets, the Court made its views clear when it conclusively stated: "We should hesitate long before adjudging that an evil of such appalling character, carried on through interstate commerce, cannot be met and crushed by the only power competent to that end.... Congress alone has the power to occupy, by legislation, the whole field of interstate commerce."

The Court in *Dagenhart* came to the opposite conclusion. In *Dagenhart*, the federal law prohibited the shipment in interstate commerce of the product of any mill, cannery, workshop, or factory that employed children under the age of fourteen, or children from fourteen to sixteen who had worked more than a limited number of hours (more than eight hours a day, seven days a week, before 6 a.m. or after 7 P.M.). The Court dismissed the dissenting opinion of Justice Oliver Wendell Holmes Jr., who argued that while a state is free to control everything within its borders, once the transportation leaves its borders and becomes interstate commerce, it is squarely within the power of Congress to regulate under the interstate Commerce Clause. The Court reasoned that the products themselves were not evil. If there was an evil, it was at the level of labor and production, which was within the police power of the state, not the commerce power of the federal government. It held that "the grant of authority over a purely federal matter was not intended to destroy the local power always existing and carefully reserved to the states in the 10th Amendment to the Constitution."

The Court also dismissed the argument that states allowing for the practice of child labor had an unfair advantage in interstate commerce, and thus, it was appropriate for Congress to address the unfair advantage. In fact, states lack the incentive to stop using child labor, because it gives them an economic advantage (cheaper prices for goods, as compared to other states that did not use child labor). The only way to ensure that any state would stop using child labor was to stop every state from using it. Thus, the conclusion in *Ames* that only the federal government could stop the evil was even truer in this case.

The decision may have rested on the fact that almost every state in the Union had some law regulating the use of child labor. The federal law simply supplemented the legislation that already existed. The Court seemed content with the fact that North Carolina (the state in question in the case) had a law forbidding child labor under the age of twelve. With respect to labor for children between the ages of twelve (state law) and fourteen (federal law), perhaps it was for the states, rather than the federal government, to decide.

Justice Holmes's dissent focused on the indirect effect of the use of legitimate Commerce Clause power (it only impacted the state if and when the product entered interstate commerce). If the product stayed within the state, then the federal law would not reach it. In contrast, the majority focused on the federal government's illegitimate use of its Commerce Clause powers to intrude into the realm of the state and its police power. For the majority, it would give Congress the power to "destroy" the local power. One might ask just how local this is if, in fact, the regulation of its transport into interstate commerce would have the effect of destroying the local power.

3. "Among the States" Revisited

In *Gibbons v. Ogden* (1824), Chief Justice Marshall held that "among the states" not only included purely interstate commerce but also intrastate commerce that impacted interstate commerce. In a number of cases during this period, the Court revisited this question. Here, the question was not whether the activity was commerce but whether commerce had a sufficient impact on interstate activities for the federal government to regulate it.

The Court, in *Houston, East & West Texas Railway Co. v. United States* (1914) (the *Shreveport Rates Cases*), narrowed *Gibbons* by upholding the Interstate Commerce Commission's decision to order the railroad to raise its in-state rates because the low in-state rates had the effect of discriminating against interstate commerce. The railroad charged higher interstate rates (between Shreveport, Louisiana, and points within Texas) than its intrastate rates (between cities within Texas). Although the case would have been easier if the Commission had decided that the interstate rates discriminated against interstate commerce, it held that the interstate rates were okay and did not need to be lowered. Rather, it was the intrastate rates (rates within the state) that were too low.

Like in *Gibbons*, this was a case that involved the instrumentalities of interstate commerce, namely, the railroad. Just as Congress could regulate ships and shipping that had an impact on interstate commerce, it could regulate trains and railroad rates that had an impact on interstate commerce. It flips the reasoning in *Dagenhart*. While the Court held that the state police powers could be invoked to limit the encroachment of the federal government in *Dagenhart* (child labor case), here, in the *Shreveport Rates Cases* the Court held that Congress could regulate intrastate (local) railway rates to protect interstate commerce. Gibbons is narrowed or clarified to the extent that *Houston* requires that the impact threaten or harm interstate commerce.

Just as *Dagenhart* was more restrictive of the Commerce Clause powers than *Ames*, the case of *A.L.A. Schechter Poultry Corp v. United States* (1935) (the *Sick Chicken Case*), was more restrictive than *Houston*. The *Sick Chicken Case* further limited *Gibbons* and *Houston* by requiring a *direct effect* on interstate commerce. In this case, the A.L.A. Schechter Poultry Corp. purchased poultry from Philadelphia and New York City and transported it to their slaughterhouses in Brooklyn, New York. The company was charged with violating the Live Poultry Code, which regulated the rights of sellers and buyers of poultry, as well as a broad spectrum of working conditions for labor in the industry. Regulations spanned collective bargaining, child labor, maximum hours, and minimum pay, but the company was prosecuted for violating only the labor provisions of the Code. The company received chickens from all over the country; however, it sold the chickens only to local retailers, mainly for local use. Thus, once the poultry arrived in Brooklyn, it stayed there. The Court held that this was not a case of chickens in the flow of interstate commerce because the violation of the Code occurred in Brooklyn, New York, and by that point, the flow of commerce had ceased. Unlike in *Houston*, the Court held that the impact on interstate commerce in this case was indirect. Simply because the chickens arrived through interstate commerce does not give Congress the authority to regulate the intrastate activities of the A.L.A. Schechter Poultry Corp.

To summarize, the Court during this period held that Congress can only regulate:

- commerce, not manufacturing, production, or agriculture (which are traditionally state concerns) (*Dagenhart, E.C. Knight Co.,* and *Carter*).
- intrastate activities that *directly*, not merely indirectly, affect interstate commerce (*Houston* and *A.L.A. Schechter Poultry Corp.*).
- evil articles within interstate commerce, not merely intrastate evils that produce goods shipped in interstate commerce (*Dagenhart*).
- intrastate transactions that are in the stream of commerce, not those that precede or follow that stream (*A.L.A. Schechter Poultry Corp.*).
- for Congress's purposes that actually carry out enumerated powers, not as a pretext for other ends or goals within the police powers of the states (*McCulloch*).

C. Postcrisis Expansion of Federal Power: 1938 to the 1990s

The Great Depression, which began with the stock market crash of 1929, made the Court's position more and more untenable. Between 1929 and 1933, the U.S. gross domestic product fell almost 30 percent, nominal income fell about 20 percent, and unemployment rose from approximately 3 percent to 25 percent. The hands-off laissez-faire approach of the *Lochner* era was not working. The Court was seen as the last holdout, striking down both state legislation and federal legislation that was backed by Congress, the President, and "the people." If anything, Congress and the people supported even more radical changes than President Roosevelt had proposed.

Roosevelt was reelected by a landslide in 1936, carrying forty-six out of the then-existing forty-eight states, with over 60 percent of popular vote and 98 percent of the electoral vote. Roosevelt's response to the above cases was to propose a Court-packing plan in 1937. Although opponents of the plan claimed it was an encroachment on the independence of the judiciary, as we learned in Chapter 1, nothing in the Constitution prohibits Congress from changing the makeup of the Court. It had done so on many occasions throughout history. Roosevelt's proposal was to add one Justice for every sitting member over the age of seventy. The maximum number of Justices was set at fifteen. Not unsurprisingly, there were six Justices over the age of seventy at the time, and this change would surely have secured the majority that he needed to ensure his legislation would not continue to be struck down by the Court.

Before the fate of the proposal was certain, Justice Roberts switched his vote in two key cases that year, making his change of opinion forever known as the "switch in time that saved nine." The two key cases were *West Coast Hotel v. Parish* (1937), in which the Court upheld a state law regulating minimum wages for women and *NLRB v. Jones & Laughlin Steel Corp.* (1937), in which the Court upheld the federal regulation of labor standards in steel manufacturing.

There were three important cases during the late 1930s and early 1940s that effectively overruled the main limiting cases of the *Lochner* era. Those case included *NLRB* (1937) (overruling the direct effect requirement in *Houston* and *Schechter*), *United States v. Darby* (1941) (overruling the prohibition on regulating the shipment of goods in interstate commerce that were produced in violation of labor laws in *Dagenhart*), and *Wickard v. Filburn* (1942) (substantially relaxing the effects doctrine in *Schechter*). These are followed by a number of cases that expanded the use of federal powers to protect civil rights and even local criminal activity.

1. NLRB v. Jones & Laughlin Steel Corp. *(1937)*

Jones & Laughlin Steel Corporation, the fourth largest steel manufacturer in the United States at the time, had plants and subsidiaries in a number of states, employed over a half a million workers, and sold its products nationwide. The National Labor Relations Board (NLRB) sued Jones & Laughlin for engaging in unfair labor practices by interfering with the rights of its employees to organize and engage in collective bargaining under the National Labor Relations Act of 1935.

Jones & Laughlin raised the challenge that the Act regulated employment conditions related to manufacturing and not commerce, and thus, this was a matter for the states under the police powers. The Court did not accept that manufacturing was not commerce, and it refused to limit Congress's authority to regulating only those activities that directly affect interstate commerce. Congress was not limited to transactions deemed to be an essential part of the flow of interstate commerce. If there were appreciable effects on interstate commerce, either direct or indirect, it was within Congress's authority to regulate it. Congress could not be denied the power to control activities within states that have "such a close and substantial relation to interstate commerce that their control is essential or appropriate to protect that commerce from burdens and obstructions."

When examining the effects, the Court accepted the NLRB's assertion that industrial strife would stop operations at the steel plant, which in turn would have a serious effect on interstate commerce. The Court concluded that the right to organize and engage in collective bargaining is often essential to industrial peace. Since the company was organized on a national scale, with interstate commerce being a dominant factor in its activities, it could not be maintained that labor relations was a forbidden field for Congress to regulate.

The Court rejected:

1. the requirement that the good or activity be in the flow or current of interstate commerce;
2. the Tenth Amendment limitation, based on the distinction between "manufacturing" and commerce; and
3. the requirement of a direct effect on interstate commerce.

2. U.S. v. Darby *(1941)*

The Fair Labor Standards Act provided minimum wages and maximum hours and established punishment for the interstate shipment of goods produced in violation of those requirements. Darby Lumber Co. was a lumber manufacturer charged with violating the wage and hour provisions of the Act and with shipping goods across state lines.

Darby raised two questions: Could Congress regulate the shipment of goods in interstate commerce that were made in violation of labor standards, and could Congress directly regulate the employment conditions if the labor was used to manufacture products destined only for interstate commerce?

Although *Darby* is similar to *NLRB*, it was not decided on the basis of the potential impact of labor practices on industrial strife, which in turn could effect interstate commerce. Rather, the first issue in Darby raised the exact issue that was raised in *Dagenhart*, namely, the regulation of the shipment of goods that although not evil in themselves, are produced using evil labor practices. The Court expressly overruled *Dagenhart*, but it went further and held that not only was the regulation of the shipment of the goods authorized under the Commerce Clause, but the Commerce Clause also authorized the direct regulation of labor practices, which produced the goods destined for interstate commerce. The Court held that through the Act, Congress had determined that goods produced under substandard labor conditions was a form of unfair competition and thus harmed interstate commerce. Therefore, it could use "the means reasonably adapted to the attainment of the permitted end, even though they involve control of intrastate activities."

This decision flips the decision in *Dagenhart*. In *Dagenhart*, the Tenth Amendment limited the means Congress could use to regulate interstate commerce. Congress could not regulate interstate commerce if it impacted and threatened the states' police powers. In *Darby*, the Court made its famous pronouncement that the Tenth Amendment was a mere truism and did not erect any barrier or limit on the exercise of congressional power. In fact, in *Darby*, the Court not only sanctioned congressional regulation of interstate shipments that would have a substantial effect on the state's police power to regulate manufacturing, the Court unanimously endorsed going directly after the manufacturing because of its effect on interstate commerce.

3. Wickard v. Filburn *(1942)*

The case of *Wickard v. Filburn* is generally considered the high-water mark on how far Congress can go to regulate local production because of its effects on interstate commerce. This case was brought under the Agricultural Adjustment Act of 1938, which permitted the Secretary of Agriculture to set quotas for growing wheat. The purpose of the Act was to limit supply to control the price of wheat in interstate commerce. The Act applied to not only commercial farms that grew and sold wheat interstate also private farms that grew wheat only for personal use. Roscoe Filburn, who owned a small farm in Ohio, was prosecuted under the Act and ordered to pay a penalty for harvesting more wheat than the quota permitted.

Filburn primarily used homegrown wheat to make flour for home consumption and to feed his livestock. He challenged the law as exceeding Congress's power to regulate interstate commerce because his production, consumption, and even limited sales were all local and at most had a minimal and indirect effect on interstate commerce.

In a unanimous decision, the Court held that the issue did not turn on whether the regulation concerned "production" or if the effects were "indirect." Rather, the question was whether the regulated activity had "substantial effects" on interstate commerce, either directly or indirectly.

The Court reasoned that because there was a large amount of wheat in interstate commerce, controlling the price and amount of wheat was important to the national economy, and homegrown wheat was the most variable factor in the wheat supply, and thus Filburn's personal consumption affected the price. Thus, even though a particular farmer's production and consumption of wheat might not directly have a substantial effect, the *cumulative effect* of regulating or failing to regulate the entire class of wheat producers had a substantial impact on interstate commerce. Thus, even local production and consumption can be regulated by Congress under the Commerce Clause, as long as it has a cumulative effect on interstate commerce.

4. Civil Rights Cases: *The Commerce Clause Goes Where the Fourteenth Amendment Cannot*

The development of precedent sometimes results in counterintuitive results. Following the Civil War, Congress passed the Civil Rights Act. The Act regulated discrimination in services and accommodations such as common carriers, hotels, and restaurants. The Act was passed to give effect to the Fourteenth Amendment and was arguably justified under Section 5 of the Amendment, which provides that Congress can pass legislation to enforce the Amendment. However, the Court, in the *Civil Rights Cases* (1883), held that the Fourteenth Amendment only applied to the states, and thus, Congress could not regulate private conduct in order to ensure equal protection under the law.

Thus, when Congress passed the 1964 Civil Rights Act, which was substantially the same as the post-Civil War Act, the Fourteenth Amendment was not available to justify the Act. Perhaps unsurprisingly, the development of the Court's Commerce Clause jurisprudence provided an alternative and more solid (if less obvious) foundation for congressional power to create the Act.

In *Heart of Atlanta Motel v. United States* (1964), the Court upheld the Act based on the Commerce Clause, even though the Act was being applied to a single local motel. The Court held that Congress could regulate local businesses if they had an impact on interstate commerce.

The motel, located in downtown Atlanta, Georgia, had refused to rent rooms to African Americans. The motel was conveniently located near two highways, derived 75 percent of its occupancy from out-of-state guests, and advertised nationally. The Court took notice of congressional findings that racial discrimination discouraged travel by a substantial portion of the African American community. They needed special guidebooks to help them in trying to find private accommodations, which were often few and far between. This had an impact on travel and, as a result, commerce; therefore, Congress could regulate to prohibit such discrimination. The Court also made clear that it did not matter that the motive for regulating the business was moral (traditionally left to the state's police powers), rather than merely economic or commercial. It was irrelevant that it was the local operation that "caused the squeeze," as long as it was interstate commerce that "felt the pinch." The only limitation on Congress is "that the means chosen by it must be reasonably adapted to the end permitted by the Constitution."

Justice William O. Douglas, in his concurring opinion, agreed that Congress had the authority to regulate the Heart of Atlanta Motel through the Commerce Clause, but he could not resist pointing out that there was a much more appropriate justification for the regulatory authority under Section 5 of the Fourteenth Amendment. He argued that the right to be free from discrimination and the right to move freely from state to state occupied "a more protected position in our constitutional system than ... the movement of cattle, fruit, steel and coal across state lines." If the decision were based on Section 5 of the Fourteenth Amendment, the Act would apply to every customer and to every place of public accommodation. This would eliminate the question as to whether the place of accommodation was within interstate commerce or whether a traveler was an interstate traveler, and it "would put an end to all obstructionist strategies and finally close the door on a bitter chapter in American History."

In *Katzenbach v. McClung* (1964), the Court went even further to uphold the Civil Rights Act. McClung was the owner of a restaurant called Ollie's Barbecue, located in Birmingham, Alabama. The restaurant was eleven blocks from the interstate highway and even further away from the train and bus station. The business mainly served local residents. Thus, it could not be said that this local restaurant caused the same "pinch" on interstate commerce that was caused by the Heart of Atlanta Hotel.

Nonetheless, 46 percent of the food purchased by the restaurant during the previous year had been bought from a local supplier, who had received it from out of state. Even though the impact of this restaurant on interstate commerce might have been slight, the Court again recognized Congress's findings that the exclusion of African Americans from restaurants had a significant impact. It restricted both interstate travel and the interstate flow of food; thus, it had a substantial cumulative effect on interstate commerce. The Court combined the reasoning from *Heart of Atlanta* and *Wickard* to find a cumulative substantial effect.

5. Organized Crime

In *Perez v. United States* (1971), the Court faced a challenge to parts of the Consumer Credit Protection Act, which made "loan sharking" a federal crime. A loan shark not only charges exorbitant rates but also seeks to collect money owed by using violence and intimidation. The Court accepted Congress's findings that loan sharking was largely under the control of organized crime, that it provided the second largest source of revenue for organized crime, and that it had an impact on interstate commerce. Thus, it was appropriate to federally criminalize loan sharking because, even though the loan shark in this case acted only within the state, the money was used to finance national operations.

Justice Potter Stewart wrote a strong dissent, pointing out the flaws in the logic. He would hold the Act unconstitutional because there is no distinction between organized crime and other crimes. All crime is a national problem that affects interstate commerce. Further, there is no requirement under the Act that the government prove that the particular defendant was involved in organized crime. If a defendant is not involved, then there is no impact on interstate commerce. Thus, for Stewart, the statute infringes on the state's police power to define and prosecute local or intrastate crime under the Tenth Amendment.

D. Modern Retrenchment? 1990s to the Present: Narrowing of the Federal Commerce Clause Power and Revival of the Tenth Amendment as a Constraint on Congress

A number of commentators have complained that since the 1990s, the Court has returned to the practices of the *Lochner* era before World War II. This argument is based on several factors: The Court has limited the scope of the Commerce Clause, it has restored the idea of state sovereignty as a substantive limitation on the reach of the Commerce Clause, it has narrowed the scope of Congress's powers under Section 5 of the Fourteenth Amendment, and it has increased the immunity of state governments from suit in state and federal court. Examined in isolation, the Commerce Clause cases during this era are not entirely unreasonable. One could argue that they simply represent the Court, once again, exercising its duty of judicial review to ensure that Congress does not exceed or abuse its power under the Commerce Clause.

1. United States v. Lopez (1995)

In *Lopez*, the Court, for the first time in nearly sixty years, invalidated a federal law as exceeding the scope of the Commerce Clause powers. The five-to-four decision included a hesitant concurrence by Justices Anthony Kennedy and Sandra Day O'Connor. Considered on its own, the decision is not wholly unreasonable. Nonetheless, it made an incremental change to the law and signaled a new era for Commerce Clause review. *Lopez* involved a challenge to the Guns Free Zone Act of 1990, in which Congress made it a federal crime "for any individual knowingly to possess a firearm at a place that the individual knows, or has reasonable cause to believe, is a school zone." The Act appeared reasonable, even to those who believe there is a constitutional right to own a firearm. The problem was that the Act has little connection with the purported constitutional source of authority for the Act. It is difficult to see the link between firearms in school zones and interstate commerce. One could argue that this case falls into what Justice Marshall called the "pretext" category of cases (*McCullough*), because it was likely that Congress was merely interested in stopping school violence, not regulating interstate commerce. The interstate commerce justification was a rationalization that occurred after Congress passed the legislation.

The Court articulated three avenues for Congress to exert legitimate Commerce Clause power. The regulation had to relate to:

1. the "channels" of interstate commerce, that is, highways, waterways, and air traffic;
2. the "instrumentalities" of interstate commerce, that is, trucks, ships, planes, and things traveling through the channels; and
3. activities that have a "substantial effect" on interstate commerce.

In this instance, Congress was not regulating an activity in interstate commerce because the Act regulated local gun possession. It clearly was not a channel or an instrumentality, and thus, the Court turned to the question of whether possession of guns at schools substantially affected interstate commerce.

There were four considerations that affected the Court's decision.

1. The Court noted that the criminal statute was unrelated to commerce.
2. It contained no jurisdictional hook or link to interstate commerce (in other words, it did not refer to guns in schools that had been shipped or sold in interstate commerce; note that the 1964 Civil Rights Act has this hook).
3. There were no congressional findings that guns in schools had a substantial impact on interstate commerce.
4. The Act was only remotely connected with interstate commerce and was more directly concerned with activities historically allocated to the states (local crimes, similar to education and family law, are historically state-law matters).

The government argued that there were substantial effects because the possession of guns in schools causes more violent crimes, which has a substantial impact on the national economy. It argued that the national economic impact was threefold: The direct costs of violent crime and insurance are spread through the population; violent crime affects the willingness of travelers to visit areas of the country believed to be unsafe; and perhaps most important, the cost of violent crime are severe in the education process, which creates less educated and thereby less productive citizens.

The Court rejected the government's argument, reasoning that if it accepted this attenuated causal argument, the Court would be "hard-pressed to posit any activity that Congress is without power to regulate." For instance, under the "costs of crime" argument, every crime could be regulated, and under the "national productivity" argument, "Congress could regulate any activity that it found was related to the economic productivity of individual citizens: family law (including marriage, divorce, and child custody), for example."

The Court noted that previous cases had extended the commerce power to great lengths, "but we decline here to proceed any further." The Court did not expressly overrule any precedent, not even *Wickard* or *Perez*, but it did make clear that the effects on interstate commerce needed to be substantial and it would not simply defer to Congress or to the government's arguments that a substantial impact existed.

Justice Kennedy, joined by Justice O'Connor, wrote a somewhat hesitant concurrence, indicating that they might decide differently if a case presented different facts. Yet Justice Clarence Thomas, in his concurring opinion, would have gone a step further and eliminated the third category of "substantial effects" altogether.

In Justice Stephen Breyer's dissenting opinion, joined by Justices John Paul Stevens and David Souter, he argued that this case was a return to the *Lochner* era because it ignored the precedent of the past sixty years. He argued that there was a substantial relation between the regulation of gun-free school zones and interstate commerce. Following *Wickard*, it was appropriate for Congress to regulate activities that have a cumulative effect on interstate commerce. Further, the Court's distinction between commercial and noncommercial activities was unworkable because Congress could easily determine that education was a commercial activity.

More important, he chastised the Court for departing from the rational basis test in this area of the law. Under rational basis, the Court defers to Congress, accepting any conceivable, rational argument that the means chosen furthers a legitimate government purpose. The question is "whether Congress could have had a rational basis for finding a significant (or substantial) connection between gun-related school violence and interstate commerce." Justice Breyer did not think that it was for the Court to determine where the line should be drawn; instead, this was a job for Congress. He reiterated the view that the states could fend for themselves through the democratic process.

Justice Stevens, in his dissent, reinforced the view that both guns and schools have a substantial impact on the economy. The future of the economy depends on "the character of the education of our children." Guns are bought and sold in interstate commerce; the fact that there is a gun market for school-age children is very troubling, and it justifies interference by Congress. Justice Stevens and Justice Souter agreed that this case had an affinity with the decisions of the *Lochner* era. Justice Souter reinforced the view that this affinity was judicial activism by the Court, evidenced by the Court's abandonment of the rational basis test and its differential standard.

For a number of years after *Lopez*, it was unclear if this was an exceptional case, due to all the factors that had combined to influence the outcome, or if it was part of a larger trend. For instance, in *Lopez*, the Court left open the possibility that it would show more deference to Congress, resulting in a different outcome, if the federal statute incuded congressional findings that the regulated activity had a substantial impact on interstate commerce.

2. United States v. Morrison *(2000)*

United States v. Morrison (2000), another five-to-four decision, addressed that possibility and a few other questions. In *Morrison*, the petitioner, Christy Brzonkala, alledged that she had been repeatedly raped and verbally abused by two football players at her college. She sued the football player and the university in a civil action under provisions of the Violence Against Women Act, which provided civil remedies for gender-motivated crimes of violence. The two defendants challenged the Act as being beyond the unenumerated powers of Congress.

The government attempted to justify the Act under both the Commerce Clause and Section 5 of the Fourteenth Amendment (the latter claim is discussed next). The Court rejected both justifications. The Act did not have any jurisdictional hook (e.g., it did not require that the violence take place across state lines or that either the victim or perpetrator cross state lines). The Court evaluated the Act under the Lopez *ruberic and found that it did not regulate the channels or instrumentalities of interstate commerce; thus, the real question was whether it regulated activities that had a substantial impact on interstate commerce.*

Here, *Morrison* could be distinguished from *Lopez* because Congress included findings that violence against women had a substantial impact on interstate commerce. It was not that the Court did not believe that there was a substantial impact on interstate commerce; rather, it did not like the fact that the impact was derived from noneconomic actvites. Again, it did not overrule *Wickard* or *Perez*, but it limited them and brought cases, such as *Heart of Atlanta* and *Katzenbach*, into question. None of these cases were overruled because the federal regulations in question regulated local *economic* activities that, when combined, had a substantial impact on interstate commerce. If everyone produced too much wheat (*Wickard*), if economic crimes such as loan sharking (an economic crime) were allowed to run rampant (*Perez*), or if African Americans were excluded from hotel accomodations (*Heart of Atlanta*) and from eating establishments across the country (*Katzenbach*), there would be a substantial economic impact, directly caused by the cumulative effects of individual or local economic impacts.

What distinguished *Lopez* and *Morisson* was that Congress regulated activities that were noncommercial in nature (i.e., possession of guns and violence against women). Even if the overall economic impact from damage to the educational system or disempowering the workforce may be substantial, for the Court, two factors put these activities beyond the reach of Congress: They were not commercial in nature, and they were traditionally within spheres regulated by the states (i.e., a limit by the Tenth Amendment). The Court also feared, legitimately or not, as in *Lopez*, that allowing the federal government to regulate the cumulative effects of noneconomic activities was a slippery slope with no end.

To be fair, the Court did not foreclose the possibility that it might uphold a future case involving the accumulation of noneconomic impacts. Rather, it held that up to this point, it had only upheld cumulative impact justifications if they were economic.

This puts *Heart of Atlanta* and *Katzenback* in some jeopardy. The activity in those cases was economic, but similar to *Lopez* and *Morrison*, Congress's primary reason for regulating the activity was to address a social issue, not an economic one. *Morrison* clearly stands for the Court abandoning rational basis review and reviving the Tenth Amendment as a limit on the reach of the Commerce Clause power. Thus, it remained an open question as to how far the Court may extend the Tenth Amendment as a limit on Congress's Commerce Clause powers.

Justice Thomas, concurred in *Morrison*, and he again urged the Court to abandon the substantial effects doctrine altogether because he thought it allows the federal government to reach into a sphere of state sovereignty. Thus, under his reasoning, all of these cases would exceed the Commerce Clause power. As will be shown in the next subsection, Justice Thomas's views did not prevail.

The dissenting opinion in *Morrison* is largely an amplified replay of the dissent in *Lopez*. The dissent believed that the Court had abandoned over sixty years of precedent, and it was reviving a view of federalism that might have been suitable for the Framers but was inadequate for today's national economy. Further, the Court was taking an improper activist role by abandoning the deferential standard of rational basis review and by taking on itself to determine what did and did not have a substantial impact on interstate commerce.

3. Cummulative Effects on Interstate Commerce

a. Regulating Commercial Loan Dispute Resolution

In *Citizens Bank v. Alafabco, Inc.* (2003), the Court dispelled possible worries that it might further constrict the cumulative effects doctrine and overrule cases like *Wickard* or *Perez*, when it upheld the application of the Federal Arbitration Act to local transactions between an Alabama bank and an Alabama construction company. Even though the debt in question was all local, the law regulated a general activity (commercial lending) that had a substantial impact on interstate commerce. The construction company, in fact, used the bank loan to engage in interstate commerce. This case was perhaps made easier by the fact that it did not raise worries that the legislation was a pretext for Congress to regulate the activity for traditional police power reasons (i.e., safety, welfare, moral or social reasons). Instead, it was for economic reasons. In other words, there was little worry that the Commerce Clause was used as a pretext to regulate what was historically or properly within the police powers of the state.

b. Regulating Personal Medicinal Production and Use of Marijuana

Although California law had carved out an exception for doctors, for other primary caregivers, and for patients who grew or possesed doctor-prescribed marijuana, this did not stop federal drug enforcement agents from taking action under the Controlled Substance Act in Gonzales v. Raich (2005). Justice Stevens wrote the majority opinion upholding the enforcement of the Act in the context of local production and use of the drug for purely medical purposes because of the possible cumulative effect on interstate commerce. It was not suprising that Justices Stevens, Souter, Ruth Bader Ginsburg, and Breyer created the core of this majority, but it was a little suprising to see Justices Kennedy and Antonin Scalia joining the opinion, leaving only Chief Justice William Rehnquist, Justice Thomas, and Justice O'Connor in the dissent. Unlike *Citizens Bank* (commercial loan dispute resolution), *Raich* involved the concern that Congress was using the Commerce Clause as a pretext to impinge on the police powers of the state. This appeared to be a very local matter involving the traditional police powers. Yet the majority not only invoked *Wickard* and the cumulative effects doctrine, it also reinstated the rational basis standard of review for Commerce Clause cases and upheld the Act.

One might have thought that *Lopez* (firearms in school zones), followed by *Morrison* (violence against women), would be hurdles, because the Court struck down federal legislation that regulated the cumulative effects of a noneconomic activity. Was the personal growth and use of marijuana any more an economic activity than the possession of guns in school zones in *Lopez*?

Because most of the Justices that dissented in *Lopez* and in *Morrison* were now members of the majority in *Raich*, it is not suprising that they would consider this activity commercial or that they would revive the rational basis test. They had argued that the Court's distinction between commercial and non-commercial regulation was unworkable, and Justice Stevens in particular had argued in his dissent in *Lopez* that possession of guns was commercial. They had all argued that the rational basis test was the proper standard of review.

The reason this group of dissenters was able to form a majority was because Kennedy and Scalia seemingly switched their positions and joined them. Justice Scalia was compelled to write a concurring opinion to explain his apparent switch from his position in Lopez and *Morrison*. Interestingly, he justified his decision with the use of the Necessary and Proper Clause (recall Justice Marshall's opinion in *McCullough* from the beginning of this chapter). His rather clever argument was that unlike in *Lopez* and *Morrison*, the regulation of the local activity here was *necessary and proper* to protect the regulation of interstate commerce. He argued that it was necessary and proper for Congress to regulate the local production and possession of medical marijuana because failure to do so "could undercut" its regulation of interstate commerce; unregulated, local marijuana could very well find its way into the channels of interstate commerce. Not regulating it would leave a local channel that could flow into interstate channels. Quoting from and distinguishing *Lopez* he argued that: "This is not a power that threatens to obliterate the line between 'what is truly national and what is truly local.'"

Though Justice Scalia's reasoning may persuasively distinguish *Morrison* (gender-motivated crimes), it is not entirely persuasive in distinguishing *Lopez* (guns in school zones). Justice Thomas, in his dissent, was emphatic that this was local and not economic; it was not "commerce ... among the several States." Looking back to the founding, he argued that "commerce" would not include "the mere possession of a good or some personal activity that did not involve trade or exchange for value. In the early days of the Republic, it would have been unthinkable that Congress could prohibit the local cultivation, possession, and consumption of marijuana."

Justice O'Connor, joined by Chief Justice Rehnquist, stressed in her dissent the importance and uniqueness of American federalism, which allowed for experimentation among the states. Respect for state autonomy is important because it promotes innovation by allowing for the possibility that "a single courageous State may, if its citizens choose, serve as a laboratory; and try novel social and economic experiments without risk to the rest of the country."

4. Channels

Just in case there were worries that Justice Thomas would gut all Commerce Clause powers if he had his way, it should be noted that he wrote the majority opinion for a unanimous Court in *Pierce County v. Guillen* (2003). In that case, the Court unanimously upheld amendments to the Federal Safety Highway Act under the Commerce Clause because it fell within the first prong of the *Lopez* framework—it regulated a channel of commerce.

The amendment to the Act required that for states to be eligible for federal funding to assist in repairing hazardous roads, they had to evaluate and implement a schedule of projects, keeping a list of the most dangerous road conditions. A woman died at a dangerous intersection, and in the subsequent civil suit, the plaintiffs wanted the information the city had collected. The city refused because the Act protected that information. The Court upheld the Safety Highway Act because the states might refuse to keep and disclose information to the federal government if they were not protected from plaintiffs using that information against them in civil suits. With a diminished threat of lawsuits and with the encouragement of federal funding, dangerous sections of highways would be fixed, and the channels of interstate commerce (the highways) would function better, facilitating the flow of the intrumentalities of commerce.

Although here the Court used the rational basis test, it is unclear whether this aspect of the decision will hold true in future cases, particularly given the weak alliance here and the arrival of two new judges on the bench (Chief Justice John Roberts and Justice Samuel Alito).

5. Avoiding the Constitutional Issue through a Limited Interpretation of Federal Legislation

In three separate cases, spanning from 2000 through 2006, the Court limited the reach of federal legislation applied by federal agencies to avoid the Commerce Clause issue. If the Court finds that the executive branch applied the statute beyond the scope of what the statute authorized, then the issue is one of federal statutory interpretation, rather than the Commerce Clause.

In *Jones v. United States* (2000), a unanimous Court held that 18 U.S.C. §844(i), which makes it a federal crime to "maliciously damag[e] or destro[y], ... by means of fire or an explosive, any building ... used in interstate or foreign commerce or in any activity affecting interstate or foreign commerce" did not apply to the private residence of Jones's cousin, and thus, Jones could not be prosecuted under the federal statute for throwng a Molotov cocktail into the house. The house was used as security on a mortgage, the owner had a casualty insurance policy with companies that conducted interstate commerce, and the house utilities were provided by an out-of-state company, but these facts were not sufficient to bring the case under the reach of the Act. If the Court had interpreted the statute to cover these facts, it may have decided that the Act went beyond the limits of the Commerce Clause.

Whereas *Jones* was an easy case, *Solid Waste Agency of Northern Cook County v. United States Army Corps of Engineers* (2001) divided the Court five to four. Congress enacted the Clean Water Act to protect water quality and eliminate pollution. The Army Corps denied the city a permit to turn a sand and gravel pit into a landfill. The Corps interpreted the phrase "navigable waters" in the Act to give it the authority to deny the permit because the gravel pit had seasonal ponds and was a habitat of migratory birds, which cross state lines. The majority held that "navigable waters" in the Clean Water Act does not include nonnavigable, isolated intrastate waters, even if used as habitat for migratory birds.

Since the Clean Water Act was within the outer limits of Congress' power, the Court required a clear statement from Congress that it intended the statute to include a sand and gravel pit. The majority reasoned that to allow the executive branch to extend the Act's scope to include nonnavigable waters would intrude into the traditional powers of the state over land and water. The Court limited the interpretation of the Act to avoid the constitutional issue.

The dissent focused on Congress's purpose for enacting the Clean Water Act. Congress intended to protect the quality of water, and therefore it was irrelevant that the water could not be navigated. Environmental regulations are within the scope of federal power, and states are not in a position to regulate migratory birds. Furthermore, the Act fell within the third category—protecting water quality has a substantial cumulative effect on migratory bird populations, and billions of dollars every year are spent on bird-watching and hunting. Thus, for the dissent, the Commerce Clause gave Congress the power to preserve natural resources that generate commerce.

In *Rapanos v. United States* (2006), the Court once again avoided the Commerce Clause question in a plurality four-one-four decision involving the Clean Water Act. *Rapanos* involved wetlands lying near ditches or man-made drains that emptied into traditional navigable waters. The Army Corps of Engineers determined that it violated the Act to fill these wetlands, based on its interpretation of the phrase "waters of the United States." It read that provision to include not only traditional navigable waters but also "tributaries" of such waters and wetlands "adjacent" to such waters and tributaries. "Adjacent" wetlands include those "bordering, contiguous [to], or neighboring" waters of the United States even when they are "separated from [such] waters ... by man-made dikes ... and the like" (§ 328.3(c)).

Four of the Justices followed *Solid Waste* (sand and gravel pit), and held that "navigable waters" includes only "relatively permanent, standing or flowing bodies of water, not intermittent or ephemeral flows of water." Wetlands must have "a continuous surface connection to bodies that are waters of the United States" to come under the Act. Justice Kennedy concurred, reasoning that the "Clean Water Act extends to non-navigable waters if there is a 'significant nexus' to waters that are navigable in fact or that could reasonably be so made." Justice Kennedy agreed with the majority that in this case, the water in question was not covered by the Act.

Most recently, in *Gonzales v. Oregon* (2006), the controversial physician-assisted suicide case, the Court held, in a six-to-three decision, that the Controlled Substance Act (CSA) did not authorize the federal government to undercut Oregon's Death with Dignity Act by suspending the authority to write prescriptions for the doctors participating in the program. The attorney general argued that providing Schedule II drugs to assist a patient in hastening death was not a "legitimate medical purpose." Thus, Oregon's act violated a 1971 federal regulation that limited prescribing Schedule II drugs only "for a legitimate medical purpose by an individual practitioner acting in the usual course of his professional practice."

The case appeared to be similar to *Raich* (medical marijuana case) because it involved a conflict between state laws and the purported enforcement of federal law under the CSA. However, the majority, led by Justice Kennedy, did not address the Commerce Clause. Rather, it held that the attorney general's interpretation of the CSA regulation did not deserve deference and that the CSA did not authorize the attorney general to prohibit doctors from prescribing regulated drugs for physician-assisted suicide.

Justice Scalia, joined by the new Chief Justice Roberts and Justice Thomas, dissented, arguing that the attorney general's interpretation of "legitimate medical purpose" was valid, and the Court should defer to his interpretation. Alternatively, even if the Court should not defer, the attorney general's interpretation was the most natural interpretation of the regulation. Finally, even if that interpretation was wrong, the attorney general's interpretations of the phrases "public interest" and "public health" should have been given deference, and it justified his actions.

III. The Taxing and Spending Powers

Article I, Section 8, Clause 1 of the Constitution sets out the taxing and spending powers of Congress. It provides:

> The Congress shall have Power To lay and collect Taxes, Duties, Imposts and Excises, to pay the Debts and provide for the common Defence and general Welfare of the United States; but all Duties, Imposts and Excises shall be uniform throughout the United States.

A. Taxing

The history of the taxing power largely follows the history of the Commerce Clause. Up until the *Lochner* era, there were few (if any) limits on Congress's taxing power. The *Lochner* era cases introduced the distinction between taxing as a penalty and taxing to raise revenues. Taxing to raise revenues was permissible under the Taxing and Spending Clause. Taxing as a penalty was impermissible because taxes that acted as a penalty were regulatory and needed to be justified by an enumerated power outside the spending power. Thus, the *Lochner* Court struck down a number of laws that were designed to address problems created by laissez-faire capitalism. For instance, the Court struck down a tax on goods produced by child labor and shipped in interstate commerce (*Bailey v. Drexel Furniture Co.*, 1922) and a tax on grain futures contracts that had not been approved by a federal trade board (*Hill v. Wallace*, 1922).

When Justice Owen Roberts created the "switch in time" that ended the *Lochner* era, the Court abandoned the distinction between taxes as penalties and taxes to raise revenues. In *Sonzinsky v. United States* (1937), the Court upheld a tax on firearms dealers, even though Sonzinsky challenged the tax as being regulatory and not revenue-generating. The Court noted that every tax was partially regulatory, and the judiciary was ill-equipped to look behind an act of Congress for illegitimate motives.

B. Spending

As discussed in the beginning of this chapter, the spending provision, along with the Necessary and Proper Clause, justified the creation of the federal bank (*McCullough*). Similar to Hamilton and Madison's debate over whether a federal bank could be created when the Constitution was silent, there was debate over whether the taxing and spending powers were limited to taxing and spending only for enumerated powers, or if the clause was a separate enumerated power that could allow for taxing and spending for the general welfare. Whereas Hamilton argued that Congress had a free hand or carte blanche to spend for the "general welfare" (unless it conflicted with other provisions), Madison argued that Congress could *only* spend to carry out one of the other *enumerated* powers listed in Article I, Section 8.

This question was not settled until *United States v. Butler* (1936), close to the end of the *Lochner* era. *Butler* involved the validity of the Agricultural Adjustment Act of 1933, a New Deal measure that sought to raise farm prices by controlling the amount of agricultural production (the same approach taken in *Wickard*). The scheme authorized the Secretary of Agriculture to contract with farmers to reduce the amount of land used for cultivation, in return for payments made from a fund that was generated by a tax on the commodity. The Court held that the spending power is an enumerated power and therefore not limited to other enumerated powers, but the spending power was to be used for spending and not regulating. In other words, Congress could not use its spending power to avoid the limits on its regulatory power (i.e., it can tax and spend outside its enumerated powers but can only regulate within its enumerated powers). Congress cannot use the Taxing and Spending Clause to tax and regulate. The Act was an unconstitutional infringement of states' rights because it sought to regulate agriculture, which was controlled locally. Just as Congress lacked the power to directly regulate agricultural production, it also lacked the power to coercively purchase compliance with a regulatory scheme through the spending power.

The Court abandoned this distinction between taxing and spending and taxing and regulating in *Chas. C. Steward Machine Co. v. Davis* (1937). This case involved a Tenth Amendment challenge to a provision of the Social Security Act, which allowed employers to receive a credit against federal taxes for any contribution to a state-enacted unemployment plan. The credit was conditioned on the state passing a plan that met congressionally defined specifications. The Court upheld the Act as a lawful exercise of Congress's spending powers to combat the national problem of unemployment.

Several cases have upheld the broad powers of Congress under the Taxing and Spending Clause. For example, in *South Dakota v. Dole* (1987), the Court upheld a federal law that conditioned the provision of highway funds on states increasing the legal drinking age to twenty-one. South Dakota attacked the statute on the grounds that this condition interfered with its own exclusive powers under the Tenth (state sovereignty) and Twenty-First (Prohibition) Amendments. The Court held that even though Congress's enumerated powers did not give it authority to set the legal drinking age itself, it had the power to indirectly encourage states to set that limit by tying the condition to the receipt of federal funds under its spending powers. While Congress could encourage states, as it did here, it could not coerce them (e.g., if too many funds for important projects were conditioned on state compliance). Further, Congress could not use its taxing and spending powers to induce the states to pass unconstitutional laws.

Thus, the test for conditional spending under *Dole* is:

1. the expenditure must be for the common defense or the general welfare;
2. the condition must be stated unambiguously;
3. there must be a relation between the purpose of the expenditure and the purpose of the condition;
4. Congress may not require the states to violate the Constitution in exchange for federal money; and
5. Congress may "induce" the states to comply, but it may not "coerce" them into doing so.

1. Conditions Must Be Unambiguous

In *Pennhurst State School and Hosp. v. Halderman* (1981), the Court held that conditions on federal funding need to be unambiguous to be enforced. The Developmentally Disabled Assistance and Bill of Rights Act of 1975 included a provision within its "bill of rights" section that called for treatment in "the setting that is least restrictive of personal liberty." The Court held that this was a mere policy objective and that for the Congress to place conditions on grants under the Act, they would need to be unambiguous (e.g., with language such as "treatment must be in the setting that is least restrictive"). Failure to make the conditions clear would mean that states were not on notice to perform the purported obligation when they accepted the federal funding.

In a similar vein, in *Gonzaga University v. Doe* (2002), the Court held that the Family and Educational Rights Privacy Act could not be read to give an implicit right of action to sue for violation of the Act. If Congress wanted to condition state funding on the right to sue under the Act, that condition must be explicit. The Court would not read it into the Act as an implied condition.

2. Extending the Power through the Necessary and Proper Clause

The Court has gone even further than *Dole* (highway funds tied to the legal drinking age) by upholding the direct regulation of third parties based on the federal funding of second parties. In *Sabri v. United States* (2004), the Court upheld a federal antibribery statute that made it a federal offense to bribe officials of organizations that receive more than $10,000 in funding from the federal government. This was not a case of conditional funding or one of regulating the conduct of the recipient of the funding; instead, the statute at issue regulated the conduct of those dealing with the recipient of the federal funds. This, again, was an instance where Congress used its powers under the Necessary and Proper Clause to extend the reach of an enumerated power—the spending power. The purpose of the law was to ensure that federal funds were not wasted through bribery and corruption. Because Congress had the power to spend, it had the power to ensure that its spending was used not for private gain but for the general welfare. The Court rejected the idea that there needed to be some jurisdictional hook as was required under the Commerce Clause in *Lopez* (gun-free school zones law struck down in part because there was no jurisdictional hook, e.g., it did not require that the guns had been sold in interstate commerce). This was not a case where Congress was seeking to achieve other ends through its enumerated powers, (i.e., it was not using the spending power as an excuse to regulate bribery). Rather, regulating bribery allowed Congress to ensure that its spending was done for the general welfare.

IV. Miscellaneous Other Domestic Powers

The Constitution gives Congress regulatory authority over a number of areas, such as interstate commerce, in which uniform national policies makes sense. Examples include powers over money, bankruptcy, the post (mail), copyrights and patents, interstate (and foreign) agreements, military facilities, federal buildings, and federal lands. Congress also has control over the District of Columbia and, as we saw from the beginning, in *Marbury v. Madison*, the power to create inferior courts and tribunals.

Most of these areas do not give rise to a great deal of constitutional dispute, and when disputes arise, the Court generally sides with Congress. For instance, the Constitution gives Congress the power over money, which includes the power to coin, regulate its value, and punish counterfeiting. Congress has the power to regulate foreign money in the United States as well as standards of weights and measures. In cases challenging the use of Treasury notes instead of coins (*Legal Tender Cases*, 1870) and challenging the abandonment of the gold standard (*Norman v. Baltimore & Ohio R.R. Co.*, 1935) the Court obviously sided with Congress.

Recently, the Court, in *Central Virginia Community College v. Katz* (2006), held that since the Bankruptcy Clause (Article I, Section 8, Clause 4) empowers Congress to establish "uniform Laws on the subject of Bankruptcies throughout the United States," then state immunity from suit does not apply in bankruptcy proceedings. Although a series of cases have held that the states are generally immune from suit in both federal and state courts unless they waive their immunity, the Court held that "Congress may constitutionally authorize suits against state government in Bankruptcy Court proceedings." There were three Justices who dissented, arguing that the states had not given up their sovereign immunity, even under the Bankruptcy Clause. (For more on state sovereign immunity, see part VII, section B.)

V. Power over Foreign Affairs

The foreign affairs powers are split between the executive and legislative branch, and those powers are often shared on particular issues, such as in the areas of treaties, the military, and war. For instance, Article II, Section 2, Clause 2 provides that the President "shall have Power, by and with the Advice and Consent of the Senate, to make Treaties, provided two thirds of the Senators present concur." The President is commander in chief of the military, but Congress has the power to declare war. Although numerous questions arise regarding the assignment of powers between the executive and legislative branch, the Court has refused to resolve many of these issues, holding that they are nonjusticiable political questions (see Chapter 1). Few questions arise with respect to the role of the states because the Constitution is relatively clear that the states have little to no foreign affairs powers.

The Constitution gives Congress a wide array of powers in the area of foreign affairs. Article I, Section 8 includes a rather extensive list. It provides, in part, that Congress shall have the power:

> To ... provide for the common Defence ... ;
> To regulate Commerce with foreign nations ... ;
> To establish a uniform Rule of Naturalization ... ;
> To define and punish Piracies and Felonies committed on the high Seas, and Offenses against the Law of nations;
> To declare War, grant Letters of Marque and Reprisal, and make Rules concerning Captures on Land and Water;
> To raise and support Armies, but no Appropriation of Money to that Use shall be for a longer Term than two Years;
> To provide and maintain a Navy;
> To make Rules for the Government and Regulation of the land and naval Forces;
> To provide for calling forth the Militia to execute the Laws of the Union, suppress Insurrections and repel Invasions;

To provide for organizing, arming, and disciplining, the Militia, and for governing such Part of them as may be employed in the Service of the United States, reserving to the States respectively, the Appointment of the Officers, and the Authority of training the Militia according to the discipline prescribed by Congress;
To exercise exclusive Legislation in all Cases whatsoever ... [and] Authority over all Places purchased by the Consent of the Legislature of the State in which the Same shall be, for the Erection of Forts, magazines, Arsenals, dock-Yards, and other needful Buildings....

Thankfully for the law student, many of these areas have not given rise to much controversy, and others have been considered nonjusticiable. Next, the treaty power, immigration and naturalization, and war powers are discussed.

A. The Treaty Power

There are three different processes for entering into binding treaties: ratification by two-thirds of the Senate, executive agreements, and preauthorization. These treaties can either be self-executing or non-self-executing. The constitutional rule that treaties must be ratified by two-thirds of the Senate is sometimes honored, particularly with multilateral human rights treaties (i.e., treaties between many countries), but the vast majority of treaties have been entered into through executive agreements. These agreements are made exclusively by the executive and do not go through the two-thirds ratification process. Over the past twenty years or so, there have been thousands of executive agreements entered into, but only a few hundred ratified treaties. It would be impossible for Congress to ratify such a large number of treaties. Nonetheless, it seems imprudent for the President to have this much power. As a result, many treaties go through a third process in which Congress preauthorizes the executive to negotiate and enter into a binding treaty (e.g., the North American Free Trade Agreement). Preauthorization does not generally include a two-thirds vote, but it does inject congressional consent and accountability, which also helps ensure that any necessary funding will likely be forthcoming.

Treaties that require domestic legislation to have force are called non-self-executing treaties. Traditionally there has been a presumption that treaties that go through the ratification procedure are self-executing unless either Congress or the treaty explicitly says that the treaty is not self-executing and requires domestic legislation, or the terms of the treaty make it clear that it needs domestic legislation (e.g., it contains a provision that states "the respective signatories agree to enact legislation to give effect to"). A treaty can also have a mixture of provisions that are self-executing and non-self-executing.

A majority of the Court in a recent decision has shifted this presumption by holding that for a treaty to be binding domestically, either Congress needs to have enacted implementing legislation or the treaty must convey the intention to be self-executing and be ratified under the understanding that it is self-executing. In *Medellin v. Texas* (2008), the Court, in a six-to-three decision, held that the President could not require that Texas implement a decision of the International Court of Justice (ICJ) (*The Case Concerning Avena and Others, Mex. v. U.S.*, 2004) because it found that the United Nations charter and the ICJ statute were not self-executing treaties. *Avena* concerned Texas's practice of ignoring the Vienna Convention on Consular Relations (VCCR), which requires that when authorities arrest a foreign national they inform the arrestee of her or his right to contact the consular office of her or his home country. The purpose of the treaty is to allow the foreign state to provide diplomatic or legal support to the arrestee. The ICJ held that a failure to notify the Mexican consulate when Texas arrested Mexican nationals violated the treaty and that those nationals had a right to review and reconsideration of their convictions and sentencing to determine if the failure to notify their consulate prejudiced their defense.

The Court did not dispute the binding nature of the decision on the United States under international law, but it did not accept that the decision was domestically enforceable as federal law. Although the United States attempted to argue that Congress had acquiesced in the President's power to require implementation of the decision, the Court rejected both that this was the case and the argument that acquiescence would be sufficient to give the President authority in this case. Instead, the Court held that congressional inaction did not amount to acquiescence and that there would need to be implementing legislation to require states to enforce a decision of the ICJ. This is because it held that the language of Article 94(1) of the UN charter, which reads, "each Member of the United Nations undertakes to comply with the decision of the [ICJ] in any case to which it is a party," was not self-executing, but simply a call to state parties to take steps to comply with ICJ decisions. Thus an ICJ decision cannot be enforced in court, even if the executive so orders. Rather, it is in the power of Congress to implement the decision. The Court further supported its interpretation by referring to the fact that the remedy for failing to comply with ICJ decisions is to refer the matter to the Security Council under Article 94(2).

In a concurring opinion, Justice Stevens noted agreement with much of the dissent's reasoning, particularly the argument that the text and history of the

Supremacy Clause and the Court's jurisprudence in treaty-related cases did not support the majority's view that there was a presumption against self-execution. Nonetheless, he could not join the dissent because he believed the language of Article 94(1) to be "perfectly ambiguous" regarding the issue of self-execution. As a result, he articulated something of a compromise position. He emphasized that even if the President did not have the authority to compel Texas to implement the decision of the ICJ, and even if the Supreme Court itself did not have the authority to compel Texas to comply, the decision was binding on the United States and on Texas through the Supremacy Clause. He read Article 94(1) of the UN charter as requiring the political branches to take further action to comply with binding ICJ decisions.

The dissent, written by Justice Breyer and joined by Justices Ginsburg and Souter, strongly attacked the majority's bright line textual test for self-execution. The strongest point made by the dissent was that it would be very rare for any treaty to embody clear language that it was self-executing because different countries had very different rules for how international treaty obligations are to become binding domestically. Whereas a number of countries, like the United States (at least up to this decision) view ratified treaties as being capable of self-execution, others, like the United Kingdom never allow for self-execution. In other words, any treaty to which the United Kingdom is a party could not contain a provision that stated that the law was self-executing because under U.K. constitutional law all treaties require domestic legislation to be binding domestically.

Drawing on the Court's previous jurisprudence, the dissent pointed to several factors, all of which contributed to an argument in favor of self-execution in this case. Those factors included the text and history of the treaty, the subject matter of the treaty, whether it concerned traditional private rights and provided for individual rights, whether the treaty set forth judicially enforceable standards, whether it created a new cause of action, and finally, if self-execution would engender constitutional controversy, or conflict between the branches.

For the dissent, the text of Article 94(1) contemplated an obligation to give the ICJ decision effect and the majority's reference to the Security Council because an enforcement mechanism was beside the point. The parties entered into a binding obligation to have disputes over the meaning or application of the VCCR resolved by the ICJ and the parties to the ICJ statute undertook the obligation to carry out those decision. The case concerned a binding provision of the VCCR that provided individual rights and judicially enforceable standards. The ICJ decision itself, which required review to determine if the denial of the right to contact one's consular office negatively impacted one's case also contained a common judicially manageable standard. It did not create a new cause of action and it did not contain subject matter that was more appropriate for the political branches. According to the dissent, it would be odd to expect Congress to either pass a blanket law that made all ICJ decisions binding domestically (e.g., under the seventy different treaties that provide for compulsory ICJ jurisdiction) or for it to intervene and pass laws on a case-by-case basis. Such a case-by-case determination is better suited to the judiciary. According to the dissent, a failure to recognize the treaty as self-executing may have serious negative practical implications for the many rights protected under the treaties that provide for compulsory jurisdiction before the ICJ. Treating the treaty as self-executing would not create conflict with the other branches because the executive favors this interpretation and Congress has not expressed any concern with regard to this interpretation.

Finally, the dissent argued that the majority has unduly hampered the power of the President under his foreign affairs powers to order the states to give effect to the ICJ decision. For the dissent, the case should have been remanded to the Texas courts to implement the President's order.

The Court has upheld the President's power to make executive agreements (*Dames & Moore v. Regan*, 1981), and it has refused to hear a challenge to the President's power to unilaterally rescind a treaty (*Goldwater v. Carter*, 1979). When President Jimmy Carter unilaterally rescinded a treaty with Taiwan (a small country that broke away when communists took over mainland China) to recognize the "other" China (mainland China or the People's Republic of China), Senator Barry Goldwater brought a claim, arguing that because the Constitution required the advice and consent of the Senate for the President to enter into the treaty, then the Senate was also needed to rescind the treaty. The constitutional text is silent on the issue, and the Court, in a plurality opinion, did not wish to enter the political thicket (see the political question doctrine in Chapter 1). The result is that the President is effectively free to unilaterally rescind treaties (without the Senate's approval) because the Court will refuse to hear the claims.

The treaty power has few limits. For instance, during the *Lochner* era, at the height of "state sovereignty" the Court held upheld a migratory bird treaty between the United States and Canada that interfered with the state of Missouri's purported sovereign rights over migratory birds (*Missouri v. Holland*, 1920). The argument was that since the Court had already held that Congress could not regulate migratory birds directly under its Commerce Clause powers because those powers were limited by the Tenth Amendment, then Congress could not regulate the birds under its treaty-making power. The Court dismissed the argument, noting that the treaty power would only be limited by an express provision of the Constitution and not the Tenth Amendment.

In *Reid v. Covert* (1957), the Court limited the effect of the treaty-making power because it violated an express constitutional provision, namely, the right to a jury trial. In that case, a treaty had provided a U.S. military tribunal with jurisdiction over all crimes committed within Britain by U.S. military personnel and their dependents. Without the aid of a jury, the tribunal convicted Clarice Covert, a dependent of a member of the U.S. armed forces, for killing her husband. The Court overruled the conviction because it violated Covert's right to trial by jury.

B. Immigration and Naturalization

The Constitution provides Congress with broad authority over immigration and naturalization (the process of becoming a citizen). Congress's power in this area preempts any state powers (*Fiallo v. Bell,* 1977). However, once a person has been naturalized and becomes a U.S. citizen, Congress loses its broad authority. Thus, the Court struck down legislation that withdrew citizenship from Angelika Schneider, a woman who moved to the United States from Germany as a child, was naturalized, and then, after graduating from college, returned to Germany and remained there for eight years (*Schneider v. Rusk,* 1964). The Court also struck down legislation that withdrew citizenship from Beys Afroyim, a Polish immigrant to the United States who voted in an Israeli election in 1951 (*Afroyim v. Rusk,* 1967).

C. War Powers

As already noted, Congress has joint authority with the executive over war powers. Even though the Constitution clearly puts the authority for deciding when to go to war in the hands of Congress, the executive has, on a number of occasions, taken it upon itself to commit troops to battle. The Court, in the case concerning *The Brig Amy Warwick* (1863), upheld the power of President Abraham Lincoln to impose a blockade on Southern states to put down the rebellion. The Court reasoned that the executive needed the authority to respond to attack or insurrection without waiting for authorization from Congress. Nonetheless, conflicts between the executive and legislative branches in this area have often been dismissed as nonjusticiable (see Chapter 1). The federal courts regularly dismissed challenges to the Vietnam War as being nonjusticiable political questions, and the Supreme Court denied the writ of certiorari to each of these cases (e.g., *Holtzman v. Schlesinger,* 1973; *Orlando v. Laird,* 1971; and *Mora v. McNamara,* 1967). Since the Court would not intervene in these cases, Congress took action through the War Powers Resolution to further limit the ability of the executive to go to war or commit troops without a declaration of war. A challenge to President Bill Clinton's use of the mil-

itary in the former Yugoslavia as exceeding the limits of the War Powers Resolution was dismissed on standing grounds in *Campbell v. Clinton* (D.C. Cir.
2000), but disputes over the Resolution would likely be dismissed under the political question doctrine as well.

VI. Congressional Enforcement of Civil Rights under the Civil War Amendments

The Civil War Amendments, the Thirteenth, Fourteenth and Fifteenth
Amendments, were designed to address the evils of slavery and discrimination. The Thirteenth Amendment prohibits slavery and involuntary servitude.
The prohibition is general and thus applies to everyone (i.e., both private persons and the states), and Section 2 of the Thirteenth Amendment provides
Congress with the power to enforce it through appropriate legislation (called
the Enforcement Clause).

The Fourteenth Amendment establishes that all people born and naturalized
in the United States are citizens and that no state can abridge the privileges and
immunities of U.S. citizens. The Amendment also provides that no state may
deprive any person of life, liberty, or property without due process of law or
deny any person equal protection of the laws. The language of the Fourteenth
Amendment ("No State shall") limits its application to the state; it does not address private persons. Thus, it is the state's duty to ensure equal protection of the
laws. What if individuals are abridging other's privileges and immunities or denying them equal protection of the laws, and the state simply stands by without
attempting to regulate this behavior? Can Congress intervene under Section 5,
which gives Congress the authority to enforce the Fourteenth Amendment through
appropriate legislation? The Court has held that it cannot. This is discussed next.

The Fifteenth Amendment states: "The right of citizens of the United States
to vote shall not be denied or abridged by the United States or by any State on
account of race, color, or previous condition of servitude." Thus, this Amendment addresses the federal government ("abridged by the United States") and
the states ("or by any State"), and it serves to guarantee U.S. citizens the equal
right to vote. The provisions of the Fifteenth Amendment are not as broad as
those of the Equal Protection Clause of the Fourteenth Amendment, which
guarantees equal protection of "the laws." The Fifteenth Amendment also has
an Enforcement Clause in Section 2. This clause is identical to Section 2 of the
Thirteenth and Section 5 of the Fourteenth, in that it affords Congress the
power to make laws to enforce the Fifteenth Amendment (e.g., the Voting
Rights Act of 1965). The Thirteenth, Fourteenth, and Fifteenth Amendments

do not require subsequent legislation to be directly enforceable. Nonetheless, Congress has passed various forms of legislation under the Enforcement Clauses each of these Amendments.

A. The Civil Rights Cases

Shortly after the passage of the Thirteenth, Fourteenth, and Fifteenth Amendments, Congress passed the Civil Rights Act of 1875, which, similar to the 1965 Civil Rights Act (which Congress enacted under its Commerce Clause power), made it illegal to deny anyone the "the full and equal enjoyment of the accommodations, advantages, facilities and privileges" of public accommodations (e.g., public places for dining, sleeping, and entertainment, and common carriers of travel accommodations). Congress passed the Act of 1875 under the Enforcement Clauses of the Thirteenth and Fourteenth Amendments (Sections 2 and 5, respectively). The purpose of the Act was to protect individuals from being denied equal protection by other individuals — for example, a privately owned restaurant that refuses service to persons based on their color or nationality. The legislation was arguably necessary because Southern states were not providing their African American citizens equal protection of the laws nor were they protecting them from the badges and incidents of slavery; states in the South allowed for other state citizens to discriminate against African Americans in providing public accommodation.

The Supreme Court, in the *Civil Rights Cases: United States v. Stanley* (1883), struck down the Civil Rights Act of 1875. Justice Joseph Bradley, writing for the majority, held that the legislation was improper under both Enforcement Clauses. It failed under Section 5 of the Fourteenth because it only allowed for legislation that regulated state conduct and not private conduct. (Recall the previous discussion; the language of the Fourteenth is addressed only to the states.) Further, it failed under Section 2 of the Thirteenth because Congress could only regulate private conduct that amounted to slavery, involuntary servitude, or the "badges and incidents" of slavery. Discriminating in the provision of public accommodations fell in between; it was neither the state denying equal protection nor individuals practicing slavery. Rather, it regulated private individuals denying access to public accommodations on the basis of race. Thus, this regulation exceeded the purposes of the Thirteenth and Fourteenth Amendments; Congress could not enact legislation under the Enforcement Clauses of those Amendments.

The Court held that the Fourteenth Amendment authorized Congress to regulate the states; it did not authorize Congress to regulate private conduct.

It was the role of the states to regulate private individuals. However, the Court noted an exception. Congress could regulate private conduct that was either sanctioned by the state or performed under the authority of the state. Yet Congress could not regulate simply because the state failed to ensure equal protection of the laws for individuals. This remains the law to this day (see discussion of *United States v. Morrison*, 2000).

Justice Harlan, the lone dissenter, wrote a powerful opinion, arguing that the Citizenship Clause in the Fourteenth Amendment ("all persons ... are citizens of the United States and of the State") guaranteed African Americans equal citizenship, which protected them from the denial of equal civil rights by either the state or by private persons. Alternatively, given that places of public accommodation had always been subject to public regulation, their owners were, in effect, agents of the state. Furthermore, he argued that Congress was correct in its determination that discrimination by owners of public accommodations, who were fulfilling public or quasi-public functions, constituted a "badge of servitude."

Although the Court thought the Act was too far a stretch to be justified under the Enforcement Clauses, the Court set the groundwork for considerable elasticity under Section 2 of the Thirteenth Amendment. The Court established that the touchstone or standard for allowing Congress to regulate under Section 2 was whether the purpose of the legislation was to abolish the "badges and incidents of slavery." Oddly enough, the Court appeared to believe that there were no badges or incidents of slavery remaining at that point in time and that "descendants of slaves" should stop asking for special treatment and stand up on their own two feet. As the Court put it:

> When a man has emerged from slavery, and by the aid of beneficent legislation has shaken off the inseparable concomitants of that state, there must be some stage in the progress of his elevation when he takes the rank of a mere citizen, and ceases to be the special favorite of the laws.

Contrary to the Court's view, as time went by, the badges and incidents evidently remained, and this eventually provided room for national legislative action. It was not until the 1960s that the Court upheld legislation governing private discriminatory conduct under Section 2 of the Thirteenth Amendment. Prior to this time, laws that attempted to protect the civil rights of African Americans to gainful employment and places of accommodation were struck down as beyond the scope of Congress's powers in Section 2 to enforce the Amendment (*Hodges v. United States*, 1906, laws prohibiting intimidation of African American employees by third parties; *Corrigan v. Buckley*, 1926, laws prohibiting racially restrictive covenants; *Hurd v. Hodge*, 1948).

The next sections address the Enforcement Clauses of the Thirteenth and Fifteenth Amendments first because there is case law only until the beginning of the 1980s. We conclude the section on the Civil War amendments with the Fourteenth Amendment because there is case law until 1997. The more recent case law under the Fourteenth Amendment potentially brings into question the stability of the case authority under the Thirteenth and Fifteenth Amendments during these earlier periods.

B. Thirteenth Amendment during the 1960s and 1970s

In *Jones v. Alfred H. Mayer Co.* (1968), the Court changed gears and decided that under Section 2, it was up to Congress to determine what qualified as the badges and incidents of slavery and determine the appropriate means to effectively eliminate them. Thus, the Court upheld 42 U.S.C. § 1982, which provides that every citizen shall have equal rights when it comes to property, including the rights to "inherit, purchase, lease, sell, hold, and convey real and personal property."

The Court used the same deferential approach to Congress's powers under Section 2 in cases involving 42 U.S.C § 1985(3), which created a private right of action to sue those involved in conspiracies to deny persons equal protection or equal privileges and immunities under the laws (*Griffin v. Breckenridge*, 1971, suit allowed by African-American victims of racially motivated assault); and the prohibition of discrimination in private contracting under 42 U.S.C. § 1981 (*Runyan v. McCrary*, 1976, private schools refusing to contract with parents of qualified African American students, i.e., refusing to admit into school).

It is unclear whether the current Court will continue to take a deferential approach under Section 2 of the Thirteenth Amendment. The Court's more recent decisions under the Fourteenth Amendment indicate otherwise.

C. Fifteenth Amendment from the 1960s to 1980

During this same period, the Court also took a deferential approach to Section 2 the Fifteenth Amendment. In *South Carolina v. Katzenbach* (1966), the Court upheld the Voting Rights Act of 1965 against challenges that certain provisions of the Act exceeded the powers of Congress and encroached on an area reserved to the states by the Constitution. The relevant parts of the Act gave the Attorney General discretion to suspend literacy tests and other voting restrictions in states that had less than 50 percent voter registration or turnout in the previous presidential election. These restrictions were suspended for five years from the last occurrence of voting discrimination, and a state would need to clear any new restriction with the Attorney General. In upholding the Act, the Court noted that previous legislation and lawsuits had been unsuccessful at remedying the problem, and given the seriousness and persistence of the problem and the evasive tactics of state officials, the Act was a proper exercise of power under Section 2 of the Fifteenth Amendment.

The Court, in *City of Rome v. United States* (1980), upheld Section 5 of the Voting Rights Act of 1965, which restricted the attorney general to approving any new voting plan or scheme only if it "does not have the purpose and will not have the effect of denying or abridging the right to vote on account of race or color." In *City of Rome*, the Attorney General could not approve changes to the election scheme in the city of Rome because they would have a discriminatory impact on African American voters (in part because the scheme included at-large elections, which have the effect of reducing representation for African Americans because their vote is spread across the whole at large district).

The Court upheld the Act as a legitimate exercise of the enforcement powers under the Fifteenth Amendment, even though it ruled the very same day in *City of Mobile v. Bolden* (1980) that a constitutional challenge to at-large elections on equal protection grounds would require proof of discriminatory purpose. Under the Act in *City of Rome*, no proof of discriminatory purpose was required. In other words, Section 2 of the Fifteenth Amendment empowered Congress to protect the right to vote by prohibiting "practices that in and of themselves do not violate ... the Amendment, so long as the prohibitions attacking racial discrimination in voting are 'appropriate,' as that term is defined in *McCulloch v. Maryland*." Section 2 serves the same function and provides the same discretion as the Necessary and Proper Clause, as interpreted in *McCulloch* (the national bank case). Thus, the Court stated that "since Congress could rationally have concluded that, because electoral changes by jurisdictions with a demonstrable history of intentional racial discrimination in voting create the risk of purposeful discrimination, it was proper to prohibit changes that have a discriminatory impact." This legislation was held to be an appropriate method to prevent the states from "undo[ing] or defeat[ing] the rights recently won" by African Americans.

D. Fourteenth Amendment

During the height of judicial deference to Congress under the Enforcement Clauses of the Thirteenth and Fifteenth Amendments, the Court also deferred to Congress's authority to legislate under Section 5 of the Fourteenth Amendment. In fact, the case of *Katzenbach v. Morgan* (1966) provided the model for *City of Rome*, which the Court decided fourteen years later.

In *Katzenbach v. Morgan* (1966) the Court upheld the Voting Rights Act of 1965, which prohibited denying the right to vote on the basis of English language competency to individuals of Puerto Rican descent who had passed the sixth grade. The law was challenged by New York voters as exceeding the parameters of the Enforcement Clause of the Fourteenth Amendment and as a violation of the Equal Protection Clause of the Fourteenth Amendment (as it singled out Puerto Rican voters from other non-English-speaking voters). The argument, in part, was that since the Court had upheld English language literacy tests in *Lassiter v. Northampton Election Board* (1959) as not violating the Fourteenth or Fifteenth Amendments, Congress could not use its power under these Amendments to prohibit such literacy tests (i.e., it could not provide more protection than the Constitution).

The Court did not accept this argument and held that the Enforcement Clause gave Congress the same powers as the Necessary and Proper Clause. Thus, Congress had the power to enact legislation that is "necessary and proper" to carry out the purposes of the Fourteenth Amendment. Similar to the Necessary and Proper Clause, Section 5 of the Fourteenth Amendment provided Congress with the authority to go beyond the floor, or minimum, set by the Court in *Lassiter*. The test for the Court was whether the law was plainly adapted to the end of furthering the aims of the Fourteenth Amendment and whether it was consistent with the letter and spirit of the Constitution. The Court viewed the Fourteenth Amendment as setting a base or floor (a minimum protection of the right to equal protection) and not a ceiling or limit (a maximum protection of the right). The Court viewed Section 5 as an authorization for building on top of that floor or base; Congress could go further and afford more protection than the Amendment afforded. Because the Act did not restrict anyone else's right to vote (which would give less protection than mandated by the Amendment) but merely cleared the way for one group to vote, it did not offend the Constitution. This was a reform measure, and Congress could take one step at a time in legislating to give full or further effect to the right. In other words, Congress did not have to clear the way for every group, but could address discrimination against one group at a time.

It is important to note that Puerto Rico was a territory of the United States and Puerto Ricans were considered citizens of the United States with a right to vote. The United States had imposed English-language-only laws on the territory after taking it over in 1898 (it had been dominated by Spain for the previous 400 years or so). The English-only laws were repealed, and Spanish was restored as the official language in 1952, when the territory became a commonwealth. This created a special situation; U.S. citizens were educated in Spanish and then later denied the right to vote by states like New York because of their lack of English skills.

Justice Harlan, in his dissent, worried that giving Congress authority to extend rights would give them license to erode rights (i.e., if it could build on top of the floor, then it could also dig under it). The majority correctly pointed out that Section 5 only gave Congress power to enact appropriate legislation to enforce or further support the Fourteenth Amendment and not tear it down or erode it.

1. City of Boerne v. Flores *(1997)*

One way of reading *City of Boerne v. Flores* (1997) is that it reversed the view taken by the majority in *Katzenbach*. At minimum, the Court rejected giving more deference to Congress's interpretation of the First Amendment, as applied to the states through the Due Process Clause of the Fourteenth Amendment, by giving more effect to the right than the Court had given it in its previous ruling in *Employment Division of Oregon v. Smith* (1990). In fact, the Court was unanimous on the point that its interpretation of the First Amendment was not a floor for Congress to build on, it was the whole building. Thus, Congress could not remodel the building or build an addition; Congress could not change or add to the right protected by the Constitution.

The case is dealt with extensively in Chapter 10, Section C. Briefly put, the case concerned the validity of the Religious Freedom Restoration Act (RFRA), which Congress had passed to overrule *Smith*. In *City of Boerne*, the Court held that generally applicable laws that burden religious freedom, protected under the Free Exercise Clause, only need to pass a rational basis test (the regulation must be rationally related to a legitimate governmental purpose). The RFRA provided that such laws needed to pass a heightened scrutiny test; in other words, they would need to be enacted for a compelling state interest. (Thus, Congress attempted to afford more protection of the Free Exercise Clause by requiring the Court to use a form of heightened scrutiny when it examined legislation that intruded on that right.)

The legislation was defended as a permissible exercise of Congress's Fourteenth Amendment enforcement powers. It was argued that, because the 1st Amendment is made applicable to the states through the Fourteenth Amendment's guarantee of due process, then Congress was authorized to create a more stringent test for the protection of religious freedom. The Court rejected this argument and vigorously defended its role in determining the parameters of the Constitution, holding that the Act had violated the separation of powers. As held in *Marbury v. Madison*, it is the province of the Court to declare

what the law is. The majority argued that allowing Congress to expand or contract the scope of constitutional guarantees would demote the Constitution
from the "supreme law" to a law, like any other, that could be altered through
the normal legislative process.

The Court distinguished the Voting Rights Cases from the present case,
holding that while the cases under the Voting Rights Act involved the enforcement of rights under the Fourteenth Amendment, the RFRA was not
designed as an enforcement measure, but as a mechanism for redefining the
right. Whereas the former was prophylactic legislation, prohibiting states
with a history of discrimination in voting rights from passing discriminatory laws, the RFRA was "so out of proportion to any supposed remedial or
preventive object that it cannot be understood as responsive to, or designed
to prevent, unconstitutional behavior. It appears, instead, to attempt a substantive change in constitutional protections." For it to be justified as remedial or preventive measure, Congress would need documentation of religious
persecution of a sufficient magnitude to justify the measure (the Court returns to this point in its recent state immunity cases, discussed in the next
section).

There is a strong argument that changing the test from rational basis to
strict scrutiny is precisely about providing more protection for the right. These
tests do not tell one what the right is, nor do they change the right. Rather,
they simply change the level of justification that the state needs to provide to
limit or infringe the right.

Although the dissent disagreed with the majority as to the correct test for
religious freedom (the dissent thought it should be a form of heightened
scrutiny), it did not disagree with the conclusion that it was for the Court, not
Congress, to decide which test to apply.

Though *City of Boerne* did not overrule the *Voting Rights Cases*, it made
clear that those cases were limited to actual enforcement of the Amendments.
At the very least, *City of Boerne* signals that the Court is unlikely to be too deferential to Congress under the enforcement sections of the Thirteenth, Fourteenth, and Fifteenth Amendments.

VII. State Sovereignty

There are a number of situations in which the notion of state sovereignty
is raised as a limit on congressional power. In some cases, it limits Congress's
power to regulate the state, and in others, it limits Congress's power to authorize suits against the state. In fact, in a number of situations, Congress may

have complete authority under an enumerated power to regulate state conduct but may be powerless to authorize suits against the state.

Part A deals with state sovereignty as a limit on the regulatory power of Congress, and part B addresses immunity from suit.

A. State Sovereignty as a Limit on the Regulatory Power

In *National League of Cities v. Usery* (1976), the petitioners challenged the 1974 amendments to the Fair Labor Standards Act, which extended the provisions of the Act to public employees. The Act provided both minimum wage and maximum hours for employees. Though there was no question that the Act was constitutional with regard to the private sector, petitioners argued that the extension to state employees was a violation of the Tenth Amendment. A majority of the Court joined Justice Rehnquist and agreed with the petitioners, holding that this interfered with the state's "traditional government functions." The Court reasoned that interfering with the wages of state employees constituted an interference with the state's budget and thus interfered with the state's ability to provide government services.

Justice William Brennan dissented and likened the holding to the Court's jurisprudence during the *Lochner* era. Justice Stevens, in his dissent, pointed out that the federal government already regulated the state and its employment activities, for example, through "environmental guidelines," "transportation limitations," and "fair hiring" requirements.

In subsequent cases during this period, the Court's invocation of the Tenth Amendment was not extended. In *Garcia v. San Antonio Metropolitan Transit Authority* (1985), the transit authority invoked *Usery* to challenge the application of the Fair Labor Standards Act to its employees. The Court took this opportunity to overrule *Usery*, holding that while the case provided some examples of what constituted a "traditional government function," the standard had proved unworkable. Justice Harry Blackmun, who wrote the majority opinion in *Garcia*, had supported the balancing of federal and states interests through the "traditional governmental functions" test in *Usery*, but found that this test resulted in chaos throughout the lower courts. Under *Garcia*, the question is not whether the state activity is a traditional governmental function, or whether the government is fulfilling a governmental or proprietary function, but whether the regulation destroys state sovereignty or is in violation of the provisions of the Constitution, for example, whether it exceeds Congress's enumerated powers. The Court held that nothing in the statute undermined state sovereignty. States can protect themselves through the political process. They are protected by Article I and by the structure of the federal government. The states have political influence in Congress, especially in the Senate, where each state is equally represented. The protection for states "is one of process rather than one of result." Thus, the Metropolitan Transit Authority is not immune from the Fair Labor Standards Act.

Justices Lewis Powell, Rehnquist, and O'Connor dissented, arguing that this decision was contrary to the Framers' intent that the states retain a separate sovereign sphere. They thought that the majority's decision undermined the federal system. The dissent questioned the majority's argument that the states were represented in the federal government and that this provided them adequate protection. For the dissent, Congress cannot choose unconstitutional means, even to obtain legitimate ends, and the judiciary should not hand over its role "to say what the law is." The Tenth Amendment should provide a limit and the federal government's chosen end should be balanced with the means that it chooses to implement that end. The dissent argued that the balance in this case was in favor of the state because mass transit was a traditional local service and displacing state and local control over labor standards in this sector would impact their ability to provide the service.

1. The Federal Government Can Regulate but Not Commandeer

In *New York v. United States* (1992), the Court held that Congress could not commandeer the states and force them to regulate nuclear waste produced within their borders. The Low Level Radioactive Waste Policy amendments included provisions to encourage states to address the problem of radioactive waste disposal. The Act provided some incentives, and it also provided significant disincentives if a state failed to deal with the waste within its borders. The Act provided federal funds for states that made such arrangements to dispose of their waste, and it denied access to certain out-of-state facilities for states that did not make those arrangements. Most important, it included a "take title" provision, which required any state that had not arranged for waste disposal to "take title" to the waste on request of the waste producer. The result would be that the state would then bear the entire responsibility of disposing of the waste and would also be liable for any damages incurred in connection with the waste disposal.

New York failed to convince its residents that nuclear waste disposal facilities would be good for their communities. The state sued, arguing that all three of the provisions, especially the take title provision, violated the Tenth Amendment because it forced the state of New York to regulate in a particular area.

The majority agreed, holding that Congress's power authorized it to regulate individuals but not the state. Congress could not simply "commandeer the legislative processes of the States by directly compelling them to enact and enforce a federal regulatory program." The program put the states between a rock and hard place, forcing them to choose between two "unconstitutionally coercive regulatory techniques." Either the state had to make arrangements for disposal of waste generated inside it, or it had to incur the liability for damages caused by those who generated the waste. The Court upheld the other incentive programs, including the denial of access to out-of-state facilities.

In *New York*, the Court distinguished *Garcia* (the transit authority case involving the Fair Labor Standards Act). In *Garcia*, the federal law applied to private parties and the state when the state occupied the same position as a private party (i.e., as an employer). The Act in question in *New York* directly regulated the state, forcing it to carry out the federal government's policy. This would allow the federal government to hide behind its policy, while the states did the dirty work of implementing it. How could New York be accountable to its electorate if it had no choice but to implement the policy for the federal government?

As Justice Byron White pointed out in his dissent, Congress was not forcing its will on the states. Rather, Congress had responded to a request by many of the states to ratify a compromise, which the states had worked out among themselves, to solve the national waste disposal problem. Congress had to force New York to cooperate under the scheme, otherwise the other states would end up with New York's nuclear waste. According to the dissent, the federal government was acting as referee between the states "to prohibit one from bullying another." In essence, it was necessary for the federal government to step in, because the states had failed to resolve the problem themselves.

For Justice Stevens, nothing in the Constitution stopped the federal government from requiring states to carry out federal policy, if it was created pursuant to Congress's enumerated powers. This was no different from *Garcia*.

New York was endorsed and extended by the Court in *Printz v. United States* (1997). When Congress passed the Brady Handgun Bill, it included provisions that required the aid of local sheriff departments to be carried out. The Act required the sheriff departments to temporarily conduct background checks on handgun purchasers until the federal government had set up its national background check system. The checks were fairly ministerial, that is, they did not require a great deal of discretion on the part of the sheriff departments. Further, unlike in *New York*, this was Act that did not commandeer the state legislature, only local officials. Jay Printz, a county sheriff in Montana, sued, arguing that under *New York*, Congress could not force them to conduct background checks on the federal government's behalf.

In *Printz*, a five-to-four decision, the Court sided with the sheriff departments and held that the federal government "may not compel the States to enact or administer a federal regulatory program." Justice Scalia, writing for the majority, concluded that the background check provision of the Brady Bill violated this prohibition and violated the separation of powers because it took away power from the President to "take Care that the Laws be faithfully executed" and put that power in the hands of local sheriffs.

Justice Scalia rejected the dissent's distinction between compelling a state to make policy and compelling state executive branch officers (the sheriff departments) to perform ministerial tasks. It was irrelevant that this case involved merely carrying out a defined function, whereas *New York* required the state to devise policy and plans to deal with nuclear waste. It did not matter that the federal government in this case did not require the state to create a policy and implement it in accordance with federal policy. Justice Scalia held:

> It is an essential attribute of the States' retained sovereignty that they remain independent and autonomous within their proper sphere of authority. It is no more compatible with this independence and autonomy that their officers be "dragooned" into administering federal law, than it would be compatible with the independence and autonomy of the U.S. that is officers be impressed into service for the execution of state laws.

Justice Stevens, in his dissent, argued that the Commerce Clause gave Congress the authority to regulate handguns and that the Necessary and Proper Clause gave Congress the right to implement its regulation by temporarily requiring local police officers to perform the ministerial step of identifying persons who should not be entrusted with handguns. For Justice Stevens, the Tenth Amendment did not bar Congress from delegating functions to local officials in this way. He stated: "The 10th Amendment provides no support for a rule that immunizes local officials from obligations that might be imposed on ordinary citizens."

These cases were distinguished in *Reno v. Condon* (2000). Under the Driver's Privacy Protection Act of 1994, states were barred from selling or disclosing the personal information they gathered from citizen who had applied for driver's licenses. South Carolina had a conflicting law, and thus, it challenged the federal law on Tenth Amendment grounds, as violating its sovereign immunity. The Court held that Congress had authority to implement the Act under its Commerce Clause powers because the records were "things in interstate commerce." Further, the Act did not implicate the Tenth Amendment. Although there was an argument that the federal government "comandeered" the state by requiring it to devote time and effort to comply with the Act, unlike *New York* and *Printz,* the state was not required to enact further legislation, nor were the states' officers required to enforce federal law. Instead, this legislation directly regulated the state on a matter within the scope of the Commerce Clause. Because it forbade the states from acting, rather than commanded them to do something, there was no "commandeering" by the federal government.

B. State Sovereignty as a Basis for Immunity from Suit

The Eleventh Amendment provides that: "The Judicial power of the United States shall not be construed to extend to any suit in law or equity, commenced or prosecuted against one of the United States by Citizens of another State, or by Citizens or Subjects of any Foreign State."

The general rule is that a state cannot be sued unless it waives its immunity or consents to being sued. In *Fitzpatrick v. Bitzer* (1976), a case involving suits against the state for employment discrimination under Title VII of the 1964 Civil Rights Amendment, the Court held that the states had implicitly consented to suit. Congress authorized Title VII under Section 5 of the Fourteenth Amendment (the Enforcement Clause). Since the Fourteenth Amendment followed and modified the Eleventh Amendment, and since the Fourteenth Amendment was aimed at state action ("no State shall"), then the states could be sued for violating Title VII.

The modern rule requires that the authorization for suit must be express and clear (versus implicit) and that it must be *proportional and congruent* to the constitutional harm. In cases under Section 5 of the Fourteenth Amendment, proportionality and congruency are determined by the level of protection afforded, given the class of persons protected under the Amendment, as well as the evidence of unconstitutional discrimination against the class of persons. If a category of persons only receives rational basis protections (i.e., in the case of age- or disability-based discrimination), there must be a history and a pattern of widespread discrimination. In cases receiving heightened scrutiny (i.e., race and gender discrimination) less proof of a history and pattern of discrimination is required.

1. The Fourteenth Amendment, but Not the Commerce Clause

There was a brief moment in time when the Court, in a plurality opinion, held that Congress could authorize suits against the states under the Commerce Clause. *Pennsylvania v. Union Gas Co.* (1989). Article I, Section 8, Clause 3 states: "The Congress shall have Power ... To regulate Commerce with foreign nations, and among the several States, and with the Indian Tribes." The idea was that the Commerce Clause powers were not complete unless Congress could back up its powers with the authorization of suits against the state.

In *Seminole Tribe of Florida v. Florida* (1996), Congress had passed the Indian Gaming Regulatory Act, which imposed a duty on states to negotiate in good faith with Native Americans, and it authorized tribes to sue the states in federal court if they failed to do so. The Seminole Tribe of Florida brought suit against the state under this Act for limiting their gaming rights.

The Court, in a five-to-four decision, held that Congress could not authorize tribes to sue the states in federal court for money damages under its Commerce Clause powers. Though it makes sense that this provision of Article I could limit preconstitutional state sovereign immunity, Article I is still subject to the provisions in the Eleventh Amendment, enacted later. Thus, to abrogate state sovereign immunity under the Eleventh Amendment, Congress would need authorization under a subsequent amendment. The Court articulated two requirements for abrogating the states' immunity from suit: (1) the authorization to sue needed to be clear; and (2) the suit needed to be authorized under Section 5 of the Fourteenth Amendment. (See section on the Enforcement Clauses.)

As the dissent pointed out, this left state citizens without a forum to bring claims against their own state for the violation of federal law. For the dissent, the Eleventh Amendment only provided immunity in diversity cases, but not in cases involving a federal question under valid federal law. (See Chapter 1, part V).

2. Denial of Intellectual Property

Florida Prepaid Postsecondary Expense Education Board v. College Savings Bank (1999) involved an agency of the state of Florida infringing on a patent. The agency had copied a college tuition plan, which the College Savings Bank from New Jersey had designed and patented. The Bank sued the agency for patent infringement under recent amendments to the federal patent laws, which authorized the suit. The argument was that the patent right was property and that the state of Florida had denied that property right without due process, as required by the Fourteenth Amendment.

Rather than deny that the state had violated the Due Process Clause of the Fourteenth Amendment, the Court held that authorization of suits against the state was not proportional to the infringement of the right. Although it is hard to imagine anything more proportional than the right to sue for the taking of one's intellectual property, the Court held that there must be a "history of widespread and persisting deprivation of constitutional rights" to justify overriding a state's immunity from suit under Section 5. The Court reasoned that because there had only been a handful of cases over the past 100 years or so, Congress's response was disproportional. Thus, this case was distinguishable from the voting rights cases, in which there was evidence of a history of widespread discrimination.

The dissent saw no justification for the majority's "history of deprivation" requirement.

3. Age Discrimination

The Court applied the same reasoning in *Kimel v. Florida Board of Regents* (2000), another five-to-four decision. This case involved the Age Discrimination in Employment Act, which made it unlawful for any employer, including a state, to refuse to hire someone based on his or her age. While the Court held that Congress did "unequivocally express" intent to abrogate state immunity, the abrogation was not justified under Section 5 of the Fourteenth Amendment.

Here, the Court reasoned that there was no widespread pattern of discrimination on the basis of age. Furthermore, since age was not a suspect class (like race or gender), Congress could not authorize suits against the states for age discrimination. The idea was that since age discrimination is only protected by a rational basis test (rationally related to a legitimate purpose), rather than heightened scrutiny, the Act was not proportional to the end. It regulated too much constitutionally protected conduct. Thus, it was disproportionate to allow Congress to interfere with state immunity in these cases. The Court reasoned that state employees could turn to their own state law and state courts for recourse.

4. Discrimination Based on Disabilities

The plaintiffs in *Board of Trustees of the University of Alabama v. Garrett* (2001) hoped to distinguish their suit under Title I of the Americans with Disabilities Act by showing that there was in fact an ample record of discrimination against the disabled and that this record was part of the Act's legislative history. Thus, they argued that unlike in *Kimel* (the Age Discrimination in Employment Act case), Congress was authorized to allow private suits for money damages against the state to enforce the "reasonable accommodations" requirements of the Act.

In yet another five-to-four decision, the Court again reasoned that the Fourteenth Amendment afforded the weakest form of protection against discrimination based on disabilities. Thus, like the Age Discrimination in Employment Act in *Kimel*, this Act also went beyond the protections afforded by the Constitution. Therefore, again, it was not proportionate and congruent to the potential constitutional harm. The majority simply dismissed the evidence of a widespread pattern of discrimination, stating that it was not supported by the legislative record. Although the dissent attached a thirty-nine-page appendix with references to discrimination against the disabled in the record, the Court again revived the legislative record from the Voting Rights Act as the standard. The record of discrimination in the Americans with Disabilities Act paled against the record of racial discrimination in the legislative history of the Voting Rights Act.

Although the federal government could still sue the states under the Act and individuals could sue to enjoin state officials, suits by individuals against the state itself for money damages did not satisfy the congruent and proportionate test.

5. Gender Discrimination

The Court in *Nevada v. Hibbs* (2003), in a six-to-three decision, upheld the right to suits against the state under the Family and Medical Leave Act. This is rather unsurprising, given that Court in the cases above heavily relied on the level of protection afforded certain classes of persons under the Fourteenth Amendment for determining whether authorization for suit against a state is proportionate and congruent.

Hibbs involved a man who was denied medical leave. Although one may question whether the Fourteenth Amendment was designed to protect men, the Court reasoned that the Act's purpose, at least in part, was to protect individuals from gender-based discrimination. Because gender discrimination receives heightened scrutiny under the Fourteenth Amendment, the Court held that it was easier for Congress to show a pattern of violations that were sufficient to justify the abrogation of state immunity. The Court held that Congress's intent to abrogate the states' immunity was clear and that the states' record of unconstitutional participation in fostering gender discrimination was weighty enough to justify the abrogation under Section 5 of the Fourteenth Amendment; it was congruent and proportional to the targeted violation.

6. Disabilities and Access to Courts

In *Tennessee v. Lane* (2004) the Court returned to the issue of suits against the state under the Americans with Disabilities Act. Here, the plaintiffs sued under Title II for discrimination on the basis of their disabilities in the provision of access to court, another fundamental right. Title II provides that "no qualified individual with a disability shall, by reason of such disability, be excluded from participation in or be denied the benefits of the services, programs, or activities of a public entity, or be subjected to discrimination by any such entity." The plaintiffs in this case were paraplegics. One had to crawl up two flights of stairs to appear for his criminal case because the courthouse did not have an elevator. It is not difficult to understand how access to the courts fundamentally impacts the right to due process and why discrimination in such cases deserves strict scrutiny. As such, it was not difficult to show that under these conditions, the abrogation of state immunity from suit was congruent and proportional.

7. Disabilities and Cruel and Unusual Punishment

In *United States v. Georgia* (2006), Justice Scalia again upheld the right to sue state governments under Title II of the Americans with Disabilities Act. In this case, Mr. Goodman sued the state of Georgia, arguing that the state's failure to give him reasonable accommodations based on his disability amounted to a violation of his right to be free from cruel and unusual punishment under the Eighth Amendment. The petitioner was a paraplegic inmate and his allegations included being "confined for 23-to-24 hours per day in a 12-by-3-foot cell in which he could not turn his wheelchair around"; and being denied assistance to shower and to use the toilet, which on several occasions resulting in him being "forced to sit in his own feces and urine while prison officials refused to assist him in cleaning up the waste." Further, he was allegedly "denied physical therapy and medical treatment, and denied access to virtually all prison programs and services on account of his disability."

The fundamental right to be free from cruel and unusual punishment has long since been incorporated into the Fourteenth Amendment, and thus, denial of a fundamental right via discrimination against the disabled justified the abrogation of state immunity from suit. Justice Scalia, writing for a unanimous Court, held that Title II of the Americans with Disabilities Act validly abrogates state sovereign immunity, at least to the extent that it creates a private cause of action for damages against the states for conduct that actually violates the Fourteenth Amendment. As he noted:

> While the Members of this Court have disagreed regarding the scope of Congress's "prophylactic" enforcement powers under § 5 of the Fourteenth Amendment no one doubts that § 5 grants Congress the power to "enforce ... the provisions" of the Amendment by creating private remedies against the States for *actual* violations of those provisions.

8. Suits against States in State Court

The Court, in *Alden v. Main* (1999), held that Congress cannot authorize suits against state governments in state court under the Fair Labor Standards Act. State governments cannot be sued in state courts, even on federal claims, without their consent. However, the Court made it clear that this immunity did not extend to state officers, municipal corporations, or nonstate governmental entities such as municipalities.

Checkpoints

- **Sources of Legislative Power**

  - Article I, Section 1, states: "All legislative Powers herein granted shall be vested in a Congress of the United States which shall consist of a Senate and House of Representatives."

  - Congress is limited to the powers enumerated in the Constitution and to what is necessary and proper to carry out those powers (*McCullough v. Maryland*).

  - Further, the notion of state sovereignty, coupled with the Tenth Amendment, limits Congress's powers. It provides: "The powers not delegated to the United States by the Constitution, nor prohibited by it to the States, are reserved to the States respectively, or to the people."

  - The Court will defer to Congress if:

    - the federal ends are legitimate and within the scope of Constitution;

    - the means (the legislation) is appropriate and clearly adapted to that end;

    - it is not expressly prohibited; and

    - it is in the spirit of the Constitution.

- **The Commerce Clause**

  - Article I, Section 8 provides that: "Congress shall have power ... to regulate Commerce with foreign nations, and among the several States, and with the Indian Tribes."

- **Early Cases: The Founding to the 1890s**

  - The Court broadly defined the Commerce Clause power, but it was rarely used.

  - "Commerce" included buying, selling, and navigation.

  - "Among the states" was defined as "intermingled with."

  - Congress could regulate things that were interstate (across states), but not matters that were completely internal to a state (intrastate), unless they affected interstate commerce (*Gibbons v. Ogden*, 1824).

- **1890s–1937: The *Lochner* Era up to the Constitutional Crisis**

  - This period is known as the *Lochner* era or the laissez-faire era.

  - The Court narrowly defined the Commerce Clause powers and used the Tenth Amendment as a limit.

  - Congress could only regulate:

    - Commerce, not manufacturing, production, or agriculture (which are traditionally state concerns) (*Dagenhart, E.C. Knight Co.*, and *Carter*).

Checkpoints *continued*

- Intrastate activities that *directly* affect interstate commerce (*Houston* and *A.L.A. Schechter Poultry Corp.*).

- Evil articles within interstate commerce, not merely intrastate evils that produce goods shipped in interstate commerce (*Dagenhart*).

- Intrastate transactions that are in the stream of commerce, not those that precede or follow that stream (*A.L.A. Schechter Poultry Corp.*).

- For Congress's purposes that actually carry out enumerated powers, not as a pretext for other ends or goals within the police powers of the states. *McCulloch.*

- **Postcrisis Expansion of Federal Power: 1938 to the 1990s**

  - The Court broadly defined Congress's Commerce Clause powers.

  - The Court refused to apply the Tenth Amendment as a limit on federal power.

  - Three important cases effectively overruled the main limiting cases of the *Lochner* era:

    1. *NLRB* overruled the direct effect requirement in *Houston* and *Schechter*.

       - The Court rejected:

         - the requirement that the good or activity be in the flow or current of interstate commerce;

         - the Tenth Amendment limitation based on the distinction between "manufacturing" and commerce; and

         - the requirement of a direct effect on interstate commerce.

    2. *Darby* (1941) overruled the prohibition on regulating the shipment of goods in interstate commerce that were produced in violation of labor laws in *Dagenhart*.

    3. *Wickard v. Filburn* (1942) relaxed the effects doctrine in *Schechter*. Local production and consumption can be regulated by Congress under the Commerce Clause, if it has a cumulative effect on interstate commerce.

  - Congress cannot protect civil rights under Section 5 of the Fourteenth Amendment(*Civil Rights Cases*, 1883), but it can regulate local businesses that discriminate under the Commerce Clause because of its impact on interstate commerce (*Heart of Atlanta Motel*, 1964, and *Katzenbach v. McClung*, 1964).

- **Modern Retrenchment? 1990s to the Present**

  - The Court has narrowed the scope of the Commerce Clause again.

  - The Court has revived the notion of state sovereignty and the use of the Tenth Amendment as a limit on Congress's power to regulate under the clause.

Checkpoints *continued*

- Congress can regulate interstate commerce in three ways:

  1. The "channels" of interstate commerce, i.e., highways, waterways, and air traffic (*Pierce County v. Guillen,* 2003).

  2. The "instrumentalities" of interstate commerce, i.e., trucks, ships, planes and things traveling through the channels.

  3. Activities that have a "substantial effect" on interstate commerce. This includes economic activities that have a cumulative substantial effect on interstate commerce (*Citizens Bank v. Alafabco, Inc.,* 2003).

- It can also regulate in-state noncommercial activities if by failing to regulate those activities that would undercut the interstate regulation of that market (*Gonzales v. Raich,* 2005, Justice Stevens's plurality opinion), or if it would be necessary and proper to regulate those activities to regulate interstate commerce (*Gonzales v. Raich,* 2005, Justice Scalia's concurring opinion).

- Per *Lopez* (1995), the Court will consider four criteria to determine whether the conduct Congress seeks to regulate has a substantial effect on interstate commerce:

  1. Is it a criminal statutes dealing with noneconomic crimes?

  2. Is there an interstate jurisdictional hook or link in the statute?

  3. Are there congressional findings that the conduct has a substantial impact on interstate commerce?

  4. Is the statute only remotely connected with interstate commerce and more directly concerned with activities historically allocated to the states?

- From 2000 to 2006, the Court avoided Commerce Clause issues by limiting the reach of federal legislation applied by federal agencies. The Court will reinterpret the federal statute if the executive applied it beyond the scope of what the statute authorized (*Jones v. United States,* 2000; *Solid Waste Agency,* 2001; *Rapanos v. United States,* 2006; *Gonzales v. Oregon,* 2006).

- **The Taxing and Spending Powers**

  - Article I, Section 8, Clause 1 provides: "The Congress shall have Power To lay and collect Taxes, Duties, Imposts and Excises, to pay the Debts and provide for the common Defence and general Welfare of the United States; but all Duties, Imposts and Excises shall be uniform throughout the United States."

  - When Congress places conditions on grants to state governments, the test under *South Dakota v. Dole* (1987) is:

    - the expenditure must be for the common defense or the general welfare;

    - the condition must be stated unambiguously (see *Pennhurst,* 1981, and *Gonzaga University,* 2002);

Checkpoints *continued*

- there must be a relation between the purpose of the expenditure and the purpose of the condition;

- Congress may not require the states to violate the Constitution in exchange for federal money; and

- Congress may only "induce" the states to comply; it may not "coerce" them into doing so.

- Further, the Necessary and Proper Clause can be used to carry out the spending power and ensure that federal money is spent properly (*Sabri v. United States,* 2004).

- **Miscellaneous Other Domestic Powers**

  - These powers include powers over:

    - money,

    - bankruptcy,

    - the post (mail),

    - copyrights and patents,

    - interstate (and foreign) compacts or agreements,

    - military facilities,

    - federal buildings, and

    - federal lands.

- **Power over Foreign Affairs**

  - **The Treaty Power**

    - There are three main processes for treaties to be binding within the United States:

      1. negotiated by the executive and ratified by two-thirds of the Senate;

      2. preauthorized by Congress by majority vote and entered into by the executive; and

      3. "executive agreements" made by the executive without Senate or congressional approval.

    - All three types of treaties are either self-executing (are directly enforceable) or are non-self-executing (i.e., they require further domestic legislation to bring them into full domestic effect).

    - Non-self-executing treaties still bind the United States to other Countries, but they can only be enforced domestically if there is further legislation incorporating them into domestic law.

    - The Court now requires that for a treaty to be self-executing it must be clear from the text that it is self-executing and that the treaty was ratified on that basis.

Checkpoints *continued*

- **Immigration and Naturalization**
  - Congress has broad authority in this area, which preempts any state powers (*Fiallo v. Bell*, 1977).
  - However, once a person is naturalized and becomes a U.S. citizen, Congress loses its broad authority (*Schneider v. Rusk*, 1964).
- **War Powers**
  - Congress has joint authority with the executive branch.
  - Conflicts between the executive and legislative branches in this area are usually dismissed by the court as nonjusticiable political questions (*Holtzman v. Schlesinger*, 1973).
- **Congressional Enforcement of Civil Rights under the Civil War Amendments**
  - **Thirteenth Amendment**
    - Prohibits slavery and involuntary servitude.
    - The prohibition is general and applies to both private persons and the states.
    - Enforcement Clause in Section 2 provides Congress with the power to enforce it through appropriate legislation.
    - The Court has deferred to the legislature's determination as to what constitutes the "badges and incidents of slavery" and the appropriate means to eliminate them (*Jones v. Alfred H. Mayer Co.*, 1968).
  - **Fifteenth Amendment**
    - Protects the right of citizens to vote.
    - Prohibits the federal government and the states from denying or abridging the right because of race, color, or previous condition of servitude.
    - Enforcement Clause in Section 2, and the Court will defer to Congress, as long as the legislation is an "appropriate" method to attack racial discrimination (*City of Rome v. United States*, 1980).
  - **Fourteenth Amendment**
    - Establishes that:
      1. all people born and naturalized in the United States are citizens;
      2. no state can abridge the privileges and immunities of U.S. citizens;
      3. no state may deprive any person of life, liberty or property without due process of law; and
      4. no state may deny any person equal protection of the laws.
    - Applies only to the states; it does not address private persons.
    - Has an Enforcement Clause in Section 5, but the scope is limited:

Checkpoints *continued*

- Congress cannot expand rights or give additional rights; the Constitution is the ceiling; and

- "enforce" means corrective legislation, that remedies violations of rights recognized by the Court (*City of Boerne v. Flores,* 1997).

- **State Sovereignty**

  - **State Sovereignty as a Limit on the Regulatory Power**

    - Old test, per *National League of Cities v. Usery* (1976), was whether Congress interfered with the state's "traditional government functions."

    - The Court overturned *Usery* in *Garcia v. San Antonio Metropolitan Transit Authority* (1985).

    - New test is whether the federal regulation destroys state sovereignty or is in violation of the provisions of the Constitution (e.g., by exceeding Congress's enumerated powers).

  - **The Federal Government Can Regulate but Not Commandeer**

    - Congress's power authorizes it to regulate individuals but not the state (*New York v. United States,* 1992).

    - The federal government "may not compel the States to enact or administer a federal regulatory program" (*Printz v. United States,* 1997).

    - Congress can forbid the states from acting; since it is not commanding them to do something, there is no "commandeering" by the federal government (*Reno v. Condon,* 2000).

  - **State Sovereignty as a Basis for Immunity from Suit**

    - The Eleventh Amendment provides: "The Judicial power of the United States shall not be construed to extend to any suit in law or equity, commenced or prosecuted against one of the United States by Citizens of another State, or by Citizens or Subjects of any Foreign State."

    - A state cannot be sued unless it waives its immunity or consents to being sued.

    - To abrogate state sovereign immunity under the Eleventh Amendment, the authorization for suit under a subsequent amendment must be:

      - express and clear (versus implicit);

      - authorized under Section 5 of the Fourteenth Amendment (not the Commerce Clause) (*Seminole Tribe,* 1996); and

      - it must be *proportional and congruent* to the constitutional harm, determined by:

        - the level of protection afforded, given the class of persons protected under the Amendment; and

Checkpoints *continued*

- the evidence of unconstitutional discrimination against the class of persons.

- Per *Florida Prepaid* (1999), if the right is only protected by rational basis (versus strict scrutiny), then the Court applies a more stringent test to justify overriding a state's immunity from suit under Section 5:

  - there must be a history of systematic and widespread deprivation, not a single instance; and

  - the remedy has to be narrowly tailored to that exact harm; proportional and congruent (not overbroad).

- Congress cannot authorize suits against state governments in state court, even on federal claims, without their consent.

- However, the Eleventh Amendment does not bar suits against state officials or local governments (*Alden v. Main,* 1999).

Chapter 3

The Federal Executive Power

Roadmap

- Express versus inherent executive powers
- Administrative power
  - Appointment power
  - Removal power
- Legislative power
- Law enforcement power
- International affairs power
  - General foreign affairs power
  - Power to recognize foreign governments
  - Treaties
  - Executive agreements
- Commander in Chief power
  - Presidential war powers
  - Power to combat terrorism
- Executive privilege and immunity
  - Executive privilege from disclosure
  - Executive immunity from suit
- Impeachment

I. Introduction

This chapter examines the federal government's executive powers. It begins by discussing the debate over whether the President has implied powers in addition to express powers, and then it describes the various areas of express executive powers that the President possesses.

One reason why the first U.S. constitution (the Articles of Confederation) failed was that it did not create an executive branch of government. When the thirteen states sent delegates to Philadelphia in 1787, they set out to ameliorate this problem. Of course, they could have designed the executive branch in a variety of ways, but they wrote in the first sentence of Section 1 of Article II: "The executive Power shall be vested in a President of the United States of America." The rest of Section 1 addresses practical issues, such as the method of electing the President (through the Electoral College); the eligibility requirements for the Presidency; the order of succession in case of the removal, death, resignation, or inability of the President; compensation; and the oath of office.

Sections 2 and 3 of Article II describe the executive powers of the President, which includes the power to:

- act as the "commander in chief of the Army and the Navy" and of the state militias;
- grant "reprieves and pardons for offenses against" the United States, except for impeachment;
- enter into treaties, with the support of two-thirds of the Senate;
- appoint ambassadors, public ministers, and consuls, Justices of the Supreme Court, and others established by law (the number of presidential appointees today exceeds 3,000 with about 600 subject to Senate confirmation);
- make recess appointments;
- "from time to time give to the Congress information of the state of the union" (annual State of the Union address);
- recommend measures (laws, policies, etc.) to Congress;
- convene both Houses of Congress "on extraordinary occasions";
- receive foreign ambassadors and other public ministers;
- commission all officers of the United States; and
- "take care that the laws be faithfully executed."

The final section of Article II provides for the removal from office of the President, Vice President, and all civil officers of the United States "on impeachment for, and conviction of, treason, bribery, or other high crimes and misdemeanors."

A. Express versus Inherent Executive Powers

The powers listed above are the express executive powers of the President. However, the first words of Article II, "the executive power shall be vested in a President of the United States of America," have produced an ongoing debate over whether they give the President inherent powers in addition to the express powers. Supporters of inherent presidential powers point to the difference in language between Articles I and II. Article I begins by stating: "All legislative powers *herein granted* shall be vested in a Congress of the United States" (emphasis added). These supporters argue that because Article II does not use the limiting words "herein granted," the President has inherent powers or powers beyond those that are specifically articulated in the Constitution. Opponents of this position argue that the Framers had no such intent and that to grant undefined and potentially substantial "inherent powers" to the President was exactly what they sought to prevent.

The primary Supreme Court case addressing the issue of inherent presidential power is *Youngstown Sheet & Tube Co. v. Sawyer* (1952). Due to a labor-management dispute, the United Steelworkers Union announced a nationwide strike at steel plants. President Harry Truman thought the strike would hurt U.S. involvement in the Korean War, as well as the national economy. To avert the strike, President Truman ordered the Secretary of Commerce, Charles Sawyer, to seize the nation's steel mills and keep steel production going. He relied on inherent executive power to take this action.

The Supreme Court rejected Truman's position by a six-to-three margin, declaring the seizure unconstitutional. Justice Hugo Black wrote the majority opinion; however, each justice who joined the majority also wrote a separate opinion and expressed views that were different from Justice Black's. Nonetheless, we can categorize the positions taken.

Justice Black argued that presidential power must come either from an act of Congress or from the Constitution. In his view, there is no inherent presidential power. After finding that Congress had not enacted legislation that authorized the President to seize the steel mills, Justice Black turned to the express powers of the executive in the Constitution. In his view, the Commander in Chief Clause authorized the President to direct military operations but not to seize private property within the United States. Furthermore, Article II's grant of authority to the President to "take care that the laws be faithfully executed" gave the President the authority to enforce the law, not to make new law on his (or her) own.

Justices Felix Frankfurter, Robert Jackson, Harold Burton, and Tom Clark, all of whom were in the majority, thought that President Truman's actions violated the express will of Congress. In their view, Truman violated the Taft-Hartley Act of 1947, which outlined procedures for dealing with a nationwide strike but did not expressly prohibit the President from seizing private property in labor disputes.

However, a majority of Justices—two from the majority and all three of the dissenters—believed that the President has some inherent executive powers to address emergencies. The dissenters thought the President has broad inherent executive powers, and two Justices from the majority believed in some inherent executive power, just not in the face of conflicting congressional acts.

The most cited and most significant opinion in this case came from the pen of Justice Jackson. In his concurring opinion, he described three zones of executive authority. The first zone is "when the President acts pursuant to an express or implied authorization of Congress." According to Justice Jackson, this is when the President's authority is at its maximum because it includes not only the executive's claim of authority but also Congress's delegation of authority. At this point, the President's acts are presumptively valid.

The second zone is "when the President acts in absence of either a congressional grant or denial of authority." Under this circumstance, the President "can only rely upon his own independent powers, but there is a zone of twilight in which he and Congress may have concurrent authority, or in which its distribution is uncertain." Of course, in this second zone of congressional silence, the President cannot violate other constitutional provisions. Otherwise, Justice Jackson said that constitutionality will "depend on the imperatives of events and contemporary imponderables rather than on abstract theories of law."

The third zone is "when the President takes measures incompatible with the expressed or implied will of Congress." In this zone, the President's "power is at its lowest ebb, for then he can rely only upon his own constitutional powers minus any constitutional powers of Congress over the matter." Because of the direct conflict between the President and Congress, presidential action will only be upheld if the courts strike down the congressional act.

II. Express Powers

A. Administrative Power

In the past century, Congress has increasingly delegated its legislative power to agencies, which are part of the executive branch. Executive agencies exercise legislative power by creating laws, executive power by enforcing them, and judicial power through administrative law judges that resolve disputes. If Congress delegates power to executive officials, then who has the power to appoint and remove them?

1. Appointment Power

Article II contains what has been named the Appointments Clause, which states:

He shall nominate, and by and with the advice and consent of the Senate, shall appoint ambassadors, other public ministers and consuls, judges of the Supreme Court, and all other officers of the United States, whose appointments are not herein otherwise provided for, and which shall be established by law: but the Congress may by law vest the appointment of such inferior officers, as they think proper, in the President alone, in the courts of law, or in the heads of departments.

This clause gives practical effect to the separation of powers doctrine. While Congress creates the federal offices, the President (with the advice and consent of the Senate), the courts, or the heads of departments appoint the individuals to the positions.

The Court has held that Congress cannot grant the appointment power to itself or to any members of Congress. In *Buckley v. Valeo* (1976), the Court struck down a federal statute that gave the President pro tempore of the Senate and the Speaker of the House the power to appoint four of the six members of the Federal Election Commission. The Court held that these two congressional leaders did not fall into any of the three categories listed in Article II that have the power to appoint (i.e., the President, the courts, or the heads of departments).

The Appointments Clause creates two types of appointed positions: principal officers and inferior officers (note that most government employees are civil servants, not subject to the Appointments Clause). Only principle officers must be confirmed by the Senate, which raises the questions of who decides whether a position is one of a "principle officer" or an "inferior officer" and how this is determined. According to the Court, Congress decides who is an inferior officer of the United States, and following the language of Article II, the President, courts, or heads of departments (who themselves are appointed by the President) have the authority to make the specific appointments of inferior officers.

The Court held in *Ex Parte Siebold* (1879) that Congress could authorize federal circuit courts to appoint election supervisors and that those courts would be excused from that duty only if there was "incongruity in the duty required." It is unclear what would constitute such an "incongruity." The Court held it did not exist in that case.

Although Congress decides who is an inferior officer, what are the grounds for distinguishing between an inferior officer and an officer? The leading case in this area is *Morrison v. Olson* (1988), which dealt with a constitutional challenge to the Ethics in Government Act, an Act created after the Watergate scandal to hold high-level officials in the executive branch accountable for breaking the law. After the Attorney General decided that an investigation was needed, the Act authorized three federal judges to appoint an independent counsel and define the independent counsel's "prosecutorial jurisdiction." If this independent counsel was an officer of the United States, then this grant of appointment power to the judiciary violated Article II. However, if the independent counsel was an inferior officer, than this appointment process was constitutional, as long as there was no "incongruity in the duty required."

The Court upheld the Act by a seven-to-one margin. The Court announced the test for determining whether an officer is a principle officer or an inferior officer:

1. whether the officer can be removed by higher executive branch official;
2. whether the officer has limited duties;
3. whether the office has limited jurisdiction; and
4. whether the office is limited in tenure.

Here, the Court found that the independent counsel was an inferior officer because he could be removed for good cause by the Attorney General, a higher-ranking official, and his duties were limited to investigating and prosecuting federal crimes (he did not make general policy). Furthermore, the independent counsel had limited jurisdiction because he was restricted to investigating officials who were suspected of crimes. Last, he had a limited tenure because his temporary role ends when the investigation ends. The Court also noted that because the independent counsel would investigate members of the executive branch, it was logical to place the appointment power in the judiciary, and not the executive branch, to ensure that the counsel was indeed independent.

2. Removal Power

Although there are no express words in the Constitution regarding the President's power to remove executive branch officials, it was arguably the Framers' intent to grant the President this authority.

In *Myers v. United States* (1926), the Court found that for purely executive officials, "the power to remove ... is an incident of the power to appoint." However, in *Humphrey's Executor v. United States* (1935), the Court upheld a provision of the Federal Trade Commission Act, which limited the President's ability to fire a commissioner to "inefficiency, neglect of duty, or malfeasance in office." The Court reasoned that Congress could create "*quasi*-legislative or *quasi*-judicial agencies" that must act "independently of executive control." The test appeared to be that if the executive official was "*quasi*-legislative or *quasi*-judicial," then the President did not have removal power.

Recently, the Court has developed a more flexible approach. In *Morrison v. Olson* (1988), the Court upheld the limits that Congress placed in the Ethics in Government Act on the Attorney General's power to dismiss an independent counsel. The limits were that removal had to be "for good cause," and the Attorney General would have to file a report with the judges who made the appointment and with the House and Senate Judiciary Committees. After asserting that it is relevant to analyze the functions of the official, the Court stated that "the real question is whether the removal restrictions are of such a nature that they impede the President's ability to perform his constitutional duty."

Consequently, to prevent Congress from impeding on the President, the Court has limited Congress's removal authority. The Court has held that Congress cannot remove an executive official except through impeachment. In *Bowsher v. Synar* (1986), the Court struck down the Gramm-Rudman-Hollings Act. The act granted the comptroller, the head of the congressional General Accounting Office, the power to impose budget cuts if spending exceeded the deficit ceiling. After stating that this constituted an unconstitutional delegation of executive power to a legislative official, who was immune from presidential removal, the Court observed that Congress cannot retain the power of removal for an executive official, other than through impeachment.

3. Administrative Agencies

The tremendous growth in the federal government over the past eighty years has come about primarily through the development of administrative agencies, almost all of which were placed within the executive branch. The breadth and depth of these agencies gives the President extraordinary power. There are a number of reasons for the rise of the administrative state, including the need for specialized expertise to draft regulations, the demand for regulations that exceeded Congress's capacity, and Congress's self-interest in passing to an agency the responsibility to draft politically sensitive regulations.

Administrative agencies are unique because they have all three powers—the power to make laws (legislative), enforce laws (executive), and adjudicate disputes (judicial). Congress has the right to create administrative agencies, but because the agencies are part of the executive branch, the President has the power to appoint and remove the officers of these agencies.

There are obvious problems regarding the principles of separation of powers and checks and balances with administrative agencies, however, it has been seventy-five years since the Court struck down a law as an unconstitutional delegation of legislative power. Practical necessity appears to have unseated those principles.

Congress creates agencies by passing a statute, which sets out the scope of the power that Congress is giving (delegating) to the agency. It is unconstitutional for Congress to give executive powers to itself or to its officers. For example, in *Metropolitan Washington Airports Authority v. Noise Abatement Citizens* (1991), Congress created an airport agency whose actions would be reviewed by a board made up of members of Congress. The Court held that this violated the separation of powers doctrine because the review board was executive power; thus, Congress had delegated executive power to itself. In *Bowsher v. Synar* (1986), Congress passed a balanced-budget act, and the President appointed a comptroller general, who would make spending cuts if the budget exceeded the limits in the Act. Although appointed by the President, Congress retained the ability to remove the comptroller through the legislature's removal power. The Court held that since Congress could remove the comptroller, he could not be given executive powers. The comptroller interpreted the statute and exercised judgment to determine where budget cuts would be made, which are executive powers. Thus, executive power cannot be given to an officer who is subject to removal by Congress without violating the separation of powers.

The Court evaluated *Bowsher* under a black-and-white perspective of separation of powers, with a clear beginning and end of legislative and executive power. Other case law shows that these powers often overlap. A complete separation of powers of the individual branches of government is a misnomer. Although the delicate balance of separated interests is fundamental to the Constitution, the Court has acknowledged that an overlap of powers can be accepted if a balance still exists.

In *Morrison v. Olson* (1988) Congress passed the Ethics in Government Act, which created a special court that had the power to appoint an independent counsel to investigate government officials for criminal offenses. The Court upheld the appointment, even though the independent counsel was not a member of the executive branch. The Court reasoned that because the executive's Attorney General had the authority to remove the independent counsel for "good cause," then the executive had enough control over the congressional appointment and it did not violate the separation of powers doctrine.

B. Legislative Power

Article II, Section 3 states that the President "shall from time to time give to the Congress information of the state of the union." Over time, this phrase has come to mean that the President gives an annual State of the Union address, delivered to a joint session of Congress in January each year. The President, "on extraordinary occasions," may convene both houses of Congress, which has been a rare occurrence.

Article II also gives the President the authority to recommend "measures" (laws, policies, etc.) to Congress. In light of the enormous size of the executive branch and all of its specialized agencies, the executive branch is well positioned to draft laws, according to the political priorities of the President. The President regularly exercises this "legislative" function because it is one of the ways Presidents seek to achieve their political agendas.

Perhaps the greatest legislative power of the President is the veto power, which is contained in Article I, not Article II. The Presentment and Objections Clauses in Article I, Section 7 state: "Every Bill which shall have passed the House of Representatives and the Senate, shall, before it becomes a law, be presented to the President of the United States; if he approve he shall sign it, but if not he shall return it, with his objections."

These clauses describe the President's options after a bill has passed both houses of Congress and is "presented" to him: (1) either sign the bill, which then makes it law; (2) return it with "objections" (veto it); or (3) not sign it at all, in which case the bill still becomes law. To override a President's veto, it takes a two-thirds vote of each house of Congress, which is a substantial and difficult hurdle to clear. The veto authority puts the President in the middle of the legislative process and gives the President tremendous bargaining power with Congress.

The line-item veto is a power that is popular among governors at the state level. In general, this allows a governor (the head of the executive branch) to veto certain provisions of a proposed law, instead of being stuck with the "all-or-nothing" option of vetoing the entire bill or signing the entire bill into law. In 1996, Congress adopted the Line Item Veto Act (LIVA), granting the President the power to veto three types of provisions of legislation. The law would otherwise go into effect as amended by the President, unless Congress voted to override the President's line item vetoes. However, in *Clinton v. City of New York* (1998), the Court struck down LIVA. The Court focused on the text of the Constitution and the meaning of the word *return*. The Objection Clause states: "If he approve he shall sign it, but if not he shall return it, with his Objections." The President's veto of a bill takes place before it becomes law, and he returns the entire bill to Congress. A line-item veto is after the bill becomes law, and the President returns only part of the bill. The Court held that the line-item veto was unconstitutional. The Court decided that the Founders intended for the President to sign or veto a law in its entirety and that the President did not have the unilateral power to repeal or amend statutes enacted by Congress. For the line-item veto to be constitutional, it must be through an amendment to the Constitution, not through legislation.

C. Law Enforcement Power

Article II grants the President the power to "take care that the laws be faithfully executed." This gives the President and the executive branch the primary authority for implementing and enforcing federal laws and the Constitution. This has given rise to the large executive bureaucracy comprised of numerous government agencies, including the U.S. Department of Justice. Of course, this involves interpreting the Constitution and the laws. Presidents usually follow judicial and legislative interpretations, although sometimes they follow their own interpretation. Enforcement of laws makes the executive branch the main source of government interaction with citizens. This involves resource allocation, which Presidents decide based on their political priorities. Funding allocation impacts law enforcement, so priority areas are enforced more rigorously, potentially leaving other areas underenforced. The line between the President not enforcing the law and underenforcing the law is difficult to draw and is mostly left to the political process.

Article II states that the President has the power to grant "reprieves and pardons" for offenses against the United States, except for impeachment. This relatively expansive presidential power allows for the chief executive to reduce or pardon any federal crime besides impeachment, but does not extend to civil liability. Arguably, the most famous instance of a President exercising this power is President Gerald Ford's expansive pardoning of all possible crimes that President Richard Nixon may have committed while in office. Though Articles of Impeachment had been drafted against President Nixon, he resigned before he was impeached. This permitted President Ford to exercise the executive right to reprieve and pardon. Due to the extremely broad nature of this presidential right, pardons such as that granted to President Nixon have been mired in controversy. Pardons by President Bill Clinton during the end of his second term in 2001 ushered in proposals to require congressional approval for the President's exercise of this right, but changing this executive privilege would require a constitutional amendment, which is a rare occurrence.

D. International Affairs Powers

Whereas many countries place the power of the chief executive (the leader of a political party with a policy agenda) in different hands than the power of the head of state (the unifier within and representative to foreign nations), the U.S. Constitution vests both powers in the President. This gives the President substantial power in international affairs, contained only by the doctrines of separation and balance of powers and express and inherent powers.

1. General Foreign Affairs Power

The express versus inherent presidential power debate is at the forefront when considering the existence of the President's foreign policy powers. This stems from the sheer lack of enumerated provisions on the subject in the Constitution. Foreign policy in the Constitution is wholly dictated through a balance of executive provisions in Article II, and the legislative provision of Article I, Section 8, which grants the Congress the powers:

> To define and punish piracies and felonies committed on the high seas, and offenses against the law of nations; To declare war, grant letters of marque and reprisal, and make rules concerning captures on land and water; To raise and support armies, but no appropriation of money to that use shall be for a longer term than two years; To provide and maintain a navy.

This provision allots the congressional powers of maintaining foreign commerce, providing the military "purse" and regulating both foreign and domestic maritime laws. Most important, the Constitution alludes to its joint foreign responsibilities with the chief executive through Congress's tremendous power to declare war.

Article II confers on the President the express powers of "commander in chief of the Army and Navy of the United States," the power to "appoint ambassadors, other public ministers and consuls," and the power, with the "advice and consent of the Senate, to make treaties." The modern trend of unequal deference to the President over Congress in the realm of foreign affairs has its roots in the Supreme Court's 1936 decision in *United States v. Curtiss-Wright Export Corporation*. In *Curtiss*, Congress had passed a Joint Resolution, which granted the President the authority to issue an executive order to prohibit arms sales to countries involved in a border dispute. An arms dealer violated this prohibition and challenged the constitutionality of Congress's delegation of authority to the President. In a majority opinion written by Justice George Sutherland, the Court upheld Congress's expansive delegation of foreign powers to the President. Further, it adopted a broad constitutional interpretation of the President's "inherent" foreign policy powers. In dicta, Justice Sutherland supported his view that the President should be given great deference regarding foreign affairs. First, the President's powers that are express, enumerated powers are limited by the Constitution; the foreign affairs power is not an express power, therefore, the Constitution does not limit this authority. Second, it is necessary for the President to have the power to speak as a representative of the nation when dealing with other countries. Though technically dicta,

Justice Sutherland's theory of the necessity for the President to act as the sole voice in foreign affairs has heavily influenced modern decisions, especially in the wake of the war on terrorism.

2. Power to Recognize and Establish Relations with Foreign Governments

The expansiveness of presidential foreign power after *Curtiss-Wright* stand in contrast to the rule established in Justice Black's opinion in *Youngstown* that the scope of the President's power is directly related to whether Congress is backing the executive office. *Curtiss-Wright's* empowered dicta looms over judicial and political decisions about the executive office, even when at odds with *Youngstown*. The public policy concerns overshadowing the question of executive authority are even more prolific in the realm of foreign policy than they are in domestic policy. However constitutional scrutiny of executive foreign policy decisions is often impossible due to the Supreme Court-created political question doctrine, which makes these matters nonjusticiable. The executive office retains control to guide foreign diplomacy under the powers to appoint U.S. ambassadors and meet other nation's ambassadors under Article II. These powers implicitly grant the President the power to select other governments with whom the United States will formally recognize and establish relations. Foreign governments not officially recognized or with whom the President does not want to establish relations fall outside the scope of judicial scrutiny and into political (not constitutional) debate.

3. Treaties

There are two types of treaties under the Constitution: Article II, Section 2 treaties require the advice and consent of the Senate; and Article VI, Section 2 treaties, usually called executive agreements, require no Senate ratification. We address the first here.

Article II treaties require involvement by both the executive and legislative branches. As opposed to executive agreements, treaties are only valid after ratification by the Senate. Even if these two political branches work together to pass a treaty, the treaty still must be constitutional. Although there is no express provision that limits a treaty's substantive power, this does not authorize a circuitous route around constitutional or statutory limitations.

There are two ways a treaty can become incorporated into U.S. law. First, if the language of the treaty clearly indicates that it is self-executing, then it becomes binding on ratification by the Senate. Second, if the treaty is not self-executing, then Congress must enact legislation implementing the content of the treaty. In *Medellin v. Texas* (2008), the Court held that the signed Protocol to the Vienna Convention did not make the treaty self-executing and therefore the treaty is not binding on state courts until Congress enacts it into law.

A validly enacted treaty supersedes existing federal law and conflicting state law. If a treaty is passed, and later Congress adopts a federal statute that rescinds the treaty, which one is valid? The Supremacy Clause, located in Article VI, states: "This Constitution, and the laws of the United States which shall be made in pursuance thereof; and all treaties made, or which shall be made, under the authority of the United States, shall be the supreme law of the land." This provision grants federal statutes and treaties coequal status as the supreme laws of the land. The Court decides conflicting authority between treaties and federal statutes by upholding the one that was drafted at the latest date. This is referred to as the "later in time rule."

If a treaty does not exceed the general substantive limitations of federal statutory language, the Court will refuse to scrutinize a challenge to a treaty. In *Goldwater v. Carter* (1979), Senator Barry Goldwater challenged the unilateral rescission of a treaty with Taiwan by President Jimmy Carter. Senator Goldwater argued that because two-thirds of the Senate must approve the creation of a treaty, then two-thirds of the Senate must also approve before one can be rescinded. The Court refused to answer this question. The divided Court found that this issue was nonjusticiable under the political question and ripeness doctrines.

4. Executive Agreements

Although the Constitution does not mention executive agreements, they have been interpreted to fall within Article VI (Section 2). Executive agreements require no Senate ratification, so they come into effect on the signature of the President and the head of the foreign state. The Supreme Court has never declared an executive agreement unconstitutional as usurping the Senate's treaty-approving function. The court has always sided with the President when there was a challenge to an executive agreement. Presidents naturally prefer executive agreements because they can be negotiated and entered into without Senate approval. Between 1980 and 1992, 4,510 new executive agreements were signed, whereas only 218 treaties were ratified. Although executive agreements do not obtain Senate ratification, the President typically is acting pursuant to congressional legislation supporting such an agreement. So the preference for executive agreements is also premised on efficiency; the Senate simply could not debate and ratify thousands of treaties.

One example of an executive agreement is *Dames & Moore v. Regan* (1981). In that case, President Carter issued an executive agreement in response to an Iranian takeover, in which hostage situation occurred at the U.S. embassy in

Iran. The executive agreement negotiated the release of the hostages in exchange for the settlement or arbitration of all litigation between the governments and the citizens of each country. The plaintiffs, who would lose pending judgments in state courts, argued that the executive agreement was an unconstitutional, invalid exercise of executive power. The Court upheld the agreement, relying on the fact that it was a long-standing practice to settle claims through executive agreements. The Court pointed to *United States v. Pink* (1942), in which an executive agreement was used to uphold the Litvinov assignment during World War II, which involved the assignment of monetary claims. New York refused to sanction the assignment, but the Court held that executive agreements have the same force as treaties, which preempt state law, due to the Supremacy Clause of Article VI. *Dames* follows the same reasoning as *Pink*—that executive agreements are constitutional because Congress implicitly authorizes them through similar federal statutes, they preempt state laws through the Supremacy Clause, and they have always been a necessary use of executive power to carry out foreign diplomacy through speed and efficiency, which is not available through treaties that must be ratified.

A more recent example of the Court upholding an executive agreement is *American Insurance Association v. Garamendi* (2003). In a close five-to-four decision, the Court found that California's Holocaust Victim's Insurance Relief Act of 1999 (HIVRA) violated an executive agreement between President Clinton and Germany. The executive agreement included provisions for Holocaust survivor compensation, which preempted provisions of the state law, HIVRA. One could argue that this decision, like *Dames*, should be narrowly interpreted as a preemption case only—both cases involved a constitutional challenge to an executive agreement that preempts state law (HIVRA in this case and the state judgment in *Dames*).

E. Commander in Chief Power

1. Presidential War Powers

As previously discussed, the executive branch's powers under Article II shares the power of the nation's defense with Congress and its powers under Article I. Although the text of the Constitution attributes more clauses regarding national defense to the legislative branch, the current interpretation of the executive branch's power is extremely broad and is swayed heavily in the President's favor. Article II, Section 2 states: "The President shall be commander in chief of the Army and Navy of the United States, and of the militia of the several states." This clause designates the President as the highest-ranking official in both foreign and domestic defense. This ranking entitles the President to certain powers, such as the ability to hire and (in certain circumstances) fire military personnel. The President's power in this area is conditional on Congress *not* having acted pursuant to its own powers under Article I, Section 8, to "make rules for the government and regulation of the land and naval forces."

During wartime, the President's role as commander in chief grants the executive office the power to directly govern military command decisions. However, the actual extent of the President's "war powers" remains a highly contested subject. Even with the judicial and legislative branch's deference to the executive office in the realm of foreign affairs, there remains a question regarding the proper balance between the Congress's war powers under Article I and the President's war powers under Article II.

The issue of executive power does not easily lend itself to judicial inquiry, which results in an absence of case law precedent. Article I, Section 8 grants Congress the right to declare war, yet the executive office has involved the nation in multiple warlike scenarios throughout history, without Congress declaring war. These situations of "war" without congressional approval have not altered the executive's use of military forces; it is identical to congressionally sanctioned war situations.

Legal precedent differentiating the executive war powers with and without congressional approval is nearly nonexistent. The Supreme Court has held that this is a nonjusticiable political question, with one exception — the *Prize Cases* (1862), where in the unusual context of the Civil War, the Court ruled that the President could mobilize forces against the Southern states, even though Congress had not yet declared war. More recently, lawsuits have challenged executive decisions regarding the use of war powers in the Vietnam, Gulf, and Iraq Wars, among others. However, the Supreme Court has not reviewed lower courts' dismissal of those cases on grounds of justiciability, opting to not interpret the war power provisions of the Constitution.

Aside from the lack of justiciability surrounding the issue of foreign affairs, even the inquiry as to what constitutes a congressionally "declared" war is uncertain when discussing the limitations of executive war powers. Congress has, at times, both formally and informally sanctioned the executive's war actions. Two examples are the informal budgetary allotments for "military force" in the Gulf of Tonkin Resolution for the Vietnam War, and the explicitly adopted declaration of war to begin U.S. involvement in World War II. Furthermore, the argument that the Constitution provides Congress with authority to limit the executive branch's war powers is supported by the War Powers Resolution of 1973, which Congress adopted during the Vietnam War. This Resolution mandates that the President may only enter the United States forces into an impending or occurring war situation if Congress has already declared war, if it is authorized by a statute, or if there is a national emergency due to an attack on the United States. The Resolution also requires the President to notify Congress before deploying forces or within two days of deployment, and it limits the President's use of armed forces to sixty days, unless Congress declares war, enacts a statute, or approves a sixty-day extension. Although these congressional limitations exist, Presidents consistently declared that they are not bound by the War Powers Resolution and in fact have failed to comply with it. The constitutionality of the War Powers Resolution has never been reviewed due to the Supreme Court's political question doctrine.

It is worth noting that if a majority in Congress strongly disagreed with a President's war effort, it could use its power of the "purse" to cut off funding for the war.

2. Power to Combat Terrorism

The sudden and unexpected nature of the September 11, 2001, terrorist attacks reignited past debates over the President's war powers and especially the executive's authority to respond to an attack. As previously mentioned, Congress may formally or informally sanction the executive's actions through resolutions. One week after 9/11, the 107th Congress passed the Authorization for Use of Military Force (AUMF), a resolution that authorized the President to "use all necessary and appropriate force" against those involved in the attacks. It stood in place of a unilateral executive decision and thus avoided a constitutional debate of the scope of the executive's power. As discussed previously in *Youngstown* (President Truman's seizure of steel mills), when the President and Congress are in agreement, the executive powers are at their height and are the least contested. Since the passage of the AUMF, the debate of unilateral executive war powers comes to the forefront with respect to its interpretation and subsequent war measures.

Fighting terrorism is more akin to fighting drug cartels or organized crime than fighting a traditional war because terrorists hide in the civilian population, emerging to fight only at strategic moments and in strategic places. Al-Qaeda, the "most serious threat" according to the National Intelligence Estimate, is comprised of autonomous underground cells in some 100 countries, making it difficult to apprehend. So although President George W. Bush led the United States to invade Afghanistan and Iraq on the grounds (among others) of combating terrorism, most of the government's efforts to combat terrorism involve working with the criminal justice system of those 100 countries. This requires collaborative criminal investigations and information sharing, negotiating extradition treaties, and developing a body of national and international antiterrorism law and criminal tribunals. The President clearly has the constitutional authority to pursue all of these undertakings. However, President Bush claimed expansive executive powers to pursue, detain, and try individuals called "enemy combatants," in some cases without the constraints of the Constitution or international law.

The constitutional challenges to President Bush's war on terrorism have dealt with the treatment of terrorist suspects (also called "unlawful or enemy combatants," "material witnesses," or "detainees"), the special judicial system set up for these detainees, and the secret surveillance in the United States, which included warrantless wiretapping. To understand the Court's opinions regarding detainees, it is important to understand the framework. First, pursuant to the AUMF, President Bush issued an executive order that created military tribunals. Second, the Uniform Code of Military Justice is the congressional set of criminal law standards, under which all martial branches of the United States must abide. Third, although the President's commander in chief decisions are political in nature, their effect on the constitutional rights of those detained is justiciable.

The military justice system exists under a separate umbrella of law than civilian justice, but it is still subject to the U.S. Constitution and Congress's power under Article I, Section 8, to "make rules for the government and regulation of the land and naval forces." However, for the military, some constitutional rights do not apply, such as the right to a grand jury under the Fifth Amendment, which states: "No person shall be held to answer for a capital, or otherwise infamous crime, unless on a presentment or indictment of a grand jury, except in cases arising in the land or naval forces." The suspension of liberty is not unlimited though, and procedural due process rights still apply to military courts and their tribunals. Military personnel can bring a procedural due process claim, directly challenging their court-martial sentences through a writ of *habeas corpus*. This is because questions of law or fact resolved by tribunals are not subject to normal appellate review.

The President's role as commander in chief places the executive office in charge of the military justice system; further, presidential powers are expanded during wartime, due to the necessity of resolving the conflict. The expansive governmental powers during wartime have historically and currently resulted in changes to the military justice system, namely, the use of President-created military courts. For example, during World War II, President Franklin D. Roosevelt issued an executive order that granted the use of a military tribunal for foreign citizens who enter the United States and commit sabotage, espionage, or other warlike acts. In *Ex Parte Quirin* (1942), Nazi soldiers dressed as civilians arrived on the beaches of Ponte Vedra, Florida, carrying explosives. The Court held that there is judicial review for a matter pending in a military tribunal. Thus, this precedent made it easier for the Court to find that the military justice arm of executive war powers is justiciable.

More recently, on November 13, 2001, the President issued an executive order, titled the "Detention, Treatment and Trial of Certain Non-citizens in the War Against Terror." This order authorized the use of military tribunals for trials of suspected terrorists. Using military tribunals circumvents general constitutional principles of military justice that normally exist during peacetime. Military tribunals remove the procedural human rights standards of the Geneva Convention; thus, they have been solely reserved for instances of martial law, military occupation of a government, and emergency war situations.

In 2004, the Court decided its first case involving the war on terror in *Hamdi v. Rumsfeld* (2004). Yaser Hamdi, a U.S. citizen born in Louisiana, moved to Saudi Arabia and then Afghanistan where he was seized by the Northern Alliance, which was working with the U.S. government to oust the Taliban government. He was eventually turned over to the U.S. military and transferred to the detention facility at Guantánamo Bay, Cuba. When they discovered that he was a U.S. citizen, they moved him to a prison in South Carolina. The government claimed that he fought with the Taliban against United States forces but charged him with no crime. The U.S. government's position in court was that because it had designated Hamdi an enemy combatant, it could hold him in prison indefinitely without bringing formal charges or proceedings against him. In short, the U.S. government's position was that Hamdi had lost, for the rest of his life, his constitutional and international human rights to a notice of charges, right to counsel, fair trial before an independent and impartial tribunal, presumption of innocence, the right to present and examine evidence and witnesses, the right to remain silent, and the right to appeal. The U.S. Court of Appeals for the Fourth Circuit agreed with the U.S. government.

On the primary issue of whether Hamdi must be accorded due process of law, the Supreme Court reversed the Fourth Circuit's decision. Writing for the plurality, Justice Sandra Day O'Connor stated that Hamdi retained his right to *habeas corpus*, to be heard in a federal court (a neutral decision maker), where he must be given notice of charges, the right to respond, right to counsel, and a meaningful factual hearing. As for the remaining procedures, the Court said that the *Mathews v. Eldridge* (1976) test for procedural due process applied.

On the question of whether the U.S. government has the authority to detain a U.S. citizen apprehended in a foreign country as an enemy combatant, the five justices answered in the affirmative. Finding that the AUMF authorized the President to use "all necessary and appropriate force" against "nations, organizations, or persons" associated with the 9/11 attacks, the Court held that this defeated Hamdi's argument that it violated the Non-Detention Act, which prohibits imprisoning U.S. citizens unless authorized by Congress.

Justices Antonin Scalia and John Paul Stevens strongly dissented, arguing that the President cannot relax constitutional protections. Instead, Congress must expressly and specifically sanction these detentions, and the AUMF was not express. Furthermore, it was improper to treat a U.S. citizen as a prisoner of war; he should be prosecuted for treason in the judicial system.

By an eight-to-one margin the Court held that the United States cannot hold a prisoner indefinitely, but only until the end of the conflict. This is controversial because, with respect to the war on terror, the conflict may go on forever.

In *Hamdan v. Rumsfeld* (2006), a Yemenite national who was Osama bin Laden's driver, was charged with conspiracy in a military commission at Guantánamo Bay. He filed a petition of *mandamus* and *habeas corpus* in federal court. The Supreme Court, after deciding that it had jurisdiction to hear the case, held that the rules of the military commission violated the Uniform Code of Military Justice and the Geneva Convention, and that Salim Ahmad Hamdan was entitled to the protections of Common Article 3 of the Geneva Convention in federal court. The Court refused to allow military tribunals for prisoners of war. It held the Geneva Convention and international rules of war afford certain protections that protect prisoners of war. The Geneva Convention requires that these minimum protections must apply in a "regularly constituted court." A military tribunal is not a "regularly constituted court," and this is not an emergency situation. Neither the Geneva Convention nor the international rules of war recognize conspiracy as a violation of the law of war. Further, Congress has not identified conspiracy as a war crime, and it is beyond the executive's power to do so by itself. The majority supported its holding by pointing to the necessity of following international war rules, so that U.S. soldiers would be afforded the same rights if captured by a foreign country.

After *Hamdan*, Congress and the President enacted the Military Commission Act of 2006, which provided statutory authority for military commissions. Among other things, this Act denied noncitizen enemy combatants access to federal courts through a writ of *habeas corpus*. Instead, such individuals had access to military proceedings with an opportunity to seek appeal to the U.S. Court of Appeals for the District of Columbia Circuit. Limiting appeals to the D.C. Circuit was important for the administration because the court could not hear claims under treaties. This meant that enemy combatants could not raise claims under the Geneva Convention relative to the Treatment of Prisoners of War or the Convention Against Torture.

In *Boumediene v. Bush* (2008), the Court decided that enemy combatants held at Guantánamo Bay do have the constitutional right to *habeas corpus*. Four years earlier in *Rasul v. Bush* (2004), the Court held that such enemy combatants had the right to statutory *habeas corpus*, but legislation was then adopted eliminating statutory *habeas corpus* jurisdiction over these claims. So the Court in *Boumediene* interpreted Article I, Section 9, Clause 2 of the Constitution, which states, "the writ of habeas corpus shall not be suspended, unless when in cases of rebellion or invasion the public safety may require it." The Court examined the ratification debates and found that the Framers deemed the writ to be an essential mechanism in the separation of powers scheme by giving courts the authority to call the jailer to account. The Court also stated that the Framers viewed freedom from unlawful restraint a fundamental precept of liberty. The Court noted that past military conflicts were of a limited duration, a feature apparently not shared with the fight against terrorism. The Court also noted that some of the petitioners had been in custody for six years "with no definitive judicial determination as to the legality of their detention."

III. Executive Privilege and Immunity

Executive privilege and immunity prevent the executive branch from being held accountable by the judicial branch. Although this appears contrary to the principle of checks and balances, it is based on the principle of separation of powers. It is considered vital to keep these branches separate in these instances for the executive branch to carry out its important executive responsibilities.

A. Executive Privilege from Disclosure

Executive privilege exempts the President from disclosing to the public information integral to the President's domestic and foreign policy making. Its purpose is to encourage open and frank discussions of policy options between the President and his or her advisors. Because this privilege competes with other constitutional values, such as openness and access to information necessary for an informed electorate, this privilege is not absolute.

In *United States v. Nixon* (1974), the Supreme Court addressed the scope of the powers inherently allowed to the President to accomplish the sensitive post as head of the executive branch. In that case, President Nixon and top executive officials were indicted for obstruction of justice for their alleged involvement in a cover-up of a burglary at the Democratic National Headquarters, located in the Watergate building in Washington, D.C. The district court issued a subpoena, requiring President Nixon to turn over audiotapes from the Oval Office. The President refused, and before the Court of Appeals considered the issue, the Supreme Court granted review.

The President claimed that the Court could not review his claim of executive privilege because of separation of powers. Furthermore, he argued that an inherent and absolute executive privilege exists, which grants complete executive discretion regarding the release of sensitive information in a criminal investigation. The Court disagreed. To refute this argument, the Court cited *Marbury v. Madison* (1803), in which it held that it is the judiciary's duty to say what the law is, and it established judicial review of executive actions. The Court stated that "separate powers were not intended to operate with absolute independence."

Although the Court rejected the notion of an absolute privilege, it recognized that the "President's need for complete candor and objectivity from advisers calls for great deference from the courts." Thus, the President's argument for implied executive privilege had merit. Confidentiality of the executive office is a true public concern, and the Court would defer in a criminal proceeding, but only if President was able to show that it was necessary to protect sensitive information of a military, diplomatic, or national security nature.

The Court recently considered the importance of the executive privilege's protection of sensitive information in a civil suit in *Cheney v. United States District Court for the District of Columbia* (2004). The executive privilege is not solely reserved for the President, but it applies to all sensitive material ascertained by the executive branch. In *Cheney*, private interest groups sued Vice President Dick Cheney, claiming that he violated the Federal Advisory Committee Act by holding secret meetings with oil companies. Vice President Cheney refused to disclose the minutes of the meetings. The Court distinguished *Nixon* because this was a civil case, which lacks the same urgency or significance as a criminal case. The Court stressed the importance of the executive privilege by stating that it should not even have to be invoked unless there are "extraordinary circumstances," as this is necessary to maintain the efficient separation of powers. The Court remanded it to the lower court, indicating that it was likely privileged, but did not give a definitive answer.

B. Executive Immunity from Suit

As with executive privilege, there exists a qualified level of immunity from criminal and civil suits for the President and other members of the executive branch. The reasons for the immunity include the need to not divert the President's energy and attention from important matters of state, to protect the President's dignity, and to avoid harassment of executive officials. These interests are balanced against the interest in presidential accountability and adherence to the Constitution.

There has been no criminal prosecution of a sitting President, so there is no judicial decision deciding whether presidential immunity would apply. On one hand, the basic principle of the rule of law is that no person is above the law, which would argue for no presidential immunity. On the other hand, the argument is that impeachment is the appropriate process for resolving allegations of presidential criminal conduct.

The Court in *Nixon v. Fitzgerald* (1982), found that a former President has "absolute immunity from damages liability predicated on his official acts." In *Fitzgerald*, President Nixon was civilly sued for alleged retaliatory termination of a Pentagon aide. The Court opined that the perpetual notion of civil liability for political acts of the office of the President would substantially handicap the decisiveness of the President. The Court's decision in *Fitzgerald* resolved the issue of civil liability immunity of a sitting President, including the preclusion of damages for any other type of conduct while in office.

However, a sitting President may be civilly liable for damages for an illegal act, if the questionable activities were not part of his official duties and occurred prior to becoming President. For example, in *Clinton v. Jones* (1997), the President attempted to invoke civil liability immunity and postponement of a sexual harassment suit, which occurred prior to the time he took office. The Court distinguished *Fitzgerald* and held that even the President is not above rightful civil proceedings for unofficial acts that began prior to the presidency. Thus, the President has civil immunity while sitting in office but is liable if the suit began prior to office.

In *Harlow v. Fitzgerald* (1982), the Court held that "for executive officials in general, ... qualified immunity represents the norm." This applies to senior presidential appointments and advisors. The court held that "government officials performing discretionary functions, generally are shielded from liability for civil damages insofar as their conduct does not violate clearly established statutory or constitutional rights."

IV. Executive Accountability: Impeachment

The primary and most common method of holding executive officials accountable is the voting booth. By electing a different candidate or party, the top executive officials change. However, the only method of removing the President, Vice President and all civil officers of the United States before a scheduled election is impeachment and removal. Article II, Section 4 states: "The President, Vice President and all civil officers of the United States, shall be removed from office on impeachment for, and conviction of, treason, bribery, or other high crimes and misdemeanors."

The mechanism for carrying out impeachment is addressed by Article I, Section 2, Clause 5: "The House of Representatives ... shall have the sole power of impeachment." If the House charges the President with impeachment, then Article I, Section 3, Clause 6 states:

> The Senate shall have the sole power to try all impeachments. When sitting for that purpose, they shall be on oath or affirmation. When the President of the United States is tried, the Chief Justice shall preside: And no person shall be convicted without the concurrence of two thirds of the members present.

So the process of impeachment is twofold. First, the House of Representatives must draft and approve articles of impeachment. Second, the Senate must try the case, with the Chief Justice presiding if the President is on trial, and convict by a two-thirds majority. These provisions have been invoked on only three Presidents and no President has been convicted of impeachment and removed from office.

The closest a President has ever come to being impeached and removed is President Andrew Johnson. Due to his reconstruction policies after the Civil War, a House majority successfully impeached the President, and the Senate nearly ended his tenure, if not for a single vote. The second instance of presidential impeachment occurred amidst the court proceedings of *United States v. Nixon* (1974), but President Nixon resigned before the House could vote on the articles of impeachment. The most recent instance of impeachment involved President Clinton. The House of Representatives passed two articles of impeachment, revolving around purported perjury by the President, but in the Senate, he was not convicted on either count.

The parameters of impeachment are explicitly laid out in the three provisions cited above, but because they have been so rarely invoked, there is little certainty over what constitutes a "high crime or misdemeanor" and what constitute the proper procedures for an impeachment trial in the Senate. In both instances, the answers are left for the political spheres to resolve, not the courts. What constitutes a high crime or misdemeanor rests solely on the shoulders of the majority of the House of Representatives. A constitutional challenge to the Senate procedure for removal was dismissed by the Supreme Court on grounds of a non-justiciable political question in *Nixon v. United States* (1993). This case involved the protests of an impeached federal judge over the procedure of his trial in the Senate. The Supreme Court held that impeachment trials are explicitly outside the influence of the judiciary because the Constitution in Article I delegates impeachment expressly to the House of Representatives and the Senate.

Checkpoints

- **Express versus Inherent Powers**

  - Express President's powers are enumerated in the Constitution, while implied presidential powers are inherent and unenumerated.

  - Justice Jackson's three zones for inherent powers, per *Youngstown Sheet* (1952) are:

    1. if the President has express or implied authorization from Congress, then the President's acts are presumptively valid;

    2. if Congress is silent, the President can only rely on his independent power in which he and Congress may have concurrent powers, and the constitutionality will depend on the imperatives of events; and

    3. if the President acts contrary to the express or implied will of Congress, then such presidential action will only be upheld if the congressional Act is unconstitutional.

- **Express Powers**

  - The Appointment Power

    - "Principle officers" are those who are nominated by the President and appointed with Senate approval. These include ambassadors and Supreme Court Justices.

    - "Inferior officers" are those officers who Congress allows to be appointed by the President, the heads of departments, or by the courts. However, Congress cannot give the appointment power to itself or to its own officials.

    - There are four factors to determine if an officer is a principle officer or an inferior officer, per *Morison v. Olson* (1988):

      - whether the officer can be removed by higher executive branch official;

      - whether the officer has limited duties;

      - whether the office has limited jurisdiction; and

      - whether the office is limited in tenure.

  - The Removal Power

    - The President has the power to remove any executive official because the power of removal is part of the power of appointment. Thus, Congress cannot limit the President's ability to remove executive officials, nor can Congress give itself the power to remove them (*Bowsher v. Synar*, 1958).

    - Congress can limit the President's removal power by statute if:

      - it is an office where independence from the President is desirable; and

      - removal is limited to good cause.

Checkpoints *continued*

- For agencies that are quasi-legislative or quasi-judicial, the President can only fire officials for cause, and the Court will read this limitation into the statute. However, Congress always has the power to impeach (*Humphrey's Executor v. United States*, 1935).

- The Legislative Power

  - The Objections and Presentment Clauses give the President three options after a bill has passed both houses of Congress and is presented to him:

    - sign the bill, and it becomes law;

    - return it with "objections" (veto it); or

    - not sign it, in which case the bill still becomes law.

  - To override a President's veto, it takes a two-thirds vote of each house of Congress.

  - The Court struck down the Line Item Veto Act in *Clinton v. City of New York* (1998). A constitutional amendment is required for the President to be given this power.

- The Law Enforcement Power of Reprieves and Pardons

  - The presidential power to reprieve may be used to pardon criminals, but not for impeachment or for civil liability.

- International Powers

  - In foreign affairs, the Constitution maintains a sense of balance by sharing the power between the executive and legislative branches.

  - The executive has the power to recognize foreign countries.

  - Executive agreements do not require Senate approval. In *Dames & Moore v. Regan* (1981), the Court held that they are constitutional because Congress implicitly authorizes them through similar federal statutes, they preempt state laws, and they are necessary to carry out foreign diplomacy through speed and efficiency, which is not available through treaties that must be ratified.

  - Treaties are equal with federal statutes, and if they conflict, the Court will uphold the one that was adopted last.

- War Powers

  - The President's role as "commander in chief" grants the President control over the military.

  - The Court will likely dismiss challenges to the President's war powers as nonjusticiable.

  - Congress has the power to declare war, but the definition of an "officially declared war" is an uncertain political question.

Checkpoints *continued*

- Congress's powers to limit and balance the President's war powers are uncertain, yet arguably exist in the War Powers Resolution of 1973.

- Power to Combat Terrorism

  - The President has a variety of ways to address terrorism, including criminal investigations, information sharing, negotiating extradition treaties, developing a body of national and international antiterrorism laws and tribunals.

  - The United States cannot hold a detainee indefinitely, but only until the end of the conflict.

  - The military may detain an American citizen as an "enemy combatant," but must provide him with due process (*Hamdi v. Rumsfeld,* 2004).

  - Enemy combatants held at Guantánamo Bay have a constitutional right to *habeas corpus.*

  - The President's role as commander in chief places the executive office in charge of the military justice system, in which the expansion of the President's war powers applies.

- Executive Privilege and Immunity

  - The executive has a qualified privilege from disclosing to the public, information integral to the President's domestic and foreign policy making. Its purpose is to encourage open and frank discussions of policy options between the President and his or her advisors.

  - The executive has a qualified level of immunity from criminal and civil suits. There is no case law on whether this immunity would apply to a criminal suit. A former President has "absolute immunity from damages liability predicated on his official acts."

  - A sitting President does not have immunity from a civil suit for unofficial acts performed prior to becoming President.

- Executive Accountability: Impeachment

  - The primary mechanism for executive accountability is the voting booth.

  - The only method of removing "the President, Vice President, and all civil officers of the United States" before a scheduled election is "on impeachment for, and conviction of, treason, bribery, or other high crimes and misdemeanors."

  - What constitutes "high crimes and misdemeanors" is left to the judgment of the House and Senate.

  - The Supreme Court held that impeachment trial procedures are explicitly outside the influence of the judiciary because the Constitution in Article I delegates impeachment expressly to the House of Representatives and the Senate.

Chapter 4

Powers Reserved to the States and Their Limits

Roadmap

- Preemption: express and implied preemption
- The three types of implied preemption:
  - conflict preemption;
  - frustration of a federal objective; and
  - field preemption.
- The dormant Commerce Clause, including the development of the law and the modern test: either an undue burden on interstate commerce or discrimination in favor of intrastate commerce to the disadvantage of interstate commerce.
- The two exceptions to the dormant Commerce Clause doctrine:
  - congressional authorization; or
  - market participation.
- Interstate privileges and immunities of citizenship, contrasted with the dormant Commerce Clause
- State taxation of interstate commerce

I. Introduction: Grant versus Limitation

The Tenth Amendment to the Constitution provides: "The powers not delegated to the United States by the Constitution, nor prohibited by it to the States, are reserved to the States respectively, or to the people."

All powers of the federal government must be expressly or implicitly granted by the Constitution. By contrast, state governments are presumed to have broad, plenary, and residual powers, limited only by the text of the Constitution, which expressly or implicitly prohibits state powers or grants powers to another branch of government. For example, in Article I, Section 10, the Constitution expressly prohibits the states from entering treaties, coining money, or granting titles of nobility. Furthermore, the Supremacy Clause states that the Constitution and federal laws are the supreme law; thus, it prohibits state laws and state conduct that conflict with legitimate federal laws. This explicit limitation of state power means that the state law is preempted by the federal law.

There are also a number of areas in which the courts have held that a power or set of powers is national in nature, and therefore beyond the reach of states. For example, although the Constitution does not explicitly forbid states from every area of foreign relations (not even from declaring war), these powers are commonly accepted as being within the exclusive competence of the national government. There are a number of areas of state and local law that are preempted in whole or in part, either expressly or implicitly.

There are two similar but distinct doctrinal areas of the law that restrict the power of states. The first is a subcategory of preemption, namely, the dormant Commerce Clause doctrine, which is invoked to limit states from passing laws that burden or discriminate against interstate commerce, even though Congress has failed to exercise its Commerce Clause power to regulate an area. The other limiting doctrine is found in Article IV, Section 2—the Privileges and Immunities Clause. This provision limits a state from discriminating against the citizens of other states. There is considerable overlap between these two doctrinal areas, given that both may be concerned with the effects of a state's regulation on other states or their citizens. Nonetheless, they are distinct not only in their source but also in the legal rules they employ and the range of applicable factual situations. These doctrines limit the ability of the state to regulate conduct, and they limit the ability of the state to tax. Whereas the Privileges and Immunities Clause analysis is the same for evaluating state regulations and taxation, the dormant Commerce Clause analysis is different in the two contexts.

This chapter addresses the issue of preemption, the dormant Commerce Clause, the Privileges and Immunities Clause, followed by state taxation of interstate commerce.

II. Preemption

Preemption occurs when Congress regulates conduct in a given area and a state law conflicts with the federal regulation. Presuming that it is constitutional for Congress to regulate the area (see Chapter 2), the Supremacy Clause of Article VI mandates that the federal law wins; the state law is preempted and therefore is invalid. In any case of apparent conflict between a state and federal law, the Court has two options: (1) It can hold that the valid federal law conflicts with state law and preempts the state law, striking the state law down; or (2) it can hold that the federal law and state law do not conflict and can co-exist, upholding both laws as constitutional. Thus, preemption is actually an issue of statutory interpretation. The Court generally decides between the two options by determining whether Congress intended for the federal law to pre-empt the state law (*Gade v. National Solid Waste Management Association,* 1992).

There are two types of preemption: express and implied. Express preemp-tion occurs when Congress expresses its intent to preempt the state law with clear language. Note that Congress can also expressly state that it does not in-tend to preempt state law. Even if Congress expresses its intent, the Court must still decide the scope of the state and federal laws to determine if there is an over-lap and, thus, a conflict. As illustrated in the cases discussed next, the Court is often divided on the scope or the reach of the statutes involved.

Implied preemption occurs when there is clear congressional intent to pre-empt the state law, or when it is implicit in the structure or purpose of the federal law. It is commonly understood that cases in the area of implied pre-emption do not have established clearly defined rules, limits, or doctrine. Nonetheless, the Court will consider whether implied preemption is appro-priate, based on whether it is an area that:

1. requires national uniformity, versus one that is more appropriate to local regulation and experimentation;
2. is traditionally regulated by the states; or
3. cannot be harmoniously regulated by both the federal and state gov-ernments (continuous conflicts will likely occur).

Express preemption is addressed in Section A, and implied preemption is ad-dressed in Section B.

A. Express Preemption

In express preemption cases, even if it is clear that Congress intended the federal law to preempt state law, there is still a question regarding the scope of the preemption. The Court must determine how broadly or narrowly to con-strue the federal law and whether any potentially conflicting state law overlaps. In other words, the issue of Congress's intent is taken off the table, so to speak, but the question remains as to where the table ends and where "off the table" begins. Assume that the tabletop is the area where federal law preempts state law. In express preemption cases, the parties are arguing over the dimensions of the tabletop and whether any given state law is on or off the tabletop.

For example, in *Cipollone v. Liggett Group Inc.* (1992), the issue concerned the scope of the Federal Cigarette Labeling and Advertising Act, which mandates that the Surgeon General's warning be printed on every pack of cigarettes. The case was brought by the son of a woman who smoked from 1942 until 1984, when she died of lung cancer. The plaintiff had several state law claims, involving torts, contracts, and fraud. In tort, he alleged design defects, failure to warn, and negligence in testing, research, sale, promotion, and advertising of the product. He also alleged that under contract law, there had been an express warranty by defendants that the product did not produce serious health consequences. Finally, he claimed that the defendant had fraudulently misrepresented the product and conspired to defraud the public regarding the medical and scientific data on the hazards of smoking.

Part of the respondent's defense was that the Federal Cigarette Labeling and Advertising Act (1965), as succeeded by the Public Health Cigarette Smoking Act of 1969, preempted the state laws that the plaintiff was relying on for his claims. The Act clearly stated that it preempted state law that imposed any "requirement or prohibition based on smoking and health ... with respect to the advertising or promotion of any cigarette ... packages" labeled in conformity with the federal rules promulgated under the Act.

Justice John Paul Stevens, writing for the plurality, held that while the federal Act preempted some of the state law claims, it did not preclude all of them. In determining which claims were preempted, the Court announced two rules of statutory construction in the area of express preemption:

1. express preemption provisions must be construed narrowly, "in light of the presumption against the preemption of state police power regulations"; and
2. the Court will not contemplate the possibility of implied preemption beyond the scope of what is expressly preempted.

In other words, the Court will interpret the tabletop to be smaller, rather than larger. Second, it will not extend the explicit dimensions of the tabletop by implying more preemption in cases where some preemption is explicit (i.e., it will not put an implied leaf in the table to extend it).

Applying these rules to the federal and state laws in question, the Court interpreted the language "requirement or prohibition" in the text of the Act to apply to both state statutory law and the common law. It reasoned that damage awards under the common law can be as effective a regulatory tool as legislation can be. It then went on to hold that the tort law claims that related to advertising and promotion (the failure to warn of the dangers of cigarettes in the marketing and advertising of the product) were preempted. Common law tort law claims that did not relate to advertising and marketing (negligent research, testing and manufacturing defects, or failure to use a safer alternative design) were not preempted. The Court held that the 1969 Act did not preempt the petitioner's claims based on express warranty, intentional fraud and misrepresentation, or conspiracy. Breach of express warranty was not preempted, because the Court held that the requirements or prohibitions that are imposed by express warranties are self-imposed through contract law, rather than under state law. They are voluntary commitments. Further, claims based on fraudulent concealment of facts are not based on duties with regard to "smoking and health," but are based on the duty "not to deceive." Conspiracy is also not preempted for similar reasons, that is, it is based on a duty not to conspire, rather than a duty regarding "smoking and health."

Two opinions, partially concurring and partially dissenting, point out the difficulty of doctrinal stability in this area of the law. Justice Harry Blackmun agreed with the Court's stated approach to preemption, as articulated in the two rules, but disagreed with the Court's application. His main criticism was that the Court did not follow its own rule and construed the statute broadly, rather than narrowly. He did not believe that the federal statute's preemptive language extended to tort law at all because tort law is primarily concerned with compensating victims, not regulating conduct. Justice Blackmun reasoned that tort law is an indirect "requirement or prohibition" and thus, should not be preempted. Based on his narrow reading, those words only applied to direct regulation, that is, through statutes and administrative rules and regulations. As he stated: "Although the Court flatly states that the phrase 'no requirement or prohibition' 'sweeps broadly' and 'easily encompass[es] obligations that take the form of common law rules,' those words are in reality far from unambiguous and cannot be said clearly to evidence a congressional mandate to pre-empt state common law damages actions." Thus, he would put all the torts claims in the nonpreemption category, along with contracts, fraud, and conspiracy.

Justice Antonin Scalia disagreed with the two rules articulated by the Court and with the Court's conclusions that not all common law claims were preempted and that the failure to warn claims were not preempted. He argued that the proper rule for statutory interpretation is to interpret the statute in light of its plain meaning, rather than through a narrow reading. Furthermore, while he agreed with the Court that express preemption excludes field preemption (because the two are incompatible), he did not agree that express preemption precludes other forms of implied preemption. Field preemption is discussed in Part B, Section 3.

The first rule of interpretation from *Cipollone* (that federal preemption provisions should be read narrowly) has endured (*Medtronic, Inc. v. Lahr,*

1996; *Bates v. Dow Agrosciences, LLC,* 2005). However, the second rule, that any express preemption precludes all implied preemption, has been brought into question.

Freightliner Corp. v. Myrick (1995) involved the question as to whether the National Traffic and Motor Vehicle Safety Act expressly or implicitly preempted state common law claims of design defect against manufacturers of trucks and trailers that were not equipped with antilock braking systems. Although the Court held that the Act neither expressly nor implicitly preempted the common law claims in this case, the Court took the opportunity to clarify, or limit, *Cipollone* by reasoning that it did not establish a categorical rule that implied preemption cannot exist when Congress has chosen to include express preemption clauses in a statute. As Justice Clarence Thomas, writing for the majority stated, "the fact that an express definition of the pre-emptive reach of a statute 'implies' — i.e., supports a reasonable inference — that Congress did not intend to pre-empt other matters does not mean that the express clause entirely forecloses any possibility of implied pre-emption."

As noted, the rule of narrowly construing express preemption clauses was adopted again in *Bates v. Dow Agrosciences, LLC* (2005). *Bates* addressed the issue of whether the Federal Insecticide, Fungicide, and Rodenticide Act preempted state law claims that the defendant's pesticide damaged the plaintiffs' peanut crops. The sharper question was whether it preempted claims of fraud and failure to warn, as well as defective design, defective manufacturing, negligent testing, breach of express warranty, and the violation of the Texas Deceptive Trade Practices Act. The Court remanded the first two claims (fraud and failure to warn) because they were not sufficiently briefed, but it held that the remaining claims were not preempted by the Act.

The preemption language in question is similar, in many respects, to the language in *Cipollone* (the cigarette advertising and promotion case), but there were some distinguishing features. The relevant language reads: "Such State shall not impose or continue in effect any requirements for labeling or packaging in addition to or different from those required under this subchapter." The distinguishing language, here, is the inclusion of "in addition to or different from those required under this subchapter." Although the regulation in *Cipollone* preempted all state-based claims related to labeling, the federal law in *Bates* allowed for state-based claims as long as they are based on or consistent with the standards in the federal Act.

Dow argued that allowing all 50 fifty to have parallel enforcement would result in a "patchwork" of different standards and thus should be preempted by the Act. The Court did not find this interpretation to be consistent with the language of the Act, but nonetheless stated: "Even if Dow had offered us a plausible alternative reading … [that was] just as plausible as our reading of that text—we would nevertheless have a duty to accept the reading that disfavors pre-emption" (*Bates,* quoting *Medtronic,* 1996). The Court explained that the reason for taking a narrow reading or one that disfavors preemption was based on the idea that "States are independent sovereigns in our federal system," and, therefore, Congress would not lightly or "cavalierly" preempt state law. This approach was reinforced when the Court stated: "The long history of tort litigation against manufacturers of poisonous substances adds force to the basic presumption against pre-emption. If Congress had intended to deprive injured parties of a long available form of compensation, it surely would have expressed that intent more clearly."

Justices Thomas and Scalia, concurring in part and dissenting in part, still argued for an ordinary meaning approach to the text, rather than one that was tilted against preemption. They also pointed out that the Court did not address any implied preemption arguments. Although they did not say that this was an implied revival of the second rule in *Cipollone,* they believed that the decision "comports with this Court's increasing reluctance to expand federal statutes beyond their terms through doctrines of implied pre-emption."

We now turn to the doctrine of implied preemption to see if Justices Thomas and Scalia's view bears out.

B. Implied Preemption

There are three situations in which the Court will imply preemption of a state law.

1. Direct conflict preemption: a direct conflict between the state and federal law, in which it is impossible to comply with both laws.
2. Frustration of a federal objective: when the state law frustrates the ends, purpose, or the objectives of a valid federal law.
3. Field preemption: when the federal regulation is so pervasive that Congress has occupied the field and there is no room left for the states to regulate it.

1. Direct Conflict: Dual Compliance Is Impossible

The clearest instance of implied preemption is when it is impossible to follow both the state and federal law. In other words, to comply with one law, one must violate the other.

In *Florida Lime & Avocado Growers, Inc. v. Paul* (1963), Florida avocado growers challenged a California law that prohibited the transportation or sale in California of avocados that contain "less than 8 percent of oil, by weight." The Florida growers argued that the California law was preempted by marketing orders approved by the Secretary of Agriculture to gauge the maturity of avocados. The federal marketing orders did not have an oil content standard for determining the maturity of the avocados. Thus, under the federal standard, avocados would be certified as mature, whereas under California's 8 percent standard, they would be prohibited from the market.

If the federal regulation is seen as an upper limit or a ceiling on the regulation, then there would be a direct conflict because at least some federally certified mature avocados are not mature under the state law standard. However, if the federal law is viewed as a minimum standard or a floor, then it is possible for the Florida growers to satisfy both standards. Leaving the avocados on the vine a bit longer would ensure that they would be mature under both standards. The stated purpose of the federal law, the Agricultural Adjustment Act, under which the federal maturity standard was created, was "to establish and maintain such minimum standards of quality and maturity ... as will effectuate such orderly marketing of such agricultural commodities as will be in the public interest." Thus, the Court held that the federal regulation was a minimum standard, and the state could impose higher standards because it was possible to comply with both. To support this interpretation, the Court noted both that this was not an area that required national uniformity and that the subject matter has been "traditionally regarded as properly within the scope of state superintendence."

The Court held that if it is physically impossible to comply with both a federal and a state regulation simultaneously, then it does not look to Congress's intent; rather, it holds that the federal law preempts the state law. It reasoned, for example, that if the federal regulation prohibited picking and marketing of avocados with *over* 7 percent oil, then a state, such as Florida, could only pick avocados that California would exclude. By contrast, in the present case, Florida could leave its avocados on the vine and comply with both standards.

If it was relatively clear that there was no direct conflict in *Florida Lime*, it is less clear that there was a conflict in *Geier v. American Honda Motor Co., Inc.* (2000). *Geier* involved the potential conflict between the federal Motor Vehicle Safety Standard rules, promulgated by the Department of Transportation under the National Traffic and Motor Vehicle Safety Act, and state tort law claims based on design defects. The federal standards allowed for either airbags or shoulder and lap seatbelts. Alexis Geier, who was seriously injured in a accident while driving her 1987 Honda, which had only seatbelts, sued under state law on the basis that the failure to install airbags was a design defect.

The regulations stated:

> Whenever a Federal motor vehicle safety standard established under this subchapter is in effect, no State or political subdivision of a State shall have any authority either to establish, or to continue in effect, with respect to any motor vehicle or item of motor vehicle equipment[,] any safety standard applicable to the same aspect of performance of such vehicle or item of equipment which is not identical to the Federal standard.

However, the Act also had a savings clause that provided, "'compliance with' a federal safety standard 'does not exempt any person from any liability under common law.'" These contradictory clauses can be resolved any of a number of ways. If both are read as applying to common law standards, then they appear contradictory, but if the preemption clause is read as applying to state statutory and regulatory standards, then there is no conflict.

The Court, in a five-to-four decision, appears to have held that the savings clause exempted state-based tort liability from the express preemption. In other words, there was no express preemption of state-based tort claims that used a higher standard than the minimum set in the federal standards.

Nonetheless, it also held that tort-based liability, predicated on a higher standard than the minimum set in the guidelines, was preempted through implied conflict preemption. As the Court stated: "Insofar as petitioners' argument would permit common-law actions that 'actually conflict' with federal regulations, it would take from those who would enforce a federal law the very ability to achieve the law's congressionally mandated objectives that the Constitution, through the operation of ordinary pre-emption principles, seeks to protect."

So where is the actual conflict? Is this not the same as the Florida avocado growers, who could satisfy both standards? If the state-based standard under tort law turned out to be airbags, could Honda satisfy this standard and the federal standard? The Court's answer was "no." As Justice Stephen Breyer, writing for the majority explained, the standards were designed to give the manufacturer a range of choices, and the mix of devices over time would have a range of benefits, from cost savings to safety, technological development, and consumer acceptance. The airbag standard would conflict with this range of choices and with the objectives of the federal regulation. The Court, in fact, declined to draw any distinction between direct or physical conflict and conflicts that frustrate federal objectives.

Justice Stevens wrote a forceful dissent, arguing that the Court was ignoring precedent, which established the presumption against preemption, and was ignoring important federalism issues involved in these cases. He noted that at the time of the decision, there was general agreement "that, to be safe, a car must have an airbag," and he believed that the question of whether Honda knew this in 1987 was to be determined by state tort law, and it was not pre-empted by federal law. He did not believe that allowing states to determine this issue in any way frustrated the federal object, much less created a direct con-flict. In fact, he noted evidence that the Secretary of Transportation favored and encouraged airbags, even though she did not require them.

Based on Justice Stevens's reading, the preemption language referred to statutory and regulatory standards and not to common law standards. The savings clause reinforced the view that the federal standards would not pre-empt or insulate manufacturers from liability based on state law standards. Unlike in *Cipollone* (cigarette advertising and promotion case), this statute had a savings clause that showed Congress's intent not to preempt state common law. For Justice Stevens, the Court basically read the savings clause out of the Act, by implying preemption where Congress expressly saved it. As Justice Stevens pointed out, the federal standards were minimum standards. He stated that the "Court completely ignores the important fact that by definition all of the standards established under the Safety Act—like the British regulations that governed the number and capacity of lifeboats aboard the *Titanic*—im-pose minimum, rather than fixed or maximum, requirements."

2. Frustration of a Federal Objective

There are many cases in which state laws will not directly conflict with fed-eral law but will nonetheless impede or frustrate the ends or objectives of fed-eral law. *Perez v. Campbell* (1971) is a classic case in the area. Adolfo Perez, after losing a lawsuit regarding his involvement in a traffic accident, was unable to pay the $2,425.98 in damages, plus court costs. As a result, under Arizona state law, his driver's license was suspended. Perez had previously filed for bank-ruptcy under federal law, and he claimed that the Arizona licensing law was preempted by the federal bankruptcy law, which discharged all of his debts. As the Court noted, one of the main purposes of the Bankruptcy Act is to provide debtors "a new opportunity in life and a clear field for future effort, unhampered by the pressure and discouragement of preexisting debt" (*Perez* quoting *Local Loan Co. v. Hunt*, 1934). For the Court, this included debt arising from tort li-ability. In other words, the Bankruptcy Act takes away the pressure of debt, yet the Arizona law puts the pressure back on by suspending the license; thus, the state law frustrated the purpose of the federal law, and it was preempted.

Although in *Perez* it is relatively clear that the federal purpose is being frus-trated, other cases are less clear. For instance, in *Pacific Gas & Electric Co. v. State Energy Resources Conservation & Development Commission* (1983), there ap-peared to be a conflict between a California law that imposed a moratorium on the construction of nuclear power plants and a federal law that encouraged nuclear energy by regulating safety. In fact, there was a strong argument, which was endorsed by the Court, that the federal government preempted the field on nuclear safety. The federal government created a scheme to promote the development of nuclear energy, while also safeguarding the public and the environment from the risks of nuclear power. The federal Atomic Energy Commission was given exclusive jurisdiction to license the transfer, delivery, receipt, acquisition, possession, and use of nuclear materials, but not to regulate electricity production, which was left to the states.

There were two ways to interpret the state's moratorium—either as a matter of ensuring public safety or as a way to ensure economic viability. The plain language of the state law providing for the moratorium said that it was for the purpose of ensuring safe disposal of nuclear waste. Nonetheless, the majority accepted California's argument that the state's objective was economics, not safety, because it was aimed at controlling the high costs of storing nuclear waste; therefore, it did not interfere with federal safety objectives. In either event, there still remained the apparent conflict with the goal of encouraging nuclear energy in general. Here again, the Court strained to limit Congress's objective to encouraging economically viable nuclear energy. It was to promote nuclear power, but this was not to be accomplished at all costs. The Court applied this limitation, in part, by reasoning that energy was an area traditionally regulated by the states, and thus it was within California's police powers.

Perhaps this case is one in which the Court demonstrated sympathy to state concerns over the development of nuclear energy. Although it may be explained in terms of sympathy for state cries of NIMBY (not in my back yard), it illustrates the flexibility of the Court to determine both the state and federal objectives and either find a conflict or create compatibility between the laws.

A more recent case of objectives preemption, *Crosby v. National Foreign Trade Council* (2000), involved a Massachusetts law barring state entities from buying goods or services from companies doing business with Burma because of its human rights violations. Although Massachusetts passed its law first, soon after, Congress imposed mandatory and conditional sanctions on Burma and empowered the President to control the economic sanctions against that country. The National Foreign Trade Council filed suit against the state officials in federal court, claiming that the state law unconstitutionally infringed on the federal foreign affairs power, violated the Foreign Commerce Clause, and was preempted by the federal law.

Justice David Souter, writing for the majority, agreed. The plenary power given to the President in the matter preempted Massachusetts law. Although both laws had similar main objectives—bringing Burma into compliance with human rights norms—those were not the only objectives that counted.

In determining if the Massachusetts law impeded federal objectives, the Court looked to Congress's "full objectives" under the federal law. This showed that the state law undermined three of Congress's objectives in three different provisions:

1. "its delegation of effective discretion to the President to control economic sanctions against Burma";
2. "its limitation of sanctions solely to United States persons and new investment"; and
3. "its directive to the President to proceed diplomatically in developing a comprehensive, multilateral strategy towards Burma."

The overall conflict was with the plenary power given to the President to use the carrots and sticks of diplomacy along with economic sanctions to bring Burma into compliance. The Massachusetts law impaired the efficacy of any actions taken and limited the President's flexibility. Massachusetts's plan also used means that conflicted with the federal statute by regulating non-U.S. citizens and existing investments. Because this was an area in which it is important that the nation speak with one voice, the Court held that the federal law preempted the Massachusetts law because it frustrated the federal objectives.

3. Field Preemption

As *Pacific Gas & Electric Co.* indicated, if the state had been regulating in the area of safety, its moratorium on the construction of nuclear power plants may have been precluded by implied field preemption. Sometimes, federal regulation schemes can be "so pervasive as to make reasonable the inference that Congress left no room for the States to supplement it" (*Rice v. Santa Fe Elevator Corp.*, 1947). Not only is it difficult to know when a scheme is so pervasive to give rise to field preemption, as *Pacific Gas* illustrates, it can also be difficult to determine the scope or the size of the field that is occupied and thus, preempted.

Hines v. Davidowitz (1941) concerned the conflict between a Pennsylvania law, which required aliens to register and carry state documentation and general federal authority over foreign affairs, immigration, and naturalization. The Court held that the Pennsylvania law was preempted, not because it conflicted with any particular legislation or federal goal but because the law affected international relations. Further, it intruded on an area that was not only traditionally regulated by the federal government but was governed by a "broad and comprehensive" federal plan that included federal registration. However, it is worth noting that nothing precluded dual registration and, in fact, the state plan might have furthered the federal objectives. Yet in the area of immigration law, federal regulations are exclusive.

Although there have been several cases upholding the preemption of state laws governing aliens, including laws regulating the granting of commercial fishing licenses (*Takahashi v. Fish and Game Commission,* 1948) and school tuition (*Toll v. Moreno,* 1982), the Court has allowed some state regulation. For instance, in *De Canas v. Bica* (1976), the Court held that the field of immigration occupied by the government did not extend to state employment laws that regulated undocumented workers for the benefit of state workers. Though it might be hard to reconcile these cases, the Court in *Bica* based its decision on congressional intent to exclude employment law within the occupied field.

In *Pennsylvania v. Nelson* (1956), the Court set up a three-part test for preemption:

1. the pervasiveness of the federal scheme;
2. the need for national uniformity; and
3. the risk of conflict between the state law and the administration of the federal program.

The case involved the Pennsylvania Sedition Act, which purported to supplement the federal Sedition Act. In other words, the objectives of both Acts were the same: to combat those advocating the violent overthrow of the government. Steve Nelson, a member of the Communist Party, was charged with and convicted of uttering sedition against the United States under the Pennsylvania law. He was sentenced to twenty years in prison. As a result, he challenged the Pennsylvania Act as contravening the Smith Act of 1940, a federal law that prohibited the knowing advocacy of the overthrow of the government of the United States by force and violence.

The Court held that because of the breadth of federal law in the area, Congress's purpose was to preempt the field of antisedition legislation. It further held that there was a predominant federal interest in the field and there was a danger of conflict between enforcement of state sedition acts and administration of the federal program. The main problem with the Pennsylvania Act was that it could interfere with delicate undercover operations. This was exacerbated by the fact that the Pennsylvania Act allowed for private individuals to initiate prosecutions. As a result, local police could be stumbling over or interfering with federal officers working surveillance or working undercover. Therefore, the Smith Act was deemed to preempt the Pennsylvania Act, precluding enforcement of the Pennsylvania Act against a person charged with acts of sedition against the federal government.

In *Uphaus v. Wymann* (1959), the Court declined to extend *Nelson* to a New Hampshire contempt order for failure to comply with a subpoena, issued as part of an investigation into possible subversive activities. Although the petitioner argued that *Nelson* applied, the Court took the opportunity to clarify that *Nelson* only preempted state law that made sedition against the United State illegal, it did not preempt a state law that prosecuted sedition against the state. The state retained the right to ensure its own safety. The state was merely preempted from trying to regulate for the purposes of national security when the federal government had already occupied that field. Unlike the interference in *Nelson*, here, there would be no fear that one investigation might impair another.

More recently, in *American Insurance Association v. Garamendi* (2003), the Court addressed the preemption of a California law that aided Holocaust survivors in obtaining information from California insurance companies, who had sold insurance in Europe at the time of the Holocaust. Although a noble cause, the Court held that the law intruded on the field of foreign relations and the President's power to enter into executive agreements with other countries on the issue. The United States already had these types of agreements with France, Germany, and Austria, and the California law, not unlike the Massachusetts law in *Crosby* (the Burma sanctions case) would tie the President's hands. The Court took the opportunity to stress that the underlying reason for preemption in both cases was the "concern for uniformity in this country's dealings with foreign nations." The Court also noted that California law could be dealt with as a matter of field preemption or conflict preemption.

If the state is regulating within its own sphere, and there is an impact on the federal field, then it should be analyzed as a conflict preemption; whereas if the state is regulating directly within the field of foreign affairs, then field preemption is more appropriate. The Court noted that there was some authority for the view that if the state was acting within its own competence under its police powers, and the effect on foreign affairs was merely incidental, then it would be allowed. Even on this basis, the majority held that the California law created more than an incidental effect. It held that there was a conflict because the existing executive agreements provided for voluntary information, and the California law contemplated coercive litigation. The Court reasoned that although there was an important interest in achieving justice for Holocaust victims, the state interest was only a fraction of the national interest. Thus, to the extent that the California law conflicted with the federal means of achieving those ends, it was preempted.

The case was a five-to-four decision, with Justices Ruth Bader Ginsburg, Stevens, Scalia, and Thomas dissenting. The dissenters reasoned that the state law did not detract in any way from the uniformity of the United States's dealings with foreign nations, because the California law was addressed to private corporations and not foreign governments. Furthermore, they did not believe that the executive had expressed any clear objectives that were directly contrary to the California law. For the dissenters, invoking the "dormant Foreign Affairs Clause" was inappropriate in this instance. In other words, it was an inappropriate case for implied preemption in the field of foreign affairs.

As one may gather from the cases discussed and the number of dissenting Justices, it is often difficult to predict what is and is not preempted. The Court is essentially balancing state and federal interests, along with its sense of what should be uniformly regulated, versus what can be regulated at both the state and federal level.

III. Dormant Commerce Clause

The dormant Commerce Clause is not in the text of the Constitution; rather, it is a doctrine that in effect works like implied preemption. The doctrine derives its force from the Commerce Clause. "Dormant" is another way of saying that the Court is not addressing federal power explicitly exercised under the interstate Commerce Clause. Rather, it is addressing the exercise of state power that intrudes onto the federal field of interstate commerce. The Commerce Clause does not preempt the entire field of interstate commerce, but even when Congress has not passed preemptive legislation under the Commerce Clause, the dormant Commerce Clause still limits what states can do in that field. The dormant Commerce Clause gives effect to the interstate Commerce Clause by protecting interstate commerce from state regulations that either have an *incidental undue burden* on interstate commerce or *discriminate* against interstate commerce.

The modern test in *incidental undue burden* cases is a balancing test, which weighs the benefits of the state law against the burden the law has on interstate commerce (called the Pike test from *Pike v. Bruce Church, Inc.*, 1970). The modern test in *discrimination* cases is a form of heightened scrutiny that comes close to the test in racial discrimination cases (see Chapter 8). It is nearly a "per se rule of invalidity" because it requires that the law be *necessary for an important governmental purpose* (*City of Philadelphia v. New Jersey*, 1978). Because it is almost always possible to achieve the same purpose in a way that has less of a negative impact on interstate commerce, most laws will not be found to be "necessary" and are, therefore, per se invalid. If the law does not discriminate against interstate commerce, the Court uses the Pike test to see if the state has unduly burdened interstate commerce.

Some commentators and members of the Court criticize the use of the dormant Commerce Clause. They usually refer to it as the "negative Commerce Clause," and their main charge is that the doctrine is an example of illegitimate judicial activism. They argue that if the Framers had wanted to give Congress exclusive powers to legislate in the area of interstate commerce, they could have put it in the text of the Constitution. Further, they reason that if Congress wants to preempt state law in the area, it can always do so by simply legislating within its Commerce Clause powers. Where it has not done so, they are hesitant to have the Court do the job for Congress.

Although the argument has some merit, there may be practical reasons why Congress does not or has not legislated to preempt state regulations that impact interstate commerce or discriminate against interstate commerce. There are simply too many areas of state regulation, which may or may not end up having an impact on interstate commerce, for Congress to see in advance. Those engaged in interstate commerce are likely to feel the pinch of state regulations before Congress can anticipate them, and they can bring their claim to court before Congress has time to respond.

There is also a strong historical and principled reason for the use of the dormant Commerce Clause. The Articles of Confederation were a failure, in part, because they did not have a mechanism that the national government could employ to regulate interstate commerce, and as a result, there was a "race to the bottom" to impose laws that discriminated against interstate commerce and favored in-state protectionism. When state after state enacts this sort of legislation to protect its internal interests, the national economy suffers. Thus, the dormant Commerce Clause helps protect out-of-state businesses and those engaged in interstate commerce, similar to the way that diversity jurisdiction helps protect those from out of state who might be discriminated against and who do not have an equal voice within the state. Although diversity jurisdiction is designed to ensure that justice both appears to be done and is actually done, the dormant Commerce Clause doctrine is designed to ensure national economic prosperity, which is hampered if the states are unduly burdening or discriminating against interstate commerce.

One vocal critic of the dormant Commerce Clause, Justice Scalia, would support the use of the dormant Commerce Clause in cases of discrimination against out-of-staters, but Justice Scalia, along with Justice Thomas, do not think it is appropriate in simple impact or undue burden cases.

A majority of the Court still finds preemption when there is either an undue burden on interstate commerce or when there is discrimination in favor of intrastate commerce and against interstate commerce. There are two exceptions to this rule: (1) when Congress itself authorizes the states to act; and (2) when the state is not regulating interstate commerce but is an active participant in the market. With respect to the first exception, Congress can authorize the states to act because of its interstate Commerce Clause powers. When the state is an active participant in the market, it is using state resources, and it should be allowed to put those resources to work in the market for its own benefit. This exception does not generally extend to cases where the state is acting as a market regulator. However, recently the Court has expanded the market participant exception to include conduct that is more regulatory (for example, providing a tax exemption) if the government's overall activity is a public function (for example, selling state and local bonds to fund government projects).

A. Approaches to Analyzing the Dormant Commerce Clause

1. The Early Cases and Approaches

a. State Police Powers versus National Powers

Before the Court settled on the foregoing modern tests, it struggled with trying to distinguish between what was within the state's police powers (i.e., the powers that were traditionally exercised by the state for the health, safety, and welfare of its citizens) and what was proper for national regulation. The distinction between local and national powers was initially raised by Justice John Marshall in *Gibbons v. Ogden* (1824) (the Commerce Clause case involving the conflict between the New York grant of monopoly over ferries and a federal grant). In cases where the state exercised such powers (e.g., through inspection and quarantine laws, health laws, and laws regulating internal commerce, such as turnpike laws and ferry laws), it was irrelevant that the state law might impact interstate commerce. The problem with this approach is that with the Industrial Revolution, the nation's economy changed from predominantly local economic transactions to a national economy; thus, local laws could severely impede national economic progress.

b. National Uniformity versus Local Diversity

In *Cooley v. Board of Wardens* (1851), the Court took a functional approach to the issue, by distinguishing between subject matter that required *national uniformity* and that which was best left to *local diversity*. The issue was, in part, whether states could regulate in the area of interstate commerce at all, even if Congress authorized them to do so. In other words, the question was whether the Constitution's Commerce Clause requires Congress to regulate the field and completely bar the states from doing so. In *Cooley*, the Court held that a Pennsylvania law that required a local ship pilot be used on all ships coming into and leaving the port of Philadelphia was constitutional. It was constitutional, in part, because of explicit congressional authorization, but it was also held to be constitutional because of the nature of the subject matter.

As the Court stated:

> Now the power to regulate commerce, embraces a vast field, containing not only many, but exceedingly various subjects, quite unlike in their nature; some imperatively demanding a single uniform rule, operating equally on the commerce of the United States in every port; and some, like the subject now in question, as imperatively demanding that diversity, which alone can meet the local necessities of navigation.

In other words, because U.S. ports are diverse, regulating who pilots ships through ports is best carried out by those familiar with local needs. National uniform rules or standards are not likely to be appropriate.

Although this functional approach was something of an improvement over the *Ogden* approach (traditional local powers versus national powers), it still did not address issues of protectionism or discrimination against interstate commerce, nor did it address local laws that impacted interstate commerce.

c. Direct versus Indirect Effects

The *direct versus indirect test*, as articulated in *DiSanto v. Pennsylvania* (1927), did not really improve on these previous tests. In *DiSanto*, the Court held that laws that had a direct effect on interstate commerce were invalid, whereas those that had merely an indirect effect were upheld. This effectively reboxed or restated the national versus local test. Laws that were local and within the state's police powers directly regulated local concerns and had an indirect effect on interstate commerce, whereas laws that directly affected interstate commerce were within the national competence.

The real problem with the direct versus indirect test, as well as the previous tests, is that they take facts that are matters of degree and place them into boxes, as if they were premade to fit in them. These approaches tend to hide the balancing of factors that goes into deciding which box the case falls. If you want the law to pass the test, then you put it in the "indirect" box, and if you want it to fail, you put it in the "direct" box. The important question is why it is placed in that box, not if it is inside it or not.

2. *The Modern Balancing Approach to Incidental Impact Cases*

The modern approach to the dormant Commerce Clause in cases that do not involve discrimination can be found in *South Carolina State Highway De-*

partment v. Barnwell Bros., Inc. (1938). South Carolina passed a law regulating the height and width of trucks using its state highways. The law would have a significant impact on interstate truckers and trucking companies that used taller and wider trucks, which were prohibited from using South Carolina highways. Although there was a significant impact on interstate commerce, Justice Harlan Stone, writing for the Court, held that that this was not a case of a state enacting legislation for the purposes of state protectionism or local advantage. The law was not designed to discriminate against interstate commerce but to ensure safety on state highways. The regulation was a matter of "great local concern." The highways in question were owned and maintained by the state, and therefore, it was legitimate for the state to regulate the height and width of vehicles on those highways.

The Court in *Barnwell* distinguished state highways from railroads, which were more centrally governed by the Commerce Clause. Thus, it is not surprising that Justice Stone, writing for the Court in *Southern Pacific Co. v. Arizona* (1945), struck down an Arizona law that limited the length of passenger and freight trains running through the state. Although the burden was similar to that in *Barnwell*, here the Court emphasized the impact on interstate commerce and the need for a national uniform standard. Arizona's standard was out of step with the standards in most states and would require trains to stop before reaching the border and break up into smaller trains. Although the justification (like in *Barnwell*) was safety, the Court accepted the trial court's finding that the regulation could actually make the situation more dangerous. Although there was a concern that longer trains caused slack action incidents (accidents that occur because of the slack between each car), the trial court found that there were just as many accidents in Arizona after imposing the restrictions as in Nevada, which did not have the restriction. Further, the increase in the number of trains would likely increase accidents, rather than decrease them.

The Arizona law mandated time and resources to break up trains and use more engines (30 percent more), and this wastefulness created a burden on interstate commerce. It required not only more trains but more manpower and energy to fuel and transport goods. These inefficient burdens outweighed the benefits to the state, and thus, the Court held the law to be unconstitutional.

As already noted, the Pike test sets out the modern balancing test. The Court, in *Pike v. Bruce Church, Inc.* (1970), stated the test as follows: "Where the statute regulates evenhandedly to effectuate a legitimate local public interest, and its effects on interstate commerce are only incidental, it will be upheld unless the burden imposed on such commerce is clearly excessive in relation to the putative local benefits." It is worth emphasizing that under *Pike*, nondiscriminatory laws are not balanced on an even scale. In cases involving discrimination, the scales are tipped heavily against the state (see following discussion); yet in nondiscriminatory cases, the scales are tipped in the government's favor. In the latter, it is the plaintiff's burden of proof to show that the burden is clearly excessive in relation to the local benefits. It is also important to note, as the cases that follow demonstrate, the mere fact that a law is facially neutral does not mean that it has only an incidental effect on interstate commerce. Discrimination can be based on facially discriminatory ends or goals, facially discriminatory means, and even a discriminatory impact that is not merely incidental.

3. The Modern Approach to Laws that Discriminate against Interstate Commerce

Discrimination against interstate commerce can either take the form of privileging intrastate commerce over interstate commerce or discriminating against out-of-state businesses or consumers in favor of in-state businesses or consumers. In the former case, the law might not discriminate against out-of-staters, in the sense that it discriminates against *both* in-state and out-of-state businesses or consumers engaged in interstate commerce. Laws of this sort may appear to have legitimate goals or ends (e.g., health and safety), but the means chosen may still be discriminatory (e.g., the law clearly puts an unequal burden for achieving the goal on out-of-staters). Laws that either have a discriminatory end or use discriminatory means are generally categorized as being facially discriminatory. In other words, the laws, on their face, impose burdens or create barriers for out-of-state businesses or consumers that are not imposed on local businesses and consumers. Other laws appear to be neutral but nonetheless have an incidental impact on interstate commerce. The burden is only incidental if, in fact, there is a nondiscriminatory and otherwise legitimate purpose for the law. Laws that fail to further legitimate ends and merely benefit in-staters are treated has having more than a mere incidental effect on interstate commerce. As noted, it is also sometimes difficult to distinguish cases involving incidental burdens from those that impose more direct burdens.

a. Discriminatory Impact: Too Direct to be Incidental

In cases where there is a significant discriminatory impact by an otherwise facially neutral law, the Court may still strike down the law, if the purported goals of the law are not furthered by the law or regulation in question. In such cases, the Court does not accept that the impact or effect is merely incidental. When the purported legitimate goal fails, the only purpose that remains is generally a protectionist or discriminatory purpose. In some cases involving facially neutral laws, the impact may be so clearly discriminatory that the Court will effectively treat it as a "discriminatory means" case and not an "incidental effect" case.

i. Freight Carriers

In *Kassel v. Consolidated Freightway Corp.* (1981), the Court addressed an Iowa law that regulated the use of sixty-five-foot double trailers. Although similar to the law in *Barnwell*, which regulated the height and width of trucks, the Iowa law applied not only to intrastate highways but also to any tractor-trailer located within the state. Similar to *Southern Pacific* (state law that limited the length of trains), the Court did not accept that the shorter double trailers were less dangerous than longer trailers. Again, like in *Southern Pacific*, there would be a large impact on interstate carriers, who would need to either drive around the state of Iowa or to stop at the border and break down loads onto to more trucks. This would not only negatively impact interstate commerce, it would also cause more safety risks because either there would be more trucks on the road or trucks skirting Iowa would be on the road for greater distances. Thus, although the law was neutral on its face, it failed the balancing test because its claims of increased safety were illusory.

ii. Apple Labels

A classic case of a law that is facially neutral but has a discriminatory impact can be found in *Hunt v. Washington State Apple Advertising Commission* (1977). *Hunt* involved a North Carolina law that required apples shipped into North Carolina from outside the state to either bear the U.S. Department of Agriculture (USDA) grade or no grade at all.

The first problem was that businesses selling Washington apples used the Washington grading system, and they purchased preprinted containers, sorted the apples, and then stored them until they needed to be shipped. Thus, to ship apples to North Carolina, the law would require them to either remove the printed labels (the product would appear damaged) or repack the apples in different containers. The major issue, however, was that the Washington grading system was superior to the USDA system, and the law required Washington to effectively dumb down their apples (or at least to dumb down their marketing).

The statutes discriminated against Washington apple growers because they (but not North Carolina growers) would have to bear additional costs for altering their labeling. More important, the regulation stripped away Washington's "competitive and economic advantage that it has earned for itself" and had an "insidious" leveling effect on the "free market forces at work."

The Court did not appear to believe North Carolina's purported purpose for the statute, which was to protect against fraud. The statute applied only to labels of closed shipping containers, and retail sales are generally not made while the apples are still in containers. Further, North Carolina did not require local growers to label their apples. Therefore, the Court held that there were other nondiscriminatory means available for ensuring that there was no fraud. One alternative was simply to allow out-of-state growers to use their state grades and also require the USDA label.

iii. Waste Processing: Protecting Local Business

The cases of *C & A Carbone v. Town of Clarkstown* (1994) and *United Haulers Association, Inc. v. Oneida-Herkimer Solid Waste Management Authority* (2007) are interesting discriminatory impact cases to contrast.

Carbone involved a town ordinance that required that all solid waste to be processed at a specific transfer station. The transfer station was privately owned, but title to the station would transfer to the town at the end of a five-year period; in the meantime, the station had a monopoly on waste processing. The law did not facially discriminate against out-of-state competitors, but it had a discriminatory effect on interstate commerce. It was also very clear that the law discriminated in favor of the one local market participant. The fact that the law discriminated against in-state waste processors, as well as out-of-state competitors, did not mean that it was nondiscriminatory. The law's impact protected the sole waste processing station and effectively squelched all competition. Again, like in *Fort Gratiot* (solid waste deposits had to fit into the county's twenty-year plan), the fact that it discriminated against both in-state and out-of-staters did not diminish the discriminatory impact.

United Haulers presented the same type of issue, with one distinction. In *United Haulers*, a waste transfer facility was operated by a state-created public benefit corporation. Chief Justice John Roberts, writing for the plurality, reasoned that trash disposal was a traditional governmental activity and that laws favoring the governmental entity to the disadvantage of in-state and out-of-state competitors alike, did not discriminate against interstate commerce. The crucial difference is that in *Carbone*, there was at least one in-state private market participant that was advantaged, while every other participant was disadvantaged. Here, all the market participants, other than the state itself, were equally disadvantaged. The Court held that: "Laws favoring local government ... may be directed towards any number of legitimate goals unrelated to protectionism." Given the rampant illegality, corruption, and environmental problems in the private market that preceded the ordinances, it was easier for the Court to find that the counties had legitimate nonprotectionist goals. Finally, the Court noted that the "the most palpable harm imposed by the ordinances—more expensive trash removal—is likely to fall on the very people who voted for the laws."

Justices Scalia and Thomas wrote separate concurring opinions, voicing their continued opposition to the use of the dormant Commerce Clause. Justice Scalia noted that he was willing to enforce the dormant Commerce Clause because of *stare decisis*, but only if a law was either facially discriminatory or indistinguishable from one previously held to be unconstitutional by the Court. For him, the law in this case did not meet either test.

Justice Thomas believed that there was no place whatsoever for the dormant Commerce Clause doctrine, and he now considered *Carbone* to be incorrect, even though he had joined that decision. Unlike Justice Scalia, Justice Thomas viewed this case as indistinguishable from *Carbone*. He viewed the state law in *Carbone* as one that also favored the local government, given that the facility was only temporarily in the hands of the private actor.

Justice Samuel Alito wrote the dissenting opinion, in which Justices Stevens and Anthony Kennedy joined. The dissenters agreed with Justice Thomas that the cases could not be distinguished, but they disagreed with his view that *Carbone* was wrongly decided. The dissent noted that the majority in *Carbone* did not take issue with the dissent's view that the waste transfer station was really a municipal facility, and by implication, the majority had adopted the view that the facility was government-owned. The dissent forcefully argued that this was the first time that the Court had ever made an exception for laws that discriminated in favor of state-owned entities. They charged the Court with confusing and misapplying the market participant exception (discussed shortly), which allows the state more leeway to discriminate against interstate commerce when it is participating in the market and not simply regulating it. As they pointed out, the ordinance in *United Haulers* regulated the market. Thus, the dissent would have applied *Carbone* to this case. For the dissent, even if the law has a legitimate end that is not related to protectionism, because the means have a discriminatory impact against interstate commerce, "the law is subject to strict scrutiny," and therefore it must be necessary for achieving those ends.

b. Discriminatory Means: Hoarding of Resources

Many cases that involve discriminatory means to otherwise legitimate ends entail the state hoarding or keeping resources for in-state businesses and consumers. This can be done either by excluding out-of-state consumers and businesses from access to resources within the state or by embargoing the export of certain resources out of the state.

For example, in *City of Philadelphia v. New Jersey* (1978), the Court struck down a New Jersey statute designed to stop the flow of solid waste from other states into New Jersey landfills. Tired of being the "garbage can" for the rest of the region, New Jersey passed the legislation to limit the use of its landfills to local waste. Though one can sympathize with the Garden State's interests in not being the "trash-dump state" and protecting the health and safety of its citizens, the discriminatory means for pursuing this end was not justified. To decrease the amount of solid waste within the state, it should have chosen other measures that did not discriminate against out-of-state waste. Justice Potter Stewart, writing for the majority, distinguished this case from other cases involving quarantine laws (e.g., laws that prevented the importation of diseased or otherwise dangerous livestock or goods into a state). Those cases involved items that could infect or contaminate local people and/or livestock. Out-of-state solid waste did not pose the same threat.

Justice William Rehnquist argued in his dissent that the regulation of state landfills for the health and safety of its citizens was within the state's police powers. He believed that the quarantine cases supported the New Jersey law in this case. He did not think that any given state should have to open up its landfills for other people's solid waste.

The Court came to the same result in *Fort Gratiot Sanctuary Landfill, Inc. v. Michigan Dept. of Natural Resources* (1992), even though the Michigan scheme also applied to other counties within the state. Michigan's law required that to deposit solid waste generated from another county, state, or country, it must fit into any given county's twenty-year plan. The mere inclusion of other counties did not negate the fact that this also discriminated against out-of-state waste and against interstate commerce. It merely meant that it also potentially discriminated against out-of-county commerce. Michigan failed to demonstrate that it could meet its health and safety concerns without the discriminatory means.

The Court also found an Oklahoma law unconstitutionally protectionist in *Hughes v. Okalahoma* (1979). The state of Oklahoma, attempting to conserve natural resources for its residents, prohibited the transportation of minnow (a fish used for bait) for sale outside of the state, if the minnow was produced in Oklahoma waters. To constitutionally preserve the minnow population, the state would have to use a nondiscriminatory means to achieve that end. *Hughes* can be distinguished from *Maine v. Taylor* (1986), a case in which the Court upheld Maine's exclusion of live-bait fish imports. In *Taylor*, the Court held that Maine had a legitimate and important governmental goal to stop the introduction of exotic parasites into the Maine ecosystem. The Court found that unlike in *Hughes*, no other nondiscriminatory means for achieving this end existed. This was the least restrictive means. It was a quarantine case, and because the out-of-state bait fish created the problem, quarantining them was an appropriate solution.

Another example of states hoarding natural resources was addressed in *Sporhase v. Nebraska* (1982), where the Court invalidated a Nebraska law that restricted the sale of groundwater for use in another state, if that state refused to reciprocate and allow groundwater to be sold in Nebraska. Although the end of conserving groundwater was legitimate and highly important, Nebraska did not show that its discriminatory means were necessary to achieve that end. In *Great A.&P. Tea Co. v. Cottrell* (1976), the Court also invalidated a Mississippi law that required reciprocity before milk could be shipped into the state from another state.

c. Does the Twenty-First Amendment Change the Scenario?

The Court in *Granholm v. Heald* (2005) addressed the issue of whether the Twenty-First Amendment, which repealed the Eighteenth Amendment (the Prohibition Amendment), displaced the dormant Commerce Clause when states regulate the transportation or importation of wine across their borders. The majority held that the Twenty-First Amendment simply returned the law to its previous position, as it existed before the Eighteenth Amendment was enacted. By contrast, the dissent, made up of Justices Stevens and O'Connor, argued that the Twenty-First Amendment removed the issue from the hands of the federal government and placed it within the hands of the state.

There was no disagreement over the fact that the laws in Michigan and New York placed higher barriers in front of small out-of-state wine producers wishing to sell wine directly to the public than the barriers for local wine producers engaging in the same activities. Though the majority held that the federal law (the Webb-Kenyon Act) and the Twenty-First Amendment gave states broad powers to regulate alcohol, those powers did not include the power to discriminate against interstate commerce. The majority did not find much merit in the purported purpose of the laws, namely, to curb underage drinking and collect taxes. The Court noted that there was no evidence that the laws would reduce underage drinking or the states would be unable to impose and collect taxes from out-of-state wineries. Thus, this level and type of discrimination was unconstitutional because the states failed to show that nondiscriminatory alternatives were unviable.

Justice Thomas also wrote a dissenting opinion, joined by Chief Justice Rehnquist, Justice Stevens, and Justice O'Connor. They argued that state regulation of alcohol was removed from the realm of the dormant Commerce Clause both by the Twenty-First Amendment and an act of Congress (the Webb-Kenyon Act). Congress had spoken, and according to the dissent, the

Act specifically allowed the states to regulate the importation of alcoholic beverages. Furthermore, the Act supported state regulation of alcohol by making it illegal under federal law to import alcohol, if it would violate existing state regulations. Although the dissenters would not allow the states to use this power in violation of the First Amendment or the Equal Protection Clause, for them, the Twenty-First Amendment and the Act made the dormant Commerce Clause inapplicable. Regardless of whether a discriminatory impact existed, the matter should be left to the states.

d. The Inexplicable Case of *Exxon Corp. v. Governor of Maryland* (1978)

In *Exxon Corp. v. Governor of Maryland* (1978), Maryland passed a law that banned oil producers and refineries from operating retail service stations in the state. There were no oil producers or refineries within the state of Maryland. Exxon transported oil into the state from its out-of-state refineries, and it claimed discrimination because it was prohibited from operating its thirty-six retail gas stations. Justice Blackmun, in his dissent, argued that the law was discriminatory and protectionist. It protected local retailers from out-of-state competition. In fact, 99 percent of the stations protected under the law were locally owned, and the unprotected stations were those run by out-of-state oil producers and refineries, like Exxon.

Although it is difficult to see how this could not be discriminatory, Justice Stevens, writing for the majority, held that the law did not discriminate against interstate commerce because it did not bar out-of-state independent dealers from competing within the state. For instance, Sears Roebuck, which did not produce or refine oil, was an out-of-state independent retailer, and it was unaffected by the ban. The law applied equally to in-state oil producers and refineries (although they did not exist), and it applied equally to independent retailers. The simple fact that the market primarily consisted of in-state service stations (99 percent), and only a small portion was from out of state, was not enough for the Court to find discrimination.

The case is very difficult to reconcile and is likely an anomaly because of the Court's recognition and appreciation of the emergency circumstances created by the 1973 oil crisis. Maryland passed the law in reaction to evidence that gas stations operated by producers and refiners had received preferential treatment during the oil shortage. During the crisis, local independent retailers were hit the hardest when producers and refiners allocated more gas to the retail stations they owned and operated because of their vertical monopoly. Thus, for example, while the Exxon stations may have been able to weather the crisis, the local mom-and-pop gas stations were severely impacted. The Court may have also sympathized with state regulations that broke up vertical monopolies, which prohibit competition and harm local, smaller competitors.

D. Exceptions to the Dormant Commerce Clause

There are two exceptions that release states from the strictures of the dormant Commerce Clause. The first is when Congress authorizes the state to regulate in a given area, and the second is when the state is a market participant rather than a market regulator.

1. Congressional Authorization

By definition, congressional authorization lifts the burdens of the dormant Commerce Clause. When Congress constitutionally acts under its Commerce Clause powers, the Clause is no longer dormant. The only issue is whether the legislation violates the Commerce Clause or other constitutional provisions, such as the Equal Protection Clause. One might argue that Congress should not be able to undermine the main purpose behind the Commerce Clause by authorizing states to discriminate against interstate commerce. However, the Court has consistently deferred to Congress, and it remains one of the few areas where Congress has clear authority to overrule a Supreme Court decision. As discussed in *Granholm v. Heald* (restriction on direct sales of wine), the Court will only exempt states from the dormant Commerce Clause when Congress has spoken clearly on the matter (e.g., *Maine v. Taylor*, 1986, regulation of baitfish to protect the ecosystem, in which the Court declined to use congressional authorization as a basis for its decision).

In both *Prudential Insurance Co. v. Benjamin* (1946) and *Western & Southern Life Insurance Co. v. State Board of Equalization of California* (1981), the Court relied on the McCarran-Ferguson Act as the basis for exempting states from scrutiny under the dormant Commerce Clause in the area of regulating and taxing insurance. The Court went so far as to state in *Prudential* that outright discrimination in the taxation of out-of-state insurance companies was exempt from dormant Commerce Clause inquiry. In *Western & Southern Life*, the Court upheld a California law that imposed a retaliatory tax on insurers from other states than imposed on California-based insurers. As detailed, the Court has struck down laws that required reciprocity or penalized nonreciprocity, both prior to and after *Western & Southern* (e.g., *Cottrell*, 1976, reciprocity required to sell milk into another state, and *Sporhase*, 1982, reciprocity required to sell groundwater to another state). Nonetheless, because Congress authorized states to regulate the insurance industry, Justice William Brennan, writing for the majority in *Western & Southern*, held that Congress, under its plenary Commerce Clause powers, can give states the power to restrict interstate commerce in ways that they could not without congressional authorization. Under *Western & Southern*, "any action taken by a State within the scope of congressional authorization is rendered invulnerable to Commerce Clause challenge."

2. The Market Participant and Public Function Exceptions

As foreshadowed by *United Hauler* (waste transfer facility operated by a state-created public benefit corporation, already discussed), there is an exception to the dormant Commerce Clause, based on the state acting as a market participant as opposed to a market regulator. When the state is participating in the market, it can discriminate in favor of its citizens. Of course, Congress itself can regulate the state, even though the state is acting as a market participant. Although the distinction is easy enough to grasp in theory, in practice, there are cases where the line between participant and regulator is quite blurry. The line is blurred further by the creation of a public function exception that the Court developed in *United Haulers* and solidified in its most recent case of *Department of Revenue of Kentucky v. Davis* (2008). The public function factor is not new and can be found as an important consideration in Commerce Clause cases, Tenth Amendment cases and in a number of the cases discussed shortly. After *Davis*, it is not merely a factor but the basis for an exception to the dormant Commerce Clause prohibition on discrimination against interstate commerce.

Justice Souter wrote for the plurality in *Davis*, which reaffirmed and extended *United Haulers*. *Davis* addressed the issue of whether Kentucky's practice (shared by forty-one other states) to exempt income taxes on bonds issued by the state of Kentucky and local authorities within the state while taxing income on bonds from out of state violated the dormant Commerce Clause. The trial court did not find that the practice violated the dormant clause, but the Court of Appeals did. The Supreme Court reversed, finding that because the law was motivated not by economic protectionism but the desire to fund traditional public functions like health, safety, and welfare through a taxing mechanism that is both traditional (over a century old) and widespread (over forty states have the same practice) it did not violate the Clause. Further, the Court held that it did not impermissibly discriminate against interstate commerce because it did not treat substantially similar entities differently. Rather, it treated itself differently, which it was allowed to do.

Though issuing bonds would clearly fall under the market participant exception, taxing them looks more like regulation than participation. Nonetheless, the plurality opinion, written by Justice Souter, held that *United Haulers* was not so much a market participant case but a case involving state and local government functions. Here, like in *United Haulers*, the state's scheme was designed to benefit the state for the purpose of serving those public functions and not as form of economic protectionism. The tax exemption here is distinguished from exempting private intrastate activities while taxing interstate activities. The exemption is solely on the income from Kentucky public bonds. Justice Souter, in fact, goes back and forth from treating this as a public function case and as a market participant case.

Davis also attempted to argue for a Pike balancing to show that the burden on interstate commerce outweighed the local interest. Justice Souter left open the question as to whether such a balancing test was appropriate in this type of case (because it is not in true market participant cases). Rather, he held that the test would not yield reliable results in the present case and could not be conclusive.

Justice Stevens, who dissented in *United Haulers* and in *Reeves, Inc. v. William Stake* (1980) (see following discussion), concurred with Justice Souter, because unlike those case which involved the state in private trade, in this case, the state and local government were merely borrowing money to finance public improvements.

Justices Roberts and Ginsburg joined the plurality but did not think it was necessary to address the case as a market participant case. Justice Scalia also did not think that it was necessary to address the case as a market participant case, and he further did not think Pike balancing was ever appropriate for the courts. For Justice Scalia, such balancing should be left to the legislative branch. Justice Thomas reiterated his view that the dormant Commerce Clause had no basis in the Constitution and should be abandoned. If Congress wished to preempt the state practice, it has had a century to do it.

Justice Kennedy was joined by Justice Alito in his dissenting opinion. The dissent emphasized that one of the Founders' primary objectives was to secure free trade unencumbered by state and local barriers. For the dissent, this was a case of explicit local discrimination that distorts the market. The dissent argued that the plurality decision was both inconsistent with precedent and will have systematic negative consequences. As the dissent aptly notes, the bonds are available on the open market and say nothing about tax-exempt status. The tax exemption comes later and affects those who hold and trade Kentucky bonds. This is simple case of protectionist differential taxation. According the dissent, this was not a case of the state treating itself differently but treating bondholders differently. Perhaps the most persuasive argument by the dissent is based on distinguishing *United Haulers*. As Justice Kennedy points out, the

Court's opinion only commanded a majority on the point of applying the government function exception from *United Haulers* to the present case. For the dissent, the decision in *United Haulers*, was based on the fact that the state had completely taken over the waste processing industry, and so the ordinance requiring everyone to process their waste through the state facility applied equally to both intrastate and interstate commerce. There was no discrimination. In this case, the whole point of the scheme is to discriminate against out of state bonds. Here, the state has "entered a competitive nonmonopolized market and, to give its bond market and advantage, has taxed out of state municipal bonds at a higher rate." The dissent warned that given the Court's opinion, there would be little basis for striking down even more aggressive discriminatory tax schemes, for example, taxing income on out of state bonds at "say, 80 percent."

In *Reeves, Inc. v. William Stake* (1980), the South Dakota Cement Commission had a policy of selling cement produced by the state-owned plant to state residents first, when there was a shortage. The plaintiff, Reeves, Inc., was an out-of-state cement distributor that sought to enjoin the state of South Dakota from continuing to give preference to South Dakota citizens over out-of-state distributors in times of shortage. Reeves, which had purchased 95 percent of its cement from the plant, was severely impacted by the clearly discriminatory plan during the 1978 nationwide cement shortage. Nonetheless, the Court held that the limitations imposed by the dormant Commerce Clause were confined to instances when the state was either regulating or taxing in a manner that impeded interstate commerce. There was no constitutional plan to limit the freedom of the state to favor its citizens when the state was participating in the market. When acting as a private actor in the market, the state had the same freedom of contract as other market participants. Justice Lewis Powell, joined by Justices Brennan, Stevens, and Byron White, dissented and argued that the dormant Commerce Clause was designed to prevent this type of economic protectionism. Though the case was one of first impression, the economic protectionism and discrimination against out-of-staters was simply too blatant for the dissent to accept. For the dissent, the market participant exception should only apply to the state when it is involved in "integral government operations in an area of traditional governmental functions" because the exception is based on the right of a state to provide for its own needs. When the state enters the market outside of these traditional governmental functions, it is too easy for it to effectively regulate the market through participatory practices. In the case at hand, the state is in effect regulating the cement market within the state to the detriment of out-of-staters. Thus, the state should not be able to do through participation what it would be forbidden to do through regulation, unless it is providing for its own needs.

Of course, one could argue that the state is providing for its own cement needs. For the dissent, this would be acceptable if it were giving preference to cement used for public projects, but not merely to supply private businesses within the state.

Even the dissent from *Reeves* would agree with the Court's holding in *United Bldg. & Const. Trades Council v. Mayor and Council of Camden* (1984). In that case, the Court examined a Camden municipal ordinance, which pressured contractors and subcontractors working on public works projects to hire city residents (at least 40 percent). The ordinance only applied to projects that were funded in whole or in part by the city. The Court held that it did not violate the dormant Commerce Clause. Similarly, the Court upheld the city ordinance in *White v. Massachusetts Council of Construction Employers* (1983), which mandated that all contractors' workforce consist of at least 50 percent city residents on any construction project financed by the city.

South-Central Timber Development, Inc. v. Wunnicke (1984) was a more difficult case because it involved restrictions on the downstream market. Alaska devised a scheme under which it sold large quantities of timber as a market participant, but it required that the purchasers agree to process the timber within the state before exporting it. Justice White, writing for a plurality, held that this additional requirement amounted to a regulation and thus was not covered by the market participant exception. Though Alaska could discriminate among buyers within the market it is participating in (the selling of timber market), it could not seek to control the downstream markets in which it is not participating (the timber processing market).

Justice Rehnquist wrote a dissenting opinion that called into question the Court's fine distinction between Alaska acting as a participant and as a regulator. Given that Alaska could have achieved the same result by any number of constitutionally permissible means that equally discriminated against out-of-state timber processors, he thought the distinction was based on form, rather than substance. For instance, Alaska could have only sold to companies that already had processing facilities within the state, or the legislation could have paid for local processing before the state sold the timber.

IV. The Privileges and Immunities Clause of Article IV

The Privileges and Immunities Clause (P&I Clause) of Article IV, Section 2 reads: "The Citizens of each State shall be entitled to all Privileges and Immunities of Citizens in the several States." Thus, regulations, in which a state is discriminating against out-of-state citizens, may be challenged under Article IV, in addition to the dormant Commerce Clause.

A. Compared and Contrasted to the Dormant Commerce Clause

The P&I Clause and the dormant Commerce Clause do not completely overlap. The P&I Clause only applies to citizens ("the Citizens of each State"), and thus, it does not apply to corporations or aliens. Aliens and (as already seen) corporations can bring claims under the dormant Commerce Clause. The advantage of bringing a claim under the P&I Clause is that the market participant exception does not apply (*United Building Council v. Camden*, 1984), and neither does the congressional authorization exception (*Dred Scott v. Sandford*, 1856). One disadvantage is that the discrimination must relate to a "privilege" or "immunity." Early cases, such as *Corfield v. Coryell* (1923), appeared to read this language broadly. In *Camden* (ordinance required 40 percent of employees to be state residents), the Court limited this language to "privileges and immunities bearing upon the vitality of the Nation as a single entity." Thus, although the doctrine applies to constitutional rights and the right to earn a living, it does not apply to recreational sporting activities that do not affect the United States's "vitality." Further, the test is somewhat weaker under the P&I Clause because the state only needs to show that the discrimination is substantially related to a substantial state interest, as compared to the dormant Commerce Clause, which requires that a regulation be necessary for an important state interest.

Although the market participant exception rendered the Camden city ordinance in *Camden* immune from dormant Commerce Clause scrutiny, it did not render the ordinance immune from scrutiny under the P&I Clause.

Although there was a good argument for a "market participant" exception under the dormant Commerce Clause, the argument did not translate into the context of the P&I Clause. The dormant Commerce Clause deals only with the regulation of commerce, and when a state acts as "market participant," it is not regulating. The P&I Clause bars any type of state conduct that discriminates against out-of-staters on matters of fundamental concern. Thus, whether the state is a participator or a regulator, it is equally subject to the P&I Clause.

In holding that the Camden ordinance discriminated against out-of-state residents, the Court addressed and rejected two other arguments: (1) that this was a municipal ordinance, thus, it was city (not state) conduct and therefore was not covered by the P&I Clause; and (2) that the ordinance did not discriminate against out-of-staters, but against anyone outside of the City, thus it did not deny a privilege to out-of-staters that was not also denied to other non-Camden residents who lived in the state (i.e., the ordinance applied to both in-state and out-of-state contractors).

Although the Court conceded that the ordinance burdens some in-staters, as well as out-of-staters, the difference was that in-staters at least had a chance to remedy the situation through state elections. The out-of-staters did not have the same chance because they could not vote to change the ordinance. Thus, the Court concluded that the ordinance affected the fundamental privilege to earn a living of one's choice, and the case would need to be remanded to determine whether the ordinance was substantially related to a substantial governmental interest. The city claimed that the purpose of the ordinance was to combat unemployment, which decreased property values and city's tax base, and resulted in middle-class residents fleeing the area. The Court did not pass judgment on whether the claimed purpose would satisfy the substantial state interest test or whether the means chosen were substantially related to that interest.

B. Analysis under the Privileges and Immunities Clause

In *Toomer v. Witsell* (1948), the Court struck down a law that required out-of-state commercial shrimping boats to pay 1,000 percent more in licensing fees than local commercial shrimping boats. Justice Fred Vinson wrote the opinion of the Court, in which it held that to justify the discriminatory treatment in this case, the state needed a substantial reason. The reason was purportedly to conserve the shrimp supply and combat the threat of excessive fishing. There was no evidence that out-of-state shrimpers were the primary cause of the problem or that they did more shrimping that local shrimping boats. Therefore, there were other alternatives, such as limiting all the shrimping boats with caps, and the means were not substantially related to the state's interest.

In *Baldwin v. Fish and Game Commission of Montana* (1978), the Court declined to apply the P&I Clause to a discriminatory Montana hunting license fee scheme. The scheme resulted in out-of-state hunters paying at least 7.5 times as much a Montana residents for a hunting license. Here, the Court held that hunting was not a privilege or immunity "bearing on the vitality of the Nation as a single entity," and therefore, the state could discriminate in favor of its citizens. The Court noted that the case involved mere recreational activities and sports and not the denial of a livelihood.

In the case of *Supreme Court of New Hampshire v. Piper* (1985), the Court addressed the New Hampshire Supreme Court rule that limited admission to the state bar to attorneys that were state residents. Kathryn Piper lived in Vermont, just miles from the New Hampshire border, and she was denied admission to the New Hampshire bar, even though she took and passed the bar exam. This was a easy case in terms of establishing that the P&I Clause applied, given that it involved Piper's livelihood and that the rule was clearly discriminatory. The more difficult question was whether the state had a substantial reason for the discriminatory treatment and whether the rule was substantially related to the state goal.

The state had several justifications for the rule, which included concerns that out-of-state attorneys:

- might be less familiar with local rules and procedures,
- may be less ethical,
- would have more difficulty showing up for urgent matters on time, and
- might not donate as much pro bono time in the state.

Although these are very important concerns, the Court did not accept the argument that out-of-state lawyers would be less familiar with local rules and procedures or that they would be less ethical. Thus, the law was not substantially related to these ends. Furthermore, concerns about timely appearances or pro bono work could be addressed through much less restrictive means, such as appointing local counsel or requiring certain levels of in-state pro bono work. Thus, again, the Court held that the rule was not substantially related to the state goals.

Justice Rehnquist argued that the case should be distinguished from other cases involving livelihoods that were interstate in nature. For Justice Rehnquist, this court rule was particularly state-based. Lawyers, like judges and legislators, are part of the state's justice system, and thus, the state had a particular interest in having residents practicing within that system. Perhaps more important, he argued that the Court was transforming the substantial interest test into a strict scrutiny test by employing the least restrictive means analysis, which is almost always fatal in application. He disagreed with the Court's approach to the problem of accessibility. The issue was not merely about being available for an emergency hearing, but about being available for clients throughout the course of litigation. The appointment of local counsel, though perhaps less restrictive, was not better suited to the end. For Justice Rehnquist, the appointment of local counsel, in addition to out-of-state counsel, could cause more problems than it fixed.

As noted, the doctrine also applies to fundamental rights. Such cases are rare, given that one can generally sue under the particular right. Nonetheless, there have been a number of cases involving discrimination against out-of-staters with regards to fundamental rights, such as:

- the right to property (*Blake v. McClung*, 1898; *Dred Scott v. Sandford*, 1856),
- access to courts (*Canadian Northern Ry. Co. v. Eggen*, 1920), and

- the right to an abortion (*Doe v. Bolton*, 1973).

Although the infamous case of *Dred Scott* is often cited as a due process case, the Court also addressed the P&I Clause in it. The Court actually held that the Missouri Compromise, a federal law that prohibited the holding of slaves in the northern territories of the Louisiana Purchase, was "obnoxious to the constitutional provision that citizens of each state shall be entitled to all the privileges and immunities of citizens of the several states." The federal law was unconstitutional because it attempted to deprive some citizens of their right to "property," namely, their right to own slaves. Thus, unlike under the Commerce Clause, where Congress can authorize state discrimination because of its plenary power over commerce, Congress has no such power with respect to fundamental rights.

V. State Taxation of Interstate Commerce

Many constitutional law courses do not cover the issue of state and local taxation, but it is nonetheless important to have some familiarity with the contours of the constitutional limitations on states' powers to tax.

Limits on the taxing authority of states can come from the dormant Commerce Clause, the P&I Clause, the Due Process Clause, and other substantive rights. The focus here is primarily on the dormant Commerce Clause, with some attention to due process. Cases involving taxing and fees under the P&I Clause are dealt with in the same way as other regulatory activities under the Clause, and therefore, there is no need to address them here. See *Toomer v. Witsell* (1948), discussed above. Taxation is treated differently under the dormant Commerce Clause and thus requires separate treatment.

The Court, in *Complete Auto Transit, Inc. v. Brady* (1977), set out the modern four-part test for when state and local taxes are permissible under the dormant Commerce Clause. A tax is permissible if:

1. the activity taxed has a substantial nexus with the taxing state;
2. the tax is fairly apportioned;
3. the tax does not discriminate against interstate commerce; and
4. the tax is fairly related to the services provided by the state.

The four prongs of the *Brady* test are addressed in order.

A. Substantial Nexus

The modern approach to the substantial nexus requirement can be found in *Quill Corp. v. North Dakota* (1992). *Quill* addressed the first prong of the *Brady* test in a case involving a North Dakota tax on a mail-order business. Because the Quill Corporation did not have any facilities or sales personnel in the state, the Court held that that there was not a substantial nexus (no substantial connection) with the taxing state. On these facts, sales in the state would meet the Due Process Clause requirement of sufficient "minimum" contacts with the state. Nonetheless, the Court held that physical presence was required under dormant Commerce Clause analysis. Congress could always authorize state taxation with less contact than in *Quill*, although not less than what is require by the Due Process Clause. In other words, Congress could use its Commerce Clause powers to override the Court's somewhat more robust requirement of physical presence, as long as it did not undermine the minimum contacts requirement of due process. The majority required physical presence, rather than minimum contacts, because the state was burdening interstate commerce with its tax. To justify burdening interstate commerce, the state was limited to taxing those with more than minimum contacts. For the dissent, the presence or absence of sales personnel in the state was too arbitrary and provided little support for allowing or disallowing a state tax.

B. Fair Apportionment

The requirement that a tax be fairly apportioned is related to the substantial nexus requirement, in that a state can only tax the portion of an activity that is connected to the state. It must apportion any tax fairly. This limits states from taking more than their fair share from a business activity, and it protects businesses from being overtaxed by multiple states.

The Court addressed this issue in *Oklahoma Tax Commission v. Jefferson Lines, Inc.* (1995). Oklahoma imposed a tax on buses by collecting a 4 percent tax on every ticket purchased in the state, without considering whether the bus was traveling wholly within the state or outside the state. On its face, the tax appear malapportioned, because more expensive tickets for buses traveling across the country would generate a greater tax revenue than cheaper tickets for shorter trips within the state. More revenue was generated by out-of-state travel, and thus, the bus lines argued that this was not fairly apportioned.

To determine whether the tax was fairly apportioned, the Court applied a test simply requiring what it termed "internal" and "external" consistency. The tax passed both requirements. Internal consistency requires that if every state imposed the same tax, there would be no unfair apportionment because interstate commerce would not be disadvantaged. Given that buses originate in one place, if every state imposed the same tax, there would be no duplicative taxes and no disadvantage on interstate commerce. External consistency requires a sufficient economic justification for the state to tax the portion it is taxing. Although interstate travel is no doubt responsible for a portion of the ticket price, the fact that the sale takes place in the state and a portion of the travel occurs within the state makes the originating state unique. No other state has the same claim to such a taxable event. In essence, it makes sense for there to be a tax at the point of sale.

C. Nondiscriminatory

States are not permitted to discriminate against interstate commerce by imposing taxes that help or advantage local businesses at the expense of out-of-state business. A state should not be permitted to fill its treasury by burdening interstate commerce with taxes that are not imposed on in-state businesses.

Thus, in *West Lynn Creamery v. Healy* (1994), the Court held that a Massachusetts law that collected a uniform tax on all dairy products sold in the state but then disbursed the revenues back to local producers was discriminatory and per se invalid. The fact that the state took two separate steps (by collecting from all dairy farmers, then providing a subsidy to local farmers) did not change the fact that it was still a discriminatory tariff on out-of-state dairy producers. The result is the same. The out-of-state dairies were taxed to subsidize the in-state dairies.

It is constitutional for a state to tax out-of-state goods that are purchased out-of-state for use within the state as a means to equalize the burden created by sales taxes imposed within the state (*Henneford v. Silas Mason Co.*, 1937). However, the use tax (the tax on goods bought outside the state for use within the state) cannot be more than the sales tax in any given county within the state even if overall the use tax is lower than the average sales tax across the state (*Associated Industries v. Lohman,* 1994). Thus, the *Lohman* Court struck down a Missouri tax scheme that had a sales tax that varied from locality to locality (4.22 percent to 7.72 percent) and a uniform use tax of 5.75 percent for goods purchased outside the state for use in the state. Even though combined local sales taxes exceeded the use tax, the Court held that in any given locality where the use tax was higher than the sales tax, the state was discriminating against interstate commerce and the tax was unconstitutional. Thus, in any given county where the sales tax was less than 5.75 percent, the tax was unconstitutional, even if the average sales tax across all the counties was greater than 5.75 percent.

It is important to note that a state tax will not be deemed discriminatory simply because it impacts interstate commerce more than local commerce. If the differential impact is based on the market, rather than the tax, then there is no discrimination. Thus, in *Commonwealth Edison v. Montana* (1981), the Court upheld a Montana severance tax on coal (a tax on coal being mined), even though 90 percent of the coal was being shipped out of state. Even though the state taxed more interstate commerce than local commerce (because of the difference in the quantity of coal leaving the state), the tax rates were the same for both local and interstate commerce, unlike the tax in *Lohman*. Furthermore, unlike the tax in *West Lynn Creamery* (the dairy product tax case), here the tax was not used to subsidize local business. It was merely the market that caused any disparity in tax revenues.

D. Fairly Related to State Services

In *Commonwealth Edison v. Montana* (1981), even though a Montana law that provided for a severance tax on coal was not held to be discriminatory, there remained the question as to whether the tax was fairly related to services provided by the state. The fourth prong of the *Brady* test requires that the state provide some benefit that renders the tax fair. Commonwealth Edison argued that the tax was excessive because it was not fairly related to the value received by the coal mining industry or to the costs to Montana, created by coal mining activities. Although the test appears to require something of this sort, the Court declined to evaluate the tax on either of these bases. Few (if any) tax schemes are based on any direct quid pro quo (exchange of a direct benefit for the tax), and the Court was not going to endorse a test that would require it to attempt to determine what were and were not acceptable tax rates. The benefits to any business are simply too varied and indirect, and they include all the benefits of living in an "orderly civilized society." They range from police and fire protection to infrastructure and a trained workforce. In effect, the Court adopted a test that looked to the first two factors of the *Brady* test, sufficient contacts and fair apportionment. As it stated:

> The relevant inquiry under the fourth prong ... is not ... the amount of the tax or the value of the benefits allegedly bestowed as measured by the costs the State incurs on account of the taxpayer's activities. Rather, the test is closely connected to the first prong of the Complete Auto Transit [*Brady*] test. Under this threshold test, the interstate business must have a substantial nexus with the State before any tax may be levied on it [and] ... the measure of the tax must be reasonably related to the extent of the contact, since it is the activities or presence of the taxpayer in the State that may properly be made to bear a "just share of state tax burden."

The Court concluded that because the tax was based on the value of the coal taken out of the state, it was proportional to the appellants activities in the state and, thereby, to the all the benefits of an "orderly civilized society."

According to the dissent of Justice Blackmun, joined by Justices Powell and Stevens, this "emasculated" the fourth prong of the test. They believed that Commonwealth Edison should have been entitled to a trial on the issue of whether the tax was in fact unfair. Under the majority's ruling, Montana, which produced 25 percent of all of the nation's coal and exported of 90 percent of it, could decide to increase taxes to any level, as long as they were proportional. This ignored the fact that Montana may have been actually shifting the tax because it was imposed largely on out-of-state business rather than in-state businesses. For the dissent, the dormant Commerce Clause may have been violated because, "the State effectively select[ed] 'a class of out-of-state taxpayers [the out of state coal purchasers] to shoulder a tax burden grossly in excess of any costs imposed directly or indirectly by such taxpayers on the State.'" Of course, as the concurrence of Justice White noted, Congress was aware of the situation and could step in at any time to limit these taxes.

Checkpoints

- **Preemption**

  - When Congress has acted, and there is an express or implied conflict between federal and state law, federal law preempts the state law, due to the Supremacy Clause.

  - There are two types of preemption: express and implied preemption.

  - Express preemption occurs when a federal law expressly preempts state law. The Court requires clear language. The issue then becomes the scope of the preemption.

  - Implied preemption occurs when preemption of the state law is implied by clear congressional intent, based on the structure and purpose of the federal law.

  - There are three types of implied preemption:

    1. Conflict preemption occurs when it is impossible to comply with both the federal and state law.

       - Consider whether the federal law set a floor, in which states can regulate more and one can comply with both laws (*Florida Lime*).

       - Consider whether Congress intended to set a ceiling and to preempt any further state regulation.

    2. Frustration of a federal objective occurs when a state law is an obstacle to accomplishing Congress's purposes (*PG&E*).

       - Consider if the regulation is within the state's traditional police powers.

Checkpoints *continued*

3. Field preemption occurs when the federal regulation is so pervasive that Congress did not leave room for the states to supplement it.

  - Examples include patent law, immigration, taxes, tariffs, and foreign relations (*Hines*).

- When Congress has not acted or when there is no preemption, a challenge can be brought under:

  - the dormant Commerce Clause; or

  - the Privileges and Immunities Clause of Article IV.

- **The Dormant Commerce Clause**

  - Prior approaches to an analysis under the dormant Commerce Clause were based on rigid categories:

    - whether the regulation was within the state's police powers or was within the federal government's national powers.

    - whether the subject matter was one that had a need for national uniformity or was best left to local diversity.

    - whether the regulation created a direct effect or indirect effect on interstate commerce.

  - The modern tests:

    1. if the law is nondiscriminatory, but imposes an incidental undue burden on interstate commerce, then balance the benefits of the law (such as safety) against the incidental burdens on interstate commerce (the Pike test).

      - The plaintiff has the burden of proof to show that the burden is clearly excessive in relation to the local benefits.

    2. if the state regulation discriminates against interstate commerce, either by benefiting intrastate commerce at the expense of interstate commerce or by discriminating against out-of-state businesses in favor of in-state business, a heightened scrutiny test applies.

      - The law is per se invalid, unless the state can prove that it is necessary for an important government purpose (*City of Philadelphia v. New Jersey*).

      - A regulation that discriminates against interstate commerce can be either:

        - facially discriminatory (has a discriminatory end or uses discriminatory means), or

        - facially neutral, but has a discriminatory impact on interstate commerce.

Checkpoints *continued*

- There are three exceptions to the dormant Commerce Clause doctrine:

  1. congressional authorization

     - Note that if Congress has acted, the Commerce Clause is no longer dormant. Evaluate whether Congress has exceeded its Commerce Clause powers or whether the law violates another constitutional provision.

  2. market participant

     - For this exception to apply, the state must be participating in the market and not regulating the market.

  3. governmental functions

     - For this exception to apply, the state must be engaged in a traditional governmental function and the Court must find that the state did not discriminate against interstate commerce by treating substantially similar entities differently.

- **Privileges and Immunities Clause of Article IV**

- This Clause limits the state's ability to discriminate against out-of-staters with respect to:

  - fundamental rights, or

  - important economic activities (such as the ability to earn a livelihood).

- To challenge a state law as violating this Clause, the law must discriminate against out-of-staters regarding privileges and immunities that the state gives its own citizens.

- The P&I Clause only applies to citizens, not aliens or corporations.

- Discrimination against out-of-staters is allowed if it is substantially related to achieving a substantial state interest (*Toomer*).

- The exceptions to the dormant Commerce Clause (congressional authorization and market participant) do not apply to the P&I Clause.

- **State Taxation of Interstate Commerce**

- The modern four-part test from *Brady*, for when state and local taxes are permissible under the dormant Commerce Clause, is when:

  1. the activity taxed has a substantial nexus with the taxing state.

     - More than the "minimum contacts" test of the Due Process Clause.

  2. the tax is fairly apportioned.

     - It must have internal and external consistency (*Jefferson Lines*).

  3. the tax does not discriminate against interstate commerce (*Commonwealth Edison*).

Checkpoints *continued*

- The tax rates are the same for both local and interstate commerce.

- The tax is not used to subsidize local businesses.

4. the tax is fairly related to the services provided by the state.

- Consider the first two prongs.

Chapter 5

Conduct Governed by the Constitution: What Is "State Action"?

Roadmap

- Introduction: The general rule is that the Constitution limits only governmental (as opposed to private) action.
- The clear exception to this rule: the Thirteenth Amendment, which applies to the state and individuals alike.
- Three further exceptions to the rule:
  - private actors performing public or *state functions*;
  - the *entanglement* or joint participation of state and private actors; and
  - the *authorization*, encouragement, or enforcement of private action by the state.
- Two modern formulations of the *authorization* exception in two separate opinions:
  - *Lugar v. Edmondson Oil Company* (1982)
  - *Blum v. Yaretsky* (1982)
- Entwinement: A hybrid exception combining incomplete elements of several exceptions

---

I. Introduction: The General Rule That the Constitution Limits Only Governmental (as Opposed to Private) Action

The general rule is that the rights and liberties granted in the Constitution only protect against action by the federal, state, or local governments, but not by private persons or entities. In other words, they only protect against "state action," the word *state* being used to mean "governmental," as it refers to the federal government or the government of a state or locality.

The conduct of federal, state, and local officials, if acting under the color of governmental authority—even if violating the law—constitutes state action. State action covers all government divisions, subdivisions, agencies, and government-created companies, for instance, Amtrak or the U.S. Postal Service. If one's rights are limited by these entities or their agents, then there is state action, but if the same action is taken with the same effect by private actors, there will not generally be state action, and the injured party will not have a constitutional claim.

The principal idea behind limiting the application of the Constitution to state actors is that the Constitution was designed to protect people from the power of the state. If private parties were also bound by the obligations of the Constitution, it would authorize further governmental intrusion into the lives and the liberties that private parties are said to hold. On this view, constitutional law regulates public power, whereas civil law (e.g., contract or tort law) and criminal law (e.g., the laws against murder or theft) protect the people from other people. These other laws may be federal, state, or local, depending on which of these jurisdictions is authorized by the Constitution and subordinate law to act in the particular area.

Thus, as a general rule, only state actors can violate your constitutional rights, because it is only against the state that one has constitutional rights. The same conduct with the same result by private actors may give rise to a legal claim under other law but would not violate your constitutional rights. For example, it is state action for the state to violate your rights to due process and freedom of expression by terminating you from a state job without a hearing because you allegedly said something unpatriotic. The same firing by a purely private employer would not constitute state action, and there would be no violation of your constitutional rights.

Further, the state action doctrine has generally been interpreted as being limited to *affirmative state* action—that is, the government's actions can violate the constitution, but the government's *failure* to act to correct private abuses does not. In other words, the Constitution is rarely read to require that the government *do* anything. It has few, if any, positive obligations, and thus, state or federal omissions are not usually enough to constitute state action. For instance, one could argue that equal protection should require states to police private discrimination and that a failure to adequately protect individuals from discrimination constitutes state action. Although this might have some appeal, the Supreme Court has not found state inaction to be the equivalent of state action. Thus, even in *DeShaney v. Winnebago County De-*

partment of Social Services (1989), where the Department of Social Services failed to protect a four-year-old child from severe abuse by his father, which resulted in brain damage, the Court did not find a violation of the Due Process Clause. The Court held that the Clause did not require affirmative state action to protect the life, liberty, or property of citizens. Thus a "mere" failure to act, or omission, on the part of the state was not enough. The private conduct of the father was to blame, and his conduct was not covered by the Constitution.

Like all general rules in constitutional law, there are ample exceptions. One exception, expressly provided by the text of the Constitution, is the Thirteenth Amendment, which prohibits both the state and individuals from engaging in slavery and involuntary servitude. There are a few other exceptions, in which the courts have determined that private conduct is subject to the requirements of the Constitution. They include situations involving:

1. private actors performing state or *public functions*;
2. the *entanglement* or joint participation of state and private actors; and
3. the *authorization*, encouragement, or enforcement of private action by the state.

The Court has developed tests for all three of these situations.

Most recently, in *Brentwood Academy v. Tennessee Secondary School Athletic Association* (2001), the Supreme Court, in a five-to-four decision, held that there had been state action when the state and private actor were *entwined*. The case did not fall neatly into a public function, entanglement, or authorization exception. The Court found that enough elements of all three were present for the Court to create a new hybrid category, called "entwinement." In fact, entwinement may be a way of capturing what is involved in all of these exceptions, namely, that state action can be found "if, though only if, there is such a close nexus between the State and the challenged action that seemingly private behavior may be fairly treated as that of the State itself." The Court in *Brentwood* found that the level of entwinement in that case satisfied the test. The Court held that it was state action when a state secondary school athletic association enforced its association rules against the plaintiff's school.

Thus, although we will break down each exception and discuss the Court's different tests for each, *Brentwood* stands for the possibility of combining the tests into factors, which the Court weighs to determine if there is state action.

II. The Beginnings: The Civil War Amendments and the *Civil Rights Cases*: Testing the General Rule and Establishing the Thirteenth Amendment as an Exception

The issue of state action did not arise until after the Civil War, when Congress attempted to address the problems associated with the institution of slavery through constitutional amendment and legislation. After the end of the Civil War, in 1865, Congress started drafting the Civil War amendments:

- the Thirteenth (prohibiting slavery and involuntary servitude) (1865; ratified 1865);
- the Fourteenth (requiring due process and equal protection and prohibiting the denial of U.S. privileges and immunities by the states) (1866; ratified 1868); and
- the Fifteenth (prohibiting discrimination in the right to vote by the states and federal government) (1869; ratified 1870).

Prior to these amendments, the Bill of Rights (the first ten amendments to the Constitution) did not have any language that bound individuals. This reflected the Framers' preoccupation with limiting public, or government, power, especially federal power. The Civil War amendments changed this by imposing certain constitutional obligations on private parties through the Thirteenth Amendment. Furthermore, they were the first amendments to explicitly bind the states, rather than merely the federal government.

This is an important point because the Civil War amendments embody the realization that it is not merely federal power that the people need protection from. As the institution of slavery demonstrated, both the states and private persons are fully capable of trampling the rights of others. It made little sense to think that the states, particularly in the South at that time, would protect the rights of African Americans, and it made even less sense to think that slavery and involuntary servitude were only problematic when a government was directly involved. Slaves were owned, sold, and used by private citizens through state property and contract laws that were enforced by the government. Thus, the institution of slavery suggested the desirability of extending at least some constitutional restrictions beyond the federal government to the states and even to private parties. As a result, the broad language of the Thirteenth Amendment ("Neither slavery nor involuntary servitude ... shall exist within the United States, or any place subject to their jurisdiction") has been interpreted to apply to both the state and to individuals. Further, Section 2 of the Amendment, which gives Congress power to enforce the Amendment by appropriate legislation (called the Enforcement Clause), is interpreted to give Congress the power to enact legislation that directly regulates the conduct of private parties. Each of the three amendments has a similar clause.

Note that the Thirteenth, Fourteenth, and Fifteenth Amendments are self-executing, or enforceable in their own right. For instance, the famous case of *Brown v. Board of Education* (1954) (desegregation of public schools) and the cases leading up to it did not require legislation under an Enforcement Clause. For this reason, the Enforcement Clauses have sometimes been interpreted as providing Congress the authority to give more effect to the rights in these amendments than the amendments would on their own. They have been likened to the Necessary and Proper Clause used by Justice John Marshall in *McCulloch v. Maryland* (1819) (the national bank case, discussed in Chapter 2).

Just after the Civil War, Congress passed the Civil Rights Act of 1875, which, similar to the 1965 Civil Rights Act (promulgated under the Commerce Clause power), made it illegal to discriminate in places of public accommodation ("inns, public conveyances on land and water, theaters, and other places of public amusement"). Congress passed the legislation under the Enforcement Clauses of the Thirteenth and Fourteenth Amendments (Sections 2 and 5, respectively), which provide that Congress can pass laws to enforce the amendments. The legislation was designed to protect individuals from the invasion of their rights by other individuals. It was deemed necessary because Southern states, by allowing Caucasian citizens to discriminate in providing public accommodations, were not providing African Americans with "equal protection of the laws," nor protecting them from the "badges and incidents of slavery," as the amendments on their face ostensibly required.

The Supreme Court, in the *Civil Rights Cases: United States v. Stanley* (1883), struck down the legislation. Justice Joseph Bradley, writing for the majority, held that the legislation was neither proper under Section 5 of the Fourteenth Amendment nor under Section 2 of the Thirteenth Amendment. It failed under Section 5 of the Fourteenth because the Amendment only allowed for legislation that regulated state conduct and not private conduct, and it failed under Section 2 of the Thirteenth because the only private conduct that could be regulated under that Section was private conduct that amounted to slavery, involuntary servitude, or the "badges and incidents" of slavery. Discriminating in the provision of public accommodations fell in between; it was neither the state denying equal protection nor individuals practicing slavery or involuntary servitude. Rather, it regulated private individuals denying access to public accommodations on the basis of race.

The Court held that the Fourteenth Amendment did not authorize Congress to regulate private conduct, as that was the role of the states. It did, however, note the exception of private conduct, which was either sanctioned by the state or performed under the authority of the state. It did not address an entanglement exception.

Justice John Harlan wrote a powerful dissent in that case, arguing that the Citizenship Clause in the Fourteenth Amendment gave African Americans equal citizenship and that this required that they not be denied equal civil rights by either the state or private persons. Alternatively, given that places of public accommodation had always been subject to public regulation, their owners were, in effect, agents of the state. Furthermore, he argued that Congress was correct in its determination that discrimination by owners of public accommodations, who were fulfilling public or quasi-public functions, constituted a "badge of servitude."

Although Justice Harlan's dissent did not win out, one will notice while reading through the cases in this area of the law that the Court appears to be more sympathetic to state action claims when those claims involve racism or racial discrimination, particularly when it appears that functions, resources, or authority are being transferred from public institutions (i.e., the state) to private institutions to avoid the Constitution's restrictions on racial discrimination. It may also be the case that because the history of slavery and racism bridged the private actor-state actor divide, the Court is more comfortable crossing that divide in finding state action. Thus, the Court might be more apt to find state action in discrimination cases than in procedural due process cases or even First Amendment cases.

As noted, Congress passed similar legislation in the 1960s under its Commerce Clause powers. Because civil rights legislation often requires private individuals to conform to constitutional standards, one may be forgiven for thinking that this also constitutes an exception to the state action doctrine. However, claims arising under civil rights laws are strictly statutory claims, and the only constitutional issue that they raise is whether the federal government has constitutional authority to pass the legislation.

III. The Other Exceptions to the General Rule

A. The Court's Willingness or Unwillingness to Find Exceptions

If one's main concern is the protection of individual rights, the distinction between private and state violation of rights is secondary. As the practice of slavery demonstrated, the abuse of private power can be just as detrimental to individual liberty as the abuse of public power. If one takes this view, then she or he would favor finding an exception to the state action doctrine whenever there is a functional equivalent of state power, state involvement, or any form of state authorization, encouragement, or endorsement that results in the violation of one's rights. The Supreme Court, during the Earl Warren Court from 1953 to 1969, appears to have been more inclined to find exceptions to the state action doctrine than the Court during the Warren Burger (1969–1986) and William Rehnquist (1986–2005) years. This may be because the Warren Court spent so much of its time dealing with the issue of racism and desegregation that cut across the public and private spheres. Further, Courts before, during, and after the Warren years have all been more likely to find an exception to the state action doctrine when racial discrimination is involved.

As noted, this may be in part because of the nature of the rights in question. The history of racism, the Civil War, the Civil War amendments, as well as the civil rights movement make it easier to find state action in race cases involving equal protection or discrimination than in cases involving other rights, like freedom of expression or the right to due process. Because the history shows how entangled the state and private actors have been in the area of race, any functional shifting from public racism to private racism, any encouragement, endorsement, or funding by the state to private racist institutions or any entanglement of the state in private racism can trigger the possibility of finding state action.

Formal general doctrine, however, expresses a fairly narrow view of state action and has only found exceptions to the doctrine when:

1. the private organization is performing *a traditional and exclusive state function* (the public function exception);
2. the level of *entanglement* has risen to a *threshold level* or the level of a *symbiotic relationship* (the entanglement exception); or
3. there is not only passive regulation but *active authorization, encouragement or enforcement,* almost to the point of requiring commandment (the authorization exception).

A number of the cases discussed next come up under more than one exception. Sometimes this is because the facts give rise to two or more of the exceptions, and sometimes it appears that the lawyers are trying a shotgun approach (i.e., trying every possible argument in the hope that one hits its mark). Though the Court generally views the tests discretely, as noted, this chapter ends with the case of *Brentwood,* in which the Court combines elements of all three tests.

B. The Individual Exceptions

The remainder of this chapter addresses the areas of public functions, entangled participation, and authorization. It concludes by looking at the notion of entwinement, which combines all three areas into factors that are balanced to determine if "there is such a close nexus between the state and the challenged action that seemingly private behavior may be fairly treated as that of the state itself."

1. The Public Functions Exception: Will Any Public Function Do? What Is a Public Function?

One exception to the state action doctrine is when private actors perform public functions. If the function is truly one that should be performed by the government, then if the government delegates or allows a private person to take over the function, there is state action. The Supreme Court recognized this exception in cases before the 1970s. Those cases held out the possibility that in a number of contexts where private actors were taking on public or quasi-public functions, state action could be found (recall Justice Harlan's dissent in the *Civil Rights Cases*). These early cases focus on the functional equivalent of state power (i.e., whether the private party is doing what the state normally does).

What counts as a public function can be interpreted broadly or narrowly. Should public functions include all the functions the state performs, or just a subset of those functions? Some of the early cases indicated the potential for a broad interpretation, but the current rule is narrow, only allowing the exception when the private actor exercises a function that is both *traditionally* and *exclusively* reserved for the government. This latter approach does not focus on the functional equivalent of state power but limits the state action doctrine to those cases where it is not only a public function that is being performed but also a uniquely governmental function that has been taken over by private actors (i.e., whether the private party is doing what only the state should do).

The remainder of this section addresses public functions in the area of elections, company towns, parks, shopping centers, and public utilities, as well as the private enforcement of liens and public funding.

a. Elections

One of the earliest sets of cases in this area most likely survives either a broad or narrow interpretation of the exception. The Supreme Court, in a series of cases from 1927 to 1953, found that the practice of excluding African Americans from Democratic primaries violated the Fourteenth and Fifteenth

Amendments. The Court easily struck down the practice, which originated under Texas state law, in *Nixon v. Herndon* (1927). Texas Democrats responded by shifting the practice from the state to political party committees (found to be state action because the committees were acting as agents of the state in *Nixon v. Condon,* 1932) and eventually to voluntary clubs of white Democrats who held preprimary elections. In *Terry v. Adams* (1953), the Supreme Court held that when a private political organization's primary determines who will run in the state primary, and thus who will be eligible to be elected in the general election, its exclusion of blacks is state action in violation of the Fifteenth Amendment. This is because such elections are "an important function relating to the sovereignty of the people." Although this case came long before the "traditionally and exclusively reserved for the government" rule, it would most likely survive that rule. It is easy to trace how the traditionally exclusive governmental function of elections was privatized to avoid the constitutional requirement that the state not discriminate in election primaries.

b. Company Towns, Parks, Shopping Centers, and Public Utilities

i. Company Towns

One of the earliest cases allowing for an exception to the state action doctrine was *Marsh v. Alabama* (1946), which involved a company-owned town. The town used general trespass law to prevent the distribution of religious literature by Jehovah's Witnesses. The use of trespass law to restrict First Amendment activities on private property is generally unproblematic. People have a right to keep others off of their property. However, in this case, the Court found that since this privately owned town was the functional equivalent of a regular governmentally run town, the streets were public forums, just like other public streets. Therefore, the First Amendment public forum doctrine was successfully invoked to defend the Jehovah's Witnesses' violation of the trespass laws.

ii. Parks

In dicta, the Court in *Marsh* also indicated that this reasoning could be extended to private parks, which serve the same function as public parks. This approach was adopted in *Evans v. Newton* (1966), a case in which African Americans were denied entrance to a park held in private trust for the city of Macon, Georgia. The will of Senator A. O. Bacon conveyed the property in trust to the city, based on the condition that it was used exclusively by whites. Justice William Douglas, writing for the majority, noted that the park fulfilled a municipal function, not unlike police or firemen, and under the Equal Protection Clause of the Fourteenth Amendment, Senator Bacon could not stopped the city from allowing African Americans to use the park. The case came back to the Court in *Evans v. Abney* (1970), after the Georgia courts had decided that the trust had failed because its purpose (to keep the park for the sole use of whites) had failed. The argument was that the park was completely private now, since the trust to the city had failed, and thus African Americans could now be excluded. By this time, Justice Warren was replaced by Justice Burger, and Justice Hugo Black, writing for the majority, declined to follow the spirit of Justice Douglas's opinion. Rather, he found that the park was no longer being held in trust for the city but was now completely private, having reverted to Senator Bacon's heirs. It was now the heirs' park for their own use and enjoyment, and they could exclude African Americans. Justices Douglas and William Brennan both dissented.

iii. Shopping Centers

Shopping centers are perhaps the closest modern equivalent to company towns in serving the public functions that municipalities generally serve. Thus, it was not a stretch when the Court decided in *Amalgamated Food Employers Union Local 590 v. Logan Valley Plaza, Inc.* (1968) that the shopping center, like the company town, was a public forum for the purposes of allowing (under the First Amendment's guarantee of free speech) informational labor picketing that was related to a store in the center. Again, however, this somewhat broad holding was narrowed during the reign of the Burger Court in *Lloyd Corp. v. Tanner* (1972). The Court distinguished *Lloyd* from *Amalgamated* on the grounds that the hand billing (passing out flyers, leaflets, or circulars) in this case was not related to a specific store or to the center itself but to the Vietnam War. Thus, the Court held "that there has been no such dedication of Lloyd's privately owned and operated shopping center to public use as to entitle respondents to exercise therein the asserted First Amendment rights." Then, the Court in *Hudgens v. N.L.R.B.* (1976) (another shopping mall case involving labor picketing) used this narrow and arguably mistaken ruling as grounds for overturning *Amalgamated*. The Court reasoned that because the distinction between the two cases was based on the content of the message (i.e., whether it was "shopping center related") and because content-based regulations of speech violate the First Amendment (discussed in more detail in Chapter 10), then *Amalgamated* was unconstitutional. Of course, the Court could just as easily have held that it was *Lloyd* that was wrongly decided because the Court introduced the content-based restriction in that case, not in *Amalgamated*. These cases demonstrate a trend of narrowly interpreting the public functions exception.

iv. Public Utilities and the Modern Formulation of the Rule

Jackson v. Metropolitan Edison (1974) is in line with this trend of narrowly reading the public function exception and seemed to narrow it even further. In this case, the plaintiff claimed that his utilities were cut off without due process of law in violation of the Fourteenth Amendment and the Civil Rights Act of 1871, 42 U.S.C. § 1983. Based on the previous cases, the Court could have held that a monopoly public utility provider with exclusive power to either allow or deny one access to electricity was not only providing a public service but wielded power that was on a par with governmental power. From this perspective, it would be reasonable to expect some level of due process before such essential services are terminated. The Court in *Jackson,* however, definitively held that the modern rule was that the public function exception only applies to functions that are "traditionally exclusively reserved to the state." Because public utilities have not traditionally been the exclusive prerogative of the state, the private public utility provider did not fall within the exception. Thus, even if there was a trend for states and municipalities to run public utilities, and even if states had traditionally used private actors to run public utilities, this would not be enough to satisfy this stringent test, which requires *exclusivity*.

c. Application of the Modern Rule in Private Enforcement of Liens and in Public Funding

The reasoning of this case was applied in *Flagg Bros., Inc. v. Brooks* (1978), where the Court held that it was not state action when the private sale of stored goods was used to enforce a warehouseman's lien, authorized under state law. The claimant's argument was that the state had delegated its traditional and exclusive power over dispute resolution to the creditor, who could now use self-help to enforce its lien. He then argued that the creditor, as a state actor, violated § 1983 of the Civil Rights Act. Because this was not the only way the dispute could have been resolved, the Court held that this was not an exclusive power delegated to the creditor by the state. Further, it is far from clear that dispute resolution, even in commercial settings, has always been monopolized by the state. Thus, the Court held that it was not a function that was "traditionally and exclusively reserved to the state."

In 1982, the Court addressed two cases involving government funding that were also (and perhaps more appropriately) argued under the entanglement exception (see next section). In *Rendell-Baker v. Kohn* (1982), the Court declined to find state action in a case where a teacher claimed that his rights to due process and freedom of expression were violated when the school terminated his employment. Although this school for problem students was heavily sub-sidized by the state (90–99 percent if its funding), it had a private board of di-rectors, was located on private property, and its function was not the exclusive province of the state. The Court came to the same result in *Blum v. Yaretsky* (1982). Patients had been discharged without a hearing from a private nursing home that received 90 percent of its funds from the state. Although Justice Brennan forcefully argued in his dissent that the decisions to discharge patients were intimately connected with state funding issues, the majority of the Court rea-soned that the day-to-day decisions of the nursing home administration were not "the kind of decisions traditionally and exclusively made by the sovereign for and on behalf of the public."

2. The Entanglement Exception: When Does Joint Participation or Symbiotic Relationships Mean State Action?

There are at least two main ways that the state (for constitutional purposes) can be involved in private action that does not meet the public function test. The first is when the state and private actors are (1) joint actors or (2) in a symbiotic relationship. This is the subject of the exception treated in this sec-tion. Here, it is commonly said that the state's and private actor's activities are "entangled." The focus is on the conduct of the participants, not on their in-tentions. The other form of state involvement, treated in the next section, is concerned with state authorization: when the state encourages, endorses, or (in certain circumstances) enforces the action. The focus here is mainly on the state's intention to authorize the action, or at least appears to have intended it. The inquiry is to ascertain whether the state appears to be putting its author-ity behind the private conduct in question. There is significant overlap in these two forms of state involvement, and some courts and commentators do not strongly distinguish the two. Of course, there are many cases where both are present, which makes a stronger case for state action. As noted, *Brentwood Academy* (2001) is something of a hybrid case using the term *entwinement*.

One of the earliest cases finding state action based on entanglement was *Burton v. Wilmington Parking Authority* (1961). In that case, a private restau-rant located in a municipal parking garage practiced racial discrimination. The plaintiff sued for declaratory and injunctive relief for racial discrimination in violation of the Fourteenth Amendment's Equal Protection Clause. The ques-tion was whether the city could be held responsible for this conduct. Justice Tom Clark, writing for the majority, held that the city was responsible because the building was owned, rented, and maintained by the city and because of the "mutual benefits" that the parking authority and the restaurant received from their joint patrons. For example, there were more restaurant customers because of the good parking, and more people used the parking garage because of the restaurant. This Warren Court decision held out the possibility of a rather expansive state action doctrine, based on the totality of state and private actor interaction.

a. Licensing and Regulation Not Enough

The plaintiff in *Moose Lodge No. 107 v. Irvis* (1972) sought an injunction under 42 U.S.C. § 1983, claiming that his right to equal protection under the Fourteenth Amendment had been violated when the Moose Lodge refused to serve him because of his race. The plaintiff attempted to extend the principle of *Burton* to this case on the basis that the lodge was a heavily state-regulated, private club and the state provided its liquor license. However, the Burger Court found that the level of involvement by the state in this case did not rise to the level of the symbiotic relationship found in *Burton* . (Compare Justice Douglas's dissent in *Moose Lodge*, discussed later, which focused on the issue of encouragement.)

b. Government Funding and Resources

Although there are early cases in which the Court found that state funds given to private schools that practiced discrimination constituted state action, the current rule is that government funding, even if critical to the existence of a private entity, is not enough on its own to create state action.

Although the early cases fall within the Burger Court era (1969–1986), they most likely have a lower threshold for finding state action because they involved racial discrimination and in particular, because they involved schools that were still practicing racial segregation into the 1970s. Here, as in the election cases (*Nixon v. Herndon*, 1927; *Nixon v. Condon*, 1932; and *Terry v. Adams*, 1953), the Court may have suspected that public functions were being privatized to avoid the requirements of the Constitution. Not only were people sending their children to private schools to escape the constitutional requirement that public schools be desegregated, they were also pulling state funds and resources into those private schools to the detriment of public schools. In this context, any funds or resources going to those schools may be seen as the state supporting these racist practices. Thus, the Court, in *Norwood v. Harrison* (1973), found that public funding for textbooks in a racially segregated school constituted state action. Again, in *Gilmore v. Montgomery* (1974), in the context of a city under a desegregation order, the Court held that allowing a segregated private school to have exclusive use of city recreational facilities amounted to state action.

However, just as the Court in *Blum v. Yaretsky* (1982) refused to find that public funding for patients made the private institution's decisions regarding the discharge of those patients a public function, it also found that it did not satisfy the entanglement exception. Again, that case involved claims that patients had been discharged without due process and that 90 percent of the patients' medical expenses were paid by the state. The argument was that the public funding considerations were entwined with and drove the discharge decisions. Nonetheless, the Court rejected the argument. Likewise, in *Rendell-Baker v. Kohn* (1982) (private high school for maladjusted students in which 90–99 percent of its funds came from the state), the Court did not find state action when a teacher was fired, allegedly in violation of his right to freedom of expression and due process of law.

These two sets of cases (*Norwood* and *Gilmore,* as opposed to *Blum* and *Rendell*) can be distinguished not only on the ground that the one set involved race but also on the basis that although the funding in the racial segregation cases may have furthered racist practices, the funding in *Kohn* and *Blum* did not further the alleged constitutional violations. But compare Justice Brennan's dissent in *Blum,* in which he argued that the decisions to discharge patients were intimately connected with state funding issues, so that the summary discharges of patients may, in fact, have been stimulated by state funding.

3. The Authorization Exception: Is More than Neutral Authorization Required?

Just as one can have either a narrow or expansive view of "public functions" and "state entanglement," one can also have a narrow or expansive view of "state authorization, encouragement, and enforcement." How much governmental encouragement, enforcement, or authorization does one need to turn otherwise private conduct into state action? Is funding, licensing, or regulating enough? Is it enough to have laws that permit private individuals to engage in behavior that denies other individuals the kind of process, equal treatment, or substantive rights they are guaranteed against the state?

At one extreme, all conduct is either allowed or forbidden by the state, and thus, everything could be said to give rise to state action. If a private employer prevented free speech on the part of his employees in some respect, and the law did not forbid it, on this theory, there would be state complicity, or state action. Furthermore, every case brought before a court or state official for sanction or approval would implicate state action. If a court upheld the firing of an at-will employee who claimed that he should have received more due process before being fired, the state, acting through the court, would have put its authority behind the firing of the individual. At this extreme, every right that individuals have against the state would be transformed into rights against other individuals. This surely goes too far, as no one thinks that at-will private employees (e.g., someone working at-will for a private company like McDonalds, Wal-Mart, or Microsoft) have a constitutional right against the employer under free speech or the Due Process Clause. We might think they should have such a right, but no one thinks it comes from the Constitution.

When the state authorizes, encourages, and/or enforces private action, the Court will find state action if it believes that the weight and authority of the state are supporting the private action. In *Flagg Bros.* (1978), the court did not find state action merely because the law authorized a private warehouse to put a lien on plaintiff's property and to refuse to return it until the plaintiff paid the amount due. By contrast, in *Lugar v. Edmondson Oil Company* (1982), the Court found state action when a creditor had the sheriff's help in executing a writ that the creditor obtained in an *ex parte* proceeding in violation of the plaintiff's due process rights. In *Lugar,* the Court stated at least one modern formulation of the state action rule, namely, that:

1. "the deprivation must be caused by the exercise of some right or privilege created by the state or by a person from whom the state is responsible"; and
2. "the party charged with the deprivation must be a person who may fairly be said to be a state actor."

This second requirement can be fulfilled in one of three ways:

a. if the person "is a state official;"
b. if the person "acted together with, or has obtained significant aid from state officials"; or
c. "because the person's conduct is otherwise chargeable to the state."

In *Flagg Bros.*, the state merely authorized the activity through law, whereas in *Lugar,* state law authorized the activity and the state (the sheriff) and a private actor carried out the activity together.

Like the cases in the other sections, the early cases and those cases involving race come closest to what we have called the "expansive view" of state authorization. More recent cases, like *Flagg* and *Lugar,* did not involve discrimination and required more than mere permissive regulation, authorization, or even encouragement. The modern cases tend to require that the state significantly encourage, command, or coerce the conduct in question. Thus, *Blum v. Yaretsky* (1982) (discharge from private nursing home case) is sometimes cited for the modern rule that the state will be responsible for private conduct:

1. if the state "has provided such significant encouragement ... that the choice must in law be deemed that of the state"; or
2. if the state's coercive power backed the private action.

a. The Earlier Expansive View

One of the earliest cases in this area took a very expansive view of the doctrine. In *Shelley v. Kraemer* (1948) the Court found state action to be present in state enforcement of a racially discriminatory deed between private parties. The deed forbade the owner of the property from selling his or her property to African American buyers. There would be no state action if white owners privately discriminated against African American buyers and only sold to white buyers. In such a case, the state would not be involved. However, in this case, a white owner wanted to sell to African American buyers, who were able and willing to buy from the owner. As a result, other white owners wanted the Court to put its coercive power behind them to stop the sale. The Supreme Court held that such judicial enforcement would constitute state action and would be unconstitutional.

The broadest reading of this decision would be that any judicial holding in favor of a private discriminatory act is state action. This would extend even to the situation where willing African American buyers could not find willing white owners to sell to them and sued to force a white owner to sell. A judicial decision refusing to do so would be discriminatory state action. The narrowest reading is that the state acts when it forces unwilling parties to discriminate by stopping willing owners from selling to African American buyers.

Although the Court has never followed the broadest reading of *Shelley*, it has adopted positions that are broader than the narrowest view. This is illustrated by the case of sit-in protests at private restaurants that practiced racial discrimination (*Lombard v. Louisiana*, 1963), and by the case of a referendum amendment to the California state Constitution (Proposition 14) which prevented the enactment of state laws to prohibit racial discrimination in renting or selling property in violation of the Equal Protection Clause of the Fourteenth Amendment (*Reitman v. Mulkey*, 1967).

In *Lombard*, both the mayor and police superintendent actively encouraged restaurant owners to refuse service to African Americans. Consequently, the Court found that *active significant encouragement* by city officials of private racial discrimination constituted state action. This state action obviously did not rise to the level of the state forcing parties to discriminate under the narrowest reading of *Shelley*. But the Court did not base its decision on the mere fact that the state, through the courts, was enforcing private trespass laws against the African

American sit-in protesters, which it could have done if it were giving *Shelley* its broadest interpretation. Rather, the Court based its decision on the active encouragement by the city officials.

In the case of *Reitman*, Proposition 14, which the Court struck down, did not require, and on its face, did not encourage, racial discrimination. This state action did not come anywhere near the level of the state forcing parties to discriminate under the narrowest reading of *Shelley*. The Proposition simply said that no laws could be passed that interfere with private discrimination. Nonetheless, given the context in which the Proposition was passed, the Court found that the "design and effect" of the amendment was not only to authorize but to "significantly encourage" racial discrimination by overturning existing fair housing laws that prohibited racial discrimination in selling and renting property.

The legislation in *Reitman* is very similar to the Colorado constitutional amendments in *Romer v. Evans* (1996), which prohibited cities, towns, and counties from taking legislative, executive, or judicial action to protect homosexual citizens from discrimination on the basis of their sexual orientation. If one is neutral about whether private individuals should be allowed to discriminate, there is an argument that both pieces of legislation are neutral. The California and Colorado amendments are neutral in the sense that they equalize the treatment of African Americans, homosexuals, and other groups that do not have protective legislation. However, they both single out a particular group, African Americans or homosexuals, respectively, and deny them the ability to seek out legislation that would protect them from private discrimination. In both cases, the state is acting to create a barrier to the group seeking protection and is opening up a door for private persons to discriminate. For the Court, that is encouragement enough.

b. The Modern, Ostensibly Narrower Approach

As noted, by the 1970s, the Court was not as willing to find state action under any of the exceptions, including the present one. Thus, in *Jackson v. Metropolitan Edison Co.* (1974) (case involving a claim of denial of due process), the Court did not find that there was state action, even though the public utilities commission had approved the tariff schedule that authorized the utility company to cut off service without notice, a hearing, or an opportunity to pay arrears. For the Court, the commission's review and approval of the tariff schedule was not active approval or encouragement by the state, but merely a failure to overturn the practice (nor did it find "entanglement" under the previous exception).

Even though in *Flagg Bros.* (1978), the state commercial code specifically allowed for the private enforcement of the warehouseman's lien without notice or a hearing for the debtor, the Court, perhaps somewhat in contrast to *Reit-*

man (California Proposition 14), found this to be a mere declaration of neutrality on the part of the state. In other words, the Court found that the state was merely saying that it would not interfere with the private sale by requiring the creditor to sell the property after notice or a hearing. The Court could have found, as it did in *Reitman*, that the "design and effect" of this legislation would encourage this kind of behavior on the part of creditors, but it did not do so.

In *Blum v. Yaretsky* (1982) (state-funded and -regulated nursing home), the Court did not find that the private nursing home's decisions regarding the discharge and/or transfer of patients were dictated by state regulations, even though pervasive regulations impacted the nursing home's funding. Justice Brennan, in a strong dissent, argued that the discharge decisions were not based primarily on professional medical judgment but were in fact based on fiscal considerations tied to the state funding. Thus, although the majority did not think that the pervasive regulations and adjustments to funding constituted "approval or enforcement," the dissent thought that the state had put its "power, property, and prestige" behind the conduct of the nursing home.

Similarly, in *Rendell-Baker v. Kohn* (1982) (state-funded private high school for troubled students), the Court did not find state action to be present when the private school fired an employee because there was no evidence that the decision was compelled or even influenced by the state or its regulations.

Again, in *Moose Lodge* (1972) (refusal to serve African American guest at a private lodge), the Court did not find state action, even though the state issued the lodge a liquor license. The Court considered this a neutral regulation rather than an endorsement. Justice Douglas, writing for the dissent, argued that when the city granted a limited resource (a liquor license) to the lodge, it not only granted the lodge the prestige of the state but also encouraged and fostered the discrimination. In fact, the liquor license required the lodge to follow its bylaws, which required that it deny service to African Americans. Nonetheless, the majority struck down the bylaws and held that there was no state action.

Thus, neutral approval, permissive regulation, or mere tolerance of practices by the state, appears to be insufficient in these cases to constitute state action. Rather, *active authorization, encouragement,* or *enforcement* is required.

c. The Principles as Applied to Racial Jury Selection through Peremptory Challenges

A series of equal protection cases extended state action to cases where preemptory challenges were used to discriminate against jurors on the basis of race (a preemptory challenge is used by either party to a case to dismiss a juror without stating a cause or reason for the dismissal). These cases included a prosecutor (*Batson v. Kentucky*, 1986), private litigants (*Edmondson v. Leesville Concrete Co, Inc.*, 1991), and defense counsel (*Georgia v. McCollum*, 1992).

The Court in *Edmondson* applied the test articulated in *Lugar* (sheriff executed a creditor's writ) and found that that there was clear statutory authorization for the use of preemptory challenges and that "in all fairness," the private litigant "must be deemed a government actor." The Court's discussion focused on "the extent to which the actor relies on government assistance and benefits, whether the actor was performing a traditional governmental function and whether the injury caused is aggravated in a unique way by the incidents of government authority." Thus, this case could perhaps have been decided under a number of the state action exceptions.

Here, there was overt significant assistance by state officials throughout the entire preemptory challenge process, resulting in the judge dismissing the potential juror. Thus, the Court found that the state had "elected to place its power, property and prestige behind the [alleged] discrimination" (citing *Burton*, 1961). Even though a criminal defense attorney is in many ways the antithesis of a state actor, the Court followed the same reasoning when it extended the doctrine to race-based preemptory challenges in *Georgia v. McCollum* (1992).

4. The Combination of Incomplete Elements of Several Exceptions: The Recent Notion of Entwinement

The Court, in *Brentwood Academy v. Tennessee Secondary School Athletic Association* (2001), a five-to-four decision, found state action in the conduct of the Athletic Association's enforcement of its rules against the plaintiff's school. The school claimed that the enforcement was state action, which violated of the First and Fourteenth Amendments. Justice Clarence Thomas, writing for the dissent, argued that the Association would fail to be a state actor under any of the existing tests for state action if they were considered individually. The Association was not exercising a traditional and exclusive state function; it did not act in a "symbiotic relationship" with the government, at least not in the narrow sense; and it was not "created, coerced, or encouraged by the government."

The majority, written by Justice David Souter, did not rely on the state function test. Instead, the Court found state action by combining the state authorization test with the entangled participation or symbiotic relation test and adding a pinch of the public function test. This resulted in the Court creating a new test, entwinement: "State action may be found if, though only if, there is such a 'close nexus between the State and the challenged action' that seemingly private behavior 'may be fairly treated as that of the State itself.'"

For Justice Souter, the level of the state's entwinement in this private association and its decision to sanction the Brentwood Academy made it "fair" to treat the Association as a state actor.

a. A Pinch of Public Function

Justice Souter noted that the Association regulated secondary school athletics in lieu of the state Board of Education's own authority "in providing standards, rules and regulations for interscholastic competition in the public schools in Tennessee." Nonetheless, there is no argument that this is a traditional and exclusive state function.

b. Elements of Entangled Participation

The Association was entangled to a large degree with state actors, because 84 percent of its members were public schools and its rule-making arm was limited to high school principals, assistant principals, and superintendents, who attended meetings during school hours. The Association's dues largely came from public schools, and its staff members were also eligible for the state retirement program, even though their salaries were not paid by the state.

c. Elements of Authorization

As these facts also indicate, the Association selected its officers from public schools and acted through public school representatives. The overwhelming majority of public school members sent their principals or faculty members to represent them and elect the members of the governing legislative council and board of control from eligible principles, assistant principals, and superintendents. Thus, most of the control and functioning of the association was done by public officials acting in their official capacity. Further, the state of Tennessee also provided state board members, who were assigned to serve in their official capacity on the board of control and on the legislative council.

d. The Case of an Interstate Athletic Association Distinguished

The Court in *Brentwood* spent a considerable amount of ink distinguishing the case of *NCAA v. Tarkanian* (1989), a case in which a basketball coach for the University of Nevada-Las Vegas was suspended. He claimed that the NCAA was a state actor because the state university had delegated its functions to the NCAA to make and apply the university's rules. Although the Court in *NCAA* had found some delegation of authority, the NCAA's policies were shaped by hundreds of member institutions, most of which were outside Nevada. In *Brentwood*, the Court pointed to dicta in *NCAA*, which indicated that if the NCAA's members were all within the state and many of them were "public institutions created by the same sovereign," then "the situation would, of course, be different."

The NCAA was, in fact, in an adversarial position to the University of Nevada on this issue, because it suspended the coach under threat of sanction by the NCAA. As the Court in *NCAA* noted, the University could have retained its coach and left the association.

Checkpoints

- As a general rule, under the federal Constitution, only state actors can be held responsible for the violation of constitutional rights.

- There are four categories of exceptions, where the courts have held there is state action, and thus, the Constitution applies to private conduct. Those categories include: *Slavery*

  1. the Thirteenth Amendment (this is the one clear exception, which applies to the state and individuals alike)

  2. private actors performing public or *state functions*;

  3. the *entanglement* or joint participation of state and private actors; and

  4. the *authorization*, encouragement, or enforcement of private action by the state.

- The narrow, modern view of state action is that the courts will only find state action when:

  - the private organization is performing *a traditional and exclusive state function*;

  - the level of entanglement has risen to the level of a *symbiotic relationship*; or

  - there is not only passive regulation but active authorization, encouragement, and enforcement, to the point of almost requiring commandment.

- In 1982, the Court articulated two similar but distinctive modern tests for the fourth exception, namely, the *Lugar* and *Blum* tests.

  - In *Lugar*, the Court stated that:

    - "the deprivation must be caused by the exercise of some right or privilege created by the state or by a person for whom the state is responsible"; and

    - "the party charged with the deprivation must be a person who may fairly be said to be a state actor."

  - In *Blum* the Court held that the state will be responsible for private conduct if:

> ## **Checkpoints** *continued*
>
> - the state "has provided such significant encouragement … that the choice must in law be deemed that of the state"; or
>
> - the state's coercive power backed the private action.
>
> • Recently, the Supreme Court created a hybrid category, *entwinement*. The Court used this in a case that would not satisfy any of the tests under the three traditional categories of exceptions, but which had aspects of state function, entanglement and authorization to such a degree that there was "such a close nexus between the State and the challenged action that seemingly private behavior [could] be fairly treated as that of the State itself."

Chapter 6

Substantive Protection of Economic Interests

Roadmap

- The freedom of contract found in the "liberty" provision of the Due Process Clause of the Fifth and Fourteenth Amendments; primarily used during the *Lochner* era.

- Economic liberties include the protection against unreasonable deprivation of property, through excessive punitive damage awards.

- The Takings Clause of the Fifth Amendment:

    - "Takings" defined.

    - Is "public use" required or is "public purpose" sufficient?

    - How does one determine "just compensation"?

- The Contracts Clause prohibits state governments from interfering with existing contracts, including both private and public contracts.

I. Introduction

Economic liberties include the rights to enter into and enforce a contract, to pursue a trade or profession, and to acquire, possess, and convey property. As seen in Chapter 4, economic liberties are protected to some degree by the dormant Commerce Clause and by the Privileges and Immunities Clause. Those clauses protect interstate commerce and out-of-state persons who are engaged in commerce or trying to make a living. Under those clauses, the state can neither discriminate against such persons or commerce nor unduly burden interstate commerce. The present chapter addresses the substantive, or direct, protection of economic liberties as found in three constitutional provisions:

- the Contracts Clause in Section 10, Article I: No state shall pass any law impairing the obligation of Contracts;

- the Due Process Clause of the Fifth and Fourteenth Amendments: Neither the states nor the federal government shall deprive a person of life, *liberty* or property without due process of law; and
- the Takings Clause of the Fifth Amendment: Nor shall private property be taken for public use without just compensation.

Although the Contracts Clause is the most explicit clause, its provisions are used the least. The reason for this is because it is directed only to the states' conduct ("No state shall"), not that of the federal government. Furthermore, the Contracts Clause prohibits the government from interfering with *existing* contracts, not *future* contracts. Since 1937, the Court has used the Contracts Clause only twice to invalidate a law. Those two cases, where the government interfered with a public contract (*United States Trust Co. v. New Jersey*, 1977) and a private contract (*Allied Structural Steel Co. v. Spannaus*, 1978), are discussed in Section D.

The Due Process Clause, found in the Fifth and Fourteenth Amendments, includes both procedural and substantive due process rights. Procedural due process concerns the right to a fair legal process and entails, for instance, the right to receive notice and a hearing. By contrast, substantive due process protects fundamental rights, and it requires the government to provide a sufficient justification for any infringement of those rights. The level of justification required turns on whether the right receives rational basis, intermediate, or strict scrutiny by the courts. If the Court applies rational basis scrutiny, the government need only show that the regulation limiting the right is rationally related to serving a legitimate state interest. Although there are a number of different ways to formulate the intermediate scrutiny test (sometimes called "heightened scrutiny"), this level of scrutiny generally requires the government to show that the regulation serves an important state interest, for which the regulation is substantially related to serving that interest. Strict scrutiny requires that the government show that the regulation serves a compelling state interest and is necessary to serve that interest. Under strict scrutiny, there must not be any other means or way to achieve the purpose that is less restrictive of the right in question.

From the time of the founding of the United States to the 1900s, economic substantive due process was rarely used because the right to due process was held as merely a procedural right (*Murray v. Hoboken Land and Dev.*, 1856; *The Slaughter-House Cases*, 1872). Thus, government was generally free to regulate. During the *Lochner* era, or laissez-faire period from the late 1800s to 1937, the Court used the notion of "freedom of contract," as found in the "liberty" provision of the Due Process Clause, to strike down government legislation. By contrast, since 1937 the Court has deferred to the government with respect to economic regulations by using the lowest level of scrutiny, rational basis. It has used the Contracts Clause twice to invalidate a law; it has also used the Takings Clause to prevent the government from "taking" private property for private use or taking it without "just compensation."

Today, substantive economic liberties are still protected by the Due Process Clause but not because of "freedom of contract." Defendants receive protection from excessive punitive damages because unreasonable deprivation of property violates procedural and substantive due process. The judiciary will only question the acts of the legislature in two areas: (1) fundamental rights, such as those enumerated in the Bill of Rights, the nonenumerated rights of the Ninth Amendment, and those protected by the concept of "liberty"; and (2) discrete and insular minorities, which are protected by the Equal Protection Clause (footnote 4 of *U.S. v. Carolene Products Co.,* 1938).

II. Foundational Cases (the *Lochner* Era)

The period from the end of the 1800s to 1937 is known as the *Lochner* era, or the laissez-faire period. During the 1800s, the Industrial Revolution created a concentration of wealth. Modern industrial capitalism caused monopolies to form; both consumers and workers tended to suffer. This gave rise to demands for legislation to regulate monopoly pricing and to regulate the hours and wages of workers. During this period, the Court generally favored the corporations, protecting them from both federal and state regulation. Recall from Chapter 2 that the *Lochner* era was a period of narrow Commerce Clause powers; the Tenth Amendment was also used to reserve power exclusively to the states. Thus, the Court struck down federal economic regulations as violating these provisions. When the states stepped in to regulate these areas, the Court invalidated the legislation on the grounds that it infringed the parties' freedom of contract and thereby their liberty interest under the Due Process Clause. Though "freedom of contract" does not expressly exist in the Constitution, the Court interpreted the liberty and property provisions of the Due Process Clause of the Fifth and Fourteenth Amendments to include freedom of contract as a fundamental right. The Due Process Clause went beyond the protections of the Contracts Clause because it limited both the state and federal governments' ability to interfere with existing contracts and regulate the provisions of future contracts. Thus, the state could interfere only to exercise its valid state police powers, and the Court scrutinized the government's interest (the ends) and the legislation's relation to that interest (the means).

In *Allgeyer v. Louisiana* (1897), a New York-based company insured property in Louisiana. Louisiana passed a state statute that prohibited an out-of-state company from doing business within the state unless the company had a place of business or an agent located within the state. The purpose of the statute was to protect Louisiana citizens from having to file suit in New York if an insurer, such as Allgeyer, denied their insurance claim. Justice Rufus Peckham, writing for the Court, held that the statute was unconstitutional because it interfered with the freedom of citizens to enter into a contract with out-of-state insurance companies.

Eight years later in *Lochner v. New York* (1905), in another decision written by Justice Peckham, the Court explicitly held that states can interfere with the fundamental right of freedom of contract, but only if the regulation has a direct relation to an appropriate and legitimate end under the state's police powers (i.e., public health and safety). For Justice Peckham, the issue before the court was: "Is this a fair, reasonable, and appropriate exercise of the police power of the state, or is it an unreasonable, unnecessary, and arbitrary interference with the right of the individual to his personal liberty?" The Court stated that the judiciary will scrutinize the ends served by the legislation and the means by which the purported goal is achieved. In that case, Joseph Lochner was convicted of violating a state statute, which limited the working hours for bakery workers to sixty hours per week and ten hours per day. The Court reasoned that although the state police powers include the power to "impose reasonable conditions for the safety, health, morals and general welfare of the public," the freedom of employees and employers to contract is a fundamental right of liberty, protected by the substantive due process clause of the Fourteenth Amendment.

The Court found the statute unconstitutional because the state lacked any reasonable ground for interfering with the bakers' rights to enter into a contract to support themselves and their families. The Court held that the law was not "necessary or appropriate as a health law to safeguard the public health, or the health of the individuals who are following the trade of a baker." Bakers are not a suspect class, and they do not need more protection by the judiciary. Thus, bakers receive only rational basis scrutiny. Furthermore, the regulation was not within the state's police powers; the statute did not protect the public with better bread, nor did it help the baker. The Court reasoned that if it upheld this legislation, then the state could regulate any trade on the basis that it would protect the public's health.

Justice Oliver Wendell Holmes dissented, stating that it is reasonable to believe that limiting the number of labor hours is rationally related to protecting the health of the bakers. He reasoned that the Constitution does not prefer one economic theory over another (paternalism or laissez-faire). Further, the people had decided through the legislature that they needed safe working conditions. Striking down this legislation perverted the true meaning of liberty. Thus,

Justice Holmes believed that the legislation survived rational basis review and that the Court should defer. Justices John Harlan, Edward White, and William Day also dissented, pointing out that bakers have a shorter life span due to the poor air quality in the bakeries, and the workers develop "white lung disease" from inhaling flour dust. Thus, for these dissenting Justices, bakers are distinctive from other workers, and it is within the traditional police powers of the state to protect the health and safety of the public.

In this period, the Court also declared that state and federal legislation protecting unionizing was unconstitutional. In *Coppage v. Kansas* (1915), the state of Kansas passed a statute that prevented employers from requiring a person to agree not to join a union as a condition of employment. The Court relied on *Adair v. United States* (1908), in which a similar federal law was held unconstitutional because it violated the freedom of contract, protected by the liberty and property provisions of the Fifth Amendment. The Court reasoned that if it is unconstitutional for Congress to deny the employers a right to enter a contract to prevent employees from unionizing, then it was unconstitutional for the states to deny the same right. The Kansas statute was not a reasonable exercise of the state's police power. However, one could argue that preventing employees from unionizing actually limits the *employees'* freedom of contract and prohibits their ability to have equal bargaining power with large employers.

Muller v. Oregon (1908) presented the rather unsurprising sexist exception to the rule in these cases. The case is famous for the Brandeis Brief. Attorney Louis Brandeis (who later became a Supreme Court Justice) submitted a 113-page brief that documented the health risks to women who worked long hours outside the home. Due to this social science research Brandeis put together, and no doubt a fair amount of bias against the equality of women, the Court upheld the Oregon law that set maximum working hours for women. Reasoning that healthy mothers are essential to preserve the human race and that hard nondomestic labor is dangerous to women's health, the Court held that it was constitutional for the state to interfere with the freedom of contract to protect women.

The Court's paternalism did not extend to protecting the morals of women. In *Adkins v. Children's Hospital* (1923), a state statute set minimum wages for women and children. The state's purpose was to protect women's morality by helping them meet the cost of living without resorting to prostitution. Justice George Sutherland, writing for the Court, struck down the statute, stating that the differences between men and women had decreased, especially in light of passage of the Nineteenth Amendment, which provided women the right to vote. Because women have equality, they should be treated as equals in the marketplace. Although the Court did not foreclose the possibility of legislation that takes into account the physical differences between men and women, it held that women no longer needed special protection in contractual relationships. Furthermore, the link between wages and morality was attenuated, because morality depends on each woman's individual circumstances. The legislation required the employer to bear the costs of ensuring the morality of its female workers, which was completely unrelated to the employer's business. Note that the Court expressly overruled this case in *West Coast Hotel v. Parrish* (discussed shortly) and upheld a minimum wage law for women and minors.

The Court also struck down legislation that protected consumers. In *Weaver v. Palmer Bros.* (1926), a state statute required sterilization of shoddy, which is secondhand clothing and rags used by manufacturers to fill duvet comforters. The Court stated there was no evidence that bacteria survived in the shoddy or that using it caused diseases; thus, the state had no legitimate interest in regulating it. The statute interfered with consumers' freedom to contract. Justice Holmes dissented, reasoning that the Court's role was to defer to the legislature and leave this type of issue to the democratic process. Because the state believed that the use of unsterilized shoddy would spread disease, and that tagging and inspection were inadequate, the Court should not interfere with the state's decision to choose sterilization as a means to rectify the problem.

Toward the end of the *Lochner* era, in *Nebbia v. New York* (1934), the Court upheld a state statute that set minimum and maximum prices for the retail sale of milk. Nebbia, a grocery store owner, sold a milk and loaf of bread combination special that brought the price of milk below the minimum price required. The legislature's purpose was to protect the livelihood of dairy farmers. This would, in turn, protect the milk supply because farmers would not be tempted to relax safeguards that prevented bacterial growth, because the safeguards greatly increased the costs of dairy production. Justice Owen Roberts wrote the opinion of the Court, which held that the statute was rationally related to a legitimate state purpose—protecting the health, safety, and welfare of the public. This case can either be viewed as exceptional because milk is an essential product that has historically been heavily regulated, or it can be seen as the first step by Justice Roberts toward his "switch in time to save nine" from President Franklin Roosevelt's Court-packing plan (discussed later).

III. Modern Approaches

A. The End of the *Lochner* Era

The Great Depression caused large-scale unemployment and low wages; it left employees with little bargaining power in the workplace. These crises, combined with society's new perception that government regulation was essential to address these problems, led to immense pressure to abandon the laissez-faire policy of the *Lochner* era. The people, Congress, and the President were all aligned against the Court. In 1936, President Roosevelt, who had been re-elected in a landslide election, reacted to the Supreme Court's consistent invalidation of his New Deal legislation by creating a Court-packing plan. The plan gave the President power to appoint an additional Supreme Court Justice for each Justice who was over the age of seventy, up to a maximum of fifteen Justices. (Note that these types of plans are constitutional and have occurred throughout history, as discussed in Chapter 1). Justice Roberts switched sides in two cases in 1937, casting the fifth vote needed to uphold the legislation. Thus, he is known as the one who "switched in time to save nine." This switch led to the end of substantive economic due process.

In 1937, the Court expressly overruled *Adkins v. Children's Hospital* (already discussed), in which the Court held unconstitutional a state law setting a minimum wage for women and children. In *West Coast Hotel v. Parrish* (1937), a hotel cleaning worker sued to recover the difference in her actual wages and the state minimum wage. In an opinion written by Justice Charles Hughes, the Court upheld the state law that provided a minimum wage for women and minors. It deferred to the legislature to protect safe working conditions and to protect women and children from oppression because of their weak bargaining positions. Reviewing the Constitution, the Court noted that the text does not say "freedom of contract," but "liberty." Freedom of contract undermines liberty; it protects the employer's liberty but not the liberty of the mass of common workers. The Court stated that the "community is not bound to provide a subsidy for unconscionable employers." In other words, society incurred the expense when individuals could not meet the cost of living because of the oppression of employers. Thus, it was constitutional for the state legislature to step in and shift the burden, and the Court should defer.

In *U.S. v. Carolene Products* (1938), a federal statute known as the Filled Milk Act prohibited shipping milk mixed with vegetable oil in interstate commerce. Justice Harlan Stone, writing for the Court, held that the legislation was constitutional and did not violate the Due Process Clause of the Fifth Amendment. The legitimate government purpose was to protect the public health by requiring a minimal nutritional value in food and preventing consumers from being defrauded into purchasing food stripped of nutritional value that is indistinguishable from the real food. The case is famous for footnote four, in which the Court set out the test for scrutinizing legislation. There is a presumption of constitutionality; with respect to economic liberties, the Court will defer to the legislature if there is any rational basis for the legislation. The Court will only second-guess Congress when the legislation in question:

1. interferes with enumerated rights (such as "liberty," "unreasonable searches and seizures," or "freedom of expression");
2. limits the political process (the right to vote, dissemination of information, or peaceful assembly); or
3. prejudices "discrete and insular minorities."

Since 1937, the Court has not found a state or federal economic regulation unconstitutional as violating the freedom of contract, protected by the liberty provision of the Due Process Clauses in the Fifth and Fourteenth Amendments. It no longer uses federalism or laissez-faire to prevent the government from regulating the economy. Economic regulations receive the lowest level of scrutiny, rational basis, and will be upheld as long as the regulation is rationally related to a legitimate government purpose. The purpose can be anything that is not prohibited by the Constitution or federal law. The government must simply use a reasonable means to achieve any conceivable purpose (not only the purported or actual purpose).

Williamson v. Lee Optical of Oklahoma, Inc. (1955) is a paradigm post-1937 case, exemplifying the Court's low level of scrutiny and high level of deference to economic legislation. In *Williamson*, a state statute prohibited an optometrist from giving a patient new frames or replacing lenses without a written prescription form. Upholding the legislation, the Court reasoned that the statute did not require a new eye exam every time frames were changed or lenses replaced, and the optometrist may have an old prescription on file. Furthermore, it was not required that the statute be logical in every respect; it could be largely wasteful and unnecessary. It was not for the Court to judge whether the statute is a good law; there only needed to be some justification for it. The legislature could have concluded that a prescription was necessary to correct vision and to detect eye problems or diseases.

The new approach was nicely summarized by Justice Hugo Black in *Ferguson v. Skrupa* (1963) (a case involving state regulation of debt adjusting):

> The doctrine that prevailed in *Lochner, Coppage, Adkins, Burns,* and like cases — that due process authorizes courts to hold laws unconstitutional when they believe the legislature has acted unwisely — has long since been discarded. We have returned to the original constitutional proposition that courts do not substitute their social and economic beliefs for the judgment of legislative bodies, who are elected to pass laws.

B. Punitive Damages: Unreasonable Deprivation of Property

Although the Due Process Clause does not protect the right to practice a trade or profession or the right to freedom of contract, this Clause has been used over the past decade or so to protect unreasonable deprivations of property. Although the Court no longer uses the Clause to strike down laws that are incompatible with an economic or social philosophy, it will invalidate unreasonably large punitive damage awards as unreasonable deprivations of property, in violation of the Due Process Clause.

In *BMW v. Gore* (1996), BMW had a nationwide policy in place to not disclose to the automobile purchaser any damage to new cars that occurred before delivery, when the cost to repair the car was less than 3 percent of the retail price. Ira Gore had purchased a $40,000 car, and nine months later, he learned that the car had been damaged and subsequently repainted. The cost to repaint the car was only $600, or 1.5 percent of the retail price. However, a repainted car is worth 10 percent less, in this case $4,000 less, than the value of a new car. At trial, it was shown that BMW had sold 1,000 refinished cars, and the jury awarded $4 million in punitive damages. On appeal, the Alabama Supreme Court reduced the punitive damages award to $2 million, pointing out that only fourteen such refinished cars were sold in Alabama.

Justice John Paul Stevens wrote the majority opinion for the Court and stated that the state interest in punitive damages was to punish and to deter unlawful conduct. Alabama could have chosen to pass a law requiring all repairs before sale of the vehicle to be disclosed to the consumer, but it could not impose punitive damages to change the conduct in other states. This would burden the interstate market for automobiles and would punish conduct that may be lawful in those states. Thus, Alabama could not impose punitive damages to change BMW's nationwide policy; it could only change its own local policy. The Due Process Clause of the Fourteenth Amendment prohibits a state from imposing a grossly excessive punishment on a tortfeasor. Procedural due process requires that a person have notice that conduct will subject her or him to punishment and the severity of the penalty. Substantive due process protects a person's right to be free from unreasonable deprivation of property. The Court laid out three guideposts to determine adequate notice (procedural due process) and reasonableness (substantive due process) of the punitive damages award:

1. the degree of reprehensibility of the defendant's conduct;
2. the ratio of the plaintiff's actual harm to the punitive damage award; and
3. comparable sanctions or remedies in other cases.

With respect to the reprehensibility of BMW's nondisclosure policy, the Court reasoned that the type of harm was only economic; it did not affect the performance of the car, safety, or even its appearance. Although BMW had *mens rea* (intent), it did not demonstrate reckless disregard for the health and safety of others.

Further, punitive damages (which address the harm likely to result from the defendant's conduct) must be reasonably related to compensatory damages (the harm that actually occurred to the plaintiff). The original punitive award of $4 million was a 1,000:1 ratio ($4 million divided by $4,000). Although the Alabama Supreme Court reduced the award to $2 million, this award was still a 500:1 ratio of punitive damages to compensatory damages ($2 million divided by $4,000).

The Court also examined comparable sanctions in other cases. In Alabama, the maximum civil penalty set by statute was $2,000. In other states, it was $5,000 to $10,000. If Alabama viewed the nondisclosure of information related to vehicle repair as a serious crime, it should have created higher sanctions. Instead, it failed to give proper notice of the risks that BMW was undertaking with its nondisclosure policy. For the Court, the severe punitive damages award failed all three guideposts; it was unconstitutional.

Justices Antonin Scalia and Clarence Thomas dissented, reasoning that punitive damages should be left to the states; this area is not for the Court to interfere. Further, the Due Process Clause does not protect against the unfairness of punitive damage awards (substantive due process). It only protects the actual process: the opportunity to contest the reasonableness of the jury award in state court (procedural due process). Furthermore, for the dissenters, the "reasonableness" of the award is a vague, subjective standard, unworkable for the courts.

The Court considered the issue of punitive damages again in State Farm Mutual Automobile Insurance Co. v. Campbell (2003). In that case, Curtis Campbell had made an unsafe pass on a highway and caused a collision, killing one driver and disabling another, although Campbell was unharmed. Campbell's insurance company, State Farm, represented him and refused to settle damages with the other drivers for the policy limit of $50,000. At trial, the jury found Campbell 100 percent at fault, and a judgment was entered against him for $185,000. Campbell entered into a contract with the injured driver and the deceased driver's estate, agreeing that if they would drop their claim against him, he would sue State Farm for bad faith, and they would receive 90 percent of the recovery. When the bad-faith claim against State Farm when to trial, the court awarded $2.6 million in compensatory damages (later reduced to $1 million) to redress the loss that the plaintiffs suffered and $145 million in punitive damages for deterrence and retribution. On appeal, the Supreme Court held that the award of punitive damages was unconstitutional, because it was an unreasonable deprivation of property in violation of the Due Process Clause of the Fourteenth Amendment.

The Court noted that the first guidepost, the degree of reprehensibility, was the most important factor. Here, the test was whether "the harm caused was physical as opposed to economic; the tortious conduct evinced an indifference to or a reckless disregard of the health or safety of others; the target of the conduct had financial vulnerability; the conduct involved repeated actions or was an isolated incident; and the harm was the result of intentional malice, trickery, or deceit, or mere accident." The harm in this case was not physical. State Farm had changed company records to make Campbell appear less at fault in the accident and had disregarded the likelihood of liability and the chance that a judgment in excess of the policy limits would be awarded. State Farm had also reassured the Campbells that their assets would be safe and then, after the judgment, told them to sell their home. There was considerable evidence that State Farm had engaged in similar unethical yet legal conduct nationwide. The Court held that the state court could not award punitive damages as a way to "expose, and punish, the perceived deficiencies of State Farm's operations throughout the country."

Examining the second guidepost, the ratio between actual harm and the punitive damage award, the Court held that although there is no bright line rule, awards must generally fall within a single digit ratio (nine to one or lower) to satisfy due process. There are exceptions, such as when the defendant's actions were particularly egregious but resulted in only a small amount of actual damages, or when there is a huge amount of actual damages. In these instances, punitive damages should be the same amount as actual damages. Although the court can consider the defendant's wealth in computing the award, the punitive damages must be reasonable and proportionate to the plaintiff's harm. Here, the ratio was 145:1 ($145 million punitive to $1 million compensatory). Furthermore, the $1 million award was for emotional distress, which, the Court reasoned, already contained a punitive award. Last, under the third guidepost, exploring comparable sanctions in other cases, the Court noted that the civil sanctions for fraud are only $10,000.

The Court recently had the opportunity to revisit the uncertainty caused in *State Farm* regarding the second guidepost in *Philip Morris USA v. Williams* (2007). It declined to address the ratio issue, but chose to address the first guidepost and limit further what harms the parties or a court may consider when calculating punitive damages. Whereas *BMW* and *State Farm* limited the harms that a court can consider to in-state harms, *Williams* further limited it to the harms caused only to parties before the court.

In *Williams*, the plaintiff's deceased spouse, Jesse Williams, smoked three packs of cigarettes a day for forty-seven years. During much of this time, Philip Morris ran a campaign touting the health benefits of smoking. Williams's estate was awarded $821,000 in compensatory damages and $79 million in punitive damages, a 96:1 ratio, clearly in excess of the 9:1 ratio required by *Campbell*. The Oregon Supreme Court upheld the punitive damages award, because it Philip Morris had "engaged in a massive, continuous, near-half-century scheme to defraud the plaintiff and many others, even when [it] always had reason to suspect—and for two or more decades absolutely knew—that the scheme was damaging the health of a very large group of Oregonians—the smoking public—and was killing a number of that group." It rejected Philip Morris's contention that the trial court had erred in refusing to instruct the jury that it could not punish the company for injury to persons not before the court. Philip Morris appealed to the Supreme Court.

The Court held that a jury may not punish a defendant for the harm caused to other, nonnamed parties. The defendant is not able to defend himself against others who are not a party to the lawsuit (i.e., by showing that the person knew that smoking was dangerous). Furthermore, there are fundamental due process concerns—arbitrariness, uncertainty, and lack of notice. Harm to others can be considered to show the reprehensibility of the defendant's conduct (i.e., that the conduct, which harmed the plaintiff, also posed a substantial risk of harm to the public), but it cannot be a direct basis for punishment. Thus, the Court invalidated the punitive damage award, based on a violation of procedural (not substantive) due process.

Justice Stevens dissented, reasoning that harm to others should be considered to address the reprehensibility of the defendant's conduct. Compensatory damages remedy the plaintiff's harm, but punitive damages can be used to sanction the defendant for public harm because such damages serve a different purpose: one of retribution and deterrence. Further, in this case the money was payable to the state; thus, the plaintiff was not being compensated for harm caused to others. Justice Stevens, as well as Justices Ruth Bader Ginsburg, Thomas, and Scalia (dissenting), criticized the Court for resting its decision on the illusive distinction between allowing the jury to look to harm to others in determining reprehensibility but not in determining the amount of punitive damages. If four Justices of the Supreme Court cannot see the distinction, it is questionable whether a jury will be able to make that type of distinction.

Justice Thomas wrote separately to emphasize that he did not believe that the Due Process Clause placed any limits on the amount of punitive damages a state could impose. He also stressed his view that these cases were not truly procedural due process cases but disguised substantive due process cases. For

Justice Thomas, because no procedures were deemed necessary to limit a jury's determination on such matters under the common law of torts at the time of the founding, there was no limit on such damages under the Due Process Clause.

Note that the Court did not address the issue of whether the award was grossly excessive and violated substantive due process. The issue of whether the nine-to-one ratio strictly applies in cases of physical harm and death (*Philip Morris*) as opposed to economic damages (*BMW* and *State Farm*) still remains an open question.

IV. The Takings Clause

The federal government and the states have eminent domain powers: namely, the power to take property for public use. This power is limited by the Fifth Amendment, which states: "Nor shall private property be taken for public use, without just compensation." This constitutional provision provides the most important protection of property rights. It requires both that the taking be for a public use, and that the government provide just compensation to the person deprived of her or his property. There are two types of takings, possessory takings and regulatory takings. A treatment of issues surrounding what constitutes public use and how to determine just compensation follows.

A. "Takings" Defined

1. Possessory/Physical Takings

A possessory taking occurs when the government physically takes or occupies the property in question. For example, in *Loretto v. Teleprompter Manhattan CATV Corp.* (1982), a New York law required landlords to allow a cable company to install equipment on the roof and the side of buildings. It provided the landlords with nominal compensation (only $1) and prohibited them from demanding more money from either the cable company or the tenant. The Court stated that whether there is a taking turns on "the character of the government action." It held that the cable installation on the landlord's building was a taking. The rule is that any permanent physical occupation is a taking, regardless of how much it benefits the public or how little it impacts the property owner. The Court relied on two earlier cases where it found possessory takings: a case involving the construction of a dam that permanently flooded an owner's property, and a case involving frequent flights directly over an owner's property. These instances had only minor physical impacts on the property, but the extent of the occupation reaches the issue of compensation, not the issue of whether a taking occurred. Thus, a permanent physical taking is a taking, regardless of other factors. This is contrasted with temporary takings, in which the government's interest is balanced with the individual's interest.

Justices Harry Blackmun, William Brennan, and Byron White disagreed with this distinction in their dissent. They reasoned that the Court should have flexibility and that the balancing test should apply to both permanent and temporary takings. The dissent argued further that this was not a possessory taking but a regulation well within the state's power to regulate the landlord-tenant relationship.

2. *Regulatory Takings*

Regulatory takings differ from physical takings. With regulatory takings, the government is not physically occupying the property; instead, a taking occurs due to a government regulation that interferes with the citizen's use of the property. There are five major concepts discussed in this section:

1. development of the law, in which the Court initially rejected a common law nuisance and property law exception;
2. the *Penn Central* balancing test, used to determine if a regulation is a taking;
3. total regulatory takings that leave "no economically viable use of the property";
4. conditions on the development of property; and
5. further development of the law where the Court held that an owner can bring a takings challenge, even if the regulation was in place before the property was acquired.

a. Development of the Law

In *Pennsylvania Coal Co. v. Mahon* (1922), the Mahons owned the surface rights of their property, built a home, and wanted to prevent Pennsylvania Coal from mining under it. However, Pennsylvania Coal owned the land underneath the Mahons' property, and the contract stated that the buyers of the surface rights to the property accepted the risk and waived any claim for damages that might result from mining. The state of Pennsylvania passed the Kohler Act, which forbade mining if it would cause damage to a structure. In a decision by Justice Holmes, the Court held that the Kohler Act was a taking because it terminated Pennsylvania Coal's interest in the land and its contract with the Mahons. The Court rejected the state's claim that the mining was a nuisance and that the Kohler Act protected public safety. The Kohler Act was not a valid exercise of police power, even to prevent mining under Pennsylvania streets or cities. If the state chose to enter into a contract for surface rights only, to forbid the coal company from mining the land underneath, it must pay compensation. Here, the state was taking property (the land underneath) from the coal company and giving it to the individuals who owned the surface rights. Thus, society should bear the expense, not the coal companies. This was not a nuisance to society generally; it was only a nuisance to those who contracted away the right to the land underneath the surface.

Dissenting, Justice Louis Brandeis argued that it was a nuisance. Although the parties had a right to enter contracts, there is no absolute right of persons to how they use their property; a property owner cannot create a public nuisance or threaten the public safety. It is within the state's police power to protect health and safety by prohibiting such uses, without paying compensation. Note that Justice Brandeis's dissent is the law today. A person cannot contract away a nuisance or a threat to public safety.

Six years later, the case of *Miller v. Schoene* (1928) involved the Cedar Rust Act, which mandated that cedar trees infected with disease must be cut down if they were located within two miles of an apple orchard. Justice Stone, writing for the Court, held that the Act was not a taking. The state faced the unavoidable choice of destroying some property (the cedar trees), to save other property (the apple orchard). The Act did not shift the costs of the orchard owners to the owners of the cedar trees; instead, it preserved the apple-growing industry, which was vital to the local economy. Furthermore, the cedar tree owners would receive the value of the lumber. This public policy choice was reasonable, and there was no taking or denial of due process.

b. *Penn Central* Balancing Test

Half a century later, the Court developed a three-prong balancing test to determine if a regulation is a taking in *Penn Central Transportation Co. v. New York City* (1978):

1. the economic impact of the regulation on the property owner,
2. the extent of the interference with the property owner's investment-backed expectations, and
3. the character of the government action.

In *Penn Central*, Penn Central wanted to add fifty stories atop Grand Central Terminal, but the application was denied because the terminal had been designated as a historic building based on New York City's Landmarks Preservation Law. The Court denied Penn Central's claim that the application denial was a taking. Here, the economic impact was only a decrease in property value. There was no interference with investment-backed expectations because the terminal could still be used in its present condition. Although the fifty-story addition application was denied, a smaller addition might be approved. Furthermore, the building was designated as a historic landmark before Penn Central tried to build the addition; thus, the company had no investment-backed expectations. Last, the character of the government action was not a complete taking; the "focus is on the parcel as a whole," not the fifty-story addition. The state had a legitimate purpose to preserve historic, architectural, and cultural landmarks and to enhance the quality of life. The Preservation Law restricted certain parcels of land, and this was an appropriate means to carry out the state's purpose. Thus, land use regulations and zoning are permissible regulations, not takings, even though they may prohibit the most beneficial use of the property.

c. Total Regulatory Takings

In *Lucas v. South Carolina Coastal Council* (1992), the Court found that a regulation may constitute a total regulatory taking. David Lucas purchased two residential lots; two years later, South Carolina passed a law that prohibited building homes along certain areas of beachfront. The lower court held that Lucas's property was "valueless." Justice Scalia wrote the Court's opinion, stating that a taking occurs when a regulation "denies an owner economically viable use of his land." In a footnote, the Court explained that if the diminution in value is less than 100 percent, then the three-prong balancing test from *Penn Central* applies. However, as long as the owner is required to "leave his property economically idle" for the benefit of "the common good," then this is a taking to which just compensation is required. Further, even if there is no economically viable use of the property, it is not a taking if the state shows that:

1. common law principles of nuisance or property law prohibit the owner from using the property (Justice Brandeis's dissent from *Pennsylvania Coal*), or
2. the use of the land was not allowed by state law at the time it was purchased (later overturned by the Court in *Palazzolo v. Rhode Island*, 2001, discussed later).

d. Conditions on the Development of Property

For the government to impose conditions on the development of property, it must show that:

1. the condition is rationally related to the government's purpose for the regulation, and
2. the burden imposed by the condition is roughly proportionate to the government's justification for the regulation (i.e., proportionate to the benefits gained by the condition)

If the condition is not rationally related and proportionate, then it is a taking.

In *Dolan v. City of Tigard* (1994), the city approved a permit for Florence Dolan to build an addition to her plumbing supply store, based on the condition that she dedicate 10 percent of this property to a storm drainage system and a pedestrian pathway. This condition was based on the state of Oregon's comprehensive land use program. Chief Justice William Rehnquist wrote for the Court, and noted that this was not simply a zoning ordinance that regulated entire areas of the city, nor was it a limitation on the use of property. Instead, Dolan was required to actually deed portions of her land to the city. Yet the Court found that the permit condition was rationally related to a legitimate government interest. The purpose was to prevent flooding with the storm drainage system and to build a walkway to reduce traffic congestion. The condition was rationally related to this interest because Dolan wanted to double the size of her building and pave an area for parking, which would necessarily increase storm water runoff. The Court remanded the case to determine if the burden created by the permit condition was roughly proportionate to the government's justification for the regulation.

Justices Stevens, Blackmun, and Ginsburg dissented, arguing that the test was too strict and that the Court should defer to the city. The public interest in avoiding floods, earthquakes, traffic, and harm to the environment outweighs any private interests. If development conditions are rationally related to fulfilling the goals of a comprehensive land use plan, then there should be a strong presumption of validity in favor of the regulation.

e. Further Development of the Law

In *Palazzolo v. Rhode Island* (2001), the Court addressed whether a property owner can challenge regulations that existed before he owned the property. Anthony Palazzolo, the sole owner of a corporation, purchased a salt marsh that flooded. He attempted to fill the land three times between 1959 and 1966. In 1979, Rhode Island passed a wetlands regulation that declared salt marshes to be protected wetlands. Palazzolo's corporation dissolved, and title of the property transferred to him. Then, in 1983, he tried to develop the property again. Thus, the issue was whether he could bring a Takings Clause challenge to the regulation, when he did not own the land (the company did) at the time the regulation was enacted. Rhode Island argued that the corporation should have challenged the taking, not Palazzolo. Justice Anthony Kennedy wrote the majority opinion, and the Court held that the state cannot "put an expiration date on the Takings Clause." Neither the passage of time nor title makes a taking constitutional.

Thus, a property owner can bring a claim, even if the regulation was in place before the property was acquired. However, Rhode Island further argued that the uplands portion of the land could still be improved and had a $200,000 value. The Court agreed with this argument, holding that Palazzolo was not deprived of all economically beneficial use. Palazzolo could still build on an eighteen-acre parcel. The regulation did not create a total deprivation of property and, thus, there was no taking.

Palazzolo does not necessarily undermine *Lucas* (after Lucas purchased the beachfront property and South Carolina passed a statute that made his property "valueless"). In *Lucas*, the Court held that a person *cannot* bring a takings claim if common law rules of nuisance and property law govern and were in place before the property was acquired. Yet in *Palazzolo*, the Court held that a person *can* bring a claim, even though regulations or statutes existed before the property was acquired. One could argue that this is simply a distinction between the common law and current statutes. The Court avoided deciding the issue of when legislation "can be deemed a background principle of state law." It held only that the passage of title does not make a taking suddenly constitutional.

In *Tahoe Sierra Preservation Council, Inc. v. Tahoe Regional Planning Agency* (2002), the Court addressed whether the temporary denial of development of property is a taking. Tahoe Regional Planning Agency imposed a thirty-two-month moratorium on land use to study the impact of development on Lake Tahoe's well-known pristine water. The plaintiffs had purchased property before the moratorium, but since they were prevented from building on their land, they sought compensation for the value of thirty-two months of use. The plaintiffs argued that *Lucas* applied because this was a complete regulatory taking and the *Penn Central* balancing test did not apply. In a majority opinion written by Justice Stevens, the Court applied *Penn Central* and added another factor to the test — the duration of the restriction. Examining the economic impact and the investment-backed expectations of the plaintiffs, the Court reasoned that the plaintiffs still had economic use of the property. The property would recover its value when the prohibition is lifted; because the moratorium helped ensure that the area will remain pristine, then property values were likely to increase in spite of the moratorium. Further, the ban was only temporary, and there was less of a risk that individuals were being singled out; instead, it was protecting the interests of all landowners. The Court also examined the type of government conduct and found that this was a regional plan, not a permit for a single parcel. The costs to agencies trying to make informed decisions should be taken into consideration. Last, considering the duration of the restriction, the Court noted that although a ban for longer than a year was questionable, the district court had found that thirty-two months was not an unreasonable amount of time. Therefore, the Court held that the moratorium was not a taking.

The dissent, made up of Justices Rehnquist, Scalia, and Thomas, believed that this was a taking. The plaintiffs were forced to leave their property economically idle. There should not be a distinction between a permanent and a temporary ban. Because this was a total deprivation of use of the property, it constituted a physical taking. The dissent criticized the majority's concern that permits and zoning changes would be considered a taking. Background principles of property law prevent delays from being a taking (but not moratoriums), and delays are part of a property owner's reasonable investment-backed expectations. The Justices agreed that Lake Tahoe needed to be protected, but they believed that the cost should be borne by society. A few landowners should not be selected to suffer losses so that everyone could receive the benefit of pristine land.

B. Public Use

The rule is that the government can use the Takings Clause to acquire property from a private owner for the good of the public as a whole, as long as it compensates the owner. A common example of the government using its eminent domain powers for the public's benefit is when the government expands a two-lane road into a four-lane road and purchases land from the owners of the houses that line the road. However, if private property is taken from private owners for private use, then the government is required to return the property because it lacks the public use requirement. Further, for the government to take private property for the benefit of another private party, it must have a public purpose to justify it, regardless of whether the owner is paid. The Takings Clause was enacted to address the Framers' concern that the government would use eminent domain to play Robin Hood and take property from rich private owners and give it to poor individuals. Yet the Supreme Court has undermined this notion by broadly defining "public use" and applying the lowest standard to takings cases, the rational basis test. Thus, the government can take private property if it is rationally related to any conceivable public purpose.

A good illustration of the government playing Robin Hood is *Hawaii Housing Authority v. Midkiff* (1984). In Hawaii, a few individuals owned over 50 percent of the land. This monopoly skewed the market, inflated the prices of land and housing, and harmed the public welfare. To address this, Hawaii enacted the Land Reform Act, which required large landowners to sell the lands they were leasing to others. The government condemned the property to save the original property owners taxes, gave the property owners just compensation, and then sold the property to the individuals leasing the land. Justice Sandra Day O'Connor, writing for the Court, held that the Land Reform Act was constitutional. It did not violate the Public Use Clause of the Fifth Amendment (which applies to the states via the Fourteenth Amendment). The Court instead laid out the test for "public use": If eminent domain is rationally related to a conceivable public purpose, then the exercise of eminent domain is not prevented by the Public Use Clause.

In 2005, the Court expansively defined "public use" as "public purpose" in the controversial case of *Kelo v. City of New London* (2005). In *Kelo*, the city of New London, Connecticut, created a comprehensive development plan to revitalize the city. It planned to create a state park and allow Pfizer, a pharmaceutical company, to build a $300 million research facility near the park. The city purchased property from the majority of affected landowners, and then used its eminent domain powers to acquire property from unwilling sellers. Although the city was economically distressed, the properties sought by the government were not blighted. In a majority opinion written by Justice Stevens, the Court reasoned that defining "public use" as "use by the public" is too narrow. Instead, "public use" should be defined as "public purpose." Thus, the city could take property from one private party and give it to another, if it is for a public purpose.

The Court examined the plaintiff's claims in light of the entire plan: A state statute authorized eminent domain for economic development, there was a comprehensive plan, it was thoroughly deliberated, and the Court had a limited scope of review of the plan. Furthermore, promoting economic development is a traditional function of the government. The Court expressly noted that the states themselves could enact more restrictions on eminent domain. The majority's opinion led to many state constitutional amendments to limit the use of the Takings Clause for economic development.

Justice Kennedy concurred in the Court's opinion. He agreed that rational basis is the proper test, but he reasoned that if the government's motives showed that the taking was intended to favor a private party, then the Court should strike it down as unconstitutional.

Justice O'Connor, who wrote the majority opinion in *Midkiff*, wrote the principal dissent in *Kelo*, joined by the Chief Justice and Justices Scalia and Thomas. Justice O'Connor objected to this type of "reverse Robin Hood taking" where property was taken from the poor and given to the rich. She worried that this type of precedent would set a new norm where those "with disproportionate influence and power in the political process, including large corporations and development firms" would reap the benefits of takings. In her opinion, the decision eliminates "any distinction between private and public use of property—and thereby effectively delete[s] the words 'for public use' from the Takings Clause of the Fifth Amendment."

Justice Thomas wrote separately in dissent to emphasize the originalist point that the Framers intended the words "Public Use" to mean public use and not "public purpose." The further extension of "public purpose" to include "any economically beneficial goal" completely undermines the public use requirement. It ensures that poor communities, which are "less likely to put their lands to the highest and best social use" and are "the least politically powerful," will see their property taken and given to developers.

C. Just Compensation

The amount of compensation due to a property owner is measured by the loss to the owner, not the gain to the taker. The owner's loss is the market value at the time of the taking. Even though the market value may increase after the taking because of the government's plan for the property, the property owner does not receive this market value increase. This is illustrated by *Brown v. Legal Foundation of Washington* (2003).

In *Brown*, the state of Washington adopted a law establishing Interest On Lawyers Trust Accounts (IOLTA) programs to pay for legal services for the poor. Attorneys were required to deposit all client funds in interest-bearing trust accounts. If funds would not earn a net interest for the client (because the account fees cost more than the amount of interest that could be made), then the account fees had to be deposited in an IOLTA. The clients in this case sought to recover the interest that accrued from their funds. The Court considered two issues: (1) whether this constituted a taking, and (2) whether it violated the Just Compensation Clause of the Fifth Amendment. The Court relied on precedent, which established that interest from the IOLTA is the property of the owner of the funds. Thus, it held that the IOLTA program was a taking because the law required that the interest payments be transferred to legal aid organizations.

Yet the Court also held that the IOLTA program did not violate the Just Compensation Clause. It stated that the Fifth Amendment does not prohibit takings; it only prohibits takings without just compensation. Furthermore, compensation must be measured by the owner's net loss, not the value of the public's gain. Here, the owner's loss after bank fees in a non-IOLTA account would be zero. The clients would not earn any interest on their funds without being joined with other funds in the IOLTA, which was created by the government program. Thus, the clients did not lose anything by not receiving the interest. This was a taking, but the owners were not due any compensation for it.

Justices Scalia, Rehnquist, Kennedy, and Thomas disagreed. In their dissent, they argued that the plaintiff's funds created the interest in the account. Without the funds, there would not be any interest; thus, the interest belongs to the plaintiffs. The Justices in dissent here likened this to a Robin Hood taking — the government was taking from the rich and giving it to indigent defendants. Here, there was no difference between the value that the plaintiffs lost and the value that the government gained.

V. The Contracts Clause

A. Introduction

Article I, Section 10, the Contracts Clause, reads: "No *State* shall ... pass any ... Law impairing the Obligation of Contracts" (emphasis added). The Clause regulates only existing contracts, not future contracts. Primarily used in the nineteenth century, the purpose of the Contracts Clause was to prevent states from adopting laws during an economic depression or recession to help debtors at the expense of creditors, which would discourage the creditors from extending credit. This provision applies only to a state or local law, not federal legislation. Furthermore, if a state passes a law regulating future contracts, it must be challenged under the Due Process Clause of the Fourteenth Amendment. Thus, in the *Lochner* era, the Supreme Court protected freedom of contract under "liberty" because it was broader: It covered existing and future contracts, and it applied to state, local and federal laws.

From 1934 to the present, the Contracts Clause is used when states interfere with private or public contracts. The tests are similar to rational basis and intermediate scrutiny tests, although in each case the test is stricter than the traditional test. In other words, the test for interference with private contracts is stricter than rational basis, but not as strict as traditional intermediate scrutiny. Likewise, the test for interference with public contracts is stricter than the traditional intermediate scrutiny test, but not as strict as the strict scrutiny test. An early example of interference with private contracts is *Home Building & Loan Association v. Blaisdell* (1934). In that case, a state law prevented mortgage holders from foreclosing on mortgages for two years. The Court upheld the law as not violating the Contracts Clause because the state had a legitimate goal, to use its police powers to temporarily protect homeowners during a catastrophe declared by legislature (the Great Depression). The legislation was reasonably related to the emergency at hand because it imposed reasonable conditions on the mortgages: Interest still accrued on the loans, the lenders could still foreclose after the two-year period ended, and the borrower had to pay rent during the two-year period. Thus, this was only a temporary interference with a contract, in response to an emergency, and not a violation of the Contracts Clause.

B. Government Interference with Public Contracts

When a state or local government interferes with a public contract—one in which the government is a party to the contract—the Court will use heightened scrutiny to examine the regulation to ensure that the state is not regulating simply to protect its own self-interest. The Court applies a three-part test, and considers:

1. the legitimate expectations of the parties to the contract,
2. whether there is an important public purpose, and
3. whether the interference is reasonable and necessary (both essential and the least restrictive means) to achieve that purpose.

In *United States Trust Co. v. New Jersey* (1977), New York and New Jersey had passed covenants agreeing to issue bonds for tunnels and prohibit the revenues from the tunnel tolls from being used for railroad passenger service. This assured investors in the Port Authority (the bondholders) that they would recover their funds and that toll revenues would not be converted to public transportation. However, due to an energy crisis, the states repealed the covenant and converted the toll revenue to improve rail transit. The Supreme Court applied a three-part test, which is similar to intermediate scrutiny. The first prong examines the legitimate expectations of the parties to the contract. The policy is that parties should not be able to enter a contract to be immune from state regulations. It is unreasonable for state law to remain static. However, in this instance, the repeal of the covenant seriously disrupted the expectations of the bondholders.

With respect to the second prong, an important public purpose, the Court held that the states' desire to protect the environment, conserve energy, and provide mass transportation was important. However, the repeal of the covenant failed the third prong. The state law must be reasonable and necessary to achieve the government's purpose. Further, for the law to be necessary, it must be essential and the least restrictive means available to achieve the purpose. The states claimed that it was reasonable to encourage travelers to use public transportation, and it was necessary to repeal the covenant because if mass transit did not receive the toll revenues, then it would be left with a deficit. However, the Court reasoned that total repeal of the covenant was not necessary and that the states had other means to achieve their goals. At the time the states adopted the covenant, they knew that mass transportation would be needed and that the railroad service would operate at a deficit, which was the reason for the contractual provision in the first place. Thus, there were no changed or emergency circumstances, and the Contracts Clause prohibited the states from repealing the covenant.

C. Government Interference with Private Contracts

When a state or local government interferes with a private contract — one in which the government is not a party — a three-part test, similar to the rational basis test, applies:

1. the plaintiff must show a *substantial* impairment of a contractual relationship,
2. the government must show a *significant and legitimate public purpose* for the interference, and
3. the means to carry out that purpose must be *reasonably related* to that goal.

Allied Structural Steel Co. v. Spannaus (1978) was the first case to address such interference since 1934, in which the Supreme Court found that a state law interfering with a private contract was unconstitutional. In that instance, Allied offered its employees a pension plan; according to the plan's terms, an employee's rights would be vested after fifteen years of service with the company. The state of Minnesota passed a law that changed the vesting period to ten years and imposed a fee if any company ended a pension plan or closed an office and was unable to pay the pensions. The purpose of the regulation was to prevent a company from opening an office within the state and then moving to another state just before the employees' rights were vested. Allied decided to close its office in Minnesota. Employees who had worked for the company for ten years did not have vested pension rights under the company's plan. The state charged Allied a fee of $185,000, and Allied sued for an injunction against the fee and law. The Court held that the Minnesota law violated the Contracts Clause because it interfered with the contract between Allied and its employees. First, there was a substantial impairment of the contract. This was an area that the state had never regulated before. Allied had calculated its contributions based on its pension plan, and it had no reason to expect that employees' pensions would be vested within fifteen years. Its contributions to the plan, which were sufficient when the company made them, suddenly became inadequate because of the state law. Most important, the regulation did not apply to every employer; it applied to those who had voluntarily set up pension plans for employees. If Allied had decided not to offer a pension plan, it could have left the state at any time without penalty.

Another case, *Energy Reserves Group v. Kansas Power & Light* (1983), demonstrates all three prongs of the private contract test. In that instance, a state law mandated that if the price of natural gas set by federal authorities increased, then the contract price could not increase. Thus, the statute overrode contractual provisions and prevented the sellers of natural gas from charging higher prices. Applying the three-part test, the Court upheld the statute. Examining the first prong, the Court noted that this involved a heavily regulated industry, and the parties knew that their contract was subject to price regulations by the state. Thus, interference with the contract was foreseeable, and the state law did not harm the parties' reasonable expectations of the contract. Furthermore, the Court held that the State had a legitimate public purpose — to set a price ceiling that would protect consumers from increasing prices caused by deregulation. Here, the statute was reasonably related to carrying out that purpose.

Checkpoints

- **Economic Liberties**

- Since 1937 and the end of the *Lochner* era, the Court has not found a state or federal economic regulation unconstitutional as violating the freedom of contract, protected by the liberty provision of the Due Process Clauses in the Fifth and Fourteenth Amendments.

- Today, when the state or federal government imposes economic regulations, there is a presumption of constitutionality.

- The Court will defer to the legislature with respect to economic liberties if there is any rational basis for the legislation.

- The Court will only second-guess Congress for certain things:

  1. if the legislation limits enumerated rights (such as liberty, unreasonable searches and seizures, or freedom of expression);

  2. if the legislation that limits the political process receives higher scrutiny (restricting the right to vote, limiting the dissemination of information, or prohibiting peaceful assembly); or

  3. if the legislation that prejudices against discrete and insular minorities (protected classes such as racial minorities or religious groups) that curtails the political process ordinarily relied on to protect minorities also receives higher scrutiny.

- **Punitive Damages Awards**

- The Court will invalidate large punitive damage awards as violating the Due Process Clause, and it will declare the government action (the state court's judgment) unconstitutional as an unreasonable deprivation of property.

Checkpoints *continued*

- There are three factors to determine adequate notice (procedural due process) and reasonableness (substantive due process) of a punitive damages award:

    1. Degree of reprehensibility — Courts consider the following factors:

        - the type of harm — economic or physical,

        - *mens rea* — intent or reckless disregard for others,

        - whether the target of the conduct was financially vulnerable,

        - repeated actions or isolated incident (if the conduct is similar), and

        - harm to others (but this is not a direct factor in determining the amount).

    2. Ratio of the plaintiff's actual harm suffered to the punitive damage award:

        - ratio between punitive damages and actual harm must be nine to one or less,

        - punitive damages award must be reasonably related to compensatory damages (harm likely to result from the defendant's conduct and the harm that actually occurred),

        - compensatory damages redress the loss that the plaintiff suffered,

        - punitive damages are used to punish and deter the defendant, and

        - consider the defendant's wealth.

    3. Comparable sanctions or remedies in other cases:

        - note that criminal penalties have more protections and a higher standard of proof, and

        - consider other civil sanctions and how other states punish similar conduct.

- The courts cannot use punitive damages to change a company's nationwide policy; this infringes on other states' policies (*BMW v. Gore*)

- **The Takings Clause of the Fifth Amendment**

- A taking can be a possessory/physical taking or a regulatory taking.

    1. Possessory taking:

        - permanent physical occupation of the property (*Loretto*).

        - temporary taking (*Lake Tahoe*).

            - Apply the *Penn Central* balancing test.

    2. Regulatory taking:

        - Total regulatory taking (*Lucas*, valueless beachfront property).

            - Justice Brandeis's trump card: common law principles of nuisance and property law (even if there is no economic use of the property left).

Checkpoints *continued*

- Note that, with respect to property law, an owner can challenge regulations that existed before he owned the property (*Palazzolo*).
- *Penn Central* balancing test used to determine if a regulation is a taking:
  - the extent of the regulation's economic impact;
  - the extent of interference with investment-backed expectations of the property owner; and
  - the type of government conduct, considering the parcel as a whole.
- Conditions on development (*Dolan*).

  The government must show that:
  - the condition is rationally related to the government's purpose for regulating; and
  - the burden created by the condition is roughly proportionate to the government's purpose
  - Public Use: Today, "public use" means "public purpose," and the Court applies rational basis (*Kelo*).
  - Just Compensation: "Just compensation" is measured by the loss to the private property owner, based on the market value at the time of the taking (*Brown*, IOLTA accounts).

- **The Contracts Clause**
- It prohibits state governments from interfering with existing contracts of private and public entities.
- It does not apply to the federal government, nor does it apply to future contracts.
- The Court has used the Contracts Clause only twice since 1937 to invalidate a state law.
- Today, it applies when:
  1. The state interferes with existing private contracts (the government is not a party) (*Allied*).

     The test in these cases is a three-part test that includes:
     - the showing of a *substantial impairment* of a contractual relationship (the plaintiff's burden of proof)
       - This is a threshold question.
       - If interference is *de minimus*, then the state does not have to justify its actions.
       - Consider whether the industry is regulated (parties cannot avoid government regulations by entering a contract).
       - Sudden and unanticipated change.

Checkpoints *continued*

- The severity of the penalties.
- Whether it applies retroactively.
- Whether it applies to other, similarly situated parties.
- the showing of a *significant and legitimate public purpose* (the state's burden of proof)
  - The interference must remedy a general problem, not special interests.
  - The interference does not have to be temporary or to resolve an emergency.
- a showing that the impairment is reasonably related to the state's public purpose
  - Conditions must be reasonable and related to the public purpose.

2. The state interferes with a public contract (*U.S. Trust Co.*).
- legitimate expectations of the parties to the contract;
- important public purpose;
- reasonable; and
- necessary (essential and the least restrictive means) to serve the state purpose.

Chapter 7

Due Process

Roadmap

- Foundational concepts: The Constitution protects a person's life, liberty, and property from government interference without due process of law.
  - The Constitutional clauses
    - The Privileges and Immunities Clause, Article IV, § 2
    - The Due Process Clauses, Amendment V and Amendment XIV, § 1
    - The Privileges or Immunities Clause, Amendment XIV, § 1
    - The Equal Protection Clause, Amendment XIV, § 1
  - The Bill of Rights and its applicability to the federal government and the states
  - The differences between substantive due process and procedural due process
- Substantive due process
  - The battle over economic substantive due process
  - The Court accepts noneconomic substantive due process
  - The right of privacy
    - Early precedents
    - The question of abortion: *Roe v. Wade* (1973), *Planned Parenthood v. Casey* (1992), *Stenberg v. Carhart* (2000), and *Gonzales v. Carhart* (2007)
    - Nonabortion privacy cases
      - Family living arrangements
      - The right to marry
      - The right to raise one's children (parental rights)
      - Sexual orientation
      - The right to die and to refuse medical care
      - The right to protect personal information
- Procedural due process: the steps the government must take before infringing a protected right
  - Proper and timely notice
  - Opportunity to be heard at a hearing

> • The balancing test the court uses to decide the specifics of the procedures.

I. The Foundational Concepts of Due Process

The Supreme Court has found that the U.S. Constitution protects many rights of individuals that are not enumerated in the Constitution through the concept of "due process," but what exactly is due process? The concept of due process is generally understood to encompass two different components: substantive due process and procedural due process. Substantive due process essentially requires the government to have a sufficiently strong interest before it can infringe a person's life, liberty, or property. Procedural due process requires the government to follow certain procedures when it deprives someone of life, liberty, or property. This dual conception of due process is not contained within the text of the Constitution. Rather, it arose through the Court's interpretation of the Constitutional provisions, which provide the underpinnings for these protections of individuals' rights. One must understand that due process is a tool by which the courts protect the rights of individuals; it is not an end unto itself.

First, this chapter explores the constitutional provisions that provide the underpinnings of due process analysis. Second, it examines the doctrine by which many of the provisions of the Bill of Rights, initially intended only to apply to the federal government, are applied to the states. Third, the chapter covers the difference between substantive due process and procedural due process. Fourth, it covers substantive due process and how that category is subdivided further into economic substantive due process, which the Court has rejected, and noneconomic substantive due process, which the Court has embraced. Finally, the chapter concludes by examining procedural due process and what requirements it places on the government to ensure that it protects our rights.

A. Constitutional Language Pertinent to Due Process

This section examines the provisions of the Constitution that relate to the concept of due process. First is the Privileges and Immunities Clause in the Constitution as originally passed. Next is the Due Process Clause of the Fifth Amendment, which expressly restrains the government from violating due process. Last are the three clauses in the Fourteenth Amendment applicable to due process.

The Constitution of the United States as originally passed only contains one provision that relates to the concept of due process: the Privileges and Immunities Clause in Article IV, Section 2, Clause 1. This clause provides: "The Citizens of each State shall be entitled to all Privileges and Immunities of Citizens in the several States." The Supreme Court understands this clause only to limit the ability of one state to discriminate regarding fundamental rights or important economic activities against those who are not its residents, such as travelers and companies based in another state. Note that although this may appear to be similar to the dormant (or negative) Commerce Clause, the Privileges and Immunities Clause is a distinct concept because the triggering condition is not the burden on interstate commerce but the presence of discrimination against the nonresident. Moreover, only "citizens" of the United States receive protection from the Privileges and Immunities Clause, thus aliens and companies (nonpersons) cannot invoke the clause on their behalf.

The main protector of due process, at least at the federal level, became part of the Constitution in the Bill of Rights. The Fifth Amendment provides that no person shall "be deprived of life, liberty, or property, without due process of law." This Amendment provides the basic requirement that the government may not violate our individual rights without complying with due process. The Fifth Amendment was ratified in 1791 and has been a part of the Constitution since shortly after the United States was formed. Notice that the Fifth Amendment does not define what due process is or how the government must comply with the requirement; it just states the requirement that the government must provide due process before it can interfere with our rights to life, liberty, and property. Moreover, this limitation only applied to the federal government because the original understanding of the Bill of Rights was that it only restricted federal action and had no application to the states. This limitation on the reach of the Fifth Amendment was remedied by the ratification of the Fourteenth Amendment in 1868.

The Fourteenth Amendment was one of the three amendments passed after the Civil War. Collectively, the three amendments are called the Civil Rights amendments. The portions of the Fourteenth Amendment pertinent to due process are contained in Section 1 of the Amendment. They read:

> No State shall make or enforce any law which shall abridge the privileges or immunities of citizens of the United States; nor shall any State deprive any person of life, liberty, or property, without due process of law; nor deny to any person within its jurisdiction the equal protection of the laws.

The first of these clauses, called the Privileges or Immunities Clause, appears to mirror the Privileges and Immunities Clause in Article IV of the Constitution. The second clause, called the Due Process Clause of the Fourteenth Amendment, expressly mimics the Fifth Amendment and applies its restrictions to the states. The third clause, the Equal Protection Clause, requires each state's laws to protect all people "within its jurisdiction" equally. Together, these three clauses form the basis of most civil rights cases and legislation, though the Privileges or Immunities Clause less so. These clauses provide the basis for the doctrine of incorporation making portions of the Bill of Rights apply against the states.

B. The Bill of Rights and its Application to Restrain the States

The Bill of Rights consists of the first ten amendments to the Constitution, which, before the ratification of the Fourteenth Amendment, were held to be inapplicable to the states. These amendments were largely proposed and ratified in an attempt to appease Anti-Federalist opposition to the ratification of the Constitution. The chief complaint of the Anti-Federalists was that the Constitution created a national government, not a federal government, and the convention that created the document had exceeded the mandate on which it was formed, namely, to amend the Articles of Confederation to correct deficiencies in the United States as it was then constituted. The Anti-Federalists saw the new nation as having too much power, which would lead to the destruction of state sovereignty, and too much national control over the citizens of the states. Thus, many states that ratified the Constitution did so only on the understanding that it would be amended to include a bill of rights to protect the rights of the people against encroachment by the new government.

Because of this origin, the Court originally held that the Bill of Rights did not restrain the power of state and local governments. It made this clear in *Barron v. Mayor & City Council of Baltimore* (1833) by holding that the Bill of Rights only restricted federal power, not state and local power. However, the early American experience with slavery served to illustrate that the state governments were just as apt to trample on basic human rights as the new federal government. After the conclusion of the Civil War, the United States permitted the Southern states that had seceded to rejoin the Union on the condition that they ratify the Fourteenth Amendment. The Fourteenth Amendment received the required ratifications in 1868, but the question of incorporation began earlier, in 1866 when Congress was debating the Amendment. The question came to a head first in *The Slaughter-House Cases* (1873).

1. Rejection of Early Attempts at Incorporation

The Slaughter-House Cases represented the first attempt to incorporate the Bill of Rights against the states, and it used the Privileges or Immunities Clause of the Fourteenth Amendment. In *Slaughter-House*, Louisiana had granted a monopoly in the slaughterhouse business for New Orleans to one company and required that the company permit anyone to slaughter their animals in the company's slaughterhouse for a set price. Several butchers sued the state, alleging that the monopoly impermissibly interfered with their ability to practice their trade. Specifically, they invoked the Thirteenth Amendment's prohibition on involuntary servitude, and all of the three provisions of the Fourteenth Amendment just discussed. The argument was that the protections of the Bill of Rights, especially the Fifth Amendment, should be considered to be privileges and immunities to which the citizens of the states are entitled, and thus, the Fourteenth Amendment's Privileges or Immunities Clause should prevent the states from abridging them. The Court rejected their contentions, narrowly construing all of the cited provisions as being directed only at protecting the rights of the former slaves. The Court expressly reserved the privileges and immunities of state citizenship to the states to administer and refused to "place [them] under the special care of the federal government." Thus, the Court refused the invitation to read the Fourteenth Amendment broadly and apply the Bill of Rights against the states.

In the twentieth century, the Court overruled the *Slaughter-House* Court's narrow construction of the Due Process and Equal Protection Clauses of the Fourteenth Amendment. However, the *Slaughter-House* Court's extremely narrow construction of the Privileges or Immunities Clause of the Fourteenth Amendment has, with one notable exception, been rendered a dead letter by the Court's decision. That exception is the protection of the right to travel by the Court's decision in *Saenz v. Roe* (1999), where it revived the Privileges or Immunities Clause to protect the right to travel between states without the destination state placing an undue burden such as treating new residents differently than established residents. The right to travel and *Saenz v. Roe* are covered in depth in the section on fundamental rights.

The *Slaughter-House* Court's extremely narrow construction of the Privileges or Immunities Clause led the Court to seek an alternative method of applying the Bill of Rights to limit state authority. The Court's alternative method was to use the Fourteenth Amendment's Due Process Clause. This time, the argument was that the provisions of the Bill of Rights protected individual liberties, and those liberties are so fundamental that the states should be proscribed from depriving its citizens of those rights. Moreover, the Equal Protection Clause would prevent states from protecting these rights for their citizens only and not extending the same protection to those temporarily in the state because the clause protected the "person" rather than the "citizen." This theory received further justification from the Court's decision in *Chicago, Burlington & Quincy Railroad Co. v. City of Chicago* (1897), where it had expressly prevented the states from taking private property without just compensation. Though it did not specifically ground its decision on the Fourteenth Amendment, this is generally regarded as the basis for the Court's decision because the Bill of Rights previously had been understood only to apply to the federal government.

2. The Development of the Incorporation Doctrine

The doctrine of incorporation began to emerge as a credible method of employing the Bill of Rights against the states in the early twentieth century. In *Twining v. New Jersey* (1908), the Court stated what the *Slaughter-House* Court refused to — that the protections of the Bill of Rights may restrain the states as well as the federal government, but if they did so it was because of their fundamental nature rather than their expression in the Bill of Rights. *Twining* involved a criminal defendant who claimed that New Jersey had violated his constitutional rights by permitting a jury to draw a negative inference from the defendant's refusal to testify at trial. The Court took a narrow view of due process and disagreed with the criminal defendant's claim, finding that by providing notice and a hearing the state had complied with due process. However, the statement that became the rule was made in Justice John Harlan's dissent: "The privileges and immunities mentioned in the [Bill of Rights were] ... secured to every citizen of the United States, and placed beyond assault by any government, Federal or state" (*Twining*, Harlan, J., dissenting). The Court continued its march toward incorporation in essence if not in name with *Gitlow v. New York* (1925), where it held that the freedom of speech was so fundamental that it was protected under the Due Process Clause of the Fourteenth Amendment.

The theory of incorporation was temporarily forestalled in *Palko v. Connecticut* (1937). *Palko* involved a criminal defendant who had been convicted of first-degree murder. After his conviction in his first trial, he appealed the conviction to the Connecticut Supreme Court of Errors, which ordered a new trial. The second trial again resulted in a conviction, and he was sentenced to death. The defendant challenged the statutory right to appeal criminal convictions on double jeopardy grounds under the Fifth Amendment. The defendant expressly claimed that the Fourteenth Amendment incorporated the entire Bill of Rights against the states, or at least that it incorporated the Fifth Amendment's proscription of double jeopardy. Justice Benjamin Cardozo, writing for the Court, rejected the total incorporation argument and reiterated the Court's position from *Twining* that if any right in the Bill of Rights also applied to the states it was only because the right was of such a fundamental nature that its violation would be contrary to the Fourteenth Amendment's Due Process Clause. However, because the Court did not view the double jeopardy protection of the Fifth Amendment as sufficiently fundamental, it rejected the defendant's claim and upheld the conviction. Thus, although the Court resisted using incorporation language, it was effectively incorporating portions of the Bill of Rights against the states.

The tide continued to turn in favor of incorporation as time passed. The Court continued its resistance to incorporation in *Adamson v. California* (1947). However, in *Adamson*, Justice Hugo Black authored a famous dissent expressing strong support for total incorporation of the Bill of Rights against the states. He explained that the line of cases beginning with *Gitlow* led the Court essentially to substitute its judgment for that of the Founders' expressed in the Bill of Rights because of an endowment of boundless power under natural law theories. Thus, he expressed the need for incorporation of the Bill of Rights to restrain the Court from trampling on legislative power of the federal and state governments.

The debate over incorporation lasted for years, involving vigorous discussion among various judges and scholars, before finally settling on the current process of selective incorporation. This process involves using the Due Process Clause of the Fourteenth Amendment, specifically that no state may deprive any person of liberty without due process of law, to hold most of the protections of the Bill of Rights as effective against the states. In *Duncan v. Louisiana* (1968), the Court expressed the test for incorporation. Under selective incorporation, a provision of the Bill of Rights is incorporated against the states if it is fundamental such that it is "a procedure necessary to an Anglo-American regime of ordered liberty." Justice Black wrote a concurrence in which he preferred total incorporation but agreed with selective incorporation as a lesser approach as long as it applied "most of the specific Bill of Rights protections" to the states. Justice Harlan wrote a dissent vigorously opposing both the Court's selective incorporation approach and Justice Black's total incorporation approach. Pointing to extensive research by one commentator, Justice Harlan explained that the original intent of the Fourteenth Amendment was not to incorporate the Bill of Rights, either in whole or in part, and that the Court should continue its "ordered liberty" analysis under which it would determine whether a procedure was fundamentally fair.

Today, the Court has largely resolved the question of incorporation by adopting the selective incorporation doctrine. However, there are still some who oppose the incorporation of certain provisions. For example, Justice Clarence Thomas urged the reconsideration of the incorporation of the Establishment Clause in *Zelman v. Simmons-Harris* (2002, Thomas, J., concurring). No other justice has agreed with Justice Thomas on that issue, which did not oppose selective incorporation, only the validity of incorporation of a certain aspect of the Bill of Rights. Therefore, the doctrine of selective incorporation appears to be well settled.

3. The Modern Understanding of the Doctrine of Selective Incorporation

The current understanding of the Bill of Rights is that certain portions of the first ten Amendments apply to restrict the power of the states by operation of the Fourteenth Amendment's Due Process Clause. However, the selective incorporation doctrine as understood today is far closer to total incorporation than the early supporters of selective incorporation would have preferred. Over time, the Court has incorporated, one by one, nearly every provision of the Bill of Rights against the states. Specifically, the Court holds that the following provisions apply to the states as well as the federal government.

- In the First Amendment: the Free Speech Clause, the Establishment and Free Exercise Clauses, and the protections afforded to the press, assembly, and the right to petition for redress of grievances.
- In the Fourth Amendment: the protection against unreasonable searches and seizures, the Warrant Clause and its probable cause requirement, as well as the judicially derived exclusionary rule that prevents admission against an accused of evidence obtained in violation of the Fourth Amendment.
- In the Fifth Amendment: the prohibition against double jeopardy, the protection from compelled self-incrimination, and the Takings Clause, which prohibits the government from taking personal property without a public use and just compensation.
- In the Sixth Amendment: the requirements of a speedy and public trial, an impartial jury, adequate notice of the charges against an accused, the Confrontation Clause requiring an accused to be able to confront the witnesses against him or her, the access to compulsory process to assist in his or her defense, and the right to counsel when facing prison.
- In the Eighth Amendment: the prohibitions against excessive bail and cruel and unusual punishment.

Though this list is quite extensive, there are several important provisions that have never been held to be incorporated and, therefore, do not restrain state power. These provisions are as follows.

- The Second Amendment: the Supreme Court has never held that the Second Amendment protects an individual right, thus it cannot apply to restrain the states.
- The Third Amendment: the protection against forced quartering of soldiers in private homes is not incorporated, largely because no case implicating it has yet reached the Court.

- The Fifth Amendment: the Court expressly excluded from application to the states the Grand Jury Clause requiring a grand jury indictment before being tried for a felony.
- The Seventh Amendment: the Court expressly excluded the right to a jury in common law civil trials from application to the states, thus states can completely eliminate civil jury trials without offending the federal Constitution.
- The Eighth Amendment: the Court has never held that the prohibition on excessive fines applies to the states.
- The Ninth and Tenth Amendments: because these do not provide specific, individual protections, they have never been incorporated against the states; additionally, the Tenth Amendment is directed solely at protecting individuals and the states from federal power, so incorporating it would be nonsensical.

Thus, although almost all provisions of the Bill of Rights are incorporated against the states, the incorporation is still technically selective. However, the Court has not adopted a single test to determine whether a provision is incorporated against the states. In *Duncan*, the Court summarized the various tests used as (1) "whether a right is among those 'fundamental principles of liberty and justice which lie at the base of all our civil and political institutions'"; (2) "whether it is 'basic in our system of jurisprudence'"; and (3) "whether it is 'a fundamental right, essential to a fair trial.'" The Court has applied each of these tests at different times to find different provisions incorporated. Regardless of the test used, the Court has found that most of the Bill of Rights is incorporated into the Due Process Clause of the Fourteenth Amendment and applies against the states.

Once a right is incorporated, the question turns to whether the incorporated right holds the states to the same standard as the federal government, or whether the Fourteenth Amendment merely applies a "watered-down, subjective version" of the right. Unfortunately, though the Court expressly rejected the watered-down, subjective version approach in *Malloy v. Hogan* (1964), it has never provided consistent direction on this crucial question. On one hand, it held in *Wallace v. Jaffree* (1985), that the states "have no greater power to restrain the individual freedoms protected by the First Amendment" than the federal government. On the other hand, the Court has held differently in the Sixth Amendment's jury requirement. In *Williams v. Florida* (1970), the Court held that states can have criminal juries consisting of fewer than twelve persons, whereas the federal government must have twelve-member juries. Furthermore, the states can convict based on nonunanimous jury verdicts (*Apodaca v. Oregon,* 1972). However, a six-member jury verdict must still be unanimous to be constitutionally sound (*Burch v. Louisiana,* 1979). Thus, while the Court has not provided consistent overall guidance, it generally holds that the Bill of Rights, except for the jury requirements just mentioned, apply to the states with equal force that they apply to the federal government.

C. Substantive Due Process and Procedural Due Process: What's the Difference?

The Fifth Amendment and the Fourteenth Amendment both make a specific reference to due process of law—a requirement that the government must meet before it can deprive a person of life, liberty, or property. As already explained, this concept of due process has a dual nature in that it embodies two separate limits on government. These limits are called substantive due process and procedural due process. Each of these two concepts are distinct, and the government must comply with both of them to infringe on the rights of any person in the United States. This section explains the differences between these two concepts.

The simpler of the two concepts to explain is procedural due process. Based on its name, one can easily understand that it governs certain procedures that the government must follow when infringing on a person's rights. The procedures that the government must follow consists of two requirements:

1. the government must provide advance notice of the intent to infringe a person's right; and
2. the government must provide the person with an opportunity to be heard so that he or she may challenge the infringement.

This means that the government must inform the person that it intends to infringe his or her rights ahead of time and then must provide some forum for the person to challenge that action. An example may help clarify these two requirements. Suppose that the state wants to build a new highway and a person's house is in the path of the proposed highway. The police cannot simply come to the house one morning, demand that the person leave it, and unceremoniously deposit the person and his or her belongings onto the street. Procedural due process requires that the state inform the person in advance of its intentions and provide him or her with some opportunity to challenge the proposed taking of the property. Thus, the government complies with the requirements of procedural due process as long as it provides notice and an opportunity to challenge an infringement before it occurs.

However, one can make a compelling argument that mere provision of notice and an opportunity to be heard does not protect one's rights adequately.

What is to prevent the government from running roughshod over some individual rights merely because it provided adequate procedures, especially when those rights are considered fundamental to our system of justice? The courts could not protect people because the government had complied with the requirements of the Constitution, for it had complied with procedural due process. This inadequacy of procedural due process to protect rights led to the development of the doctrine of substantive due process.

Simply put, substantive due process is a judicially developed doctrine that requires the government to have a sufficiently strong reason for infringing a person's rights to life, liberty, or property. Absent a sufficiently strong reason, the government is not permitted to infringe on a person's rights. The Court adopted this concept of due process in *Allgeyer v. Louisiana* (1897). *Allgeyer* involved a state law requiring property owners in the state to insure their property with policies issued from insurance companies licensed by the state. The Court read the liberty portion of the Due Process Clause broadly and found that the state lacked a sufficiently strong interest in its requirement, which the Court found to be unconstitutional. The question then becomes how one determines what rights are deserving of this protection. The answer is that it depends on the level of scrutiny the Court applies to the right in question. Some rights are considered so fundamental to our system of justice that strict scrutiny is required and the law will only be upheld if it is necessary for achieving a compelling government interest. Other rights are not so fundamental; the Court only requires intermediate scrutiny, and the law will be upheld if it is narrowly tailored to achieve an important government interest. Still other rights only receive rational basis scrutiny, which means that the law will be upheld if it is rationally related to the achievement of a legitimate government interest. These levels of scrutiny are covered in more detail in the chapter on fundamental rights, but for the present purposes, understand that the level of scrutiny applied to the right dictates the strength of the government's interest required as well as how targeted it is at achieving that interest.

D. Threshold Issues in Due Process Analysis

Before one embarks on an analysis of either procedural or substantive due process, there are three threshold issues that must be resolved.

- First, there must be state action, for without state action there can be no need for due process.
- Second, the state action must lead to the deprivation of an individual's right.

- Third, the individual right must be one of life, liberty, or property.

State action was covered in Chapter 5, so it is not discussed here. Rather, this chapter focuses on the other two issues—whether an individual's right was infringed, and whether the right is an individual's right to life, liberty, or property. These three requirements must all be present to trigger the need for procedural and substantive due process; remove any one of them, and the Constitution no longer mandates the need for due process. This section of the chapter explores what the Constitution means by "deprive" and what qualifies as life, liberty, and property.

1. The Deprivation Requirement

Both Due Process Clauses prohibit the federal and state governments from depriving a person of life, liberty, or property unless the government observes the requirements of due process. Hence, this protection turns on what the word *deprive* means or what constitutes a deprivation. Clearly, government action can cause a deprivation that must be protected by due process, but must the government act intentionally, or is recklessness or even negligence sufficient? Similarly, can government inaction be sufficient to cause a deprivation? Finally, can the availability of remedies provided by the government prevent government action or inaction from constituting a deprivation? Each of these three questions is considered.

First, the Court has held that an affirmative act intended to cause a deprivation is sufficient to cause such a deprivation and that negligence is not sufficient. In *Daniels v. Williams* (1986), the plaintiff, who was a prisoner, tripped over a pillow that a prison guard negligently left on the stairs. The prisoner claimed that the guard had infringed his right to be free from bodily harm caused by the state's negligence. The Court explained that negligence by a government actor is not sufficient to cause a deprivation because "the word 'deprive' in the Due Process Clause connote[s] more than a negligent act," and that the federal courts should not be opened "to lawsuits where there has been no affirmative abuse of power." Though the Court has clearly ruled out the negligence of a government actor as causing a deprivation, it has not expressly done so for recklessness or deliberate indifference. However, in *County of Sacramento v. Lewis* (1998), the Court found that deliberate indifference in an emergency situation by a government actor was not sufficient to cause a deprivation. Rather, in emergency situations, for unintentional acts to cause a deprivation, they must "shock the conscience." The Court explained that deliberate indifference by its own terms requires the kind of deliberation that is not plausible in an emergency situation. This statement by the Court may indicate that in nonemergency situations deliberate indifference may cause a deprivation, however, a strict reading of the holding in *Daniels* would seem to imply that anything less than an "affirmative abuse of power" would not rise to the level of a constitutional deprivation requiring the application of due process of law.

Addressing the second question, the Court has held that the Constitution imposes no duty to protect private individuals from harmful acts by other private individuals; rather, the government is only liable for inaction where it has created the injury-causing danger or the person is in the government's custody and that inaction must be due to more than negligence. In *Davidson v. Cannon* (1986), a prisoner claimed that the government deprived him of his right to be free from bodily harm without due process because the prison authorities had negligently failed to protect him from attack by another prisoner. The injured prisoner told the prison guards that he had been threatened by the other prisoner and the authorities had forgotten about the message. The Court held that the negligent inaction by the prison officials did not constitute a deprivation. Later, in *DeShaney v. Winnebago County Department of Social Services* (1989), the guardians of a child claimed that the Department of Social Services had violated the child's right to be free from bodily harm without due process because it had failed to protect the child from her father's beatings, despite being informed of the father's abuse of the child for more than two years. The Court found that the state had not deprived the child of any protected right and explained that the government's "failure to protect an individual against private violence simply does not constitute a violation of the Due Process Clause." However, in dissent, Justice Harry Blackmun argued that the Court had relied on an overly formalistic distinction between action and inaction and would have held that on opening the investigation into the case the state had assumed the duty to protect the child and that it had to carry out that duty with care and competence. The Court recently followed *DeShaney* in *Town of Castle Rock, Colorado v. Gonzales* (2005), finding that the permissible exercise of discretion by state authorities to enforce a domestic violence injunction is not a deprivation of life, liberty, or property.

Addressing the third question, the Court has held that the availability of state remedies is insufficient to prevent the finding of a deprivation of life, liberty, or property. However, the provision of state remedies will preclude the finding of a deprivation when:

1. the loss is only of liberty or of property;
2. the loss resulted from a "random and unauthorized act by a state employee";
3. the complaint is only for the failure to provide procedural due process;
4. no hearing could have been provided despite the foreseeability of the loss; and

5. the state's postloss remedy is adequate.

In *Parratt v. Taylor* (1981), the Court found that the loss by prison guards of a prisoner's hobby kit did not constitute a deprivation because the property was lost due to a "random and unauthorized act" by the guard, and that the state provided a tort claims remedy that was adequate. Subsequently, the Court simultaneously expanded and limited the scope of the *Parratt* exception in *Zinermon v. Burch* (1990). The *Zinermon* Court expanded the reach of the *Parratt* exception to the loss of liberty as well as property, and it also limited the exception only to complaints of the failure to provide procedural due process, not the violation of a substantive right, and where the officials could not have provided a hearing even where the loss was foreseeable.

2. What Constitutes Life, Liberty, or Property?

Having addressed what constitutes a deprivation, the next requirement for a due process claim is that it be a deprivation of life, liberty, or property. Although the definition of life for the purpose of the due process requirement appears to be fairly clear, it arises in a few other contexts that are addressed in the sections about abortion and the right to refuse medical treatment. This section focuses on the more difficult question of what constitutes an interest in liberty or property. It is important to understand that the property interest referred to here is not the right to possess actual property, be it real or personal, but the right to certain intangibles, such as a job or the right to assistance from government. The Court's early decisions limited the definition of liberty and property such that it only required due process when the government infringed a right and not a privilege. Today, however, the Court has expanded the requirement of due process substantially and provides broad definitions of property interests and liberty interests.

Until the latter portion of the twentieth century, the Supreme Court defined liberty and property narrowly, drawing a sharp distinction between a right and a privilege. Under this scheme, a right was an interest not granted by the government and that was also protected from government infringement, such as the freedom of speech or private ownership of property. In contrast, a privilege was an interest granted by the government that was not protected from government infringement, such as one's occupation or the receipt of government welfare. Thus, to infringe a right, the government must comply with due process, whereas the infringement of a privilege did not require due process. This scheme came to an end in the early 1970s.

In 1970, the Court decided *Goldberg v. Kelly* (1970), followed closely by *Board of Regents v. Roth* (1972), which eliminated the Court's sharp distinction between rights and privileges concerning due process rights. In *Goldberg*, the Court addressed the termination of an individual's welfare rights finding, contrary to established precedent, that once the government bestows the right to receive welfare, a property right arises in that recipient and his or her receipt of welfare cannot be terminated without due process. In his opinion for the Court, Justice William Brennan expressly stated that today's climate made it more realistic to consider welfare to be a property right rather than a mere gratuity. Two years later, the *Roth* Court expressly declared the "wooden distinction between 'rights' and 'privileges'" to be "fully and finally rejected." The main benefit provided by the distinction between rights and privileges was the ease with which one could determine whether a particular interest was protected. Following the demise of that tool, the Court has struggled to define adequately protected property interests and protected liberty interests. In the process, it has created different standards by which the three interests protected by due process, life, liberty, and property, are determined. Each of these is addressed in turn.

The Court's definition of a property interest revolves around that provided in *Roth*. In *Roth*, the Court explained that a property interest is more than a desire or a need for the property in the abstract. Rather, it requires the person to have "a legitimate claim of entitlement to it." Thus, the Court has equated a property right with an entitlement. However, its definition of an entitlement in *Roth* was problematic. There, the Court defined an entitlement in two different ways. First, it defined an entitlement as that which people "rely [on] in their daily lives, reliance that must not be arbitrarily undermined." This is a subjective definition of an entitlement—as long as a person has a sufficient reliance on the interest in his or her daily life, it would be an entitlement. Then, the Court stated that entitlements "are not created by the Constitution," but by "existing rules or understandings" derived from independent sources that "secure certain benefits and that support claims of entitlement to those benefits." This is an objective definition of an entitlement—as long as a person reasonably expects to receive the benefit in the future, the interest is an entitlement. Though the Court has yet to expressly conform to one definition of an entitlement over another, its decisions have tended to favor the objective definition of an entitlement. Thus, where a person has a reasonable expectation to continue to receive a benefit provided by the government, that person has an entitlement and a property interest, which is protected by due process.

While the Court's definition of a property interest became less definite, its definition of a liberty interest has become even less definite. In *Roth*, the Court tried to provide a definition of liberty. In his majority opinion, Justice Potter Stewart stated that liberty encompasses more than the mere freedom from bodily restraint. Rather, it encompasses "those privileges long recognized ... as essential to the orderly pursuit of happiness by free men." Though he did not limit the liberty interest to them, Justice Stewart expressly included the rights to contract, engage in an occupation, acquire useful knowledge, marry, establish a home and raise children, and worship according to one's conscience. Under this definition, liberty rights enumerated in the Constitution are clearly protected as liberty interests; moreover, the Constitution expressly protects unenumerated rights from infringement in the Ninth Amendment. Thus, the Court's broad definition of a liberty interest clearly protects not only freedom from physical restraint but other enumerated and unenumerated fundamental rights protected by the Constitution as well as other rights that the Court undertakes to protect. The scope of the liberty interest is explored under the substantive due process rights discussed in Part III of this chapter.

II. Substantive Due Process

As explained at the beginning of this chapter, the concept of due process is divided into substantive and procedural due process, and when due process is required, the government must comply with both forms. This part deals with substantive due process, the concept that the government must have a sufficiently strong reason to interfere with an individual's rights to life, liberty, and property. It first covers the rise and decline of the concept of economic substantive due process, followed by the Court's acceptance of noneconomic substantive due process. This section concludes by exploring the privacy rights protected under the Constitution — the umbrella under which most substantive due process litigation occurs today.

A. The Battle over Economic Substantive Due Process

Economic substantive due process is the concept that the Constitution prevents the government, federal or state, from interfering with the economic rights of individuals, such as the right to contract and to acquire and dispose of property, as well as to be free from government regulation of the economy. This concept has its roots in natural rights theory, holding that the government is powerless to interfere with the natural rights of individuals. For example, in *Calder v. Bull* (1798), the Court upheld a state law that reversed a state court ruling denying inheritance to designated beneficiaries under a will. Justice Samuel Chase expressly stated that because governments exist to protect certain rights, especially property rights, the state governments may not infringe the very rights they were created to protect. This view of the supremacy of natural rights continued into the nineteenth century. However, the Court initially enforced these protections based on natural rights theory rather than any provision of the Constitution.

Over the course of the nineteenth century, the influence of natural rights theory waned, and those seeking protection of economic rights began to rely on the Constitution as the source of the limits on government. Initially, proponents of constitutional protection of economic rights turned to the Due Process Clauses of the Fifth and Fourteenth Amendments. However, the Court at that time rejected those claims because it did not conceive of a substantive aspect of due process. For example, in the *Slaughter-House Cases*, decided in 1872, the Court denied the existence of substantive due process in a challenge to a Louisiana law granting a legal monopoly in the slaughterhouse business to a private company. Specifically, the Court emphasized that due process only required that procedural due process be followed, and because the state had complied with the required procedures, no relief could be awarded. However, two justices authored vigorous dissents where they found what amounted to a substantive aspect to the Due Process Clauses. Specifically, they argued that those clauses prevented the federal and state governments from interfering with economic rights, such as the right to engage in a chosen occupation, by arbitrary laws and to deny such protection is to deny a person his or her very freedom. Although this was not the majority view of the Court at the time, it soon became so.

The 1870s saw a substantial increase in government regulation as the economy became more industrialized and less agrarian. However, the legal community still held a deep-set belief in a laissez-faire approach to government regulation: Less is more. As such, although the Court generally upheld various economic regulations by state governments, it consistently indicated in its dicta that it would invalidate any regulations that interfered with natural rights. These intimations finally took hold with a majority of the Court. In 1897, the Court decided *Allgeyer v. Louisiana,* in which it invalidated a state law for violating substantive due process that prohibited making payments on marine insurance policies made outside of the state to insurance companies not licensed in the state. This position stated the Court's substantive due process standard, which it followed for four decades.

Most notably in the economic substantive due process cases are those cases from the Court's decision in *Lochner v. New York* (1905) to when the tide began to turn against economic substantive due process in *Nebbia v. New York* (1934). *Lochner* involved a state law that set the maximum work hours for bakers at sixty hours per week and a maximum of ten hours per day. The state legislature passed the law out of concern for the health of those working in the baking profession because of the exposure to flour dust. Not only could bakery companies not require more hours, the bakers themselves could not decide for themselves whether to contract to work for more hours than limited by the law. Addressing the challenge to the law founded in violation of substantive due process, the Court rejected the state's contention that the law was a valid exercise of the state's police power. Specifically, the Court found that regulating the work hours of bakers bore no relationship to public health and that the bakers themselves were sufficiently competent to negotiate their own hours. Additionally, the Court showed concern that the states would enact more rigorous laws regulating the hours of other workers (even of employers themselves) if it were to uphold this law. Thus, the Court determined that the state law passed beyond permissible regulation under the state police power and found the law to be unconstitutional.

Though this decision garnered a majority of the Court, it was supported by only five of the nine justices, and Justices Harlan and Oliver Wendell Holmes authored strong dissents. Justice Harlan urged judicial deference to the legislature and argued that it is not for the courts to inquire into the wisdom of laws. He stated that the test should be whether there is a "real or substantial relation between the means" to achieve the end and the end itself—an echo of the rational basis test developed later. Similarly, Justice Holmes urged judicial deference and argued that the Court had substituted its preference of a laissez-faire economy and the theory of social Darwinism for the wisdom of the legislature. He wrote that the "Constitution is not intended to embody a particular economic theory." Justice Holmes then argued that the regulation was a legitimate legislative end because the bakers found themselves at a disadvantage in bargaining power with the employers. To avoid the conflation of the predilections of the justices with the legitimate limits on state power, Justice Holmes advocated a reasonableness test and reserved a stricter scrutiny only for those laws that would infringe on fundamental principles of freedom as traditionally understood by Americans.

The *Lochner* doctrine thus espoused the theory that the government could not interfere with freedom of contract because it was protected by the Due Process Clauses, and that the Court would carefully examine any such laws to ensure that they served a valid police purpose—the protection of the health, safety, or morals of the public. The contrary position, articulated by Justices Harlan and Holmes, remained in the minority until 1937. During that period of more than thirty years, the Court used the *Lochner* concept of economic substantive due process to invalidate many state and federal regulations as impermissible overreaching of government power. These included laws protecting the unionization of workers, laws setting minimum wages, consumer protection laws, and laws regulating the entry of new businesses into a given field. However, the Court was not necessarily consistent in its application of *Lochner*-style economic substantive due process. For example, in *Muller v. Oregon* (1908), and again in *Bunting v. Oregon* (1917), the Court upheld maximum hours laws for women and men, respectively, out of concern for the workers' welfare. *Lochner* and its progeny were criticized for being inconsistent in their application of economic substantive due process, for constitutionalizing one economic theory for the benefit of one segment of society and to the detriment of another, and for being an improper exercise of judicial power.

The era of the *Lochner*-style economic substantive due process came to a close in the late 1930s, but not without a fight. In the mid-1930s the Court was generally hostile to President Franklin Roosevelt's New Deal programs, which increased federal regulation of the economy in an effort to recover from the Great Depression. However, by 1934, the Court showed signs that it was willing to back away from the *Lochner* theory, though it was not yet ready to abandon it. In *Nebbia v. New York* (1934), the Court upheld a law establishing minimum prices for milk as a valid exercise of the state's power to protect the public welfare. The Court explained that a law that is reasonably related to a valid legislative purpose satisfies due process when it is not arbitrary and not discriminatory. Additionally, the *Nebbia* Court's opinion questioned some of the foundations of the *Lochner* doctrine—specifically, that the government has the power to promote the general welfare and the call for judicial deference. However, the Court proceeded to invalidate several key pieces of New Deal legislation until 1937. In response, the President threatened legislation permitting him to appoint one new Justice for every Justice over age seventy who had served on the Court for at least ten years. The Court finally relented in 1937 with its decisions in *West Coast Hotel Company v. Parrish* (1937), *NLRB v. Jones & Laughlin Steel Corporation* (1937), and others, where two justices switched sides, leading to the abandonment of the *Lochner* doctrine of economic substantive due process.

Since the switch in 1937 and the concomitant judicial deference to the legislature, no state or federal law regulating the economy has been invalidated on economic substantive due process grounds. This deference was clearly illustrated in *United States v. Carolene Products Co.* (1938), where the Court upheld the 1923 Filled Milk Act, which prohibited shipping in interstate commerce any skimmed milk that was then "filled" with any fat other than milk fat. The Court first found that the regulation was a valid exercise of Congress's power under the Commerce Clause before addressing the question of economic substantive due process. In his majority opinion, Justice Harlan Stone unambiguously stated that the Court would no longer scrutinize Congress's goals in enacting any legislation because that is not the function of the courts. Then, Justice Stone explained that because the legislation was rationally related to Congress's power to regulate interstate commerce, the Filled Milk Act was valid. Interestingly, in a footnote to his opinion, Justice Stone indicated that the Court's focus would change from the protection of economic rights to the protection of personal liberties. This change in focus eventually provided the basis for much of the Court's modern protection of personal liberties as well as the protection of "discrete and insular minorities."

Today, the Court generally reviews all legislation impacting economic rights, including the right to contract, under the rational basis standard established in *Carolene Products*. However, the scholars and judges are not unanimous in condemning the *Lochner* line of decisions — there are some who find that freedom of contract and other elements of economic substantive due process should still be vigorously protected by the Court. However, after the abandonment of the *Lochner* doctrine in 1937, the Court has shown no indications that it would return to *Lochner*-style economic substantive due process.

B. The Court's Use of Substantive Due Process to Protect Fundamental Rights

In stark contrast to its rejection of economic substantive due process beginning in 1937, the Court has used substantive due process to protect many of what we consider to be fundamental rights, especially after the decision in *Carolene Products*. The Court's approach to the protection of fundamental rights has tended to follow the pattern in the fourth footnote of its *Carolene Products* decision. Specifically, the Court scrutinizes legislative acts that violate an individual's fundamental rights under the strict scrutiny standard. The strict scrutiny standard means that the Court will hold the law to be invalid unless it is necessary to the achievement of a compelling government interest. Similarly, where the legislative act is otherwise constitutional but discriminates against a "discrete and insular" minority group, the Court uses an intermediate scrutiny standard to review that act. All other laws are examined under the very deferential rational basis test. Analysis under substantive due process follows the following pattern.

- Is there a fundamental right?
- Is that fundamental right infringed by state action?
- Is there a sufficient state purpose for the infringement?
- Is the state action sufficiently related to the state purpose?

In approaching the first question, the most common source of fundamental rights are the Equal Protection Clause of the Fourteenth Amendment
and the Due Process Clauses of the Fifth and Fourteenth Amendments. The
Ninth Amendment is sometimes mentioned concerning fundamental rights
because it provides that the rights outlined in the Constitution and its amendments are not the only rights that receive the protection of the Constitution.
However, the Court very rarely invokes the Ninth Amendment as a source
of fundamental rights; rather, the Court uses it primarily to justify its protection of nonenumerated rights. Once the right is identified as fundamental, the second question in the analysis determines whether the government
has infringed on the right. Specifically, the Court finds that there is an infringement where the challenged act either (1) directly prohibits the right at
issue, or (2) burdens the ability to exercise the right. To determine whether
the government act has burdened a right, the Court examines how directly
the act impacts the fundamental right and how substantially the act impacts
the exercise of the right. However, the Court has provided precious little
guidance beyond that to determine when a government act burdens a fundamental right.

The last two questions examine the level of scrutiny. Where the right is a fundamental right, strict scrutiny generally applies, but where the right is not fundamental, rational basis applies to review the act. Thus, for the third question,
strict scrutiny requires that the government act be designed to further a compelling government interest; in other words, the goal must be a vital interest
of the government. In contrast, under the rational basis test, the government
act must merely be designed to further a legitimate government interest. The
fourth question then examines the "fit" of the government act to the end it
seeks to obtain. Under strict scrutiny, this fit must be very close; the end must
not be achievable by any means that are less restrictive of the right being infringed. Under rational basis, the fit requirement is very loose; the end must
only be rationally related to the achievement of the objective.

Beyond these four questions, it is important to note where the burden of proof
lies for these levels of scrutiny. For the strict scrutiny standard, the government bears the burden of showing that the act is necessary to achieve the compelling interest. In contrast, the rational basis standard places the burden on
the challenger of the government act to prove that the government act is not
rationally related to the achievement of a legitimate government interest. Under
the strict scrutiny standard, it is very difficult for the government act to survive scrutiny, whereas under the rational basis standard it is very difficult for
the government act to be found invalid. Thus, the categorization of a challenge is very important to its eventual success.

Most of the fundamental rights protected by the Court fall under the category of privacy. The development of this protection of the right of privacy, and many of the important categories of privacy protected by the Court are explained in the next section.

C. The Right of Privacy

The right to privacy protected by the Constitution is unrelated to the torts protecting a person from an invasion of privacy. Instead, it protects an individual's right to participate in certain activities of a highly personal nature, which the government must have a very strong reason for infringing. The right of privacy underlies many of the protections of individual fundamental rights afforded by the Constitution. However, there is no express provision in the Constitution protecting an individual's right to privacy, which has led many judges and scholars to dispute the existence of a right to privacy. Because of the lack of an express protection for privacy, the Court had to create the protection of the right over time by the development of case law protecting many apparently discrete individual rights. The majority of these developments occurred in the area of procreation and abortion rights, but the right of privacy is not limited to these areas. This section focuses on the development of the right of privacy and major areas where the right has been held to curb federal and state governmental authority.

1. Early Precedents

Although today the Court recognizes a right of privacy that protects several guarantees of fundamental freedoms, it did not always do so. In 1927, the Court decided *Buck v. Bell* (1927), where it upheld a state's decision to involuntarily sterilize a mentally retarded woman. In his majority opinion, Justice Holmes found that the state was acting for the benefit of society by preventing the procreation of the mentally retarded. However, in 1942 the Court reversed its position and invalidated a similar forced sterilization program in another state. In *Skinner v. Oklahoma* (1942), the Court found that forced sterilization intruded impermissibly on "one of the basic civil rights of man." In his majority opinion, Justice William Douglas described the right impacted by the legislation was "a sensitive and important area of human rights," and "basic to the perpetuation of a race." The Court explained that forced sterilization could have consequences that are hard to detect and yet have pervasive effects on humankind. Though the Court did not expressly overrule *Buck v. Bell*, *Skinner* shows the beginning of a concern for individual privacy in the form of personal autonomy. The majority of the initial development of a right of privacy occurred in the context of procreation and abortion rights. These decisions, in turn, relied on constitutional provisions and prior decisions of the Court respecting privacy in specific contexts.

Chief among the specific provisions of the Constitution concerning some form of protection of an individual right of privacy are found in the Bill of Rights, specifically the First, Third, Fourth, and Fifth Amendments. In the First Amendment, the right of assembly has been interpreted to protect a right of association, which is a form of privacy because the government cannot interfere with one's choice to associate (or not) with another. The Third Amendment's prohibition on quartering of soldiers in an individual's home without his or her permission and the Fourth Amendment's prohibition on unreasonable searches and seizures are more explicit guarantees of privacy in that they maintain the integrity of the home against invasion by the police or the military. Last, the Fifth Amendment protects an individual from being forced to testify against him- or herself and also protects private property from being appropriated without a public use and just compensation; each of these involves an implicit recognition of a right of privacy. The Court used these constitutional bases when it crafted the general right of privacy.

Nearly a decade before the infamous *Roe v. Wade* (1973) case, the Court's decision in *Griswold v. Connecticut* (1965) expressly relied on these constitutional provisions when it held that there was a right of privacy that protected the ability to purchase and to use contraceptives. The defendants in *Griswold* had been convicted for furnishing contraceptives to a married woman in violation of a state statute proscribing the use of "any drug, medicinal article or instrument for the purpose of preventing conception" as well as assisting, abetting, or counseling a person to violate the statute. The Court overturned the state statute and the conviction, finding that it violated the defendants' right of privacy. However, in his majority opinion, Justice Douglas rejected the argument that the right of privacy was found within the Due Process Clause of the Fourteenth Amendment and sidestepped the question of *Lochner* in the process. Rather, he found not only that the First, Third, Fourth, and Fifth Amendments protect their specific textual rights but that their protections radiate out as penumbras from those specific rights to protect other rights "that help give them life and substance." Within these penumbras, Justice Douglas found the right of privacy.

Two aspects of Justice Douglas's opinion are interesting. First, he did not couch his decision in terms of reproductive autonomy, but in the nontextual constitutional right to privacy. Second, Justice Douglas's use of penumbras was largely unique to this opinion and was not the basis for further decisions concerning a right to privacy. With regard to the first aspect, because he focused on a right to privacy, this case set the Court on the path that would eventually recognize a general right of privacy that encompasses both reproductive rights and non-reproductive rights. In a concurring opinion, Justice Arthur Goldberg supported a right to privacy couched in terms of the Ninth Amendment, rather than the penumbras of other guarantees from the Constitution. Concerning the second aspect, the Court abandoned Justice Douglas's use of penumbras and has used substantive due process and equal protection to invalidate violations of the right to privacy. Justices Hugo Black and Stewart dissented. Each explained that there was no textual basis for a right to privacy. Justice Black even famously wrote, "I like my privacy as well as the next one, but I am nevertheless compelled to admit that the government has a right to invade it unless prohibited by some specific constitutional provision."

Seven years after *Griswold*, the Court decided *Eisenstadt v. Baird* (1972) and invalidated a state statute that prohibited selling contraceptives to people who were not married. Relying on *Griswold*, Justice Brennan's majority opinion found that the statute was flawed for two reasons. First, it violated the right to privacy established in *Griswold* using language that echoed substantive due process as the basis for the protection. Second, the statute discriminated against unmarried persons by preventing them from having the same access to contraceptives as married persons. The Court determined that a legitimate government purpose for such a statute would be the prevention of premarital sex or even prevention of disease. However, the statute was directed at neither of these problems, and even if it were, the Court found that it would not sufficiently further the achievement of those goals. Thus, *Eisenstadt* expanded on *Griswold* to state that the Constitution protects the right to privacy and that right is fundamental.

2. The Question of Abortion and Privacy: Roe v. Wade *and Its Progeny*

The year after it decided *Eisenstadt*, the Court issued its landmark ruling in *Roe v. Wade* (1973) where it recognized a constitutionally protected right for a woman to obtain an abortion. In *Roe*, the defendant challenged a state law that proscribed all abortions save those necessary to protect the life of the mother. Writing for the Court, Justice Blackmun explained that the state statute was unconstitutional because it violated a woman's right to privacy. To support this, he traced the history of abortion from ancient times to the then-present day, including technological advancements that increasingly enabled abortions to be performed safely. He then traced the development of the right to privacy in case law and found that the right of privacy "is broad enough to encompass a woman's decision whether or not to terminate her pregnancy." He also stated that the right of privacy encompassed a woman's decision to abort her unborn child regardless of the source of the right of privacy. However, in making his determination, his argument was structured as a substantive due process argument based in the Fourteenth Amendment's Due Process Clause. He found that the Due Process Clause protected a woman's right to terminate her pregnancy because to force her to bring the baby to term would be to force maternity and motherhood on her against her will. Moreover, a woman could suffer psychological harm and future distress if she were forced to have an unwanted child. To support his decision, Justice Blackmun found that a fetus is not a child within the meaning of the Fourteenth Amendment's Due Process Clause, thus there was no compelling state interest in protecting the potential of an unborn child to develop into a life. However, he also explained that the right to abortion, like all other rights protected by the Constitution, is subject to limitations and qualifications.

The primary limitation, expressed in the decision itself, is that the right to an abortion is not protected from proscription by the state after a certain point in time. Specifically, the Court divided pregnancy into three trimesters and limited what the states could do to restrict abortions in each of them. In the first trimester, the Court stated that the government could not ban abortions outright; rather, it could only regulate abortion as it does any other medical procedure, including licensing requirements. The Court similarly restricted the government's power to proscribe second-trimester abortions but permitted the government to regulate abortions to facilitate the health of the fetus or the mother. However, the Court permitted the government to completely outlaw abortions in the third trimester, after the fetus had achieved viability, unless the procedure was necessary to protect the life or health of the mother.

The critics of *Roe* have focused primarily on the source of the right to an abortion. Specifically, the greatest criticism of the decision has come from the lack of a textual basis in the Constitution for the Court's decision (nor was it intended by the Founders). The Court attempted to insulate itself from this attack by finding that it saw that its decision in *Roe* was merely an extension of the other privacy-connected reproductive autonomy cases decided before *Roe*. The ultimate resolution of this criticism largely depends on the interpretive mode that one applies to the Constitution — a strict textualist would find that *Roe* was not supported by the Constitution because there was no textual basis for it, whereas a "living constitutionalist" would find that the modern world necessitated the protection of the right to an abortion and that the government has no right to restrict a woman's right to an abortion. Other critics, including Justices William Rehnquist and Byron White in dissent to *Roe*, find that *Roe* was an exercise in judicial legislation. These critics find that the Court should not have decided the issue and should have left the question to the deliberative bodies of our democratic republic. However, despite these criticisms,

Roe has stood for thirty-five years, though not without objection by several Justices, and its protection of abortion has developed substantially over that period of time.

Much of the development in abortion law since *Roe* has focused not on the decision itself but on defining the limitations on the right to abortion. In 1992, the Court decided *Planned Parenthood of Southeastern Pennsylvania v. Casey*, in which it examined several state regulations restricting access to abortion. Specifically, the Court upheld Pennsylvania's requirements of a twenty-four-hour waiting period before a woman could obtain an abortion, that a physician must provide information to the woman about her fetus, and that an unmarried minor must obtain parental consent before she could obtain an abortion. However, it found unconstitutional Pennsylvania's requirement that a married woman notify her husband of her intent to seek an abortion. In making its decision, a majority of the Court reaffirmed that the government cannot limit the right to an abortion before the viability of the fetus. However, seven Justices, though not in a majority opinion, rejected *Roe*'s rigid trimester framework, and a plurality of the Court replaced it with an undue burden test. Under this undue burden test, the government cannot place an undue burden on a woman's decision to have an abortion before the fetus is viable. However, the government may restrict access to abortion after viability provided that the procedure is not necessary to preserve the life or health of the mother. The plurality defined an undue burden as a regulation that "has the purpose or effect of placing a substantial obstacle in the path of a woman seeking an abortion of a nonviable fetus." Thus, a regulation places an undue burden on a woman's right to seek an abortion if it would prevent a woman from having an abortion of a unviable fetus.

This undue burden test developed by *Casey* remains the modern test the Court has used to examine the constitutionality of many abortion regulations. Many of these regulations are targeted at either imposing hurdles on the woman seeking an abortion or imposing certain requirements on the physicians themselves. These are addressed briefly below:

- Waiting periods: In *Casey*, the Court held that a twenty-four-hour waiting period was not unconstitutional. The plurality reasoned that it did not impose an undue burden on a woman's ability to obtain an abortion.
- Informed consent requirements: In *Casey*, the Court held that it was not unconstitutional to require a woman seeking an abortion to be informed about the potential effects an abortion may have on the woman, as well as the availability of materials describing the characteristics of an unborn child at various stages of development. The plurality reasoned that this was not an undue burden. However, *Casey* contradicts earlier decisions that

found it unconstitutional (under the *Roe v. Wade* standard requirements) to inform the mother with more detailed information. Thus, to what extent the states can require information be provided is still uncertain.

- Requirements on physicians: The Court generally has upheld various requirements on physicians performing abortions, such as requiring them to record and report information on abortions they perform and testing for the viability of the fetus. These requirements have been found not to place an undue burden on access to abortions; however, any information recorded and reported must preserve the confidentiality of the patient. One exception concerns laws governing the actual abortion procedures; prior to *Casey*, they had been found unconstitutional under the *Roe v. Wade* standard. However, these types of laws have not yet been tested, with the exception of the partial-birth abortion (discussed separately) under the *Casey* undue burden test.

- Notification and consent requirements: The Court has refused to permit the government to require the notification or the consent of the woman's spouse before a woman can obtain an abortion. However, the Court found constitutional the requirement that a minor seeking an abortion notify or obtain the consent of a parent as long as the regulation provides for a judicial bypass where the child may appear before a judge who can approve the abortion if the judge finds that the abortion is in the minor's best interest or that the minor is mature enough to make the decision for herself. Without a judicial bypass, the Court has found parental notice or consent requirements unconstitutional.

Recent years have seen the Court struggle with the questions of funding of abortions with public funds and the ability of states to regulate the medical procedures for performing an abortion, including the difficult question of bans on partial-birth abortions. Turning first to the question of using government money to fund abortions, the Court repeatedly has held that the Constitution does not require federal, state, or local governments to subsidize abortions. There are two aspects to this question, turning on whether the abortion is necessary to protect the life or health of the mother. If it is necessary, it is called a therapeutic abortion; it is called a nontherapeutic abortion if it is not necessary. The Court has found expressly that the Constitution does not require public subsidization of either type of abortion.

In 1977, the Court was faced by different issues in three cases, all of which were related to the question of public funding of abortions. *Beal v. Doe* (1977) and *Maher v. Roe* (1977) both addressed the question of whether the federal Medicaid program required states to subsidize nontherapeutic abortions; *Poelker v.*

Doe (1977) addressed whether local governments were required to subsidize non-therapeutic abortions in their local public hospitals. In all three cases, the Court held that there was no constitutional requirement that government subsidize nontherapeutic abortions, even when the same government chooses to subsidize childbirth. Three years later, the Court expanded this principle and found that the Constitution did not require public subsidization of abortions even when such abortions were medically necessary, except when necessary to save the mother's life. The Court's holding in these public funding of abortion cases is consistent with the constitutional principal that the government has no duty to facilitate rights protected by the Constitution; in other words, refusal to facilitate the exercise of a right does not effect a denial of that right and is not the imposition of a substantial burden under the *Casey* test.

Regarding medical procedures used to perform an abortion, the Court generally has found such regulations to be unconstitutional. These include regulating the specific procedures used, as in *Planned Parenthood of Central Missouri v. Danforth* (1976), where it invalidated a law prohibiting saline amniocentesis as a method of performing an abortion, and laws requiring all abortions on fetuses that had grown past the first trimester to be performed in hospitals (*City of Akron v. Akron Center for Reproductive Health, Inc.,* 1983). However, the Court found a state law constitutional that required two physicians to be present during the abortion of a postviable fetus in *Planned Parenthood Association of Kansas City, Mo., Inc. v. Ashcroft* (1983), though the constitutionality of such a statute requires it to contain an emergency exception for the life and health of the mother or to imply one sufficiently. However, these decisions all preceded the Court's decision in *Casey*, which announced the new substantial burden test— whether these decisions are still viable after *Casey* is questionable and has yet to be tested in court.

What has been tested in court is the legality of the ban on a procedure commonly called the partial-birth abortion. This procedure generally involves a partial vaginal delivery of the unborn child before the physician kills the partially delivered child and then finishes the delivery. Initially, the Court found laws banning this procedure to be unconstitutional by a five-to-four decision in *Stenberg v. Carhart* (2000). In his majority opinion, Justice Stephen Breyer reasoned that such a statute placed an undue burden on a woman's ability to obtain an abortion in violation of the *Casey* test. However, in 2003, Congress enacted a federal ban on partial-birth abortions, the Partial-Birth Abortion Ban Act, which essentially banned the same procedure that the Court had found unconstitutional in *Stenberg*. This federal law faced an immediate challenge, but the Court upheld it by a five-to-four decision in *Gonzales v. Carhart* (2007). Writing for the Court, Justice Anthony Kennedy found that the statute was not beyond Congress's power under the Commerce Clause and that the statute did not offend current abortion jurisprudence of the Court. In response to the argument that the law was unconstitutional because it failed to include an emergency exception provision, Justice Kennedy deferred to Congress's findings that the partial-birth abortion procedure was never necessary and found such an exception unnecessary. However, Justice Kennedy was careful not to overrule the prior decision in *Stenberg*. Instead, he distinguished it by stating that the state law had been too vague, whereas the federal law was not. Thus, the Court upheld the congressional ban but left intact its decision in *Stenberg* finding the state law unconstitutional.

3. Nonabortion Privacy Issues

The abortion question both relied on and has contributed to the expansion of the right of privacy protected by the Constitution. The seminal case in the Court's abortion jurisprudence, *Roe v. Wade*, depended on the preexisting privacy-related decisions of the Court. Since *Roe*, the Court has found several other situations where it applied the right of privacy. These privacy issues that are not related to abortion, both preceding and following *Roe*, are the subject of this section. The following discussion examines the right to privacy in the context of family living arrangements, the rights to marry and to raise one's children, homosexuality, the right to die, and the right to keep personal information private.

a. Family Living Arrangements

The question of privacy as it relates to families living together was a later-developing issue, rising to the level of the Supreme Court in the 1970s. However, the issue did not arise in the context of laws targeted at families but in how generally applicable laws restricting the number of persons who could live in one household affected families. Today, the Court recognizes a fundamental right of family members to live together in the same household. That right goes beyond the immediate family to the extended family.

The first decision in this line of cases came in 1974 when the Court decided *Village of Belle Terre v. Boraas* (1974), finding constitutional a zoning ordinance that limited the number of unrelated persons who could live together in the same household. The constitutional challenge was made by a group of college students who wanted to live together in the same house but ran afoul of the zoning ordinance. In finding the ordinance to be constitutional, the Court emphasized that the ordinance provided an exception for persons "related by 'blood, adoption, or marriage.'" Thus, the ordinance by its own terms applied only to nonrelatives, which the Court found not to violate the Constitution.

A few years later in 1977, the Court heard two other cases involving the right of family members to live together. In *Moore v. City of East Cleveland, Ohio* (1977), the Court addressed a zoning ordinance that also prevented unrelated persons from living together but essentially limited the reach of family relations only to the immediate family. The ordinance at issue defined unrelated persons such that a grandparent was not considered to be related to his or her own grandchildren. Although there was no majority opinion, the plurality opinion written by Justice Lewis Powell proved to be influential in protecting the right of extended family members to live together. Specifically, Justice Powell explained that due process under the Constitution protects the right of family members to live together because the responsibility of bringing up children has long been shared among parents and grandparents.

However, the Court has limited the reach of this right to persons related by blood. In *Smith v. Organization of Foster Families for Equality and Reform* (1977), the Court addressed the rights of foster parents. The state was taking foster children from their foster parents without a preremoval hearing when they had been placed there for less than eighteen months but providing a hearing once the eighteen-month threshold had been met. The Court found that this did not violate the foster parents' due process protections. The Court did not argue that the attachment between foster children and foster parents was insignificant. Rather, the Court noted that the entire reason that the relationship existed was due to the efforts of the state and that the state could remove the children before eighteen months without a preremoval hearing without offending the Constitution. Thus, the Court has recognized that the fundamental right of family members to live together does not extend beyond family members who are actually related to each other.

In addition to the requirement that the persons be actually related to each other, the Court has found that there is no constitutional issue unless the government has directly and substantially infringed with the right. In other words, a law is not unconstitutional if it only incidentally burdens the right of related family members to live together. For example, in *Lyng v. Castillo* (1986), the Court addressed a challenge to the federal food stamp program. The federal program provided food stamps to a household rather than to individuals within the household, essentially grouping together all related persons into one household but keeping unrelated persons separate. This caused an incidental burden on the right of family members to live together by treating relatives differently than nonrelatives. The Court found that this was not a direct burden on the right of relatives to live together and found the law to be constitutional. Thus, unless a law directly burdens this right of relatives to live together, it is unlikely to be unconstitutional.

The Court holds that the Constitution protects the right of family members to live together under a due process theory. That right is extended beyond the immediate family to those actually related to each other, at least by blood and marriage; foster relationships receive lesser protections. Additionally, unless a challenged law places a direct and substantial interference with the right, the law will pass constitutional muster. This direct and substantial interference standard also applies to the Constitution's protection of the right to marry.

b. The Right to Marry

The Court has recognized the entry into marriage as a fundamental right under the Due Process Clauses of the Fifth and Fourteenth Amendments since 1967. The Court first announced this protection for marriage in *Loving v. Virginia* (1967). *Loving* involved a state statute that prohibited miscegenation, the marriage by people of different races, called an antimiscegenation statute. Specifically, Virginia's antimiscegenation statute prohibited a white person from marrying anyone who was not also a white person. The Court found the freedom to marry to be "long recognized as one of the vital personal rights essential to the orderly pursuit of happiness by free men." It characterized marriage as a "basic civil right ... fundamental to our very existence and survival." Having found that marriage is such a basic civil right, the Court found that the state statute violated the Constitution's protection of equal rights under the Fourteenth Amendment because it was a discriminatory classification based on race, and it also violated the Fourteenth Amendment's due process clause because it deprived interracial couples of the ability to marry without due process of law.

Although the Court protected the right to enter into marriage in *Loving*, the case only addressed the question of a law banning entry into marriage outright; it did not address whether the government could burden the exercise of that right. The Court did not decide this issue until 1971 with its decision in *Boddie v. Connecticut. Boddie* involved a state law that required the payment of a filing fee to obtain a divorce. The Court found that this placed a burden on an individual's ability to exercise his or her right to marry because one cannot legally enter into multiple marriages simultaneously, thus to enter into a subsequent marriage, the first marriage must be terminated. Because the state statute in *Boddie* did not permit waiver of the filing fee for indigents, those who could not afford to pay the filing fee were denied the ability to exercise their right to marry without due process of law. Therefore, the Court held that requiring a filing fee for divorces without permitting waiver of that fee for indigent persons was unconstitutional. However, the Court has emphasized that its decision in *Boddie* does not require a waiver of filing fees for indigents in all cases, only for those impacting the ability to exercise a fundamental right.

Specifically, the Court has found that a filing fee for bankruptcy and appealing the denial of welfare benefits do not require a waiver for indigents.

To emphasize the strength of the protection of the right to marry, the Court has even found that the right extends even to prisoners in *Turner v. Safley* (1987) by striking down a state law that proscribed prisoners from marrying without the permission of the prison superintendent. However, the Court did find that the government may interfere with the rights to marry if reasonably related to the achievement of a legitimate penal interest. Specifically, the government can regulate the time of the marriage ceremony and the circumstances surrounding it, and it can prohibit the married couple from living together in the same cell.

However, though the Court finds that the right to marry is protected strongly by the Constitution, that right is not without limitations. Specifically, the Court has found that a law will not violate this right if it does not constitute a direct and substantial interference with the exercise of the right. Thus, if the law only indirectly impacts the right to marry or its impact is insubstantial, it will not violate the Constitution's protection of the right to marry. For example, in *Califano v. Jobst* (1977), the Court found to be constitutional a portion of the Social Security Act that eliminated certain benefits for a person who was disabled before turning eighteen and who marries another person who is working and earning a wage unless that other person is also eligible for the same benefits. In his opinion for the Court, Justice John Stevens recognized that the provision would likely impact the choices of some individuals to marry. However, that impact was neither direct enough nor substantial enough to render it unconstitutional. This direct and substantial effect test has found many different provisions to be constitutional, including the provision of food stamps to households as opposed to individuals, and the inclusion of all income from all members of a household in determining eligibility for federal welfare programs such as Aid to Families with Dependent Children.

c. The Right to Raise One's Children

Just as the Court has found that due process as required by the Constitution protects the right to marry as a fundamental right, it also protects the right of parents to raise their own children. This protection developed in the context of the education of children in the 1920s, beginning with *Meyer v. Nebraska* (1923) and *Pierce v. Society of Sisters* (1925). In *Meyer*, the Court addressed a state law that prohibited teaching in any language other than English. The Court found this prohibition to be unconstitutional, but it did so by using a substantive due process analysis and not a First Amendment freedom of speech or freedom of association analysis. Specifically, the Court found that the Constitution protected the right of parents to make decisions for the upbringing of their children. Similarly in *Society of Sisters*, the Court found that a state law requiring all children in the state to attend public schools to be unconstitutional because it violated the right of parents to make choices for their children. The Court expressly found this to be a fundamental liberty on which the governments of the states and of the Union rest and that it was stronger than the state's interest in standardizing the education of children. Moreover, the Court noted that children are "not the mere creature[s] of the state," but of their parents, and their parents "have the right, coupled with the high duty, to ... prepare" their children for life.

However, this right is also not without its limits and is subject to regulation by the state, provided that the state has a sufficiently powerful interest. Such a sufficiently powerful interest has been found where necessary to protect children. For example, in the early twentieth century child labor was a large and growing national problem that resulted in the exploitation of and harm to many children throughout the United States. States attempted to get this practice under control and ban it by passing child labor laws, which the Court has found to be constitutional. Similarly, the Court found that states could compel school attendance by children without infringing on the rights of parents to raise their children.

The analysis turns on when the state's interest is sufficient to override the parental right protected by the Constitution. The Court repeatedly has demonstrated that it is willing to defer to the judgment of parents, and this deference is quite substantial. For example, the Court has found that a state has a strong interest in ensuring that its citizenry is sufficiently educated. However, in *Wisconsin v. Yoder* (1972), the Court found that there are situations where even that interest was outweighed by the right of parents to control the upbringing of their children. In reaching this decision, the *Yoder* Court relied in part on *Meyer v. Nebraska* to carve out an exception to a state law, which required that all children in the state attend school until they reach the age of sixteen (for Amish parents of fourteen- and-fifteen-year-old children). In its analysis, the Court weighed the strength of the state's interest against that of the parents' given the strong cultural and religious reason for taking their children out of school and found that the parents' interest outweighed that of the state. Thus, when considering whether a state law infringes on the parental right to raise one's own children, the Court balances the relative strengths of the interest of the parent against the interest of the state and generally grants substantial deference to the parent.

d. Sexual Orientation

In recent years, the question of whether the Constitution protects individuals from discrimination based on sexual orientation has begun to arise. There are still very few cases decided by the Supreme Court addressing the extent to which these protections exist, however, the Court appears to track the attitudinal changes in society at large. The context in which the Court has considered this question is with private sexual relations between consenting adults of the same sex. Although the Court initially found that the states had the power to restrict or even prohibit this type of activity, today the Court has reversed that position and found that the Constitution protects consensual sexual activity between adults of the same sex.

When first presented with this question, the Court upheld a state statute that criminalized consensual homosexual activity between adults within the confines of a private residence. In *Bowers v. Hardwick* (1986), the Court addressed a state law that proscribed sodomy, finding that it was not unconstitutional. Under the state law, "a person commits the offense of sodomy when he performs or submits to any sexual act involving the sex organs of one person and the mouth or anus of another." The plaintiff at trial had been arrested for engaging in sodomy in his own bedroom, and although the state decided not to prosecute the case, the plaintiff sought relief under the Constitution in federal court. On appeal, the Court upheld the state sodomy statute in a five-to-four decision. Writing for the Court, Justice White found that homosexual conduct was not protected by the Court's privacy jurisprudence. Specifically, he found that the Constitution protects as fundamental only (1) those rights that are supported by the text of the Constitution or the intent of the Founding Fathers, or (2) those rights that traditionally have enjoyed protection. Finding that any right to engage in consensual homosexual conduct was not supported by either of the prongs, he concluded that the Constitution did not extend any protection for that conduct. Interestingly, the state statute in question was not directed at homosexuals, but prohibited all sodomy—by heterosexual as well as homosexual persons.

However, early in the twenty-first century the Court reversed its position on homosexual conduct and overruled *Bowers* with its six-to-three decision in *Lawrence v. Texas* (2003). In *Lawrence*, the state statute at issue clearly was aimed at homosexual conduct because it only proscribed certain acts of sexual intercourse between persons of the same gender. The defendant had been arrested and prosecuted after he was found to be engaging in homosexual conduct in his residence by police who had responded to a report of a weapons disturbance. On appeal to the Supreme Court, the appellants argued that the state law under which they were convicted violated their right to privacy protected by the Constitution. Writing for the Court, Justice Kennedy based the Court's decision in its long-standing recognition of the protection afforded by the Constitution to "the most intimate and personal choices a person may make in a lifetime." Justice Kennedy expressly referred to "marriage, procreation, contraception, family relationships, child rearing, and education" among these choices that enjoy this protection. For these reasons, Justice Kennedy argued that the state statute violated the constitutional protection of due process in these personal and intimate choices of life.

Though the Court's decision overruling the state statute was by a vote of six to three, Justice Kennedy's majority opinion only garnered the support of five justices. Justice Sandra Day O'Connor concurred in the judgment only and wrote her own opinion, in which she found the statute unconstitutional but for different reasons, and she would not have overturned *Bowers* to do so. Specifically, Justice O'Connor argued that the Equal Protection Clause of the Fourteenth Amendment, rather than the Due Process Clause, was the applicable provision. Justice O'Connor argued that the statute created a classification because it only proscribed certain sexual acts between persons of the same gender, leaving the same acts between persons of different genders permissible. The state had argued that this classification only needed to endure rational basis scrutiny because it was not a classification based on a suspect or a semi-suspect class and that the classification was rationally based on the state's interest in promoting morality. Justice O'Connor argued that moral disapproval standing alone is not a sufficient state interest to survive rational basis scrutiny in a classification, especially one that makes its classification by criminalizing the very conduct that defines the members of the class. For these reasons, Justice O'-Connor would have found the state law unconstitutional but would not have overruled *Bowers*, which applied to both homosexual and heterosexual sodomy.

In his dissent, Justice Antonin Scalia found several problems with the Court's decision. He argued that the decision was an assault on its own application of *stare decisis*, that it was bowing to the winds of political change, and that the Court was unwilling to pronounce homosexual conduct as a fundamental right but at the same time was willing to determine that the state had no legitimate state interest in criminalizing certain sexual practices that the people of the state considered to be immoral. He argued that this analytical method could be used by the courts to overturn laws against "bigamy, same-sex marriage, adult incest, prostitution, masturbation, adultery, fornication, bestiality, and obscenity"; laws that have long been found to be constitutional because of the moral disapproval by the people.

This decision is a landmark case for gays and lesbians because it recognizes their right to equal treatment under the Constitution, but it is also an important decision because it applies the right to privacy to sexual activity between consenting adults performed in the privacy of their homes as deserving constitutional protection from government intrusion.

e. The Right to Die and to Refuse Medical Care

The Court has also considered whether the Constitution protects two closely related rights. First is whether an individual has a constitutionally protected right to refuse medical care. Second is whether the Constitution protects an individual's right to die. Additionally, the Court has examined whether the government has an affirmative duty to provide medical care. Regarding an individual's right to refuse medical care, the Court has found that there is a constitutionally protected right to do so. However, the Court refused to go further and find that the Constitution protects any right of an individual to end his or her life affirmatively by assisted or unassisted suicide.

i. The Right to Refuse Medical Treatment and the Right to Die

The Court repeatedly has found that the Constitution protects an individual's right to refuse medical treatment. It bases these decisions in the liberty aspects of the Due Process Clauses of the Fifth and Fourteenth Amendments. However, this constitutional protection is not without its limits, and the Court has upheld certain forced treatments over the objections of the patient. For example, the Court has found that the state's interest in stopping and preventing communicable diseases from spreading is compelling enough to overcome the individual's right to refuse treatment and to force vaccinations. In contrast, the Court found that an incarcerated person has a liberty interest in preventing the forced administration of antipsychotic drugs, though it found that that interest was protected by providing notice and a hearing before the administration of the drugs. The case of *Cruzan v. Director, Missouri Department of Health* (1990) reinforced the right of individuals to refuse medical treatment but also found that the state may intervene in cases of incompetent persons to ensure that he or she truly desired to refuse or to terminate the treatment.

In *Cruzan*, the Court directly addressed an individual's right to refuse medical treatment. *Cruzan* involved a woman who had been put into a permanent vegetative state by head injuries received in a car accident. Because she was in a permanent vegetative state, she was unaware of her environment and was unable to feed or care for herself. The doctors had informed her parents that there was virtually no hope that she would recover, and the parents wanted to terminate the life-supporting food and hydration being provided to her. This would effectively end her life because she would starve to death, and the state of Missouri acted to prevent this. On appeal, a substantial majority of the Court's holding had three important aspects. First, it held that competent adults have the constitutionally protected right to refuse medical treatment. Second, the Court held that a state could temper that right by requiring proof by clear and convincing evidence of that intent before the treatment is terminated. Last, it held that the state could prevent family members from ending the treatment of a family member.

Regarding the first aspect of the Court's holding, Chief Justice Rehnquist's opinion for the Court found that "a competent person has a constitutionally protected liberty interest" to refuse medical treatment that he or she does not want. This aspect of the Court's holding was supported by eight of the nine Justices, with only Justice Scalia disagreeing. However, five Justices went further and found that this liberty interest expressly extended to the refusal of such life-saving treatment as was at issue in *Cruzan*. Justice Scalia argued that the courts have no power to adjudicate in this area because U.S. courts have traditionally upheld the power of the state to prohibit suicide, even when such suicide results from "refus[al] to take appropriate measures necessary to preserve one's life."

The other two aspects of the Court's holding enforce the intensely personal nature of the right to refuse medical treatment because it carries with it the ultimate finality: death. To do so, the Court held that:

- states can require a greater showing to permit one individual to enforce the alleged decision of another to terminate medical treatment; and
- states can prohibit family members from ending the life-saving treatment of another family member.

Specifically, the majority found that the right rests with the individual and not his or her family members. Because the "view of close family members will [not] necessarily be the same as the patient's would have been" if he or she had been faced with the situation while still competent and able to make the decision. Therefore, the intensely personal nature of the right to refuse medical treatment permits states to regulate the power of family members to make such a decision for an incompetent family member in an effort to protect his or her liberty under the Constitution.

In contrast to the patient's right to refuse medical treatment, the Court has found that there is no right protected by the Constitution to end one's life, with or without the assistance of a physician. In so doing, the Court essentially upheld the relevant laws in virtually every state in the Union. The Court addressed both of these issues in 1997 when it decided *Washington v. Glucksberg* (1997) and *Vacco v. Quill* (1997). These two decisions came out of the Ninth Circuit and the Second Circuit, respectively.

The Supreme Court heard both *Glucksberg* and *Vacco* because each had interpreted the Constitution, especially in light of *Cruzan*, to protect an individual's right to commit suicide. The Ninth Circuit's decision in *Compassion in Dying v. Washington* (1996), renamed on appeal as *Washington v. Glucksberg*, had held that the Constitution protected an individual's right to commit suicide. Specifically, the Ninth Circuit found that substantive due process protected an individual's right to "control the time and manner of one's death." Similarly, the Second Circuit's decision in *Quill v. Vacco* (1996) found that the Equal Protection Clause protects a right to commit suicide with the help of a physician because patients on life support have the right to refuse medical treatment, including the right to be taken off of life support.

Reviewing both of these cases, the Supreme Court held that the Constitution does not protect any right to physician-assisted suicide. Writing for the Court in each of these two cases, Chief Justice Rehnquist emphasized that a right is fundamental under the Due Process Clauses only when that status is borne out by history or by legal tradition. He explained in *Glucksberg* that the rights declared by the Ninth and the Second Circuits ran contrary to "over 700 years [of] Anglo-American common-law tradition" under which suicide and attempted suicide had been not only disapproved but also punished. Hence, there was no fundamental right to commit suicide, either individually or with the assistance of a physician. Without suicide being a fundamental right, Chief Justice Rehnquist found that the state law was valid because it was rationally related to legitimate state interests, such as protecting life. Similarly, in his majority opinion in *Vacco*, the Chief Justice held that laws proscribing physician-assisted suicide do not violate the Equal Protection Clause. Chief Justice Rehnquist explained that there was no suspect or quasi-suspect class, and there was no fundamental right violated. Thus, under equal protection analysis, the state law at issue withstood scrutiny because it was rationally related to legitimate state interests. With these two decisions, the Court has stated emphatically that there is no fundamental right to suicide, with or without the assistance of a physician.

ii. The Government Has No Affirmative Duty to Provide Medical Care

Just as there is no constitutionally protected right to commit suicide, the Constitution generally does not mandate that the government must provide medical services to those in need of them. The Court explained in *DeShaney v. Winnebago County Department of Social Services* (1989) that its jurisprudence found that the Constitution does not provide any affirmative right to the aid of the government. This holding even extends to situations where the aid would be needed to "secure life, liberty, or property interests" of which the government is prohibited from depriving a person. Thus, the Court has found that the refusal to provide aid to a person is not a deprivation of a right.

However, the Court explained in *DeShaney* that such aid might be required in extraordinary circumstances; however, the Court has limited these extraordinary circumstances to those in which the government has taken a person into its custody, such as incarceration or institutionalization. The Court has not yet found another situation in which the Constitution would require the government to provide medical aid.

f. Keeping Personal Information Private

In today's world there is an often repeated phrase: "Information is power." To that end, people wish to have their private information kept private, to prevent others from having power over them. Surprisingly, opinions by the Supreme Court in this area of the law are quite rare. However, whereas the Constitution limits the ability of the government to acquire private information in certain circumstances, the Court has made it clear that the Constitution generally does not protect a right to keep information private. The seminal case in this field is *Whalen v. Roe* (1977). In *Whalen*, the Court found that a state-maintained central prescriptions database that included the names and addresses of patients as well as the doctors prescribing medication was not a violation of privacy. Writing the majority opinion, Justice Stevens found that when private information is collected for a legitimate purpose, that collection "does not automatically amount to an impermissible invasion of privacy." The Court's decision in *Whalen* followed closely its decision in *Paul v. Davis* (1976), in which the Court found no violation of privacy in the publication of the name of a person who had been arrested for shoplifting but who had not yet been tried for the crime. More recently, the Court emphasized in *Department of Justice v. Reporters Committee for Freedom of Press* (1989) that neither the Constitution nor the common law protected an individual, fundamental right to privacy. However, this does not preclude the states and Congress from granting a statutory right of privacy, though such a statutory right of privacy could be rescinded at any time and for any reason.

III. Procedural Due Process

Procedural due process is the flip side of the coin of substantive due process, and it is concerned chiefly with fairness. It is also the more traditional notion of due process, and the only form envisioned at the time the Constitution was written. However, these two aspects of due process are complementary, and the government must comply with both before it can deprive a person of life, liberty, or property. Whereas substantive due process requires the government to have a sufficiently powerful interest before it engages in such a deprivation, procedural due process requires the government to jump through certain hoops before it actually can deprive a person of life, liberty, or property. These procedural hoops generally require the government to provide proper and timely notice to the person whose rights will be infringed as well as an opportunity to be heard and challenge the infringement.

When a court must perform a procedural due process analysis differs from when that same court would perform a substantive due process analysis, although there is some overlap. The latter applies whenever a government act would deprive a person of life, liberty, or property, whereas the former applies only when there are factual determinations to be made in conjunction with the deprivation. For example, if a federal employee does not challenge the facts that form the basis for his or her discharge from employment, then the employee does not have a right to any procedural due process. However, if that same federal employee did challenge those facts, then he or she would be entitled to procedural due process to determine the accuracy of those facts. Thus, procedural due process applies only when there is a need for a factual determination.

Once the question of whether procedural due process is owed, two things must happen. First, there must be proper and timely notice of the deprivation of life, liberty, or property. Second, the government must provide a sufficient opportunity to be heard, generally at some form of a hearing. Of the two, the form of notice is the easier question. The difficult questions arise in the context of the hearing itself regarding the form that the hearing should take and what procedural safeguards must be provided at the hearing.

A. Proper and Timely Notice

The notice to which a person is entitled before he or she may be deprived of life, liberty, or property, like the rest of due process analysis, focuses on fairness. The Constitution does not require that the person be directly and completely informed that action is pending. In other words, the Constitution does not demand actual notice. Rather, it only requires that the notice be designed reasonably to ensure that all interested parties will learn of the pending action. Specifically, the Court stated in *Mullane v. Central Hanover Bank & Trust Company* (1950) that a "fundamental requirement of due process" is that the notice of a pending action must be "reasonably calculated, under all the circumstances, to apprise interested parties" that the action is pending and to give those interested parties the opportunity to object. This means that the notice must not only be of a form designed to apprise of the pending action, it must also be delivered in sufficient time to permit the recipient to respond and participate in the associated hearing. The Constitution requires no more and no less.

B. Opportunity to Be Heard

In addition to proper and timely notice, the Constitution requires that the government provide a hearing so that those aggrieved by the government's action can have their objections heard. The timing of the hearing is also an important consideration. Ideally, the hearing should precede the deprivation. However, there are situations where the hearing cannot reasonably precede the deprivation, such as emergency injunctions to prevent an immediate harm and temporary restraining orders.

There is no one form of hearing that is appropriate for every deprivation. The Court has defined a balancing test to determine what procedures are sufficient to meet the Constitution's requirement for an opportunity to be heard. In *Mathews v. Eldridge* (1976), the Court outlined this test as the balance of three factors:

1. the private interest affected by the government action;
2. the degree of risk that the procedures used will result in an erroneous deprivation of the private interest coupled with the relative value of other additional or substitute safeguards to reduce that risk; and
3. the strength of the government's interest, including the governmental function involved, and the burdens that additional or other substitute safeguards would impose.

The first two factors focus on the individual, and the third factor focuses on the government. The courts balance the first two factors against the third to determine whether the procedures provided are sufficient to comport with due process. Specifically, courts use the balancing test to determine what procedures are required, whether a formal adversarial hearing is necessary, and what standard of proof is required to justify the deprivation.

Because of the inherent unpredictability of a balancing test of this type, there is no general rule by which one can determine what procedures are required. As a result, the Court deals with each situation on a case-by-case basis. The major areas where the Court has addressed what procedures are required are summarized next.

1. Receipt of Government Benefits

When revoking an individual's government benefits, the Court balances the *Eldridge* factors to determine what procedures are necessary. *Eldridge* itself involved the revocation of Social Security disability benefits. Reviewing the factors, the Court found that all three factors balanced in favor of a postdeprivation hearing. Specifically, the first factor did not require a predeprivation hearing because the recipient of the benefits could still obtain income from other sources, including need-based welfare programs. Similarly, the second factor supported a postdeprivation hearing because any hearing would be primarily based on neutral and unbiased reports of doctors. Last, a predeprivation hearing would result in substantial costs to the government in time and resources because it would permit the recipient to continue to receive benefits while exhausting the appeals process. However, the Court emphasized that a predeprivation hearing may be required where there would be no other source of income, or the decision would turn on contested factual questions, as was the case in the earlier case of *Goldberg v. Kelly* (1970).

2. Rights of Government Employees

The Court has held that the government need not provide a full hearing before terminating an employee for misconduct. Specifically, the Court found that a review of the situation by the department before termination was sufficient as long as the termination was followed by a hearing to determine the propriety of the termination. The Court has repeatedly applied the *Eldridge* factors and found that a posttermination hearing is sufficient in the face of misconduct by a public employee.

3. Family Rights

The Court's decisions in what process is necessary to deprive a parent of his or her rights as to his or her children has lacked consistency. For example, the Court has held that the state cannot terminate parental rights without a predeprivation hearing, and the state must make its proof by clear and convincing evidence. In contrast, the Court has found that states need not provide counsel for indigent parents at these hearings to terminate a parent's rights to his or her children. In *Lassiter v. Department of Social Services* (1981), the Court stated that it recognizes a right to automatic appointment of counsel for indigent litigants only when the litigation could result in the loss of physical liberty. In his dissent in *Lassiter*, Justice Stevens argued that providing procedural protections against the deprivation of liberty by the government is worth any cost.

4. Rights of Children

The Court has found that the government generally owes children less due process than it does adults for the deprivation of rights, even if the deprivation is substantially the same. This is especially true when the parents are acting to deprive the children of their rights. The Court presumes that parents act in the best interest of their children and generally does not require substantial procedural protections, even when seeking the civil commitment of their children. An important distinction here is that in such situations, there may be no state action because the parent is seeking the deprivation and not the government. However, when the government is causing the deprivation, the Court will examine the *Eldridge* factors to find out what procedures are necessary, though it tends to find that the procedures required for children are less than those required for adults.

5. Rights in Schools and Other Educational Institutions

When a school seeks to deprive children of their interests in property and liberty, the Court generally accords such actions with considerable deference. Initially, however, the Court found in *Goss v. Lopez* (1975) that expelling or suspending a child from school required due process. However, the Court found that the due process owed depended on the degree of interference: In the case of a short suspension, such as for ten days or less, it was sufficient to provide notice of the allegations and permit the child to explain the situation. However, the Court found that longer suspensions or expulsions required greater and more formal proceedings. Interestingly, the Court has not required any due process procedures before a school may utilize corporal punishment; instead, it appears satisfied with the remedies in tort to deter abuse of such punishment measures. The Court generally defers to the educational institution because of the unique nature of the learning environment and the school's strong interest in maintaining an orderly environment that is conducive to learning.

6. Rights of Prisoners

Although prisoners do not check their constitutionally protected rights at the jailhouse door, their rights are substantially curtailed. Due to this limitation on their rights, prisoners are only owed a hearing when the deprivation of their rights is intentional; negligence is not sufficient. Moreover, the hearing can occur after the deprivation—it need not be held beforehand. The Court generally determines what procedures are necessary by considering the severity of the infringement on the prisoner's rights. For example, in a hearing to revoke parole or probation, the Court requires advance notice so that the person has the opportunity to present evidence on his or her behalf, as well as a formal hearing before an independent decision maker. The person also has a right to a written report of the proceeding. However, the person has no automatic right to the assistance of counsel; rather, a court determines whether there is a right to counsel on a case-by-case basis. Similarly, the Court has held that there is no right to counsel when the government attempts to revoke a prisoner's credits for good behavior. In contrast, the Court has found that a prisoner being transferred to a mental hospital is entitled to the assistance of counsel at the hearing on the propriety of the transfer.

Checkpoints

- **Foundational Concepts of Due Process**
  - Five Clauses of the Constitution implicate the requirement for due process:
    - The Privileges and Immunities Clause of Article VI, Section 2
    - The Due Process Clauses of the Fifth and Fourteenth Amendments
    - The Privileges or Immunities Clause of the Fourteenth Amendment
    - The Equal Protection Clause of the Fourteenth Amendment
  - Incorporation of the Bill of Rights against the states
    - The Court has held that most of the provisions of the Bill of Rights apply against the states.
    - The Court uses a procedure called "selective incorporation" to incorporate the Bill of Rights into the Fourteenth Amendment's Due Process Clause and apply them against the states.
    - Under selective incorporation, the Court examines whether the right is sufficiently fundamental that it should apply to the states.
    - The following provisions of the Bill of Rights have been incorporated:
      - all of the First, Fourth, and Sixth Amendment protections;
      - all of the Fourth Amendment protections;
      - all of the Fifth Amendment protections, except for the grand jury requirement; and
      - the Eighth Amendment prohibitions of excessive bail and cruel and unusual punishments.
    - The following provisions of the Bill of Rights have never been incorporated:
      - all of the Second, Third, Seventh, Ninth, and Tenth Amendment protections; and
      - the Eighth Amendment's prohibition against excessive fines.

Checkpoints *continued*

- The Court generally holds the states to the same standards as the federal government respecting the incorporated rights, except that:
  - the states need not have twelve-person juries; and
  - the states need not require a unanimous jury verdict for a criminal conviction except in the case of six-person juries, which must be unanimous.
- The difference between procedural and substantive due process
  - Procedural due process simply requires that the government follow certain procedures before it can deprive an individual of his or her right to life, liberty, or property.
  - Substantive due process requires the government to have a sufficiently strong reason to deprive an individual of his or her right to life, liberty, or property.
    - The required strength of the government's reason depends on the right infringed.
    - There are three levels of scrutiny that the Court uses when examining the necessary strength of the government's reason, which are discussed further in the chapter on fundamental rights:
      - strict scrutiny;
      - intermediate scrutiny; and
      - rational basis scrutiny.
    - Under strict scrutiny, the challenged government act must be necessary to achieve a compelling government interest, and the government bears the burden to prove that it is. Strict scrutiny is nearly always fatal to the government act.
    - Under intermediate scrutiny, the challenged government act must be substantially related to achieving an important government interest, and the government bears the burden to prove that it is. Intermediate scrutiny is almost always fatal to the government act.
    - Under rational basis scrutiny, the challenged government act must be rationally related to some legitimate government interest, and the challenger bears the burden to prove that it is not. Rational basis scrutiny is almost never fatal to the government act.
- Prerequisites to a finding of a violation of due process
- Before the government can deprive a person of his or her right to life, liberty, or property, it must satisfy both procedural and substantive due process requirements.

Checkpoints *continued*

- Before due process is required, there must be:
  - state action;
  - an infringement of an individual's right; and
  - the right infringed must be the right to life, liberty, or property.
- When a right is infringed
  - The Court generally applies a three-part test to determine whether there was an infringement.
  - First, the Court requires that the alleged infringing act must be intentional; a negligent act is not sufficient.
  - Second, the Court requires that the act be an act by a government entity; acts of private parties are not sufficient to cause a deprivation.
  - Third, the availability of state remedies will generally not preclude the finding of a deprivation, except where:
    - the loss is only of liberty or of property;
    - the loss resulted from a "random and unauthorized act by a state employee";
    - the complaint is only for the failure to provide procedural due process;
    - no hearing could have been provided despite the foreseeability of the loss; and
    - the state's postloss remedy is adequate.
- Infringement of a liberty interest
  - The Court defines liberty interests broadly, to encompass more than simply freedom from physical restraint.
  - The Court's definition of liberty interest includes all of the fundamental rights enumerated in the Constitution's text. However, it also includes unenumerated rights, which the Court determines are protected by the Constitution, particularly under the Ninth Amendment and those that it recognizes under the Due Process Clauses.
- Infringement of a property interest
  - Whether the infringement is of a property interest depends on whether a person has a legitimate claim of entitlement to the interest.
  - The Court has endorsed both a subjective and an objective definition of a property interest, though it generally favors the objective definition.
    - Subjective: A person has a legitimate claim of entitlement where people rely on the interest in their daily lives such that the reliance must not be undermined arbitrarily.

Checkpoints *continued*

- Objective: As long as a person reasonably expects to continue to receive the benefit in the future, the person has an entitlement to that benefit.

- **Economic Regulations under Substantive Due Process**
  - Under the *Lochner* line of decisions, the Court would closely scrutinize the goals of a piece of legislation to determine whether it violated economic substantive due process.
  - However, today the Court applies a rational basis test to all economic regulations as long as they are enacted according to a valid source of power.

- **Protection of Fundamental Rights under Substantive Due Process**
  - The fundamental rights are those which are specifically enumerated in the Constitution and its amendments as well as those that involve personal liberty as protected by the Due Process Clauses of the Fifth and Fourteenth Amendments.
  - Analysis under substantive due process involves determining whether:
    - there is a fundamental right involved;
    - the state action has infringed that right either directly or by burdening that right;
    - there is a sufficient government interest in infringing the right; and
    - the infringing act is sufficiently related to the government interest.
  - To determine whether a government act burdens a right, the Court examines the directness of the impact on the right and how substantially government act interferes with the right.
  - The inquiry into the sufficiency of the relationship between the act and the interest is called the "fit" of the act to the interest.
  - If the right involved is a fundamental right, then the Court applies the strict scrutiny test to determine if the act is constitutional.
  - If the right involved is not a fundamental right, then the Court only applies the rational basis test to determine if the act is constitutional.
  - The strict scrutiny test
    - Under the strict scrutiny test, the Court requires:
      - the government interest to be compelling; and
      - the government act be necessary to achieve that compelling interest.
    - An interest is generally compelling where it is a vital interest of the government.
    - An act is only necessary when the interest cannot be achieved by any means less restrictive of the right in question.

Checkpoints *continued*

- Under strict scrutiny, the government bears the burden of proof, and this level of scrutiny is generally fatal to any challenged act.

- The rational basis test

  - Under the rational basis test, the Court requires:

    - the government interest must only be legitimate; and

    - the government act must only be rationally related to that interest.

  - Under rational basis scrutiny, the challenger bears the burden of proof and this level of scrutiny generally results in the finding that the act is constitutional.

- **Economic Substantive Due Process versus Noneconomic Substantive Due Process**

  - The Court generally does not recognize any substantive due process protection for purely economic matters.

  - In the *Lochner* era, the Court aggressively protected an individual's economic rights from infringement by the government. However, beginning in 1937 the Court completely reversed its position and has stoutly refused to provide any such protection since then.

  - In contrast, the Court recognizes noneconomic substantive due process, particularly in the area of fundamental liberties.

  - To infringe on one's fundamental liberties, the Court requires the government act to pass strict scrutiny, but where the infringement is not of a fundamental right the government act must only pass rational basis scrutiny.

- **The Right of Privacy**

  - There is no right of privacy found within the text of the Constitution.

  - However, the Court has developed a generalized right of privacy based on the Court's decisions in cases involving certain provisions of the Constitution, such as the Fourth Amendment.

  - The exact contours of such a generalized privacy right are rather indistinct, and the Court has to address new potential areas as they arise, as there is no general rule by which one can determine whether it would receive protection.

- **Abortion and the Right of Privacy**

  - Generally, the Court has found that the generalized right of privacy protects a woman's ability to obtain an abortion.

  - The Court recognizes that the right to an abortion is not without its limits.

Checkpoints *continued*

- A state cannot place an undue burden on a woman's right to an abortion before the fetus achieves viability. An undue burden is a substantial obstacle to the exercise of the right.

- After viability, a state may restrict or even prohibit a woman's ability to have an abortion as long as the abortion is not necessary to protect the mother's life or health.

- Specific situations and their constitutionality

  - Waiting periods: A twenty-four-hour waiting period is not unconstitutional because it does not impose an undue burden on a woman's ability to obtain an abortion.

  - Informed-consent requirements: Requiring a woman seeking an abortion to be informed about the potential effects as well as the making available of materials that describe the characteristics of an unborn child at its various developmental stages is not an undue burden.

  - Requirements on physicians: Requiring physicians to record and report information on abortions is not an undue burden, as long as the information recorded protects the patient's confidentiality. Requiring a physician to test a fetus for viability is also not an undue burden. However, it is an open question whether laws controlling the actual abortion procedures constitute an undue burden.

  - Notification and consent requirements: Requiring the consent of the spouse, or notification of the spouse, does represent an undue burden on the ability to obtain an abortion. However, the same requirements are not an undue burden on a minor's ability to obtain an abortion as long as the law provides for a judicial bypass.

- **Nonabortion Privacy Concerns**

  - Family living arrangements

    - Generally, family members have the right to live together without infringement.

    - However, only direct infringements on this right of relatives to live together are protected. For example, a federal law that granted food stamps on a household basis, and not an individual basis, is not unconstitutional, whereas an ordinance that would prevent a grandparent from living with a grandchild would be unconstitutional.

  - The right to marry

    - Generally, the Court recognizes that the right to marry is a fundamental right protected by due process and the Equal Protection Clause of the Fourteenth Amendment if the law makes a classification based on a protected class of persons.

Checkpoints *continued*

- A challenged law is unconstitutional if it imposes a direct and substantial interference with the fundamental right to marry.
- The right to raise one's children
  - The Court protects parental rights to control the upbringing of their children as a fundamental right.
  - However, the Court refuses to extend these rights to grandparents; essentially, grandparents do not have any rights to their grandchildren.
- Homosexuality
  - Initially, the Court found that the state was within its power to prohibit any and all homosexual conduct between adults, even where it occurred within the confines of the home.
  - Today, the Court finds that consensual, private homosexual conduct between adults is protected where it occurs within the confines of the home.
- The right to refuse medical care
  - Individuals have the right to refuse medical care, even when that medical care is necessary to preserve the life of that individual.
- The right to die
  - There is no fundamental right to commit suicide, either with or without the assistance of a physician.
  - Laws proscribing suicide and physician-assisted suicide must only pass rational basis scrutiny to be valid.
- Government provision of medical care
  - The Constitution generally does not require the government to provide affirmative aid to individuals, even if that aid is necessary to protect interests of which the government is prohibited from depriving an individual.
  - However, the Court has recognized that the government has a duty to provide medical care for an individual that the government takes into custody, whether by incarceration or by institutionalization.
- The right to protect personal information from disclosure
  - The Constitution does not protect any right to keep private information private; however, the states and Congress may provide such a right by passing appropriate legislation.
- **Procedural Due Process**
  - Before the government may deprive a person of life, liberty, or property, it must provide him or her with procedural due process.

Checkpoints *continued*

- Unless there are factual issues to be resolved involving the deprivation, the due process provided by the creation of the law at issue is all that is required.

- If there are factual issues to be resolved, then the government must provide (1) notice to those affected, and (2) opportunity to be heard and to challenge the deprivation.

- The notice required must be designed to apprise reasonably the interested parties that there is an action pending and provide them with an opportunity to object.

- What procedures must the government provide?

  - The Court prescribes a three-factor balancing test to determine what procedures are required.

  - If the procedures require a complete adversarial hearing, the factors must be balanced again to determine the burden of proof necessary to justify the deprivation.

  - These three factors as outlined in *Matthews v. Eldridge* are:

    1. the private interest affected by the government action;

    2. the degree of risk that the procedures used will result in an erroneous deprivation of the private interest coupled with the relative value of other additional or substitute safeguards to reduce that risk; and

    3. the strength of the government's interest, including the governmental function involved, and the burdens that additional or other substitute safeguards would impose.

  - The Court has balanced these factors in many different contexts. The major situations are summarized here.

    - Receipt of government benefits:

      - Generally, the Court will balance the *Eldridge* factors.

      - The Court generally requires at least a postdeprivation hearing.

      - The Court has found that a predeprivation hearing is not necessary where the recipient of benefits has (1) alternative means of receiving the benefits, (2) a hearing would largely be based on unbiased reports of neutral witnesses, and (3) the costs of providing the benefits while the hearing proceeds would be substantial.

    - Termination of government employment:

      - Termination of an employee for misconduct only requires a post-termination hearing as long as there was a pretermination review by the department.

Checkpoints *continued*

- However, termination of an employee for reasons other than misconduct may require a hearing, especially if the employee has a vested right to the job such as when he or she is under an employment contract.

- Family rights

  - The Court's decisions in this area have been remarkably inconsistent.

  - States may not terminate parental rights without proving that it is necessary by a preponderance of the evidence at a pretermination hearing. However, there is no automatic right to the assistance of counsel if the parent is indigent.

- Rights of children

  - When the state seeks to deprive a child of rights, the Court will examine the *Eldridge* factors but generally requires less process than it would for the same deprivation of the same liberty in an adult.

  - However, when it is the parent of a child seeking the deprivation, the Court presumes that the parent is acting in the child's best interests and does not require any procedures.

- Rights in schools and other educational institutions

  - The Court generally defers to the determinations of schools in depriving their pupils of their interests in property an in liberty.

  - Where the deprivation is slight, such as a short suspension from school of ten or fewer days, the Court has found that providing notice to the student and an opportunity to explain the situation is sufficient process to satisfy the Constitution.

  - Where there is a substantial deprivation, as in the expulsion of a child from the school, the Court will require more formal proceedings.

  - Interestingly, the Court finds that there is no requirement for due process before a school may impose corporal punishment. The Court appears to be satisfied with the remedies in tort to deter abuse.

- Rights of prisoners

  - Prisoners generally have fewer rights than do children in schools, however, the Court has found that they do not lose all their rights on incarceration.

  - Because of this, a deprivation of a prisoner's rights must be intentional to require any due process — a negligent deprivation is not sufficient.

Checkpoints *continued*

- Moreover, usually the Court finds that a postdeprivation hearing is sufficient and does not require a hearing before the deprivation occurs, though the Court will balance the *Eldridge* factors and require more process where the deprivation is more severe.

- For example, the Court requires advance notice and a predeprivation hearing before revoking parole or probation, but there is no automatic right to the assistance of counsel in such a hearing.

- However, the Court will require a predeprivation hearing with the assistance of counsel when a prisoner is being transferred to a mental hospital.

Chapter 8

Equal Protection

Roadmap

- Equal protection is established by the Fourteenth Amendment and is binding on the states.
    - It is binding on the federal government through the Fifth Amendment Due Process Clause.
- Types of Governmental Discrimination:
    - Facial
    - Impact
- Three major judicial tests and the classifications that fall under them:
    - Strict scrutiny
        - Suspect classes
            - Race
            - National origin
            - Alienage
    - Intermediate scrutiny
        - Quasi-suspect classes
            - Gender
            - Legitimacy
    - Rational basis
        - Everything else
            - Virtually all economic and social regulations
- Reasons for the different tests
    - Historical discrimination
    - Immutable characteristics
    - Unfair and unreasonable as a general rule
- Fundamental rights
    - Subject to strict scrutiny

- Right to travel
- Right to vote
  - Nonfundamental rights
- Right to justice
- Right to education

I. Overview

Although today equal rights are seen as fundamental to U.S. constitutional democracy, throughout most of the history of the Constitution, no right to equality existed. The Declaration of Independence in 1776 contained such inspirational language as "we hold these truths to be self-evident, that all men are created equal," yet, it took nearly 100 years and the Civil War for a constitutional amendment to be passed (the Fourteenth Amendment in 1868). Even once passed, the Amendment was rarely invoked and was considered as only applying to African Americans (*The Slaughter-House Cases,* 1872; *Bradwell v. Illinois,* 1873). In fact, it took a separate amendment, fifty years later, to give women the right to vote (the Nineteenth Amendment in 1920).

This is not to say that the Fourteenth Amendment did much for African Americans even after its passage. Some of the more fundamental milestones in equal rights jurisprudence, even for African Americans, did not take place until the 1950s with *Brown v. Board of Education* (1954) (requiring the dismantling of segregation in schools "with all deliberate speed") and its progeny and *Loving v. Virginia* (1967) (striking down laws that made it a crime for whites and nonwhites to marry). Although the Court indicated that it should perhaps invoke some form of heightened scrutiny in cases involving discrete and insular minorities in footnote 4 to *U.S. v. Carolene Products Co.* (1938), not until *Korematsu v. U.S.* (1944) did the Court articulate the strict scrutiny test for discrimination on the basis of race or national origin. Despite the invocation of strict scrutiny in *Korematsu,* the Court upheld the evacuation and internment of Japanese Americans during World War II.

A. Neither the States nor Federal Government Can Deny Individuals the Equal Protection of the Laws

The Fourteenth Amendment provides: "No state shall make or enforce any law which shall deny to any person within its jurisdiction the equal protection of the laws." The provision is clear that it binds states, but is equally clear that it does not bind anyone else, including the federal government. Though there is no similar provision that explicitly forbids the federal government from denying equal protection, the Court has interpreted the Fifth Amendment's Due Process Clause in such a way as to provide essentially the same equal protection. *Bolling v. Sharpe* (1954) was a companion case to *Brown*, with the same claims as *Brown*, but in the context of schools in Washington, D.C., a federal territory. It would have been inconsistent (and outrageous) to allow discrimination in federal schools but not in state schools. Thus, the Court held that the denial of equal protection by the federal government is a violation of one's due process rights under the Fifth Amendment. The analysis in either federal or state discrimination is the same (*Buckley v. Valeo,* 1976).

B. What Does the Equal Protection Clause Protect Against?

The text of the Equal Protection Clause does not clearly tell us what it means to "deny someone the equal protection of the laws." If the Clause is read broadly to forbid all discrimination, then almost no law would meet the test, for most every law provides benefits or rights to one group of people and not another or restricts the rights, liberties, or entitlements of one group but not another. Laws routinely make distinctions based on income, property ownership, and myriad other things. For instance, the law often distinguishes between people based on age (voting rights, right to drive, drink, smoke, work, etc.), and most would not think that this violates the Equal Protection Clause. Most view these laws as reasonable and fair. The government could barely function if no discrimination was allowed. As a result, the clause has been interpreted to provide that neither the state nor federal government may make or enforce any law that *unreasonably or without adequate justification* denies persons within its jurisdiction the equal protection of the laws. This, in effect, shifts the idea from discrimination or making distinctions (which every law must do) to unreasonable discrimination, or discrimination that lacks a sufficient justification.

Discrimination can take place in one or both of two general ways. Either government can discriminate in terms of how it treats categories of people (e.g., discrimination based on race, gender, age) or it can discriminate in what it provides or burdens (e.g., rights or entitlements or burdens on rights and entitlements). In many cases, the discrimination will involve both an issue of who is discriminated against and what is being denied or burdened. For instance, denying the right to vote based on race could be treated through either the lens of racial discrimination or discrimination in the provision of the right to vote. Most of the treatment of equal protection below focuses on discrimination based on categories or characteristics of persons, ranging across race and ethnicity, gender, alienage, illegitimacy, disabilities, sexual orientation, age, socioeconomic status, or class. When the government discriminates in the provision of fundamental rights (e.g., the right to interstate travel, access to courts, and the right to vote), one can bring a claim under either the Equal Protection Clause or the Due Process Clause. In many cases, plaintiffs present both claims and members of the Court often split in their opinions on the basis of the more appropriate analysis to follow. Although many cases present both avenues, this chapter focuses only on equal protection claims.

The Court has determined that when the government discriminates in terms of some of these categories (e.g., race and gender), the government has a heavy burden to show that the discrimination is justified. The Court is very suspicious of the use of such categories, and there is almost a presumption that discrimination on these bases is unfair. The government's burden varies, depending on the basis for the discrimination or the category of the person being discriminated against. With certain bases and characteristics (disability, sexual orientation, age, and class), there is no presumption that the discrimination is unfair, and the plaintiff has the burden to show that the government acted irrationally. In fact, the presumption in these cases is that the government is acting rationally within its powers (the reasons for this are controversial and are addressed below in Section D). This presumption holds true unless the government is discriminating in the provision, or the burdening, of a right that is deemed fundamental and thereby should, as general rule, be provided to everyone. Discrimination in the provision of fundamental rights, even if based on a nonsuspect classification, gives rise to strict scrutiny, and the government has a heavy burden to show that the discrimination in the provision of the right is fair. Thus, after addressing discrimination on the basis of categories or characteristics of persons, this chapter addresses discrimination in the provision of certain rights like this.

C. What Are the Mechanisms for Governmental Discrimination? Facial Discrimination versus Impact Discrimination

The government can discriminate in a variety of ways, such as through legislation, governmental rules, regulations, policies, and the application of legislation. This discrimination can take place in two ways: (1) by discriminating against persons or groups of persons on the face of the legislation; or (2) by discriminating through the impact of the legislation. Facially discriminatory laws clearly discriminate based on their language. For example, a law that excluded African Americans from certain health benefits would be facially discriminatory on the basis of race, which is considered a suspect class (the Court deems discrimination against certain classes as suspect for the reasons articulate in Section D). On the other hand, the legislature could simply pass a law that denied coverage for certain diseases, like sickle cell anemia. On its face, the legislation does not discriminate against a suspect class (those who suffer from sickle cell anemia), yet this is a disease that disproportionately affects African Americans compared to Caucasians. Thus, such legislation would have a serious discriminatory impact. Nonetheless, proving discriminatory impact is not sufficient for a successful Equal Protection Clause challenge. One must also show that government had the purpose of causing the discriminatory impact. It is not sufficient that the government was negligent or even that it knowingly discriminated; it must have been the government's purpose to discriminate.

Discrimination in the provision of health services to those suffering from a disease or syndrome that is closely associated with race makes it difficult to imagine that bias or racial discrimination is not the actual purpose. Nonetheless, it is easy to imagine other laws or policies that impact the provision of health services that would have a discriminatory impact without a discriminatory purpose. Unfortunately, due to a range of factors, African Americans have a shorter average life expectancy and are at higher risk for contracting a range of diseases and disorders than the average Caucasian. Thus, any reduction in health services would have a discriminatory impact. It does not follow, however, that the discriminatory impact was the government's purpose. Other examples of governmental conduct that have a discriminatory impact include tests or exams with cultural biases, physical requirements that have a discriminatory impact on women (e.g., for service in the police or military), or the provision of goods and services to the poor (who are statistically overrepresented by minorities and single mothers). In each case, one must show not only that the state knew or should have known about the impact, but that the state had the actual purpose of bringing about the discriminatory impact.

D. Tests Applied by the Court

Although nothing in the Equal Protection Clause distinguishes any particular type of discrimination as being more pernicious, or any given group or category of persons as being more deserving or in need of equal protection, the Court has developed a range of equal protection tests that effectively provide more protection to certain categories of persons than others, or that at least treat discrimination on the basis of certain characteristics more strictly than others. The strict scrutiny test is applied to discrimination on the basis of *race, national origin,* and *alienage* (with a number of exceptions to alienage) and to discrimination in the provision of *fundamental rights.* Discrimination based on *gender* and on the marital status of one's parents (*legitimacy*) receives *intermediate scrutiny,* and every other basis for discrimination receives the deferential *rational basis* test.

1. The Strict Scrutiny Test

Currently the strict scrutiny test applies to discrimination with regard to *fundamental rights* and discrimination on the basis of race, national origin, and alienage (with a number of exceptions in this last category). Strict scrutiny requires the state to demonstrate that it has a compelling interest and that its chosen means are necessary to further that interest. In other words, the discrimination or the infringement of a fundamental right must be necessary to achieve a compelling governmental interest. The state can show that it was "necessary" by demonstrating there were no other means to achieve the end that are less restrictive of the fundamental right or that are less discriminatory. Although this is the highest level of scrutiny, there are a number of cases in which laws or governmental conduct have survived the test. Note that even overbroad legislation might satisfy the test if the legislation is absolutely necessary. The Court's jurisprudence under this test is explored in Section III.

2. The Intermediate Scrutiny Test(s)

The Warren Burger Court (1969–1986) introduced the idea of intermediate scrutiny, which is a test (or a range of tests) that falls in between the deferential rational basis test and the strict scrutiny test. There are a number of different intermediate scrutiny tests in the area of First Amendment protections (see Chapter 9), but for equal protection, intermediate scrutiny only applies to discrimination on the basis of *gender* and *legitimacy* (which protects the children of unmarried parents). The most common formulation of the test is that the discrimination must be substantially related to an important governmental interest. The interest need not be compelling, but it must be important. Further, the means chosen do not need to be the least restrictive means (unlike strict scrutiny) but must be substantially related to achieving or furthering the government's interest. The Court's jurisprudence under this test is explored in Section IV.

3. The Rational Basis Test

The rational basis test applies to all other types of discrimination not covered by the strict and intermediate scrutiny tests. It also applies to social and economic legislation. It requires legislation be rationally related to a legitimate governmental purpose. As indicated, it is the test that is most deferential to government. When the rational basis test applies, there is a strong presumption, in favor of the government, that the law is reasonable and justifiable. Instead of the government bearing the burden of proof (as in strict scrutiny), here the challenger of the law has the burden of proof. The Court's jurisprudence under this test is explored directly in Section II.

E. Reasons for the Tests

We will briefly canvas a range of reasons or explanations for the different tests—namely, historical discrimination, the need to protect those who are at a disadvantage in the political process, the unfairness of discriminating on the basis of immutable characteristics, and the idea that, as a general rule, discrimination on any given basis is likely to be reasonable and justifiable. It may be that this last factor is a rough conglomeration of all of the foregoing, coupled with the speculation regarding the likelihood of a legitimate reason for discriminating.

One reason for having two tests (rational basis and strict scrutiny) that are nearly always determinative of the outcome is judicial efficiency; the Court does not need to work very hard to determine whether the legislation is in any way rationally related to a legitimate purpose under the rational basis test, or whether the government has shown that its legislation is necessary for a compelling governmental interest under the strict scrutiny test. This is much easier than determining whether legislation is reasonable and justifiable on a case-by-case basis.

1. Historical Discrimination and the Need to Protect Those Who Are Disadvantaged in the Political Process

Due to America's history with slavery and the Civil War, it makes sense that the Fourteenth Amendment provides the most protection to African Americans. However, without question, other ethnic and racial groups have also suffered from discrimination throughout U.S. history. If the clause is meant to embody generally applicable principles, they too should be protected. Footnote four in *U.S. v. Carolene Products* (1938) provides some compelling reasons for the

Court to abandon its deferential posture toward governmental conduct in certain cases. The Court held that in cases where the legislature is regulating economic liberties, the Court will defer to the legislature if there is any rational basis for the legislation. Yet in footnote four, the Court identified three areas that may require the Court to abandon the presumption of constitutionality and to apply a more searching judicial inquiry, namely, when the legislation in question:

1. interferes with enumerated rights (such as "liberty," "unreasonable searches and seizures," or "freedom of expression");
2. limits the political process (the right to vote, dissemination of information, or peaceful assembly); or
3. prejudices "discrete and insular minorities."

With regard to this last category, the Court noted that "prejudice against discrete and insular minorities may be a special condition, which tends seriously to curtail the operation of those political processes ordinarily to be relied upon to protect minorities."

It is not difficult to justify the strict review of legislation that infringes on fundamental rights or that will tend to undermine the political process. One of the main reasons for a Constitution and a justiciable (i.e., judicially enforceable) Bill of Rights was to ensure that fundamental rights would not be subject to the whims of the majority, acting through the legislative process. The courts have a special function in ensuring that rights are not trampled on and that majorities do not entrench and insulate themselves from the democratic process. If the majority, through the legislature, is undermining fundamental rights, distorting the political process and/or trampling on the rights of those with the least voice in the process, there is no other institution, apart from the judiciary, that can step in to protect those rights, protect democracy, and protect those in the minority. Discrete and insular minorities are, of course, the most vulnerable in a majoritarian system, and thus, they are most in need of the Court's equal protection powers.

Recall from Chapter 6 that footnote four to *Carolene Products* also signaled the end of the *Lochner* era (1887–1937), a time in which the Court routinely struck down social and economic legislation on the grounds of due process. As the Court noted in footnote four, this type of legislation now carries a strong presumption of constitutionality.

During the Warren Court era (1953–1969), the Court followed the footnote four line of reasoning and applied strict scrutiny to discrimination with respect to fundamental rights and on the basis of race or national origin. Everything else, including economic and social welfare legislation, received little or no scrutiny under the rational basis test. The footnote four line of reasoning, coupled with the history of the Fourteenth Amendment, support protecting African Americans and other minorities, but not necessarily Caucasians. Nonetheless, the Court applies strict scrutiny when race or ethnicity is the basis of the distinction, regardless of which race or ethnicity is burdened by the classification.

It is reasonable to argue that other groups, like the young or old, the poor, those with certain disabilities, and those whose sexual or gender identity falls in the minority, might also be in need of protection by the courts. No doubt, the history of discrimination against some of these groups, along with the Court's reasoning in footnote four, would appear to justify a more vigilant test than the deferential rational basis test. Nonetheless, in many of these cases, the Court has applied (and still applies) rational basis. It was not until 1973 that the Court abandoned the rational basis test in cases involving gender-based discrimination (*Frontiero v. Richardson*, 1973, applying strict scrutiny). It finally settled on the current intermediate scrutiny test for gender discrimination in *Craig v. Boren* (1976). Although the Court sometimes gives the rational basis test more bite, it has not explicitly invoked a higher level of scrutiny for any of these other categories.

2. Immutable Characteristics (Characteristics beyond One's Control)

The Court has routinely provided heightened scrutiny based on the policy that one should not discriminate against people due to immutable characteristics, that is, characteristics that are beyond one's control. This indicates there may be other reasons affecting this area of the law than those embodied in footnote four and the history of oppression or discrimination of a particular group. Though this is an effective justification for providing strict scrutiny for racial discrimination and only rational basis for economic status, it does not fully account for withholding heightened scrutiny in cases involving discrimination on the basis of age, disability, sexual orientation, and other "immutable" characteristics.

3. Unfair and Unreasonable as a General Rule

What would justify applying strict scrutiny to cases in which a Caucasian majority passes a law that benefits a minority group while putting the majority at a disadvantage (e.g., through some form of affirmative action)? Nothing in the history of footnote four justifies heightened scrutiny in such a case, and it is not clear that the concept of immutable characteristics is what really drives the issue. If one wishes to apply strict scrutiny to the case, one must think that generally it simply is not fair; it is not reasonable and justifiable to discriminate on that given basis. Note that under the current range of tests, if the majority passes affirmative action for African Americans, women, and homosexuals, the legislation will be reviewed under three different tests. There will be less scrutiny of legislation that discriminates in favor of the homosexual and more scrutiny of discrimination in favor of the African American.

At the end of the day, the different tests represent a rough rule of thumb that discrimination on any given basis is more or less likely to be reasonable and justifiable. For example, using the strict scrutiny test to evaluate discrimination based on race embodies a judgment call that discrimination on the basis of race is rarely ever justified. There is a presumption against the discrimination, and there is thus a heavy burden on the government to rebut the presumption. The use of rational basis review embodies the complete opposite general rule, namely, that the law or conduct is not suspect and is presumed to be reasonable and justifiable. Up until the 1970s, it was presumed that discrimination on the basis of gender was reasonable and justifiable, and this view continues with respect to discrimination on the basis of sexual orientation. In cases involving rational basis review, there is a heavy presumption in favor of the legislation and a heavy burden on the plaintiff to rebut the legitimacy of one law.

One may take issue with the Court as to which groups or categories should get what level of protection and whether the same tests should apply in cases of affirmative action. There has been a recent trend to give more bite to the rational basis test in cases involving gay and lesbian persons, and as we shall see, the government does not always win when this deferential test is applied. Furthermore, the government does not always lose when strict scrutiny is applied.

F. What Are the Three Tests Testing? Ends and Means (Purpose and the Relation of the Means to That Purpose)

The different levels of scrutiny used are tools for scrutinizing two separate things: (1) the ends, goals, or purpose that government is trying to achieve; and (2) how well the means further that end goal or purpose. Strict scrutiny requires a very important, compelling, or overriding purpose. Intermediate scrutiny (sometimes referred to as heightened scrutiny) merely requires an important or substantial purpose. Rational basis review allows for any conceivable legitimate purpose. Legitimate governmental purposes include the police powers (regulating for the safety, health, welfare, and morals of the people). The means for achieving these ends or purposes is often through legislation but can include other governmental rules, regulations, or conduct. The levels of scrutiny also differ as to how well the given means (e.g., the legislation) must further or achieve the end. The tests range from requiring the means be necessary to achieve the purpose (strict scrutiny), they be narrowly tailored to achieve the purpose (intermediate scrutiny), or that they be rationally related to the given end or purpose (rational basis). All three levels will be explored in detail in the rest of this chapter.

The means (usually a law, regulation, or policy) can either be overinclusive (overbroad) or underinclusive (too narrow). A law is underinclusive if it does not apply to similarly situated individuals; a law is overinclusive if it includes more people than are necessary for the government to achieve its goal. A law that is neither overinclusive nor underinclusive is one that achieves its purpose by having no more of a negative affect than is absolutely necessary. Overinclusive legislation may achieve the goal, but it has an unnecessary negative impact. For example, a law that requires judges or professors to retire at age sixty might attain the legitimate goal of keeping senile judges off the bench and senile professors from behind the podium. Nonetheless, it will also exclude many competent and experienced judges and professors. Setting the age at eighty would likely be more narrowly tailored and much less overbroad. Note that if the age were set at ninety-five, the law would not likely be overbroad because it would exclude few academics or judges that are willing and able to serve. It does not follow, however, that a law with the age limit of ninety-five is more narrowly tailored than a law set at age eighty. While the age ninety-five law may exclude fewer people, it is too underinclusive (too narrow) and will not achieve the goal of weeding out senile judges and professors. Thus, any law with an age restriction will likely be both overinclusive and underinclusive to differing degrees. Of course, other mechanisms, such as performance reviews or competency tests, would be individually tailored and would be more effective than age restrictions. However, individualized review might negatively impact on other goals or interests, such as judicial independence or academic freedom.

The Court is generally more sympathetic to underinclusive legislation for two reasons: (1) The only negative impact is that a person or a group that should have been included in the regulation was not included; and (2) a government should be able to tackle problems one step at a time. Though overinclusiveness can be illustrated by the teacher punishing the entire class because one student cheated, underinclusiveness is illustrated by the child who argues that because others were not punished for cheating, then he should not be punished. The latter argument is less convincing, and the court is more concerned with the former. Thus, although the government needs a stronger justification for an overinclusive law, this does not mean that all underinclusive laws will be reasonable and justifiable (*Allegheny Pittsburgh Coal Co. v. County Commission*, 1989, discussed later in this chapter).

Stop Points

- **Authority for Equal Protection**
  - The Fourteenth Amendment's Equal Protection Clause expressly prohibits the states from denying people the equal protection of the laws.
  - No express provision imposes a similar restriction on the federal government.
    - However, the Supreme Court has interpreted the Fifth Amendment's Due Process Clause as containing an equal protection component that also prohibits the federal government from denying people the equal protection of the laws.

- **Interpreting Equal Protection**
  - The Equal Protection Clause appears to bar the government from engaging in any type of discriminatory conduct.
  - However, if it prohibited all discrimination on the part of the government, practically all laws would be unconstitutional because every law classifies by imposing burdens or conferring benefits on a selective basis, singling out some people or activities for treatment different from that accorded to others.
  - Therefore, the Clause has never been interpreted as outlawing all forms of discrimination.
  - The Clause has been interpreted to prohibit the government from making or enforcing any law that unreasonably or without adequate justification denies persons the equal protections of the law.
  - Government discrimination can take place in one or both of two general ways:
    - discrimination in terms of how it treats categories of people; or
    - discrimination in what it provides or burdens.

- **Mechanisms for Governmental Discrimination**
  - The state can discriminate in a variety of ways, such as legislation, governmental rules, regulations, policies, and through the application of legislation. This discrimination can take place in two ways:
    1. By discriminating against persons or groups of persons on the face of the legislation
       - Clearly discriminates based on its language
    2. By discriminating through the impact of the legislation
       - Legislation that does not expressly discriminate by its language but has a serious discriminatory impact
       - Proving discriminatory impact is not sufficient to prove an equal protection violation

- Must also show that the government had the purpose of causing the discriminatory impact
- **Three Major Tests**
  - The Supreme Court applies three different tests depending on what categories of persons or certain characteristics a law is claimed to be discriminating against:
    1. Strict Scrutiny Test
       - Applies to government action that intentionally discriminates against "suspect" classes, which include:
         - Race
         - National origin
         - Alienage (with a number of exceptions)
         - Discrimination in the provision of fundamental rights
           - Right to vote
           - Right to travel
       - Test: is the government action necessary to achieve a compelling government purpose?
    2. Intermediate Scrutiny Test
       - Applies to discrimination on the basis of:
         - Gender
         - Legitimacy
       - Test: is the government action substantially related to an important government purpose?
    3. Rational Basis Test
       - Applies to every other basis for discrimination
       - Test: is the government action rationally related to a legitimate government purpose? (Note: There are other formulations of this test.)
- **Reasons for the Different Tests**
  - Historical discrimination and the need to protect those who are disadvantaged in the political process
  - Immutable characteristics (characteristics beyond one's control)
  - Unfair and unreasonable generally
- **What the Three Tests Are Testing: Ends and Means (Purpose and Relation of the Means to that Purpose):**
  - The different levels of scrutiny used are tools for scrutinizing two separate things:
    1. The ends, goals or purpose the government is trying to achieve:

- Strict scrutiny requires a very important, compelling, or overriding purpose.
- Intermediate scrutiny merely requires an important or substantial purpose.
- Rational basis review allows for any conceivable legitimate purpose.

2. How well the means further that end-goal or purpose:

- The means for achieving these ends or purposes is often through legislation, but can include other governmental rules, regulations or conduct.
  - Strict scrutiny requires the means to be necessary to achieve the purpose,
  - Intermediate scrutiny requires the means to be narrowly tailored to achieve the purpose,
  - Rational basis requires that the means be rationally related to the given end or purpose.

II. Rational Basis Review

The use of the rational basis test makes the most sense in cases where there is little worry the discrimination is based on animus toward a given group, the result of some flaw in the democratic process, or where the Court concludes it is in no better position than the legislature or government to second guess the law, for example, in cases of general economic and social welfare legislation, and in cases where discrete and insular minorities are not affected. As already noted, the test embodies a presumption that in most cases discrimination on that given basis or in the regulation of a given thing or activity is reasonable and justifiable.

The most extreme view of the test can be found in *Federal Communications Commission v. Beach Communications* (1993). In that case, the Court held that any *conceivable* legislative purpose for the law was sufficient. The government only had to state a legitimate purpose at the time the law was challenged; it was irrelevant that this was not the legislature's true purpose for passing the law or that the legislature had not even considered the purported purpose. Thus, the plaintiff had the burden to negate or disprove "every conceivable basis" for the law's rationality.

Justice John Stevens and former Justices William Brennan, Thurgood Marshall, and Harry Blackmun have criticized this approach. Justice Stevens noted in his concurring opinion in *Beach Communications* that this form of review is "no review at all." Justices Brennan and Marshall, in their dissenting opinion to *U.S. Railroad Retirement Board v. Fritz* (1980), drew attention to a line of precedent that supported examining the government's actual purpose and scrutinizing stated purposes that appear to be incompatible with the legislative intent. Justice Blackmun, in *Logan v. Zimmerman Brush Co.* (1982), declared the test was not toothless and there must be some objective basis for asserting a connection between the government's chosen means and the end it seeks to further.

In general, the Court is highly deferential to the government, both in accepting any conceivable legitimate purpose and in refusing to scrutinize the relation between the means and the purpose or end. There have been, however, a number of cases in which the Court appears to *really* test whether there is an actual legitimate purpose and if the legislation is, in fact, rationally related to it (as opposed to the purpose being a mere facade and the means being arbitrary and unreasonable). Those cases include discrimination against unrelated cohabitants (hippies), people with disabilities, and gays, lesbians, and bisexuals (GLBs). Though these categories of persons do not usually get heightened scrutiny, in some contexts, the courts may more closely scrutinize whether there is a legitimate governmental purpose and whether the means are rationally related to furthering that purpose.

A. Cases of Exceptional Deference

In *Railway Express Agency (REA) v. New York* (1949), New York City passed an ordinance that regulated advertising on the sides of trucks. The law discriminated between business owners who advertised their own business on their own trucks and all other businesses that did not have their own trucks or who simply wished to advertise on other trucks. Further, the law discriminated between those who wished to advertise on billboards and those who advertised on trucks they did not own.

The Court held the government's stated purpose for passing the regulation, traffic safety, was legitimate. The plaintiff argued the ordinance was not rationally related to the purpose because it turned on ownership of the truck, not on the type of advertising. Though one can accept that traffic safety is a legitimate purpose, it is unclear how advertising on another's truck causes more traffic safety problems than advertising on one's own truck or on billboards. The Court chose to defer to the city by holding that although the law was underinclusive, the city may have reasonably concluded that the latter did not present the same problems as the former.

Why did the Court decide to defer to the city when the ordinance appears to arbitrarily discriminate? Our introductory materials provide a number of reasons.

1. The case did not involve discrete and insular minorities.
2. There was little concern that the discrimination was due to a flaw in the democratic process.
3. The case did not involve fundamental rights.
4. The case involved economic regulation for the purpose of health and safety.
5. The case involved an underinclusive ordinance that is rationally related to the problem of traffic safety (even if it does not include the other forms of advertising that contribute to the problem).

Thus, there is little reason for the Court to step in and substitute its judgment for that of the city of New York.

Similarly, in *Fitzgerald v. Racing Ass'n of Central Iowa* (2003), the Court upheld a state law that imposed higher taxes on slot machines at race tracks than on riverboats. The state was not required to allow slot machines at racetracks; thus, for the state to allow the slots and tax them at a higher rate than those on riverboats was rationally related to helping the struggling racetrack business. Nothing requires the state to support every area of the economy equally. The state can reasonably choose to help out riverboats more than racetracks.

In a case involving the New York City Transit Authority, the Court upheld a law that was overbroad in its exclusion of all methadone users from employment with the Authority even though many of those on the treatment were just as employable as people who were not on the treatment program (*New York City Transit Authority v. Beazer*, 1979). The policy treated those on the program as if they would relapse into illicit drug use even though 70–80 percent of them would not. Although debatable, the Court held "because it does not circumscribe a class of persons characterized by some unpopular trait or affiliation, it does not create or reflect any special likelihood of bias on the part of the ruling majority." Thus, rational basis applied. The Court held that the plaintiffs were not able to show that there was another way to excluding those who would relapse (between 20 and 30 percent) that was just as cost-efficient and effective as excluding everyone. As a result, even if the law could have been more narrowly tailored with regards to a subclass of the group, "the Constitution does not authorize a federal court to interfere with that policy decision." Narrow tailoring simply was not required.

Can a law be rationally related to a legitimate governmental purpose, if the law itself undermines "the purpose" articulated in the legislative history? As noted, in *United States Railroad Retirement Board v. Fritz* (1980), the Court held that laws do not need to serve some clearly articulated purpose set forth by the legislature. Rather, any conceivable legitimate purpose would suffice. This is partially due to the fact that in the United States, as opposed to some other countries, the legislature is not required to agree on any one given purpose for a particular piece of legislation. Although this might be helpful, searching for one purpose and limiting legislation to one purpose would be too intrusive on the legislature's prerogative to pass legislation that may have many different purposes.

For years, the retirement fund for railroad employees provided almost anyone who ever worked at the railroad a pension on retirement, even if they retired from some other business years after working at the railroad. The original railroad retirement fund allowed workers who had worked for the railroad at some point in their careers to receive a railroad pension, plus Social Security, plus a pension from another employer. This created a windfall payment to retired railroad workers. By 1974, it was clear that if the practice continued, the system would be bankrupt by 1981. As a result, Congress passed legislation to reduce the costs and make the program financially viable. The Railroad Retirement Act of 1974 required that to receive a pension, one needed twenty-five years of railroad experience, or to have retired from the railroad (not another company) after ten years of experience, or to simply be working at the railroad in 1974.

The result was that one who worked for the railroad for twenty-four years, left before 1974, and planned to retire from another company would not receive a pension, whereas a person who had only worked for ten years at the railroad would get the pension, as long as she or he retired from the railroad.

There is no question that the overall purpose of reducing costs and keeping the pension afloat were legitimate state interests, but what could be the legitimate interest that would justify this seemingly irrational and unjust distribution of benefits? As Justice Brennan, joined by Justice Marshall, argue in their dissent, Congress's stated purpose was not "to deprive retirees of any portion of the benefits they had been promised and that they had earned under the prior law."

The law completely undermines this purpose by giving the windfall to employees who happen to be working at the railroad in 1974. This indicates that something may have gone wrong in the democratic process. In fact, as the dissent pointed out, the only people on record who advocated for the Act were current railroad management and employees. Former employees were underrepresented in this case and during the legislative process. Because their interests were not adequately represented, the language that undercut the stated purpose and discriminated against former employees was likely a mistake that slipped through the legislative process. (Note that it is not uncommon for members of Congress to vote on legislation that they have not carefully read.)

Justice William Rehnquist, writing for the majority, held Congress could properly determine that those who had reached retirement while still working in the railroad industry had a greater claim to those benefits than those who had become eligible while working for a different company. In other words,

providing those with a "current connection" to the railroad with more benefits was not arbitrary and would serve a legitimate state interest.

Thus, even though the law appears to have undermined Congress's stated
purpose of not depriving retirees of any portion of the benefits they had been
promised and had earned under the prior law, there were other conceivable
legitimate purposes the law could serve, and thus the Court upheld the law.

The idea that the Court will defer to any conceivable governmental purpose
was vehemently reaffirmed in *Federal Communications Commission v. Beach Communications* (1993). In that case, Justice Clarence Thomas, writing for the majority, held that "those attacking the rationality of the legislative classification
have the burden to negate every conceivable basis which might support it." As
noted, Justice Stevens criticized this approach as amounting to no review at all.

B. Cases Involving Some Level of Scrutiny

1. Too Arbitrary

Justice Rehnquist wrote the opinion in *Fritz* and joined the unanimous decision in the tax case of *Fitzgerald*, two cases in which the Court was deferential
to the government. By contrast, in *Allegheny Pittsburgh Coal Co. v. County Commission* (1989), the Court was more willing to scrutinize the government. In *Allegheny*, Justice Rehnquist, writing for a unanimous Court, did not defer to a county
tax assessor in West Virginia. The assessor's practice resulted in gross disparities
in the valuation of and subsequent tax imposed on newly purchased land as opposed to previously purchased land. While Justice Rehnquist acknowledged that
different types or classes of property could be taxed at different reasonable rates,
here the assessment practice resulted in comparable neighboring properties
being valued from between eight and thirty-five times more or less, depending
on whether it was a newer purchase or an older purchase. The Court did not accept the state's argument that the assessment scheme was rationally related to the
state's legitimate purpose of assessing property at its true current value.

All of the reasons for taking a deferential approach appear to be present in
this case. New property owners are not a discrete and insular minority group.
Furthermore, the tax assessment policy was underinclusive; the argument was
not that the new houses were not being assessed properly but that the re-
assessment of old houses did not reflect their market values. The incremental
changes to old property values simply did not keep up with the market, and
new property owners were carrying the bulk of the tax burden.

There are three possible reasons the Court gave the rational basis test some
bite in this case:

1. The county tax assessor's practices seemed to conflict with the state constitution's mandate that taxes be apportioned according to the property's value;

2. members of the Court may have sympathized with the new property owners; and

3. the assessment scheme resulted in disparities that were simply too gross or extreme for the Court to defer to the assessor.

The first point is important because the Court is less likely to defer to a government official (the executive branch) and his or her method of implementing of the law, particularly if it appears that it is not supported by the law passed by the legislative branch (here, the state constitution). The other points are important because there is nothing in the rational basis test that guarantees the Court will give the government a "free pass" of constitutionality. The Court is always free to decide whether the law, policy, or practice really is, in fact, rationally related to a legitimate state interest. Following are three more instances where the Court has chosen to aggressively apply the rational basis test. All three cases involved the Court's determination that the government's real or primary purpose for the law, ordinance, or amendment was animus toward a given group.

2. Illegitimate Purposes: Animus or Ill Will toward a Given Group of People

a. Animus toward Hippies: *U.S. Dep't of Agriculture v. Moreno* (1973)

In 1971, the U.S. Department of Agriculture amended the food stamp law to exclude households consisting of unrelated adults. Among those excluded were Jacinta Moreno, a fifty-six-year-old diabetic, her live-in caregiver, Ms. Sanchez, and Ms. Sanchez's three children. The Court, in *United States Department of Agriculture v. Moreno* (1973), held that this exclusion did not rationally further the Act's stated purposes, which was to alleviate hunger and malnutrition among the needy and stimulate the agricultural economy by purchasing surplus farm supplies (as stated in Congress's "declaration of policy").

As a result, the Court examined whether there existed other legitimate governmental interests. The Court noted the legislative history that existed on the amendment to the food stamp law indicated its purpose was to prevent "hippies" and "hippie communes" from participating in the food stamp program. The Court held that "if 'equal protection of the laws' means anything, it must at the very least mean that a bare congressional desire to harm a politically unpopular group cannot constitute a legitimate governmental interest." The state attempted to argue there were other legitimate interests, such as combating fraud, but the Court did not accept the notion that unrelated people were more likely to defraud the government than related people. The Court found the Act contained other effective ways of dealing with fraud, and thus, it doubted that fraud was the real purpose for the legislation.

Justice Rehnquist, joined by Chief Justice Warren, dissented, arguing the majority went beyond merely determining whether Congress had a rational basis for discriminating between related and unrelated persons. Justice Rehnquist argued that "reasonable men" could find the amendment was rationally related to preventing fraud, caused by unrelated groups pooling their resources. The fact that there could be unintended consequences did not make the amendment unconstitutional.

Here, the Court found it necessary to more closely scrutinize the amendment to protect discrete and insular minorities, who are disadvantaged in the political process. When members of Congress have stated on the legislative record that the law's purpose is to remove benefits from a politically unpopular minority group (here, hippies), the Court should scrutinize the government's purported purpose to determine if it is merely a facade.

Furthermore, in this instance, the legislation was grossly overbroad because it arbitrarily denied people government assistance. Here, Ms. Moreno lost her food stamps, along with Ms. Sanchez and her three children. Even if the government's purpose was to target fraud by hippies, the scope of the law reached everyone who was unrelated and lived together, not just hippies. The amendment did not further any of the government's purported purposes, and it had the effect of arbitrarily depriving hippies and nonhippies of government assistance.

b. Animus toward Those with Mental Disabilities: *City of Cleburne, Texas v. Cleburne Living Center, Inc.* (1985)

An ordinance for the city of Cleburne, Texas, required a special permit for group homes consisting of the mentally disabled, but not for other group homes, such as apartments, sororities, fraternities, hospitals, nursing homes, and homes for the elderly. The city denied a special-use permit to the Cleburne Living Center, which sought to establish a group home for people with mental disabilities. The Court of Appeals of the Fifth Circuit determined that the "mentally retarded" was a "quasi-suspect" class and that the ordinance violated the Equal Protection Clause because it did not survive intermediate scrutiny. The Supreme Court, in *City of Cleburne, Texas v. Cleburne Living Center, Inc.* (1985), held that the "mentally retarded" were not a suspect class but nonetheless struck the ordinance down under the rational basis test.

At first glance, those with mental disabilities appear to be a discrete and insular minority in need of the Court's intervention because they have historically been discriminated against, and their ability to further their interests through the political process may be questionable. Nonetheless, the Court articulated four reasons this group should not be treated as a suspect class.

1. As a class, the "mentally retarded" often require different or special treatment because of their special needs, and thus, it will often be reasonable and justifiable to discriminate on this basis.
2. The legislative branch, at both the federal and state level, has recently responded by passing legislation singling out this group for special positive treatment (benign discrimination).
3. The fact that the legislature has passed legislation, favoring those with mental disabilities, indicates that they are not politically powerless.
4. If this group were considered to be a suspect class, this would lead to a slippery slope of including other groups, such as "the aging, the mentally ill, and the infirm."

Further, the Court was concerned that heightened scrutiny would make it more difficult for the legislature to intervene to positively help those with disabilities.

The city council put forward a number of reasons for requiring such a permit:

1. the negative attitudes of nearby property owners;
2. the proximity to a high school with students that might mistreat the residents;
3. the fact that the home was on a flood plain;
4. concerns over the number of people within the house, given its size; and
5. avoiding the overpopulation of and lessening congestion on the streets.

After debunking all of these purported justifications, the Court held that "requiring the permit in this case appears to us to rest on an irrational prejudice against the mentally retarded." Most of these purported reasons either were completely arbitrary, were farfetched, or required one to hold irrational, prejudicial beliefs. Although individuals in society may hold such beliefs, it is improper for the Court to give them effect.

c. Animus toward Gays, Lesbians, and Bisexuals: *Romer v. Evans* (1996)

A number of cities in the state of Colorado (Aspen, Boulder, and Denver) passed ordinances that prohibited discrimination on the basis of sexual orientation in the provision of housing, employment, education public accommodation, and health and welfare services. Similar legislation exists at the state and federal levels to protect these classes from discrimination on the basis of race, gender, and disabilities. The city ordinances in question met strong opposition throughout the state, and in 1992, a Colorado constitutional amendment was passed in a statewide referendum. The referendum went beyond simply repealing the ordinances; it prohibited "all legislative, executive or judicial action at any level of state or local government designed to protect the named class, … homosexuals or gays and lesbians." Under the amendment, there would be no protection against discrimination in "housing, sale or real estate, insurance, health and welfare, services, private education, and employment" or against discrimination by any level of government in the state of Colorado. These protections are disallowed no matter how public or private and regardless of how local or widespread the discrimination. Further, it forbade all levels of government from protecting the group from discrimination.

The state of Colorado attempted to argue that this merely put gays and lesbians on equal footing as other persons, but the Court, in *Romer v. Evans* (1996), rejected this argument. The Court found that the amendment put homosexuals "in a solitary class with respect to transactions and relations in both the private and governmental spheres." The Court held the amendment singled out this group and took away the legal protection against discrimination they had gained in various cities in the state and forbid any future protection. No other group was treated this way, and no other group would need a state constitutional amendment to seek protection against discrimination.

As the Court noted, the protections taken away are not special but are the kind of protections most people either do not have or do not need. Although the Court did not explicitly mention it, Caucasian males are protected from discrimination on the basis of their gender and race as much as the African American female. The Court's equal protection jurisprudence does not merely protect women or minorities, and the city ordinances would not only protect gays, lesbians, and bisexuals but heterosexuals as well.

The Court acknowledged that homosexuality was not a suspect class; thus, it would uphold the classification, if it bore a rational relation to some legitimate end. Yet here, the amendment not only failed, it defied "this conventional inquiry." The Court pointed out two reasons:

1. The legislation imposed "a broad and undifferentiated disability on a single named group"; and
2. the amendment is so overbroad and discontinuous with the reasons offered by the state that the only thing that can explain the amendment is animus toward the group.

Elaborating on the first reason, the Court noted that the legislation was both grossly underinclusive in its singling out of a single group and grossly overinclusive in that it "denies them protection across the board." The state's proffered reasons for the amendment included freedom of association for those who may not wish to associate with homosexuals and conserving resources to fight other forms of discrimination. The Court found the sweeping nature of the amendment was simply too overbroad and discontinuous with these purposes to be credible.

The Court concluded that animus was the sole reason for the amendment, and animus is not a legitimate state purpose. The Court quoted *Department of Agriculture v. Moreno* (1973) (discrimination based on animus toward hippies): "If 'equal protection of the laws' means anything, it must at the very least mean that a bare ... desire to harm a politically unpopular group cannot constitute a legitimate governmental interest." The majority concluded its opinion by stating: "A State cannot so deem a class of persons a stranger to its laws."

Justice Antonin Scalia, joined by Chief Justice Rehnquist and Justice Thomas, dissented and viewed the amendment as simply denying preferential treatment; it did not deny equal treatment or equal protection. He made a rather powerful argument that if the state can criminalize homosexual conduct (which the Court upheld in *Bowers v. Hardwick,* 1986), then the state can pass laws disfavoring homosexual conduct, and thus, it can certainly pass a law that merely prohibits providing them special protection. Justice Scalia charged the Court with imposing its elite views on the rest of America without any constitutional authority for doing so, even arguing that the Constitution is silent on the subject.

Justice Scalia's argument is sound if one accepts that the amendment merely withholds special treatment or that the law in *Bowers,* which covered homosexual conduct or behavior, is indistinguishable from a law that allows for private and governmental discrimination and entrenches it in its constitution. For the majority, the legislation was too overbroad because it did not target specific behavior but mere status. The amendment did not merely allow for discrimination based on conduct; it also allowed one to discriminate against a minister or priest who was openly homosexual yet practiced celibacy. Even with this example, it is admittedly difficult to reconcile this case with *Bowers,* and it is unfortunate that the majority did not take the opportunity to strike down *Bowers.* Finally, seven years later, the Court overruled *Bowers* in *Lawrence v. Texas* (2003). Without *Bowers,* and in light of *Lawrence,* Justice Scalia's rather strong argument loses most if not all of its thunder. In other words, even if Justice Scalia's opinion was a better reflection of the law in 1996 when *Romer* was decided, it would not follow that it is still a better reflection of the law now that *Lawrence* has been decided.

Stop Points

Rational Basis Review

- Test: is the government action rationally related to a legitimate government purpose?

- The government action will be presumed as constitutional unless the challenging party can prove that the government classification is not rationally related to a constitutionally permissible government interest.

- **Cases of Exceptional Deference:** any conceivable legislative purpose for the law is sufficient. The government only needs to state a legitimate purpose at the time the law is challenged; it is irrelevant that it was not the legislature's true purpose for passing the law. The plaintiff has the burden to negate or disprove every conceivable basis for the law's rationality.

- **Cases Involving Some Level of Scrutiny:** although the Court is highly deferential to the government under this test, there have been a number of cases in which the Court appears to really test whether there is an actual legitimate purpose and if the legislation is, in fact, rationally related to it.

  - In these cases the Court found that the classification was invidious, wholly arbitrary, or capricious. These cases include discrimination against unrelated cohabitants, people with disabilities, and gays, lesbians, and bisexuals.

III. Strict Scrutiny: Race, National Origin, Ethnicity, Ancestry, and Alienage (Including Segregation and Affirmative Action)

A. Introduction

As noted at the outset, classifications based on race, national origin, and ethnicity receive strict scrutiny from the Court. These three categories often overlap, and the Court's jurisprudence generally treats them the same (e.g., even native Hawaiian ancestry was considered a proxy for race in *Rice v. Cayetano*, 2000). Alienage is a slightly different category and refers to one's status as either a citizen or a noncitizen. The federal government has the power to regulate this area of the law; thus, the Court is more deferential to Congress in this arena than to the states. The Court generally applies strict scrutiny to state discrimination on this basis, unless it involves an issue that is core to state governance; for example, eligibility to serve in a political office, as a police officer, or as a teacher. However, the Court did not articulate the strict scrutiny test until 1944, in *Korematsu v. U.S.* Finally, in 1995 in *Adarand Constructors, Inc. v. Pena*, the Court settled on applying the test in cases of affirmative action, sometimes called "benign discrimination," by the federal government.

Strict scrutiny only applies if the law or governmental conduct is (1) discriminatory on its face; or (2) it has both a discriminatory impact, and the government's purpose was to have the discriminatory impact (*Washington v. Davis*, 1976).

In the context of voting districts, the rule is slightly different. The Court, in *Shaw v. Reno* (1993), established that for strict scrutiny to apply to political gerrymandering (the manipulation of voting district lines to make it easier for one party to get elected), the district must either appear on its face to be gerrymandered based on race (have a very irregular shape, e.g., like a Chinese dragon or a river with numerous tributaries), or the plaintiff must show that race was the predominant factor or reason for drawing the district boundaries. In other words, it is not enough that the government's purpose included racial considerations; race must have been the most important purpose.

The remainder of this section covers the history of Court's jurisprudence from before and after the Civil War and the Civil War amendments (the Thirteenth, Fourteenth and Fifteenth Amendments). It will cover the rise and fall of the doctrine of "separate but equal" as well as the issue of laws that have a discriminatory impact yet are neutral on their face. It will also cover the rise and fall of efforts to remedy segregation and affirmative action. It will end with a look at discrimination in the context of voting districts and discrimination on the basis of alienage.

B. History: Pre-Civil War

As already noted, the original Constitution did not give effect to the broad principles stated in the Declaration of Independence (except as to white males, who owned property). The Constitution avoided referring to slaves, but there was nothing color-blind about its provisions affecting slaves. States that allowed for slavery were awarded extra representation through Article I, Section 9, which allowed those states to count three out of every five slaves, for the purposes of increasing slaveholders' representation in Congress. The Constitution also set out to protect the institution of slavery and rights of slave owners by:

1. preventing Congress from banning the importation of slaves for the next twenty-one years (Article I, Section 9),
2. not allowing the above item to be changed, even by constitutional amendment (Article V), and
3. by requiring that fugitive slaves (those who escaped to free states and territories) be returned to their owners or those to whom they owed service or labor (the Fugitive Clause, Article IV, Section 2).

The constitutional text did not provide much hope for abolitionists or slaves. There was very little color-blind language in the text that would allow the courts room to combat the institution of slavery, even if that was their desire.

The Court's decision in *Dred Scott v. Sandford* (1857) is often cited as one of the low points in constitutional history. That case involved the issue of slavery within the new territories of the Louisiana Purchase (the purchase of French territories within the United States running from Louisiana all the way northeast to Montana and comprising almost a quarter of the country's current landmass). The controversy over slavery in the territory came to a head when Missouri wished to join the Union as slave state within the territory. This lead to the Missouri Compromise (1819), which allowed Missouri to join the Union as a slave state but prohibited slavery in the northern part of the new territories that were obtained through the Louisiana Purchase. Let's take a quick look at *Dred Scott*.

A Southern plantation owner named John Emerson owned a slave named Dred Scott in Missouri and took him to Illinois, a free state. After Emerson died, Dred Scott sued the administrator of Emerson's estate, John Sandford, and claimed his freedom as resident of Illinois. The Court held that because Dred Scott was a slave, he was not a citizen; instead he was property. As a noncitizen, he did not have standing to bring a diversity suit against Sandford.

Furthermore, the Court held the Missouri Compromise was unconstitutional. Since the Fugitive Slave Clause, in Article IV, Section 2, affirmed the right of property in slaves, then Congress lacked the power to pass the Missouri Compromise and deny slave owners their property rights. Slave owners did not lose their right to property just because slaves, such as Dred Scott, were moved into a free state.

Although the Court perhaps missed an opportunity to limit the institution of slavery, it is questionable whether the law would justify a different result. The Missouri Compromise was in conflict with the Constitution, which at its worst protected the institution of slavery, and at its best did not empower Congress to forbid states from instituting slavery. The Court's decision further exacerbated the tensions between the North and South and fueled the debate, leading to the Civil War from 1861 to 1865. In 1865, Congress passed the Thirteenth Amendment, which outlawed slavery and involuntary servitude. The Amendment effectively overruled *Dred Scott* by making former slaves citizens of the United States. It also empowered Congress to pass further legislation to enforce the Amendment.

C. History: The Early Period to Post-Civil War

Along with the Thirteenth Amendment, which made slavery unconstitutional, Congress also passed the Fourteenth and Fifteenth Amendments. Although the war was fought, in part, to stop the South from seceding from the Union, Congress passed the Fourteenth Amendment without Southern representation. After several Southern states rejected the Amendment, Congress passed a law in 1867 that put ten Southern states under martial law and removed their legislators from office. Thus, the Fourteenth Amendment was ratified in 1868 without the approval of three-fourths of the states.

The Fifteenth Amendment, which was ratified in 1870, granted former male slaves the right to vote. It provides the "right of citizens of the United States to vote shall not be denied or abridged by the United States or by any State on account of race, color, or previous condition of servitude." This right was not given much effect until the late 1960s, after the passage of the Voting Rights Act of 1965.

In 1883, the Court considered an Alabama law that provided more severe penalties for the crimes of adultery and fornication if those committing the crimes were of a different race. Mixed-race offenders were to be sentenced between two and seven years, whereas same-race offenders could serve no more than a year. In *Pace v. Alabama* (1883), the Court upheld the law on the ground that the law affected both races equally. The Court stated:

> Section 4189 applies the same punishment to both offenders, the white and the black. Indeed, the offense against which this latter section is aimed cannot be committed without involving the persons of both races in the same punishment. Whatever discrimination is made in the punishment prescribed in the two sections is directed against the offense designated and not against the person of any particular color or race. The punishment of each offending person, whether white or black, is the same.

Thus, from the start, the Court not only accepted, but enforced the notion that separation of the races was a valid state interest or purpose. The same year, in *The Civil Rights Cases* (1883), the Court struck down the Civil Rights Act of 1875, which Congress enacted under the authority of the Civil War amendments to eradicate the badges and incidents of slavery. The Act imposed sanctions on private persons for interfering with the rights of African American citizens. The Court held that the Fourteenth Amendment's Enforcement Clause, which empowered Congress to give effect to the Amendment, only applied to the states, not private individuals ("No State shall ..."). Although Congress could enforce the Thirteenth Amendment by passing laws that would bind private persons, those laws were limited to "slavery" or "involuntary servitude," which did not include civil rights. Thus, the Civil Rights Act of 1875 was unconstitutional because it was beyond the scope of Congress's powers.

Further, in *U.S. v. Harris* (1883), the Court struck down the criminal provisions of the Civil Rights Act of 1871, otherwise known as the Ku Klux Klan Act, which was passed to combat the nation's first terrorist organization, the KKK. The Act made it a crime to "conspire or go in disguise upon the highway or on the premises of another for the purpose of depriving" any person of the equal protection of the laws. The Court applied the same reasoning it used in the *Civil Rights Cases* and held that the Act went beyond Congress's powers. Due to the development of its Commerce Clause powers, Congress finally enacted the Civil Rights Act of 1964. Remarkably, it also was not until 1964 that the Court overruled *Pace*, in *McLaughlin v. Florida* (1964) (striking down a law that made it a crime for a black person and a white person to live together or share a room at night).

The first successful equal protection claim was in *Yick Wo v. Hopkins* (1886). The Court held that San Francisco's enforcement of an ordinance that banned laundries in wooden structures violated the Equal Protection Clause. Although the ordinance itself was not discriminatory, the authorities implemented it with an "evil eye and an unequal hand." Although they universally denied every petition for an exemption by Chinese launderers, they granted exemptions from the ordinance to almost everyone else. In 1879, in *Strauder v. West Virginia*, the Court struck down a West Virginia statute that excluded all African Americans from serving on juries. Although the Court in *Strauder* found that discrimination against African Americans in serving on juries was unconstitutional, in *Virginia v. Rives* (1879), the Court declined to take the next step and acquit a black defendant convicted by an all-white jury.

D. Post-Civil War: "Separate but Equal" under Jim Crow

As the foregoing cases illustrate, the end of the Civil War did not bring racial harmony. The laws that criminalized mixing of the races in private were strongly echoed by laws and policies that segregated black from white in most aspects of public life, including public schools, transportation, restrooms, and parks. The government designed these laws and policies to exclude African Americans from restaurants, hotels, and voting. At the very least, the laws had the effect of providing separate (but unequal) access to schools, parks, public transportation, and accommodations.

The laws and institutions that developed during this period are often referred to as Jim Crow laws. Jim Crow was a caricature of the African American male, depicted him as a foolish, clownish simpleton; it often appeared in minstrel shows as a singing and dancing buffoon. This, along with other caricatures of African Americans, no doubt helped justify in the stereotypical mind the need and desirability of providing separate and inferior services to those who were freed by the Civil War.

The Court placed its stamp of approval on the doctrine of "separate but equal" in *Plessy v. Ferguson* (1896). Homer Plessy was denied a seat in the whites-only railway car because one of his great-grandparents was black. He had one-eighth African blood. The state of Louisiana had passed legislation that provided a "separate but equal" car for blacks. Under this law, there was to be no commingling of the races in the same car, unless a partition was provided. The Court upheld the legislation and denied Plessy a writ of prohibition, which would have prohibited prosecution for violating the statute.

The Court held the Fourteenth Amendment could only abolish inequality of the law but could not reach social inequality. Thus, it was within the state's police powers to require separate but equal accommodations. With somewhat strained reasoning, the Court considered the issue to be whether people could choose to segregate themselves; the Court would not force people together. Of course, this view is from the perspective of a white majority who did not want to be forced to allow African Americans into their railway cars. In addition, the Court stated that separating the races did not "stamp the coloured race with a badge of inferiority." If blacks felt that way, the Court reasoned, it was because of their own doing and not because of the legislation itself.

In fairness to the Court, it recognized that to decide otherwise would have wide-ranging effects. It was not merely the states, or even the South, that provided "separate but equal" services for African Americans; Congress's own school district in the District of Columbia was also segregated by race at the time. The Court was not convinced it could decide that separate train cars were unconstitutional without also deciding that separate schools were as well. It was not until the death of Chief Justice Fred Vinson in 1953 and the Court's decision in *Brown v. Board of Education* (1954) that the era of separate but equal finally ended.

Plessy was not a unanimous decision; Justice John Harlan wrote one of the most famous and prophetic opinions in Supreme Court history. He argued that the Constitution was color-blind and the Court's decision would "prove to be quite as pernicious as the decision made ... in the *Dred Scott* case." Justice Harlan did not accept that "separate but equal" provided equal treatment under the law, as required by the Fourteenth Amendment. He convincingly picked apart the majority's argument that the law somehow respected the choice of people to remain separate. He pointed out "that everyone knows" the purpose of the statute was to exclude "coloreds" from entering railroad cars occupied by whites. There was no equal treatment here, but a law based on color that created separate classes.

E. The Introduction of Strict Scrutiny

As previously noted, *Korematsu v. United States* (1943) was the first case to introduce the strict scrutiny test for discrimination based on race or national origin. The Court was unanimous in adopting the strict scrutiny test, although it split six to three on the issue of whether California's forced exclusion of Japanese Americans from certain parts of California during World War II satisfied the test. Although the Court did not articulate the test in its exact modern form, Justice Hugo Black, writing for the majority, held that legal restrictions on the civil rights of a single racial group are "immediately suspect" and to be subject to the "most rigid scrutiny." Such restrictions would not be upheld if they were based on "racial antagonism," but would be upheld if they were based on "pressing public necessity." The Court held that the treatment of Fred Korematsu was not due to animus toward his race but because of the pressing national security interest in protecting the country during a time of war with Japan. Three Justices strongly dissented on this last point, arguing that the danger was not so imminent and severe as to justify the discriminatory treatment toward American citizens of Japanese descent.

F. The Challenge to *Plessy:* Can Separate Really Be Equal?

The dismantling of legally imposed segregation in America was largely the product of a long series of legal challenges brought by the National Association for the Advancement of Colored People (NAACP). The NAACP began by attacking secondary school systems that were separate but not equal in the 1930s. These challenges focused on the clear and tangible provision of unequal facilities and/or resources. In the case of *Murray v. Maryland* (1936), the NAACP successfully argued before the Maryland Court of Appeals that the exclusion of African Americans from the University of Maryland School of Law violated Donald Murray's equal protection rights because the alternative state schools that would admit him were clearly unequal to the University's law school. This resulted in the desegregation of the University of Maryland School of Law.

In *Missouri ex rel. Gaines v. Canada* (1938), the NAACP challenged the state of Missouri's policy of excluding African Americans from its law school yet providing funding for African Americans to go to law schools outside the state. The Court sided with the NAACP and held that a legal education in another state was too separate to be equal; Missouri could not meet its obligation to provide an equal education by outsourcing the obligation to another state. It would need to provide that opportunity within the state.

Sweatt v. Painter (1950) marked the first Supreme Court decision in which the Court ordered a segregated white university to admit an African American student. The University of Texas School of Law had denied Herman Sweatt admission on the grounds that he could attend the newly formed Prairie View Law School. The University of Texas had sixteen full-time faculty members and substantial facilities. At the time Sweatt was denied admission, Prairie View had no full-time faculty or library. By the time the Court heard the case, there were five full-time professors and a small library. Nonetheless, the two schools were clearly unequal. As the Court noted, "it is difficult to believe that one who had a free choice between these law schools would consider the question close." Most important, the Court acknowledged it was more than the tangible differences that made the schools unequal; the intangibles, such as reputation and the alumni connections, were important considerations as well.

In *McLaurin v. Oklahoma State Regents* (1950), decided on the same day as *Sweatt*, the Court held that the University of Oklahoma's practice of segregating African American students within the law school adversely affected George McLaurin's ability to obtain an equal education. Here again, the Court noted the tangible and intangible effects of segregation on the ability to obtain an equal education.

Sweatt and *McLaurin* set the groundwork for *Brown v. Board of Education* (1954). In the former two cases, the segregation could perhaps be remedied by better facilities, but the latter could not. Brown was the named plaintiff in consolidated cases involving numerous school-age children across Kansas, South Carolina, Delaware, and Virginia who wished to attend whites-only schools. Some of these cases could have been decided in favor of the plaintiffs under the *Plessy* doctrine of separate but equal, due to the clear tangible inequalities in the education being provided to African American children. This likely would have been the grounds for the decisions, had it not been for former Chief Justice Vinson passing away and being replaced by Chief Justice Warren. In a unanimous decision, written by Chief Justice Warren, the Court overruled *Plessy* by holding that the doctrine of separate but equal had no place in realm of public education. The Court recognized that even if the tangible facilities were equal, segregated education labeled African American children as inferior and thereby denied them equal educational opportunities. In making its decision, the Court relied on social science studies to show that segregation had negative psychological effects on African American children.

Although the use of social science studies to defend the Court's decision has been criticized by numerous authors, the Court identified the correct problem: Segregation is not merely an issue of resources or facilities, but of the deeper message sent when the state separates on the basis of race. Because the decision was based in part on social science, it left open the possibility that at a different time and in a different context, some forms of separate educational opportunities may not carry a badge or mark of inferiority or superiority and thus might not offend the equal protection guarantee.

Brown did not answer the questions of segregation in other contexts. However, in a series of *per curium* decisions after *Brown*, the Court held that the segregation of public facilities was unconstitutional, for example, beaches and bathhouses in *Mayor and City Council of Baltimore City v. Dawson* (1955), golf courses in *Holmes v. City of Atlanta* (1955), bus systems in *Gayle v. Browder* (1956), airport restaurants in *Turner v. City of Memphis* (1962), and courtrooms in *Johnson v. Virginia* (1963).

More recently, in *Johnson (Garrison) v. California* (2005) (note that that there are two different *Johnson v. California* cases from 2005—this case involved Garrison Johnson), the Court held that the state of California must meet the strict scrutiny test to justify the segregation of prisoners on the basis of race. The Court rejected arguments by the state that the segregation applied equally to all and thus, was not discriminatory; it rejected similar arguments in *Brown v. Board of Education* (1954). In a five-to-three decision, the Court remanded the case to the court below to determine if in fact the segregation was necessary to achieve a compelling state interest. In his dissent, Justice Stevens argued that there was no need to remand the case because it was clear that California did not meet the strict scrutiny test. Justice Thomas's dissent, joined by Justice Scalia, was based on the argument that the Court should show deference to prison officials and follow precedent that lowered the threshold standard of review in cases involving the constitutional claims of prisoners. They argued that the test should be whether the policy was "reasonably related to a legitimate penological interest" (a legitimate interest tied to incarceration). The majority distinguished those cases as not involving racial discrimination, much less express racial classifications. According to the majority, the use of express racial classifications made the policy immediately suspect and subject to strict scrutiny review.

G. Laws Punishing Intimate Relations between the Races: Punishing Both Races Is Not Race Neutral

As noted, it took over eighty years for the Court to overrule *Pace v. Alabama* (1882). In *Pace*, the Court upheld a law that imposed harsher penalties for acts of fornication and adultery by interracial couples than by couples of one same race. As the Court stated in that case, the law "applies the same punishment to offenders, the white and the black." In *McLaughlin v. Florida* (1964), the

Court rejected this reasoning and struck down a law that made it a crime for a black person and a white person to live together or share a room at night. Although the law applied to everyone, it was still a race-based law with a race-based purpose. If the law was designed to thwart premarital sex, that goal could be met with a race-neutral law.

In *Loving v. Virginia* (1969), the Court also rejected the idea that a racially motivated law or policy did not offend the Equal Protection Clause if it applied to people of all races. It is remarkable that it took fifteen years after *Brown* and five years after *McLaughlin* before the Court struck down antimiscegenation laws (laws forbidding marriage between the races). Antimiscegenation laws are probably the most pernicious form of segregation because they proscribe perhaps the most fundamental and important arena of association. *Loving* involved an interracial couple that had married in Washington, D.C., and moved to Virginia. They were both convicted of violating a Virginia statute that prohibited mixed-race marriages. From one vantage point, the law treated all races equally—neither a white person nor a nonwhite person could marry a person from a different race, and both parties were subject to punishment. The Court rejected this argument because the law clearly distinguished between those who could marry and those who could not on the basis of race. The Court concluded that the law was meant to maintain white supremacy, and because the state of Virginia could not show a legitimate overriding purpose for the law, it was struck down (in other words, there was no compelling state interest).

The Court came to the same conclusion in *Palmore v. Sidoti* (1984) when it held a natural mother could not lose custody of her child simply because the mother was part of an interracial marriage. Though the Court acknowledged that private biases might expose the child to social stigmas because she lived with interracial parents, the Court held the Constitution forbids public officials from directly or indirectly giving those biases effect.

H. Race-Neutral Classifications with a Discriminatory Impact

Although the text of the Equal Protection Clause does not contain a *mens rea* requirement, the Court has consistently held that governmental classifications that are facially neutral only violate the Equal Protection Clause if there is both a discriminatory purpose and discriminatory effect. Congress can (and has) passed civil rights laws that lower this requirement and allow for a statutory claim based on discriminatory impact alone (e.g., Title VII of the 1964 Civil Rights Act and the 1965 Voting Rights Act, as amended in 1982). Under both the Constitution and statutory claims, there must be a discriminatory impact; a discriminatory purpose alone is not enough to bring the claim, unless that purpose is clear on the face of the law.

Although never expressly stated by the Court in an Equal Protection Clause claim, the case of *Mt. Healthy City School District Board of Ed. v. Doyle* (1977), stands for the proposition that the plaintiff must show that the purpose of the law was causally related to the discriminatory impact. *Mt. Healthy* involved a First Amendment claim by Fred Doyle, who had been fired in part because of comments he made to a radio station regarding the dress code at his school. In that case, the Court held that although the school district's bias against the protected speech caused the plaintiff's termination, it had not been established that this was the cause of the school district's refusal to hire him back. In that instance, the plaintiff needed to show that the purpose of the law (the bias against his speech) was causally related to the discriminatory impact (failing to be rehired). The school may have declined to hire him back for any number of reasons.

For a plaintiff to successfully bring an Equal Protection Clause claim, she or he must show that it was the government's purpose to bring about the result of discrimination. It is not sufficient to show a reckless disregard of the risk that a discriminatory result may occur, nor is it sufficient to show there was knowledge that the result will occur (*Personnel Administrator of Massachusetts v. Feeney*, 1979).

Discriminatory purpose can sometimes be gleaned from the history and circumstances leading up to the enactment of a law or from a clear discriminatory impact of a law that makes it difficult to discern whether a legitimate purpose motivated the law (*Village of Arlington Heights v. Metropolitan Housing Development Corp.*, 1977). The Court held that the pattern must be stark and pointed to the stark patterns of discrimination found in the cases of *Yick Wo v. Hopkins* (1886) and *Gomillion v. Lightfoot* (1960).

One of the earliest cases where the Court dealt with a facially neutral law was in *Yick Wo v. Hopkins* (1886). Although the law was race-neutral, it had a discriminatory impact because the authorities implemented it with an "evil eye and an unequal hand." The Court held that San Francisco's enforcement of an ordinance that banned laundries in wooden structures violated the Equal Protection Clause because the authorities denied every petition for an exemption by Chinese launderers, while they almost universally granted exemptions from the ordinance to non-Chinese petitioners. Thus, although the law itself did not have a discriminatory purpose, the city administered the law in such a way that it gave effect to a discriminatory purpose. The pattern of discriminatory application was stark.

Gomillion v. Lightfoot (1960), as well as *Yick Wo*, are often cited as examples of cases in which the discriminatory impact is so clear as to make it difficult to imagine a nondiscriminatory purpose for the law. In *Gomillion*, the city of Tuskegee, Alabama, redrew what was a square-shaped voting district into something that resembled a Chinese dragon with twenty-eight sides. The new district managed to leave almost every African American outside of the city limits.

In another series of cases, the Court did not find the discriminatory impact to be the motivating reason for the law or practice. For instance, in *Washington v. Davis* (1976), the petitioners, two black men, failed the written test to become Washington, D.C., police recruits. They claimed the test was racially biased. They pointed to the facts that African American applicants had higher failure rates than whites and that the test was unrelated to the job performance of police officers. The Court held that a test that is neutral on its face and rationally related to a legitimate state interest is constitutional, even though it may disproportionately impact one race. Here, the test was administered generally to all applicants, and it was used to determine verbal ability, vocabulary, and reading comprehension. Justice Brennan wrote a strong dissent that Justice Marshall joined. The dissent focused on the fact that there was no evidence the test had any validity as a predictor of job performance. Justice Brennan argued that this fact, coupled with the test's discriminatory impact, should have resulted in the Court holding the policy invalid.

The same rule was applied and the same result obtained in *Village of Arlington Heights v. Metropolitan Housing Development Corp* (1977), a case in which the zoning law had a discriminatory impact on racial minorities because it affected the ability of those with low incomes to obtain housing. In this case, the village denied the petitioners a permit to rezone a parcel of land from single family to multifamily, low-income housing. The Court held that discriminatory impact was not sufficient; there must have been a motivating discriminatory purpose. Although the case was questionable on the facts, the Court held that there simply was not sufficient evidence of a racially motivated purpose. Similarly, in *City of Mobile v. Bolden* (1980), the Court upheld an "at-large" election scheme that had the impact of making it very difficult for minority representatives to get elected to the city council.

The Court came to a different result in *Rogers v. Herman Lodge* (1982), when it held, given the history of discrimination in the jurisdiction, that the at-large election scheme was motivated by racial considerations. *Rogers* is an example of how history and circumstances, leading up to the enactment of a law, may be used to prove purpose when facial discrimination is not present.

The case of *Personnel Adm. of Massachusetts v. Feeney* (1979), which involved the preferential hiring of veterans, is commonly cited for the rule that laws that are not facially discriminatory require both a discriminatory impact and discriminatory purpose. In *Feeney*, the discriminatory impact was based on gender, because the vast majority of veterans were men at the time. Although the discriminatory impact was clear, similar to *Yick Wo* (ordinance that banned laundries), there were numerous legitimate, nondiscriminatory purposes for the law, such as the desire to reintegrate veterans back into society and provide them with benefits that were commensurate with the sacrifices they made for the country.

There is a lower threshold for showing a discriminatory purpose in the area of preemptory challenges during jury selection. Most jury selection rules allow both the prosecution and defense to exclude people from sitting on a jury based on cause and to exclude a limited number of people for no stated reason. These are called challenges for cause and preemptory challenges, respectively. In *Johnson, Jay Shawn v. California* (2005), the Court held that the criminal defendant, Jay Shawn Johnson, was only required to provide enough evidence for the trial judge to draw an inference that jurors of the defendant's race were dismissed because of their race. This lower threshold for establishing a prima facie case is due to the gravity of harm caused to the justice system and criminal defendants, should a defendant be convicted by a jury selected based on racial considerations.

Showing a discriminatory purpose merely establishes a prima facie case that discrimination was the purpose for the law, policy, or practice. The burden then shifts to the government to show that a legitimate purpose motivated the law, policy, or practice (*Arlington Heights*). *Batson v. Kentucky* (1986), a case involving racially motivated jury selection by using preemptory challenges, articulated a three-step test: (1) the plaintiff must establish a prima facie case of discrimination; (2) the burden then shifts to the government to present evidence that it had race-neutral reasons for the preemption; and (3) the trial court must decide if the government's reasons are persuasive or if the plaintiff has made her case.

The three-step process was established through a series of cases involving allegations of racial discrimination in jury selection. *Batson v. Kentucky* (1986), which overruled the earlier case of *Swain v. Alabama* (1965), was the first case to find that a criminal defendant could establish a prima facie case of discrimination without showing a stark pattern of discrimination. In *Batson*, the Court held that the defendant could establish a prima facie case (step 1) if he showed that he was a member of a cognizable racial group and the prosecution used preemptory challenges to remove members of the defendant's race from the jury pool. As noted, *Johnson, Jay Shawn v. California* (2005) established that to build a prima facie case, the criminal defendant need only present enough evidence for the trial judge to draw the inference that jurors of the defendant's race were dismissed on account of their race. The Court has also held that in the second step, the government does not need to provide a persuasive or even plausible race-neutral explanation (*Purkett v. Ellem*, 1995). Nonetheless, if it does not, this will certainly affect the Court's weighing of the evidence in the third step. The Court in *Purkett*, a *per curium* decision, held that the state need only provide a legitimate reason for the Court to find in its favor. In other words, the question is not how good or wise the reason was for the law, as long as the Court is satisfied it was the reason. Nonetheless, as the Court recently stated in *Miller-El v. Dretke* (2005): "Some stated reasons are false, and although some false reasons are shown up within the four corners of a given case, sometimes a court may not be sure unless it looks beyond the case at hand." In *Dretke*, the Court emphasized the need to scrutinize both the record in the case as well as historical patterns. It is not enough to focus merely on the stated reason given by government.

One of the more troubling cases in this area is *McCleskey v. Kemp* (1987). In this case, the petitioner sought to use a study by Professor David Baldus and colleagues that showed gross discrepancies in the application of the death penalty to black defendants. The starkest results were based on differences in the race of the victim. For example, the death penalty was imposed 22 percent of the time when a black defendant was convicted of killing a white victim, but only in 3 percent of the cases involving a white defendant killing a black victim. The petitioner, Warren McCleskey, was a black man convicted of murdering a white police officer. After being sentenced to death, he claimed his sentencing was administered in a discriminatory manner. For McCleskey to succeed, he needed to show more than general discriminatory impact; he needed to show that the sentencing in his particular case was motivated by racial bias. Further, it was not enough that the state of Georgia knew its death penalty statute had a discriminatory impact, or even that in spite of this knowledge it failed to repeal the statute. Rather, to bring a successful Equal Protection Clause challenge, McCleskey needed to show that the state maintained the statute because of its racial impact. Because he was unable to do this, his petition failed.

Perhaps the most infamous case in which the Court held there was no discriminatory impact is *Palmer v. Thompson* (1971). Although it was clear that the city of Jackson, Mississippi, chose to close its public swimming pools to avoid desegregating them, the Court held that the denial of access to public facilities to all citizens does not violate the Equal Protection Clause because the impact was not discriminatory. Justice William Douglas, in his dissent, argued that the government should not be allowed to avoid integration by eliminating all of its public services, such as school, parks, or pools. According to Justice Douglas, government may not close facilities for the purpose of "perpetuating or installing apartheid." Although there was an equal denial of access to the public facility, there was not an equal impact on Caucasian and African American citizens. The number of Caucasians who could afford access to private, segregated pools was undoubtedly much greater than the number of African Americans with those resources. This latter point was abundantly clear in the case of *Griffin v. County School Board* (1964), where Prince Edward County, Virginia, chose to close its schools rather than desegregate. The Court ordered the county to reopen the schools, explaining that "whatever nonracial grounds might support a state's allowing a county to abandon public schools, the object must be a constitutional one, and grounds of race and opposition to desegregation do not qualify as constitutional." If these two cases are distinguishable, it is due to the importance of access to primary education, as contrasted to access to swimming pools.

I. Remedying Segregation in Schools

The Court's holding in *Brown v. Board of Education* (1954) (called *Brown I*), that legally mandated segregation violated the Equal Protection Clause, raises numerous difficulties, given the complex relationship between legal or *de jure* segregation (segregation imposed by government) and social or *de facto* segregation (segregation that is the result of private actors). Although the former version of segregation violates the Equal Protection Clause, the latter does not. In some cases, one can effectively have the same degree of segregation, and as long as the segregation is not based on governmental action, the courts are not empowered to remedy the situation. However, if it is found that a school district engaged in *de jure* segregation, and the Courts are seized of the matter (the district is under a court order or court supervision), then a policy that the courts might have considered race-neutral will often be treated as race-conscious in violation of the Equal Protection Clause.

In *Griffin v. County School Board*, the school board's decision to close the schools instead of desegregating them is an example of what might be considered a race-neutral policy of simply not providing public school education. However, given that the decision was made in response to the order to desegregate, the Court would not accept the school board's attempt to claim that its *de jure* segregation of public schools was only *de facto* segregation in private schools. The problem is that even if school districts are ordered to take affirmative measures to undo the effects of *de jure* segregation, as long as *de facto* segregation based on racism and socioeconomic inequality persists, there may be no clear point at which one can tell whether a remedy has been provided. The history of the law in this area is something of a pendulum. The Court began with a rather mild or weak approach to desegregation, followed by a period of aggressive and far-reaching responses. Now the Court appears to be abandoning its attempts to chase down and eradicate the effects of *de jure* segregation.

As already discussed, the cases leading up to *Brown v. Board of Education* (1954) were largely brought against graduate or professional schools. For example, in *Sweatt v. Painter* (1950), which involved segregated laws schools in Texas, the Court held there was a straightforward right of the otherwise qualified but excluded African American student(s) to attend the school in question. This remedy, in the context of postsecondary education, was affirmed in the *per curium* decision of *Florida ex. rel. Hawkins v. Board of Control* (1956).

In *Brown v. Board of Education II* (1955) (called *Brown II*), the Court addressed the issue of how to give effect to the decision that separate education was not equal from *Brown I*. In other words, *Brown II* addressed the remedy issue. The Court did not provide the same remedy for the primary school children seeking admittance to white schools as they did in graduate school cases, because the admission of a few students at the graduate school level did not present the same social or practical obstacles as integrating segregated school children across the South. Social and political resistance aside, there would be significant logistical hurdles to integrating children in schools when they were also segregated geographically. Thus, in *Brown II*, the Court did not provide the schoolchildren with a right to attend the schools from which they had been excluded, but ordered the school districts to make a "prompt and reasonable start towards full compliance [with the decision in *Brown* I]." The Court ordered the remedy to be carried out with "with all deliberate speed" and included an order to the local and district courts to use their equitable powers to balance the duty to integrate schools with the logistical difficulties of integration. The Court ordered, and no doubt hoped, the districts to carry out the orders in good faith. Instead, there was massive resistance, which ranged from street-level violence to retaliatory legislation that either declared the Court's decision null and void or simply passed legislation to override the school districts' desegregation plans.

A prime example of this resistance can be found after the Little Rock school system was ordered to desegregate in 1957. The order resulted in the state's governor ordering National Guard troops to prevent African American students from entering whites-only schools, and President Dwight Eisenhower ordering federal troops to make sure that they could attend those schools. The school district then petitioned the courts to stay the integration plan. The Court responded with a unanimous decision in *Cooper v. Aaron* (1958), holding that the students' rights could not be sacrificed because of the violence and disorder caused by the state governor and legislature. The Court drew on Chief Justice John Marshall's words in *Marbury v. Madison*, which "declared the basic principle that the federal judiciary is supreme in the exposition of the law of the Constitution." The Court held that to war against the Court's decision in *Brown II* was tantamount to violating one's oath to support the Constitution. The Court was emphatic that *Brown II* could not be nullified either directly or indirectly through evasive schemes.

Nonetheless, evasive schemes persisted. Although the most common tactic was delay, the county school board in *Griffin* (1964) attempted to shut down its public schools instead of integrating, and other districts created voluntary transfer programs that gave children and their parent(s) the choice of whether to return to their segregated schools (*Goss v. Board of Ed.*, 1963). In 1964, Congress passed the Civil Rights Act and amended it in 1965 to deny funding for public schools that continued to segregate. This conditional funding motivated school to desegregate in the following years.

At the time the Court considered *Griffin*, it was already tired of delays, and it stated, "the time for mere deliberate speed had run out." When it decided *Alexander v. Holmes County Board of Ed.* (1969), the Court held, "the continued operation of segregated schools under a standard of 'all deliberate speed' for desegregation is no longer constitutionally permissible." In *Holmes*, the Court ordered dual school districts to immediately terminate, requiring all school districts to operate and maintain unitary districts.

By 1971, the Court was prepared to authorize broad remedial powers to the district courts to combat segregation in schools. In *Swann v. Charlotte-Mecklenburg Board of Education* (1971), the Court authorized the following methods to integrate students: the use of numerical ratios as a starting point for achieving unitary schools; the redrawing of attendance zones within school districts; and the busing of students, as long as the distance and time of travel did not endanger the students' health or education.

About two years later, in *Milliken v. Bradley* (1973), the Court pulled back on its holding in *Swann* by limiting remedial measures to those within the school district. In *Milliken*, the district court had found that the city of Detroit had a segregated system, and it ordered the school district to end *de jure* segregation and take affirmative measures to reintegrate. However, this remedy had failed in the face of the *de facto* segregation brought on by the "white flight" out of the inner-city district and into the suburban districts. Thus, the district court ordered interdistrict busing between the predominantly white suburbs and predominantly back inner city. The Supreme Court reversed, holding that the district court could not impose an interdistrict remedy if an interdistrict violation had not taken place. Here, only the city had engaged in segregation, so the district court was limited to ordering a remedy for Detroit but not the suburbs. This case represents the beginning of the end of the Court's approval of creative remedies, designed to pursue *de jure* segregation into the realm of *de facto* segregation.

A few years later, in *Pasadena City Board of Ed. v. Spangler* (1976), the Court pulled back on the ability of district courts to redraw attendance zones. The Court held that it was beyond the district court's power to order the annual re-drawing of attendance zones to maintain a unitary school district. It is impor-tant to note that the school district had been found to be a unitary district but had returned to a segregated district within five years of being found unitary.

By the 1990s, the Court was weary of continued attempts to desegregate. In *Board of Education of Oklahoma City Public Schools v. Dowell* (1991), the Court held that the district courts' authority over school districts extended only until the school districts before the court complied with the injunctions for a long enough time to reasonably redress past segregation. In the early 1970s, the district court imposed a desegregation plan for the Oklahoma City Public School System. The plan proved to be successful, and by the mid-1980s the district court dissolved the desegregation decree. The court of appeals re-versed because the school district's proposed new plan, although not discrim-inatory on the basis of race, arguably would result in backsliding into a segregated district. In his majority opinion, Chief Justice Rehnquist noted that the lower courts had been inconsistent in defining a "unitary" school system because some courts had required a district to remove all vestiges of segregation, whereas others merely required that a district desegregated its assignment policies. The Court held that a district court's authority to enjoin a school district only ex-tends to the point necessary for the district to remedy past discrimination to the extent practicable, as long as the district was making a good faith effort to remedy the situation.

In *Freeman v. Pitts* (1992), the Court held that when a district court's de-segregation order had multiple requirements, and the school district had met one or more of them, the district court could not continue a standing order for those requirements already met but only for the ones that had not yet been fulfilled. For example, in *Pitts*, the school district had satisfied the order's re-quirements regarding student assignment and facilities but not that regarding the assignment of teachers. Thus, the district court was not allowed to revisit the impact of future programs or policies on student assignments and facili-ties, but only on teacher assignments. This required district courts to lift or-ders one step at a time, and once lifted, the district court could not revisit those areas, unless it was proven that *de jure* segregation had taken place. This takes the effect of segregationist policies out from under the *de jure* umbrella and places them out in the *de facto* rain, where those who suffer from those effects do not receive protection under the Equal Protection Clause.

In the same year, the Court decided *United States v. Fordice* (1992), in which it addressed the issue of historically black colleges in the state of Mississippi. As noted, the previous remedy for the exclusion of qualified African Americans from postsecondary educational institutions was direct and immediate admittance. The tension in *Fordice* was how the state determined whether an applicant was qualified to attend the previously white schools as opposed to the historically black schools. The state both maintained duplicated schools and programs, and made it more difficult for everyone to be admitted into the historically white schools by requiring higher test scores. This had the effect of perpetuating the segregated colleges. *Fordice* reinforced the rule that the adoption of race-neutral policies was an insufficient means to remedy segregation. Thus, the Court held: "If the State perpetuates policies and practices traceable to its prior system that continue to have segregative effects ... and such policies are without sound educational justification and can be practicably eliminated, the State has not met its burden of proving that it has dismantled its prior system."

Justice Thomas argued in his concurrence that the Court's decision did not foreclose the possibility of sound educational justifications for maintaining historically black colleges that, although open to all, had programs that were more appealing to a given race (separate and equal). However, the majority made it clear that "separate but more equal" did not satisfy the requirements of *Brown*. In other words, although Justice Thomas wanted to leave open the possibility of separate but equal colleges, the majority opinion appears to foreclose that possibility.

In *Missouri v. Jenkins* (1995), the district court had ordered a school district to incur expenditures to improve facilities and increase teachers' salaries as a mechanism to lure white students back to the city's "magnet schools." The Supreme Court held that this was an *interdistrict* remedy, which was not justified by the finding of *intradistrict de jure* segregation. In other words, the Court held that this case fell under the rule in *Milliken*. Although the remedy in *Milliken*, which involved redrawing school district lines and busing children from the suburbs, was radically different from the order in *Jenkins*, which simply made it more attractive for white students to move back, the Court held that the remedy exceeded the nature and the scope of the violation. The violation was intradistrict (in the Kansas City, Missouri, school district), and thus, the remedy could not be designed to reach outside the district (interdistrict) and lure people back to the district. The Court made it clear that the district court's broad, equitable, and creative remedies, which the Supreme Court had previously authorized in *Brown II*, were to be reined in. The Court held that the remedies for segregation must be tailored to the nature and scope of the violation, to return the victims to the position they would have been in, but for the violation.

J. Affirmative Action: Benign Discrimination for the Benefit of Minorities?

Affirmative action, or action taken by the state to benefit minorities when there has not been a finding of *de jure* discrimination, raises a number of important and controversial issues. The first question is whether race-based laws or policies that are not strictly remedial of *de jure* discrimination can be classified as benign discrimination or whether they are always presumptively malignant or invidious and, thereby, suspect. This issue arises in arguments regarding what level of scrutiny should be applied in cases where it appears the state is acting to help a minority. Recall in *City of Cleburne v. Cleburne Living Center* (1985) that the Court refused to allow heightened scrutiny for discrimination on the basis of "mental retardation," in part because the Court found that this would jeopardize the many legislative efforts to positively help those with disabilities. In other words, the Court thought that for the most part, government discrimination on this basis was benign and using a stricter level of scrutiny might undermine those benign efforts. The same argument can be made with regard to legislation that is clearly passed to help other specific groups, such as African Americans or women. Subjecting such legislation to strict or even heightened scrutiny makes it much more difficult to pass. After a considerable period of uncertainty, the Court has settled on requiring strict scrutiny for all race-based discrimination, whether purportedly benign or not. This applies to affirmative action on the local, state, and federal level. Under the Constitution, it does not apply to affirmative action by private actors, although private affirmative action in some contexts is governed by civil rights legislation.

The next question is what is sufficient to constitute a compelling state interest. Remedying past *de jure* discrimination is a compelling state interest, but remedying *de facto* discrimination is not. As mentioned previously, the line between *de facto* and *de jure* discrimination is often difficult to draw. In a recent set of cases involving affirmative action in schools, the Court held that diversity in higher education can be a compelling state interest if there is an individualized evaluation of each student that does not focus on race alone, but on "all factors that may contribute to student body diversity" (*Parents Involved in Community Schools v. Seattle School District*, 2007).

Finally, even if the government can show a compelling state interest, it must also demonstrate that the actions taken are narrowly tailored to achieve that interest. Although there have been a few cases in which the Court has upheld the use of quotas or numerical set-asides as a remedy for past discrimination, they usually fail to satisfy the narrowly tailored requirement, particularly if the compelling state interest is only diversity.

As noted, the Court took some time to settle on strict scrutiny as the test for race-based affirmative action. The first case to directly address the issue, *Regents of the University of California v. Bakke* (1978), failed to produce a majority view on the issue. The case involved a challenge to numerical se-asides for the University of California, Davis Medical School admissions. The university used set-asides (i.e., quotas) that reserved 16 spots out of 100 in each entering class for disadvantaged minorities. Five Justices viewed the case as raising a constitutional issue, while the other four addressed it as a violation of Title VI of the Civil Rights Act of 1964.

With respect to the constitutional issue, four of the five Justices dissented, arguing that intermediate scrutiny was the proper standard, so the issue was whether the quota policy was substantially related to an important governmental interest. Recall in footnote 4 to *Carolene Products,* one finds little justification for applying strict scrutiny when a white majority passes a law or creates a policy for the benefit of minorities. Caucasians are not a discrete and insular minority, and they are adequately represented in the political process. Thus, there is little reason to think that racial animus is likely to be the motive when the law is truly beneficial to minorities. Further, the Caucasian majority is unlikely to create policies that disadvantage themselves more than is necessary, and thus, there is little fear the policies or laws will be overbroad. If both of these statements are true, then there is little reason for strict scrutiny.

Justice Lewis Powell wrote the only concurring opinion and disagreed with the application of intermediate scrutiny. According to Justice Powell, ethnic and racial distinctions are inherently suspect, whether for the purported purpose of benefiting minorities or not. Racial animus is not required to trigger strict scrutiny, there merely needs to be race-based discrimination. Thus, the policy must be necessary for a compelling governmental interest.

Justice Powell's opinion was prophetic in two ways: (1) A majority of the Court later found that strict scrutiny is the appropriate test, and (2) the Court recognized diversity as a compelling state interest. Although Justice Powell thought that quotas were not a legitimate means for achieving diversity, he believed that academic freedom, which is protected under the First Amendment, mandated that diversity is a compelling state interest at the university level. Further, race could be considered as one factor in achieving the goal of diversity.

In yet another decision without a majority opinion on the issue, the Court upheld a federal law that required local governments receiving federal funds for public works projects to set aside 10 percent of their budget for minority-owned businesses (*Fullilove v. Klutznick,* 1980). A plurality of the Court upheld the set-aside as remedy for past discrimination, but the Court was equally split regarding which level of scrutiny to apply.

Finally, nine years later, in *City of Richmond v. J.A. Croson Co.* (1989), a bare majority of the Court adopted the strict scrutiny test. In *City of Richmond,* African Americans represented the majority of the population and the majority of the city council members. The city set aside 30 percent of its public works funding for minority-owned businesses, which arguably represented an instance of the majority passing race-based legislation to benefit itself. A plurality of the Court agreed that "a state or local subdivision ... has the authority to eradicate the effects of private discrimination within its own legislative jurisdiction." However, the Court found there was insufficient evidence to conclude that remedial action was necessary. The 30 percent set-aside failed the strict scrutiny test because the city could not show that minority-owned businesses were underrepresented in public works due to racial discrimination.

Furthermore, the remedy was not narrowly tailored to the government interest in remedying discrimination. Generally, the 30 percent set-aside was not narrowly tailored because the percentage, 30 percent, was arbitrary. More important, "minority-owned businesses" was defined to specifically include "Eskimos or Aleuts" (note the term "Eskimo" is sometimes considered derogatory), yet there was no evidence these groups had ever resided in Richmond or had been discriminated against in the Richmond area. Thus, this was also not narrowly tailored.

Justice Marshall, joined by Justices Brennan and Blackmun, dissented, arguing that the decision to apply strict scrutiny in the affirmative action context was a "deliberate giant step backward." He could not agree with the Court that the record of discrimination in the construction industry was insufficient. Justice Marshall argued that the former seat of the Confederacy had a long history of racial discrimination and this history, along with the fact of gross underrepresentation in the industry, was sufficient to establish the discrimination.

Justice Stevens, in his concurrence, wanted to leave open the possibility that the use of affirmative action that was not strictly remedial could be valid in a future case. He stated in the first footnote: "In my view, the Court's approach to this case gives unwarranted deference to race-based legislative action that purports to serve a purely remedial goal, and overlooks the potential value of race-based determinations that may serve other valid purposes." He did not focus on what test should be applied, in part because he did not like the fact that the different tests were often determinative of the outcome in these cases. In fact, Justice Scalia argued in his concurrence that race-conscious classifications that were not strictly remedial could never survive strict scrutiny.

Just one year later, in *Metro Broadcasting, Inc. v. Federal Communications Comm.* (1990), the Court flipped back to intermediate scrutiny and distinguished *Croson.* In a five-to-four decision, the Court held that congressionally mandated race-conscious measures that were not remedial were constitutionally permissible if they were substantially related to an important governmental purpose. The decision was partially based on the idea that more deference should be given to Congress's enforcement powers in the Fourteenth Amendment to give effect to the Equal Protection Clause.

A somewhat radical change in the Court's composition resulted in overruling *Metro* in *Adarand Construction Inc. v. Pena* (1995). Justice Sandra Day O'-Connor, in her plurality opinion, attempted to soften the harshness of the strict scrutiny test by dispelling the myth that application of the test is always fatal. Justice Scalia, in his concurring opinion, could not resist arguing otherwise; he believed the test was fatal because the state could never have a compelling interest in remedying discrimination with more discrimination. Justice Stevens, in his dissent, argued that the Court was ignoring precedent and failing to properly distinguish between benign and invidious discrimination and between federal and state benign discrimination. He argued that cases involving federally imposed affirmative action or benign discrimination did not warrant strict scrutiny.

Justice O'Connor justified using strict scrutiny on the basis that the Constitution protected individual rights, not group rights; therefore, one could not sacrifice any given individual's rights for the mere benefit of a group. She argued that because of the potential for stigma and racial hostility that accompanies distinctions based on race, the strict scrutiny test was needed to "smoke out" illegitimate uses of race. Further, it would ensure that both the state interest was compelling enough to justify the use of such a suspect tool and that the tool was necessary for achieving those interests.

She argued: "Despite lingering uncertainty in the details ... the Court's cases through *Croson* had established three general propositions with respect to governmental racial classifications." Regardless of whether these general propositions were truly established by the time of *Croson*, Justice O'Connor solidified them in *Adarand*. Those propositions were: (1) skepticism of any preference based on race or ethnicity (i.e., skepticism that race-conscious discrimination could be benign); (2) consistency across any person of any race that is burdened by a classification (e.g., classifications that burden Caucasians were treated the same as those that burden African Americans); and (3) congruence between the analysis of local, state, and federal discrimination under the Fifth and Fourteenth Amendments.

The resulting rule was that all race-conscious discrimination is subject to strict scrutiny, regardless of whether it is benign or invidious, burdens a majority or minority, or is promulgated by the local, state, or federal government. After laying out these three principles, the Court remanded the case to the district court to determine if strict scrutiny was satisfied.

K. Diversity, Critical Mass, and Individualized Assessment

As noted, Justice Powell's opinion in *Bakke* was prophetic in recognizing that diversity in higher education could be a compelling state interest, that quotas were not narrowly tailored to achieving that interest, but that race could be used as one factor in an individualized assessment of applicants. In addition to quotas failing the narrowly tailored requirement, a plurality of the Court, in *Wygant v. Jackson Board of Ed.* (1986), struck down the school board's policy of laying off white teachers before black teachers. Justice Powell wrote the plurality opinion and did not clearly endorse nor foreclose faculty diversity as a compelling state interest. Nonetheless, he rejected the idea that providing role models for students was a compelling state interest. But he accepted that remedying societal discrimination (as opposed to governmental discrimination) was a compelling state interest. Here, the school board's means of achieving and maintaining racial diversity was not narrowly tailored to that end. Although there was some indication that the Court might uphold the less restrictive means of preferential hiring, laying off teachers on the basis of their race was too blunt a tool for achieving racial diversity.

The Court squarely revisited the issues raised in *Bakke* in a pair of cases in 2003, *Grutter v. Bollinger* and *Gratz v. Bollinger*. The former case involved affirmative action in admissions to the University of Michigan Law School, and the latter involved affirmative action in admissions to the university's undergraduate programs.

In *Grutter*, Justice O'Connor wrote the majority opinion for the Court and firmly endorsed Justice Powell's opinion in *Bakke*, holding that diversity in student admissions at the university level was a compelling state interest and that it justified the use of race as a factor in admissions. Similarly, she also emphasized the link between diversity and academic freedom and the deference given to the university to exercise that freedom in determining its mission. This deference was predominately based on the connection between academic freedom and the First Amendment. The Court accepted that diversity was important to the learning process and to preparing students to practice law in a diverse world, demonstrate leadership, and serve in the military.

The University of Michigan Law School's mechanism for achieving diversity resulted in Barbara Grutter's application being denied, even though she had a 161 LSAT score and a 3.8 GPA in undergraduate school. The mechanism used in *Grutter* was not a numerical set-aside or a quota as in *Bakke*, but the law school did have the goal of achieving a "critical mass" of each minority group. The law school provided an individualized review of each student, and racial diversity was one factor among many. Unlike a quota system, which is rigid and mechanical, this system was individualized and holistic. The majority found that the goal of achieving a critical mass, coupled with an individualized assessment, demonstrated that the school respected and sought to further the idea that all minorities were not the same, but that diversity within diversity is more important than mere balancing.

By contrast, Chief Justice Rehnquist and Justice Scalia argued in their dissents that this was not narrowly tailored and amounted to racial balancing. Chief Justice Rehnquist focused on how closely the percentages of minorities tracked the percentages of applications. In his view, this showed that the mechanism was actually a quota or racial balancing, not an individualized assessment. Furthermore, if achieving a critical mass was really necessary to providing diversity within diversity, then one would have expected much larger numbers of other minorities, such as Native Americans and Hispanics.

In his dissenting opinion, Justice Scalia argued that diversity was not a compelling state interest when diversity is used to recruit students into universities; if it was, then it would be equally compelling across the public sector, from grade school to high school and public employment. His slippery slope argument started with the premise that diversity, or as he put it "playing well with others," is not part of any examination in a class or part of any state bar exam. As such, if one can argue that universities have a compelling interest in such a tangential or peripheral goal, then surely that interest is as compelling in a whole range of other contexts. Of course, one might find Justice Scalia's argument compelling without being concerned by his predicted result. Perhaps diversity in all these other contexts is a compelling state interest. If one is not convinced that this is so, there still may be legitimate ways to distinguish the goal of diversity in these different contexts.

Justice Anthony Kennedy, in a separate dissenting opinion, argued the Court had failed to apply truly strict scrutiny in the case. Justice O'Connor's majority opinion did not require that the means chosen be the absolute least restrictive means, or that "every possible race-neutral alternative" be exhausted before adopting a race-conscious plan. For Justice O'Connor this was consistent with the narrow tailoring requirement for strict scrutiny, whereas for Justice Kennedy, it was not.

Justice Thomas's opinion called into question what most Justices took for granted — namely, the need for Michigan to maintain an elite law school. Justice Thomas argued somewhat persuasively there was no compelling state interest in such an elite and exclusive law school. For him, the fact that most of the students did not even remain in the state of Michigan for work after law school showed that there was no pressing public need for the school to exist. If the school was not elite, then its need to recruit critical masses would likely dissipate, as would its need to exclude people like Grutter. In rather personal language, he argued that such programs were based on aesthetics and that many African Americans brought into these elite schools were out of their depth. He indicated that such students would be better served in institutions that did not give them a handout.

In his opinion, Justice Thomas appears to regret his experience at Yale University and resent the idea that he was given a handout through race-based affirmative action. He is on record for being surprised when he found out that he was admitted based on affirmative action, as he believed he was admitted based on the level of adversity that he needed to overcome to get to where he was.

Under the Michigan Law School admittance scheme, these two separate factors for admittance significantly overlap. A student with Justice Thomas's background may be admitted both because he or she overcame significant adversity and because of race, even if a white student or another African American had a higher LSAT score and higher GPA. The point is that an individual with a diverse and adverse background may be accepted over another student who is either less diverse in terms of race or who overcame less adversity.

In *Gratz*, the Court struck down the university's undergraduate admissions policy. The crucial difference between *Gratz* and *Grutter* was that due to the volume of students applying to the university's undergraduate programs, a truly individualized assessment was simply not possible. The mechanism used by the university to achieve diversity was a point system, which awarded students points based on certain factors, such as a merit factor (up to 100 points) and a race factor (20 additional points) out of a total possible of 150 points. While points were assigned for legacy, personal achievement, and work experience, these factors only received four or five points each. According to the majority, as applied, the system guaranteed that "virtually every minimally qualified underrepresented minority applicant" was accepted. Although later in the process some individualized assessment took place, by this point, most of the acceptance offers had already been made.

The Court held that the point system was not narrowly tailored, given that each candidate did not receive an individualized evaluation, as opposed to the system in *Grutter*. The Court may have found differently if fewer points were awarded based on race, or if points were more proportionate to other non-race factors. Justice O'Connor, in her concurring opinion, seemed to espouse this view. She argued that assigning such a great weight to membership in a racial group without any individualized assessment was tantamount to a quota system, which was not narrowly tailored to achieving racial diversity. If the points given for race would have been fewer, it might not have amounted to a quota system.

It should be noted that twenty points could also be awarded for socioeconomic disadvantage, for athletic scholarship recipients, and at the Provost's discretion. Thus, even though legacy students only received four points, a Provost could bump this up by twenty more points.

Parents Involved in Community Schools v. Seattle School District (2007) combined two cases challenging the race-conscious assignment of students, one in Seattle, Washington, and one in Jefferson County, Louisville, Kentucky. Seattle had never used a segregated system, and Jefferson County had already achieved a unitary system. As such, the question for the Court was "whether a public school that had not operated legally segregated schools or has been found to be unitary may choose to classify students by race and rely upon that classification in making school assignments."

In Seattle, the plan allowed for students across the district to choose the school they wanted to attend. If a school was over its capacity, then students with siblings who already attended a given school were given preference. If a school was still oversubscribed and was unbalanced in its racial composition as compared to the general population by more than 10 percent, then race would be the deciding factor. If the school was not racially unbalanced or if there was still a tie after race was considered, then geographical proximity between the student's home and the school would be the deciding factor.

Jefferson County's scheme mandated that African American attendance at any nonmagnet school could not deviate more than 50 percent from the percentage of the local population. African Americans comprised approximately 34 percent of the population and the mechanism was designed to keep the racial balance of African Americans between 15 percent and 50 percent of the population in any given school.

In *Seattle School District*, the Court rejected Justice Scalia's slippery slope argument made in *Grutter*. Chief Justice John Roberts wrote the plurality opinion, which was joined by Justices Scalia, Thomas, Samuel Alito, and Kennedy in part. The Court limited its holding in *Grutter* by refusing to recognize diversity as a compelling state interest in primary and secondary school admissions in these districts. Justice Kennedy, in his concurring opinion, did not join the other four Justices of the plurality who argued that governmental decisions needed to be color-blind and that diversity at the primary and secondary level could not be a compelling state interest. In his opinion, he left open the possibility that diversity at this level could be a compelling state interest under the right conditions. Justice Kennedy also concurred with the majority that the school districts' formulation of diversity was not compelling and the means used by the school districts were not sufficiently narrowly tailored. Thus, *Seattle School District* only has a majority for these last two points as binding law.

The plurality noted that it had recognized two compelling interests to justify race-conscious admissions: (1) the interest in remedying past discrimination, and (2) the interest in diversity in higher education. The present case did not fall under the first category because Seattle had never segregated and Jefferson County was determined to have a unitary district in 2001. Chief Justice Roberts, writing for the majority, emphasized that in *Grutter*, the admissions program focused on each applicant as an individual and the classification of an applicant by race was part of holistic review. He sharply contrasted this with the systems under review where "race is not considered as part of a broader effort to achieve 'exposure to widely diverse people, cultures, ideas, and viewpoints'; race, for some students, is determinative standing alone."

The school districts argued that race was only one factor, used along with students' preferences, sibling attendance, and geographic proximity, but the Court disagreed. The Chief Justice reasoned that not only was race the deciding factor but the schools districts' form of racial balancing between whites and blacks was a very limited view of diversity. The Court would not accept, without proof, that diversity based on race alone would provide the educational benefits the schools districts claimed. According to Chief Justice Roberts, this was racial balancing and "the principle that racial balancing is not permitted is one of substance, not semantics. Racial balancing is not transformed from 'patently unconstitutional' to a compelling state interest simply by relabeling it 'racial diversity.'" The majority used the school districts' argument that racial considerations did not have a large impact to show the means chosen were not narrowly tailored to achieving the purported end. A lack of impact undermined any argument the means were necessary. Finally, the Court held neither school district had evaluated the use of less restrictive means.

In his dissenting opinion, Justice Stevens pointed out that the Chief Justice concluded his opinion by drawing a strained analogy to *Brown*. In the Chief Justice's words:

> Before *Brown*, schoolchildren were told where they could and could not go to school based on the color of their skin. The school districts in these cases have not carried the heavy burden of demonstrating that we should allow this once again ... the way "to achieve a system of determining admission to the public schools on a nonracial basis," is to stop assigning students on a racial basis. The way to stop discrimination on the basis of race is to stop discriminating on the basis of race.

Justice Kennedy in his concurrence could not agree with the plurality's assertion that "the way to stop discrimination on the basis of race is to stop discriminating on the basis of race." He thought that this was insufficient to decide the case and seized the opportunity to argue that while the idea of a "colorblind" Constitution was admirable in the context of a dissenting opinion in *Plessy v. Ferguson* (1896), it would not work as a universal constitutional principle in the real world. In rather moving words, he stated:

> This Nation has a moral and ethical obligation to fulfill its historic commitment to creating an integrated society that ensures equal opportunity for all of its children. A compelling interest exists in avoiding racial isolation.... Likewise, a district may consider it a compelling interest to achieve a diverse student population. Race may be one component of that diversity, but other demographic factors, plus special talents and needs, should also be considered. What the government is not permitted to do, absent a showing of necessity not made here, is to classify every student on the basis of race and to assign each of them to schools based on that classification. Crude measures of this sort threaten to reduce children to racial chits valued and traded according to one school's supply and another's demand.

Although he could not accept the school districts' race-conscious policies in the present case, he outlined a number of race-conscious policies achieving diversity that would avoid the need for strict scrutiny, including "strategic site selection of new schools; drawing attendance zones with general recognition of the demographics of neighborhoods; allocating resources for special programs; recruiting students and faculty in a targeted fashion; and tracking enrollments, performance, and other statistics by race." For Justice Kennedy, the virtue of these mechanisms is that they do not classify or tell a student they are defined by race, and thus, "it is unlikely any of them would demand strict scrutiny to be found permissible."

Justice Stevens wrote a very short and sharp dissent, noting the cruel irony in the Chief Justice's reference to *Brown*. It reminded him of Anatole France's observation that: "The majestic equality of the la[w], forbid[s] rich and poor alike to sleep under bridges, to beg in the streets, and to steal their bread." As Justice Stevens further observed, "the Chief Justice fails to note that it was only African-American schoolchildren that were so ordered [not to attend schools preserved for white children]; indeed, the history books do not tell stories of white children struggling to attend black schools."

Justice Stephen Breyer wrote the main dissenting opinion, which Justices Stevens, David Souter, and Ruth Bader Ginsburg joined. He argued that the plurality had ignored precedent "that recognized that the public interests at stake in such cases are 'compelling'... and that ... approved of 'narrowly tailored' plans that are no less race-conscious than the plans before us." The dissent's main focus was on the recent history in Seattle and Jefferson County that had resulted in the resegregation of schools. He explicitly questioned the distinction between *de jure* and *de facto* desegregation, arguing that the distinction was meaningless in the present context.

He argued it was well established that "the Equal Protection Clause permitted local school boards to use race-conscious criteria to achieve positive race-related goals, even when the Constitution does not compel it." Quoting from the unanimous decision in *Swann*: "School authorities are traditionally charged with broad power to formulate and implement educational policy and might well conclude, for example, that in order to prepare students to live in a pluralistic society each school should have a prescribed ratio of Negro to white students reflecting the proportion for the district as a whole." Although he argued that a case like this did not require strict scrutiny, nonetheless, the schools districts had met the test.

Not only was ending segregation compelling, the broad range the school districts used as guidelines were narrowly tailored. He argued that the ends served were remedial, educational, and in the service of democracy, given our pluralistic society. He further argued that the means chosen were not only narrowly tailored; they were more narrowly tailored than the plan in *Grutter*. As he stated, "the race-conscious criteria at issue only help set the outer bounds of broad ranges. They constitute but one part of plans that depend primarily upon other, nonracial elements. To use race in this way is not to set a forbidden 'quota.'" They were narrower than in *Grutter* because race only becomes a factor in a fraction of students' non-merit-based assignments. Further, the effects of reassignment are much less severe than being denied admission to the

University of Michigan Law School. Finally, the plans at issue here were tailored by the local communities, based on their history of segregation.

L. Voting

1. *Invidious Race-Based Discrimination in the Provision of Voting Rights*

Although discrimination in the provision of voting rights will be addressed separately in section V, it is worth addressing a handful of cases that deal with discrimination in voting on the basis of race. As we saw in Chapter 5, when addressing state action, the Supreme Court, in a series of cases from 1927 to 1953 (the all-white primary cases), found the practice of excluding African Americans from Democratic primaries violated the Fourteenth and Fifteenth Amendments. The Court struck down the practice, which originated under Texas state law, in *Nixon v. Herndon* in (1927). When Texas democrats responded by shifting the practice from the state to political party committees, the Court still found the practice to be a violation of the Fourteenth Amendment (*Nixon v. Condon,* 1932). Texas then attempted to move the practice from the political party to "voluntary clubs of white Democrats," but again the Court struck down the exclusionary practice in *Terry v. Adams* (1953).

The all-white primary cases involved practices that were discriminatory on their face. Most of the cases in this area involve impact discrimination, which requires further proof of discriminatory purpose. As we saw in the case of *Gomillion v. Lightfoot* (1960) (where the voting district was redrawn from a square to a twenty-eight-sided figure that excluded almost every African American from the district), governmental conduct will be found to have a discriminatory purpose if the nature of the discriminatory impact makes it too difficult to imagine a nondiscriminatory purpose for the law. In that case, it was impossible to discern a purpose for the Chinese dragon-shaped district other than the purpose it achieved, namely, the removal of African Americans from the district. In *City of Mobile v. Bolden* (1980), the Court upheld the at-large election scheme that had the impact of making it very difficult for African American representatives to get elected to the city council. If the three-member council was elected in three distinct geographical districts, it would be more likely that at least one council member would be elected to represent African American voters. The at-large scheme meant that the majority would always be able to elect all three members. The Court came to a different result on the facts in *Rogers v. Herman Lodge* (1982). The Court determined that given the history of discrimination in the jurisdiction, the at-large election scheme was motivated by racial considerations. In other words, the requirements of impact and purpose were satisfied.

In many cases, however, it is not clear that the mere fact of a discriminatory impact on a racial minority is enough to show that the voting policy or plan had a racially discriminatory purpose. This is because it is often the case that race and political party affiliation have a strong correlation. Policies that impact racial minorities might equally impact party members, and it is not unreasonable to assume that politicians are more interested in discriminating against the other party or parties than against people on the basis of race. Thus, in *Easley v. Cromartie* (2001) the defenders of the North Carolina legislature's voting redistricting successfully appealed a judgment of the district court that had found the legislature used race as the predominant factor in drawing a district's boundaries. The Court found the district court's determination rested on findings such as the district's shape, its splitting of towns and counties, and its high African American voting population. However, given undisputed evidence that racial identification was highly correlated with political affiliation, such facts could not, as a matter of law, support the judgment. Because there was so much overlap between African American voters and Democratic Party affiliation, it would be very difficult to distinguish between creating minority safe districts and Democratic Party safe districts.

Thus, the Court articulated the rule in these cases as,

> those who claim that a legislature has improperly used race as a criterion, in order, for example, to create a majority-minority district, must show at a minimum that the "legislature subordinated traditional race-neutral districting principles ... to racial considerations." Race must not simply have been "*a* motivation for the drawing of a majority-minority district," but "the *predominant* factor" motivating the legislature's districting decision. (Internal citations removed)

References to racial balance by a senator and staff member were not persuasive to the Court, and charts summarizing evidence of voting behavior tended to refute the argument that the districting was based on race and not politics. Writing for the majority, Justice Breyer held that for the appellees to have been successful, their expert would need to have shown that the legislature could have achieved its legitimate political objectives through the use of traditional districting principles and that the alternatives would have resulted in significantly less racial compacting (or more racial balance) than the present plan. They did not, and thus Justice Breyer held that the legislature drew its plan to protect incumbents, which is a legitimate political goal.

2. Benign Race-Based Districting? Creating Majority-Minority Districts to Benefit Minorities

What would happen if a city or state redrew districts to correct the type of problem that one found in *Mobile v. Bolden* (1980), namely, the problem that minorities have a difficult time electing any representatives if either the election is at large, or if minorities are dispersed among districts? If left alone, racial minorities, who are voting minorities, will be outvoted. However, if one redraws the districts so that racial minorities are the majority in at least one or more district, they should have a much better chance of electing representatives in those districts. This is arguably a laudable goal, particularly if the redistricting is designed to merely give the minority proportional representation (as apposed to overrepresentation). This is arguably benign discrimination.

However, benign or laudable, the Court has applied strict scrutiny in such cases. *Shaw v. Reno* (1993) is a prime example. *Shaw* involved drawing an irregularly shaped district for the purpose of making it a majority minority district. Writing for a five-to-four majority, Justice O'Connor compared such plans to political apartheid. She warned that the practice "reinforce[d] the perception that members of the same racial group—regardless of their age, education, economic status, or community in which they live—think alike, share the same political interests, and will prefer the same candidate at the polls." This, she noted, amounted to impermissible stereotyping. The rule is the same as was articulated in *Easley* (2001),; namely, that if race is the predominate factor in redistricting (even to create districts in which minorities are a majority), then strict scrutiny applies.

Similarly to the affirmative action cases, the Court has held that remedying the effects of voting discrimination is a compelling state interest (*Shaw v. Hunt,* 1996). Further, the Court has indicated complying with Sections 2 and 5 of the Voting Rights Act of 1965 might also satisfy strict scrutiny. *Bush v. Vera* (1996) (a case involving the creation of majority-minority districts). The Court in *League of United Latin American Citizens v. Perry* (2006) explained Section 2 violations:

> A State violates § 2 if, based on the totality of circumstances, it is shown that the political processes leading to nomination or election in the State or political subdivision are not equally open to participation by members of [a racial group] *in that its members have less opportunity than other members of the electorate to participate in the political process and to elect representatives of their choice.* (emphasis added)

Creating majority-minority districts, in at least some situations, can be seen as a way to ensure equal opportunity for minority voters. While satisfying Section 2 might be a compelling state interest, the mechanism still needed to be narrowly tailored. Thus, the Court in *Bush v. Vera* (1996) held the state could not subordinate traditional districting principles more than was reasonably necessary to satisfy Section 2.

Section 5 of the Voting Rights Act provides a more aggressive mechanism for dealing with states and counties that were found to have a history of systematically discriminating against minority voters. The Act established a mechanism to ensure that those jurisdictions found to have discriminated did not slide back into racial gerrymandering (the manipulation of voting district lines to make it easier or harder for a given racial group to elect representatives). This mechanism requires covered jurisdictions to get what is called preclearance (prior authorization) from either the U.S. Department of Justice or the U.S. District Court for the District of Columbia before they can make any changes to their voting practices or procedures (including changes to voting districts). The practice of creating minority-safe districts is a mechanism for insulating minorities from vote dilution or backsliding into a gerrymandered district. Nonetheless, the Court in *Bush* held that Section 5 would justify the use of mechanisms that prevented vote dilution, or the suppression of minorities' electoral rights, but not their augmentation or enhancement. Majority-minority districts could not be created to enhance minority representation unless it was remedial.

M. Discrimination on the Basis of Alienage

1. Introduction

Discrimination on the basis of alienage is not the same as discrimination on the basis of national origin (i.e. discrimination against individuals because of the country a person, or that person's ancestors, came from). Alienage refers to one's status as either a citizen or a non-citizen. Aliens are non-citizens, and while non-citizens are not protected by rights in the Constitution that are strictly reserved to citizens (e.g. the Fourteenth Amendment Privileges and Immunities Clause) they are protected by both the Equal Protection Clause and the Due Process Clause of the Fourteenth Amendment, which simply refer to "persons."

Aliens, perhaps more than any other group, are the clearest example of a discrete and insular minority in need of constitutional protection, because they do not have the right to vote or run for political office. Thus, it would be logical for discrimination on this basis to receive strict scrutiny; when states or local government discriminate on this basis strict scrutiny is applied as a general rule. The exception to this rule on the state and local level is when the government requires that one be a citizen for the purposes of either participating in the political process or occupying posts with political functions (i.e., when the discrimination relates to state governance, e.g., voting, running for political office, the police services, and even eligibility to serve as a teacher). The idea that supports this exception also supports the rule that rational basis review is the test to be applied when the federal government discriminates on this basis, namely, judicial deference to other branches or levels of government when they are addressing issues within their competence.

Aliens who are illegally present in the country present a different issue, because the status of being illegally present is not an immutable characteristic but an illegal choice. Thus, discrimination against aliens who are illegally present does not receive strict or heightened scrutiny. Nonetheless, the state cannot place a discriminatory burden on innocent children as a way of regulating the conduct of the illegally present alien parent. See *Plyler v. Doe* (1982), discussed later.

The federal government only receives rational basis review because the Constitution gives Congress broad powers over immigration and naturalization (citizenship) in Article I, Section 8, Clause 4. As a result, the judicial branch shows deference by applying rational basis review. Often state and local laws that discriminate against aliens can be challenged on preemption grounds, under the Supremacy Clause, as well as for violating equal protection (see Chapter 2). When states intrude in this field, deference is not automatic, but only comes into play in those cases that touch on state governance. The types of issues that would allow a state to avoid preemption by federal law are also the types of issues that have convinced the Court to give deference to the state.

2. State-Based Discrimination: The General Rule

From the 1800s up to almost 1950, discrimination on the basis of alienage was allowed at the state level in the areas of natural resources and land ownership and use, as well as employment or occupational licensing. Discrimination in these areas was allowed based on the idea that they related to "special public interests." This doctrine was challenged in 1948 in *Takahashi v. Fish and Game Commission* (1948), a case in which California sought to deny commercial fishing licenses to people who were ineligible for citizenship. Being of Japanese descent, Torao Takahashi fell under this category at the time. The state defended the limitation based on the special public interest doctrine, in particular the ownership of fish by the state as a natural resource. The Court did not fully accept that the state of California had title to the fish off its coast, and furthermore, it did not accept that ownership was sufficient to deny lawful resident aliens the ability to earn a living.

It was over twenty years before another state-based alienage discrimination case came before the Court. In *Graham v. Richardson* (1971), Arizona required its residents to either be U.S. citizens or residents of the United States for fifteen years to be eligible for state welfare benefits. Carmen Richardson was denied welfare benefits solely on the basis of being a resident alien who has resided in the country for less than fifteen years. The Court noted that the special public interest doctrine had been brought into question in *Takahashi* and declined to extend that doctrine to include welfare benefits as a scarce resource to be protected under the doctrine. Rather, the Court held that restrictions based on alienage by a state are akin to classifications based on race or nationality and subject to strict scrutiny. The Court further held that the state's "desire to preserve limited welfare benefits for its own citizens" was not a compelling government interest, and thus the statute was unconstitutional.

The Court again applied strict scrutiny in two 1973 cases, one involving civil service jobs, and the other involving licensing for the practice law. In *Sugarman v. Dougall* (1973), the Court declared unconstitutional a New York law that prevented aliens from holding civil service jobs. New York defended the exclusion on the basis that it only wanted to employ civil servants who had undivided loyalty to the United States. In effect, the Court held that the exclusion was overbroad because many of the civil service jobs had no function related to national loyalty. The Court held that excluding aliens denied them equal protection and a "flat ban on the employment of aliens in positions that have little, if any, relation to a state's legitimate interest, cannot withstand scrutiny under the 14th Amendment."

In *Application of Griffiths* (1973), the Court invalidated a Connecticut law that excluded aliens from being admitted to the state bar. The Court reaffirmed that strict scrutiny was the appropriate test for discrimination against aliens (although it did use the phrase "substantial state interest") and held it was impermissible for states to require citizenship as a condition for practicing law. The Court did not find the state's argument that citizenship was an important factor in being fit for the practice of law. As Justice Powell wrote for the Court, "It in no way denigrates a lawyer's high responsibilities to observe that the powers 'to sign writs and subpoenas, take recognizances, [and] administer oaths' hardly involve matters of state policy or acts of such unique responsibility as to entrust them only to citizens." Again the law was overbroad, or not narrowly tailored. Although some aliens may not be fit for the practice of law, this could not justify a total ban.

3. State-Based Discrimination: The Exception

Although the doctrine of "special public interests" has been carved down, the core of the exception still exists when the state is regulating matters that deal with the political process or important political functions. In these cases, the Court has adopted rational basis review.

In *Foley v. Connelie* (1978), New York state law prohibited noncitizens from being appointed state police officers. Edmund Foley, who was an alien, was refused the opportunity to sit for the state police exam. If aliens cannot be denied the chance to become lawyers (who after all are officers of the court), then one would think that they cannot be denied the chance to become police officers either. As compelling as this logic may be, the Court held that the police (as law enforcement agents) carry out functions that are "at the heart of our political institutions." As such, regulating access to this profession on the basis of alienage would only receive rational basis review.

The dissent, written by Justice Marshall and joined by Justices Stevens and Brennan, emphasized police officers do not make broad public policy but are charged to carry out policy and enforce the law. They, like most civil servants, merely implement policy created at a higher level. Thus, their function is not a core political function and discrimination on the basis of alienage in their recruitment should receive strict scrutiny. The dissenting opinion of Justice Stevens, joined by Justice Brennan, would have applied *Griffiths* and required that ineligibility to serve in the police force, like fitness to practice law, should be evaluated individually. As Justice Stevens wrote, "Unless the Court repudiates its holding in *In re Griffiths,* it must reject any conclusive presumption that aliens, as a class, are disloyal or untrustworthy." These Justices did not see how alienage was more relevant to the police services than to the practice of law. As Justice Stevens asked, "Are untrustworthy or disloyal lawyers more tolerable than untrustworthy or disloyal policemen?"

In *Ambach v. Norwick* (1979), the Court went even further and held the denial of teaching certificates to the respondents on the basis that they were aliens would also receive deferential rational basis review. Writing for a five-to-four majority, Justice Powell stated that education, like the police power, represents a "fundamental obligation of [state] government." The Court held that preparing children to be active citizens was a governmental function, and thus, discrimination in the access to this function on the basis of alienage would only receive rational basis review. The fact that public school teachers, unlike attorneys and engineers, are employees of the state, allowed the majority to distinguish previous case law to the contrary.

Justice Marshall, writing for the dissent, argued that teachers were not engaged in broad public policy making. As such, discrimination on this basis should not receive mere rational basis review.

In *Cabell v. Chavez-Salido* (1982), the Court upheld discrimination on the basis of alienage in eligibility to become a probation officer. The Court reasoned that the probation officer served both the functions of a police officer and as a teacher. They both enforce the law and prepare former convicts for civic life. They have considerable discretion in how they supervise the people under their charge, as the probationers attempt to reintegrate into the community.

The Court did not extend the exception to a state law that made citizenship a prerequisite for being a notary public in *Bernal v. Fainter* (1984). The Court clarified that the exception pertained to positions that required the "formulation, execution or review of broad public policy" and notary publics do not perform such functions. Thus, the law was subjected to strict scrutiny and failed to meet the test.

4. Undocumented Aliens and Their Children

In *Plyler v. Doe* (1982), the Court addressed the issue of a Texas state law that discriminated against the children of undocumented aliens by denying them free public education. The Court rejected Texas's assertion that the Equal Protection Clause only protected aliens who were in the country lawfully. While the Court held that undocumented aliens (who are often wrongly labeled "illegal immigrants") are protected by the Fourteenth Amendment as persons, it declined to recognize them as a suspect class. Because being undocumented or in the country illegally was not an immutable characteristic but was in fact the result of illegal conduct, discrimination on this basis was not suspect and did not merit strict scrutiny. However, the law in this case discriminated against the children of undocumented aliens who, in most cases, would have no control over their presence or their parent's status in the United States. Even if the law was designed to impact the decision of parents to immigrate illegally, it did "not comport with fundamental conceptions of justice" to place the discriminatory burden on the children by effectively denying them the opportunity to learn to read and write.

Although the majority did not articulate a standard of review in this case, the review was something more than rational basis and something less than strict scrutiny. The dissent argued that because the case did not involve a suspect class or a fundamental right, rational basis should have been applied in this case and the Court should have deferred to the Texas legislature.

5. Congressionally Approved Discrimination

As already noted, the idea that motivated the political function exception in the state level also animates the rule that rational basis review is the test to be applied when the federal government discriminates on this basis—namely, deference to other branches or levels of government to address issues within their competence. Since the Constitution gives Congress near plenary power to address issues of immigration and naturalization, the Court is deferential to that power and applies rational basis review. The treatment of aliens also implicates the federal government's broad powers in the area of foreign relations, where neither the states nor the courts have a particular competence.

It is worth noting that although the Court was highly divided in many of the foregoing decisions regarding the political function exception, the Court was unanimous in applying rational basis review to Congress's limitation on the eligibility of aliens to receive federal medical insurance benefits in *Mathews v. Diaz* (1976). The Court unanimously upheld the limitation that required aliens to legally reside in the United States for a continuous five years before being eligible for the benefit. The Court held that it was rational to limit these benefits to aliens with a stronger affinity to the United States, and it was within Congress's discretion to decide how long one should live in the United States as evidence of affinity.

It is worth noting that administrative agencies will only receive this level of deference if there is a clear mandate from Congress or from the President for the discrimination. Thus, in the same year that *Mathews* was decided, the Court in *Hampton v. Mow Sun Wong* (1976) declined to give the federal Civil Service Commission the same deference it gave Congress in *Mathews*. The Commission adopted a regulation that denied employment to aliens. The Court noted that if Congress or the President had mandated the regulation, it might reasonably be presumed that they did so for purposes that were rationally related to foreign policy or to encourage aliens to naturalize and become citizens. However, since the Commission was not mandated to engage in policy decisions regarding either area of competence (either foreign policy or naturalization) its regulation was subjected to strict scrutiny.

Stop Points

Strict Scrutiny Review

- Test: government action that draws distinctions on the basis of race or national origin must be necessary to achieve a compelling government purpose.

- A classification is necessary when it is narrowly tailored so that no alternative, less burdensome means are available to accomplish the state interest.

- Strict scrutiny only applies if the law or governmental conduct is:

  - Discriminatory on its face; or

  - It has both a discriminatory impact and the government' purpose was to have the discriminatory impact.

    - The strict scrutiny test for suspect criteria requires that the government action have a discriminatory purpose; that is, intentional or deliberate discrimination must be shown, which can be found in three ways:

      - On the face — *Korematsu v. United States* (1944)

- By application — *Batson v. Kentucky* (1986)
- By its discriminatory motive — *Gomillion v. Lightfoot* (1960)
- **Racial segregation** — legally mandated segregation violates the Equal Protection Clause — *Brown v. Board of Education* (1954)
- Remedying Segregation in Schools: schools have an affirmative duty to eliminate intentional racial segregation of schools. The remedy in any given case must be determined by the nature and the scope of the constitutional violation. It may not extend beyond the conditions produced by that violation.
- **Affirmative Action:** even benign (government action that favors racial or ethnic minorities) is subject to strict scrutiny.
  - Court held remedying the present effects of identified past discrimination qualifies as a compelling interest.
    - The classification must seek to rectify the effects of identified racial discrimination within the entity's regulatory jurisdiction.
    - The entity adopting the remedial scheme must have a strong basis in evidence to conclude that remedial action was necessary before it implements the program.
  - Court held higher education institutions have a compelling interest in attaining a diverse student body.
    - Race considerations may not be permanently a part of admission policies, but only should be used until they are no longer needed.
    - Race and ethnicity may be considered as a plus, but may not be the predominant criteria for deciding whether a particular applicant is accepted.
- **Discrimination on the Basis of Alienage**
  - Discrimination on the basis of alienage is not the same as discrimination on the basis of national origin. *Alienage* refers to one's status as either a citizen or a noncitizen.
  - Generally strict scrutiny applies when a state or local government discriminates on the basis of alienage.
    - Exception: the general rule does not apply when the state and local government requires that one be a citizen for the purposes of either participating in the political process or occupying a post with political functions.
    - Rational basis review is the test that is applied when the federal government discriminates on the basis of alienage.
      - The federal government only receives rational basis review because the Constitution gives Congress broad powers over immigration and naturalization. The judicial branch shows deference by applying this lower standard.
    - Discrimination against aliens who are illegally present does not receive strict or heightened scrutiny.

• State cannot place a discriminatory burden on innocent children as a way or regulating the conduct of the illegally present alien parent.

IV. Intermediate Scrutiny: Gender-Based Discrimination and Discrimination against Children Born out of Wedlock (Illegitimacy)

A. Introduction to Gender-Based Discrimination

Gender-based discrimination has been a feature of American life since before the founding, and it has been an accepted (if not applauded) feature of American life for most of U.S. history. As noted in the introduction to this chapter, gender discrimination was still acceptable long after the Civil War and the enactment of the Civil War Amendments. Women's equality was not launched with the Fourteenth Amendment, and their right to vote was not brought on by the Fifteenth Amendment. It wasn't until 1920 when women won the right to vote under the Nineteenth Amendment, and it was not until 1971 that a successful gender-based discrimination claim was brought in *Reed v. Reed* (1971). It was only in 1973 in *Frontiero v. Richardson* (1973) that rational basis review for gender based discrimination was abandoned.

If one recalls the arguments for strict judicial review, it is unquestionable that many of those factors apply to gender-based discrimination. Sex changes and gender-bending aside, gender strongly tracks sex, which is only mutable at a very high cost. Further, women have a long history of discrimination, be it in terms of the right to vote, the right to choose a profession, the right to equal pay, and rights to own property, enter into contracts, and even sue in court. Although these factors indicate a need for strict scrutiny, the fact that women are not a minority and that there are some differences between the sexes that may call for different treatment (e.g., concerning pregnancy), indicate that strict scrutiny might not be appropriate. The Court in fact adopted strict scrutiny review in *Frontiero* but eventually settled on intermediate scrutiny in *Craig v. Boren* (1976).

Although the use of the intermediate scrutiny test for gender-based discrimination has its critics, the test has been comfortably adopted by a very strong majority of the Court since 1976. This is due in part to the flexibility of the test or range of tests. Intermediate scrutiny (sometimes called *heightened scrutiny*) can occupy the entire range of review between strict scrutiny and rational basis. Although the most common formulation of the test requires that the governmental law, policy, or conduct be substantially related to an important governmental interest, there is considerable flexibility in what counts as important and what suffices as being substantially related. This is one of the main criticisms of the test by people like former Chief Justice Rehnquist and Justice Scalia.

There are cases after *Boren* in which the test is either watered down to look more like rational basis review or strengthened to look more like strict scrutiny. For instance, Justice Rehnquist's plurality opinion in *Michael M. v. Superior Court of Sonoma County* (1981) required the law to be "sufficiently related to a strong interest," whereas Justice Ginsburg's opinion in *U.S. v. Virginia* (1996) required the state to provide an "exceedingly persuasive justification" for its discrimination. Both cases and their inconsistent tests are addressed.

It should be noted, as a preliminary matter, that gender discrimination is proven in the same way that discrimination based on race is. One will recall from the foregoing treatment of racial discrimination that the discrimination either needs to be clear on its face, or there needs to be both a discriminatory impact, and it needs to be proven that the state had the purpose of causing the discriminatory impact. As we noted, the case of *Personnel Adm. of Massachusetts v. Feeney* (1979), which involved the preferential hiring of veterans, is also commonly cited for the rule that laws that are not facially discriminatory require both a discriminatory impact and discriminatory purpose. In *Feeney*, the discriminatory impact was based on gender, given that the vast majority of veterans were men at the time. Although the discriminatory impact was clear (the vast majority of those receiving the benefit were men and not women), there were numerous legitimate, nondiscriminatory purposes for the law, including the desire to reintegrate veterans back into society and provide benefits that were commensurate with the sacrifices they made for the country. Thus, the Court held that gender-based discrimination had not been proven.

This section of the chapter addresses the early case law before 1971, which largely reinforced gender stereotypes, and then turn to the development of the modern test after 1971. Then the section addresses cases in which the Court has upheld law or rules that discriminate on the basis of gender based on the idea that those laws or rules track or closely follow "real" differences between the sexes. After that, the chapter turns to a number of cases across many areas of social life where the Court has struck down laws or rules on the ground that they are based on role stereotypes or overgeneralizations that tend to perpetuate inequality. Finally, the section covers cases in which the law discriminates on the basis of gender as a means to correct or remedy past discrimination before turning to the topic of illegitimacy, which also receives intermediate scrutiny.

B. Case Law before 1971

Perhaps unsurprisingly, the first case to be brought alleging gender discrimination was brought by a woman wishing to enter the legal profession. Myra Bradwell (who had studied under her husband in his firm and who passed the Illinois bar), was denied the opportunity to practice by the state of Illinois. In *Bradwell v. Illinois* (1871), the Court upheld the exclusion, holding that the practice of law was not a privilege of citizenship protected under the Privileges and Immunities Clause of the Fourteenth Amendment. On the question of discrimination, Justice Joseph Bradley argued in his concurring opinion that "the paramount destiny and mission of women are to fulfill the noble and benign offices of wife and mother." According to Justice Bradley, this role was ordained by God and natural law, and the civil law should follow it, and not make exceptions, even for exceptional women. Illinois later changed its laws, and in fact, Bradley was admitted to the Illinois bar before the Supreme Court heard its second case involving the exclusion of women from a state bar in *In re Lockwood* (1894). This time, the plaintiff was already admitted to the bar in the District of Columbia and the Supreme Court. Nonetheless, the Court upheld its decision in *Bradwell*, holding that it was within the province of the state of Virginia to decide if women should be allowed to practice within its jurisdiction.

The view that a woman's place was in the home and they were the weaker sex in need of protection supported these decisions, as well as most of the decisions by the Court in this area during the first three quarters of the twentieth century. For example, this view informed decisions such as *Muller v. Oregon* (1908), upholding a maximum hours law for women (even though a similar law for men was struck down in *Lochner v. New York,* 1905); *Radice v. N.Y.* (1924), upholding a New York law that restricted women from working between 10 P.M. and 6 A.M.; *Goesaert v. Cleary* (1948), upholding a law that restricted women from being bartenders unless their husband or father owned the bar; and finally, *Hoyt v. Florida* (1961), upholding a law that exempted women from jury duty unless they waived the exemption, and that required men to serve unless they applied and were granted an exception from serving. Although *Hoyt* is more progressive because it allowed women to opt in for jury duty, the law still presumed that a woman's place was in the home. The Court stated that women were the "center of the home and family life" and they should be able to decide if jury duty was consistent with duties in that respect.

C. Articulating the Modern Test(s)

Finally, in *Reed v. Reed* (1971) the Court struck down a law that discriminated on the basis of gender. Idaho passed a law that set out the priority ordering of who was eligible to administer any given intestate estate (the estate of someone who dies without a will). People were ranked in terms of their relation to the decedent, but if a man and a woman were tied within a given ranking, the tie went to the man (e.g., if both of one's parents were alive, the father would be preferred over the mother even though they were both at the same rank). The Court held "a classification must be reasonable, not arbitrary and must rest on some ground of difference having a fair and substantial relation to the object of the legislation, so that all persons similarly circumstanced shall be treated alike." Though it is reasonable to have some form of tie breaker, the Court could find no rational basis for the uniform preference of a man over a woman for the role of administrator. This preference was arbitrary.

The Court in this case did not apply strict scrutiny or even intermediate scrutiny as we know it today, but it did give the law more scrutiny than is customary under the rational basis test. While it did not question the end of administrative efficiency, it required that the classification be more than rational. It required that the classification be *reasonable* and have a *fair and substantial relation to the object of the legislation*.

In *Frontiero v. Richardson* (1973), four members of the Court (Justices Brennan, Douglas, Marshall, and Byron White) adopted the strict scrutiny test for gender in their plurality opinion. They were joined by four other Justices in their decision to strike down a federal law allowing male members of the uniformed services to automatically claim their spouses as dependants for the purpose of receiving added benefits, whereas female members were required to prove that their spouses were dependants. All the remaining justices, save Justice Rehnquist, joined the plurality in the conclusion that the law should be struck down but disagreed that strict scrutiny was the appropriate test. Justice Rehnquist followed the reasoning of the district court, arguing that the rational basis test should have been applied. According to Justice Rehnquist, in his dissent, given that the vast majority of male uniformed service members had spouses that were dependent and the vast majority of female service members had spouses who were not, it was rational and efficient to require the female members to prove the dependency of their spouses to obtain the benefits.

It should be noted that if strict scrutiny had become the test for all gender-based discrimination, then attempts to recognize, accommodate, or even remedy differences related to gender and sex would need to pass the test. This would be the case whether it be in terms of affirmative action to redress the history of discrimination against women or measures to accommodate physical differences related to the reproductive capacity of women. Given the difficulties faced by minorities with regard to affirmative action, it is not clear that the often inflexible strict scrutiny test would best serve a society wishing to achieve gender equality.

Over the next few years, several cases were decided with no clear test coming from the Court. It was not until *Craig v. Boren* (1976) that the Court settled on the intermediate scrutiny test that we have today. *Boren* involved an Oklahoma law requiring that men be twenty-one before they could buy 3.2 percent beer, whereas women were allowed to buy the beer at the age of eighteen. The Court held that the law must serve important governmental objectives and be substantially related to those objectives to survive. The state defended the law on the basis of traffic safety, citing statistics that young men were arrested more often for drunk driving than women. The cited statistics showed 0.18 percent of females and 2 percent of males in the eighteen- to twenty-one-year-old group were arrested for the offense. Justice Brennan writing for the majority found the 2 percent difference to be inadequate as a justification for the discrimination. He claimed it was an "unduly tenuous fit."

Justice Rehnquist, joined by Justice Burger, dissented, arguing against the introduction of a new test he called "diaphanous and elastic." According to Justice Rehnquist, "both of the phrases used are so diaphanous and elastic as to invite subjective judicial preferences or prejudices relating to particular types of legislation, masquerading as judgments whether such legislation is directed at 'important' objectives or, whether the relationship to those objectives is 'substantial' enough." Justice Rehnquist further argued that men did not need the extra protection that came with the intermediate scrutiny. In his view, rational basis should have been applied and the law in question should have been found to be rationally related to traffic safety. Justice Rehnquist cited statistics that showed ratios of up to eighteen to one for male drunk driving to female drunk driving. Given that more young men drank beer and drove, he found it rational to have different age requirements.

A majority of the Court in *U.S. v. Virginia* (1996) adopted a version of the intermediate scrutiny test on the stricter side of the spectrum. In an opinion written by Justice Ginsburg addressing the exclusion of women from the Virginia Military Institute (VMI), the Court required that the state show an "exceedingly persuasive justification" for the exclusion.

According to the opinion, VMI was an elite training ground for military leaders. Founded in 1839, it was the only single-sex collegiate institution run by the state of Virginia. It had a long tradition of providing a rigorous, military-style college experience to its students. It applied harsh "adversative" training, and the state argued that it could not include women within its program without changing the training to such a degree that the advantages of a VMI education could be saved. It argued that those advantages would be lost, in fact, to both men and women.

After a negative ruling at the circuit court level, the state could have either integrated the school or privatized the school. Instead, it chose to create a separate women's school at the Mary Baldwin College, the Virginia Women's Institute for Leadership (VWIL). This case is very similar on the facts to the case of *Sweatt v. Painter* (1950) in which Texas attempted to create a "separate but equal" law school for blacks. One may recall that not only were the facilities and the faculty inferior, so were intangibles such as reputation, alumni networks, and the overall experience. In the present case, Mary Baldwin's overall student population had much lower SAT scores, it had significantly fewer doctorates on the faculty (who were paid much less), and it did not offer the same range or depth of programs as VMI. More important, VWIL did not have the same reputation, history, and network of committed alumni. There were no generals or members of Congress from VWIL. This separate institution had little hope of even becoming equal.

Nonetheless, the state attempted to argue that VMI was suited for men and VWIL was suited for women. It argued it was engaged in benign discrimination by providing a diversity of institutions catering to women and men.

The Court did not accept that the state's purposes were actually benign, but found that they were rationalizations after the fact, used to justify the exclusion of women. It also did not accept the arguments that VMI was suited to men and VWIL suited to women, and that VMI would need to radically change to accommodate women, and thus undermine the benefits of the institution for both men and women.

Justice Ginsburg found that while many women (and men for the matter) would not choose VMI and its adversarial method of education, the issue was not whether the state could force it on women but whether it could deny that training to women who wanted it. The case was not about men and women in general but about women wishing to be admitted to VMI. As equal citizens, women should not be categorically denied such opportunities regardless of their individual merit. Justice Ginsburg concluded by noting that in contrast to generalizations the state of Virginia rests its case on, there are women who would perform well under the VMI method of training, who are both mentally and physically capable of meeting the standards of VMI, and who would wish to attend VMI. According to Justice Ginsburg, it is for them that the United States had instituted this suit and it is for them that there must be a remedy.

It may be that in another context a separate institution could be equal, but separate cannot be equal if, as here, women are denied the unique educational opportunities afforded to men.

Justice Scalia, the sole dissenter in the case, attacked Justice Ginsburg's opinion on two separate but related grounds. First, he argued that that Justice Ginsburg had distorted the intermediate scrutiny test, making it much stricter than it had traditionally been. Justice Scalia argued there was no support for requiring an "exceedingly persuasive justification" as opposed to requiring that the discrimination be substantially related to an important governmental interest. Second, he argued that the Court should not have taken it upon itself to disrupt the long-standing practice of having men's military colleges. He believed that the Constitution did not take sides on the question of whether there was substantial educational value in an all-male military academy. For him this was not an issue for the Court, but for the state of Virginia, and thus the Court should not have removed the choice of having such institutions from the democratic process.

There are a number of ways for dividing up the case law on gender discrimination. Gender-based discrimination can be observed across a number of different areas of life — for example, discrimination with regard to education, military service, property rights, marital property, parental rights, dependant benefits, and worker's compensation benefits. Discrimination in these areas can also fall under one or both of two categories: discrimination designed to benefit women and discrimination that perpetuates inequality. As we saw in *VMI*, there are often arguments that the two types overlap. Not unlike in the context of race, gender-conscious governmental conduct designed to aid women may be based on stereotypes that tend to perpetuate inequality. There are in fact not many cases where the Court has struck down laws that had the purpose of disadvantaging women. Like in *Craig v. Boren* (1976), many cases are brought by men who are disadvantaged by a law (in that case, it was a bar owner). Nonetheless, if the Court finds that the distinction is based on stereotypes that perpetuate inequality, the Court will likely strike the law down. The Court is more likely to uphold discriminatory laws that it feels closely track what it considers to be "real" differences between the sexes. Of course these decisions can also be brought into question, for it is always debatable when the "real" or "natural" differences give out and when the societal stereotype kicks in. Most biological differences do not apply in relevant part to every woman or man, and often technology can mitigate what differences still remain for any given person. After addressing the cases where the Court has determined that the law is tracking "real differences," we address the cases in which the law or rule discriminates to compensate for past discrimination. Finally, the section will turn to the numerous cases in which the Court has found that the discrimination in question is tracking overgeneralizations or societal stereotypes.

D. Discrimination that Tracks "Real" Differences

In 1981, the Court decided two cases in which it upheld laws that clearly discriminated on the basis of gender. Both cases disadvantaged men. The cases were *Michael M. v. Superior Court of Sonoma County* (1981), which involved a California statutory rape law that reserved the crime for men only, and *Rostker v. Goldberg* (1981), which involved the Military Selective Service Act, which empowered the President to require only men to register for the draft. The main opinion in each case was written by Justice Rehnquist; it is worth remembering that Justice Rehnquist did not believe that gender-based discrimination should receive heightened scrutiny. *Michael M.* is a plurality decision because Justice Rehnquist could not get a majority to agree with him on his watered-down version of the intermediate scrutiny test. In *Rostker*, it is clear Justice Rehnquist believes that the law passes intermediate scrutiny under *Craig v. Boren*.

In *Michael M.*, Michael M., a seventeen-year-old male who had sexual intercourse with a sixteen-year-old female, was charged with statutory rape. He argued that the law violated equal protection because it discriminated against him on the basis of his gender. There was no provision in the law making it illegal for a woman to have sexual intercourse with a male or female minor.

Justice Rehnquist, writing for a plurality, ruled that the finding by the California Supreme Court that the prevention of pregnancy was the justification for the statute and should be given great deference, because the state had a strong interest in this objective. In his plurality opinion, Justice Rehnquist ruled that providing punishment only for males was "sufficiently related to the state's objective [to deter teenage pregnancy] to pass constitutional muster." Thus the test appears to be a "sufficiently related to a strong interest" test. For Justice Rehnquist, the law passed the test because teenage women already had a sufficient deterrent from getting pregnant: namely, pregnancy and all of its negative effects. As there was no "similar natural sanction" to deter males, the criminal sanction "serve[d] to roughly 'equalize' the deterrents on the sexes."

Justice Blackmun concurred in the result, but did so under application of the standard intermediate scrutiny test. For Justice Blackmun, the law was substantially related to the important governmental interest in deterring teenage pregnancies.

Justice Brennan wrote a dissent that was joined by Justices White and Marshall. Justice Stevens wrote a separate dissenting opinion. Justice Brennan applied intermediate scrutiny and arrived at the opposite result of Justice Blackmun. Although he agreed that preventing teenage pregnancy is an important objective, he did not believe that California met its burden of demonstrating that the gender-based statute was more effective at decreasing teenage pregnancies than a gender-neutral statute. The state did not show that a gender-neutral statute would be less effective than the gender-based statute.

Justice Stevens, in his dissent, argued that it was perverse to only punish the male when both parties were equally guilty of the risk-creating conduct. In fact, on his view, the fact that the risk of harm falls on the teenage female is all the more reason to apply the prohibition to her. He made the somewhat persuasive argument that a parent of twins of the opposite sex would not "forbid the son and authorize the daughter to engage in conduct that is especially harmful to the daughter." Finally, he argued that even if this logic was flawed, he thought that the constitutional mandate to dispense justice impartially and even-handedly would trump any speculative basis for treating the equally guilty party differently.

The plurality decision can either be critiqued for perpetuating the stereotype that men are aggressors and women victims, or it can be viewed as an accommodation of the "reality" of the causes, incidents, and mechanisms for deterring teenage pregnancy. No doubt the law was based in part on the idea that teenage females would not have sex (given the deterrent of risk of pregnancy) unless males were "pushing" them into it. Undoubtedly, there is a great deal of gray area when it comes to the consent of teenage women to sex. Perhaps the same is true for young men. Nonetheless, statutory rape laws remove the gray by taking away the consent defense.

It is very unclear that were the Court to hear a case like this today, in an age of contraception and infamous predatory female teachers, the law would be held to be substantially related to the interest in preventing teenage pregnancy. Note that if the purpose was to prevent the spread of STDs or HIV/AIDS, the gender difference largely fades away.

As noted, *Rostken* addressed the Military Selective Service Act (MSSA), which authorized the President to require that men between the ages of eighteen and twenty-six register for the draft. Justice Rehnquist, this time writing for a majority, began his opinion by noting the great deference the Court should give to the decisions of Congress, particularly in the area of national defense and military affairs. Justice Rehnquist did not have a hard time arguing that the purpose of the law—namely, to provide a supply of combat troops in times when a military draft is necessary—was an important government interest, satisfying the test in *Craig v. Boren*.

The means chosen to further this end were substantially related because only men are eligible for combat duty. Because of this, registering all women would be an administrative inconvenience for little benefit. Men and women are thus differently situated for purposes of a draft. Furthermore, most non-combat positions are filled by combat-ready troops who are rotated with other troops, further diminishing the payoff from the registration of women.

The dissent, written by Justice White and joined by Justice Brennan, did not address the issue of whether excluding women from combat positions offended the Constitution, since it was not raised. Assuming it was constitutional, it did not follow that women would not be needed in case of war. If the purpose of the law was merely providing combat troops, the law was substantially related to that end. However, the dissent did not see the law having merely that purpose. For the dissent, the purpose was to provide military personnel, both combat and noncombat, in a time of war. If the combat-ready troops would need to and could fill all the noncombat positions, there would be no reason for women in the military at all. However, the district court findings were that the military would need to conscript 80,000 persons to fill noncombat jobs. It could not rely on volunteers for these jobs. There was no reason women should not be registered to be conscripted to fill their share of these positions. As Justice White concluded, "I discern no adequate justification for this kind of discrimination between men and women."

The entire decision in this case relies on the notion that women are not equipped to perform combat duties. Although this may be true of some women, it is not clear that it is true of all women. Of course mandatory conscription is different from volunteering to perform combat duty. It is unclear, however, why women could not be conscripted for general duty, and allowed to then volunteer for combat duty if found to be individually fit for job.

In *Nguyen v. Immigration and Naturalization Service (INS)* (2001), Justice Kennedy, writing for a five-to-four majority, upheld an INS rule that made it easier for the foreign-born offspring of U.S. women to obtain citizenship than foreign-born offspring of U.S. men. If the father is an American but the mother is not, one of three additional steps is required to establish paternity and for the child to become a citizen. Before the person turns eighteen, it is required that either:

"(A) the person is legitimated under the law of the person's residence or domicile,

(B) the father acknowledges paternity of the person in writing under oath, or

(C) the paternity of the person is established by adjudication of a competent court."

In the case of children born to American women abroad, this is not required. Thus, on its face, the law discriminates against men on the basis of gender. Although Tuan Anh Nguyen's father brought him to the United States to live with him in 1975 at the age of five and he subsequently became a legal permanent resident, his father did not satisfy any of the three requirements before Nguyen turned eighteen. As a result, and because Nguyen had been found guilty of a deportable offense, he was subject to deportation.

Justice Kennedy quoted *U.S. v. Virginia* (1996) for the intermediate scrutiny test, but interestingly did not quote Justice Ginsburg's more robust version of the test. Rather, he quoted language that "for a gender-based classification to withstand equal protection scrutiny, it must be established 'at least that the [challenged] classification serves important governmental objectives and that the discriminatory means employed' are 'substantially related to the achievement of those objectives'" (*United States v. Virginia*, 1996). He ruled that this test was satisfied and stated, for this reason, the Court did not need to decide if a weaker test were appropriate. According to Justice Kennedy, the test was satisfied because of the government's interest in ensuring that there was a biological as well as parental relationship between parent and child. It was not enough that a formal relationship exist, there must be an opportunity for some type of bonding or a meaningful relationship. He ruled that the law was substantially related to these important objectives, because while women's biological and parental relationships take place through the pregnancy and birth, this is not the case with men. Men do not have the same obvious biological link to the child, and a man overseas may not even know he has fathered a child. The mother may not even be sure who the biological father is.

Justice O'Connor wrote the dissent, joined by Justices Souter, Ginsburg, and Breyer. The dissent argued that the government should have been required to provide an exceedingly persuasive justification for the discriminatory rule as articulated in *U.S. v. Virginia* (1996). The dissent took issue both with the Court's rendition of the important governmental objectives at stake and of the relationship between the rule and those objectives. According to the dissent, INS stated that the rule's objectives were "first, ensuring that children who are born abroad out of wedlock have, during their minority, attained a sufficiently recognized or formal relationship to their United States citizen parent—and thus to the United States—to justify the conferral of citizenship upon them; and second, preventing such children from being stateless." The majority stated the objectives as requiring both a biological relationship and more than a formal or sufficiently recognized relationship. According to the dissent, given the state of the art of paternity tests, there were much better means than those stated in the rules for establishing paternity.

As to the second objective, the dissent questioned whether it was an important governmental interest, and argued that there was no guarantee that a mother would have more of a relationship to the child than a father. After all, a father could become the primary parent and the mother could abandon her child after birth. Perhaps more important, the requirement that proof of paternity take place before the child turns eighteen does not substantially further the interest. In the present case, even though the child was raised by his father from at least age six onward, a DNA test showed a 99.98 percent probability of paternity, and the father obtained an order of parentage from a Texas court, all of this proof of a relationship came too late.

Finally, the majority failed to address the second object of the rule put forward by INS. The object of not rendering children stateless is only furthered by the lax requirements for mothers but is substantially impaired by the somewhat draconian requirements for fathers. Here there can be no question that any number of gender-neutral means for reaching the stated objective would be better.

It is worth noting *Nguyen* followed other earlier cases in which the law had a bias toward mothers over fathers. For instance, in *Parham v. Hughes* (1979), the Court upheld a law requiring men establish paternity over a nonmarital child to sue for the wrongful death of the child. The mother was not required to establish maternity. Also in *Lehr v. Robert* (1983), the law required that fathers either live with the mother and child or register their intent to claim paternity to have the right of notice that the mother intended to give the child up for adoption. The Court in these cases, as in *Nguyen*, assumed the mother's biological and substantive relation to the child. Again, like in *Nguyen*, the Court treated the discrimination as discrimination between fathers who had established those relations and those that had not. The mother's nature was assumed to be static while the father's nature could change. Nonetheless, fathers would need to demonstrate that they had changed their nature to have the same rights as mothers.

1. Is a Failure to Track Real Differences Discriminatory?

If potential for pregnancy is generally one of those characteristics that mark a "real" or "natural" difference between the sexes, then arguably equal treatment under the law would require this difference not be ignored. This was the argument put forward by the plaintiffs in *Geduldig v. Aiello* (1974) in their challenge to the California disability insurance system, which excluded normal pregnancy-related disabilities from the plan. The state argued the limited coverage was based on the desire to save costs for all members of the plan, both men and women. They argued that the plan did not discriminate against women in favor of men but rather distinguished between pregnant and nonpregnant women. This is very similar to the Court's reasoning in *Parham, Leher,* and *Nguyen*—namely, that the laws and rules in those cases discriminated between men (in terms of their relationship to their biological offspring) and not between men and women.

Justice Brennan, joined by Justices Marshall and Douglas, dissented, arguing that because the plan covered the risk of disabilities that were male-related (e.g., prostatectomy and hemophilia), and yet excluded this female-related risk (the risk of disability as a result of pregnancy), it violated the Equal Protection Clause. The law did not simply discriminate between women, but treated risks to men and women differently.

Congress addressed the issue by effectively siding with the dissent and prohibiting discrimination against pregnant persons with the enactment of the Pregnancy Discrimination Act, 42 U.S.C. § 2000e(k).

E. Discrimination Based on Overgeneralizations/Stereotypes

1. Mothers and Fathers

In *Caban v. Mohammed* (1979), a case decided the same year as *Parham*, the Court struck down a law that allowed for an "illegitimate" child to be adopted with the consent of the mother but without the consent of the father. In *Caban*, the Court found the law to have violated the Equal Protection Clause because it was based on the stereotype that the unwed mother-child relationship is fundamentally different from the unwed father-child relationship. The Court held that unwed fathers could have a relationship with their children that was fully comparable to that of mothers to their children. The law deprived all unwed men that right, regardless of their actual relationship to the child. This distinguishes this case from *Nguyen*, *Parham*, and *Lehr*. Although the laws and rules in the cases of *Nguyen*, *Parham*, and *Lehr* assumed the mother-child relation and required fathers to prove their relationships to their children, they at least gave the fathers that opportunity. In *Caban*, there was no opportunity to show that one did not fit the stereotype.

2. Breadwinners and Dependants

In *Orr v. Orr* (1979), the Court struck down an Alabama law that exempted women from the duty to pay alimony, while authorizing the courts to require men to pay under the correct circumstances. The Court did not accept Alabama's assertion that sex was an appropriate proxy for financial need. Although financial need was an important governmental interest, there was no need for the proxy because the divorce proceedings included an assessment of individual financial need. Thus, the law failed to be substantially related to the end. Similarly, the Court in *Wengler v. Druggist Muy Ins. Co.* (1980) invalidated a workers' compensation law that presumed a wife's dependency for the purposes of benefits under the scheme.

3. Marital Property

Kirchberg v. Feenstra (1981) involved a Louisiana law allowing husbands to unilaterally dispose of joint spousal property, whereas wives were required to obtain the consent of their husbands to dispose of such property. The case was easily decided, as no one could come up with an important governmental interest that would be served by the law. It was simply a vestige of paternalistic male privilege that could not be justified.

4. Occupational Education

Long before the case of *VMI* (exclusion of women from the Virginia Military Academy), the Court addressed a case in which a man was excluded from the Mississippi University for Women (MUW). In *MUW v. Hogan* (1983), the plaintiff, a male who wished to obtain a baccalaureate degree in nursing, was denied admission to the all-female School of Nursing on the basis of his gender. Justice O'Connor, writing for a five-to-four majority, could not accept the argument that the practice was designed to remedy past discrimination because there was no shortage of women in the nursing profession and there was no shortage of gender-neutral training opportunities for women. The fact that the school allowed men to audit nursing classes significantly undermined any argument that women needed single-sex education and completely undermined any argument that the exclusion of men from being enrolled in the program was substantially related to the end. Rather, the exclusion of men from the nursing program perpetuated the stereotype that nursing was a female profession and not a male one.

There were four dissenters in the case and three different dissenting opinions. Justice Powell's dissent was the most comprehensive. In it, he argued that the plaintiff had not suffered harm because the state offered other co-ed programs that were not inferior to the program at MUW. Furthermore, he argued that single-sex education had its benefits and having a diversity of educational opportunities had benefits. Finally, Justice Powell warned that the ruling had the potential to eliminate all women-only institutions of higher education. In this point, Chief Justice Burger emphasized that the majority opinion only applied to the nursing college and not to the university as a whole or other institutions of higher education.

Justice O'Connor's opinion was limited to the nursing college, and her reasoning was tailored to the peculiarities of the nursing profession and the fact that the school allowed for male auditors. Thus, other programs or institutions that did not perpetuate stereotypes, but served a remedial or other important educational interest, might survive intermediate scrutiny.

F. Discrimination as a Means to Compensate for Past Discrimination

In three cases in the mid- to late 1970s, the Court upheld laws that discriminated on the basis of gender because they were designed to compensate for past discrimination. For instance, in *Kahn v. Shevin* (1974), the Court upheld a state law giving a property tax exemption for widows, but not widowers, based on the fact that past discrimination against women made it more difficult for widows to support themselves than widowers. Similarly, the next year in *Schlesinger v. Ballard* (1975), the Court upheld a law giving female military officers four more years to achieve a promotion before being discharged than their male counterparts. If a male officer was passed over twice for promotion after nine years of service, he would be discharged, whereas the female officer would only be discharged if she was passed over twice after thirteen years. The Court upheld the distinction because it tracked the inequality of opportunity for female officers to gain the types of experience needed for promotion, particularly combat-related experience. The extra time was needed to redress the past discrimination in terms of opportunity for experience. Finally, in *Califano v. Webster* (1977), in a unanimous decision, the Court upheld a provision in the Social Security Act that had a formula making it easier for women to get more benefits for their age and earning history than their male counterparts. The Court upheld the discriminatory law because it was not based on "archaic and overbroad generalizations" about women but was designed to compensate for the discrimination that women had suffered in the employment market. It should be noted that *Webster* was decided just shortly after *Califano v. Goldfarb* (1977). In *Goldfarb*, the Court struck down parts of the Social Security Act that it found were based on overgeneralizations, in particular the section giving widows automatic benefits as surviving dependants, but requiring widowers to prove dependency.

It is worth noting that it is unlikely that *Webster* would survive the strict scrutiny test required for cases involving race. Remember that in *City of Richmond v. A.J. Croson Co.* (1989), the Court held that generalized allegations of past racial discrimination were not sufficient to justify remedial legislation. They did not provide a compelling state interest. This is one advantage of intermediate scrutiny. The state need only show an important governmental interest and show that the law substantially furthers that interest.

G. Discrimination against Children Born Out of Wedlock: "Illegitimate" Children

The status of being born to unmarried parents has all the hallmarks of a discrete and insular minority in need of the Court's protection from the democratic process. There has been a long history of discrimination against such children; their status is immutable and out of their control, and they are a minority that does not have a great deal of power in the political process. Even if there is some value in morally condemning parents for extramarital sex, there is something fundamentally unfair about visiting those "sins" on an innocent child. The Court has distinguished illegitimacy from race and gender in terms of both the degree of discrimination throughout history and the obviousness of the characteristic (*Mathews v. Lucas*, 1976). The fact that outside of certain narrow contexts, one cannot easily determine if someone was born in or out of wedlock has the effect of limiting the extent to which such children are discriminated against. Nonetheless, it is difficult to see why this makes the discrimination that does occur any less problematic. In spite of the many reasons for applying strict scrutiny to discrimination on this basis, the Court has never recognized the group as a suspect class deserving of strict scrutiny. It was not until *Clark v. Jeter* (1988) (striking down a law that required a child to establish paternity by age six to receive child support from the father), when the Court firmly settled on adopting the intermediate standard of review for discrimination on this basis.

As early as 1968, the Court struck down a law barring the unacknowledged illegitimate child from recovering for the wrongful death of its mother as violating the Equal Protection guarantee (*Levy v. Louisiana*, 1968). In that case, the Court found the legitimacy was not related in any way to alleged wrongful death of the mother. Likewise, in the companion case of *Gloria v. American Guarantee & Liability Insurance Co.* (1968), the Court struck down a law barring parents from bringing wrongful death suits that involved their illegitimate children.

These cases can be distinguished from the case of *Jimenez v. Weinberger* (1974), in which the Court upheld a law requiring a father to have either legitimated or formally acknowledged the child to bring a wrongful death suit. In this case, the law discriminates between fathers who have "done the right thing" and those who have not. It simply denies the right to sue to those fathers who have failed to legitimate or acknowledge their child. Rather than discriminating against "illegitimate" children, the law encourages fathers to take responsibility for them.

In another Louisiana case, the Court in *Weber v. Aetna Casualty & Surety Co.* (1972) struck down a workers' compensation law that discriminated against unacknowledged dependent surviving illegitimate children. (An unacknowledged illegitimate child is a child whose father has not acknowledged paternity.) Although the law did not bar them from recovering in every case, the children could only receive benefits under the scheme if there were still funds left after legitimate children and acknowledged surviving illegitimate children were paid out. The Court held that the discriminatory treatment of unacknowledged illegitimate children did not bear a significant relationship to the objectives of the workers' compensation statute.

The Court decided a number of cases in the 1970s that appear very easy by today's standards. The Court struck down a New Jersey law excluding single-parent families from receiving public assistance designed to aid the working poor in *New Jersey Welfare Rights Organization v. Cahill* (1973); a Texas law that only required fathers to pay child support for their legitimate children and not their illegitimate children in *Gomez v. Perez* (1973); and an Illinois law that barred illegitimate children from inheriting from a father who died without a will in *Trimble v. Gordon* (1977). There simply was no justification for punishing these children by denying them the benefits or rights in question.

In *Mathews v. Lucas* (1976), in a six-to-three decision, the Court confronted a slightly more difficult set of facts. The Social Security Act provided benefits for dependent survivors, and presumed that legitimate children and illegitimate children who could inherit under state law were dependent, whereas illegitimate children who could not inherit under state law were required to prove dependency. At first blush, the law seems to unfairly discriminate against illegitimate children, but it really discriminates between illegitimate children. The class of illegitimate children who can inherit under state law would include the bulk of illegitimate children who were dependent, for that class would include acknowledged illegitimate children, illegitimate children whose parent had been established by Court order, or those whose parent was ordered to pay support and whose parents later married. Thus, the Court held that the classifications were "reasonably related to the likelihood of dependency at death." Given the administrative costs of proving dependency, the Court found that it was reasonable to presume that this class of illegitimate children and the class of legitimate children were dependent and require other illegitimate children to show proof of dependency.

Justice Stevens, writing for the dissent, attacked the majority opinion for failing to truly apply heightened scrutiny. He argued that "the reason why the United States Government should not add to the burdens that illegitimate children inevitably acquire at birth is radiantly clear: we are committed to the proposition that all persons are created equal." The dissent did not believe that "administrative convenience" was a sufficient justification for the discrimination. The dissent called into question the actual relationship between the different classifications and actual dependency. They argued that a father could just as easily sever relations with a legitimate child as an illegitimate child, and there may be numerous illegitimate children who were dependent on fathers who supported them who did not meet their state's requirements for inheritance. In cases where the father was giving support, the father may never have had a reason to officially acknowledge paternity, much less have gone through any of the other procedures required by the state for eligibility of inheritance. Rather than accept the state's purported interest in "efficiency," the dissent suspected that the law was based on the idea that illegitimates were "less deserving persons than legitimates."

The Court has struck down a number of statutes of limitations involving paternity suits. The Court struck down a statute requiring that paternity claims be brought before the child is one year old in *Mills v. Habluetzel* (1982), before the child is two years old in *Pickett v. Brown* (1983), and before the child is six years old in *Clark v. Jeter* (1988). In each case, the Court determined that the statutory limit was not substantially related to the purposes of the statute of limitations, namely, to avoiding fraudulent or stale claims.

Nonetheless, in an earlier case, the Court upheld a law that only permitted illegitimate children to inherit by intestate succession (the process of inheritance when there is no will) from a deceased father if paternity had been legally established during the father's lifetime (*Lalli v. Lalli,* 1978). Here, a plurality of the Court held that the law did further the state interest in having a just and orderly disposition of the property. Justice Powell, writing for the plurality, used language that sounded more like rational basis review than intermediate scrutiny when he stated, "our inquiry under the Equal Protection Clause does not focus on the abstract 'fairness' of a state law, but on whether the statute's relation to the state interests it is intended to promote is so tenuous that it lacks the rationality contemplated by the 14th Amendment."

Justice Brennan was joined by Justices White, Marshall, and Stevens in his dissent. The dissents' primary argument was that "the state interest in the accurate and efficient determination of paternity can be adequately served by requiring the illegitimate child to offer into evidence a 'formal acknowledgment of paternity.'" The dissent drew attention to the fact that in cases where a father had acknowledged his paternity and actually provided support, it would be unlikely that a court determination would take place. Court orders are generally sought when a father denies paternity and/or fails to provide support for the child. The injustice is demonstrated by the facts of *Lalli*. The father formally acknowledged the paternity of his son and supported him. Thus, no one involved saw a need for a court order of paternity. Nonetheless, the son was denied his share of his father's estate merely because there was no judicial order.

Given the state of the art of DNA testing for paternity claims, it is difficult to see how any statutes of limitations would be substantially related to the purposes of these types of statutes (unless the DNA was simply not available). However, DNA testing was not available when these cases were decided. It only became available in the mid-1980s. Though DNA testing can exclude 99.99 percent or more of the population, the test that was available in the 1970s only reliably excluded about 80 percent of the population.

Stop Points

Intermediate Scrutiny Review

- Test: classifications based on gender and legitimacy violate equal protection unless they are substantially related to important government objectives.
- Gender
  - For sex discrimination to be upheld, the important government objective must be genuine, and its justification cannot be based on overbroad generalizations about males or females.
  - Laws compensating women for past discrimination have been upheld as being substantially related to an important government objective.
- Legitimacy
  - Most state laws that discriminate against nonmarital children have been invalidated, because the state's concern over illicit relationships cannot be the foundation for penalizing the children who are the product of such relationships.
  - Some discrimination against nonmarital children has been upheld as a reasonable effort to serve administrative convenience.

V. The Protection of Fundamental Rights under Equal Protection

The Court generally protects fundamental rights by subjecting governmental infringement of those rights to strict scrutiny. The same basic strict scrutiny test applies whether the Court is protecting rights through a due process analysis or an equal protection analysis. If the Court uses due process, otherwise known as substantive due process, it asks whether there is a compelling state interest that justifies the infringement, and if there are ways of achieving that interest that would have less impact on the right. If the Court uses equal protection, the analysis is slightly different, in that it asks whether discrimination in the provision of or the burdening of the right can be justified. Again, the discrimination must be necessary for a compelling state interest. Of course, if the right is equally denied or infringed on. then the equal protection analysis is inappropriate. Also under equal protection, the law need not be struck down, if the government is willing to treat everyone equally. If the government treats everyone equally by infringing too much on the right, it will be struck down under substantive due process.

Rights not deemed fundamental, such as economic liberties, receive only rational basis review, and the Court has applied a balancing test in cases where it does not think the right has been significantly burdened. The balancing test is a flexible test that balances the state interest against the burden imposed by the state to further the interest.

Though the Constitution does contain the Bill of Rights, it does not mention the notion of fundamental rights. To add to the possible confusion, most of the rights the Court has deemed fundamental are not listed in the Bill of Rights, or explicitly listed as a right anywhere in the text of the Constitution (e.g., travel, voting, and access to justice). Most of the rights deemed fundamental arguably flow from or derive from one or more rights or liberties mentioned in the text. These rights flow both from multiple textual references and the structure, logic, tradition, and objectives of the U.S. constitutional republic. The text of the Ninth Amendment opens up the possibility of recognizing a host of rights not found in the text of Constitution. It reads: "The enumeration in the Constitution of certain rights, shall not be construed to disparage others retained by the people."

Although there is considerable debate concerning the legitimate sources for fundamental rights, the Ninth Amendment appears to recognize that there are other rights that are part of our history and tradition that could be deemed fundamental. Arguably the Court has recognized rights that are new or novel and thus, by definition, are not part of the text or American tradition. Whether this is legitimate depends on one's view of rights and the Constitution. If the Constitution is a living document, meant to develop in step with the progressive development of rights and social norms, then perhaps it is best for the courts to breathe life into those provisions that have breathing room. If the Constitution is viewed as a document that derives its force and legitimacy from those who enacted it, then perhaps the courts should leave any updating to the political institutions entrusted to formally amend the Constitution. In any case, the Court should be hesitant in taking on such a task unless there is good reason to believe that the democratic process is not working and the Court is helping safeguard the democratic process.

As we saw in Chapter 7, some of the most controversial fundamental rights are those concerning the right to privacy, including family autonomy, marriage, reproductive freedom, sexual conduct and orientation, and decisions regarding medical care and the right to die. Although these cases are sometimes treated under equal protection, the rights that fall out of or under the right to privacy are more commonly seen as part of the substantive due process tradition.

Somewhat less controversial are the rights and interests related to travel, access to courts, and voting. Although the Court has recognized the importance of education, it has not recognized it as a fundamental right. Of course, rights under the First Amendment are among those deemed fundamental, but they are addressed in a separate chapter.

The remainder of this chapter addresses the rights to travel, vote, access to justice, and the interest in receiving an education.

A. The Right to Travel

The Articles of Confederation contained a right of ingress and egress from the various states, but such a right was left out of the Constitution. On the one hand, it can be argued that the omission should be read to undermine any claim that such a right exists. Few have held this view, largely because the Constitution was designed to correct the flaw of a weak federal government under the Articles of Confederation. A right to interstate travel was seen as a necessary right for the new Union to survive. As Justice Potter Stewart stated in *United States v. Guest* (1966), regarding the absence of the express provision in the Constitution, "the reason ... is that a right so elementary was conceived from the beginning to be a necessary concomitant of the stronger Union that the Constitution created. In any event, freedom to travel throughout the United States has long been recognized as a basic right under the Constitution."

The Court adopted this reasoning as early as *Crandall v. Nevada* (1867), when the Court struck down a state law imposing a per person tax on carriers transporting people out of the state. The Court held that the tax would effectively be a tax on individuals wishing to leave the state. Although the Court did not use the phrase "right to travel," it held that the federal government had a right to call citizens from anywhere in the United States, and citizens had a correlative right to go to the seat of government to assert claims, transact business, seek protection, and participate in government. The Court further held that citizens also had the right to access seaports and the governmental offices and courts of the several states. The Court reasoned that the right of the citizen to interstate travel was essential to the federal system of government, and if states could interfere with the right, they could undermine the entire federal system.

Notice that there is nothing in this logic that would extend the scope of the right beyond interstate travel to international travel. It may extend to travel within the state, but only so far as intrastate travel was necessary for interstate travel. In other words, the logic would not extend to zoning laws that kept certain people and/or their activities from living, traveling, or doing business within certain areas. In fact, the Court has not found or created a fundamental right to either foreign travel or intrastate travel.

Although the Court generally applies strict scrutiny to equal protection claims involving the right to interstate travel, there are some cases in which the Court appears to apply a lesser standard. It perhaps goes without saying in some cases the Court does not find there has been an infringement or denial of the right to interstate travel. In these cases, strict scrutiny is not applied.

In *Saenz v. Roe* (1999), the Court revived the dormant Privileges and Immunities Clause of the Fourteenth Amendment to strike down a California law that violated the right to interstate travel by giving out different levels of welfare benefits based on the duration of one's residency. The clause provides that states cannot deny the privileges and immunities of citizens of the United States. Although it would make sense that many fundamental rights, and those rights in the Bill of Rights, could be seen as privileges and immunities of citizenship, the Court closed down this interpretation of the text in the *Slaughter-House Cases* (1872). The clause was basically a dead letter until Justice Stevens, along with a majority of the Court in *Saenz*, revived the clause. Given the justification for the right to travel, the clause fits like a glove. The right is not a right to travel abroad, or even to travel within a state, but is a right to travel between states. Thus, it makes sense to view the right as a privilege of U.S. citizenship that states cannot abridge. Most of the cases that follow could be addressed as violations of the clause. Little turns, however, on whether the right is protected through equal protection, as a fundamental right, or as a privilege or immunity.

1. Residency and Durational Residency Requirements

Though the Court has struck down many laws that condition benefits on durational residency, it has upheld laws that simply require genuine residency. In fact, the Court has held that simply requiring residency before one receives a benefit does not violate the right to interstate travel. Thus, in *McCarthy v. Philadelphia Civil Service Com'n* (1976), the Court upheld an ordinance requiring Philadelphia employees to actually reside in the city of Philadelphia. Similarly, in *Martinez v. Bynum* (1983), the Court upheld a law that required residency to receive free public education. Because the Court held that neither the Equal Protection Clause nor the right to travel were infringed, the laws in question did not have to survive strict scrutiny.

In a number of cases, the Court has found that conditioning rights or benefits on one's length or duration of residency violates the fundamental right to interstate travel, yet in others, it has not. There does not appear to be a hard-and-fast rule in these cases, but something of a balance of how significant the burden is on both the right to interstate travel and the underlying benefit. The two go hand in hand because the more significant the deprivation of the benefit, the larger the deterrent to entering the state.

The Court has held in various cases that one-year residency requirements violate the right to interstate travel and fail to survive strict scrutiny under equal protection. Those contexts include access to welfare assistance in *Shapiro v. Thompson* (1969), eligibility to vote in *Dunn v. Blumstein* (1972), and eligibility for indigents to receive medical treatment in *Memorial Hospital v. Maricopa* (1974). Although there is a fundamental right to vote, there is no fundamental right to receive medical treatment or welfare assistance.

It is somewhat difficult to reconcile these cases with the Court's decisions in *Sosna v. Iowa* (1975), upholding a one-year residency requirement to obtain a divorce in Iowa. The Court distinguished this case on the basis that the right to access the courts was not lost but only delayed. In these cases, the harm of not being able to access welfare assistance, vote in a given election, and obtain medical treatment in any given case were more severe deprivations. Although one can presumably delay a divorce, it is much more difficult to delay the basic necessities of life that welfare assistance and medical treatment provide. If one cannot vote in any given election, the state does not delay the vote until one has satisfied his or her residency requirement. That opportunity is lost and irreparable. In *Sosna*, the Court also accepted the state's argument that one-year residency helped ensure that the parties to the divorce had genuine contacts with the state, and therefore would reduce collateral attacks on the proceedings from courts in other jurisdictions.

Just one year after *Blumstein*, the Court decided two cases that would appear to significantly limit that case. In *Martson v. Lewis* (1973), the Court upheld a fifty-day durational requirement for voting on the basis that this was narrowly tailored to administering the electoral system. This would allow the state to check rolls and prevent fraud. In dicta, the Court in *Blumstein* stated that thirty days would be sufficient for such purposes. However, in the present case, the Court held that given the special problems both caused and faced by Arizona's system of volunteer voting officials, fifty days was appropriate.

Although this case could be squared with *Blumstein*, it is much more difficult to square *Blumstein* with the result in *Rosario v. Rockefeller* (1973), in which the Court upheld a New York law that "required a voter to enroll in the party of his choice at least 30 days before the general election in November in order to vote in the next subsequent party primary." This requirement amounted to registration of between eight and eleven months depending on the election. Nonetheless, the Court held that the law was "a permissible deterrent against the practice of primary election 'raiding' by opposing party members." Election raiding takes place when members of one party designate themselves as voters of another party, to influence or determine the results of the other party's primary. Although the effects of *Rosario* would appear to severely limit *Blumstein*, the cases are not actually on point. *Rosario* was brought by residents of New York who could have registered with the party but simply failed to do so. Although the claimants argued that their rights to vote and association were violated, neither the five-person majority nor the four-person dissent ever addressed the right to travel. The dissent's main criticism of the majority opinion was that it did not strictly scrutinize the law as is required when the fundamental right to vote is infringed. Rather, the majority held that the registration requirement was "not an arbitrary time limit unconnected to any important state goal."

In *Zobel v. Williams* (1982), the Court struck down an Alaska law that distributed proceeds from the Alaska pipeline based on the length of one's residency in the state. The impact on interstate travel is somewhat difficult to see in this case. The law was designed to encourage people to come and set up residence, and the state argued that the benefits paid out were designed to recognize the differing degrees of past contributions by those residing longer in the state. Although on its face the law does not seem to greatly burden interstate travel or be unreasonable or grossly unfair, the Court held that recognizing past contributions was not a legitimate state interest, and the distinction based on length of residency was not rationally related to the state's legitimate interest in the prudent management of resources and the funds derived from them.

The real impetus for the decision, and the reason the Court appears to apply rational basis, can be explained by the slippery slope on which such schemes lie. The fear is that if a scheme such as this passed constitutional muster, then why not all government benefits? (better education, health services, etc., the longer one resides in the state). The problem is, when taken to their logical conclusion, such schemes create a range of classes of citizens with the first class being the longest residents and the last being new residents. By holding that the main justification for such schemes (some notion of fairness based on length of stay and contribution) is not a legitimate purpose and that other more mundane legitimate purposes, like efficiency, are not rationally related to such schemes, the Court forecloses most every possible scheme of this type. If such schemes do not pass rational basis, they could never pass strict scrutiny.

In two other cases during the 1980s, the Court struck down laws that discriminated between veterans on the basis of residency. The first, *Hooper v. Bernalillo* (1985), provided a property tax exemption to veterans who had become residents before May 8, 1976, but not after. The Court held that this distinction should be subject to strict scrutiny, but like in *Zobel*, did not even pass rational basis. Again following *Zobel*, the Court held that rewarding past contributions to the state was not a legitimate state interest. The state could not treat veterans who arrived before, during, or shortly after the war better than those who established residency later. The state was not allowed to treat new residents as less than "their own" than older residents. Similarly, in *Atty. Gen. of N.Y. v. Soto-Lopez* (1986), the Court struck down a New York law providing affirmative action in hiring veterans who had established residency before going to the war but not after. Justice Brennan's four-justice plurality opinion held that the law failed strict scrutiny review. The two separate concurring opinions argued that the law failed even rational basis review. The plurality did not question the purposes in this case, namely:

> (1) the encouragement of New York residents to join the Armed Services; (2) the compensation of residents for service in time of war by helping these veterans reestablish themselves upon coming home; (3) the inducement of veterans to return to New York after wartime service; and (4) the employment of a "uniquely valuable class of public servants" who possess useful experience acquired through their military service.

Nonetheless, the law failed because it was not narrowly tailored to these purposes. According to the plurality, the state could have adequately accomplished these goals with the less restrictive means of treating all otherwise qualified veterans the same. Giving all otherwise qualified veterans the same number of extra points when considering their job applications would equally (if not better) achieve these stated goals.

2. Foreign Travel

Although some early cases indicated that there was a fundamental right to travel abroad, the Court in *Califano v. Aznavorian* (1978) made it clear that although there was a fundamental right to interstate travel, the right to travel abroad was not fundamental. Rather, it was merely an aspect of liberty protected by the Due Process Clause. In this case, certain provisions of the Social Security Act denied benefits otherwise available for the needy, aged, blind, and disabled, for any month that the recipient spent entirely outside of the United States. The Court upheld the provisions, stating both that they were rational and that they merely had an incidental effect on international travel. Thus, even if the right was fundamental, the law did not substantially burden the right.

Subsequent cases have also applied rational basis review to limitations on the right to international travel. The Court in *Haig v. Agee* (1981) (upholding the authority of the Secretary of State to revoke a passport for national security reasons) and *Regan v. Wald* (1984) (upholding federal regulations prohibiting travel to Cuba) applied rational basis analysis in their decisions. The Court in both cases noted that deference should be given to political branches of the federal government in the areas of foreign policy.

B. The Right to Vote

Although several provisions in the Constitution address aspects of voting rights, the text does not contain a right to vote. Article I, Section 2 requires that anyone who can vote for the "most numerous branch" of their state legislature can vote for members of Congress. This has been read to require strict population proportionality in congressional elections. From the time of the founding until relatively recently, the right to vote was denied to African Americans, to women, to the poor, and to young adults. Several amendments to the Constitution helped remedy this. It was not until after the Civil War that discrimination in access to the polls on the basis of race, color, or condition of previous servitude was banned (Fifteenth Amendment), and it was not until the Nineteenth Amendment in 1920 that discrimination based on gender was banned. The Seventeenth Amendment, passed in 1913, provided Senators were to be elected by the people in their state rather than being appointed by the state. The bulk of African American voters were kept from the polls until the mid-1960s, with the passing of the Voting Rights Act of 1965 and the ratification of the Twenty-Fourth Amendment in 1964, which prevented states from imposing taxes on individuals wishing to vote for candidates running for federal office. Finally, the Twenty-Sixth Amendment, ratified in 1971, extended the franchise to citizens who were age eighteen and older.

Although the text does not provide for a general right to vote, the Court has determined that the right is fundamental. The right not only draws from the textual provisions but from the First Amendment freedoms of expression and association. The right to vote is considered fundamental, because it is essential to our democracy and to our "Republican form of government." Article IV, Section 4 states, "the United States shall guarantee to every state in this Union a Republican Form of Government." Although the Court has held that the clause is nonjusticiable because of its political nature, there is no dispute over the fact that representative democracy is what is meant by "a republican form of government." The general rule that the courts should defer to the political branches of government is premised on the idea that the political branches are democratically elected and accountable. This also underlies the exceptions to the rule (e.g., when the courts have reason to fear that the democratic process is not functioning well, for instance, when it comes to laws that discriminate against discrete and insular minorities). Without a right to vote, there would little to justify the Court's deference to the other branches of government.

The cases in this area of the law often fall under one of two large areas. The first set of cases deal with limiting access to the polls, and the second set of cases addresses how votes are counted once people have gone to the polls. One's right to vote can either be directly interfered with by limiting one's access to the polls, or one's vote can be diminished after it is cast by either diluting it, gerrymandering it, or simply doing an arbitrary job of counting it. A related set of cases address limitations on the right to run for election. In effect, limiting who can run for office also limits one's vote, for it limits who one can choose from in casting her or his vote.

1. Access to the Polls

Shortly after the Constitution was amended to prohibit the use of poll taxes in federal elections (Twenty-Fourth Amendment), the Court struck down a Virginia poll tax (*Harper v. Virginia State Board of Elections,* 1966). Justice Douglas wrote for a majority at a time when the Court took discrimination on the basis of wealth seriously. As a result, the decision to apply strict scrutiny was based in part on treating poverty as a suspect class, and in part on discrimination in the provision of a fundamental right. Although poverty did not remain a suspect class, the right to vote did remain a fundamental right. The Court in *Harper* held that classifications that restrained the right to vote needed to be "closely scrutinized and carefully confined." The poll tax in this case was only $1.50, yet the Court held that fee paying had no relation to one's ability to participate in the electoral process.

Because schools are often funded by local property taxes, it follows that property owners have an interest in school district affairs. They and the parents of school district children are arguably the largest stakeholders and the most interested in school district affairs. The school district in *Kramer v. Union Free School District* (1969) argued that this was the justification for limiting those who can vote in school district elections to parents of children enrolled in a school in the district and to those who own taxable real estate in the district. The Court rejected this argument because almost every member of the community has an interest in its school system. Some property owners may have little interest in a school district, whereas some renters may have a great interest in the school district (e.g., a teacher who has no children). The law was both overbroad and underinclusive, and thus the Court struck it down, holding that these requirements were not narrowly tailored enough to the goal of limiting the vote to those who were primarily interested.

A number of decisions followed *Kramer*, striking down property owner-ship limits on the franchise in the context of governmental bonds; for exam-ple, approving municipal revenue bonds, *Cipriano v. City of Houma* (1969); general revenue bonds, *Phoenix v. Kolodziejski* (1970); and the sale of bonds for a city library, *Hill v. Stone* (1975). Again, the reasoning was it was not merely prop-erty owners who had an interest and a stake in such decisions, and thus the ex-clusion of nonproperty owners was not narrowly tailored.

It is difficult to reconcile these cases with *Salyer Land Co. v. Tulare Lake Basin Water Storage Dist.* (1973) and *Ball v. James* (1981). In *Salyer*, the Court upheld a law that restricted the right to vote in the water storage district to property own-ers. The law in *Salyer* not only limited the right to vote to property owners, it weighed those votes according to the assessed value of the property. The Court distinguished this case on the grounds that the election was for something that the landowners had a special interest. The Court emphasized that the water district was a special public entity that did not exercise general governmental authority but only provided limited services. The Court in *Ball* extended *Salyer* to a water district that controlled and delivered water and sold electricity to over 200,000 residents in central Arizona. The law in *Ball* required that one own at least one acre of land to vote for the directors of the district. In addi-tion to the water and electricity authority, the entity had authority to condemn land and sell tax-free bonds and had an important role to play in flood and en-vironmental management. Nonetheless, the Court held that the district did not have the kind of governmental power that required an open election. The Court found it sufficient that property owners were the most affected by the entities power to tax them, and the entity would not likely have come into existence if property owners were not given sufficient input into electing the directors.

The Supreme Court of Missouri took *Ball* to its logical extreme by upholding a provision of its Constitution that limited membership on a board (which had the authority to draft a plan to restructure local government), to people who owned property. The provision read: "the governments of the city of St. Louis and St. Louis County may be reorganized by a vote of the electorate upon a plan of reorganization drafted by a 'board of freeholders.'" The Supreme Court of Missouri held that the restriction did not violate the Equal Protection Clause of the Constitution, because the board, like the water district author-ity in *Ball*, did not exercise general governmental powers. The Supreme Court, in *Quinn v. Millsap* (1989), a unanimous decision by Justice Blackmun, over-ruled the Missouri Supreme Court and distinguished *Ball* on the grounds that the water district in that case had a very narrow function. In *Quinn*, the board would be proposing the reorganization of local government. This was a very broad function affecting the general population, and thus the Court held that it was "a form of invidious discrimination to require land ownership of all appointees to a body authorized to propose reorganization of local government."

Thus, after *Quinn*, it appears that the Court will take two things into consideration: (1) whether the election is for a special or limited purpose, and (2) whether the result of the election, or the functions of the entity, primarily impacts property owners.

As we saw under the right to travel, the Court has struck down durational residency requirements in *Dunn v. Blumstein* (1972) (striking down a one-year residency requirement) unless:

1. they are narrowly tailored to administering the electoral system as in *Martson v. Lewis* (1973) (upholding a fifty-day durational requirement for voting on the basis that this was narrowly tailored checking rolls and preventing fraud), or
2. they are narrowly tailored to preventing primary election raiding by rival parties as in *Rosario v. Rockefeller* (1973) (upholding a New York law that "required a voter to enroll in the party of his choice at least 30 days before the general election in November in order to vote in the next subsequent party primary" as a permissible deterrent to party raiding).

Remember that *Rosario* was not so much a right to travel case because the petitioners were not new immigrants to the state. Rather, their claim fell squarely on the right to vote and freedom of association, because they were denied the vote based on their failure to register with the party in time. Though limiting election manipulation through party raiding is an important state interest, it is not clear that the majority of the Court adequately protected the right through the standard of review it articulated. The Court merely held that the registration requirement was "not an arbitrary time limit unconnected to any important state goal." Under more strict review, there were surely less restrictive means available.

The importance attached by the Court to the ability of parties to prevent raiding, to associate, and to exclude nonparty members was brought to the forefront in *California Democratic Party v. Jones* (2000), where in a seven-to-two decision the Court struck down a California voter initiative allowing voters to vote in either party's primary. This would amount to an open invitation to election manipulation and denied parties their right to association, because it opened up the very real possibility that a party's candidate would be chosen not by party members but by opponents.

Although the Court has upheld restricting the franchise to nonfelons, in *Hunter v. Underwood* (1981), it unanimously struck down a provision of the Alabama constitution that denied the franchise to anyone convicted of a crime involving moral turpitude. The law was struck down, not because it denied criminals the right to vote but because the Court found that the law had both the purpose and effect of disenfranchising African Americans.

a. Voter ID laws

In one of its most recent decisions, the Supreme Court decided a case challenging Indiana's strict voter identification law. The law, which requires a valid government-issued photo identification to vote in person, was challenged on its face before the election rather than after, as an applied challenge. A plurality of the Court, in a three-to-three-to-three decision, upheld the law in *Crawford v. Marion Election Board* (2008). The three-judge plurality written by Justice Stevens and joined by the Chief Justice and Justice Kennedy, held that the law survived a facial attack but may be vulnerable to an as applied attack if it was shown that the law substantially impacted the right to vote (for instance, if elderly voters or the disabled brought a claim based on their actual inability to vote). It was of particular importance that the Indiana identification was provided free of charge. This allowed the state to avoid the holding in *Harper v. Virginia State Board of Elections* (1966), striking down the Virginia poll tax under strict scrutiny review. Rather, the Court held that under *Anderson v. Celebrezze* (1983) (striking down an Ohio statute that required that independent candidates for President file long before the Republicans and Democrats) "evenhanded restrictions that protect the integrity and reliability of the electoral process" are not considered invidious. The plurality held that *Anderson* and subsequent cases such as *Burdick v. Takushi* (1992) (upholding a Hawaii law that prohibited voters for adding and voting for write-in candidates) established a balancing approach for cases involving reasonable nondiscriminatory laws. The plurality held that on its face, the law was an even-handed restriction that was justified by the sufficiently weighty state interest in protecting the "integrity and reliability of the electoral process." Although there was no evidence of voter fraud in the state, the Court found the state's interest in only counting eligible voters' votes and its interest in voter confidence to be sufficient to justify the law.

The concurrence of Justice Scalia, joined by Justices Thomas and Alito, argued that under the *Burdick* balancing test, the Indiana law should be subjected only to a "deferential 'important regulatory interest'" standard of review. They would have held that because the overall burden on voters was minimal, it should not matter that there was a special burden on some voters. For the concurrence, the extra burden here is not a significant burden over and above the normal burdens associated with voting.

The three-person dissent, written by Justice Souter, also used the *Burdick* balancing test, but the dissent completely inversed the majority's reasoning. While the majority demanded concrete proof of a substantial interference with the right, the dissent would have held that the state had the burden of making a factual showing that the threat to its interests (even if compelling) actual outweighed the impediments imposed. Although the plurality found the burden on the right to be speculative at best, the dissent argued that the burden on the right was concrete and serious. The burden included costs associated with the need to travel to a limited number of Bureau of Motor Vehicle offices; the cost for obtaining the identification required in many cases to get the Indiana photo identification (i.e., a birth certificate); and the problems associated with provisional ballots. These costs amounted to a serious burden on the 43,000 voting-aged residents of Indiana who lacked appropriate identification and who were predominantly poor. Further, according to the dissent, the plurality failed to adequately scrutinize the state's interests in the case. First, voter fraud, which is documented as a problem in the state of Indiana in absentee ballot cases, is untouched by the law, whereas in-person voter fraud, which has not been documented as being a problem in the state, is addressed. Second, the state itself was being sued by the national government for failing to remove ineligible voters from its list, so it is perverse that it should be able to justify burdening the right to vote to correct its own wrongful practice. Finally, the only evidence that there was a lack of voter confidence was linked to the state's negligent conduct with regard to its voter list. Thus, for the dissent, the state of Indiana should end its official negligence rather than burden the right to vote.

In sum, the plurality balanced the case in favor of the state, through a form of heightened scrutiny, but left open the possibility of an applied challenge; the concurrence would make the balance more deferential to the state; and the dissent would balance the case in favor of the voters whose right to vote was seriously burdened.

2. Discrimination in the Weight or Counting of One's Vote: Vote Dilution (Not Always Strictly Scrutinized)

a. Malapportionment: Representation that Is Disproportional to the Population

As noted, the right to vote can either be infringed on through an impediment to reaching the polls or by diluting the strength or weight of one's vote once cast. Vote dilution generally takes place through disproportionate representation. Proportional representation takes place if representatives are apportioned according to population. For example, if a state has 100,000 eligible voters with ten districts and ten representatives, then each district should contain 10,000 people. In this way, each person's vote counts equally. If instead of having ten proportional districts (10,000 each), the district is malapportioned, so that there are five districts with 1,000 eligible voters each, and five districts with 19,000 voters each, then the voters in the districts with the large populations are having their votes diluted. Five thousand voters have had their votes concentrated to such a degree that their votes carry as much weight as the other 95,000 voters.

In many cases, state voting districts were malapportioned simply as a result of people moving from the country into larger and larger cities. This shift started with the Industrial Revolution in the late eighteenth century as we shifted from an agricultural society to an industrial society. While at one time, roughly equal geographical districts might have had roughly equal populations, with the movement to big cities, those districts fell out of proportion. Densely populated areas had their votes diluted, whereas sparsely populated areas had their votes concentrated. This is one area in which the normal democratic process is not likely to correct itself, for the simple reason that those elected to office were elected based on the existing districts. Representatives have no reason to fix the apportionment, because, in many cases, this would result in making it very unlikely that they would get reelected. Although this was an area ripe for judicial intervention, the Court consistently held that claims based on malapportionment were nonjusticiable political decisions.

It was not until *Baker v. Carr* (1962) that the Court held that such claims were justiciable and *Gray v. Sanders* (1963) that the Court held that an election scheme was unconstitutional because of malapportionment. In *Gray,* Justice Douglas, writing for the majority, held that the Georgia electoral system for its U.S. Senator primary and its statewide officers (i.e., the state executive and judicial officers) was unconstitutional. The system was based on existing counties with large discrepancies in size. In fact, rural counties, which held about one third of the population, had a majority of the representatives. Justice Douglas held that everyone participating in an election should have an equal vote, regardless of race, sex, occupation, income and place of residence within the geographical unit. In grand language, he held that "the Conception of political equality from the Declaration of Independence to Lincoln's Gettysburg Address, the 15th, 17th and 19th Amendments can only mean one thing—one person, one vote."

In *Reynolds v. Sims* (1964), the Court extended *Gray* to the state of Alabama's plans for the apportionment of seats to its two houses of representatives. Applying the "one person, one vote" rationale of *Gray*, Chief Justice Warren held that the Alabama scheme violated the Equal Protection Clause because the seats were not apportioned on a population basis. Although the Court recognized that exact proportionality was not practically possible, states were required to make a good-faith effort at proportional representation. The Court also allowed for the possibility that a desire to keep political subdivisions in tact may justify some deviation.

The Court has been more lenient in cases involving state legislators and offices than in cases involving U.S. congressional seats. In *Karcher v. Daggett* (1983), the Court struck down a scheme that resulted in 0.7 percent of a deviation from the perfect population proportionality in a congressional districting case, while in the same year in *Brown v. Thomson* (1983), the Court held that deviations under 10 percent were to be considered minor and would require no justification at all. Those over 10 percent were to be considered *prima facie* discriminatory and would require justification. The Court held that the state in these cases would need to show that the "plan may reasonably be said to advance a rational state policy." The standard articulated in *Karcher* was that the plaintiff would need to show that the districts "could have been reduced or eliminated by a good faith effort to draw districts of equal population." Once shown, the burden shifted to the state to prove "that each significant variance between districts was necessary to achieve some legitimate goal." Although neither test is exactly strict scrutiny, it is fairly clear that congressional elections must approximate strict scrutiny while state elections need only satisfy something close to rational basis review. In fact, in *Brown*, the Court upheld Wyoming's county based districting plan which had an average deviation of 16 percent and a maximum deviation of 89 percent from proportional representation. The Court accepted the plan as reasonably related to Wyoming's consistent "one county, one representative" policy, which it had adopted since its founding. The law was not discriminatory but followed traditional political subdivisions. If the plan were made proportional, small counties would lose their representatives.

The explanation for the difference lies in the fact that Article I, Section 2 of the Constitution requires proportionality, whereas the Fourteenth Amendment does not clearly require it. At the state and local level other considerations, like traditional subdivisions, have a role to play that they do not play in congressional elections.

It is worth mentioning that while the Court has numerical standards for how to apportion based on populations, it has not articulated a standard for how to count the population. It would be fairest to count only eligible voters, but in many cases, districts are drawn on the population as a whole.

b. Supermajorities

Requiring a supermajority vote does not violate equal protection or amount to vote dilution even though in some sense it gives a minority the power to veto the law (*Gordon v. Lance*, 1971) (upholding a law requiring a 60 percent approval for political subdivisions to incur bonded debts and to increase taxes).

c. At-Large Elections

A minority party, or minority voting block, may have their votes effectively diluted if the state puts several representatives in one large district, sometimes called "multimember districts." When representatives run in "at-large" elections, the minority party or minority voting block will often lose all of the seats in that district. If the district was split up, a minority, if geographically compact, would have a better chance of getting at least one seat. Nonetheless, as we saw in the section on race-based discrimination, the Court has not found such schemes to be discriminatory merely because of their impact (*City of Mobile v. Bolden*, 1980). However, as we also saw, if a racially discriminatory purpose can be show in addition to the impact, then strict scrutiny will apply (*Rogers v. Lodge*, 1982).

d. Political Gerrymandering

The manipulation of districts to skew the vote in favor of one party or another is referred to as political gerrymandering. The way it works is by packing large numbers of a party's voters into a few districts and cracking the rest up into a large number of districts; an incumbent party can thus protect its representatives. Take the example of a ten-district state with 100 registered voters equally split between the two parties. If the districts are apportioned fairly and are fairly drawn, then each party should get five representatives. If the incumbent party gerrymanders the districts by packing two districts with ten members, each of the opposing party, and then split up the rest equally, the opposing party would win those two districts ten to zero, ten to zero, but would lose all the other eight districts by either six to four, seven to three, or eight to two. Thus, political gerrymandering is a powerful tool for skewing the weight of votes. The result is that in recent elections for the U.S. House of Representatives, less than 10 percent of incumbent seats are actually contestable. In other words, the election results for 90 percent of the seats are known before the election because of the way the districts have been drawn. In the same way that those elected to office in malapportioned districts are not likely to correct the system, those elected through gerrymandered districts are not likely to change the system. In fact, they have every incentive to entrench their power through further refinement of the political gerrymander. Nonetheless, the Court has struggled to find such claims even potentially justiciable.

Although six members of the Court in *Davis v. Bandemer* (1986) held that such claims are justiciable, the Court could not form a majority to agree on a standard for determining when political gerrymandering was unconstitutional. By the time of *Vieth v. Jubelirer* (2004), it was only five members of the Court who held out the possibility that such claims were justiciable, and they too could not agree on a standard. The other four judges would overrule *Bandemer* because they did not think a judicially manageable standard existed. The most recent case, *League of United Latin American Citizens v. Perry* (2006), did not change the situation very much. Here, too, a majority of five judges held that such claims are still justiciable. Two Justices, Justices Thomas and Scalia, would hold that there is no judicially manageable standard for such cases, while the new Justices, Chief Justice Roberts and Justice Alito, have chosen to remain agnostic on the issue.

The most common overall standard is very similar to the standard in malapportionment claims, namely, a standard of partisan symmetry that would require that the electoral system treat similarly situated parties equally, by making votes for the party overall proportional to the legislative seats. Thus, if Republicans received 60 percent of the vote, they should get 60 percent of the seats. Of course, exact proportionality is never possible, and approximating it may require sacrificing other goals like geographical compactness, protecting minority safe districts, and so on. Thus, the Justices disagree over what level or degree of asymmetry is required to violate the Constitution. Justice Kennedy, who is the swing voter, has not settled on a justiciable test but has indicated that the threshold might be met in cases where a party received a minority of votes yet obtained a majority of seats in an election. Thus, if Republicans received 60 percent of the vote but only 49 percent of the seats, this may satisfy Justice Kennedy.

Justice Stevens, joined by Justice Breyer, would rule, at a minimum, that if the desire for partisan gain was the sole factor motivating the decision to redistrict and the redistricting did result in harm to other parties, then this would violate the Equal Protection Clause. Justice Stevens argued that the standard follows from both the First Amendment and from the Court's equal protection jurisprudence, namely, that one cannot be penalized on the basis that they choose to associate with a political group and that the desire to harm a politically disfavored group is not a legitimate state interest. Justice Souter, joined by Justice Ginsburg, did not revisit the test he articulated in *Vieth*, because it was clear that there would be no majority for a single test. Nonetheless, he did indicate that he thought more work on the idea of partisan symmetry might result in a test that could command a majority of the Court in the future.

e. Racial Gerrymandering

As we saw in the subsection covering discrimination based on race, race-based gerrymandering is justiciable and does receive strict scrutiny (*Easley v. Cromartie*, 2001). However, because there is often considerable overlap between race and political affiliation, the standard for establishing racial gerrymandering is

> those who claim that a legislature has improperly used race as a criterion ... must show at a minimum that the "legislature subordinated traditional race-neutral districting principles ... to racial considerations." Race must not simply have been "*a* motivation for the drawing of a majority-minority district," but the "*predominant* factor" motivating the legislature's districting decision. (Internal citations removed)

If race is not the predominant factor, but politics is, then the case is treated as a political gerrymandering case.

f. Arbitrary Vote Counting

Bush v. Gore (2000), which effectively decided the 2000 presidential election, was a controversial decision for a number of reasons, not the least of which is the fact that the *per curium* opinion explicitly limited itself to the particular circumstances of the case before it. Thus, it is difficult to say if the decision has much value in terms of precedence. It is worth noting that the Supreme Court has not cited *Bush v. Gore* in any of its election decisions over the past eight years.

Bush v. Gore addressed the Supreme Court of Florida's order to recount the votes in certain contested counties. The problem was that there was considerable disagreement between and even within counties on how to count the ballots. Disagreement arose because there were many ways in which a ballot that was meant to be punched might look. There may be indentations, partial punches, or pieces of the pushed-out part "just hanging on" (the "hanging chad"). The only standard for conducting the recount was to be "guided by the intent of the voter." Without uniform rules for the recount, there was no assurance that votes would be treated equally. Similar cases would not necessarily be treated alike, and this was a violation of the Equal Protection Clause.

In sum, the Court applied a vague form of heightened scrutiny to the counting of votes that lacked uniform rules. Although this appears uncontroversial, if this approach were applied to recounts and to elections throughout the country, or even to elections within any given state, including Florida, it is doubtful that many elections would pass the test. Many states, including Florida, delegate the administration of elections to local authorities. Those authorities not only have different standards for counting votes, but in many cases they have different mechanisms for recording votes.

The subject of much of the disagreement between the majority and the dissent centered on issues of deference to the Florida state Supreme Court on issues of Florida law.

On the issue of the equal protection claim with regard to standards, several Justices took issue with the majority. Justice Stevens argued that the standard was sufficient given that a single magistrate was charged to adjudicate all disputes regarding the recount. He considered the decision by the majority as an affront to the impartiality of the judiciary, both because of the judicial activism of the Court and because it assumed that the Florida magistrate could not impartially resolve potential disputes. Several Justices criticized the majority for failing to remand the case back to the Florida Supreme Court to articulate a uniform standard for the recount. This criticism was made by Justice Stevens as well as Justices Ginsburg and Breyer in their separate dissents. The response by the majority was that this would put the recount past the due date for resolving election disputes under Florida law, and thus could not be an appropriate remedy. The dissent argued that this was for the Florida courts to decide.

3. Restriction on Running for Office

Just as the Court has held that restrictions on access to voting require strict scrutiny, it has held that many forms of restricting access to inclusion on the ballot need to survive strict scrutiny. Many of the restrictions have also been used to limit access to running for office. The basis for the restrictions include race, wealth, property ownership, and the number of supporters for independent parties.

It should come as little surprise that the Court struck down a Louisiana law that required one's race be listed on the ballot when running for office. The Court in *Anderson v. Martin* (1964) struck down such a law because it amounted to the state encouraging racial prejudice at the polls by reducing the candidate's qualification to their race; this was the only information listed other the candidate's name. The Court did not accept the state's contention that it was nondiscriminatory because it applied to white and black candidates, and Louisiana could find no legitimate purpose for the requirement.

Cases involving filing fees and property ownership requirements have been struck down as failing to satisfy strict scrutiny. For example, in *Bullock v. Carter* (1974) the Court held that the state of Texas had failed to show that its $1,000 filing fee as applied to indigent candidates was necessary for the funding of elections. The Court in *Lubin v. Panish* (1974) held that California's filing fee was not narrowly tailored to a candidate's support or to her or his seriousness for running for office. Note that in the context of a right to vote, the Court held that all fees were unconstitutional; in these cases, the Court merely held that there must be a waiver of the fee for indigent candidates. As we saw in *Quinn v. Millsap* (1989), the Court unanimously held that it was "a form of invidious discrimination" to require landownership as a condition for being appointed to a governmental body. Presumably, the Court would decide the same way if property ownership was a condition for running for elected office.

The Court has upheld restrictions on access to the ballots for small parties without demonstrated support. For instance, in *Jenness v. Fortson* (1971), the Court upheld a Georgia law requiring that candidates who had not won a primary submit a petition with signatures totaling 5 percent of the number of votes cast in the previous election for the desired post. This would be waived if the candidate's party had received over 20 percent of the vote in the previous gubernatorial election. This case was distinguished from *Williams v. Rhodes* (1968) in which the Court struck down an Ohio law requiring signatures totaling 15 percent of the previous gubernatorial race. The Ohio law also required that the petitions be filed early. The Court held that the law failed strict scrutiny because it was not narrowly tailored to preventing voter confusion and electing majority candidates. The law was overbroad in its suppression of new political parties and was struck down.

The Court in *Anderson v. Calebrezze* (1983) struck down another Ohio statute that required that independent candidates for President file their petitions well before Democrat and Republican candidates were required to name their candidates. The law denied independent candidates access to the ballot and infringed on the ability of voters to sign petitions for candidates of their choice. The state offered three justifications for the early deadline: voter education, equal treatment for partisan and independent candidates, and political stability. The Court accepted the first as a compelling interest, but found that the law was not narrowly tailored to that end. It found no relationship between the law and equal treatment because the law resulted in the unequal treatment of independent parties; the Court held that "political stability," which was merely another way of saying that the state wished to protect the Republican and Democratic parties, was not a legitimate state interest.

The perfect blend of denying the right to vote and to run for elected office can be found in the Hawaiian law that banned all write-in votes in its elections. Nonetheless, the Court upheld the law in *Burdick v. Takushi* (1992) on the grounds that it was narrowly tailored to preventing party raiding and factionalism. The Court did not apply strict scrutiny in the case, but a balancing test, because it did not consider the burden on the right to be substantial and it considered the law to be reasonable and nondiscriminatory. It only prevented write-in ballots, and because it was very easy to get on the ballot in Hawaii, this would only impact candidates who had virtually no demonstrated support and a small fraction of voters who wished to vote for candidates with no demonstrated support.

C. Access to Justice

Cases involving access to justice are sometimes decided on equal protection grounds and sometimes on substantive due process grounds. It is difficult to imagine a right more fundamental to the rule of law and fair administration of justice or one more closely tied to the need for equal protection. *Griffin v. Illinois* (1956) illustrates the point. The state of Illinois provided for a right of appeal, but the right was only accessible in many cases if one had a transcript of the trial from the trial court. Illinois did not provide such transcripts for free unless one was sentenced to death. As a result, all other defendants who could not afford the transcript were denied access to the appellate court. The Court held that if Illinois provided appellate review, it needed to provide it without discriminating against the poor. As Justice Black, writing for the plurality stated, "appellate review has now become an integral part of the Illinois trial system for finally adjudicating the guilt or innocence of a defendant. Consequently at all stages of the proceedings, the Due Process and Equal Protection Clauses protect persons like petitioners from invidious discriminations." Thus, Illinois would need to provide such transcripts to those who could not afford them.

The Court has also held that indigent defendants have a right to appointed counsel for appeals that are provided as a matter of right (*Douglas v. California*, 1963). Unfortunately for the poor, equal access to justice stops there. The Court in *Ross v. Moffitt* (1974) did not extend the right to discretionary appeals to the state's highest court or the U.S. Supreme Court, and the Court in *Murray v. Giarrantano* (1989) declined to extend the right to collateral attacks, even in cases where the defendant faced the death penalty. Thus, there is no right for the poor to have free counsel to bring a writ of *habeas corpus*.

The Court has extended the *Griffin* right to be provided free necessary transcripts to other criminal justice contexts, including judicial discretion over the provision of transcripts to the indigent (*Eskridge v. Washington*, 1958) and for the writ of *habeas corpus* (*Long v. District of Iowa*, 1966). The Court has also extended *Griffin* to cases involving appeals against the termination of parental rights (*M.L.B. v. S.L.J.*, 1996). Although there is no general right for the indigent to access the civil justice system, cases involving the termination of parental rights are different. Here, the Court held that because that the state was intruding on the family relationship and the mother could lose her child, the state was required to provide access to the transcripts without regard to her ability to pay.

Similarly, the Court has held that states are required to waive filing fees for the indigent in divorce proceedings (*Boddie v. Connecticut*, 1971). Because divorces touch on the fundamental right to marry and the state has a monopoly over divorces, it violates the Equal Protection Clause to deny access to the courts for the purposes of divorce on the basis of one's income. *Boddie*, like *Douglas*, has been severely limited. The Court refused to extend *Boddie* to filing fees in bankruptcy cases (*United States v. Kras*, 1973) and for judicial review of administrative decisions regarding welfare entitlements (*Ortwein v. Schwab*, 1973). Both of these cases were five-to-four decisions with the dissent arguing that *Boddie* controlled. The majority opinions in these cases distinguished *Boddie* on the grounds that fundamental rights were not involved and there were alternative ways of settling the issues. For the majority, access to the courts in these cases was likened to cases of discretionary appeal. The dissent argued that bankruptcy and welfare benefits for the poor were not discretionary but often a matter of survival. There is something particularly odd about denying the poor access to the courts to address issues intimately tied to their state of poverty. The dissents in both cases argued that there were no other effective mechanisms for resolving these issues for these claimants. The dissent in *Ortwein* split in part over whether the case was about the taking of an established right to welfare without due process.

There are few contexts in which one is more vulnerable to a denial of access to the courts than when one is in prison. For instance, in *Ex parte Hull* (1941), the Court addressed a Michigan state prison rule denying prisoners the right to apply to the federal courts for a writ of *habeas corpus*. Officials in that case not only refused to notarize or send Mr. Hull's petition for a writ of *habeas corpus*, they went as far as confiscating one copy that he gave to his father to mail and intercepting one copy from the mail. Unsurprisingly, the Court held that the rule was unconstitutional. Later cases went further and provided for access to law students and paralegals (*Procunier v. Martinez*, 1974). The Court in *Bounds v. Smith* (1977) held that either the state needs to provide access to trained legal advice, or if that was not available, then access to law libraries for self-help as a means for preparing cases and accessing the Courts.

The view that prisoners are particularly vulnerable members of our society in need of protection by the Courts took a serious blow in *Turner v. Safley* (1987) when the Court laid down the rule that it would only apply rational basis review to the denial of rights to inmates within the prison context. The Court cited deference to prison authorities in determining prison policy. Thus, prison regulations impinging on inmate's rights need only be rationally related to legitimate penological interests (interests related to incarceration) to survive.

With this in mind, it is not surprising that the Court would take a more narrow view of prisoners' rights to access legal advice and libraries after 1987. For example, the Court in *Lewis v. Casey* (1996) held that to bring a claim under *Bounds*, one would need to show that the infringement of the right actually caused a denial of access to justice (e.g., caused an inmate to miss a filing deadline, present a claim, or present a sound legal argument). Further, even if one could show this, the practice could still be upheld if it was rationally related to a legitimate penological interest. Thus, the Court held that the district court had failed to show proper deference to the choice of prison officials to delay access to law materials to prisoners on lock-down because such a decision was rationally related to the interest in safety and security.

It should be kept in mind that a large amount of this case was related to the systemwide remedy imposed by the district court on the Arizona Department of Corrections. The remedy was a twenty-five-page injunction, proposed by a special master and adopted by the Court, that set out to "provide meaningful access to the Courts for all present and future prisoners." The injunction covered library hours, the qualifications of librarians, access for those on lockdown, and accommodations for non-English-speaking inmates. It effectively put the Court in charge of the Arizona prison systems libraries. Like in the context of remedying past racial discrimination above, the Court held that the remedies need to be limited to actual harm. The Supreme Court found only a few instances of actual harm in this case, and these few instances could not justify the systemwide remedy imposed by the district court.

D. Education

Although it is difficult to imagine anything more fundamental to human survival in the modern world than a good education, there is no federal right to an education. As a general rule, the states do not need to provide free education, nor do they need to provide equal education. Of course, if a state discriminates on the basis of race or gender in the provision of education, this is subject to strict and intermediate scrutiny, respectively. However, if the state simply discriminates between rich and poor by financing individual school districts through local property taxes, only rational basis review applies. Thus, in *San Antonio Ind. School Dist. v. Rodriguez* (1973), the Court held that the financing scheme was rationally related to the state's interest in promoting local control of schools. It is important to note that the state did not completely deny the right to an education to the poor. According to the Court, the poor still received a minimally adequate education. Again in *Kadrmas v. Dickenson Public Schools* (1988), the Court upheld a fee for using the school bus in districts that had not reorganized, even though the law clearly discriminated against the poor. The law was designed to benefit school districts that agreed to reorganize, and because the law only discriminated on the basis of income, it only received rational basis review.

These cases involving the poor can be distinguishable from *Plyler v. Doe* (1982) (addressed under discrimination based on alienage) because the law in *Plyler* discriminated against the innocent children of undocumented aliens. Although discrimination by states against aliens who are in the country legally receives strict scrutiny, discrimination against so-called illegal aliens only receives rational basis. This law discriminated against a group that arguably fell in-between. Although the children of undocumented aliens are sometimes in the country illegally, some are born in the United States and are U.S. citizens under the Constitution. In either event, the Court held that the state could not punish the innocent children of undocumented aliens by denying them access to free education. As already noted, the Court applied a form of intermediate scrutiny, holding that the state had failed to show a substantial state interest to justify the discrimination.

Stop Points

Fundamental Rights

- Laws that classify in ways that infringe on the exercise of a fundamental constitutional right will be upheld only if they survive the same strict scrutiny test that is applied to suspect classifications.

- The classification must be necessary to serve a compelling governmental interest.

- For strict scrutiny to be triggered when a law discriminates with respect to a constitutional liberty, the Court requires that there be a substantial impairment of the liberty.

- **The Right to Travel**

  - One has a right to move to a state and establish residence there. Laws that discourage or penalize exercise of this right by discriminating against newcomers to the state are subject to strict scrutiny.

  - What is protected is the right to migrate and change one's domicile and to then be treated as an equal with other residents of the state.

  - Not all laws discriminating against new residents of the state are subject to strict scrutiny. It comes into play only if the state's adverse treatment of newcomers was sufficient to discourage or penalize migration to that state.

- **The Right to Vote**

  - Although the text of the Constitution does not provide for a general right to vote, the Court has determined that the right is fundamental.

- The Equal Protection Clause right to vote is the right to participate in the election process equally with other qualified voters. It is only a right to participate in the elections on an equal basis with other citizens in the jurisdiction; it does not confer the right to vote in an absolute sense.

- **Access to Polls**

    - States and cities may restrict the vote to those who are citizens and bona fide residents of the jurisdiction.

    - Durational residency requirements for voting are subject to strict scrutiny, because they temporarily deny the vote to persons who are, in fact, residents of the jurisdiction.

    - The rule that selective denials of the right to vote are subject to strict scrutiny applies only to elections for public entities that perform normal governmental functions.

    - For special limited-purpose entities that do not exercise governmental power, the Court will apply rational basis review to those people who are primarily affected by the entity's actions.

- **Vote Dilution**

    - This is implicated by employing an electoral scheme in which some people's votes count less than others.

    - Vote dilution typically results from the fact that electoral districts are drawn in such a way that they do not include the same number of people even though each district elects the same number of officials. As a consequence, those who live in larger population districts cast a vote that is diluted in relation to the vote of those residing in smaller districts.

    - The fact that voting districts contain unequal populations does not necessarily mean that there is individual vote dilution. The key lies in whether there is a disparity between districts in terms of the ratio of elected officials to population.

    - Individual vote dilution is subject to strict scrutiny. Each person is entitled to cast a vote that carries substantially the same weight as that of other voters in the same election.

- **Access to Justice**

    - Under very limited circumstances, the Equal Protection Clause may require that indigents be provided with equal access to the courts.

    - Here the government may be obligated to furnish counsel, waive fees, or pay litigation costs for those who would otherwise be unable to participate effectively in the legal process.

    - The Court has not recognized a broad-based fundamental right of equal access to the judicial process.

- **Right to an Education**

- There is no federal right to an education.
- As a general rule, the states do not need to provide a free education, nor do they need to provide equal education.

Checkpoints

- **Authority for Equal Protection**
  - The Fourteenth Amendment's Equal Protection Clause expressly prohibits the states from denying people the equal protection of the laws.
  - No express provision imposes a similar restriction on the federal government.
    - However, the Supreme Court has interpreted the Fifth Amendment's Due Process Clause as containing an equal protection component that also prohibits the federal government from denying people the equal protection of the laws.
- **Interpreting Equal Protection**
  - The Equal Protection Clause appears to bar the government from engaging in any type of discriminatory conduct.
  - However, if it prohibited all discrimination on the part of the government, practically all laws would be unconstitutional because every law classifies by imposing burdens or conferring benefits on a selective basis, singling out some people or activities for treatment different from that accorded to others.
  - Therefore, the Clause has never been interpreted as outlawing all forms of discrimination.
  - The Clause has been interpreted to prohibit the government from making or enforcing any law that unreasonably or without adequate justification denies persons the equal protections of the law.
  - Government discrimination can take place in one or both of two general ways:
    - discrimination in terms of how it treats categories of people; or
    - discrimination in what it provides or burdens.
- **Mechanisms for Governmental Discrimination**
  - The state can discriminate in a variety of ways, such as legislation, governmental rules, regulations, policies, and through the application of legislation. This discrimination can take place in two ways:
    1. By discriminating against persons or groups of persons on the face of the legislation
       - Clearly discriminates based on its language

Checkpoints *continued*

2. By discriminating through the impact of the legislation

- Legislation that does not expressly discriminate by its language but has a serious discriminatory impact

- Proving discriminatory impact is not sufficient to prove an equal protection violation

- Must also show that the government had the purpose of causing the discriminatory impact

- **Three Major Tests**

- The Supreme Court applies three different tests depending on what categories of persons or certain characteristics a law is claimed to be discriminating against:

  1. Strict Scrutiny Test

     - Applies to government action that intentionally discriminates against "suspect" classes, which include:

       - Race

       - National origin

       - Alienage (with a number of exceptions)

       - Discrimination in the provision of fundamental rights

         - Right to vote

         - Right to travel

     - Test: is the government action necessary to achieve a compelling government purpose?

  2. Intermediate Scrutiny Test

     - Applies to discrimination on the basis of:

       - Gender

       - Legitimacy

     - Test: is the government action substantially related to an important government purpose?

  3. Rational Basis Test

     - Applies to every other basis for discrimination

     - Test: is the government action rationally related to a legitimate government purpose?

- **Reasons for the Different Tests**

- Historical discrimination and the need to protect those who are disadvantaged in the political process

Checkpoints *continued*

- Immutable characteristics (characteristics beyond one's control)

- Unfair and unreasonable generally

- **What the Three Tests Are Testing: Ends and Means (Purpose and Relation of the Means to that Purpose):**

  - The different levels of scrutiny used are tools for scrutinizing two separate things:

    1. The ends, goals or purpose the government is trying to achieve:

       - Strict scrutiny requires a very important, compelling, or overriding purpose.

       - Intermediate scrutiny merely requires an important or substantial purpose.

       - Rational basis review allows for any conceivable legitimate purpose.

    2. How well the means further that end-goal or purpose:

       - The means for achieving these ends or purposes is often through legislation, but can include other governmental rules, regulations or conduct.

         - Strict scrutiny requires the means to be necessary to achieve the purpose,

         - Intermediate scrutiny requires the means to be narrowly tailored to achieve the purpose,

         - Rational basis requires that the means be rationally related to the given end or purpose.

- **Rational Basis Review**

  - Test: is the government action rationally related to a legitimate government purpose?

  - The government action will be presumed as constitutional unless the challenging party can prove that the government classification is not rationally related to a constitutionally permissible government interest.

  - **Cases of Exceptional Deference:** any conceivable legislative purpose for the law is sufficient. The government only needs to state a legitimate purpose at the time the law is challenged; it is irrelevant that it was not the legislature's true purpose for passing the law. The plaintiff has the burden to negate or disprove every conceivable basis for the law's rationality.

  - **Cases Involving Some Level of Scrutiny:** although the Court is highly deferential to the government under this test, there have been a number of cases in which the Court appears to really test whether there is an actual legitimate purpose and if the legislation is, in fact, rationally related to it.

Checkpoints *continued*

- In these cases the Court found that the classification was invidious, wholly arbitrary, or capricious. These cases include discrimination against unrelated cohabitants, people with disabilities, and gays, lesbians, and bisexuals.

- **Strict Scrutiny Review**

  - Test: government action that draws distinctions on the basis of race or national origin must be necessary to achieve a compelling government purpose.

  - A classification is necessary when it is narrowly tailored so that no alternative, less burdensome means are available to accomplish the state interest.

  - Strict scrutiny only applies if the law or governmental conduct is:

    - Discriminatory on its face; or

    - It has both a discriminatory impact and the government' purpose was to have the discriminatory impact.

      - The strict scrutiny test for suspect criteria requires that the government action have a discriminatory purpose; that is, intentional or deliberate discrimination must be shown, which can be found in three ways:

        - On the face — *Korematsu v. United States* (1944)

        - By application — *Batson v. Kentucky* (1986)

        - By its discriminatory motive — *Gomillion v. Lightfoot* (1960)

        - Racial segregation — legally mandated segregation violates the Equal Protection Clause — *Brown v. Board of Education* (1954)

- **Remedying Segregation in Schools:** schools have an affirmative duty to eliminate intentional racial segregation of schools. The remedy in any given case must be determined by the nature and the scope of the constitutional violation. It may not extend beyond the conditions produced by that violation.

- **Affirmative Action:** even benign (government action that favors racial or ethnic minorities) is subject to strict scrutiny.

  - Court held remedying the present effects of identified past discrimination qualifies as a compelling interest.

    - The classification must seek to rectify the effects of identified racial discrimination within the entity's regulatory jurisdiction.

    - The entity adopting the remedial scheme must have a strong basis in evidence to conclude that remedial action was necessary before it implements the program.

  - Court held higher education institutions have a compelling interest in attaining a diverse student body.

Checkpoints *continued*

- Race considerations may not be permanently a part of admission policies, but only should be used until they are no longer needed.

- Race and ethnicity may be considered as a plus, but may not be the predominant criteria for deciding whether a particular applicant is accepted.

- **Discrimination on the Basis of Alienage**

  - Discrimination on the basis of alienage is not the same as discrimination on the basis of national origin. *Alienage* refers to one's status as either a citizen or a noncitizen.

  - Generally strict scrutiny applies when a state or local government discriminates on the basis of alienage.

    - Exception: the general rule does not apply when the state and local government requires that one be a citizen for the purposes of either participating in the political process or occupying a post with political functions.

  - Rational basis review is the test that is applied when the federal government discriminates on the basis of alienage.

    - The federal government only receives rational basis review because the Constitution gives Congress broad powers over immigration and naturalization. The judicial branch shows deference by applying this lower standard.

  - Discrimination against aliens who are illegally present does not receive strict or heightened scrutiny.

  - State cannot place a discriminatory burden on innocent children as a way or regulating the conduct of the illegally present alien parent.

- **Intermediate Scrutiny Review**

  - Test: classifications based on gender and legitimacy violate equal protection unless they are substantially related to important government objectives.

  - Gender

    - For sex discrimination to be upheld, the important government objective must be genuine, and its justification cannot be based on overbroad generalizations about males or females.

    - Laws compensating women for past discrimination have been upheld as being substantially related to an important government objective.

  - Legitimacy

    - Most state laws that discriminate against nonmarital children have been invalidated, because the state's concern over illicit relationships cannot be the foundation for penalizing the children who are the product of such relationships.

Checkpoints *continued*

- Some discrimination against nonmarital children has been upheld as a reasonable effort to serve administrative convenience.

- **Fundamental Rights**

  - Laws that classify in ways that infringe on the exercise of a fundamental constitutional right will be upheld only if they survive the same strict scrutiny test that is applied to suspect classifications.

  - The classification must be necessary to serve a compelling governmental interest.

  - For strict scrutiny to be triggered when a law discriminates with respect to a constitutional liberty or right, the Court often requires that there be a substantial impairment of the liberty or right.

  - **The Right to Travel**

    - One has a right to move to a state and establish residence there. Laws that discourage or penalize exercise of this right by discriminating against newcomers to the state are subject to strict scrutiny.

    - What is protected is the right to migrate and change one's domicile and to then be treated as an equal with other residents of the state.

    - Not all laws discriminating against new residents of the state are subject to strict scrutiny. It comes into play only if the state's adverse treatment of newcomers was sufficient to discourage or penalize migration to that state.

  - **The Right to Vote**

    - Although the text of the Constitution does not provide for a general right to vote, the Court has determined that the right is fundamental.

    - The Equal Protection Clause right to vote is the right to participate in the election process equally with other qualified voters. It is only a right to participate in the elections on an equal basis with other citizens in the jurisdiction; it does not confer the right to vote in an absolute sense.

    - **Access to Polls**

      - States and cities may restrict the vote to those who are citizens and bona fide residents of the jurisdiction.

      - Durational residency requirements for voting are subject to strict scrutiny, because they temporarily deny the vote to persons who are, in fact, residents of the jurisdiction.

      - The rule that selective denials of the right to vote are subject to strict scrutiny applies only to elections for public entities that perform normal governmental functions.

      - For special limited-purpose entities that do not exercise governmental power, the Court will apply rational basis review to those people who are primarily affected by the entity's actions.

Checkpoints *continued*

- **Vote Dilution**

  - This is implicated by employing an electoral scheme in which some people's votes count less than others.

  - Vote dilution typically results from the fact that electoral districts are drawn in such a way that they do not include the same number of people even though each district elects the same number of officials. As a consequence, those who live in larger population districts cast a vote that is diluted in relation to the vote of those residing in smaller districts.

  - The fact that voting districts contain unequal populations does not necessarily mean that there is individual vote dilution. The key lies in whether there is a disparity between districts in terms of the ratio of elected officials to population.

  - Individual vote dilution is subject to strict scrutiny. Each person is entitled to cast a vote that carries substantially the same weight as that of other voters in the same election.

- **Access to Justice**

  - Under very limited circumstances, the Equal Protection Clause may require that indigents be provided with equal access to the courts.

  - Here the government may be obligated to furnish counsel, waive fees, or pay litigation costs for those who would otherwise be unable to participate effectively in the legal process.

  - The Court has not recognized a broad-based fundamental right of equal access to the judicial process.

- **Right to an Education**

  - There is no federal right to an education.

  - As a general rule, the states do not need to provide a free education, nor do they need to provide equal education.

Chapter 9

Freedom of Expression and Association

Roadmap

I. Introduction

The exploration of the First Amendment begins with its text: "Congress shall make no law respecting an establishment of religion, or prohibiting the free exercise thereof; or abridging the freedom of speech, or of the press; or the right of the people peaceably to assemble, and to petition the Government for a redress of grievances." This chapter focuses on the freedoms of expression and association that are contained in the First Amendment, whereas the next chapter explores the freedoms protected by the clauses concerning "an establishment of religion" and protecting the "free exercise" of religion, collectively referred to as the Religion Clauses.

Like many constitutional provisions, the language of the First Amendment is vague and broadly stated. The Constitution and its Amendments do not expressly define the terms, use, or boundaries of the freedoms they protect. Thus, it is incumbent on the courts, especially the Supreme Court of the United States, to give meaning to these words. The Court's exercise of judicial review on the First Amendment did not commence meaningfully until the twentieth century. While the language of the First Amendment is broad, the language prohibiting Congress from adopting a law abridging these freedoms is unequivocal and absolute. Does this mean that whenever the right to free speech confronts another right, free speech always wins? Although the absolutist approach to free speech has had its supporters on the Court, notably Justice Hugo Black, the Court has never interpreted the First Amendment in such a fashion. Justice Black consistently pushed for a literal reading of the First Amendment language, "Congress shall make no law ... abridging the freedom of speech." He argued that these clear and plain statements indicated that the Amendment's drafters performed all the balancing of expressive liberty versus the other needs of society that was necessary. He found that by adopting the First Amendment, the founders intended "to put the freedoms protected there completely out of the area of any congressional control" (*Konigsberg v. State Bar of California*, 1961). However, Justice Black drew a powerful distinction between expression and conduct. To him, the former was protected absolutely, whereas the government could regulate the latter.

Early in the Amendment's history, the question was whether it protected *all* speech. Some, such as President John Adams and the early Federalist-controlled Congresses, determined that "false, scandalous and malicious writing" against the federal government or its officers was unprotected, as evidenced by the passage of the Alien and Sedition Acts. However, the Court never addressed this issue because the Acts were repealed before they could be tested in court. Clearly today the Court would strike down the Alien and Sedition Acts.

The Court's early jurisprudence determined that speech contrary to national security could be punished. Hence, the Court determined that the First Amendment protection of speech and expression did not extend to such speech. By the middle of the twentieth century, this restriction of speech was challenged, most powerfully by Justice Black and Justice William Douglas. Over time, the Court recognized a spectrum ranging from no protection to varying levels of protection. No speech is protected absolutely by the Court; even protected speech is subject to regulation by the government if its interest is sufficiently strong. The Court also permits the government to regulate speech if the regulation is not targeted at the speech itself, but rather at the so-called secondary effects incident to the speech. Driving the decision of what speech is protected or unprotected, and if protected, to what extent, are the history, theory, and methodology of the First Amendment.

II. History, Theory, and Methodology of Freedom of Speech

The first ten Amendments to the Constitution, known as the Bill of Rights, protect many of the fundamental freedoms that today are considered basic international human rights. By definition, as amendments, they were not included in the original text as ratified by the states. However, they were as essential to the ratification of the Constitution as was the Constitution itself. Many Americans were afraid of a strong central government because of their perceived mistreatment by the English government. Those Americans saw the proposed Constitution as placing too much power in the hands of the federal government and felt that they needed written guarantees of rights that the federal government could not take away without their permission. Several states, particularly New York and Massachusetts, made it clear during their ratification of the Constitution that they expected proposed amendments addressing a number of individual rights to be forthcoming shortly.

The First Amendment was most likely a reaction to the English suppression of speech and the press. For much of its history, there was a pervasive system of licensing of speech in England. Existing until 1694, this comprehensive system prevented the publication of any material not licensed by the government. The colonists in America were not the only Englishmen disenchanted with the status quo. In his famous commentaries on the laws of England, William Blackstone wrote that freedom of the press consisted not of freedom from criminal sanctions after the publication of material but in eliminating "*previous* restraints upon publication." To him, subjecting the press "to the restrictive power of a licenser" subjects all expression to the whims of, at worst, one person and makes the government the "arbitrary and infallible judge of all controverted points in learning, religion, and government."

However, even after the system of licensing was abolished, the English government continued to prosecute speakers for seditious libel. The Court of the Star Chamber in England held that any public criticism of the king or the government was forbidden and could be prosecuted criminally. These prosecutions were an effective method of silencing and intimidating critics. In these prosecutions, truth was not a defense because the goal was to prevent criticism of the government, even if true. The aim of this policy was to show the government only in a positive light. A true criticism could be even more damaging than a false one. Hence, truth could actually be considered an aggravating factor in prosecutions for seditious libel. In the American colonies, seditious libel was considered a breach of the peace and a criminal offense. It was defined as any criticism directed against the government or a government official, and as in England, truth was not a defense.

A. History of Foundational Ideas

One method of interpreting the Constitution, including the First Amendment, is to investigate the drafters' and ratifiers' intent. On close examination, this is a difficult task. Given the English government's restrictions both prior to and after publication of speech at the time of the American Revolution, one can argue that at least two goals of the First Amendment were to eliminate the system of prior restraints and the prosecutions for seditious libel. However, if that were the case, why did many of the drafters and ratifiers of the Amendment vote to adopt the Alien and Sedition Act of 1798 after they became members of Congress? This dearth of evidence of the Framers' and ratifiers' intent has made the task of the Supreme Court more difficult in interpreting the reach of the protections of the First Amendment. The situation is aggravated further because there is very little in the historical record as to what degree of protection the First Amendment was supposed to provide for freedom of expression and association. Additionally, many of the Founders felt that the First Amendment and the Bill of Rights in general, were unnecessary because the Constitution created, by definition, a federal government of limited power. Many of those founders thus opposed the Bill of Rights until it became clear that the Constitution would not be ratified without express limits on the power of the government such as those provided by the Bill of Rights.

There is also virtually no debate in Congress or other legislative history about why the Amendment was adopted and what it was intended to mean, probably because of the strong sentiment in favor of freedom of expression. This stark lack of evidence means that the Court has to interpret the First Amendment without substantial guidance from the founders. Thus, the Supreme Court focuses less on the intent of the Founders when interpreting the First Amendment's protection of freedoms of expression, association, and the press than it does when interpreting other constitutional provisions.

B. Competing Theories of the Meaning and Application of the First Amendment

The broad language of the First Amendment and the general lack of information about the Framers' intent make the Court's job concomitantly more difficult and controversial, forcing the Court to balance competing values in its First Amendment decisions. Thus, an accurate and thorough analysis and prediction of the Court's decisions requires an understanding of the goals and underlying values of freedom of expression. There is no unified theory of the goals and values of the First Amendment, so they sometimes compete. In addition to eliminating prior restraints and prosecutions of seditious libel, other goals include enhancing self-government, seeking truth, encouraging self-fulfillment, balancing stability and change, and promoting tolerance in a pluralistic society. These goals and values are not mutually exclusive, though the theory to which one adheres will influence or even determine one's views on many First Amendment issues.

1. Enhancing Self-Government

This goal assumes that freedom of speech is crucial in any democratic society, such as our democratic republic. At its foundation, it emphasizes that for a person to make an informed political decision, he or she must be able to hear all points of view from all political candidates as well as about issues of public concern. This permits the citizenry to hold their public officials accountable for their actions and their inactions.

Virtually no one would dispute with any credibility that freedom of political speech is a core concern of the overall freedom of expression. To do so would be to deny the historical underpinnings of the founding of our country. The Supreme Court has even described the ability to speak freely in the political context as "the central meaning of the First Amendment" (*New York Times Co. v. Sullivan,* 1964). This concept is enshrined further in this republic's founding documents by the statement in the Declaration of Independence that governments "deriv[e] their just Powers from the Consent of the Governed." Alexander Meiklejohn said that without effective protection of political free speech, self-government cannot exist. Meiklejohn went further, including education, philosophical and scientific knowledge, literature and the arts, as well as public discussion of issues of public importance, in what must be protected to safeguard self-government.

Some have proposed the idea that only political speech should be within the protection of the First Amendment. A famous proponent of this view is Judge Robert Bork, who argues that constitutional protection should only be extended to speech that is explicitly political. Adherents to this theory base their position on the lack of historical evidence that the Framers of the First Amendment intended any great protection of speech in general and because many of the founders aggressively fought to suppress speech that they thought was inimical to government. However, the Court has never taken the position that only political speech should be protected. Rather, the Court has included a wide array of speech within the protections of the Constitution. This may be partly due to the difficulty of determining what speech is and is not political. However, the Court has also indicated a desire to include other areas of speech within the Constitution's protections because of the importance of information in making all manner of informed decisions.

2. Seeking Truth (the Marketplace of Ideas)

This concept is founded on the idea that freedom of expression is important to society and is the most effective manner of evaluating the truth of ideas. Justice Oliver Wendell Holmes called this concept the marketplace of ideas. He wrote that testing ideas in a marketplace where free competition reigned was the best "test of truth" (*Abrams v. United States*, 1919). This theory holds that truth results most accurately and efficiently from the presentation of competing ideas in a purely competitive environment.

Holmes's theory has many adherents, including the philosopher John Stuart Mill. In 1859, Mill expressed his view of this theory in his book *On Liberty*. To him, suppressing the expression of an opinion would rob the human race, both present and future, of something of great value. He viewed the suppression of a false idea to be just as bad as the wrongful suppression of a true one because although the suppression of a true idea is wrong, humanity is deprived of enlightenment by the public refutation of the false idea.

Under the marketplace of ideas, no idea should be suppressed. Rather, every idea should be expressed regardless of its accuracy. History appears to bear this out when one looks at the travails of Isaac Newton, Galileo Galilei, Nicolaus Copernicus, and Albert Einstein in challenging ideas widely believed by their contemporaries to be absolutely and unquestionably true. In fact, most if not all significant advancement, including scientific, philosophical, and political, emerged from the clash of the new ideas with the old. This clash results in a paradigm shift that is necessary to bring about advancement.

However, this theory is also heavily criticized. Many scholars have claimed that the marketplace of ideas fails as a theory because all ideas do not enter the marketplace and among those that do, some will win not because they are the better idea but because they are shouted the loudest and the most often. Further, they argue that the true idea will not necessarily win out over the false idea. Rather, because people often tend to be ruled by emotion rather than reason, whatever idea provides the greater appeal to the greater number of people will win, regardless of the veracity of the idea. In response to these criticisms, advocates of the theory acknowledge its flaws. However, they maintain that permitting the alternative, that is, permitting the government to decide what ideas are worth expressing and what ideas are not, is worse than enduring the flaws of letting ideas compete in an open marketplace.

3. Self-Fulfillment and Personal Autonomy

Providing personal self-fulfillment and advancing personal autonomy rests on the idea that men and women are naturally expressive beings. However, although this expression often communicates ideas to others, sometimes the expression is more for the person's own fulfillment rather than communicating any ideas. Additionally, the expression of ideas, even to oneself, can be critical to understanding oneself or to working out solutions to problems. This self-actualization is exemplified by the antiwar protester who, knowing full well that expressing her opposition to a war will not likely bring about any change in the country's policy, still participates in the protest as a method of defining herself internally and to the world.

This theory views state suppression of expression not as suppression of a person's ability to convince one person that his or her idea is the correct one. Rather, it views censorship as the state's interference with a person's individual autonomy and ability to define him- or herself. Thus, whereas adherents to this view recognize the benefits of the power of expression in communicating ideas to others, they hold the power and right to define oneself both personally and publicly to be of paramount importance and immune from stifling by the government.

Those who find no difference between speech and other conduct that could be claimed to be part of individual autonomy or self-fulfillment have also criticized the theory of self-fulfillment and personal autonomy. The critics find that there is nothing inherently special about speech that would militate in favor of granting it greater protection than other activities.

4. Balancing Stability and Change

Governments may choose to suppress ideas as a means to achieve and maintain a preferred social norm. However, such suppression essentially substitutes the use of force for the application of rational debate. This inevitably does little more than mask the underlying social problems and conflicts of a society. Thus, while permitting the government to choose what speech is permissible and what is not permissible may slow the pace of social change, it cannot completely stop it. It also fails as a method of ensuring loyalty among the people. Rather, it could even exacerbate the problems that the suppression masks because they cannot be addressed openly and are therefore neglected. Hence, when the social problems eventually break through the facade, they will do so in a far more violent fashion.

Suppression of expression cannot eradicate that expression but will only drive the expression underground. The benefits of permitting expression, that is, permitting the people to voice their grievances and to let off steam, outweigh the long-term effects of suppressing expression. Permitting expression enables the government to channel the energy (that would otherwise be pent up and repressed) into avenues that are consistent with lawful activity. It also enables the government to understand the issues facing the people and to be able to deal with them effectively.

5. *Promoting Tolerance in a Pluralistic Society*

This theory is based on the idea that our society should protect freedom of speech to promote tolerance of others' viewpoints and that such tolerance should be a basic value of society. The arguments in favor of this theory follow closely with those for the enhancement of self-government except instead of debating policies, a pluralistic society must respect the ideas of others. To be effective, this tolerance must be extended not only to popular ideas but also to those ideas that are unpopular or distasteful. Furthermore, this tolerance of others' ideas also engenders a general respect for others and a toleration of people who are different from the norm.

In comparison with the other theories concerning the freedom of speech, this theory is relatively new. Despite its recent pedigree, this theory also has its detractors. They assert that there must be a limit on the tolerance that must be afforded to speech, particularly when the speech at issue is itself intolerant of others. When speech expresses a lack of tolerance of others, it is likely to injure others, either emotionally or by inciting physical violence against them. Critics of absolute tolerance of speech maintain that preventing harm to others from intolerant speech outweighs the benefits of tolerating the harmful speech. The recent rise in advocacy for the punishment of "hate speech" is one particular example where some would place a limit on the tolerance of speech for the sake of enhancing tolerance of others in general.

C. Defining Speech

Before one can analyze whether a particular expression is or should be protected, it is necessary to define speech. Clearly, oral communication of information, ideas, or emotions from one person to another, or to a group of people is speech. Similarly, the written communication of information, ideas, or emotions also clearly constitutes speech. However, speech is not limited to oral or written communication; conduct can be speech as can symbolic expressions. Denying protection to these nonverbal expressions would result in the loss of some of the most effective forms of speech.

The Supreme Court has extended First Amendment protections to communicative conduct, also called symbolic speech, for more than seventy years. In the seminal case of *Stromberg v. California* (1931), the Court declared a state law unconstitutional that prohibited the display of a red flag as a "sign, symbol or emblem" representing opposition to the government. The Court also struck down a law requiring public school students to salute the flag because saluting or refusing to salute the flag is communicative conduct (*West Virginia*

State Board of Education v. Barnette, 1943). The Court explained that the use of symbols is a valid method of communication that is essentially a "short cut from mind to mind." However, although some conduct communicates and thus is protected, not all conduct can be considered communicative, else no law could prohibit any conduct without violating the First Amendment's protection of expression.

Hence, the question becomes "what is communicative conduct, or when does conduct become communicative?" The Supreme Court has explained that one can find "some kernel of expression in almost every activity a person undertakes ... but such a kernel is not sufficient" to render the activity within the protective arms of the First Amendment (*City of Dallas v. Stanglin*, 1989). The Court has identified two factors that although mildly helpful are problematic to apply. Conduct becomes communicative when (1) the actor intended to communicate a particularized message, and (2) the circumstances were such that there was a great likelihood that the message would be understood by those who viewed the conduct (*Spence v. Washington*, 1974).

Spence involved a person who was convicted for affixing a peace sign to an American flag following the death of students at Kent State University who were killed while protesting the American invasion of Cambodia. After several failed attempts to disperse the protesting students, the Ohio National Guard opened fire, killing four and wounding nine others. Spence argued that his conduct, taping the peace sign on the flag, was intended to communicate his opposition to the killings at Kent State and in Cambodia. The Court agreed and reversed his conviction. In a *per curiam* opinion joined by five Justices, the Court stated that Spence's action was "not an act of mindless nihilism. Rather, it was a pointed expression of anguish by appellant about the ... domestic and foreign affairs of his government." Thus, the Court found that by taping the peace sign to the flag, Spence intended to communicate a message of displeasure about the United States's activities in Cambodia and on Kent State's campus and that the circumstances surrounding the act created a great likelihood that the message would be understood.

The Court has found conduct to be communicative in many other cases and situations. Some examples include students wearing black armbands to protest the war in Vietnam, an individual's burning of his selective service registration certificate on the steps of a courthouse, defacing a vehicular license plate, civil disobedience, and in some cases desecration or burning of the American flag. In each of these cases, the Court focused on whether conduct was communicative, generally based on the presence of a particular message to be conveyed by the conduct. When there was a particular message, the conduct was deemed to be communicative and when there was no such message, the conduct was deemed noncommunicative. However, the inquiry does not end there.

Once a court determines that the conduct at issue was communicative, then the conduct falls within the reach of the First Amendment's protections. However, that does not mean that the symbolic speech and regulation of such conduct must comport with the regulation of so-called pure speech, nonsymbolic or verbal speech. The *O'Brien* test provides a useful four-part test for determining when the government's interest in regulating communicative conduct is sufficient to overcome First Amendment protections. In *O'Brien*, the Court stated that a government regulation of expressive conduct is permissible if:

1. it is within the constitutional power of the government;
2. the regulation furthers an important or substantial government interest;
3. the government interest is unrelated to the suppression of free expression; and
4. the restriction on First Amendment freedom "is no greater than is essential" to further the government interest (*United States v. O'Brien*, 1968).

O'Brien involved an individual who burned his selective service registration certificate on the steps of the South Boston Courthouse and was subsequently convicted for violating the Universal Military Training and Service Act of 1948. The version of the Act in force at the time, as amended through 1965, criminalized the "forg[ing], alter[ing], knowingly destroy[ing], knowingly mutilat[ing,]" or changing the selective service registration certificate in any manner.

The Court found that the Act as amended in 1965 met the four-part test it promulgated and upheld the conviction. The Act met the first part of the test because it is within Congress's power to raise and support armies and, by the Necessary and Proper Clause, to enact any legislation necessary to achieve that end. The Court determined that the second prong was satisfied because the Act furthered several government interests that were at least important, including quick determination of persons who failed to register, facilitating mobilization in emergency situations, and deterring deceptive use of the certificates. Because the Act was related to regulating all conduct related to desecration of the certificates, not just public or contemptuous conduct, it was of general applicability and not aimed at suppression of expression, thus meeting the third prong. Fourth, the Court determined that the law imposed no greater a restriction on First Amendment freedoms than necessary to achieve the Act's purposes and met the last part of the test.

The *O'Brien* test has found significant application in cases concerning laws prohibiting the desecration or burning of the American flag. In the first of these cases, the Court protected desecration and burning of the flag. However, those early cases were decided on narrow grounds and did not reach the ultimate issue of the communicative aspects of the conduct. For example, the Court reversed the conviction of a man who burned a personally owned flag in public and said, "We don't need no damn flag." The statute he was convicted under proscribed public "mutilat[ion], defac[ing], defil[ing], or defy[ing], trampl[ing] upon," or casting contempt upon the American flag by words or actions (*Street v. New York,* 1969). The Court reasoned that the statute was too vague and the man could have been convicted merely for uttering the words and not for destroying the flag.

The Court finally decided the question of symbolic speech in flag burning cases in *Texas v. Johnson* (1989). There, it invalidated a Texas statute prohibiting a person to "deface, damage, or otherwise physically mistreat" a flag in such a manner that the person knows would offend at least one person observing his actions. The five-to-four decision, written by Justice William Brennan, distinguished *O'Brien* because in *Johnson* the law specifically criminalized communicative conduct, unlike the statute in *O'Brien.* Chief Justice William Rehnquist dissented, stating that he would accord the American flag special treatment because it is such an important national symbol and that there were other methods by which a would-be flag burner could convey his or her message.

In an attempt to circumvent the Court's decision in *Johnson,* Congress adopted the Flag Protection Act of 1989. The Act criminalized the knowing mutilation, defacement, defilement, burning, or trampling of the flag, without the qualifying language in the Texas statute. However, the Court ruled that statute unconstitutional in *United States v. Eichman* (1990), with the same split in the Court that existed in *Johnson.* Justice Brennan again wrote for the majority, finding that the federal law suffered from the "same fundamental flaw" as did the Texas statute in *Johnson.* Hence, the Court clearly protects the desecration and burning of the American flag, at least as far as it is communicative. However, based on Rehnquist's dissent in *Johnson,* it is hard to find legitimate instances of flag burning that are not communicative, and thus the government is attempting to protect an important national symbol of patriotism while prohibiting specific expressions of dissent. This is clearly a distinction based on the content of the message and as will be explored later, such laws must meet strict scrutiny.

In sum, expression includes what most would consider to be expression — spoken or written words communicating any idea. It also includes nonverbal artistic expressions as well as communicative conduct. Conduct is communicative if it is intended to communicate a particular message. The *Spence* test also requires the Court to consider whether the attendant circumstances would indicate a great likelihood that the message would be received and understood by those who viewed the conduct. If the conduct is noncommunicative, the government generally may regulate it. However, if the conduct is communicative, the analysis diverges depending on whether the statute is aimed at suppression of free speech. If so, then the law is generally unconstitutional unless it passes strict scrutiny. However, if it is not aimed at suppression of free speech, the law generally must pass scrutiny under the four-part *O'Brien* test, or else it is unconstitutional.

D. Vagueness and Overbreadth

Two powerful weapons for the enforcement of constitutionally protected freedoms, especially for First Amendment free speech protections, are the doctrines of vagueness and overbreadth. As will be explained, these doctrines often overlap, but it is important to understand that they are distinct and address different statutory infirmities. There are two important commonalities of these doctrines. First, they both permit a person to bring a facial challenge to the law, rather than a challenge to the application of the law to a specific situation. Second, they both operate as an exception to the standing doctrine, thus allowing a person to challenge a law without having to suffer a personal injury. Although both doctrines could apply in some cases, it is important to understand their differences and how they apply individually to provide a complete analysis of the issues.

1. Vagueness

A law is void for vagueness if a reasonable person would have to guess at what speech is proscribed. Vagueness can void any law, not just those limiting free speech. However, these issues arise frequently in the free speech context so judges particularly scrutinize laws criminalizing the freedom of expression for vagueness. Any law that does not adequately inform a reasonable person as to what speech or conduct is prohibited and what is permitted violates due process. This vagueness doctrine is supported by several rationales. First, it is necessary for a criminal law to place a person on notice as to what he can or cannot do. Second, a criminal law must provide adequate guidance to the government and limit the discretion of law enforcement officers to avoid arbitrary enforcement. Additionally, because the freedom of speech is a fundamental freedom that requires breathing room, governmental regulation on expression must be drawn narrowly and specifically. The regulation of free speech also raises the danger that the speech could be "chilled" by the criminal proscriptions and that otherwise protected, and socially valuable, speech would be suppressed because the statute was not drawn sufficiently clearly. This last danger provides extra motivation to the courts in requiring that laws regulating speech receive exacting scrutiny.

A classic example of an unconstitutionally vague law not in the context of free expression is *City of Chicago v. Morales* (1999). Chicago had adopted a statute making it a crime to loiter, defined in the law as "remain[ing] in any one place with no apparent purpose." Because the statute was aimed at preventing gang activity, the Chicago police were empowered to order a group of loiterers to disperse, and failure to do so was a misdemeanor. The Court overturned the law with Justice John Stevens writing an opinion that was a majority opinion in part. Justice Stevens found that the law was vague and unconstitutional because a person could not be certain as to what behavior would subject him or her to arrest. This ambiguity in the guidance that the law provided, both to the people of Chicago and to the police, rendered the law void for vagueness. Similarly, vagueness in the context of free speech is illustrated in *Baggett v. Bullitt* (1964). In *Baggett*, the Court addressed the loyalty oath imposed on state employees that prevented any "subversive person" from being a state employee. The state also required its employees to swear that they are not "subversive person[s]" and that they are not part of any subversive organization. The Court found the oath and the requirement unconstitutional because of the inherent ambiguity in the word *subversive* and the ambiguous language in the statute. Those ambiguities did not give adequate guidance as to what speech and personal associations were proscribed.

The Court has never prescribed any bright-line test to clearly delineate when a statute is unconstitutionally vague. It is simply impossible for the Court to do so, especially given the inherent ambiguities in language. However, the Supreme Court case law indicates that it treats criminalization of expression with increased scrutiny. If a law fails to provide a reasonable person with guidance as to what speech is proscribed or if a law fails to adequately and effectively limit the power of the police in enforcing the law, then that law will probably be held to be void for vagueness. Thus, this doctrine is a powerful tool to challenge a law placing any restraints on freedom of speech.

2. Overbreadth

A close cousin of vagueness, the doctrine of overbreadth is also a powerful tool when challenging any law, especially one abridging the freedom of speech. A law is overbroad if it regulates more conduct than is necessary to achieve its ends. Applying this to the First Amendment, a law regulating speech is unconstitutionally overbroad if it (1) regulates substantially more of the challenger's speech than the Constitution permits; or (2) regulates substantially more of a third party's speech than the Constitution permits, regardless of its constitutionality as applied to the person raising the challenge. Like the vagueness doctrine, the ability of the overbreadth doctrine to permit one to raise the rights of another is an exception to standing that holds regardless of whether the law is constitutional in the case at bar.

The ability to challenge the constitutionality of a law because of its effect on a party not before the court exists because of the dangers of overbroad regulations of speech. Specifically, an overbroad law tends to chill the speech of others by preventing them from speaking in the first place. Because this could be seen as a prior restraint on speech, the Constitution will not tolerate such a chilling effect. The power of the overbreadth doctrine is illustrated in *Kunz v. New York* (1951). *Kunz* involved a city ordinance that proscribed religious gatherings and meetings on the streets without a permit from the city police commissioner. The defendant, a Baptist minister, had obtained a one-year permit in 1946, which was later revoked because he had "ridiculed and denounced other religious beliefs" in a meeting. He reapplied for permits in 1947 and 1948, but both applications were rejected. Following the 1948 rejection, the minister held a meeting on the street without a permit and was arrested. The Court overturned the conviction, holding that the permitting ordinance was too broad and operated as a prior restraint on speech. Writing for the majority, Chief Justice Fred Vinson explained that the ordinance vested too much power in the police commissioner because it did not provide sufficient guidance concerning the issuance and revocation of the permits. The Court found such a requirement incompatible with the aims of the First Amendment. The Court invalidated the ordinance based on its effects on third parties not before the Court. Justice Robert Jackson's dissent explained that the ordinance should only be considered as applied in the case at bar and would have sustained the conviction.

The common component of the overbreadth doctrine is that the challenged law must regulate substantially more speech than the Constitution permits. Before finding the law unconstitutionally overbroad, the Court requires the law to regulate substantially more speech because the doctrine is such "strong medicine." As an example, in *Broadrick v. Oklahoma* (1973), the Court refused to find a law facially invalid that prohibited political activities by government employees. The Court acknowledged that the law was overbroad but found it was not substantially overbroad. It further explained that any problems with the reach of the law could be addressed in as applied challenges on a case-by-case basis. This requirement of substantial overbreadth applies in all challenges based on the freedom of speech, even if the speech is communicative conduct and not pure speech.

Substantial overbreadth cannot be reduced to an exact definition. However, the Court does not find substantial overbreadth merely because one can conceive of some applications of the law that would be unconstitutional. Rather, in *Members of the City Council of Los Angeles v. Taxpayers for Vincent* (1984), the Court explained that "there must be a realistic danger" that the law "will significantly compromise recognized First Amendment protections" of third parties. Thus, one method of showing substantial overbreadth is demonstrating a significant set of situations where the law could be applied to prohibit constitutionally protected speech.

For example, in *Houston v. Hill* (1987), the Court held a law unconstitutionally overbroad that proscribed citizens from interrupting police officers when performing their duties. The defendant was convicted for shouting at police officers in an attempt to prevent them from arresting his friend. The Court explained that the law was unconstitutional because it was only enforced selectively despite it being violated numerous times per day. Because the law reached a substantial amount of constitutionally protected speech and because it conferred too much discretion on the police in when to enforce it, the law was substantially overbroad. Similarly, in *Board of Airport Commissioners v. Jews for Jesus, Inc.* (1987), the Court invalidated a resolution that banned all "First Amendment activities" from the Central Terminal Area in the Los Angeles International Airport. The lower courts had invalidated the resolution because the Central Terminal Area was a traditional public forum, but the Court invalidated the resolution because it was unconstitutionally overbroad. Writing for the Court, Justice Sandra Day O'Connor explained that the statute "reache[d] the universe of expressive activity" prohibiting all forms of protected expression. The statute did not limit its prohibitive activity to those who could interfere with operations of the airport or who could cause a disruption or a disturbance. It prohibited every form of expression, including simple conversations between travelers or reading. Thus, the Court found that the law was clearly and unconstitutionally overbroad because "no conceivable governmental interest would justify such an absolute prohibition of speech."

In contrast, if a law only proscribes a relatively small amount of constitutionally protected speech, the Court will not find it unconstitutionally overbroad. This was the case in *New York v. Ferber* (1982), where the Court upheld a statute prohibiting child pornography. Recognizing that the law could apply to material that had serious value in the literary, scientific, or educational fields, the Court explained that such situations would amount only to a "tiny fraction of the materials within the statute's reach."

Even if a law is held unconstitutionally overbroad, it can still be saved in two ways. First, if the statute could be given a construction that would limit its application, the Court may find the statute constitutional as limited by the construction. Second, the law could be saved if it contained a severability clause and the unconstitutional portion(s) could be severed from the law without undermining the reason the law was enacted in the first place. The limiting construction method of saving a law was considered in *Jews for Jesus* where the Court found that the resolution's language was not susceptible to any construction that would remove its unconstitutional aspects. The severability method was applied in *Brockett v. Spokane Arcades, Inc.* (1985). There, the state law contained a severability clause that permitted the Court to declare only a portion of it unconstitutional and sever that portion from the law.

3. Comparing and Contrasting the Vagueness and Overbreadth Doctrines

From these discussions, one can see the similarities and differences between the two doctrines. Both permit a person to challenge a law based on the rights of a third party not before the court, and neither of the boundaries can be clearly and definitively defined. However, vagueness is aimed at providing clarity as to what conduct is proscribed and providing guidance to law enforcement, whereas overbreadth targets laws that permissibly regulate some speech but whose reach extends too far by proscribing otherwise protected speech. Understanding and being able to apply these similarities and differences is important to providing a complete analysis of the constitutionality of laws regulating speech.

E. Content-Neutral Laws versus Content-Based Laws

The Court repeatedly has held that the First Amendment fundamentally prevents the government from regulating speech based on its content. This is a basic concept in free speech law. For example, the Court stated that, "above all else," the First Amendment prevents the government from restricting expression "because of its message, its ideas, its subject matter, or its content" (*Police Department of the City of Chicago v. Mosley*, 1972). This concept is so fundamental that the Court has based many of its decisions on the distinction between content-based and content-neutral laws.

Generally, a law that proscribes speech because of its content is unconstitutional. The Court has explained that such laws are "presumptively invalid" (*R.A.V. v. City of St. Paul, Minnesota*, 1992). The Court requires that laws prohibiting speech based on its content to pass strict scrutiny, whereas a content-neutral regulation must only pass intermediate scrutiny. Note that the Court has created several categories of speech that are unprotected and less protected, many of which are necessarily content-based. However, aside from these categories, content-based regulations must survive strict scrutiny and the Court requires that content-based restrictions within the unprotected and less-protected categories survive strict scrutiny.

The restrictions on content-based regulations are intended to prevent the government from targeting specific messages and viewpoints that it deems undesirable. Without such restrictions, the government could use speech regulations effectively to control thoughts by driving undesired viewpoints from the public consciousness. This is most effectively accomplished by restricting a particular viewpoint directly or by restricting the subject matter of speech. Thus, the First Amendment requires the distinction between content-based and content-neutral regulations.

How, then, does the Court determine whether a given regulation is content-based or content-neutral? As explained, the requirement that the government's regulation of speech remain content-neutral requires that any restrictions on expression not regulate based on (1) the viewpoint expressed, such as the ideas or the message; or (2) the subject matter or topic of the speech. Any such content-based regulations generally must pass strict scrutiny. As an example of a content-based restriction, the Court in *Boos v. Barry* (1988) struck down an ordinance of the District of Columbia that prohibited displaying signs within 500 feet of an embassy if those signs were critical of that embassy's government. The Court found that the proscription only of critical signs was an impermissible viewpoint-based regulation and ran afoul of the First Amendment.

Regulation of the topic of speech, the subject matter, is similarly restricted. For example, in *Carey v. Brown* (1980), the Supreme Court invalidated a Chicago ordinance that prohibited all non-labor-related picketing in residential areas. The Court explained that while no specific viewpoint was attacked, the ordinance restricted the subject matter of the speech. Therefore, the ordinance was held unconstitutional. In contrast, a law is content-neutral if it regulates all speech, regardless of the viewpoint or the subject matter. Thus, if a law prohibits some speech because of its viewpoint or its topic, then the law is content-based and must satisfy strict scrutiny, otherwise it is content-neutral and must only survive intermediate scrutiny.

Once a law is determined to be content-based, that does not completely determine the level of scrutiny to apply to the regulation. A law that is facially content-based may still be deemed content-neutral if it is aimed at achieving a permissible content-neutral goal (*City of Renton v. Playtime Theaters, Inc.*, 1986). In *Renton*, the permissible content-neutral goal was the secondary effects of the speech, not the speech itself. The case involved an ordinance that prohibited locating adult movie theaters from displaying sexually explicit content within 1,000 feet of an area zoned residential, a residence, a church, a school, or a park. The Court held that the ordinance was justified because it was not aimed at the speech but the undesirable social elements (secondary effects) associated with theaters of that kind.

However, *Renton* and its holding have been roundly criticized both by commentators and by some Supreme Court Justices. The Court sometimes has applied *Renton*, and at other times it has distinguished it. For example, in the fairly recent case of *City of Erie v. Pap's A.M.* (2000), the Court applied *Renton* to uphold a city ordinance prohibiting public nudity. Writing for the majority, Justice O'Connor found that although the ordinance was aimed at shutting down a nude dancing club, the law was still content-neutral because it was aimed at the secondary effects of that type of establishment rather than at suppressing "the erotic message conveyed by nude dancing." However, the Court distinguished *Renton* in *City of Cincinnati v. Discovery Network, Inc.* (1993). Cincinnati had passed an ordinance prohibiting the distribution of commercial publications by way of news racks placed on public property. The city was concerned about the impact of the newsracks on the safety and aesthetics of the property on which they were located. Writing for the majority, Justice Stevens found that the regulation was content-based because whether a given newsrack was banned from public property depended entirely on the content of the publication inside it—commercial publications were banned, whereas noncommercial ones were not. Justice Stevens distinguished *Renton* by stating that there is no set of secondary effects caused by the presence of the commercial newsracks that are not also implicated by the newsracks the city permitted to remain on public property. Therefore, he refused to transform the clearly content-based ordinance into a content-neutral one.

In sum, a law that facially regulates speech based on its viewpoint or its subject matter is presumed to be content-based, but the government can rebut the presumption by proving that the law has a purpose independent of the content of the speech. To do so, the government must show that the law was targeted at the secondary effects associated with the speech. If the government is successful in rebutting the presumption, then the law is deemed content-neutral. In contrast, when a regulation is facially content-neutral, the inquiry ends and the law is deemed to be content-neutral. Finally, a content-based regulation must pass strict scrutiny, else it is struck down, whereas a content-neutral regulation must only pass intermediate scrutiny to survive.

F. Prior Restraints

1. Introduction

Governments have long recognized the power of information and have sought for an equally long time to control the dissemination of information, often by using prior restraints on speech. A prior restraint is a restriction and sometimes a prohibition on expression that takes effect before the expression is even communicated, rather than after the speech has occurred. At English common law, prior restraints on speech were common and came in many forms, the most prominent of which was the old licensure provisions. Because prior restraints prevent speech from occurring, the Supreme Court views them as "the most serious and least tolerable" infringements on the protections of the First Amendment.

The Court's distaste for prior restraints is well documented. Generally, the Court views prior restraints with an extremely jaundiced eye, and they are burdened with a heavy presumption of invalidity (*Bantam Books, Inc. v. Sullivan*, 1963). As introduced elsewhere, the Court's attitude against prior restraints partly derives from the fact that the First Amendment was largely a reaction against the licensing requirements present in England at the time. Although the Court's attitude toward prior restraints is fairly clear, there is no good, clear definition as to what constitutes a prior restraint.

2. Finding a Definition of a Prior Restraint

Justice Anthony Kennedy, in *Alexander v. United States* (1993), stated that "the term prior restraint is not self-defining." Further, devising a workable definition is a difficult but necessary task because of the special disfavor in which the Court holds them. Though it is true that a prior restraint prevents speech from occurring, it paints the concept with too broad a brush to say that all laws preventing speech from occurring are prior restraints. Such a definition would cause all laws regulating speech to be considered as prior restraints because they are generally aimed at discouraging certain forms of speech by the threat of post speech punishment. The clearest definition from the Court is that a prior restraint is a judicial order or an administrative scheme that prevents speech from occurring.

However, sometimes the Court finds that something that appears to have all the hallmarks of a prior restraint is not in fact a prior restraint. There have been several examples of laws that appeared to be prior restraints, yet the Court refused to hold that they were. An example from the latter portion of the twentieth century is *Pittsburgh Press Co. v. Pittsburgh Commission on Human Relations* (1973). An administrative agency ordered newspapers to cease publishing gender-based advertisements for employment opportunities, but the Court found the order not to be a prior restraint. The Court explained that the particular evil of a prior restraint is that it would stop speech before the speaker could adequately determine whether the speech was protected by the First Amendment. It found that the order was not a prior restraint because it did not stop any "arguably protected speech" and that the conduct at issue was "a continuing course of repetitive conduct" and the Court did not have to speculate "as to the effect of publication." Furthermore, the Court emphasized that the order was clear and did not reach more speech than necessary to achieve its ends. Yet the Court's reasons are not clear as to why the agency's order would not amount to a prior restraint when it is very likely that a similar court order would be a prior restraint. The only distinction it provided was in a footnote where it indicated that the administrative agency would not be able to punish a violator with a contempt citation, which a court could have done.

Another, more recent, example that muddied the waters even more is *Madsen v. Women's Health Center, Inc.* (1994). There, a court issued an order that restricted speech within a buffer zone of thirty-six feet around an abortion clinic. The Court refused to find the lower court's order to be a prior restraint. It based this on the fact that the order did not prevent protesters from speaking outside the buffer zone and that the area had been created not because of their conduct but because of their prior illicit activities. The buffer zone was created to protect the ingress and egress of staff and patients to the facility with which the protesters had previously interfered.

These cases indicate that the Court's definition of a prior restraint is not very clear. The definition put forth in *Alexander* is the clearest one the Court has provided. However, it is inconsistent with some of the Court's other decisions, especially those illustrated here.

3. The Evils of Prior Restraints

In his famous commentaries, Blackstone forcefully stated that freedom of speech comes not from freedom from censure of criminal prosecution of speech, but in countenancing "no *previous* restraint upon publication." The primary purpose and the primary evil of a previous restraint, or prior restraint, is that it prevents speech before the speech can occur. However, laws that punish speech after it occurs can have just the same effect through means of deterrence. Why are prior restraints so much worse than post speech laws having the same effect, especially when there is generally some amount of due process before the prior restraint occurs and in a licensing scheme? The problem is that by preventing speech before it is spoken, the government invades and scrutinizes a far greater range of speech than it would if it could only react to speech. The proactive nature of prior restraints avoids the procedural protections and publicity that a post speech criminal trial provides. Additionally, government censorship of speech is antagonistic to a free society because with this power governments are prone to suppress speech critical of the government and thereby eliminate dissenting views from political discourse. The government's argument that prior restraint can prevent a possible violent response is both conjecture as well as a failure to distinguish between speech and violent action.

Another negative aspect of prior restraints is the collateral bar rule. The collateral bar rule prevents a person from challenging a court order's legality after the person has violated the order. A court order must be followed until it is set aside, so a person who violates a court-ordered prior restraint would not be able to challenge the constitutionality of the order in his subsequent trial for criminal contempt, even if the order was illegal. In contrast, a speaker who is criminal prosecuted for violating a law proscribing speech, can challenge the constitutionality of the law at trial. For example, in *Walker v. City of Birmingham* (1967), a Birmingham court ordered several civil rights protesters, including Dr. Martin Luther King Jr. and other ministers, to not protest on the streets unless the city issued them a permit. The protesters violated the order and were held in contempt of court. The Supreme Court upheld the contempt convictions, finding that the protesters were barred from challenging the legality of the court order because they had violated it. The Court explained that "respect for judicial process is a small price to pay for the civilizing hand of law," and that a person cannot take the law into his or her own hands and ignore the legal procedures. The only exception to the collateral bar rule that the *Walker* court permitted was an order that was "transparently invalid" or lacked even a tenuous claim to being a valid order.

However, the Court has limited the reach of the collateral bar rule by restricting its application only to court orders that follow proper procedures. For example, if the court order fails to provide due process, the Court will not require it to be obeyed. This was the situation in *Carroll v. President and Commissioners of Princess Anne* (1968), where a court order preventing demonstrations for a ten-day period resulted from an *ex parte* proceeding where the protesters received no notice of the hearing and no attempt was made to contact them. The Court explained that the procedure by which the order was issued was fatally defective and that the First Amendment had no room for a violation of such a basic freedom. One could credibly argue that the limitation in *Carroll* was merely an example of the exception in *Walker*, because such a procedural defect would cause the order to have no viable claim to validity. Hence, the collateral bar rule requires a person to obey a court order unless it is so obviously invalid that it has no realistic claim to validity, and it prevents a person from challenging a contempt conviction for violating any other order regardless of its constitutionality. Note that the Court has sometimes enforced the collateral bar rule in systems of licensing, but only when the law requiring licensing is valid and contains due process protections. However, enforcement of the collateral bar rule in such administrative situations does not carry the same policy reasons as it does in the judicial context.

The dangers of prior restraints are clear. One who violates an unconstitutional law is free to challenge that law and under the doctrine of standing, that may be the only situation in which a person could challenge the law. In contrast, a person is bound to obey an unconstitutional court order until it is set aside. She cannot challenge her conviction for contempt if she violates the order, unless the order is so obviously defective that it has no realistic claim to validity. It seems unduly harsh to punish a person for making constitutionally protected speech, but such is the situation with prior restraints, especially in the form of judicial orders.

4. Forms of Prior Restraints

Prior restraints come in different forms. Clearly, an outright ban on a particular mode of speech would be a prior restraint, such as the seizure of every copy of a periodical. However, prior restraints are most commonly found as either an administrative licensing scheme or a court-ordered injunction against speech. Laws restricting speech must be scrutinized with an eye that they arguably may be prior restraints on speech.

a. Administrative Licensing Schemes

Licensing schemes grew to prominence following the invention of the printing press. Before that time, information could be spread to a wide audience only with the expenditure of time and great effort. Because of the ease with which people could disseminate speech following the development of the printing press, the English government required publishers to submit manuscripts to the government for approval before they could be published. The license to publish the manuscript could be denied completely or granted as long as objectionable information was deleted. This is the licensing scheme against which Blackstone railed, and it is still occasionally encountered today.

Generally, license-based prior restraints are invalid unless (1) the government has an important reason for the licensing, and (2) there are clear criteria for the denial of a license such that the licensing authority essentially has no discretion in the matter. The Court also requires the licensing scheme to provide procedural safeguards, such as (a) prompt action on the license application; and (b) judicial review of the denial of a license application. A licensing scheme that failed to meet these requirements was held unconstitutional in *Lovell v. City of Griffin, Georgia* (1938). There, an ordinance prevented the distribution of all literature, regardless of the time, place, or manner of distribution without first obtaining a permit from the city manager. The Court determined that the ordinance was an unconstitutional prior restraint and was facially invalid. Writing for the Court, Chief Justice Charles Hughes explained that the character of the licensing scheme strikes at the heart of the freedom of the press and that the struggle to achieve that freedom was "primarily directed against the power of the licensor."

Without an important reason for the license requirement, a licensing scheme is invalid. Examples of such important reasons are content neutral time, place, and manner restrictions designed to manage access to scarce public resources, such as a protest march in a public park or a parade. For example, in *Cox v. New Hampshire* (1941), the Court upheld a licensing scheme that required people wishing to hold a parade or protest to obtain a permit and only permitted such an application to be denied if another group was already using the venue at the same time. These restrictions are considered important because they ensure public safety, promote order, and prevent confusion by overlapping events and ensure that other travelers can conveniently use the streets. In contrast, the Court invalidated a North Carolina law requiring professional fundraisers to get a license before making a solicitation but placed no such restriction on volunteer fundraisers. The Court explained that just because a person receives payment for speaking does not vitiate the protections afforded that speech. North Carolina claimed that it had an important interest in regulating people who solicit money. However, the Court found the state's argument unpersuasive, especially when it is not accompanied by other protections, such as prompt determination on the application. Justice O'Connor dissented, finding North Carolina's argument persuasive. She explained that the law in no way burdened charities' ability to speak, it just required them to hire licensed fundraisers, recognizing the important interest that solicitors of money be licensed by the state. Thus, unless there is an important reason for the licensing scheme, it will most likely be found to be invalid.

Additionally, a licensing scheme must clearly spell out the standards by which a license may be rejected and it must leave essentially no discretion in the licensing authority. This was violated in *City of Lakewood v. Plain Dealer Publishing Co.* (1988), where an ordinance regulated the placement of newsracks on public property by requiring a license from the mayor. The ordinance listed several criteria that the mayor was to use in determining whether to grant a license. However, one criterion permitted the mayor to require the licensee to agree to any "other terms and conditions [he] deemed necessary and reasonable" before granting the license. The Court held the ordinance to be an unconstitutional prior restraint that essentially gave the mayor unfettered discretion to deny a license application. Thus, a licensing scheme must provide clearly delineated standards to the licensor, leaving virtually no discretion, else it is an invalid prior restraint.

Moreover, a valid licensing scheme must have at least some procedural safeguards to ensure that licenses are dealt with fairly and efficiently. Generally, valid safeguards include a prompt determination on the license application and a full and fair hearing subject to prompt judicial review before the denial of the license becomes final. The Court considered a law requiring a license before publicly exhibiting a motion picture, unanimously finding that the law was unconstitutional (*Freedman v. Maryland,* 1965). Writing for the Court, Justice Brennan explained that the Maryland law lacked sufficient procedural safeguards. Under the scheme, once a license was denied, the applicant would have to begin judicial proceedings and persuade the court that the speech was protected. Furthermore, after being denied, the law prohibited exhibiting the movie until a judicial determination of the denial was made, but it placed no time restrictions on the judicial action so it could conceivably drag on for some time. The Court refrained from specifying what specific procedural safeguards were required, leaving that up to the lawmaker, but it did provide a model of what it considered to be valid safeguards.

Thus, to be valid, a licensing scheme must meet specific criteria. There must be an important reason for the scheme, it must delineate specific criteria for the denial of a license, and it must provide sufficient procedural safeguards to ensure that denials are fair and applications are considered in an expedient manner. If the scheme is missing any of these criteria, it is most likely an unconstitutional prior restraint.

b. Court-Ordered Injunctions against Speech

In addition to administrative licensing schemes, the other common form of a prior restraint is a judicial order that prevents speech. Court orders restricting speech have been addressed in several areas, specifically national security, protecting fair trials and the integrity of the judicial system, and preventing obscene speech. However, a major question is whether a judicially imposed prior restraint is more tolerable than one issued by an administrative official.

The Court clearly answered the question as to whether a judicial order preventing speech constituted a prior restraint in *Near v. Minnesota* (1931). There, Minnesota considered "malicious, scandalous and defamatory newspaper[s], magazine[s] or other periodical[s]" to be public nuisances that could be abated. The trial court issued an injunction against a newspaper preventing it from publishing any "malicious, scandalous and defamatory" matter. The Court reversed the injunction, finding it to be an unconstitutional prior restraint. Writing for the Court, Chief Justice Hughes explained that the main purpose of the First Amendment was to prevent prior restraints on speech and that the proper way to punish publication of restricted and unprotected speech was an after-the-fact punishment, rather than preventing it from occurring. The Court also stated that the prohibition of prior restraints was not absolute but that certain "exceptional cases" could permit the use of prior restraints. Among the exceptional cases, the Court included speech that is dangerous to national security, obscene publications, and incitements to violence or the forcible overthrow of the government. In dissent, Justice Butler explained that the injunction in *Near* was not a prior restraint because it was a judicial remedy invoked after the speech had already occurred. Justice Pierce Butler further explained that an injunction to prevent future speech does not "authorize administrative control [of speech] in advance," a key feature of prior restraints, but is merely an equitable remedy. Thus, *Near* established the proposition that injunctions preventing future speech are unconstitutional prior restraints on speech, even when they come after the speech initially occurred.

The first of the exceptional situations announced by the Court is speech that threatened national security, such as publishing troop movements and operational details, including where a military action will occur. However, the government bears a very substantial burden in showing the need for the injunction even when national security would be jeopardized by the speech. The Court established this very heavy burden in *New York Times Co. v. United States* (1971), commonly called the Pentagon Papers case. In that consolidated case involving both the *New York Times* and the *Washington Post*, the United States sought to prevent two newspapers from publishing classified documents about the nation's involvement in the Vietnam War. The lower courts had refused to issue the injunctions against the publications, but on appeal one court reversed, issuing the injunction against the *New York Times*, and one affirmed. In a *per curiam* opinion, the Supreme Court affirmed regarding the *Washington Post* and reversed concerning the *New York Times*. The opinion did little more than explain that the government had failed to meet its burden to sustain the injunction. Each Justice in the six-to-three ruling wrote an opinion.

In their concurrences, Justices Black and Douglas took an absolutist view that prior restraints on the news were never appropriate. They explained that the language and history of the First Amendment were crystal clear and that the press "must be left free to publish news, whatever the source, without censorship, injunctions, or prior restraints." Additionally, they decried any use of injunctions to silence the press in a representative government because secrecy was inherently incompatible with open government and the government wielding any power over the press would damage the country irreparably. Justice Brennan took a slightly less absolutist position. He explained that the Court would only countenance injunctions against the press in time of war when the government must be able to act to prevent actual threats to national security, such as to prevent obstruction of its troop recruitments or the publication of the sailing dates of vessels or the strength and location of a deployment. Short of that limited scope, Justice Brennan would find no support for judicial prior restraints on the media. Justices Potter Stewart and Byron White found a separation of powers issue, explaining that the courts are not competent to issue injunctions in this arena, and that that power belongs solely to the executive and legislative branches of government, but here Congress had not acted and the President had failed to meet his burden. Justice Thurgood Marshall noted that there was no statutory authority for an injunction but even if there was one, if might violate the First Amendment.

The dissenters focused on the issue of time, finding that the Court had acted too quickly and that it should not have decided the case on the record before it. Chief Justice Warren Burger explained that the Court had no appreciation for the facts of the case when it ruled, partly because of the speediness of the appeals and partly because of the delay of the *New York Times,* which had possessed the papers for some time before demanding such a quick resolution to the issue. Justice John Harlan described exactly how quickly the case had progressed. The courts of appeals had issued their opinions on June 23. By 11 A.M. on June 24, the *New York Times*'s petitions were filed with the Court and the *Washington Post* was only slightly slower, getting its petitions in by about 7:15 P.M. on the same day. The Court held oral argument on June 26 at 11 A.M., having only received the briefs a little before 1 P.M. on June 25. The time between the decisions of the courts of appeals to oral argument lasted only three days. The Court issued its opinions on June 30, one week after the courts of appeals. Justice Harry Blackmun agreed in his dissent. He explained that the Court's handling of the case was altogether too fast and lacked the standards to evaluate the cases properly, as well as the tools of a properly developed record.

The rushed nature of the decision in *New York Times* prevented the Court from establishing standards by which the government might stop the press from publishing material that could damage national security. Justice Stewart found the executive and legislative branches competent to prevent such publication, not the judicial branch, but he did not provide any clear guidance on the matter. Justice White also explained that some circumstances could countenance such an action by the government, but also did not clearly explain the circumstances that would need to exist before the government could prevent such information from being published. Additionally, the Court did not provide any insight into whether the Congress could pass a law permitting such an injunction, though Justices White and Marshall indicated that such a law might permit the challenged act. Unfortunately, the Court has never been presented with these issues since *New York Times,* so it has yet to clarify the questions.

Only two other cases could have presented this issue before the Court. One was *United States v. Progressive, Inc.* (1979), but it was dismissed before reaching the Supreme Court because the challenged information was published in other outlets. The other was *Snepp v. United States* (1980). There, an ex-CIA agent published a book on the fall of Vietnam. While an agent, he had signed an agreement with the CIA that permitted it to demand that the book be submitted to them for review before publication. The former agent violated the agreement, and the Court found that the agreement was enforceable. It also explained that national security concerns would have permitted the CIA to demand such prepublication review even without an agreement or any proof that the book could damage national security.

The second major area where the Court has addressed injunctions as prior restraints concerns orders to control pretrial publicity to preserve the integrity of the judicial process and ensure that the defendant receives a fair trial. In *Nebraska Press Association v. Stuart* (1976), the Court created a three-part test before a court could issue a gag order preventing the press from publishing information about a criminal defendant prior to the trial. For a gag order to be valid, the court must find that (1) the extensive pretrial publicity that would occur without the injunction would jeopardize the ability to find and select a fair and impartial jury; (2) other, less extreme, measures would be unlikely to mitigate the effects of the pretrial publicity; and (3) the injunction would be effective in protecting against the danger of pretrial prejudice against the defendant.

Nebraska Press involved a court order preventing the publication of "accounts of confessions or admission made by the accused or facts 'strongly implicative' of the accused" in a multiple murder prosecution. The district court's order was a response to the widespread coverage that the murder received in the press and represented that court's attempt to preserve the defendant's right to a fair trial. On review, the Supreme Court held that the injunction was invalid because it failed to meet the three-prong test. Writing for the Court, Chief Justice Burger found that the trial court's order satisfied the first prong because it concluded that there would be "intense and pervasive pretrial publicity" that it could reasonably find might impair the defendant's right to a fair trial. The Chief Justice also found that the record did not support a finding that other, less extreme, measures would be unlikely to mitigate the effects of the publicity. He expressly stated several other alternatives that are available, such as (a) change of venue; (b) postponing the trial to let the publicity die down; (c) searching questioning of the jurors in *voir dire*; (d) "emphatic and clear instructions" to the selected jurors to consider only evidence admitted in open court; and (e) sequestration of the jury. Further, the Court determined that the injunction was not likely to be effective because of the nature of the small community of 850 people and the probability that the information would spread by word of mouth. The Court was careful to state that it did not ban absolutely all such injunctions, but it is difficult to imagine a situation where all three prongs would be satisfied. The purpose of the Court's test in *Nebraska Press* is to keep gag orders limiting press coverage of criminal trials to a minimum, thereby maintaining the First Amendment protection of the freedom of the press. This protection is not extended to lawyers— the courts have the inherent right to regulate the legal profession because lawyers are officers of the court. It is important to note that the Court has never upheld a prior restraint to protect a defendant's right to a fair trial since *Nebraska Press*.

However, the Court has upheld the ability of courts to limit the access of the press and the general public to court proceedings. In *Richmond Newspapers, Inc. v. Virginia* (1980) and *Globe Newspaper Co. v. Superior Court* (1982), the Court explained that although the First Amendment protects the press's and the public's right to be present at a criminal trial, the court may close the proceedings when there is a compelling state interest. However, the closure must be narrowly tailored to achieve that interest. *Globe Newspaper* involved a Massachusetts case where the court closed the trial of a defendant accused of committing sex crimes against minors. The court had acted pursuant to a state law that mandated closure in those instances. On review, the Court found the statute unconstitutional because it mandated closure, even when the victim does not seek the closure and the victim would not be injured by the presence of the press and the public. Thus, while the Massachusetts law was supported by a compelling state interest, it was not narrowly tailored to achieve that interest.

The third major area where the Court has addressed judicial prior restraints is in the area of obscene speech. The Court has held that an injunction preventing obscene speech is constitutionally permissible. It announced this decision in *Paris Adult Theatre I v. Slaton* (1973) . However, it has limited the application of this rule only to enjoining the expression of specific material, and the Court does not permit the injunction to be used to close down an establishment merely because it is used to exhibit obscene materials. This area will be more fully explored in the next section on unprotected and less protected speech, but because it involves injunctions to prevent speech before it occurs, it also qualifies as a prior restraint on speech.

Generally, the Court is suspicious of prior restraints and applies a very strict standard when determining their validity. Some Justices have even advocated an absolute prohibition on prior restraints based on the history behind the adoption of the First Amendment. Finally, it is important to remember that prior restraints, administrative or judicial, come to the court with a heavy presumption of invalidity.

Stop Points

- **Interpreting the First Amendment**
  - Despite the language of the First Amendment, "Congress shall make no law ... abridging the freedom of speech," the court had never adopted a literal interpretation.
  - The First Amendment was likely a reaction to the English suppression of the press and speech through licensing (prior restraints) and the crime of seditious libel.
  - Free speech is vital to democracy because it allows the voters to hear and discuss a variety of viewpoints and hold public officials accountable.
  - Free speech is necessary to evaluate the truth of ideas. We arrive at the truth most accurately and efficiently when we allow ideas to openly compete in the marketplace.
  - Free speech is necessary to achieve personal autonomy and self-fulfillment.
  - Free speech offers a safety valve for releasing pent-up frustration in a lawful activity.
  - Free speech promotes tolerance of different viewpoints which engenders a respect for others, an important component to a pluralistic society.

- **Defining Speech**
  - Clearly oral and written communication of information, ideas and emotions is speech.
  - Conduct is speech when (1) the actor intended to communicate a particularized message, and (2) the circumstances are such that there is a great likelihood that the message would be understood by those who viewed the conduct.
  - Under O'Brien, government regulation of expressive conduct is permissible if:
    1. The government has the power to regulate the field;
    2. The regulation furthers an important or substantial government interest;
    3. The government interest is unrelated to the suppression of free expression; and
    4. The restriction on First Amendment freedom "is no greater than is essential" to further the government interest.
  - If the conduct at issue is speech (thus invoking the First Amendment), and the state's regulation was unrelated to suppression of free expression, then the O'Brien test applies. If the regulation is related to suppressing expression then strict scrutiny applies.

- **Vagueness and Overbreadth**
  - Vagueness and overbreadth both permit a person to facially challenge a law rather than to challenge based on a specific application, and both operate as an exception to the standing doctrine by allowing a person to challenge a law without having to suffer a personal injury.
  - A law is void for vagueness if a reasonable person reading the law would not know what speech is illegal.
  - A law regulating speech is unconstitutionally overbroad if it regulates substantially more speech than the constitution permits.
- **Content-Based Regulation and Prior Restraints**
  - Except for several categories of speech which are unprotected or less protected, government regulation of speech based on its content must pass strict scrutiny.
  - A prior restraint is a judicial order or administrative scheme which prevents speech from occurring.

III. Unprotected and Less Protected Speech: Permissible Content-Based Restrictions

The First Amendment's language contains no qualification in the mandate that "Congress shall make no law ... abridging the freedom of speech, or of the press." However, the Court has interpreted the Free Speech Clause to protect most speech (but not all) from abridgment. To facilitate the analysis of the protected nature of speech, the Court has identified several categories of speech that it considers to be "unprotected" and "less protected." These categories are (a) advocacy of illegal action; (b) fighting words and the hostile audience; (c) true threats; (d) hate speech; (e) sexually oriented speech; (f) defamation; (g) disclosure of private information; (h) speech of public employees; and (i) commercial speech.

For speech that is not protected by the First Amendment, a law regulating or outlawing that speech need only be rationally related to the achievement of a legitimate government purpose. A regulation of less protected speech, generally must be substantially related to the achievement of an important government purpose. Last, if the speech is protected by the First Amendment, then any regulation of it must be narrowly tailored to achieve a compelling government purpose. The quick rule of thumb is that generally, unprotected speech must only survive rational basis scrutiny, less protected speech must survive intermediate scrutiny, and protected speech must pass strict scrutiny. Thus, it is of critical importance to understand the definitions required to place speech within a category because such a categorization of speech will determine what level of scrutiny to apply.

Note, however, that a law distinguishing between speech in the same grouping must pass strict scrutiny, even if the speech is less protected or unprotected. This was the holding in *R.A.V. v. City of St. Paul, Minnesota* (1992). Before *R.A.V.* it was widely believed that a regulation distinguishing between speech in the same grouping need only meet rational basis scrutiny. The decision in *R.A.V.* invalidated a city ordinance banning so-called hate speech based on race, color, religion, or gender if that speech was likely to anger or alarm others or cause resentment against the target group. The Court found that the speech banned by the ordinance was in the fighting words category and thus unprotected by the First Amendment. However, because the ordinance drew a content-based distinction between different forms of hate speech, the ordinance must pass strict scrutiny. Finding that the ordinance did not pass strict scrutiny, the Court struck it down. Thus, for example, a law that bans only the public exhibition of homosexual pornography but does not ban the public exhibition of heterosexual pornography must pass strict scrutiny, else it is invalid.

A. Advocacy of Illegal Action

Few would dispute that a government inherently can protect itself against actions that are illegal, but when the government may act is the crucial question. The boundaries of what expression the government could regulate were born from the forge of national security concerns in times of actual war or the Cold War. The early cases dealt with speech opposing war or advocating social, economic, or political change using methods that were violent and illegal. Initially, the Court read the First Amendment narrowly. This led to a constricting of the language of the Amendment such that laws punishing protesters or advocates of communism, lawlessness, or other revolutionary ideologies were upheld. However, over time, the Court's jurisprudence gradually shifted from a narrow construction to a more expansive interpretation whereby the Amendment was seen to protect considerably more speech. Today, although advocacy of illegal action is an unprotected category of speech, the Court uses a strict definition of what speech falls in this category; much speech that would have fallen into the category in the earlier formulations will not do so today. The current test to determine whether speech is an incitement to illegality requires the speech to be (1) directed at causing imminent illegal activity, and (2) likely to produce the illegal activity.

1. The Development of the Clear and Present Danger Test

Initially, the Court focused on what has been called the Clear and Present Danger test—whether the speech posed a clear and present danger that would cause the very evils that Congress intended to prevent when it made the advocated action illegal. This test was initially announced in *Schenck v. United States* (1919). *Schenck* arose during World War I for a violation of the Espionage Act of 1917. The defendant had printed a pamphlet he distributed to men who had been drafted and were qualified for service in the armed forces. The pamphlet decried the draft, likening it to indentured servitude or slavery prohibited by the Thirteenth Amendment and exhorted the draftees to stand up and resist. He was charged with "causing and attempting to cause insubordination" in the ranks of the military and Navy of the United States. He asserted the First Amendment as a defense but was convicted. On review, the Supreme Court explained that the content of the speech is not solely determinative of the outcome and that the circumstances of the speech are relevant. Writing for the majority, Justice Holmes explained that, just as yelling "Fire!" in a theater is not protected, speech is unprotected that is "used in such circumstances and [is] of such a nature as to create a clear and present danger" that it will cause illegal activity. Justice Holmes went on to state that "it is a question of proximity and degree," and that words that may not permissibly be regulated in peacetime may be regulated in a time of war. Thus, the Court found that speech advocating illegal activity may be regulated if it (1) poses a clear and present danger (2) of inciting illegal activity. This result would be reached even if no illegal activity ever occurred.

Justice Holmes further refined his clear and present danger test in his dissent in *Abrams v. United States* (1919), where several self-described "anarchists," "revolutionaries," and "socialists" were convicted for violating the Espionage Act of 1917. Finding that the leaflets had the "obvious effect" of frustrating the American effort in World War I, the Court affirmed the convictions. Justice Holmes disagreed for two reasons. First, he found that the circulars were intended not to interfere with the American war effort but to help Russia and promote the Russian Revolution, and thus were not within the reach of the statute. Second, addressed the constitutional issue, he found that the defendants "had as much right to publish [two of the leaflets] as the Government has to publish the Constitution of the United States," and that their publications were protected by the First Amendment. In support of his second point, he further explained the Clear and Present Danger test, stating that speech should not be punished as an advocacy of illegal action unless (1) there was a "present danger of immediate evil[,]" or (2) the speaker intended to bring about the immediate evil. This reinforced the fact that the evil never need actually occur and explained there were two ways in which the test could be satisfied.

2. Revising the Clear and Present Danger Test

In the years following *Abrams*, the states passed "criminal syndicalism" statutes that punished the advocation of communism, anarchy, or revolution and the Court was called on to decide their constitutionality. Though this concept may be anathema today, during the Great Red Scare it was seen as necessary to protect the American government and way of life, and the laws were generally held to be constitutional as long as the speech had a "bad tendency." In *Gitlow v. New York* (1925), the defendant had been convicted of violating New York's criminal anarchy statute for advocating criminal anarchy. He had published a leaflet called "The Left Wing Manifesto" and a paper called "The Revolutionary Age," which advocated the violent overthrow of the government. Finding that the New York statute did not punish abstract opinions or doctrine, only the advocating of actual violent means to overthrow the government, the Court upheld the convictions. Justice Edward Sanford, writing for the Court, recognized that the First Amendment, as applied against New York through the Fourteenth Amendment, protected free speech. However, he explained that the speech outlawed by the statute posed such a substantial danger to the peace and the well-being of the government that New York was justified in punishing it. To hold otherwise would require the state to hold off until the seeds of revolution had been sown, germinated, and bore the fruit of the beginnings of violent overthrow. Thus, the Court held that a person could be punished for advocating the violent overthrow of the government, even in general terms and even if not addressed to specific individuals.

Justice Holmes dissented. He found that the Court's characterization of the publications to be an incitement was without basis, for all ideas are incitements. He explained that the manifesto and the paper simply advocated a general viewpoint and were protected by the First Amendment. However, had the publications exhorted immediate uprising against the government rather than one at some indefinite point in the future, Justice Holmes explained that the result would likely be different. However, that not being the case, Justice Holmes wrote that the convictions should have been reversed.

In *Whitney v. California* (1927), the Court upheld a conviction under a California criminal syndicalism statute. The defendant had attended an organizational meeting of the Communist Labor Party, which advocated radical methods, whereas she herself advocated more moderate methods. The Court upheld the conviction. Writing for the Court, Justice Sanford expressed extreme deference to the California legislature. He found that the state was within its valid police powers when it enacted the statute because of the extreme danger to the public order posed by the advocation, teaching, or aiding and abetting of violent means of overthrow of the government. He explained that the California law would only be illegal if it was an arbitrary or unreasonable exercise of the state's police power. Finding that it was not, and that the defendant's rights of free speech and association had not been infringed, the Court affirmed the defendant's conviction. Justice Louis Brandeis concurred. He explained that, while the First Amendment guarantees the freedoms of speech and assembly, it did not protect the acts advocated by the Communist Labor Party because they were designed to effect the violent overthrow of the government. However, he explained that what saved the California law was that it essentially only created a rebuttable presumption that the speech presented an immediate danger and that the defendant was free to show that the speech did not present such a danger. Because the defendant failed to show the lack of danger, and that credible evidence had been presented showing the imminent danger of illegal activity, Justice Brandeis saw no need to disturb the state's judgment.

This phase in the development of the incitement to illegality category is generally called the reasonableness phase. In these cases, the Court generally upheld the convictions because they were reasonable given the facts and the circumstances. This reasonableness was buttressed by the need to protect the public order and for the governments to protect themselves from illegal acts intended to bring them down. However, the tide began to turn slowly after these cases.

In several post-*Whitney* and post-*Gitlow* cases, the Court overturned convictions under criminal syndicalism statutes, not because of applying the Clear and Present Danger test but because it found that the convictions were unreasonable. For example, in *Fiske v. Kansas* (1927), and in *De Jonge v. Oregon* (1937), the Court overturned the convictions under the state criminal syndicalism laws because the convictions were unreasonable. In both cases, there was no indication that the defendants or the organization actually advocated illegal acts at the meetings that led to the convictions. Although couched in terms of reasonableness, students today will recognize this as being a form of rational basis review where the Court grants deference to the legislative determination and only overturns a conviction if it was arbitrary or unreasonable.

The changes to the Clear and Present Danger standard continued into the Cold War era, slowly evolving into a more speech-protective formulation. But the evolution was very slow and generally represented an awakening to the points expressed in Holmes's and Brandeis's dissents and concurrences in the *Abrams*, *Whitney*, and *Gitlow* cases, among others. A key turning point occurred in 1951 when the Court reformulated the test into an analysis of the risk bordering on a formulaic approach. During the McCarthy era, in *Dennis v. United States* (1951), the Court affirmed the convictions of defendants who taught from books written by Karl Marx and Friedrich Engels, Vladimir Lenin, and Josef Stalin. Specifically, the defendants were charged with violating the Smith Act, essentially a federal criminal syndicalism law. Writing for the Court, Chief Justice Vinson explained that the question was not whether the Congress had the power to punish those who advocate the violent overthrow of the government, but whether the means that Congress chose conflicted with the First Amendment. He analyzed the Clear and Present Danger test, finding that it did not require the government to wait until the revolution is imminent before it can act. Chief Justice Vinson adopted the formulation of Chief Judge Billings Learned Hand (Second Circuit Court of Appeals) that the "gravity of the 'evil,' discounted by its improbability, justifies [the] invasion of free speech as is necessary to avoid the danger." Finding that the danger of overthrow existed and that its occurrence was likely because of the highly organized character of the Communist Party, the Court then concluded that the infringement on the freedom of speech was justified by the danger. Justice Felix Frankfurter concurred, finding that the Congress was well within its power when it enacted the Smith Act and that the Court was not empowered to overturn the law when it was not unconstitutional, but that did not mean that the Justices necessarily agreed with the law and its implications.

In dissent, Justice Black explained that by affirming the convictions, the Court had "repudiated" the Clear and Present Danger test, not merely restated it as the Court claimed. Justice Douglas also dissented, explaining that the defendants had merely taught abstract doctrine and did not advocate actual illegal acts such as sabotage, assassination, bombing, and street warfare. Instead, all the defendants did was teach books that were completely legal to buy and read. Justice Douglas wrote that in certain situations speech loses its constitutional immunity, such as when "conditions are so critical that there will be no time to avoid the evil that the speech threatens," however, the record in *Dennis* did not present such a situation. Thus, without such circumstances or actual advocacy of illegal acts, the convictions should not have stood.

Dennis did not represent the only case used in reformulating the Clear and Present Danger test. However, the Court began to distinguish between the advocation of violent overthrow and mere expounding of abstract doctrine. In *Yates v. United States* (1957), the Court overturned the defendants' convictions for conspiracy to violate the Smith Act. In doing so, the Court reexamined its holding in *Dennis* and required actual "advocacy to action" that Justices Black and Douglas had advocated in their dissents in *Dennis*. Under this new formulation of *Dennis*, the Court upheld the conviction of a defendant in *Scales v. United States* (1961) for being a member of an organization that advocated the overthrow of the government by extralegal means. Thus, the reformulation in *Yates* of the *Dennis* test did not mark the end of prosecutions under the Smith Act, but it did require that the person or the organization actually advocate the overthrow of the government. Although not a great expansion of the protections of the First Amendment, these cases clearly afforded greater protection to the advocation of unpopular ideas, even if the ideas were inherently incompatible with the existing government, as long as the speaker did not call for illegal means of overthrowing the government.

3. The Modern Test

The Court continued its evolution of the test in the late 1960s, changing it so that it afforded greater protection to speech, even when it encouraged subversion of the government. Moving away from condemning the mere advocacy of illegal activity, the Court paralleled its development in the hostile audience context, explored in the next section, and moved toward a requirement that there be proof that the speech was imminently about to cause harm. Today, the Court requires a three-prong test to determine if speech falls into the unprotected advocacy of illegal actions category. The next step in the evolution of the test was *Watts v. United States* (1969).

With its decision in *Watts*, the Court signaled its willingness to change its standard and indicated that it would require proof that the speech would imminently cause harm. The defendant had been convicted of willfully threatening the life of the President while participating in a rally on the grounds of the Washington Monument. Specifically, he stated that he had been drafted, that he refused to report for his physical, and that "if they ever make [him] carry a rifle the first man I want to get in my sights is L.B.J." In a *per curiam* opinion, the Court reversed his conviction, though it found the statute under which the defendant was convicted to be constitutional on its face. However, because the statute criminalized pure speech, it was subject to the strictures of the First Amendment. Thus, the Court found that because the defendant's speech neither incited violence toward the President nor did it contain an actual threat of violence, it did not constitute a "true" threat as required by the language of the statute. Instead, the Court characterized the statement as mere "political hyperbole." Thus, the defendant's admittedly crass condemnation of the President did not pose an imminent danger of illegality and he could not be convicted for making the statement.

The Court completed its progress toward the modern test with its decision in *Brandenburg v. Ohio* (1969). *Brandenburg* involved a leader of the Ku Klux Klan who was convicted under the Ohio criminal syndicalism law for advocating unlawful methods of terrorism to effect political or industrial reform and for meeting with others for the purpose of such advocacy. The Court explained that "abstract teaching" of the propriety or necessary of violent action against the government is not sufficient. It pointed to the prior decisions that required advocacy "directed to inciting or producing imminent lawless action" and that the advocacy must be likely to produce that action. Thus, the Court formulated the modern test: the speech must be (1) directed at producing imminent lawless action and (2) the likely to bring about the imminent lawless action. In so doing, the Court expressly overruled *Whitney* and afforded greater protection for speech critical of the government; however, the majority opinion avoided discussing the Clear and Present Danger test.

Justice Black and Justice Douglas concurred and agreed that the old Clear and Present Danger test has no place in First Amendment jurisprudence. Specifically, Justice Douglas explained that the test was inapposite in times of peace and expressed doubt that it had any utility in times of war. He further explained that the cases applying the test showed that it left too much power in the government to undermine the protections of the First Amendment. However, Justice Douglas explained that the Court should have gone further by expressly overruling the Clear and Present Danger test and the line of cases derived from that flawed test. However, the Court's failure to do so is a serious ambiguity left by its decision in *Brandenburg*.

The ambiguities left by the *Brandenburg* decision were illustrated in *Hess v. Indiana* (1973), where the Court was divided over the imminence of the alleged harm, but it also showed that the Court reads the *Brandenburg* test strictly. In *Hess*, antiwar demonstrators blocked the street and the police cleared the street without violence. However, in the process, the defendant said either "We'll take the fucking street later" or "We'll take the fucking street again." The police arrested him for disorderly conduct, of which he was convicted at trial. In a *per curiam* opinion, the Court reversed his conviction. It found that the statement by the defendant was, "at worst, ... nothing more than advocacy of illegal action at some indefinite future time." Because the statement was not directed at any identifiable person or group of people, the Court found that he could not be advocating any action. Thus, the Court found that the statement did not advocate any action, much less any imminent lawlessness, and his conviction could not stand. Justice Rehnquist dissented, joined by the Chief Justice and Justice Blackmun, and explained that the Court had overstepped its permissible scope of review and conducted an independent weighing of the evidence. However, the key from *Hess* is that it strengthened the *Brandenburg* test, essentially requiring the speaker to actually advocate imminent violence or illegal action; merely advocating violence or illegality without the language being directed at causing imminent violence or illegality is not sufficient under the *Branden-burg* test as enhanced by *Hess*.

The modern test as applied by the Court in *Hess* is what the Court would use today. Remember, the importance of the test is that if the speech meets the test then it falls into the unprotected category of advocacy of illegal activity and the government's action must only pass rational basis review.

B. Fighting Words and the Hostile Audience

The next category of unprotected speech that we discuss is a clear content-based restriction that involves speech considered to be "fighting words" or speech that is directed to an audience that is hostile to the speaker. The degree of protection afforded to speech is based on the value that the Court attributes to the speech. Because the Court considers this category to be of low value, if it has any value at all, it is virtually unprotected.

1. The Fighting Words Doctrine

The fighting words doctrine encompasses speech that is so patently offensive or insulting that it would provoke a violent reaction from even a reasonable person. This means that the words (1) are directed at a specific individual, and (2) their mere utterance is likely to inflict emotional injury or would tend to incite an immediate breach of the peace. Clearly, this kind of behavior cannot be tolerated in a civilized society and the government is free to regulate such speech because of the inherent injury and volatility that it creates in the listener. However, the Court carefully polices laws restricting this category of speech to ensure (1) that the regulation is not overbroad such that it reaches more speech than necessary, and (2) that a hostile response by the audience is the speaker's or the audience's responsibility.

The Court first clearly defined fighting words as unprotected speech in *Chaplinsky v. New Hampshire* (1942). At issue in *Chaplinsky* was a New Hampshire statute that prohibited any person from "address[ing] any offensive, derisive or annoying word to any other person" in public, "nor call him by any offensive or derisive name, nor make any noise or exclamation in his presence and hearing with intent to deride, offend or annoy him," or that interferes with the conduct of his business. The defendant, a Jehovah's Witness, was distributing his church's literature on the public streets on Saturday afternoon. After a disturbance arose because of the defendant's words, the police took him to the police station. On the way, the defendant encountered the city marshal and, in response to the marshal's warning about his speech, the defendant told the marshal that he was "a God damned racketeer" and "a damned Fascist." The Defendant admitted that he made those statements, except for using the word "God," after the marshal warned him. The defendant was convicted for violating the New Hampshire statute.

The Court upheld the conviction because it deemed the defendant's words to be "fighting words." The Court defined *fighting words* as words that "by their very utterance inflict injury or tend to incite an immediate breach of the peace." Writing for the majority, Justice Frank Murphy explained that such words are not protected by the First Amendment because they are not essential to the expression of any ideas and that they "are of such slight social value as a step to truth that any benefit … from them is clearly outweighed by the social interest in order and morality." Furthermore, this use of personal verbal abuse and epithets is not essential to the communication of information or opinion, which the First Amendment was designed to protect, and punishing such speech would not be questioned under the Constitution. Justice Murphy explained that the statute was not overly broad because the highest court in New Hampshire put a limiting construction on the statute that expressly stated that the test is not how any given hearer would react but how men of "common intelligence" would understand words that would cause the average person to respond to them in a violent manner. It explained that the only words prohibited are those that, when delivered face to face, would tend to cause the listener to breach the peace. The Court also explained that the statute did not infringe on otherwise protected speech because the proscribed words were not intended to communicate opinions or ideas. Rather, the words falling within the reach of the statute could properly be considered epithets that would be likely to cause a violent response by the average listener.

In the half century since *Chaplinsky* was handed down, the Court has yet to uphold a conviction under a fighting words statute. However, in no case has the Court overturned *Chaplinsky*. In overturning convictions that may otherwise seem to fall within the reach of the fighting words doctrine, the Court has found the applicable laws to be unconstitutionally overbroad and vague, has held that the laws were impermissible content-based regulations of speech, and has narrowed the reach of the fighting words doctrine. Although this doctrine has essentially lain dormant, the Court has never overturned the decision, so it is likely still good law.

The Court narrowed the reach of the doctrine with its decision in *Street v. New York* (1969). There, the Court explained that there was only a "small class of 'fighting words'" that fit within the definition in *Chaplinsky*. In *Street*, a man was convicted of burning an American flag and exclaimed, "We don't need no damn flag…. If they let that happen to [James] Meredith we don't need an American flag." The Court explained that the speech did not qualify as fighting words unprotected by the First Amendment, despite the fact that some might have found the speech to be inherently insulting and provocative. In 1971, the Court explained the doctrine further in *Cohen v. California* (1971). There, the Court held that to qualify as fighting words they must not only be likely to inflict injury or incite the listener to a violent reaction, they must be directed at an individual person. In *Cohen*, the defendant was convicted for wearing a jacket with the words "Fuck the Draft" in a courthouse. Writing for the majority, Justice Harlan explained that the words on the jacket did not qualify as fighting words because they were not directed at any individual person. Thus, no person present who read the words would be likely to consider them a personal insult or affront.

The Court continued this narrow interpretation in *Gooding v. Wilson* (1972), finding that a Georgia statute banning opprobrious words and abusive language was unconstitutionally broad and vague. Writing for the majority, Justice Brennan explained that the language of the law reached more speech than was permitted under the fighting words doctrine. Relying on the definition of *Webster's Third New International Dictionary* from 1961, the Court explained that the definitions of *opprobrious* and *abusive* were broader than that of the fighting words doctrine as explained in *Chaplinsky*. Hence, the statute permitted too much speech to be regulated and gave too much latitude to juries. The Court also found that the courts of Georgia had not placed the same limiting interpretation on its statute that the highest court of New Hampshire did in *Chaplinsky*. Therefore, the Court found that the statute was unconstitutionally overbroad and vague and overturned the defendant's conviction. In dissent, Chief Justice Burger and Justice Blackmun stated that the Court's decision to find the statute facially invalid was not based on the language of the statute but on the fact that the courts of Georgia had not limited the interpretation or reach of the statute.

Thus, a statute banning fighting words must be narrowly tailored so that it only reaches unprotected speech, else it will be overturned for being either too broad or unconstitutionally vague. However, any such regulation must not be written too narrowly, or the Court will find that the statute is unconstitutional for drawing an impermissible content-based restriction. In *R.A.V. v. City of St. Paul, Minnesota* (1992), a municipal ordinance banned symbols, objects, or graffiti, which included a burning cross or a Nazi swastika, from being on public or private property when one knows or reasonably should know that the banned communication would arouse "anger, alarm or resentment in others on the basis of race, color, creed, religion or gender." The Court unanimously found the ordinance to be unconstitutional. Writing for the majority, Justice Antonin Scalia explained that the government was limited in its ability to draw content-based distinctions between speech within categories of unprotected speech. He clarified the meaning of unprotected speech by explaining that it was not that the speech was "entirely invisible to the Constitution," but that the content of the speech could be constitutionally proscribed. However, distinctions within categories of such speech must still pass strict scrutiny. Thus, the government can criminalize libel because its content is constitutionally proscribable; however, the government cannot criminalize only libel against the government unless that distinction is necessary to achieve a compelling government interest.

The Court explained two exceptions to the requirement of strict scrutiny for content-based distinctions within a category of unprotected speech. First, such a distinction is permitted if it directly promotes the rationale behind classifying the speech as unprotected in the first instance. Second, if the law is directed at the secondary effects of the speech rather than the content of the speech itself, then the distinction will not be considered to be based on the content of the speech. Justice Scalia applied the test to the ordinance at issue in *R.A.V.* and found that it was unconstitutional. Because it only applied to invective language that would be likely to injure or provoke a violent response based on a few topics (specifically race, religion, creed, or gender), and not all such language, the ordinance drew a content-based distinction within the fighting words category. Additionally, the ordinance did not advance a compelling government interest, especially because other topics (such as homosexuality and political affiliation) were not covered. The Court also found that neither exception applied to these words, thus the ordinance failed the strict scrutiny test.

Thus, to qualify as fighting words, the statute must be narrowly drawn to proscribe only those words (1) directed at an individual; and (2) that simply by their utterance would tend to injure the listener or provoke her to a violent reaction. However, the regulation must not be too narrowly drawn, else it would be invalid for drawing a content-based distinction within the unprotected category. However, that invalidation would not occur if the law (1) passed strict scrutiny, (2) directly advances the reason that the category of speech was unprotected, or (3) was aimed at remedying the secondary effects of the speech rather than regulating the content of the speech.

2. The Hostile Audience

Unlike the fighting words doctrine, which applies to unprotected speech, the hostile audience doctrine is a category of lesser protected speech that is used when speech otherwise protected by the First Amendment either provokes or has a tendency to provoke the audience to violence. Today, the Court appears to require the police to make every effort to protect the speaker before invoking this doctrine to silence him or her. This doctrine intersects with the concept of advocacy of illegal action, already discussed. The difference between the two doctrines lies in the fact that advocacy of illegal action is focused on speech that calls for the listener to act contrary to the law, whereas the hostile audience doctrine is concerned with a hostile reaction by the audience because the speech is unpopular or offensive but does not advocate illegal activity.

The development of the hostile audience doctrine came to a head in the 1940s and 1950s. The Court addressed cases that involved speech that led the audience to act out in a breach of the peace. In early cases, such as *Cantwell v. Connecticut* (1940), and *Terminiello v. Chicago* (1949), the Supreme Court applied a Clear and Present Danger test, similar to the one applied in the advocacy of illegality. In *Cantwell*, the defendant had been convicted for playing a record attacking the Roman Catholic faith on the corner of a public street. The Court overturned the conviction because although a clear and present danger of "riot, disorder, interference with traffic on the public streets, or other immediate threat to public safety, peace, or order" would clearly permit the government to intervene, such a danger was not present based on the speech at issue. Thus, the government cannot use the guise of such authority to punish speech that is otherwise protected simply because it is unpopular. There must be an actual likelihood of imminent illegality based on the speech itself. The Court reached a similar conclusion in *Terminiello*, where the defendant had been convicted for calling his opponents names. In reaction to the defendant calling his opponents "slimy scum," "snakes," and "bedbugs," several disturbances arose despite a substantial police presence. The Court overturned his conviction for disturbing the peace because the speech did not pose a clear and present danger of imminent lawless action. The Court explained that to be regulated, the speech must pose a clear and present danger of causing "a serious substantive evil that rises far above public inconvenience, annoyance, or unrest." Because the speech itself did not pose that danger, the conviction could not be sustained.

The Court applied the same standard in *Feiner v. New York* (1951). There, the defendant was addressing a gathering crowd of blacks and whites through a loudspeaker system attached to a vehicle. He was trying to get people to attend a meeting he was holding that evening, but in the process he made derogatory remarks about various public officials, including President Harry Truman, the American Legion, and the mayor of Syracuse. The police made no attempt to interfere with the speech, but the crowd began to grow restless when he appeared to be exhorting the blacks in the audience to rise up and fight for equal rights. Some in the crowd threatened the police with violence if they did not control the crowd, and the police asked the defendant to stop speaking and come down from his soap box. After he refused several times, the police arrested him. He was convicted of disorderly conduct for "ignoring and refusing to heed and obey reasonable police orders." The disorderly conduct statute proscribed, *inter alia*, gathering with others on a public street and refusing to move when ordered by the police. Relying on its reasoning in *Cantwell*, the Court upheld the conviction. Writing for the majority, Justice Vinson explained that although the hostile audience doctrine could not be used if the crowd was merely murmuring and objecting to the speech, it is an entirely different situation when the speech is going beyond "the bounds of argument or persuasion and undertakes incitement to riot." Because the defendant refused to stop speaking at the request of the police, which was made after the crowd began to threaten violence, the Court held that the statute was not unconstitutional as applied.

Justice Black, writing in dissent, argued that the facts of the case did not show an imminent threat of a riot or other uncontrollable disorder. The scene as found in *Feiner* was not far from any similar scene where the crowd disagrees, sometimes violently, with a speaker. Justice Black found that the assertion that the police had no duty to protect the speaker's right to speak unfathomable. He explained that before silencing the speaker in the name of preserving order, the police must make all reasonable efforts to protect the speaker. Only after all reasonable efforts to protect the speaker have been made may the police then silence the speaker to prevent the public disorder. Here, the police immediately jumped to silence the speaker rather than to attempt to protect his right to speak and protect him from the crowd. Furthermore, the speaker's refusal to comply with the police did not rise to the level of deliberate defiance because his speech was protected by the Constitution. He was entitled to know why he had to stop when his actions were lawful. He went on to describe that the Court's holding amounted to permitting the government to silence unpopular speakers.

A difficult question in the hostile audience doctrine is that the speaker is punished for the reactions of his or her audience. This essentially permits a crowd to have the power to silence an unpopular speaker by their actions. Additionally, because the police themselves are likely to agree with the crowd, their own attitudes may shade the perception of the threat of disorder, causing them to act prematurely. In more recent rulings, the Court appears to have followed Justice Black's dissent in *Feiner*. In *Edwards v. South Carolina* (1963), the Court explained that the police protection at the scene was sufficient to prevent any foreseeable disorder. The Court emphasized the ability of the police to control the crowd in overturning a conviction in *Cox v. Louisiana* (1965), where the speaker protested racial segregation at lunch counters and urged a sit-in, and some in the audience found the speech inflammatory. The Court reached a similar result in *Gregory v. City of Chicago* (1969), even where the crowd became angry with the speaker and began throwing rocks.

Thus, the hostile audience doctrine still exists as a form of less protected speech. To qualify, the speech must cause or be imminently about to cause a disturbance of the peace. However, it also appears that the police must make all reasonable efforts to control the crowd before they can invoke the doctrine and silence the speaker.

C. Hate Speech

Laws that prohibit the expression of hate, commonly called hate speech, against individuals or groups based on national or ethnic origin, sex, race, sexual orientation, or religion are common outside the U.S. Justifications for these laws include protecting the dignity of the individual, avoiding discrimination, and lowering societal tensions that lead to violence. In the U.S. free speech interests prevail so there is no judicially or legislatively created category of unprotected or less protected speech that is called hate speech. So hate speech in the U.S. is only proscribed to the extent that it falls under one of the existing categories of less or unprotected speech such as advocacy of illegal action, fighting words, hostile audience or the true threats doctrine. Although legally classifying speech as "hate speech" is of relatively recent vintage, it goes without saying that hate speech has been around for time immemorial.

The questions of what constitutes hate speech and how such speech should be handled is still a developing area of the law. The most active attempts to curb hate speech involve the hate speech codes passed on college campuses. This revival of hate speech codes began in the 1980s and continues today. However, every time these codes are challenged in court, they are struck down as an infringement on the First Amendment.

1. Group Libel

The Court has addressed several approaches to the problem of hate speech. In 1952, the Court addressed a challenge to an Illinois law proscribing the portrayal of "depravity, criminality, unchastity, or lack of virtue of a class of citizens" based on race, creed, color, or religion if the portrayal would expose such citizens to contempt, derision, or which would cause a breach of the peace or riots. In that case, *Beauharnais v. Illinois* (1952), the Court upheld the convictions of several people under that statute. Specifically, the individuals had called for the whites in Chicago to unite and for the city to "protect" white neighborhoods from blacks, whom they saw as invading, harassing, and encroaching on their neighborhoods. The Court held that the government can proscribe defamatory language directed at a defined group of individuals. The Court based its decision on the government's power to make defamation illegal, seeing the speech by the defendants as essentially the same as libelous defamation directed at an identified group and not an individual. Justice Frankfurter's majority opinion also explained that the Court did not need to apply the Clear and Present Danger test because the speech was essentially defamatory and as such was already within the government's power to control.

The Court's decision in *Beauharnais* established the rule that one can libel an identified group, called group libel, and this decision has never been overruled. However, intervening decisions have called its holding into question and it is debatable whether it would hold up today. One reason is that courts have repeatedly refused to follow the Court's holding in *Beauharnais*. A classic example is the case of *National Socialist Party of America v. Village of Skokie* (1977). There, the Court upheld the right of Nazis to march in Skokie, Illinois, a town populated mostly by Jews, including many survivors of concentration camps. After the case was remanded, the Seventh Circuit found attempts by the town to prohibit publication and distribution of material that promoted and incited hatred of others based on their religion or race and to ban the display of the swastika to be unconstitutional. In its decision, the Seventh Circuit expressly stated that it no longer regarded *Beauharnais* as good law.

Another reason that the *Beauharnais* holding may no longer be good law is that its underpinnings have since been eroded. When it decided the case in 1952, the Court expressly based its decision on the government's unlimited ability to proscribe defamation. However, in *New York Times Co. v. Sullivan* (1964), the Court rejected this unlimited power and placed rather strong limits on the ability of the government to curb defamatory speech. This is explored more in the section on defamation.

Thus, while the Court upheld government proscription of group libel in *Beauharnais*, it is an open question whether it would do so today. Additionally, applying the doctrines of void for vagueness and overbreadth, it is likely that statutes similar to that in *Beauharnais* would be deemed overbroad or vague. If not, it is also likely that the content-based distinction within a given classification, as presented in *R.A.V.*, would overturn the statute unless it passed strict scrutiny. Therefore today hate speech probably cannot be successfully proscribed under the group libel theory.

2. Fighting Words and True Threats

Other avenues that may apply to hate speech are the fighting words doctrine and the concept of a true threat. As already discussed, fighting words are in a category of speech that is not protected by the First Amendment. Following the analysis in *Chaplinsky*, words that are directed at an individual and that by their utterance are likely to provoke a violent reaction are unprotected. Thus, hate speech that falls into this definition could be proscribed; in fact, many colleges and universities have based their hate speech codes on this foundation.

However, this avenue of attacking hate speech faces difficulty. First, the Court has not upheld a statute banning fighting words since *Chaplinsky*. Second, the statutes must be crafted with care, or they will likely be held void on grounds of vagueness or overbreadth, or they will fail under *R.A.V.*'s application of strict scrutiny to content-based distinctions within a category of unprotected speech. Third, the courts have yet to uphold hate speech laws or university hate speech codes against constitutional challenge. In fact, the courts have overturned every hate speech code that has been challenged.

Another tool to combat hate speech is the true threats doctrine. Although the Court has never defined what constitutes a true threat, numerous federal statutes have, the broadest of which makes it a crime to transmit in commerce any communication containing any threat to injure another person. As interpreted by the lower courts, the speaker need only intend the threatening communication, he or she need not actually intend to carry the threat out or even have the ability to carry it out. Though this doctrine is often linked to hate speech, it is not limited to hate-based threats. In fact, it was initially developed to address threats made against the President or Vice President of the United States. In *Watts v. United States* (1969), the Court explained that the Constitution did not protect speech that was intended as a threat to the life of the President and upheld a federal statute banning such speech. However, the Court also explained that the threat must be an actual threat of illegal, violent harm, and not merely a "very crude offensive method of stating a political opposition to the President." In making its determination, the Court looked at the totality of the circumstances. In *Watts*, the defendant, protesting the draft and police brutality, stated that he received his draft classification as 1-A and that he had to report for his physical on Monday. He then said, "I am not going. If they ever make me carry a rifle the first man I want to get in my sights is L.B.J." In a *per curiam* opinion, the Court explained that, when taken in context, the speech only indicated the speaker's disagreement with the President and that it did not actually threaten him with illegal violent harm.

The seminal case addressing true threats in the context of hate speech is *Virginia v. Black* (2003). There, the Court addressed a Virginia statute banning cross burning with the intent to intimidate a person or a group of persons. However, the statute went further and found that the mere fact of cross burning raised a presumption that the burning was with the intent to intimidate, requiring the defendant to rebut that presumption. The Court struck down the Virginia statute because of the presumption it permitted based on the defendant's conduct. Justice O'Connor's opinion, a majority opinion in part and a plurality opinion in part, explained that without the presumption that burning a cross was prima facie evidence of intent to intimidate, the statute would not have been unconstitutional. Justice O'Connor also explained that the statute need not ban all intimidating speech to be constitutional. Rather, she explained that cross burning is especially intimidating given its history with the Ku Klux Klan and that because of its especial virulence, the government could ban only that speech if it chose. Specifically, Justice O'Connor expressed that such intimidating hate speech is intended to be a threat of illegal violent harm to the hearer, and burning a cross has traditionally been used to communicate that threat. Thus, under the logic of *Black*, hate speech may be proscribed without offending the First Amendment because it is intended to threaten and instill fear in the hearer, rather than communicate ideas.

Another possible avenue that is being explored by legislatures around the country is tacking on additional penalties to crimes involving hate as a motivation. Commonly known as hate crimes laws, the Court has lent at least a measure of legitimacy to these enhancements. For example, in *Wisconsin v. Mitchell* (1993), the Court upheld a statute that provided for greater criminal punishments when the victim was chosen on grounds of race. Chief Justice Rehnquist, writing for a unanimous Court, explained that the nature of crimes committed based on hatred for another due to race involves a greater harm to society in general and also inflicts "distinct emotional harms on their victims," and they have a greater likelihood of provoking a breach of public order or riots. Note that hate crimes laws are not aimed directly at preventing hate speech. However, the trend is to use hate speech as an indication of the animus behind the crime and as evidence of the hateful motivation. Thus, although not directly targeting hate speech itself, hate crimes legislation may have the side effect of deterring hate speech to avoid the penalty enhancements created by the legislation.

Another approach to proscribing hate speech involves the doctrines of incitement to imminent illegality and the hostile audience. These two doctrines were already discussed, but they are also applicable in the context of hate speech. First, under the *Brandenberg* test, the government enjoys the ability to protect itself from change caused by "violence, revolution, and terrorism." The ability to protect the citizenry from violence and to preserve the peace are also valid exercises of the police power of the state. However, under the *Brandenberg* test, the bar is set very high: The speech must present a threat of imminent violence. To be proscribed under these doctrines, the hate speech must be intended to cause imminent violence or it must be provoking a crowd against the speaker to the point that, absent silencing the speaker, will lead to imminent lawlessness. Recall that, the Court seems to follow Justice Black's dissent in *Feiner v. New York* (1951), which would require the police to take all reasonable steps to control the crowd first and only permit silencing the speaker if the police are unable to do so. Thus, the bar on using these doctrines is high but not insurmountable.

Based on the foregoing, hate speech in itself is likely protected under the First Amendment. The Court's method of banning it by group libel theory in *Beauharnais* will probably not hold up today and treating hate speech as fighting words will be difficult due to *R.A.V.* and the tests of vagueness and overbreadth. That said, speech that incites to imminent violence or is clearly intended to threaten or intimidate may be proscribed, and hate crimes legislation may succeed in combating hate speech. However, this is still an active and developing area of free speech law.

D. Sexually Oriented Speech

The regulation of sexually oriented speech is always a hot topic in First Amendment law. The Court has long recognized that the government could regulate such speech. In 1948, the Supreme Court affirmed a conviction for violating Philadelphia's criminal obscenity statute. In that case, *Doubleday & Co., Inc. v. Pennsylvania* (1948), the defendant had published a book that contained two scenes where he described sexual intercourse. The Court ended up affirming the conviction only because they were deadlocked four to four with one Justice not participating. The next year, a bookseller was charged with violating a Pennsylvania criminal statute but was acquitted (*Commonwealth v. Gordon*, 1949). The bookseller was acquitted because, although the judge found that the Court, in dicta, had endorsed the idea that obscene speech could be punished merely because it was obscene, he found that there was no nexus between the publication of the material and any actual criminal behavior or threat of imminent criminal behavior due to the publication.

In finding that the Court had endorsed punishment of obscenity *qua* obscenity, the judge relied on several statements by the Supreme Court. In *Chaplinsky v. New Hampshire* (1942), the Court stated that there were "certain well-defined and narrowly limited classes of speech" that were not protected by the First Amendment and included "lewd and obscene" material in such a class. The Court's endorsement of prosecuting obscenity continued after the acquittal in *Gordon*. For example, Justice Murphy included the "lewd and obscene" among the speech that has no value to society in *Beauharnais*. The Court has since refined its position on sexually oriented speech by dividing it into three groups: obscenity, child pornography, and language that is profane and indecent. The

Court finds that the first two categories, obscenity and child pornography, are not protected by the First Amendment; the third category is generally protected, but there are exceptions.

1. Obscenity

Although it has not shied away from permitting the regulation of obscene speech, the Court has found it extremely difficult actually to define what obscene speech is. In fact, its attempt to define obscenity led to the famous quote from Justice Potter Stewart's concurrence in *Jacobellis v. Ohio* (1964), "Perhaps I could never succeed in intelligibly ... [defining hard-core pornography]. But I know it when I see it." Although the Court has progressed from this and provided substantial guidance as to what constitutes obscenity, sometimes it appears that the Court just "know[s] it when [it] see[s] it."

The Court first addressed obscenity directly in *Roth v. United States* (1957), and this case still forms the core of the Court's obscenity jurisprudence today. In *Roth*, the Court expressly held that obscenity was not protected by the First Amendment. In so holding, the Court relied on its past dicta in *Chaplinsky* and *Beauharnais* and, in his majority opinion, Justice Brennan noted that it had always assumed that obscene speech fell outside the protections of the First Amendment. He explained that this accorded with history because the Court had long held that ideas with at least some redeeming value, no matter how slight or how unpopular, were protected by the Constitution unless the speech infringed on "more important interests."

After finding that obscenity was not protected, Justice Brennan went further and divorced sex from obscenity. He explained that to be obscene, the material must "deal with sex in a manner appealing to prurient interest," and that displays of nudity or sex in art, literature, science, and similar forums were not obscenity. Justice Brennan then qualified the "prurient interest" language, explaining that the theme of the work must be judged as a whole by applying contemporary community standards from the viewpoint of the average person in the community. He then stated that generally, there would be no violation of due process if a statute banning obscenity were found to be less precise than desirable, as long as the statute provided "adequate warning" as to what conduct was proscribed. Thus, under *Roth*, the Court articulated a three-part test for obscenity. To qualify as obscene, the material must (1) appeal to a prurient interest in sex; (2) have no redeeming artistic, scientific, literary, or other similar value; and (3) on the whole, be offensive to the average person applying contemporary community standards.

The Court has continually held that obscene speech is not protected by the Constitution, however in the years after *Roth*, the Court struggled with how to define obscenity and how to justify its finding that obscenity was not protected speech. In *A Book Named "John Cleland's Memoirs of a Woman of Pleasure" v. Attorney General* (1966), the Court overturned a conviction based on a finding that the book had at least some "social value" and thus was not obscenity. The Court was badly fractured however, and could not muster a majority opinion in the case. However, Justice Brennan's opinion stated that the three elements of the *Roth* test were independent of each other, and material was not obscene if it passed any of the three elements. The confusion continued with *Ginzburg v. United States* (1966). There, the Court found commercial publications devoted to sex to be obscene because they were commercial ventures that exploited erotica solely for their prurient appeal. With his decision in *Ginzburg*, Justice Brennan ran directly counter in his opinion in *Memoirs* because he never considered any potential social value of the publications. Thus, the Court seemed to indicate that if the material is intended to appeal solely to prurient interests, that intent outweighed any social value that the material may have had.

The Court eventually came through the fog of its own creation with its decision in *Miller v. California* (1973). Again, the Court reaffirmed that obscene material was not protected by the First Amendment. It also created the test for obscenity that is still used today. First, it abandoned the post-*Roth* approaches of treating the *Roth* elements independently and that material intended to appeal solely to prurient sexual interests would override any vestige of redeeming social value. The *Miller* test was based on the *Roth* elements but expanded on them. Under *Miller*, material is obscene if (1) the average person applying contemporary community standards would find that, viewed as a whole, the work appealed to the prurient interests; (2) the work describes or depicts sexual conduct defined by the applicable law in a patently offensive way; and (3) as a whole, the work lacks serious literary, political, scientific, or artistic value. As examples, the Court explained that patently offensive depictions or descriptions of ultimate sex acts would fall within the *Miller* test, as would patently offensive descriptions or depictions of masturbation, excretion, and lewd exhibition of genitalia. The dissents decried the new test as one that endorsed censorship by permitting suppression simply based on individual predilections and permitted statutes that would otherwise be void on vagueness or overbreadth grounds.

The Court reaffirmed *Miller* in *Paris Adult Theatre I v. Slaton* (1973). There, the challenge was to the legality of adult theaters in Georgia that prohibited minors from entering. The Georgia Supreme Court described the films being displayed at the theater as "hard core pornography" which left "little to the imagination." The defendant argued that the films were protected speech because they were shown for adult consumption only. However, the Court rejected that argument, recognizing the longstanding and legitimate interest of states to regulate obscene material in local commerce and "in all places of public accommodation." However, the Court went further and explained that because depictions of obscenity could have a "corrupting and debasing impact" that may lead to antisocial behavior, states could ban such depictions under legitimate police powers. The fact that the speech was only made to adults did not lend it talismanic immunity under the First Amendment. The Court went further and emphasized the governmental interest in avoiding the negative effects on a community by such establishments congregating in a single community.

In other decisions, the Court addressed the issues of possessing obscene material and distinguished it from commerce involving obscenity. In *Stanley v. Georgia*, (1969), before *Miller*, the Court upheld the right to possess obscene materials because the states only have a legitimate interest in regulating obscenity in commerce and public discourse. It found that the First and Fourteenth Amendments protected private possession of obscene materials. However, in *United States v. Reidel* (1971), the Court explained that although a person cannot be prosecuted from possessing obscene materials under *Stanley*, there is no constitutionally protected right to sell or deliver those materials to that person.

Thus, the Court has upheld an individual's right to possess obscenity, but no one has a right to buy or sell such materials. Further, the government is not prohibited from banning obscenity as long as regulation law passes the three-prong *Miller* test. However, the *Miller* test is not limited only to material that potentially could be viewed by children. Under *Paris Adult Theatre I*, the fact that minors are not permitted in to view material in a publicly accessible place does not shield the speech from being regulated, especially given the effects that such places have on the community. Thus, the government generally has the right to regulate the dissemination of obscene speech but not the naked possession of such materials.

2. Child Pornography

Child pornography is a category of unprotected speech, but because it is a content-based restriction of obscenity, it must pass strict scrutiny. As a category of unprotected speech recognized by the Supreme Court, it is of relatively recent vintage. It developed as one branch of the outgrowth of the Court's creation and application of the strict scrutiny test to content-based restrictions on speech. The doctrines of vagueness and overbreadth had developed sufficiently by the 1980s such that any new test would have to survive scrutiny under their requirements. Thus, when the Court recognized the category of child pornography as unprotected speech in 1982, it not only considered the state interest involved and the fit of the law to the interest but also ensured that the law not be unconstitutionally vague or overbroad.

The seminal case where the Court recognized this category was its decision in *New York v. Ferber* (1982), where it held that the government could prohibit the advertising, selling, display, and distribution of pornographic materials involving children. Specifically, it upheld a New York law that prohibited the promotion of "a sexual performance by a child." It defined such a sexual performance as one "which includes sexual conduct by a child less than sixteen years of age," and sexual conduct as "actual or simulated sexual intercourse, deviate sexual intercourse, sexual bestiality, masturbation, sado-masochistic abuse, or lewd exhibition of the genitals." The defendant was the owner of a bookstore specializing in sexually oriented materials sold two films depicting young boys masturbating. The Supreme Court unanimously upheld the conviction.

The Court based its finding on the compelling need to protect children, listing five supporting premises. First, it recognized the state's compelling interest in protecting the physical and psychological well-being of children, stating that preventing sexual abuse and exploitation is a "government objective of surpassing importance." It further observed that the use of children as subjects of pornographic productions harms the children physiologically, emotionally, and mentally, and that virtually all states have statutes prohibiting "child pornography." Second, distribution of child pornography is directly related to the state's compelling interest because (a) the materials are a permanent record of the child's participation in the activity with the distribution exacerbating the harm to the child, and (b) the distribution network encourages the distribution and thus the exploitation and abuse of children. Third, the advertising and sales of this material provides an economic incentive which, in turn, feeds the growth of the industry and the exploitation of the children. Fourth, the value of such materials, if any, is "exceedingly modest, if not *de minimis*" and, if there were any artistic, literary, scientific, or educational value, it could be met by activity by a person of legal age who appears to be younger. Fifth, recognizing child pornography as a category of unprotected speech is not contrary to existing case law precedent.

Additionally, the Court expressly held that the test for validity of child pornography laws is different than the obscenity test as enunciated by the *Miller* court. Specifically, the validity of laws proscribing child pornography need not appeal to the prurient interest of the average person, it need not be portrayed in a patently offensive manner under community standards, and the work need not be considered as a whole. However, the Court noted one specific exception. It retained First Amendment protection of distributing descriptions or other nonobscene depictions of sexual conduct that do not involve live performances, photographic, or other visual reproductions of live performances. Further, the Court emphasized that criminal responsibility cannot be imposed without having to prove some element of scienter against the defendant.

The Court's decision in *Ferber* is important for three main reasons. First, it delineated the standard by which the constitutionality of anti-child pornography laws would be judged. Second, the Court did not actually define child pornography. Rather, it merely passed on the constitutionality of the definition provided in the New York statute. Third, it provided that the doctrines of vagueness and overbreadth could be applied to such laws but found that they were not applicable to the New York law under its scrutiny. Justice O'-Connor's concurring opinion stressed that although New York's law was not facially unconstitutional, it may be found unconstitutional as applied in certain situations because it may proscribe acts that do not threaten the harms against which the state may legitimately protect. Specifically, she found that the statute may criminalize clinical depictions of adolescents like those that may have a place in medical textbooks, and that there may be other applications that do not implicate the "kiddie porn" market that New York was attempting to control.

Recently, the Court addressed the question of the use of simulations of adolescents in sexual positions. In *Ashcroft v. Free Speech Coalition* (2002), the Court struck down portions of the Child Pornography Prevention Act of 1996 (CPPA) that proscribed "virtual pornography" by outlawing sexually explicit images that purported to depict minors. The content at issue used adults who looked like minors or computer-generated images. Analyzing the statute under *Ferber*'s protection of children, the Court found that when no actual minors were used in the creation of what appeared to be child pornography, the state's interest in preventing child abuse was not implicated because no children were harmed. Further, the Court explained that the CPPA was not saved by the *Miller* test because it did not require that the material appeal to the prurient interest, it need not be patently offensive, and it did not permit work that had serious literary, social, or scientific value when considered as a whole. Thus, the *Ferber* standard is a more permissive one than the *Miller* standard, but it only applies when actual children are used in producing the material.

The government may regulate and proscribe child pornography without meeting the requirements of *Miller*, but only when actual minors are used in the production of the challenged material. When the material uses youthful-looking adults, computer-generated images, or other simulated minors, the Court applies the *Miller* test. When actual minors are used in the production of the material, *Ferber*, a much more lenient and deferential standard, applies.

3. Profanity and Indecency: Protected but Low-Value Speech

Speech that does not meet the definition of either obscenity under the *Miller* test or qualify as child pornography under *Ferber* but is otherwise profane or indecent is generally protected by the First Amendment. The Court finds that such speech, even if it is of only low value to society, is protected. It bases this on the difficulty of separating the speech from the ideas that it is intended to express. To hold otherwise would essentially open the door to censorship because the speech was unpopular or generally offensive.

The classic case is *Cohen v. California* (1971), where the Court held that the government may not punish expression simply because those to whom the speech is expressed may find it offensive. In *Cohen*, the defendant was arrested and convicted for wearing a jacket that read "Fuck the Draft." In overturning the conviction, Justice Harlan wrote that one cannot forbid speaking certain words without inherently suppressing the ideas that the words were intended to convey. He was concerned that once the state has the ability to proscribe specific words because others may find them offensive, there would be no rational boundary between those words and other words that may be offensive.

A similar rational prevents the general proscription of speech that has sexual content but is not obscene. The Court addressed this issue in *Erznoznik v. City of Jacksonville* (1975). *Erznoznik* involved a challenge to a Jacksonville, Florida, ordinance proscribing drive-in theaters from exhibiting motion pictures depicting nudity if the images are visible from any public street or public place. The Court found that statute was underinclusive because it did not protect people from all movies that might offend them. Further, Justice Lewis Powell, writing for the Court, explained that the ordinance was overinclusive because it would ban motion pictures that would not be considered obscene, such as educational movies, including those about peoples for whom public nudity is common, war documentaries showing nude victims of the war, and a film that shows a baby's unclothed bottom. The Court also stated that such an ordinance could be saved if the state courts had given it a narrowing construction. However, the state courts of Florida had not done so, and the plain language of the ordinance was not amenable to such a construction. Thus, because the material banned was not obscene, the Court found that it was within the protection of the First Amendment, and the Jacksonville ordinance was invalid.

The Court has found two exceptions to this protection. First, speech in schools that may offend others may be proscribed if it is inconsistent with the educational mission of the school. In *Bethel School District No. 403 v. Fraser* (1986), a student had been punished for giving a nominating speech at a school assembly that, while it did not contain profane language, was replete with sexual innuendo. The Court upheld the student's punishment because the speech was "wholly inconsistent with the 'fundamental value' of public school education."

Second, the Court has recognized the government's ability to prohibit profanity and indecency broadcast over the airwaves. In *FCC v. Pacifica Foundation* (1978), the Court upheld the ability of the Federal Communications Commission to punish indecent speech broadcast over radio or television. The Court explained that although the government could not ban all indecent speech, it could do so over the radio, especially where the speech was patently offensive, because the speech accosts the individual at his or her home, where a person has a right to be left alone. The Court found that the expectation of privacy, insofar as being left alone, overrode the First Amendment rights of the intruder. It explained further that placing warnings bookending the different segments of the speech would not be sufficient because that would not protect a person who happened to tune in between the warnings.

The Court has refused to extend these exceptions to other forms of media, including telephones, cable television, and the Internet. First, in *Sable Communications v. FCC*, (1989), the Court addressed a federal statute that was targeted at banning the "dial-a-porn" industry by banning indecent or obscene speech over the telephone. The Court explained that the speech could not be banned merely because it was indecent or obscene. Further, the speech was not made to a captive audience because, except for wrong numbers, the caller generally intended to encounter the speech.

The Court ruled along similar lines in *Denver Area Educational Telecommunications Consortium, Inc. v. FCC* (1996), where it addressed the Cable Television and Consumer Protection and Competition Act of 1992 (CTCPCA). Several provisions of the CTCPCA were challenged. One proscribed material on cable television that was considered patently offensive and sexually oriented. Another required that cable systems permitting such material segregate it on a single channel and require the subscriber request access to the channel in writing. The last provision permitted cable systems to prohibit material on public, educational, or governmental channels that was sexually explicit. Though it could not muster a majority opinion, the Court upheld the first provision and invalidated the last two.

Finally, the Court has refused to apply *Pacifica* to the Internet. In *Reno v. ACLU* (1997), the Court, by a vote of seven to two, invalidated several portions of the Communications Decency Act of 1996. Writing for the Court, Justice Stevens recognized the importance of protecting minors from access to this material but found that the government could not restrict access by adults to achieve that end. The Court addressed the issue again in *Ashcroft v. ACLU* (2004), where it considered the Child Online Protection Act (COPA). Justice Kennedy, writing for the majority, explained that this second attempt to "make the Internet safe for minors," failed the strict scrutiny test. The Court recognized the state's interest in protecting minors from exposure to profanity and indecency over the Internet. However, it found that preventing access to such material by adults or making it difficult using methods like filtering software were not narrowly tailored to protecting children. Justice Kennedy explained that the Congress could pass a law encouraging the use of filtering software, not mandating it, which would give parents the ability to protect their children without criminalizing protected speech.

Thus, the Court has found that speech that may be offensive or indecent because of its near-obscenity or its profane content is generally protected by the First Amendment. However, it recognizes exceptions to the general rule for speech in schools that are contrary to the mission of the school and such speech broadcast over the radio or television waves. However, the Court has refused to extend that proscription beyond those two exceptions. Thus, obscene or indecent speech over the telephone lines, cable television, and the Internet are protected under the First Amendment.

E. Defamation

Defamation is the issuance of a false statement about another person, which injures the reputation of that person. Defamation is divided into spoken defamation (slander) and written defamation (libel). Traditionally, states had the ability to define and punish defamatory speech through tort law without implicating the First Amendment because the Court had long recognized such speech to be outside the protection of the First Amendment. For example, as recently as the 1950s, in *Beauharnais v. Illinois* (1952), the Court explained that libelous speech is not protected by the First Amendment because it is of "such slight social value as a step to truth" that the social interest in social order and morality outweighed any benefit provided by such speech. However, today, defamatory speech has been found to fall within the protections of the First Amendment, especially when the speech concerns a public official or a public figure. As we will see, the tendrils of the First Amendment do reach speech concerning private persons. The ongoing tension in this area is the protection of the right of free speech with a person's right not to have his or her dignity besmirched by the exercise of another's right of free speech.

The Court began to constitutionalize defamation with its decision in *New York Times Co. v. Sullivan* (1964). Before *New York Times*, states were free to define and punish the tort of defamation as they saw fit. In *New York Times*, the

Court held that the ability to recover against a tortfeasor for defamatory speech was circumscribed by the First Amendment. In doing so, the Court supplemented the all states' tests for defamation when the speech was about a public official with the requirement that the speech be made with "actual malice." The Court defined actual malice as publication of the speech "with knowledge that it was false or with reckless disregard of whether it was false or not."

New York Times involved a defamation suit by a city commissioner of Montgomery, Alabama. The defendant, the petitioner in the Court, had published a advertisement containing an allegation that after black students had protested at the Alabama state Capitol by singing "My Country, 'Tis of Thee" the Alabama state college expelled their students and "truckloads of police armed with shotguns and tear-gas ringed" the campus. Further, the advertisement alleged that the police sought to "starve [the students] into submission" by locking them in the dining hall after the entire student body refused to reregister. The plaintiff was responsible for supervising the police and fire departments of the city, and he claimed that this reference to the police defamed him. At trial, he won and was awarded $500,000 in damages, which the Supreme Court of Alabama affirmed. The Supreme Court granted *certiorari* and reversed.

Writing for the Court, Justice Brennan began with Alabama law providing that once a plaintiff established that the speech was libelous *per se*, the defendant's only defense is to prove that the speech was "true in all [its] particulars." If he cannot prove that the speech was true, then damages were presumed and the plaintiff could be awarded damages without proof that his reputation was actually damaged. Justice Brennan examined this law against the policies underlying the First Amendment, that public debate should be "uninhibited, robust, and wide-open," and that that debate will sometimes involve unpleasant attacks on public officials. The Court then focused on the fact that in free and vigorous public debate, erroneous statements are inevitable and that they must be protected to ensure that free speech has the "breathing space" that the First Amendment intended it to have. As such, putting the onus of proving truth on the speaker in the face of libel *per se* does not comport with the protections of the First Amendment when the speech involves a public official. Hence, the defamatory content of speech nor factual error suffice to "remove the constitutional shield" from criticizing official conduct of public officials.

Justice Brennan then explained that states cannot use the civil law of libel to accomplish what it cannot do with criminal law. Furthermore, the Alabama law permitted damages *per se* that was 1,000 times greater than a criminal fine and 100 times greater than that under the Alien and Sedition Acts. Under this scheme, the threat of successive civil judgments against a publisher would have a substantial chilling effect on free speech and would risk silencing public debate over crucial issues. Finding that the *New York Times* published the advertisement without checking its own files and that a reasonable examination of the files would have turned up the false nature of the allegations are not sufficient to show that it knew that the publication was false. Further, the paper was not reckless as to the falsity of the advertisement because it did not have a substantial reason to suspect the false nature of the claims because they had come from sources with a strong reputation for accuracy. The Court found that at most, the paper's actions constituted negligence that failed to meet the standard required to show actual malice.

New York Times dealt with a public official plaintiff against a private party, but it did not address situations involving defamation of private persons who have achieved fame and notoriety. It also did not distinguish between speech relating to purely private concerns and speech on matters of public issues. In *Rosenblatt v. Baer* (1966), the Court explained that all public employees are not public officials. Rather, it applies, at a minimum, to public employees who have or are perceived to have "substantial responsibility for or control over the conduct of governmental affairs." The Court's constitutionalization of defamation continued over the next three decades as it clarified the test and its application to situations, including those above.

Three years after it crafted and applied the actual malice standard to public officials, the Court extended it to public figure plaintiffs in *Curtis Publishing Co. v. Butts* (1967), but it could not muster a majority opinion. *Curtis* was a consolidated case involving the former head football coach at the University of Georgia, the incumbent athletic director at the school at the time of the suit, and a former general in the U.S. Army. Articles were published claiming that the athletic director had fixed a football game while he was the head coach and that the former general had commanded a crowd in a racial protest, orchestrating an assault on federal marshals. Writing for the plurality, Justice Harlan explained that the actual malice standard applied to public figures because, like public officials, they command "sufficient continuing public interest" and they have sufficient access to channels of communication to combat the statements in the media. Further, he differentiated public figures into two forms: (1) the person who is a public figure merely because of his position, and (2) the person who injects himself into the "'vortex' of an important public controversy."

The Court solidified its actual malice standard in *Gertz v. Robert Welch, Inc.* (1974). Writing for the majority, Justice Powell explained that the actual malice standard developed in *New York Times* was applicable only to public officials and public figures and not private plaintiffs. Furthermore, he used the distinction, introduced in *Curtis*, between people who are public figures for all purposes and those who are public figures solely because of their intentional involvement in a controversy of public importance. The first form of a public figure was called a public figure for all purposes, and the second form was called a public figure for the limited issues into which she injected herself. The Court explained that the lessened protection of public officials and public figures was balanced by their access to the channels of communication to use self-help to combat the defamatory statements. Because private persons do not generally command the same access, they need additional protection. To that end, the Court held that the states are free to define defamation as it applies to publishers or broadcasters of defamatory material that harms a private individual. Further, it placed two important limits on the states' ability to permit recovery for defamation. They cannot provide liability without fault, and they cannot permit recovery of presumed or punitive damages without meeting the actual malice standard as defined in *New York Times*. Additionally, the Court refused to adopt the content-based distinction suggested by the plurality in *Rosenbloom v. Metromedia, Inc.* (1971), where a private individual would have to meet the actual malice standard if the issue was one of public interest even if she did not inject herself into the controversy.

Thus, today there is a substantial distinction between the protection that states can provide to victims of defamation that is based solely on their status in the public eye. A public official or a public figure is accorded less protection because of access to the media to refute the defamatory statements. Consequentially, one must show that the publication or broadcast was made with actual malice that is, knowing that the statement was false or acting in reckless disregard of the falsity of the statement. A person may become a public figure by either (1) holding a position that by its nature, generates public interest in that person, or (2) injecting him- or herself into the forefront of a public controversy. However, a person who is not a public official and who is not a public figure enjoys the greatest protection. The state is free to permit her to recover under the traditional common law tort of defamation as long as it does not (1) permit strict liability, or (2) permit recovery for presumed or punitive damages without meeting the actual malice standard.

F. Disclosure of Confidential Information and Other Speech-Related Torts

The Court has addressed the application of the First Amendment to the government's ability to provide relief for other speech-related torts aside from defamation. The Court holds that the *New York Times* standard limits the ability of the government to permit recovery by public officials or public figures for intentional infliction of emotional distress and for false light invasion of privacy. Regarding public disclosure of private facts, the Court holds that the First Amendment prohibits recovery for information that is not of legitimate public concern if (1) it was obtained from public records, (2) it was not obtained unlawfully, and (3) it was reported truthfully.

1. Intentional Infliction of Emotional Distress

The Court definitively applied its First Amendment jurisprudence regarding intentional infliction of emotional distress in *Hustler Magazine v. Falwell* (1988). The plaintiff, a nationally known Christian minister and active commentator on politics and public affairs, was the subject of an advertisement in the defendant's magazine. The ad was a parody of another ad that featured a transcript of a fictional interview with the plaintiff that portrayed him as a drunk and immoral and suggested that he only preached when he was intoxicated. The Court held that public officials and public figures may only recover for intentional infliction of emotional distress when the publication was made with actual malice as defined in *New York Times*. Writing for the majority, Chief Justice Rehnquist explained that such parodies are protected by the First Amendment for the same reasons that defamatory speech is protected. He traced the long and storied history of parodical publications in American political and public debate, finding that the quality of American political dialogue "would have been considerably poorer without them."

2. False Light Invasion of Privacy

The tort of false light invasion of privacy involves the (1) publication, (2) of private information, (3) that is reasonably believed to be factual, and (4) places the person in a false light. The Court addressed this tort in the context of public officials and public figures in *Time, Inc. v. Hill* (1967). *Hill* involved the publication of an article about a play that closely mirrored the plaintiff's experience in which his family was held prisoner by three escaped convicts. The article expressly drew the comparison between the play and the plaintiff's ordeal, which had been widely reported in the media when it happened. Foreshadowing its later decision in *Rosenbloom v. Metromedia, Inc.* (1971), the Court held that because the article involved events of public concern, the tougher *New York Times* standard applied and required the plaintiff to meet the actual malice standard. However, the modern standard for false light invasion of privacy mirrors the standard from *Gertz*. Private persons may recover actual damages as long as the state does not permit strict liability, but they may only recover presumed and punitive damages if they meet the *New York Times* actual malice standard; public figures must meet the *New York Times* actual malice standard to recover actual damages.

3. Publication of Private Facts

The tort of publication of private facts involves the (1) publication, (2) of private facts, (3) that are not of legitimate public concern, and (4) would be offensive to a reasonable person. The Court holds that the First Amendment prevents recovery when the facts were obtained from public records, were not obtained unlawfully, and were reported truthfully. The leading case is *Cox Broadcasting Corp. v. Cohn* (1975). *Cox Broadcasting* involved the publication of the name of a rape victim. The information was true, and it was publicly available because it was contained in court documents that were a matter of public record. The Court found that the First Amendment prevented recovery in this situation. Justice White, writing for the majority, explained that once information had been disclosed to the public by its inclusion in court documents that are open to public inspection, the press could not be punished for reporting it. To hold otherwise "would invite timidity and self-censorship" that would likely lead to suppression of information that should be available to the public.

In *Bartnicki v. Vopper* (2001), the Court addressed a similar issue but one step removed. *Vopper* involved the situation in which the published information was obtained by lawful means, was truthful, and involved matters of public concern. However, the information was obtained by an intermediary third party who got the information unlawfully. The information at issue dealt with negotiations between the Pennsylvania State Education Association, a teachers' union, and the local school board. The negotiations had been contentious and received wide coverage in the media. During one conversation between the president of the teacher's union and the union's chief negotiator, the president of the union said that if the board did not move, the union would go to the homes of the board members and "blow off their front porches," because they had "to do some work on some of those guys." The Court held that because the information was a matter of such public concern, the defect in the chain between the source and the publisher was not sufficiently tainted to remove the First Amendment's protection of that speech.

In sum, the Court has applied the First Amendment to speech-related torts other than defamation. The First Amendment requires *New York Times* actual malice standard to limit recovery for the torts of intentional infliction of emotional distress and false light invasion of privacy, holding public officials and public figures to a higher standard of proof than private plaintiffs. The ability of states to permit recovery for the tort of public disclosure of private facts has also been circumscribed by the First Amendment such that once otherwise private information has been disclosed in public documents, the information may be published with impunity as long as the information was lawfully acquired.

G. Speech of Public Employees

Thus far, we have considered freedom of speech in the context of private persons. However, does the First Amendment extend the same protection to the speech of government officials and public employees as it does to the private sector? The Court has addressed this question in two distinct areas. First, the Court has held that the government can prohibit participation in political activities by government employees. Second, the government may prohibit its employees from speaking on matters of public concern if its interest in efficient operations outweighs the employee's interest in such speech.

1. Prohibition of Participation in Political Activities

The Court upheld the government's power to prohibit its employees from participating in partisan political activities in *Union Public Workers of America (C.I.O.) v. Mitchell* (1947). The plaintiffs sought to enjoin the enforcement of Section 9(a) of the Hatch Act based on the First Amendment's protection of free speech. Section 9(a) of the Hatch Act read, "No officer or employee in the executive branch of the Federal Government [shall] take any active part in political management or in political campaigns." Writing for the majority, Justice Stanley Reed explained that the government has the ability to regulate the political conduct of its employees, including regulation of political contributions of money. He then compared the provisions of the Hatch Act with statutes regulating political contributions of money by public employees, finding that the Hatch Act was a regulation of political contributions of time and energy. The Court held that the government can "regulate the political conduct of government employees" so long as the regulations fall "within reasonable limits." Thus, the government has the power to prohibit its employees from participating in partisan political activities as long as the regulations are reasonable.

Justice Black wrote in dissent that there was no rational distinction between First Amendment protections of private citizens and those of government employees. Further, he argued that while a few high-ranking government employees may abuse their positions to coerce citizens, "muzzl[ing] millions of citizens" was not an appropriate response.

2. Speech by Government Employees in the Workplace

The Court has addressed the government's ability to punish its employees for their speech in the workplace. In *Connick v. Myers* (1983), the plaintiff, an assistant district attorney, was terminated because she created and distributed a survey among her co-workers about the office's transfer policy, its morale, and the need for a committee to address employee grievances. The plaintiff distributed the survey because she had been informed that she would be transferred to a different section. Shortly after she distributed the questionnaire, she was terminated for insubordination and because she refused to accept the transfer. The Court held that the government's interest in efficient operation outweighed the First Amendment interest implicated by the termination.

Writing for the majority, Justice White expanded on the Court's decision in *Pickering v. Board of Education* (1968). He explained that the Court must weigh the government's interest in efficient operation against the speaker's interest because her questionnaire contained a question involving a matter of public interest. However, because it only contained one question, it only touched on matters of public concern in a very limited context. Rather, Justice White characterized it as an employee's grievance regarding an internal policy of the district attorney's office. Balancing against the plaintiff's slight interest in the speech was the fact that the speech occurred at the office, it involved the application of the policy at issue to the speaker, and the plaintiff had to disrupt her own work to distribute the questionnaire. Thus, the Court found that the government's interest in efficient operations and avoidance of disruptive activities outweighed the plaintiff's relatively slim interest in speaking. Justice Brennan's dissent, joined by Justices Marshall, Blackmun, and Stevens, wrote that the Court's decision would deter public employees from making statements critical about the operation of government agencies.

The Court addressed the same issue in *Rankin v. McPherson* (1987), and it applied *Connick* in reaching its decision. The plaintiff, a low-level probationary employee who could be fired at any time and for any reason, including no reason, had been fired because of a racially charged remark she made about her own race when conversing with a co-worker. The remark concerned the attempted assassination of President Ronald Reagan and was made in the presence of another employer whom the plaintiff did not know was present. The Court found that the plaintiff's interest in making the statement outweighed the government's interest in efficient operations and held that her discharge was improper.

Writing for the Court, Justice Marshall found that the statement addressed a matter of public concern and that the test outlined in *Pickering* and expanded in *Connick* applied. Weighing in favor of the government was the fact that the plaintiff made the statement at work in the government office. However, the plaintiff's statement did not disrupt the office's operation, it had not disturbed or interrupted other employees, and she did not bring disrepute onto the office because she spoke in the office and not in public, and nobody else heard the statement. Furthermore, Justice Marshall pointed out that the plaintiff had been fired because of the content of the speech and that her position in the office was not sufficiently high to subject the content of her speech to such scrutiny. He also explained that to uphold the plaintiff's discharge would unnecessarily burden other similarly situated employees by causing them to censor themselves because their boss could overhear them and deem them unworthy to serve in the office. Therefore, the Court found that the plaintiff's interest in speaking outweighed the government's interest in maintaining an efficiently operating agency. Justice Scalia, in a dissent joined by the Chief Justice, Justice White, and Justice O'Connor, wrote that the statement by the plaintiff was so close to words that receive no protection from the First Amendment that it should not enjoy protection in this context.

Hence, speech by public employees is substantially less protected than speech by private persons. The First Amendment does not protect such speech unless it is about a matter of public concern. Once the speech is found to be a matter of public concern, then the Court balances the employee's interest in speaking against the government's interest in efficient government operations. If the government's interest outweighs the employee's interest, the speech may be regulated.

H. Commercial Speech

Traditionally, the government was permitted to regulate commercial speech without regard to the First Amendment. Commercial speech was thus a completely unprotected category of speech. However, in the mid-1970s the Court began to extend the protections of the First Amendment to commercial speech. The level of protection afforded to commercial speech is less than that of the fully protected categories, thus commercial speech is a less protected category of speech. The analysis of protection of commercial speech first requires the court to determine whether the speech is commercial speech. Once the speech is found to fall in that category, the court must determine whether the speech is protected. For commercial speech to be regulated, the Court uses a four element test: (1) the speech must be about lawful activities and it must not be misleading, (2) the government interest must be substantial, (3) the law must advance the interest directly, and (4) the regulation must only be as extensive as necessary to achieve the interest.

1. What Is Commercial Speech?

The Court has developed a definition that, although appearing to be specific, fails to provide sufficient clarity to be a bright-line test. Its definitions are focused on speech that advertises. However, it has yet to fully consider what speech, other than advertisements, would or would not qualify as commercial speech. The current test consists of three elements: (1) the speech must be an advertisement, (2) the speech must refer to a specific product, and (3) there is an economic motive behind the speech.

When the Court indicated that the First Amendment protected commercial speech in *Virginia State Board of Pharmacy v. Virginia Citizens Consumer Council, Inc.* (1976), the Court defined commercial speech as speech that only proposes a commercial transaction. Unfortunately, this definition proved difficult to apply in practice because it was understood to mean advertisements, but there were advertisements, such as political campaign ads, that were clearly not commercial. The Court altered the definition of commercial speech in *Central Hudson Gas & Electric Corp. v. Public Service Commission of New York* (1980). In *Central Hudson*, the Court expanded commercial speech to include expression that solely concerns the economic interests of the speaker and its audience. However, this definition was more extensive than necessary because it could reach the content of publications or broadcastings, which, although being solely concerned with the economic interests of the speaker and the audience, would fall within the protections of the First Amendment.

The Court expressed the modern test for whether speech is commercial speech in *Bolger v. Youngs Drug Products Corp.* (1983). *Bolger* involved a condom manufacturing company that also published informational pamphlets about sexual topics. Some of the brochures dealt with condoms in general, and others addressed the specific products made by the company. The Court examined the pamphlets and determined that they constituted commercial speech. The Court explained that its previous tests were not sufficient, and it formulated the modern test. It said that just because the pamphlets were advertisements was not sufficient to find that the speech was commercial, thus it rejected *Virginia State Board of Pharmacy*. Further, the Court rejected *Central Hudson* and stated that because the pamphlets were produced under an economic motive would not suffice on its own. The Court concluded that the proper test was the combination of all of these characteristics. Thus, commercial speech is (1) advertisement, (2) referring to a specific product, (3) motivated by economics.

2. The Test for Regulation of Commercial Speech

As stated in the previous section, the Court began to lend some protection to commercial speech in its decision in *Virginia State Board of Pharmacy v. Virginia Citizens Consumer Council* (1976). A few years later, the Court announced the test that has survived until today. In *Central Hudson Gas & Electric Corp. v. Public Service Commission of New York* (1980), the Court's four-part test for regulating commercial speech requires: (1) the speech must not be misleading and must concern lawful activity, (2) the government must have a substantial interest in regulating the speech, (3) the regulation must directly advance the government interest, and (4) the regulation must be no more extensive than necessary to serve the government interest. Stated another way, the Court applies intermediate scrutiny to regulations of commercial speech regarding lawful activities that are not misleading. Although this test has generally survived, there is still some debate over the degree of deference to be accorded the government in determining its compliance with the last two elements of the test.

The debate has centered around whether the Court requires that the regulation be the least restrictive alternative in achieving the government interest. In addressing this question, the Court has not provided clear and consistent direction. However, as of today, it appears that although the Court does not require that the regulation be the least restrictive means of advancing the government interest, it must still be narrowly tailored to achieve that interest.

Board of Trustees of the State University of New York v. Fox (1989) involved a challenge to the state's regulation of commercial solicitations on college campuses. The majority rejected requiring the regulation be the least restrictive alternative. Rather, the Court interpreted the restrictions of the last two prongs of the test to require only that the regulation be narrowly tailored to achieve the government interest. Writing for the majority, Justice Scalia expressly drew a distinction between commercial speech and noncommercial speech. He stated that the former enjoys " 'a [more] limited measure of protection' " than noncommercial speech because it held a " 'subordinate position in the scale of First Amendment values.' "

The Court appeared to take a less deferential view of the extent to which the regulation advances the government interest and the breadth of the regulation in *Rubin v. Coors Brewing Co.* (1995). In *Rubin*, the Court required the regulation to directly and materially advance the asserted government interest. Writing for the Court, Justice Clarence Thomas further required the government to prove that the dangers that it asserts are posed by the commercial speech to be regulated are real and that the regulation " 'will in fact alleviate them to a material degree.' " This language is clearly inconsistent with the language in *Fox*. The Court continued to struggle with the formulation of the last two elements of the *Central Hudson* test over several years, producing two plurality opinions with diametrically opposed viewpoints on the question.

However, the Court appeared mostly to settle the issue in its recent decision in *Lorillard Tobacco Co. v. Reilly* (2001). *Lorillard Tobacco* involved a Massachusetts regulation on the advertising and sale of cigarettes, smokeless tobacco, and cigars. The regulations placed various restrictions on advertising and promotional materials placed outdoors and at the point of sale, product samples, cigar labels, and retail and mail order transactions for tobacco products. The Court expressly rejected the petitioners' request to jettison the *Central Hud-*

son test and replace it with a strict scrutiny test. Instead, it reaffirmed *Central Hudson* and explained that the First Amendment only requires that the regulation be narrowly tailored to achieve the government's objective. While the Court mustered a majority behind the *Central Hudson* test, four Justices dissented in part. This reveals that there is still some indecision in the application of the last two elements of the *Central Hudson* test. For now, the Court holds that the last two elements only require the regulation to be narrowly tailored to achieving the substantial government interest.

3. Application to Specific Situations

a. Commercial Speech about Illegal Activities or That Is Misleading or False

The Court has held that commercial speech about illegal activities, or that is misleading or false, is not protected by the First Amendment. The Court has only addressed the advertisement of illegal activity in *Pittsburgh Press Co. v. Pittsburgh Commission on Human Relations* (1973). There, the Court explained that commercial speech advertising illegal activity could be regulated without offending the Constitution. Note that this case was decided before the Court extended any protection to commercial speech and before the Court announced the *Central Hudson* test. However, because the *Central Hudson* test expressly excludes illegal speech from its reach, the Court's later decision clearly excluded this speech from the reach of First Amendment protection.

The same analysis holds for commercial speech that is deceptive or misleading. This is because such speech does not contribute to the public dialogue in any meaningful manner. Though the First Amendment protects false, deceptive, and misleading speech in the noncommercial context, as discussed in the section on defamation and other speech-related torts, it does not protect such speech in the commercial context.

b. Solicitation of Clients by Attorneys and Accountants

Though the Court initially held that attorney advertising could not be regulated, it has since held that attorneys may engage in truthful advertisement of their services so long as the advertisement is not deceptive, subject to regulation. It is permissible to regulate the in-person solicitation of potential clients by attorneys if motivated by profit. Yet lawyers may solicit potential clients where they will represent the client for free and may not be punished for doing so. In *Ohralik v. Ohio State Bar Association* (1978), the Court found that Ohio's punishment of an attorney for in-person solicitation of the victim of a car accident was permissible when the solicitation was in person and in the hospital. The Court reasoned that personal solicitation of legal services for profit inherently risked fraud, undue influence, or misrepresentation. On the same day that it decided *Ohralik,* the Court decided *In re Primus* (1978), where it found that the punishment of an attorney for in-person solicitation of a potential client violated the First Amendment because the lawyer offered to represent the person free of charge. Thus, in-person solicitations by attorneys are not protected when they are motivated by profit, but are protected when the representation will be for free.

The Court stopped this permissible regulation of attorney solicitation at the personal level. Any solicitation by targeted, direct mail is protected, whether the representation would be for free or was motivated by profit. In *Shapero v. Kentucky Bar Association* (1988), the Court invalidated a Kentucky law that prohibited such solicitation because the parties are at less of a risk of deceptive or unfair practices by the attorney because the solicitation was in writing and there would be a paper trail for a court to follow. Although it may not be prohibited, it may still be regulated. In *Florida Bar v. Went For It, Inc.* (1995), the Court upheld a Florida law prohibiting direct mail solicitations of potential personal injury or wrongful death clients within thirty days of the accident leading to the cause of action. The Court found that such direct solicitation was invasive and intended to preserve the public's confidence in the profession. The dissent disagreed, finding that such solicitation was not invasive and could harm the victims by delaying their ability to get representation. Therefore, attorneys may make direct mail solicitations of clients, but that may be regulated to some degree.

In contrast to the regulation of in-person solicitation of clients by attorneys where the solicitation was motivated by profit, the Court prevents such regulation of solicitation by accountants. In *Edenfield v. Fane* (1993), the Court held invalid a state law prohibiting certified public accountants from soliciting business in person. The Court distinguished *Ohralik,* finding that such solicitations by accountants did not pose the same dangers as in-person lawyer solicitations for profit. Thus, states may not regulate in-person solicitation of accounts like it can for lawyers.

c. Regulating the Trade Names of Businesses

The Court has found that the use of trade names by a business was not protected by the First Amendment. It considered the speech to be commercial speech "and nothing more." The Court found that a state law constitutional that prohibited optometrists from advertising or offering their services under a trade name in *Friedman v. Rogers* (1979). The Court justified this because it found that the use of trade names inherently risked deception. A bad optometrist could simply change the trade name under which he practiced, hiding his true identity. This would permit him to assume the identity of a good optometrist who retired or went out of business and then fool the public into thinking he was the good optometrist. Because the Court couched its decision in the inherent deceptiveness of trade names, it seems likely that other speech that is inherently deceptive can be regulated. One could even analogize this with the Court's decision to allow regulation of in-person attorney solicitations for money, just discussed, because the overreaching it feared would be a form of deception. Thus, governments have the ability to regulate trade names for businesses and, arguably, any other speech that inherently risks deceiving the public.

d. Regulation of Commercial Speech as a Means to Combat Other Problems

The Court generally prohibits states from limiting commercial speech where the laws were enacted under the theory that people will be better off without the information. This theory generally runs counter to the First Amendment value that people are better off when they have more information. However, the Court has upheld some restrictions on commercial speech that is truthful advertising of legal activities when the restrictions are aimed at addressing other problems.

One example of where the Court has upheld such restrictions on speech is where the speech would negatively impact traffic safety, but this is an unsettled field. An example of a case upholding this type of regulation was *Railway Express Agency v. New York* (1949). There, it upheld a city ordinance that banned advertisements on trucks where the advertisement was not related to the usual business of the truck owner. The Court applied what was later called rational basis scrutiny and found that the city may have determined that those who advertise their own business on their own trucks do not pose the same traffic problems as those whose trucks contain the advertisements of others.

More than thirty years later, the Court upheld a city ordinance banning all outdoor advertisements in *Metromedia, Inc. v. City of San Diego* (1981), to the extent that it only applied to commercial advertisements. Noncommercial advertisements, such as by candidates for political office, could not be banned. The Court explained that the restriction on commercial speech was permissible because it was a less protected category of speech and the city could regulate it to combat traffic problems, but that the city could not regulate other, protected speech even to deal with traffic issues.

However, the Court reached the exact opposite conclusion in an earlier case, *Lehman v. City of Shaker Heights* (1974), where it permitted restrictions on advertisements for political candidates but did not permit restrictions on commercial advertising. The confusion is further shown by the Court's invalidation of a city ordinance prohibiting the distribution of commercial newspapers on newsracks but permitting the sale of noncommercial papers on the same newsracks in *City of Cincinnati v. Discovery Network, Inc.*(1993). The Court explained that because the law was a content-based distinction that was unrelated to the asserted other purpose, it was unconstitutional. Because it is very difficult to reconcile *Discovery Network, Metromedia, Lehman,* and *Railway Express,* the Court has provided very little direction in this vein.

The Court has also generally limited the ability of the government to regulate certain activities or products with the goal of reducing participation in the activities or consumption of the products. The Court addressed this question regarding alcohol at the federal level in *Rubin v. Coors Brewing Co.* (1995) and at the state level in *44 Liquormart, Inc. v. Rhode Island* (1996). In both cases, the law ran afoul of the *Central Hudson* requirement that the regulation be narrowly tailored. Similarly, the Court struck down a state regulation of tobacco advertising in *Lorillard Tobacco Co. v. Reilly* (2001) because it also failed the narrow tailoring requirement of the *Central Hudson* test.

However, the Court has permitted states to regulate gambling advertisements to reduce gambling in the state. In *Posadas de Puerto Rico Associates v. Tourism Company of Puerto Rico* (1986), the Court upheld a law prohibiting casino advertisements. The Court explained that the regulation was a valid exercise of the state's police power to protect the health, safety, and welfare of its citizens. It also found that the law was narrowly tailored to achieve the ends. The Court extended these findings in the context of a law banning advertisements for lotteries. In *United States v. Edge Broadcasting Co.* (1993), a federal law prohibited the advertisement of one state's lottery by a station located in another state that did not have a lottery. The Court followed *Posadas* and upheld the law because of the government's interest in discouraging gambling and the law advanced the policies of states that chose not to have lotteries. However, such regulations must still be narrowly tailored to advance the asserted state interest. In *Greater New Orleans Broadcasting Association, Inc. v. United States* (1999), the Court struck down a federal law banning advertising by casinos because it was not narrowly tailored to achieve the goal of reducing gambling because of the many exceptions permitting advertisements by casinos on Native American reservations.

The Court has also clearly held that the government may not restrict advertising of abortion services or of contraceptives. The Court has held that such advertising is strictly within the protection of the First Amendment and that prohibiting such advertisements because they may offend or embarrass others, as claimed in *Carey v. Population Services International* (1977), was not permitted. Similarly, the Court has long held that truthful advertisements by lawyers that are not deceptive are protected by the First Amendment. Although direct, in-person solicitations may be banned when motivated by profit, as discussed, truthful advertising by lawyers may not be banned and the content may not be regulated as long as it is not deceptive. For example, in *Zauderer v. Office of Disciplinary Counsel of the Supreme Court of Ohio* (1985), the Court held that such advertisements are protected by the First Amendment as long as they are not deceptive. The attorney had been disciplined because his advertisement contained information about a specific legal problem, it included an illustration, and the advertisement was deceptive. The Court struck down the first two bases for the discipline but upheld the third.

Similarly, the Court has held that signs advertising property for sale may not be proscribed by the government. In *Linmark Associates, Inc. v. Township of Willingboro* (1971), the Court addressed an ordinance banning the display of "for sale" or "sold" signs to deter white flight. White flight is a phenomenon where the vast majority of the white people living in an area move out of the area in close temporal proximity to each other. The Court accepted as valid the ordinance's goal of preventing white flight from a racially integrated community. However, it held that the government could not achieve that goal by "restricting the free flow of truthful information." The Court unanimously held that such restrictions based on the theory that people are better off with less information were invalid and violated the First Amendment.

Stop Points

- **Unprotected and Less Protected Speech**
  - Advocacy of Illegal Action
  - Fighting Words and the Hostile Audience
  - Hate Speech
  - Sexually Oriented Speech
    - The Court has created three categories of sexually oriented speech: (1) obscenity; (2) child pornography; and (3) profanity and indecency.
    - Obscenity and child pornography are unprotected speech and laws prohibiting them need only pass the rational basis test.
      - Under *Miller*, material is obscene if:
        - (1) the average person would find that the work appeared to the prurient interests when viewing the work as a whole and applying contemporary community standards;

- (2) the work describes or depicts sexual conduct defined by the applicable law in a patently offensive way; and

- (3) as a whole, the work lacks serious literary, political, scientific, or artistic value.

- Under *Miller*, no one has a constitutionally protected right to produce, distribute, or sell obscene materials.

- However, under *Reidel*, one has a constitutionally protected right to possess obscene materials.

- Under *Ferber*, the government may regulate or proscribe child pornography without applying the *Miller* test when the material depicts minors in sexual acts and actual minors were used.

- However, under *Ashcroft v. Free Speech Coalition*, where the material purports to depict children engaging in sexual acts, but no actual children were used, the *Miller* standard applies.

- Profane and indecent speech are protected by the First Amendment, thus laws punishing this speech must pass strict scrutiny.

- However, the Court has identified limited exceptions to this protection for such speech in schools and on the broadcast media.

- But the Court has refused to extend those exceptions to First Amendment protections to telephones, cable television, and the Internet, thus they are protected under the First Amendment.

- Defamation

  - The First Amendment requires that a public official or a public figure cannot recover for defamation without proving that the publication was made with actual malice, defined as knowing that the publication was false or acting with reckless disregard of its falsity.

  - A public official is a public employee who controls, or is perceived to control, the conduct of governmental affairs.

  - There are two kinds of public figures:

    - A person who, by virtue of her position, generates public interest in her, is a public figure for all purposes and in all contexts; and

    - A person who injects himself in the forefront of a public controversy becomes a public figure for the limited purposes of that controversy and related issues.

  - A private person still enjoys protection from defamation under the traditional definition, except that states cannot permit a private person to recover on a strict liability theory.

  - Further, a private person may not recover presumed or punitive damages without meeting the amplified actual malice standard.

- Speech-Related Torts Other Than Defamation

- The *New York Times* standard applies to the ability of public figures and public officials to recover for intentional infliction of emotional distress and for false light invasion of privacy.

- The First Amendment prevents recovery for publication of true information that is private, once that information is released to the public, such as through publication in court documents.

- Speech by Public Employees

  - The government can prohibit participation in political activities by government employees.

  - The government may prohibit its employees from speaking on matters of public concern if its interest in efficient operations outweighs the employee's interest in such speech.

- Commercial Speech

  - Commercial speech is (1) an advertisement; (2) that refers to a specific product; and (3) is motivated by economic motives.

  - The First Amendment protects commercial speech, but it protects it less than noncommercial speech.

  - The Court applies a four-part test to determine the validity of regulations of commercial speech. This test requires: (1) a substantial interest in regulating the speech; (2) the regulation must directly advance the interest; (3) the regulation must be no more extensive than necessary to serve the interest; and (4) the speech must not be misleading and must concern lawful activity.

  - The last two prongs of the test are understood only to require that the regulation be narrowly tailored, not the least restrictive means, to achieve the government interest.

  - The First Amendment does not protect commercial speech that is misleading, deceptive, or false or concerns illegal activities. Thus, a regulation of such speech need only pass rational basis scrutiny.

  - Attorneys may engage in truthful advertisement of their services as long as the advertisement is not deceptive, subject to regulation.

    - Any solicitation by targeted, direct mail is protected, but may be regulated to some degree.

    - In-person solicitations by attorneys are not protected when they are motivated by profit, but are protected when the representation will be for free.

  - The use of trade names by a business is not protected by the First Amendment.

  - States generally cannot limit commercial speech where the laws were enacted under the theory that people will be better off without the information.

- However, the Court has upheld some restrictions on commercial speech that is truthful advertising of legal activities when the restrictions are aimed at addressing other problems, like traffic safety.

- The Court has struck down regulations of certain activities or products with the goal of reducing participation in the activities or consumption of the products.

  - But the Court has permitted states to regulate gambling advertisements to reduce gambling in the state.

IV. In Which Locations Does Free Speech Apply?

The First Amendment is not only implicated when the government interferes with free speech because of its content. It also applies to protect when and where speech may occur because there can be no speech without a place to speak or a medium through which to speak. Generally, these issues arise when people try to use public property for their speech. However, they also arise when people try to speak on private property that they do not own. The typical use of property for speech, whether the property is public or private, involves an attempt to stage a rally in a public place to generate or to show substantial support for a certain position, or to distribute or post fliers, pamphlets, or other publications. This section examines the Court's decisions regarding the places where speech occurs. It covers speech on public property, private property, and finally speech restricted environments, which are certain environments the Court finds to be substantially less protected by the First Amendment, such as schools or the military.

A. Government Properties

Initially, the Court rejected that the public had any right to speak on public property. It refused to recognize that there was any difference between speech on public property and speech on private property. In the early cases involving speech on public property, the Court held that the government can control speech on public property just as strictly as a private person may control speech on his or her property. In *Davis v. Massachusetts* (1897), the Court upheld the conviction of a minister for preaching in Boston Common without a license. In so holding, the Court expressly stated that the government has the power to control the manner in which the public may utilize public property and analogized the government's power to that of the owner of a private residence. To the *Davis* court, this power was inherent in the government's role as the representative of the public, and it could not logically be limited unless it interfered with proprietary rights.

This attitude persevered until 1939 when the Court began to recognize that the public had the right to speak on at least some public property that had been traditionally opened for and used by the public for the exchange of ideas. This revolution in thought began with *Hague v. Committee for Industrial Organization* (1939), when the Court found a Jersey City, New Jersey, ordinance facially invalid. The ordinance prohibited all public meetings in the streets and other public places unless a prior permit had been obtained. In his plurality opinion, Justice Owen Roberts wrote that regardless of the ownership of streets and public parks, they have, since time immemorial, "been held in trust for the use of the public and, time out of mind, have been used for purposes of assembly, communicating thoughts between citizens, and discussing public questions."

The revolution in the Court's jurisprudence continued in *Schneider v. New Jersey* (1939). In that consolidated case, a majority of the Court invalidated city ordinances from different states that prohibited the distribution of pamphlets by individuals on public property. The cities attempted to validate their ordinances as valid exercises of the police power because they were motivated by prevention of littering in the streets and that permitting such distribution of pamphlets would encourage littering. Justice Roberts, writing for the majority, rejected this argument. He explained that the government may regulate the use of the streets to protect the health, safety, and welfare of the public as long as it does not infringe with the right of free speech or other fundamental liberty interests. He contrasted the ordinance with other methods of controlling the public's use of the streets such as blocking traffic on the streets or prohibiting the act of littering by explaining that such regulations would not necessarily have any relationship to the freedom to write, speak, or distribute information. To hold otherwise would be to permit the police to determine what ideas may be expressed and what ideas may not be expressed. However, Justice Roberts was very careful to state that the holding in *Schneider* did not extend to commercial solicitations or canvassing, which could be regulated by the state as necessary, even under the ordinances at issue in the case.

The Court's decision in *Hague* began the legal recognition of the concept of a public forum. A public forum is a public place that has either traditionally been open to the public to use for speech or a place that is specifically designated by the government as being open for the public to use for speech.

The Court expressly articulated the concept of a public forum and provided three categories of public spaces—public forums, limited public forums, and nonpublic forums—in *Perry Education Association v. Perry Local Educators' Association* (1983). There, the Court described the streets and parks as "quintessential public forums" because they have "by long tradition or by government fiat ... been devoted to assembly and debate." These public spaces enjoy the greatest free speech protection. The Court then explained that places that the government has "voluntarily opened" for the public to use for communication also receives substantial protection, but they are more limited because the government may close down these limited public forums. Finally, the Court described those places that are not traditionally considered public forums, nor does the government open them for purposes of communication. In these nonpublic forums, the government is free to reserve the space for its intended use and may more readily restrict the speech that occurs there. The constitutionality of a speech regulation on public property depends on the characterization of the public space. Thus, whether a public place is a public forum, a limited public forum, or a nonpublic forum is the threshold question in analyzing restrictions of speech in public spaces, and that determination may be determinative of the regulation's constitutionality.

1. Public Forums

Under *Perry Education Association*, the Court recognized that the public's interest in speaking in public forums is very strong. The public forums are those public places that have been traditionally devoted to speech and assembly or have been so designated by government fiat. Sidewalks and parks are the archetypical public forums. In public forums, the government's ability to regulate speech is sharply curtailed by the First Amendment.

The *Perry Education Association* court expressly stated that the government cannot prohibit all expressive activity in public forums. To determine the constitutionality of a regulation of speech in a public forum, the law must be either a reasonable content-neutral time, place, and manner restriction, or it must pass strict scrutiny. If the restriction is a content-neutral time, place, and manner restriction, it must also serve an important government interest and leave adequate alternative venues for the speech. Finally, the restriction must be narrowly tailored to achieve the government interest, but it need not be the least restrictive alternative.

a. Content-Neutral Speech

To be content-neutral, the regulation must not regulate either the viewpoint of the speech or the subject matter of the speech. As an example, *Boos v. Berry* (1988), discussed elsewhere, the Court invalidated a city ordinance prohibiting signs critical of a foreign government to be displayed within 500 feet of that government's embassy. The Court held that the regulation targeted political speech on sidewalks, traditionally recognized as public forums. However, the Court upheld another aspect of the ordinance that permitted the police to disperse crowds within 500 feet of the embassy of a foreign government if the crowd threatened the peace or public safety. This latter aspect of the ordinance was sustained because it was a valid exercise of the police power that applied regardless of the subject matter or the viewpoint expressed in the speech.

Regulations of demonstrations provide difficult questions and can lead to different results on apparently similar facts. Contrast *Carey v. Brown* (1980) with *Hill v. Colorado* (2000). In *Carey*, the Court invalidated a state statute prohibiting people from picketing or demonstrating around an individual's residence unless the residence was used either as a place of business or as a place of employment and was involved in a labor dispute. The Court found that the statute was not content-neutral because it treated certain views on a certain subject differently than others. However, the Court took a different view of demonstrations and protests outside an abortion clinic. In *Hill*, the Court sustained the regulation of protests within 100 feet of any health care facility, finding that the regulation was content-neutral. The regulation prohibited any person from knowingly approaching within eight feet of another person, without that person's consent, for the purpose of passing literature, showing a sign, or orally protesting, educating, or counseling the other person. The Court explained that the law was content-neutral because it applied regardless of the subject matter of the speech or the viewpoint it expressed. The dissent argued that the law was clearly content-based because it had the purpose of curtailing a specific message. One could reconcile *Carey* and *Hill* by noting that the Court appeared to focus on whether the law could be justified on some content-neutral grounds, regardless of the intent and effect of the law.

b. Time, Place, and Manner Restrictions

The Court has long held that the government has the power to regulate the time, place, and manner in which the public may use a public forum to speak. This is a crucial aspect to the police power because it helps the government ensure that the public's use of the space for nonspeech purposes, such as transportation in the case of the streets, is not hampered by the speech that occurs there. Furthermore, it helps the government regulate the use and availability of scarce public resources. However, the regulation must be content-neutral, and it must be reasonable. If the regulation is content-based or is an unreasonable restriction, then the regulation must pass strict scrutiny; otherwise, it is invalid.

In *Cox v. New Hampshire* (1941), the Court addressed a state statute that forbade unlicensed parades, processions, and other public performances on a public street. The statute set out the requirements for licensure in the margin of the statutory text. Sixty-eight people were arrested for violation of the statute. They along with twenty others had met, divided into groups, and marched on the sidewalk, each carrying a staff with a religious message written on it, and some carrying placards with another religious message. The marchers also passed out religious leaflets. On review, the Court found that the statute was a content-neutral and reasonable time, place, and manner restriction. The Court explained that the licensing provision was not a prior restraint on speech because of the limiting guidelines the statute provided. It also explained that requiring the permit enabled the authorities to have sufficient prior notice of the event "to prevent confusion by overlapping parades or processions, to secure convenient use of the streets by other travelers, and to minimize the risk of disorder." Because the statute was not discriminatory and was not applied as such, and it was a reasonable restriction on the time, place, and manner of the use of the public streets, the Court found the statute to be constitutional.

In *Heffron v. International Society for Krishna Consciousness, Inc.* (1981), the Court upheld a state regulation restricting to designated areas any group distributing literature, selling materials, and soliciting donations at a state fair. This rule applied to all groups — nonprofits, charitable organizations, and commercial vendors — equally. Although the representatives of a group could walk around the fairgrounds and communicate orally with the patrons, distribution and sales could only occur at a booth leased from the fair. The booths were leased on a first-come, first-served basis and in a nondiscriminatory fashion. The state fair in question was located on a 125-acre tract of public property. In the preceding five years, the twelve-day fair had attracted an average of 115,000 people on weekdays and 160,000 people on weekends. The Court found the regulation to be a valid time, place, and manner restriction. Justice White explained that the regulation did not discriminate based on the content of the speech. Furthermore, it did not prohibit speech, only where and how it could occur at a certain time. Finally, the regulation was directed at an important government interest: protecting public safety and ensuring orderly conduct at the fair. Justice White emphasized that the restriction need not be the most reasonable restriction to achieve the interest, it must merely be a reasonable restriction.

In contrast, consider *Police Department of Chicago v. Mosley* (1972). There, the Court addressed the constitutionality of a Chicago ordinance prohibiting disorderly conduct. The statute expressly defined disorderly conduct to include "picket[ing] or demonstrat[ing] on a public way within 150 feet of any ... school" during school hours. However, the statute expressly excluded "peaceful picketing of any school involved in a labor dispute." The respondent, a frequent picketer of a Chicago high school because it practiced racial discrimination, challenged the ordinance as violating his right to picket the school. The Court found the statute unconstitutional because it provided for different treatment of speech based on the content of that speech. Picketing in a labor dispute with the school was permissible, but no other picketing or demonstrating was. The Court explained that this violated the Equal Protection Clause of the Fourteenth Amendment as well as the First Amendment. Justice Marshall explained that the ordinance designated certain speech as impermissible by its content, not by how, when, or where the speech occurred, which "is never permitted." That the ordinance permitted peaceful labor picketing did not save the ordinance as an attempt to prevent disturbing school activities because it did not permit all peaceful picketing, only peaceful picketing on a certain subject. Therefore, the Court found the ordinance to be unconstitutional.

The time, place, and manner restriction must also serve an important government interest. Such interests include maintaining good public order, preventing public disturbances, and maintaining good order and discipline in schools. In *Heffron*, the Court upheld the prohibition of distributing literature or soliciting money at a state fair, except in a booth, to control foot traffic and ensure public safety. Similarly, the use of loudspeakers on trucks or other devices to amplify sound could be controlled to prevent disturbing the public. The Court has also permitted the regulation of speech outside a school during school hours to preserve from disruption the "peace or good order" of a school. All of these restrictions were valid time, place, and manner restrictions because they did not ban all such speech, they did not permit some speech but forbid other speech based on content, and they were intended to achieve an important government interest.

Thus, the test for a valid time, place, and manner restriction is threefold. First, it must be content-neutral, both on the subject matter and the viewpoint. Second, the regulation must reasonably restrict the time speech can occur, where it can occur, and how the speech can be made. This kind of restriction can also protect licensing schemes, as shown by *Cox*. Finally, the restriction must serve an important government purpose.

2. Limited Public Forums

The Court has also determined that speech on public property that is not a traditional public forum is protected by the First Amendment. According to the Court in *Perry Education Association*, a limited public forum is a place that the government has opened to the public to use for expressive activities. The distinguishing factor between a limited public forum and a traditional public forum is that because the government opened the limited public forum to the public to use for speech, it can close that access at any time. However, that factor is relevant only to the fact that a limited public forum can be closed to the public's speech, whereas a traditional public forum cannot be so closed. During the time the limited public forum is open for the public to use for speech, the Court has held that that speech enjoys the same protection as that made in traditional public forums. In *Good News Club v. Milford Central School* (2001), Justice Thomas explained that although the government may limit the speech that can be made in a limited public forum, it cannot discriminate based on the viewpoint of the speech, and that the restriction must be reasonable when considering the purpose for which the forum is used. Thus, the crucial inquiry is whether the public property is a limited public forum.

Unlike traditional public forums, limited public forums must be opened by the government to the public for purposes of speech. As such, they can and do take many different forms. Public schools and universities who open their property for use by students have been held to be limited public forums. Clearly, public schools and universities are not traditional public forums, but once opened for speech, they become limited public forums. More difficult questions are government spaces that are opened to the public, even if not expressly for speech, such as an airport.

In *International Society for Krishna Consciousness, Inc. v. Lee* (1992), the Court addressed just this situation. The case involved a regulation adopted by the Port Authority that prohibited the "repetitive solicitation of money" as well as the distribution of literature. The regulation only governed speech inside the airport terminals and was inapplicable to the sidewalks outside the terminal buildings themselves. The parties did not dispute that the solicitation at issue in the case was speech protected by the First Amendment. The question was the character of the airport terminals—were they public forums or not? The Court held that they were not public forums. Writing for the majority, Chief Justice Rehnquist began his analysis by recognizing that the public streets and parks are traditional public forums because they have been made available for speech since time immemorial. He clarified that statement by describing the traditional public forum as one that has the free exchange of ideas as a principal purpose of the space.

Chief Justice Rehnquist then explored the limited public forum concept. The government must affirmatively act to create a limited public forum. Government inaction by failing to proscribe or restrain speech cannot cause a nonpublic forum to become a public forum. Similarly, by permitting people to visit or use freely a place owned or operated by the government is not sufficient to promote it to the status of a public forum. Rather, the government must "intentionally open a nontraditional forum for public discourse." He also found that the location of property is relevant to the public forum inquiry because the separation of property from "acknowledged public areas" may indicate that the separated property is "a special enclave" and speech there enjoys less protection.

Applying these distinctions, the Court explained that airport terminals are not public forums or limited public forums. Airport terminals are not traditional public forums because they have only recently become places where great numbers of people come; thus, even if they have been held out for speech, they have not been so held out for a sufficiently long time. Further, it is only within the recent history of airports that they have been used by religious and other nonprofit groups to distribute literature, solicit funds, recruit members, and similar activities. Similarly, airport terminals are not limited public forums. The government has not opened them to public access to use for speech purposes. Rather, they are opened for use as transport hubs. Furthermore, the fact that the government has not objected to the use of these airport terminals by religious and other nonprofit groups for speech purposes does not create a limited public forum. Therefore, the Court found that airport terminals are not public forums, either traditional or limited. Accordingly, the Court upheld the ban on solicitation activity in airport terminals. However, the Court overturned the ban on distribution of literature, finding that the ban was not a reasonable restriction on speech in the nonpublic forum.

3. Nonpublic Forums

Unlike public forums and limited public forums, the nonpublic forum receives substantially less protection. As explained in *Perry Education Association*, a nonpublic forum is public property that is neither a public forum nor a limited public forum. Under the test in *International Society for Krishna Consciousness*, a nonpublic forum is a space that is not:

1. traditionally available to the public to use for speech, or
2. opened by the government for the public to use for communication.

Thus, if the space is not traditionally open for speech, and the government did not expressly open access to the space for speech, it is a nonpublic forum and speech receives a lesser degree of protection in the forum. However, the restrictions must generally still be reasonable and nondiscriminatory to be valid.

Presented in the immediately preceding subsection on limited public forums, the Court held in *International Society* that airport terminals were nonpublic forums. The reduced protection of speech in the nonpublic forum thus permitted the airport to prohibit solicitation of airport patrons as a reasonable restriction on speech there. However, the Court refused to permit the airport to prohibit distribution of literature by the same group. The *International Society* court based its holding on several precedents finding several other places to be nonpublic forums, including advertisement space on buses and military bases.

In *Lehman v. City of Shaker Heights* (1974), the court found a "car card space" on a public transportation bus to be a nonpublic forum because it was not an area traditionally held out to the public for communication. It distinguished the car card space from traditional public forums such as "open spaces, ... meeting hall[s], park[s], [and] street corner[s]." The Court analogized advertisement in the car card space to advertisements in newspapers, explaining that such advertisement was not the primary purpose of either venture, and thus, both ventures could exercise discretion in what advertisements they selected. Therefore, the car card space on the public transportation bus was not a public forum.

The Court determined that military bases were not public forums in *Greer v. Spock*, (1976). At the time, Fort Dix permitted the public access to nonrestricted areas of the military installation but prohibited them from certain forms of expression, including demonstrations, political speech, and protest marches. The Court explained that the primary purpose of the military installation was to provide for the training of soldiers, not to provide a public forum for communicative purposes. The Court explained that a the commanding officer of a military installation has had the "historically unquestioned power ... summarily to exclude civilians from the area of his command." Thus, the military installation has not traditionally been held out for the public's use in communication, and the installation in this case was not opened to the public for the purpose of communication. Therefore, the military base was a nonpublic forum, and the speech restriction was upheld.

The Court upheld the ability for a state to restrict the use of its property and prohibit its use for communication by the public in *Adderley v. Florida* (1966). There, civil rights demonstrators had been convicted for holding a rally outside a jail and failing to disperse at the order of the police. As long as it did not act in a discriminatory manner, the divided Court found that the state could exclude the public from using its property to communicate. Four dissenters explained that a jail is a seat of government, like an "executive mansion, a legislative chamber, [or] a courthouse," and when the public feels that a prisoner is being unjustly held the public should be permitted to demonstrate to that effect outside the jail.

4. Private Property

All of the foregoing discussion about public forums, limited public forums, and nonpublic forums applies only to property owned by the government; there is no right to use private property for speech. This is because most protections of the Constitution, including free speech, require state action. When an individual person acts of his or her own accord, there is no state action because such action is definitionally not action by the government. Thus, the owner of private property can restrict the speech of others while they are on that owner's property without running afoul of the Constitution.

However, in the past, the Court had found that some types of property that, although private, were open to the general public and to which the Constitution's protections of speech extended. The Court held in *Marsh v. Alabama* (1946) that a company-owned town could not constitutionally prevent Jehovah's Witnesses from distributing literature within its borders. The Court found that although the town was owned by a company and was private property, the company essentially acted as a government in running the town. The company had assumed the duties and functions of a government in its management of the town and therefore was a *de facto* government. Thus, the company's actions represented state action, and it was restrained by the First Amendment. Following this decision, the Court analogized a shopping mall to the company town in *Marsh* and found in *Amalgamated Food Employees Union Local 590 v. Logan Valley Plaza, Inc.* (1968) that the Constitution's speech protections extended to a labor dispute on the mall's property. The Court essentially considered the shopping mall, an important place where a substantial amount of the public gathered to conduct commerce, to be a microcosm of the town in *Marsh*.

However, the Court has retreated from this position; today, there is no constitutionally protected right to use others' private property for speech. It began the retreat in *Hudgens v. National Labor Relations Board* (1976), when it examined a prior decision that permitted a shopping mall to exclude speakers based on content and found that that was a content-based distinction that was not supportable under the First Amendment. Finding that it could not square that decision with *Logan Valley*, the Court reversed its position and held that the First Amendment does not apply to privately owned shopping malls. The Court later created an exception for state constitutions in *PruneYard Shopping Center v. Robins* (1980). In *PruneYard*, the Court held that a state could create a right to speak in public places that was protected by the state constitution without violating the rights of the property owner under the federal Constitution. Specifically, the plaintiff contended that such a right created under a state constitution violated the plaintiff's rights under the First Amendment and also constituted a taking under the Fifth Amendment that required just compensation. The Court emphatically disagreed. Therefore, today, there is no right to speak on private property that is protected by the federal Constitution, though any state is free to create such a right protected by its constitution.

5. *Restricted Environments*

The relevance of where the speaker speaks or wishes to speak extends to other contexts as well. There are some places that the government controls to which the Court has nevertheless granted great deference to the regulation of speech. These places include schools, prisons, and the military. Although each of these environments has unique characteristics that differentiate them, they share some similarities that have led the Court to treat them similarly. Because these environments are places (1) where people are often involuntarily present, and (2) that are generally authoritarian environments out of necessity, the Court tends to accord great deference to regulation of speech and expressive activities in them. However, the restrictions still must be appropriate and the deference must not be too extreme.

a. Speech in Public Schools

Public schools are the least restrictive of these three settings, and many argue that restriction of speech in the school is antithetical to the school's purpose of education. Two main issues arise under the First Amendment in the context of public schools. First is the question of the freedom of students to express their thoughts and ideas. Second, the school's ability to control student access to "objectionable" materials is at issue.

Concerning student speech, the Court has recognized that there is some need for order and discipline in the school setting. As a result, the Court generally defers to the school's determination of what speech is permissible and what would tend to disrupt the order and discipline necessary to further the educational objectives of the school. Early Court decisions were strongly protective of the right of students to speak while in school. In *West Virginia State Board of Education v. Barnette* (1943), students refused to salute the flag at the beginning of the school day. Though it rested its argument primarily on the Religion Clauses of the First Amendment, the Court found that saluting the flag was a form of speech, and it upheld the right of students not to be forced to speak in school. Furthermore, in *Tinker v. Des Moines Independent Community School District* (1969), the Court upheld the right of students to protest the Vietnam War by wearing black armbands. Writing for the Court, Justice Abe Fortas made the famous statement that "neither students [n]or teachers shed their constitutional rights to freedom of speech or expression at the schoolhouse gate." To hold otherwise would be to turn public schools into "enclaves of totalitarianism." Because the wearing of the armbands was a silent protest, it did not disrupt the school's educational efforts. Thus, the Court held that speech was protected by the First Amendment unless it would "materially and sub-stantially interfere with the requirements of appropriate discipline in the op-eration of the school." *Tinker* was decided in the context of a public secondary school, and the Court extended *Tinker* to postsecondary colleges and univer-sities in *Papish v. Board of Curators of the University of Missouri* (1973). In *Pa-pish*, the Court overturned the expulsion of a student for publishing a political cartoon in a school newspaper.

However, in recent years, the Court has evinced a greater trend of deferring to school authorities. Hence, it has become far less protective of the rights of students to speak in the school environment. For example, in *Bethel School District No. 403 v. Fraser* (1986), a student was punished for nominating another student for a position in the student government in a speech filled with sexual innuendo that was delivered at a school assembly. The Court upheld the pun-ishment. Chief Justice Burger, writing for the Court, emphasized the need for deference toward the judgment of school officials. Further, he distinguished *Tinker* because *Tinker* involved curtailment of political expression, whereas the student's speech in *Fraser* did not. The Court extended its deferential treat-ment of the determinations of school officials in *Hazelwood School District v. Kuhlmeier* (1988). In *Hazelwood*, a school journalism class published a news-paper that was to include articles about three students' experiences with preg-nancy and the effect of divorce on students but would preserve the students' anonymity by withholding their names. The newspaper's faculty advisor and the class's teacher allowed the stories to be included in the draft sent to the principal. The principal deleted the stories and published the remainder of the newspaper. The Court upheld the principal's decision, rejecting the students' challenge under the First Amendment. Writing for the Court, Justice White quoted *Fraser* to explain that the "First Amendment rights of students in the pub-lic schools 'are not automatically coextensive with the rights of adults in other settings.'" He emphasized that the school newspaper was a nonpublic forum pro-duced as part of the curriculum of the journalism class and that schools have the power to control the curriculum of their classes. Thus, the principal had acted within his authority and the Court upheld the principal's decision.

Concerning the ability of the school to control student access to "objec-tionable" materials, the Court has held that the First Amendment protects the right to receive information as well as the right to express it. In *Board of Edu-cation, Island Trees Union Free School District No. 26 v. Pico* (1982), the Court addressed the ability of a school library to remove "objectionable" books from its collection. The Court explained that such action by the school authorities directly implicated the First Amendment rights of the students to receive in-formation. Additionally, the unique characteristics of a school library—that it is part of a scholastic institution and is designed to provide student access to materials — make the First Amendment's protections especially applicable. However, if the school library can show a reason for removing or not purchasing certain materials that is not based on content, such as budgetary concerns or that the books were damaged and unreadable, then the library would not violate the First Amendment.

b. Prisons

The need for order and discipline in a prison is substantially greater than that in the public schools. As a result, the Court has held that the First Amendment does not protect speech by prisoners that is inconsistent with status as a prisoner or would interfere with the legitimate penological interests of the prison system. The Court generally defers to the regulation of prisoners' speech by the government by application of an analogue of the rational basis test. If the regulation is rationally related to the achievement of a legitimate penological interest, then the regulation will be upheld. As a result of the high deference this test provides, most restrictions of inmate speech are upheld. This deference has also generally extended to restrictions of access to prisoners by members of the press for interviews or to observe conditions in the prison and to receipt of hardback books by prisoners not sent by bookstores or publishers out of concern that they could contain contraband.

In one instance, the Court has overturned a regulation on the content of mail sent by prisoners to recipients outside the prison. In *Procunier v. Martinez* (1974), a prison prohibited inmates from mailing letters that either would "magnify grievances" or were "lewd, obscene, defamatory; ... or otherwise inappropriate." The Court explained that this regulation was not rationally related to a legitimate penological interest because it was unrelated to maintaining order and discipline within the prison itself. The prison did not have a legitimate interest in preventing prisoners from airing their grievances to noninmates or in censoring what prisoners wrote to those outside the prison. However, later decisions have called this holding into question, and it is doubtful whether the decision in *Procunier* is still good law. For example, in *Turner v. Safley*, (1987), the Court upheld a prison regulation restricting the ability of those in one facility to write to prisoners in another facility. The Court agreed that such correspondence could lead to comparisons between the two facilities that could cause dissatisfaction with a facility and cause unrest in the prison. Thus, the Court generally exhibits a high degree of deference to regulations of the speech of inmates in a prison facility.

c. The Military

The deference accorded to the military in regulating the speech of service members generally has exceeded even that of the deference accorded to prisoners. For example, in *Parker v. Levy* (1974), the Court upheld the conviction of an officer by a general court-martial for making statements to enlisted personnel that were critical of the Vietnam War. Furthermore, the officer had stated that black soldiers should refuse deployment in Vietnam because they were being used for the most hazardous duty in the conflict. In upholding the conviction, Justice Rehnquist explained that the military establishment "is, by necessity, a specialized society separate from civilian society." Thus, although service members are not barred from receiving the protections of the First Amendment, those protections must be applied differently because of the special nature of the military community and its mission. Justice Douglas dissented from the decision in *Parker*, explaining that the officer's words and actions expressed his own deeply held personal beliefs and was not an attempt at subversion. As such, Justice Douglas argued that his expression should have been protected under the First Amendment.

This extreme deference to the military in regulating the speech of service members has led to restrictions being imposed on the military that the Court would not sanction in most other contexts. These include political speech, actions intended as communication, and possession of child pornography, which are found to be prejudicial to good order and discipline. For example, in *Brown v. Glines* (1980), the Court upheld an Air Force regulation that prohibited the posting or distribution of printed materials on an Air Force base without the prior permission of the commanding officer. The Court upheld this prior restraint on publication because the base commander is charged with maintaining the essential military characteristics of "morale, discipline, and readiness, he must have authority over the distribution of materials that could affect adversely" those characteristics. Therefore, the speech of military service members is subject to substantial regulation to which the Court grants greater deference than in virtually any other context.

Stop Points

- **Impact of Location on Freedom of Speech**
  - Public Forum, Limited Public Forum and Nonpublic Forum
    - A regulation of speech in a public forum must be: (1) a reasonable. (2) content-neutral. (3) restriction on the time, place, or manner of speech, (4) that achieves an important government purpose.

- A limited public forum is a public space opened by the government specifically to be used for speech.

- A limited public forum is not created simply by opening a public space for use by the public; it must be opened specifically for speech.

- Additionally, the failure of the government to prevent speech in a public space does not create a limited public forum because the creation of a limited public forum requires the government affirmatively to open the public space for speech.

- Regulations of speech in limited public forums must meet the same test as regulations of speech in traditional public forums.

- A nonpublic forum is government property that is neither a public forum nor a limited public forum.

- The government may place reasonable and nondiscriminatory restrictions on expression in nonpublic forums.

- Private Property

  - There is no right to speak on others' private property protected by the federal Constitution.

  - However, a state is free to create such a right protected under that state's constitution without violating the property owner's First Amendment rights or effecting a taking under the Fifth Amendment.

- Restricted Environments

  - Public Schools

    - Public school officials may restrict student speech if that speech would materially and substantially interfere with the need for discipline in the school's operation.

    - The Court generally defers to the determination of school officials about what speech is a material and substantial interference with discipline in the school's operation.

    - However, that deference is not absolute, and the actions taken by the school officials must be reasonable in light of the speech.

    - Public school libraries have the ability to control their collections, but the First Amendment prevents them from removing materials from their collections based on the content of the materials.

  - Prisons

    - The Court has developed a rational basis-like test for regulation of speech by prisoners: The regulation will be upheld if it is rationally related to the achievement of a legitimate penological interest.

    - Generally, the Court defers to the judgment of the facility concerning virtually all aspects of speech by prisoners, including between prisoners of different facilities and the access of the press to prisoners for interviews or to observe the conditions.

- The Military

  - Military service members are subject to greater regulation of their speech, including prior restraints on publication at a military installation, than are civilians or even prisoners because of the risk of prejudice to the good order and discipline of the military.

  - The Court generally evinces extreme deference to the judgment of the military because of the special, unique character of the military and its mission.

V. Freedom of the Press

The First Amendment to the Constitution specifically mentions the freedom of the press separately from the freedom of speech: "Congress shall make no law ... abridging the freedom of speech, or of the press." Although the freedom of the press clause initially applied only to infringements by the federal government, the Court incorporated the clause through the Fourteenth Amendment in 1931 which made it applicable to state and local government as well. The general protections afforded for speech are also afforded to the press because the press also speaks when it publishes information, and many of the protections afforded for speech in general were developed by laws and government acts restricting the freedom of the press. However, the separate mention of the press in the First Amendment has given rise to two competing views of the amendment's protection of the press.

The first view argues that the press is accorded greater protection than that provided by the Freedom of Speech clause. This view derives from the role that the press plays in a democratic society by providing a check on the government through publication of its actions to the people. Under this view, restricting the press would injure the republic by depriving it of valuable information critical to the functioning of the republic. Justice Powell expressed this viewpoint in his concurring opinion in *Branzburg v. Hayes* (1972). He argued that the press has a preferred position in our constitutional scheme. This additional protection is because information is crucial to the proper functioning of our democratic republic, not because the press seeks profitability or because the press is a privileged class. It is important to note that this view is not generally followed by the Court.

The second view argues that the press clause does not confer any additional protections beyond that of the speech clause. There are two main reasons underlying this viewpoint. First, the historical evidence indicates that the Founding Fathers generally viewed "speech" and "the press" synonymously. The second reason is the extreme difficulty of providing a complete and accurate definition of the press as a separate group of persons. Any distinctions could easily run afoul of the Equal Protection Clause or work to deny protections afforded by the First Amendment. This viewpoint was expressed by Chief Justice Burger in his concurrence in *First National Bank of Boston v. Bellotti* (1978). He explained that the historical record does not bear out that the Founders intended to afford any special protections to the "institutional press." This second view is the one that represents the position most often taken by the Court.

This section examines four topics and how they affect the press. First, it examines attempts to treat the press differently from the general public. Next, it examines the press's access to public facilities and documents. Then, it addresses differences in the regulation of the broadcast media and the print media. Finally, it examines the press clause in light of new technologies, such as delivery over cable, satellite, and the Internet.

A. Efforts to Treat the Press Differently

The separate proclamation of protection for the press in the First Amendment has led to many attempts to treat the press differently from the general public. Some of those attempts have been to the benefit of the press and some to its detriment. These issues have arisen in the context of taxation, providing additional protections for the press, and protection of confidentiality of reporters' sources. Generally, the Court has refused to find that the attempted differentiation of the press from the general public, regardless of any additional benefit or detriment to the press.

On the issue of special taxes for the press, the Court has been consistent in finding such taxes to be unconstitutional, but the press may be subjected to generally applicable taxes. Discriminatory taxes, even if apparently benign at first, could easily transform into either retaliatory measures to punish the press or a form of licensing or prior restraint. The Court has overturned two notable attempts at taxes aimed at the press. First, in *Grosjean v. American Press Co.* (1936), the Court invalidated a state's attempt to levy a tax on advertisements in publications with more than 20,000 issues circulated per week. The Court found that the tax could have the effect of chilling the press and that such taxes directed at the press were unconstitutional. Second, in *Minneapolis Star & Tribune Co. v. Minnesota Commissioner of Revenue* (1983), the Court invalidated a state's attempt to tax paper and ink used for publications but exempted the first $100,000 from the tax. Writing for the majority, Justice O'Connor explained that such a tax directed at the press would have a chilling effect on the press and must be justified by a "counterbalancing interest of compelling importance" that the state could not achieve without the special tax. Thus, the press cannot be the target of a tax without such a compellingly important interest; however, the press is within the reach of generally available taxes. Interestingly, in the case of *Leathers v. Medlock* (1991), the Court upheld a tax that distinguished between members of the press.

The question of additional protections for the press has arisen in two different contexts. First, the press has attempted to stake a claim to greater speech protections than are available to the general public through exemptions from generally applicable laws. Second, it has tried to claim that the press clause provides it with greater protection from searches and seizures. However, in both cases, the Court has refused to find that the press should be treated differently than the general public.

The Court stated its determination that the press is not exempt from generally applicable laws most strongly in the case of *Cohen v. Cowles Media Co.* (1991). *Cohen* was a breach of contract case because a newspaper revealed a source despite its promise not to do so. The newspaper argued that the First Amendment protected them from liability for breach of contract. The Court disagreed. It explained that the law governing contract breaches applied to all persons and was not intended to interfere with the activities of the press. Thus, enforcing generally applicable laws against the press does not offend the First Amendment, even if the enforcement incidentally affects the press' ability to perform its function. Similarly, in *Zurcher v. Stanford Daily* (1978), the Court clearly held that the press was not entitled to greater protections against searches and seizures than the general public. In *Zurcher*, the police searched a student newspaper pursuant to a valid warrant. The newspaper claimed that the search violated the newspaper's rights as protected by the First Amendment, but the Court was not convinced. Writing for the Court, Justice White explained that the First Amendment lends newspapers no greater protection than what is generally applicable under the Fourth Amendment. Thus, the First Amendment conveys no new protections to the press from generally applicable laws than are available to the general public.

Finally, the press has tried to claim that it has a right to protect the confidentiality of its sources from discovery by the government. Members of the press frequently claim that the protection of their news sources is crucial to their ability to gather the information communicated to the public and that this immunizes them from complying with subpoenas requiring the disclosure of sources. However, the Court rejected this claim in *Branzburg v. Hayes* (1972). Justice White, writing for the Court, explained that the public's interest in effective law enforcement overrode the press's interest in protecting the identity of its sources. Justice White also explained that were the Court to find that the press was so protected, determining who constituted the press would cause a definitional problem that would be difficult (if not impossible) to overcome. Thus, the First Amendment extends no special shield to the press protecting them from being lawfully compelled to reveal their sources.

B. Access to Government Property

The function of the press is crucial in a democratic republic, and this critical function is recognized by the First Amendment guarantee of the freedom of the press. The previous section showed that the First Amendment does not protect the press from generally applicable laws and taxes. However, freedom of the press also necessitated freedom of access to information, for without access to information, the press's ability to perform its crucial function would be hindered or even exterminated. The Court has not yet addressed this question in the form of a general rule; however, it has addressed it in the specific contexts of access to judicial proceedings and access to prisons. In the former, the Court has found that the press enjoys considerable access to judicial proceedings, but in the latter the Court has found that the press is not entitled to greater access to prisons than the general public.

Concerning access to judicial proceedings, the Court has found that the Sixth Amendment's guarantee of a fair and public trial requires that the press have access except in very limited circumstances. In *Globe Newspaper Co. v. Superior Court* (1982), the Court explained that restrictions imposed on the press's access to criminal trials are subject to the very stringent strict scrutiny standard. In *Globe Newspaper*, Massachusetts prohibited the press and the general public from being present at a trial for certain sexual offenses where the victim was under age eighteen. Justice Brennan, writing for the Court, explained that the press's access to criminal trials is constitutionally protected but not absolute. Any restriction on the press's access to such trials must be narrowly tailored to achieve a compelling state interest. However, the Court has yet to address whether the press's access is coextensive with that of the general public or whether the First Amendment affords the press greater access.

Contrary to the protection of access to judicial proceedings, the Court has held that the press has no greater right of access to prisons than does the general public. Here, the leading case is *Pell v. Procunier* (1974). In *Pell*, the California Department of Corrections prohibited the press from interviewing inmates when the press requests to interview "specific individual inmates." The Court found that the press was generally not entitled to special access to information that was not generally available to the public. It extended this determination to access to prisons and found that the press's right of access to inmates was the same as that enjoyed by the public in general. Thus, because the press's right was no less than that of the general public, the California regulation did not infringe on any rights protected by the First Amendment.

C. Broadcast Regulation

The technology available to the press has advanced considerably since the time that the First Amendment was authored, passed, and ratified. At that time, the press was limited to street corners and printing presses. In the intervening time, the broadcast media developed that had the potential to reach far more people because it was generally available for free. Specifically, the broadcast media refers to radio and television broadcasting. The Court struggled to adapt First Amendment law to cope with the newer technology, which differs in two main ways from the more traditional press. First, broadcast signals penetrate the homes and businesses of the public without being requested, making it harder to control who is exposed to what broadcast information, especially young children. Second, there are only a limited set of channels available for broadcasting, and the Court found that the scarcity of channels required government regulation to ensure an efficient allocation and use of the broadcasting spectrum and to prevent one broadcaster from intruding onto another. Eventually, the Court determined that the differences between the broadcast media from the more traditional media required greater regulation of the broadcast media than is appropriate for the more traditional press.

In *Red Lion Broadcasting Co. v. FCC* (1969), the Court upheld the FCC's fairness doctrine. The fairness doctrine required broadcasters (a) to "give adequate coverage to public issues," and (b) to present such issues fairly such that it "accurately reflects the opposing views." The Court analyzed the differences between the broadcast media and the print media and found that the broadcast media was entitled to less protection than the print media. Writing for the Court, Justice White explained that this was necessary because there are only a limited set of broadcast frequencies, that the government had the responsibility to allocate the frequencies, and that without governmental assistance many would not have access to the frequencies to voice their viewpoints. Similarly, in *FCC v. Pacifica Foundation* (1978), the Court upheld the power of the FCC to regulate and punish the broadcast of indecent material over the airwaves even if that material is not obscene. Writing for the majority, Justice Scalia explained that the specific regulation of broadcast media was appropriate because sending "patently offensive, indecent material" over the airwaves made that material "uniquely accessible to children" and invaded the public's right to be left alone.

D. Advancing Technology

Recent years have seen the emergence of new technologies for communication. Chief among these new technologies are cable television and the Internet. Just as it struggled to address the broadcast media when it was a new medium, the Court is currently struggling with the degree of constitutional protection to which these media are entitled. These media are different from the broadcast media in a few key ways. First, both cable and the Internet require intentional access to the information, either through a subscription to a service provider or by specifically requesting the information disseminated. Second, cable and the Internet are discrete communications media: There is no risk of interference as there is with the broadcast media. The Internet is also substantially easier and cheaper to establish a presence in than the other types of media, and it is frequently used to disseminate ideas that many find objectionable or are otherwise unpopular. These differences have caused the Court to reconsider its deferential attitude toward regulating the new forms of media. The Court generally requires a regulation of cable to satisfy a form of intermediate scrutiny:

1. be content-neutral;
2. be narrowly tailored; and
3. serve an important government interest.

However, the Court generally has been reticent to uphold any regulations of content on the Internet, essentially applying strict scrutiny to such regulations.

The Court's position concerning regulation of cable was most clearly expressed in *Turner Broadcasting System, Inc. v. FCC* (1994). *Turner Broadcasting* involved a challenge to the Cable Television Consumer Protection and Competition Act of 1992, which required cable operators to carry local stations operating within the same market, called the "must-carry" provisions. On direct appeal, the Supreme Court vacated the district court's judgment upholding the must-carry provisions and remanded the case back to trial. Writing for the Court, Justice Kennedy explained that cable programming and its operators are entitled to the protections of the First Amendment because they engage in speech. He explained that the differences between cable and the broadcast medium make application of the broadcast precedents inapposite and that the must-carry provisions were not a content-based restriction. Instead, the provisions were intended to keep the broadcast media alive to ensure free access to television. Justice Kennedy explained that because they were content-neutral, the regulations must be narrowly tailored to achieve a "substantial government interest" that would not be achieved as efficiently without the regulation. Concurring in part and dissenting in part, Justice O'Connor, joined by Justices Scalia, Ginsburg, and Thomas, found that the must-carry provisions were content-based because they indicated preferential treatment for certain content and were impermissible restraints on speech.

The Court first addressed restrictions of content on the Internet in *Reno v. ACLU* (1997). *Reno* involved a challenge to the Communications Decency Act of 1996 (CDA), which prohibited the distribution of indecent material over the Internet. In a decision supported by seven Justices, the Court overturned the CDA. Writing for the Court, Justice Stevens explained that the statute was so vague and overbroad that it would prohibit "serious discussion about birth control practices, homosexuality, ... or the consequences of ... rape." Recognizing that the government has a compelling interest in protecting children from exposure to sexually explicit materials, Justice Stevens explained that the government cannot prohibit communication of materials to adults to protect children.

In response to *Reno*, Congress passed the Child Online Protection Act (COPA), which was challenged in *Ashcroft v. ACLU* (2004). The COPA required commercial Web site operators to restrict access to material which "the average person 'applying contemporary community standards, would find, ... is designed to pander to, the prurient interest." On appeal, a divided Court explained that although the statute was not unconstitutionally vague and overbroad like the CDA, it was not the least restrictive means for achieving the compelling interest of protecting minors from sexually explicit materials. Writing for the majority, Justice Kennedy explained that filters could be more effective because they would not be limited to one method of content distribution, Web sites, but would cover email and forms of distribution yet to be developed.

Stop Points

- **Freedom of the Press**
    - Differentiation between the Press and the General Public
        - Generally, the press is subject to generally applicable laws and is not entitled to any special exemption from them.
        - The press is not entitled to any specific protection from either searches pursuant to valid warrants or subpoenas requiring the divulging of news sources.
        - The press is also subject to generally applicable taxes and does not receive any specific protection from them.
        - However, the press is protected from taxes directed at the press, and such efforts to tax only the press are generally found to be unconstitutional.
    - Access to Government Property

- The Court has yet to provide a general rule on this question but has addressed it with respect to access to judicial proceedings and access to prisons.
- The press enjoys a substantial ability to observe and report on judicial proceedings; any limitations on that ability must meet exacting standards. Any restriction on the press's access to criminal trials must be narrowly tailored to achieve a compelling state interest.
- However, the press enjoys no greater access to prisons than the general public.
- Regulation of Broadcast Media versus Print Media
  - Generally, the broadcast media is subject to greater regulation than the print media because of (1) the scarcity of the broadcast frequencies; and (2) the government is responsible for allocating the channels and without government assistance some persons would not have access to the channels to express their viewpoints.
- Regulation of New and Emerging Technologies
  - Cable companies and programming providers are less regulated than are the broadcast media.
  - The Court has endorsed a form of intermediate scrutiny for regulations of cable companies and programming, requiring the regulation: (1) to be content-neutral; (2) to serve a substantial government interest; and (3) to be narrowly tailored to serve that interest.
  - The Court has generally been hostile to regulations of content on the Internet.
  - Regulations of content on the Internet must pass strict scrutiny else they are invalid.

VI. Freedom of Association, Political Parties, and Campaign Finance

The First Amendment contains no express protection of a freedom of association. However, it does expressly protect the "right of the people peaceably to assemble." The Supreme Court has held that the right to associate is protected by the combination of this right, "peaceably to assemble," when read in the context of the other rights in the First Amendment and in conjunction with the Fourteenth Amendment's Due Process Clause. In so doing, the Court has announced that the right to associate is a fundamental right protected by the First Amendment, especially when such association involves speech that is more effective when spoken collectively. Because of the fundamental nature of the right, any state action infringing on that right must pass strict scrutiny or fail.

The Court emphatically announced the protection of freedom of association in *NAACP v. Alabama* (1958). At the time, Alabama required foreign corporations to qualify by registering with the state before conducting any business within the state. The attorney general of Alabama sought to enjoin the NAACP from conducting activities within the state and to oust the organization, a non-profit corporation organized under New York law, from the state for failure to register. When the NAACP refused to comply with a court order to produce its membership rolls, the court held the NAACP in civil contempt and fined them. On appeal, the Supreme Court reversed the trial court's contempt citation and fine. Writing for the majority, Justice Harlan explained that although Alabama had not taken any affirmative action to restrict the freedom of association, the production order "entail[ed] the likelihood of a substantial restraint" on the ability of the citizens of Alabama to exercise that right. Finding that the Fourteenth Amendment protected the right of the NAACP's members to associate freely, the Court held that the production order was state action infringing that right. Furthermore, because the state had not shown a "controlling justification" for the infringement, the Court invalidated the order, the contempt citation, and the fine.

A. Defining Association

The threshold question in analyzing the right of association is what associative activity is protected by the First Amendment? The Court has found that the right of association generally protects the right of a group of people to form an association and determine its membership, as long as its membership is not determined in a discriminatory manner. However, the Court has upheld discriminatory membership policies in one of two cases. First, it has permitted discrimination in determining the membership of an "intimate association," a small and private gathering. Second, it has permitted discrimination if the discrimination is integral to expressive activity.

The leading case announcing these minor exceptions to the nondiscriminatory requirement of the right of association is *Roberts v. United States Jaycees* (1984). In *Roberts*, the Jaycees, a national organization comprising young men between the ages of eighteen and forty, brought a right of association challenge to the Minnesota Human Rights Act. The Act proscribed discrimination based, *inter alia*, on race and gender. The Jaycees claimed that the freedom of association permitted the group to exclude women from its membership. The Court disagreed. In his opinion for the Court, Justice Brennan recognized that forcing a group to accept members that it does not wish to accept was the "clear[est] example of an intrusion into the internal structure or affairs of an association." However, he explained that the freedom of association was not inviolable and held that an infringement of that freedom was not unconstitutional if its reach is only so far as is necessary to accomplish a legitimate government purpose. However, the Court announced two exceptions to the general rule prohibiting discriminatory practices concerning association memberships — discriminatory membership policies were permitted if the association (1) is an "intimate association," defined as a small and private gathering, or (2) is an integral part of expressive activity. Because the Court found that the Jaycees were too large to be an "intimate association," and that the association was not an integral part of expressive activity, it found that the discriminatory membership policy was not protected by the First Amendment and upheld the law.

Applying *Roberts*, the Court upheld discriminatory membership practices in *Boy Scouts of America v. Dale* (2000). The respondent, James Dale, was a Boy Scout who had risen through the organization to the rank of Eagle Scout and had become an assistant Scoutmaster. During college, he became involved with gay rights advocacy and was the co-president of the Gay/Lesbian Alliance at Rutgers University in New Jersey. After seeing an article that quoted Dale in his position with the Alliance, a Boy Scout official wrote Dale and informed him that he could no longer participate in the Boy Scouts. Dale sued, claiming that the action violated the New Jersey law proscribing discrimination by places of public accommodation. The Boy Scouts claimed that their association had an antigay message and the Court agreed in a five-to-four decision. Chief Justice Rehnquist's majority opinion found a sufficiently expressive message in the Boy Scouts' interpretation of its Scout Oath and its position taken during litigation. He explained that just because the message is not "trumpet[ed] ... from the housetops" does not remove the expression from the protection of the First Amendment. Thus, the majority found that the Boy Scouts were an association tied to a message and forcing them to permit homosexuals to be members would undermine that message, and they upheld the practice of the Boy Scouts. In dissent, Justice Stevens noted that there was nothing in the Boy Scouts' literature to support this position.

B. Electoral Process

Another area where freedom of association issues arise is in the electoral process. Many laws regulating campaign financing methods require disclosure of the contributors to candidates. Recognizing the potential to chill contributions by forcing such disclosures, the Court has upheld the disclosure requirements as being narrowly tailored to stop corruption. However, the Court has found an exception where such disclosures may chill contributions to a minor party candidate and will permit such groups to withhold the information. Two cases are instructive.

In *Buckley v. Valeo* (1976), the Court reviewed a provision of the Federal Election Campaign Act of 1971. The provision at issue required campaigns (1) to maintain lists of the names and addresses of all donors contributing more than $10; and (2) to provide access to those lists to the Federal Election Commission for public inspection and copying. The Court upheld the provision, finding that the interest it served, preventing corruption was significant and the possibility of disclosure helped discourage corruption and encouraged public faith in the electoral process. However, the Court stated an exception for minor parties in its dicta in the case. It explained that minor parties were protected because of the substantially reduced likelihood that such parties would be successful in an election. The Court applied this dicta in *Brown v. Socialist Workers '74 Campaign Committee* (1982), finding that it did not have to obey state disclosure laws. It based this determination on the fact that the party was a minor party and that historically it had been unpopular. Thus, the disclosure requirements would probably chill contributions to the party and would not serve a significant purpose because of the reduced likelihood of the party's electoral success.

Checkpoints

· **Interpreting the First Amendment**

- Despite the language of the First Amendment, "Congress shall make no law ... abridging the freedom of speech," the court had never adopted a literal interpretation.

- The First Amendment was likely a reaction to the English suppression of the press and speech through licensing (prior restraints) and the crime of seditious libel.

- Free speech is vital to democracy because it allows the voters to hear and discuss a variety of viewpoints and hold public officials accountable.

- Free speech is necessary to evaluate the truth of ideas. We arrive at the truth most accurately and efficiently when we allow ideas to openly compete in the marketplace.

- Free speech is necessary to achieve personal autonomy and self-fulfillment.

- Free speech offers a safety valve for releasing pent-up frustration in a lawful activity.

- Free speech promotes tolerance of different viewpoints which engenders a respect for others, an important component to a pluralistic society.

Checkpoints *continued*

- **Defining Speech**

  - Clearly oral and written communication of information, ideas and emotions is speech.

  - Conduct is speech when (1) the actor intended to communicate a particularized message, and (2) the circumstances are such that there is a great likelihood that the message would be understood by those who viewed the conduct.

  - Under O'Brien, government regulation of expressive conduct is permissible if:

    1. The government has the power to regulate the field;

    2. The regulation furthers an important or substantial government interest;

    3. The government interest is unrelated to the suppression of free expression; and

    4. The restriction on First Amendment freedom "is no greater than is essential" to further the government interest.

  - If the conduct at issue is speech (thus invoking the First Amendment), and the state's regulation was unrelated to suppression of free expression, then the O'Brien test applies. If the regulation is related to suppressing expression then strict scrutiny applies.

- **Vagueness and Overbreadth**   → fundamental Rt.

  - Vagueness and overbreadth both permit a person to facially challenge a law rather than to challenge based on a specific application, and both operate as an exception to the standing doctrine by allowing a person to challenge a law without having to suffer a personal injury.

  - A law is void for vagueness if a reasonable person reading the law would not know what speech is illegal.

  - A law regulating speech is unconstitutionally overbroad if it regulates substantially more speech than the constitution permits.

- **Content-Based Regulation and Prior Restraints**

  - Except for several categories of speech which are unprotected or less protected, government regulation of speech based on its content must pass strict scrutiny.

  - A prior restraint is a judicial order or administrative scheme which prevents speech from occurring.

- **Unprotected and Less Protected Speech**

  - Advocacy of Illegal Action

  - Fighting Words and the Hostile Audience

Checkpoints *continued*

- Hate Speech

- Sexually Oriented Speech

  - The Court has created three categories of sexually oriented speech: (1) obscenity; (2) child pornography; and (3) profanity and indecency.

  - Obscenity and child pornography are unprotected speech and laws prohibiting them need only pass the rational basis test.

    - Under *Miller*, material is obscene if:

      - (1) the average person would find that the work appeared to the prurient interests when viewing the work as a whole and applying contemporary community standards;

      - (2) the work describes or depicts sexual conduct defined by the applicable law in a patently offensive way; and

      - (3) as a whole, the work lacks serious literary, political, scientific, or artistic value.

    - Under *Miller*, no one has a constitutionally protected right to produce, distribute, or sell obscene materials.

    - However, under *Reidel*, one has a constitutionally protected right to possess obscene materials.

    - Under *Ferber*, the government may regulate or proscribe child pornography without applying the *Miller* test when the material depicts minors in sexual acts and actual minors were used.

    - However, under *Ashcroft v. Free Speech Coalition*, where the material purports to depict children engaging in sexual acts, but no actual children were used, the *Miller* standard applies.

  - Profane and indecent speech are protected by the First Amendment, thus laws punishing this speech must pass strict scrutiny.

  - However, the Court has identified limited exceptions to this protection for such speech in schools and on the broadcast media.

  - But the Court has refused to extend those exceptions to First Amendment protections to telephones, cable television, and the Internet, thus they are protected under the First Amendment.

- Defamation

  - The First Amendment requires that a public official or a public figure cannot recover for defamation without proving that the publication was made with actual malice, defined as knowing that the publication was false or acting with reckless disregard of its falsity.

Checkpoints *continued*

- A public official is a public employee who controls, or is perceived to control, the conduct of governmental affairs.

- There are two kinds of public figures:

  - A person who, by virtue of her position, generates public interest in her, is a public figure for all purposes and in all contexts; and

  - A person who injects himself in the forefront of a public controversy becomes a public figure for the limited purposes of that controversy and related issues.

- A private person still enjoys protection from defamation under the traditional definition, except that states cannot permit a private person to recover on a strict liability theory.

- Further, a private person may not recover presumed or punitive damages without meeting the amplified actual malice standard.

- Speech-Related Torts Other Than Defamation

  - The *New York Times* standard applies to the ability of public figures and public officials to recover for intentional infliction of emotional distress and for false light invasion of privacy.

  - The First Amendment prevents recovery for publication of true information that is private, once that information is released to the public, such as through publication in court documents.

- Speech by Public Employees

  - The government can prohibit participation in political activities by government employees.

  - The government may prohibit its employees from speaking on matters of public concern if its interest in efficient operations outweighs the employee's interest in such speech.

- Commercial Speech

  - Commercial speech is (1) an advertisement; (2) that refers to a specific product; and (3) is motivated by economic motives.

  - The First Amendment protects commercial speech, but it protects it less than noncommercial speech.

  - The Court applies a four-part test to determine the validity of regulations of commercial speech. This test requires: (1) a substantial interest in regulating the speech; (2) the regulation must directly advance the interest; (3) the regulation must be no more extensive than necessary to serve the interest; and (4) the speech must not be misleading and must concern lawful activity.

Checkpoints *continued*

- The last two prongs of the test are understood only to require that the regulation be narrowly tailored, not the least restrictive means, to achieve the government interest.

- The First Amendment does not protect commercial speech that is misleading, deceptive, or false or concerns illegal activities. Thus, a regulation of such speech need only pass rational basis scrutiny.

- Attorneys may engage in truthful advertisement of their services as long as the advertisement is not deceptive, subject to regulation.

  - Any solicitation by targeted, direct mail is protected, but may be regulated to some degree.

  - In-person solicitations by attorneys are not protected when they are motivated by profit, but are protected when the representation will be for free.

- The use of trade names by a business is not protected by the First Amendment.

- States generally cannot limit commercial speech where the laws were enacted under the theory that people will be better off without the information.

  - However, the Court has upheld some restrictions on commercial speech that is truthful advertising of legal activities when the restrictions are aimed at addressing other problems, like traffic safety.

- The Court has struck down regulations of certain activities or products with the goal of reducing participation in the activities or consumption of the products.

  - But the Court has permitted states to regulate gambling advertisements to reduce gambling in the state.

- **Impact of Location on Freedom of Speech**

  - Public Forum, Limited Public Forum and Nonpublic Forum

    - A regulation of speech in a public forum must be: (1) a reasonable. (2) content-neutral. (3) restriction on the time, place, or manner of speech, (4) that achieves an important government purpose.

    - A limited public forum is a public space opened by the government specifically to be used for speech.

    - A limited public forum is not created simply by opening a public space for use by the public; it must be opened specifically for speech.

    - Additionally, the failure of the government to prevent speech in a public space does not create a limited public forum because the creation of a limited public forum requires the government affirmatively to open the public space for speech.

Checkpoints *continued*

- Regulations of speech in limited public forums must meet the same test as regulations of speech in traditional public forums.

- A nonpublic forum is government property that is neither a public forum nor a limited public forum.

- The government may place reasonable and nondiscriminatory restrictions on expression in nonpublic forums.

- Private Property

  - There is no right to speak on others' private property protected by the federal Constitution.

  - However, a state is free to create such a right protected under that state's constitution without violating the property owner's First Amendment rights or effecting a taking under the Fifth Amendment.

- Restricted Environments

  - Public Schools

    - Public school officials may restrict student speech if that speech would materially and substantially interfere with the need for discipline in the school's operation.

    - The Court generally defers to the determination of school officials about what speech is a material and substantial interference with discipline in the school's operation.

    - However, that deference is not absolute, and the actions taken by the school officials must be reasonable in light of the speech.

    - Public school libraries have the ability to control their collections, but the First Amendment prevents them from removing materials from their collections based on the content of the materials.

  - Prisons

    - The Court has developed a rational basis-like test for regulation of speech by prisoners: The regulation will be upheld if it is rationally related to the achievement of a legitimate penological interest.

    - Generally, the Court defers to the judgment of the facility concerning virtually all aspects of speech by prisoners, including between prisoners of different facilities and the access of the press to prisoners for interviews or to observe the conditions.

  - The Military

Checkpoints *continued*

- Military service members are subject to greater regulation of their speech, including prior restraints on publication at a military installation, than are civilians or even prisoners because of the risk of prejudice to the good order and discipline of the military.

- The Court generally evinces extreme deference to the judgment of the military because of the special, unique character of the military and its mission.

- **Freedom of the Press**
  - Differentiation between the Press and the General Public
    - Generally, the press is subject to generally applicable laws and is not entitled to any special exemption from them.
    - The press is not entitled to any specific protection from either searches pursuant to valid warrants or subpoenas requiring the divulging of news sources.
    - The press is also subject to generally applicable taxes and does not receive any specific protection from them.
    - However, the press is protected from taxes directed at the press, and such efforts to tax only the press are generally found to be unconstitutional.
  - Access to Government Property
    - The Court has yet to provide a general rule on this question but has addressed it with respect to access to judicial proceedings and access to prisons.
    - The press enjoys a substantial ability to observe and report on judicial proceedings; any limitations on that ability must meet exacting standards. Any restriction on the press's access to criminal trials must be narrowly tailored to achieve a compelling state interest.
    - However, the press enjoys no greater access to prisons than the general public.
  - Regulation of Broadcast Media versus Print Media
    - Generally, the broadcast media is subject to greater regulation than the print media because of (1) the scarcity of the broadcast frequencies; and (2) the government is responsible for allocating the channels and without government assistance some persons would not have access to the channels to express their viewpoints.
  - Regulation of New and Emerging Technologies
    - Cable companies and programming providers are less regulated than are the broadcast media.

Checkpoints *continued*

- The Court has endorsed a form of intermediate scrutiny for regulations of cable companies and programming, requiring the regulation: (1) to be content-neutral; (2) to serve a substantial government interest; and (3) to be narrowly tailored to serve that interest.
- The Court has generally been hostile to regulations of content on the Internet.
- Regulations of content on the Internet must pass strict scrutiny else they are invalid.

- **Freedom of Association**
  - Generally, the First Amendment protects the right to associate, though it is not expressly stated in the Amendment.
  - The freedom of association has been incorporated against the states through the Fourteenth Amendment.
  - Infringements on the freedom must be narrowly tailored to achieve a legitimate government interest.
  - Defining Association
    - Generally, freedom of association does not protect a group that has discriminatory membership policies.
    - However, the freedom of association does protect a group with discriminatory membership policies if:
      - The group is an intimate association, defined as a small, private gathering, or
      - The group is an integral part of an expressive activity.
  - The Electoral Process
    - Generally, campaigns can be required to disclose lists of donors because of the government's substantial interests in preventing corruption and preventing the appearance of corruption.
    - However, a minor party may refuse to comply with disclosure requirements because of the risk that the disclosure requirement could chill contributions to the party and because the party is unlikely to win at the ballot box.

Chapter 10

The Religion Clauses

Roadmap

- The religious prohibition of Article IV, Clause 3 of the Constitution.
- What is religion?
- When did the court start applying the Religion Clauses to the states?
- Three analytical frameworks for Establishment Clause:
    - Strict Separation;
    - Neutrality; and
    - Accommodation
- The three-part *Lemon* Test for analyzing Establishment Clause cases:
    - whether the government act has a secular purpose;
    - whether its primary effect neither advances nor inhibits religion; and
    - whether it does not create an excessive entanglement between government and religion.
- Areas of Establishment Clause jurisprudence: school prayer, school curricular decisions, religious displays, equal access to public facilities, financial aid to religious institutions, and school vouchers
- The Free Exercise Clause
- The Religion Clauses and free speech

I. Introduction

It is important to know that the body of the Constitution contains a religious prohibition. Article VI, Clause 3 of the Constitution states:

> The Senators and Representatives before mentioned, and the Members of the several State Legislatures, and all executive and judicial Officers, both of the United States and of the several States, shall be bound by Oath or Affirmation, to support this Constitution; but no religious

Test shall ever be required as a qualification to any Office or public
Trust under the United States.

Thus, even before the First Amendment was added to the Constitution, the government could not establish religion as a condition for holding federal office.

The First Amendment, which opens the hallowed Bill of Rights, begins with the often quoted words: "Congress shall make no law respecting an establishment of religion, or prohibiting the free exercise thereof." This portion of the First Amendment is commonly broken down at the comma into two Religion Clauses, the Establishment Clause and the Free Exercise Clause, respectively. These two clauses were designed to protect liberty of conscience, freedom of religious expression, religious equality and pluralism, and separation of church and state. These clauses appear to be simple and clear. In application, they are complex and vague and are some of the most contested words in the whole Constitution.

To fully appreciate the application of the Religion Clauses, it is crucial to understand two basic points. First, to comprehend when the First Amendment applies, one must know the Court's definition of what constitutes a "religion." Second, for most of the history of the United States, the Court did not apply the Religion Clauses to the states. In changing their applicability, the Court uses the Fourteenth Amendment to apply the Religion Clauses to the states.

A. Definition of Religion

What is "religion?" This is a central question when interpreting and applying the Religion Clauses. Any definition must account for the variety of different spiritual beliefs and practices in the United States. This diversity, which any workable definition must embrace, shows that the apparently simple task conceals an extremely complex reality. Some commentators have suggested that providing a bright-line definition is an unworkable goal because it is impossible to bring all religions within the scope of the definition without also encompassing practices that are not religious.

One theory called for two different definitions of religion, one for the Establishment Clause (which prevents the government from establishing a religion) and one for the Free Exercise Clause (which protects the freedom of to practice religion). The theory is that a narrow definition of religion for the Establishment Clause would restrict the limits on government, and a broader definition of religion for the Free Exercise Clause would increase the protections for religious conduct. The theory was illustrated in *Malnak v. Yogi* (3d Cir., 1979), where a school offered classes in transcendental meditation. A broad definition of religion for the Free Exercise Clause would protect transcendental meditation as a religious practice, but for a public school to provide the class, one would need a narrow definition of religion to prevent the class from running afoul of the Establishment Clause. This theory has never been accepted by the Supreme Court. In fact, Justice Wiley Rutledge expressly rejected this concept of a dual definition in his concurrence in *Everson v. Board of Education* (1947). He stated that although the word *religion* appears only once in the First Amendment, the same word "governs two prohibitions and governs them alike."

Because of the diversity of beliefs and practices that any definition must encompass, the Court has directly addressed the issue in a relatively few cases. The Court has successfully avoided the issue by deciding cases on independent grounds, which make reaching the question unnecessary. However, when the Court has dealt with defining religion, its rulings provide some insight, but little guidance.

In 1890, the Court, in *Davis v. Beason*, adopted a substantive definition of religion — a practice that involves "the belief in and the worship of a deity." The Court ruled that "the term 'religion' has a reference of one's views of his relations to his Creator, and the obligations they impose of reverence for his being and character, and obedience to his will."

In 1961, in *Torcaso v. Watkins*, the Court abandoned the substantive approach and moved toward a functional definition of religion. The case involved a provision of the Maryland Constitution, which had been used to deny a secular humanist an appointment as a notary public. The Court struck down the provision, unanimously holding "that the term religion did not apply solely to those beliefs which were based upon the existence of a deity." This ruling prevented the government from aiding a religion, even if that religion does not encompass a belief in a "God." Thus, the government could not avoid the prohibition of the Establishment Clause by claiming that the religion does not include "worship of a deity." Justice Hugo Black wrote: "Among religions in this country which do not teach what would generally be considered a belief in the existence of God are Buddhism, Taoism, Ethical Culture, Secular Humanism and others."

The Court reiterated the functional approach in *United States v. Seeger* (1965), which involved the interpretation of the Universal Military Training and Service Act of 1948. The Act allowed an individual to be a conscientious objector and avoid the military draft if such individual, "by reason of religious training and belief, is conscientiously opposed to participation in war in any form." Under the Act, the definition of "religious training and belief" was "an individual's belief in relation to a Supreme Being involving duties superior to those arising from any human relation, but not including essentially political, sociological, or philosophical views or a merely personal moral code." The trial court denied Daniel Seeger's claim of conscientious objector status because his belief was not based on a Supreme Being as required by the Act.

The crux of the issue focused around whether the term "Supreme Being" meant the orthodox God or the broader concept of a power or being to which all else is subordinate. The Court chose the latter, formulating a functional definition of religion and citing theologian Paul Tillich's view of God not as a projection "out there" or beyond the skies but as the ground of our very being. The Court stated that a "person's belief can be classified as religious if such belief is 'sincere and meaningful ... [and] occupies in the life of its possessor, a place parallel to that filled by God.'"

Thus, in *Seeger*, the Court abandoned the substantive definition of religion to prevent the judiciary from being in the position to decide the truth of a religious belief. As Justice William Douglas stated in *United States v. Ballard* (1944): "Men may believe what they cannot prove. They may not be put to the proof of their religious doctrines or beliefs. Religious experiences which are as real as life to some may be incomprehensible to others." In fact, the truth of religious views cannot properly be presented to the jury because doing so would open the door to converting prosecutions into religious persecutions. Courts are also not competent to determine whether a party has interpreted the tenets of his or her faith correctly. Since its early nineteenth-century decision in *Watson v. Jones* (1872), the Court has generally left these internal issues to the relevant religious tribunals, and courts must accept a religion's highest tribunal's interpretation of doctrine as binding.

In response to the court's decision in *Seeger*, Congress amended the Universal Military Training Act and deleted the reference to a "Supreme Being." But the Act continued to provide that "religious training and belief" does not include "essentially political, sociological, or philosophical views, or a merely personal moral code." In *Welsh v. U.S.* (1970), the Court reexamined the Act and stated that purely ethical and moral considerations may be viewed as religious.

The following year, in *Wisconsin v. Yoder* (1971), Amish parents were convicted under Wisconsin's compulsory attendance laws for failing to send their children to school. The parents refused to send their children because the Amish way of life is based on their religion and is incompatible with education beyond the eighth grade. The parents successfully challenged their convictions under the First Amendment. The Court characterized "a religious belief or practice entitled to constitutional protection" as "not merely a matter of personal preference, but one of deep religious conviction, shared by an organized group, and intimately related to daily living." The parties in *Seeger* and *Welsh* did not claim to be part of an organized religious group, yet the Court found that their beliefs fell within the definition of religion, so no one factor appears to be determinative for the court.

B. Applicability of the Religion Clauses to the States

For most of the nation's history, the Constitution's references to religion did not apply to the states. Article IV, Clause 3 prohibits religious tests for government office, and it only applied to the federal government until *Torcaso v. Watkins* (1961), when the court applied it to the states. The very language of the First Amendment refers only to the federal government: "Congress shall make no law respecting an establishment of religion, or prohibiting the free exercise thereof." The Court used the Fourteenth Amendment to apply the Religion Clauses to the states. It incorporated the Free Exercise Clause in *Cantwell v. Connecticut* (1940) and the Establishment Clause in *Everson v. Board of Education* (1947). This incorporation of the Religion Clauses into the Fourteenth Amendment for application against the states is the law today. Therefore, states, like the federal government, are forbidden from employing religious tests for public office as well as establishing religion or prohibiting the free exercise thereof.

II. The Establishment Clause

The First Amendment begins with the phrase: "Congress shall make no law respecting an establishment of religion." Although it is a prohibition directed at Congress, it has since been applied to the states through the incorporation doctrine of the Fourteenth Amendment. But what is a "law respecting an establishment of religion?" Clearly, the Establishment Clause prevents the government from aiding or formally establishing a government-sponsored religion. However, even acting neutrally would "aid" religion in some manner, even if the government provided fire and police protection for religious buildings and nothing more. Thus, the government can completely avoid aiding religion only by actively acting against religion, but that is proscribed by the Free Exercise Clause, which is discussed in the next major section.

A. Three Major Analytical Frameworks: Strict Separation, Neutrality, and Accommodation

Three major frameworks have developed to carry out the requirements of the Establishment Clause. Each has its promoters on the Court and among the commentators, and each is visible in the Court's decisions. The first is commonly called the "wall of separation" or "strict separation." The second major framework advocates the government taking a neutral approach to religion.

The third framework advocates an accommodation approach to balance the relationship between government and religion.

1. Wall of Separation or Strict Separation Approach

The wall of separation approach maintains that the government should be separated from any and all religion as much as is practically possible. This approach is based on a remark made by Thomas Jefferson in a letter to the Danbury Baptist Association in Connecticut. Jefferson wrote that the Religion Clauses of the First Amendment erected a wall of separation between the government and religion. It requires the government to take an active stance to avoid interaction with religion as much as possible. Whether the motivation is to protect the state from the evils of religion (hostility toward religion), protect religion from the evils of the government (hostility toward the government), or create an environment where both flourish best, strict separationists will do their best to keep state and religion completely out of each other's realms. However, as mentioned before, some government functions, such as police and fire protection, cannot realistically be denied to religious institutions, even though, on some level, they can be viewed as aiding religion. Thus, even a strict separation approach is not an absolutist position.

The Court first promulgated the wall of separation doctrine in *Everson* (1947). In that case, a school board in New Jersey created a program to reimburse parents for the costs of using public transportation to send their children to Catholic schools. In his majority opinion, Justice Black wrote that the Establishment Clause constructed a wall that separates the government from religion and that the "wall must be kept high and impregnable." He also said that the Court could not accept or permit any breach of the wall, no matter how *de minimis*. However, the Court did not find that the reimbursement program breached that wall because providing public transportation was not related to religion but was a public function. Justice Black compared public transportation to other public functions, such as providing police and fire protection. Further, the Court said that although providing the reimbursement did not violate the Establishment Clause, the Free Exercise Clause did not require the government to provide reimbursement for public transportation costs.

The Court was unable to fully explore its new strict separation doctrine, due to the limited facts available to the Court in *Everson*. However, the Court made it clear that even in a strict separation approach, compromises must be made. It would be untenable for the government to refuse to do anything that could be remotely construed as benefiting religion. That would cause the government to become openly antagonistic to religion, which would arguably impinge the Free Exercise Clause. At the same time, the strict separation doctrine requires the government to do everything practical to avoid piercing the wall of separation.

2. Neutrality Approach: The Endorsement Test

The second major framework focuses on maintaining neutrality between government and religion. This means that the government cannot give or indicate a preference of religion over secularism or a preference of one religion over another. The neutrality approach is supported by the Court's decision in *Everson*, which prohibited state power from being used to either handicap or favor religions. Others have expressed that neutrality requires the government to keep its promotion or discouragement of religious observance, belief, or activity to a minimum.

The difficulty arises in how to evaluate whether a government program or activity violates the neutrality requirement. In *Lynch v. Donnelly* (1984), Justice Sandra Day O'Connor expressed the view that the neutrality approach mandates that every government act be examined under the totality of the circumstances to determine whether it amounts to an endorsement or disapproval of religion. The difficulty of measuring the neutrality of government action led to the development of an "endorsement test"—whether the government action endorses either a specific religion or its symbols or endorses religion over secularism in general. This test has been promoted by several Justices, including Justice O'Connor.

In *Capitol Square Review & Advisory Board v. Pinette* (1995), the Court addressed (without a majority opinion) which government actions will violate the endorsement test and when it should be applied. Seven Justices agreed that if the state government had allowed the Ku Klux Klan to place a large cross in a ten-acre public park, across from the statehouse in Columbus, Ohio, it would not have violated the Establishment Clause. In the separate opinions in *Pinette*, the Justices articulated three different approaches to applying the test. Justice Antonin Scalia, writing for the majority, opposed applying the test when the issue is private speech delivered on public property. Justice O'Connor, joined by two other Justices, concurred, stating that the endorsement test is applied from the perspective of a reasonable person, similar to that in tort law, but possessing some knowledge that may not be held by the general public. This removes the focus from examining whether a particular person would be offended by the potential religious character of the government's action and from examining whether a reasonable person would think that the action endorses religion. Justices John Stevens and Ruth Bader Ginsburg advocate the third approach, agreeing with Justice O'Connor that endorsement depends on the perception of a reasonable person, but without any special knowledge and simply from the perspective of a passerby. Thus, the government could allow the Ku Klux Klan to place/burn the cross, without endorsing the Klan or its symbols (the cross) and without endorsing the Klan over another religion or secularism.

3. Accommodation of Religion Approach

The third major framework, accommodation of religion, is based on the belief that the Establishment Clause recognizes the societal importance of religion. Supporters of accommodation argue that the presence of religion in society should be accommodated, as long as the government does not directly aid a religion in its religious function. Under the accommodation framework, government action only violates the Establishment Clause if it establishes a state religion, forces people to participate in religion, or favors one religion over another. Anything else would not run afoul of the Establishment Clause.

Justice Stanley Reed applied this approach in his dissent in *Illinois ex rel McCollum v. Board of Education* (1948). *McCollum* involved a program releasing public school students from class for a short period to attend optional religious classes on the school premises. The Court held that this program was unconstitutional because the classes occurred on public school premises; thus, the state's laws compelling student attendance at school were used to teach religion. In his dissent, Justice Reed argued that the Founding Fathers, including Thomas Jefferson and James Madison, had approved of requiring students at the University of Virginia to attend religious services. Thus, because education was a public function, and not a religious one, Justice Reed said that the requirement did not support a religion itself.

The Court addressed a similar situation in *Zorach v. Clauson* (1952). In that instance, the program was upheld because the religious classes were not held on public school property. The Court stated, "When the state encourages religious instruction or cooperates with religious authorities by adjusting the schedule of public events to sectarian needs, it follows the best of our traditions. For it then respects the religious nature of our people and accommodates the public service to their spiritual needs." Justice William Douglas's majority opinion stated that complete separation between church and state would interfere with many societal traditions based on religion, such as chaplains in legislatures, religious holidays off from school, and oaths in the courtroom. The dissenting opinions, by Justice Robert Jackson and Justice Black, criticized the majority's distinction based merely on the location of the religious classes. They argued that it would not violate the Establishment Clause only if the religious instruction occurred outside of school hours. Justice Black also reiterated his wall of separation view and explained that the majority's decision represented a balancing test that strayed too far into the realm of religion and that a categorical approach is more appropriate.

B. The *Lemon* Test for Analyzing the Establishment Clause

In 1970, the Court implemented a three-part test for deciding cases under the Establishment Clause, and it held that a law is constitutional if:

1. it has a secular purpose;
2. its primary effect neither advances nor inhibits religion; and
3. it does not create an "excessive entanglement" between government and religion.

Lemon v. Kurtzman (1971) involved a challenge to Rhode Island and Pennsylvania statutes that subsidized salaries for teachers in private schools. Chief Justice Warren Burger, writing for the majority, reasoned that the Establishment Clause not only forbade establishing an official religion but also prohibited government actions that were steps in that direction. Chief Justice Burger acknowledged that the Court's prior decisions did not call for a total separation between church and state, and that the "wall" of separation had become "a blurred, indistinct, and variable barrier." The Chief Justice then created what has been called the *Lemon* test. This test provides that a law that provides for "sponsorship, financial support, [or] active involvement" in religious activity violates the Establishment Clause, unless it has a secular legislative purpose, its primary effect neither advances nor inhibits religion, and it avoids creating "excessive entanglement" between government and religion. The analysis under the excessive entanglement prong involves these three factors:

1. the "character and purposes" of the particular religious institutions;
2. the nature of the governmental aid; and
3. and the relationship between the two that results from the aid.

The Court applied its new test and held the state statutes unconstitutional as violative of the Establishment Clause. The state laws required substantial oversight and intervention of "an intimate and continuing" character to ensure that the schools receiving the government aid did not violate the neutral stance on religion mandated by the First Amendment. This oversight and intervention would require entanglement between the government and the institution of the character and nature prohibited by the Religion Clauses. As a result of this entanglement, the Court held that the entanglement required by the acts would violate the Establishment Clause.

Although the *Lemon* test was announced in the context of financial aid to religious institutions, it is used as a general framework for analyzing laws under the Establishment Clause, and its very terms indicate that it has broader application. It is important to note that the Court is not restricted to the *Lemon* test; it has since decided several cases without using it. The test is a favorite of those Justices who favor the wall of separation framework, including both of its subcategories of strict separation and neutrality; whereas Justices who favor the accommodation framework have pushed for the Court to overrule the *Lemon* test. Recent developments have called the vitality of the test into question, although it has never been expressly overruled. Some fairly recent decisions have even invoked the test with approval. However, several Justices on the Court (if not a majority) disapprove of the test and have advocated replacing it with other alternative approaches, such as those discussed next.

C. Other Tests Proposed, but Not Adopted

One prominent test, the symbolic endorsement test, is a reformulation of the *Lemon* test. Over the past few decades, several Justices have adopted this test; most recently, Justice O'Connor applied it in her concurrence in *Lynch v. Donnelly* (1984), which is discussed shortly. Nevertheless, it has remained a minority test, and it has never been adopted expressly by the Court. The symbolic endorsement test examines whether the challenged government act expressed government endorsement or disapproval of religion. This endorsement or disapproval can either be direct (intent to endorse or disprove) or indirect (the act's effect is endorsement or disproval). The symbolic endorsement test differs from the *Lemon* test by deemphasizing the secular purpose prong and reformulating the other two prongs into an analysis of the endorsement or disapproval of religion.

Another alternative test to the *Lemon* test is called the coercion test. This test has also received substantial support from some Justices, and Justice Anthony Kennedy has applied it in several cases, such as *County of Allegheny v. ACLU* (1989) and *Lee v. Weisman* (1992). The coercion test examines the government action for the coercive effect it has on participation in state-sponsored or state-initiated religious activity. This test is typically applied in the context of primary and secondary schools, but it has been applied in other situations as well. The coercion that it examines can be either obvious or subtle. Subtle coercion, such as peer pressure, is more insidious because it is harder to detect. However, similar to the symbolic endorsement test, the coercion test has remained a minority approach, and the Court has never expressly supported it.

D. Government Support for Religious Beliefs

1. School Prayer and Other Government-Sanctioned Prayer

Since the 1960s, a common Establishment Clause battleground has been prayer in public schools. The Supreme Court has held that prayer in public schools is unconstitutional if it is initiated or sanctioned by school officials. The Court reached this decision in *Engel v. Vitale* (1961), where a New York school district wrote a prayer and required the students to recite it at the beginning of every school day. The Court held that this was a clear violation of the Establishment Clause. Relying on historical arguments, Justice Black, writing for the majority, explained that the First Amendment precludes the government from being able to prescribe any official prayer in any program of state-sponsored religious activity. Justice Douglas concurred, relying on the neutrality framework and reasoning that government interference in spiritual matters would be a divisive force.

In his dissent, Justice Potter Stewart advocated the accommodation framework. He wrote that denying children the ability to pray interferes with the nation's spiritual heritage. This heritage has included several government-sponsored invocations of religion, such as the Supreme Court's invocation of God's protection at the beginning of every day's session, the provision in the Pledge of Allegiance that the United States is "one nation under God," and the National Day of Prayer, which Congress established in 1952. He reasoned that this instance was similar to *Zorach* (students allowed to leave school for religious classes) because the school district's prayer is merely an expression of our national heritage. Several constitutional amendments have been proposed to authorize prayer in public schools. However, none of these amendments have received the required two-thirds vote to pass Congress.

Similarly, in *Abbington School District v. Schempp*, the Court struck down a state law that required public school students to read Bible verses at the beginning of the day and recite the Lord's Prayer. Unlike *Engle*, the state did not write the content of the prayer. Yet the Court held that the school curriculum, which required students to read Scripture and recite a prayer from a specific religion, was an inherently religious activity and a violation of the Establishment Clause. The Court was careful to limit its holding; it did not extend it to preclude the study of any religion's scripture in literature or religion courses.

The Court's holding in *Engle* and *Abbington* make it clear that the Establishment Clause prohibits government-prescribed prayer in public school. In *Wallace v. Jaffree* (1984), the Court expanded this holding to an Alabama statute that provided for prayer led by teachers for *willing* students only, and the Court struck it down as unconstitutional. What about a period of silence in public schools that can be used for meditation or prayer? In *Wallace v. Jaffree* (1985), the Court considered two other Alabama statutes that authorized a one-minute period of silence for meditation (1978 statute) and a period of silence for "meditation or voluntary prayer" (1981 statute).

The majority took a stance reminiscent of the neutrality framework in its analysis of the statute before the Court. Justice Stevens, writing for the majority, applied the *Lemon* test and held that the statute violated the first prong, which requires the legislative act to have a secular purpose. The Court held that the law lacked a secular purpose because the legislature intended to return voluntary prayer to Alabama public schools. The Court further reasoned that the only purpose was religious because the statute had the same effect as the 1978 statute, except that it added prayer as an accepted activity. This statute was an endorsement of a religious activity and violated the complete neutrality required by the First Amendment.

Justice O'Connor, in her concurrence, also took a neutrality stance while balancing the competing values of the Religion Clauses. She reasoned that nothing in the Constitution prohibits students from engaging in completely voluntary prayer. A state law that provides for a moment of silence, without mentioning prayer, was sufficient to protect the students' rights to voluntary prayer and to avoid impermissible government involvement in religion.

Chief Justice Burger dissented and advocated the accommodation framework. He argued that the statute merely stated that prayer was a permitted activity, and because it did not require prayer, it was not an endorsement of prayer. Justice Byron White agreed with this position, reasoning that the statement was necessary, otherwise a teacher would not be able to confidently say that prayer was permitted, if a student so inquired.

In *Lee v. Weisman* (1992) the Court considered the issue of prayer at graduation ceremonies. It held that public schools could not invite clergymen to deliver invocations and benedictions at middle school and high school graduations. The majority opinion, written by Justice Kennedy, stated that the government may not coerce the support of religion or participate in the exercise of religion. It may also not act in a manner that establishes or tends to establish a state religion. The Court held that the law violated the Establishment Clause because it permitted the school principals to select and invite clergymen to pray at school-sponsored graduations, it controlled the content of the prayer by telling the clergymen that it must be nonsectarian, and peer pressure could force unwilling students to participate. Justice David Souter concurred, expressing the concern that students participating in the graduation ceremony would be a captive audience to any prayer delivered. He distinguished presidential proclamations and addresses because they are not addressed at any person in particular but are impersonal, and the audience is free to leave.

The Court also examined prayer at school-sponsored activities that are not academically related—football games. In *Santa Fe Independent School District v. Doe* (2000), the Court held that student-led nondenominational prayer at high school football games were unconstitutional, even though the students voted on whether to have the prayer and which student should deliver it. Justice Stevens wrote the majority opinion, stating that this was not private speech because the public school endorsed and facilitated the prayer. It endorsed the prayer by encouraging it and following the tradition of praying at football games. The school facilitated prayer by providing the facilities where they were delivered and permitting their broadcast over the school's public address system. Additionally, the fact that the students voted to have the prayer did not make it constitutional because fundamental rights cannot be removed by majority vote. Justice Stevens noted that the proper question was whether an objective observer would perceive the prayer as state endorsement of religion, similar to the "symbolic endorsement" test offered by Justice O'Connor and others.

Recently, in *Elk Grove Unified School District v. Newdow* (2004), the Court had an opportunity to address whether the phrase "under God" in the Pledge of Allegiance constituted prayer in school when a teacher led public school students in reciting it. However, the Court sidestepped the issue and unanimously disposed of the case on standing grounds. The Elk Grove Unified School District's policy required elementary school teachers to lead their students in reciting the Pledge. The father of a student sued on the grounds that the policy violated the Establishment Clause, and he claimed that he had standing himself and that he could sue on his daughter's behalf. The Court disagreed and held that because he did not have custody of his daughter, he lacked standing to sue on her behalf.

Justice Stevens wrote the plurality opinion for the Court and concluded that the Pledge is a common pronouncement of the ideals represented by the flag of the United States. Stevens noted that the Pledge was originally created over 100 years ago, that Congress adopted it in 1942, and in 1954 Congress amended the Pledge to include "under God." Rather than decide the First Amendment issue, Justice Stevens dismissed the case on standing grounds.

Three Justices, Chief Justice William Rehnquist, Justice O'Connor, and Justice Clarence Thomas, wrote concurring opinions. Chief Justice Rehnquist believed that the Court should not sidestep the issue. Rather, it should hold that reciting the Pledge, including the phrase "under God," does not violate the Establishment Clause. For Chief Justice Rehnquist, the phrase is not sufficient to transform reciting the Pledge into a religious exercise because it only recognizes the founding history of the country.

Justice Thomas reiterated his argument that the Establishment Clause is a federalism provision, and thus, it is not incorporated into the Fourteenth

Amendment. He argued that regardless, the school district's policy did not create, maintain, or lend governmental authority to any religious establishment or religion. Justice O'Connor again advocated the endorsement test and its application to speech and public displays sponsored by the state. She considered the Pledge to be "ceremonial deism," which is ceremonial references to the divine in certain circumstances without offending the First Amendment. Other examples include the imprint of "In God We Trust" on the currency, traditional patriotic songs, and the Court's invocation of God before beginning each session. Justice O'Connor explained that the phrase "under God" is a generic reference to the divine, not a specific reference to any certain deity or religion. Furthermore, even if some of the members of Congress, who approved the phrase, had religious purposes, it is not controlling because they also had valid secular purposes.

These cases—*Engel, Jaffree, Lee,* and *Doe*—clearly indicate that prayer in the public schools is generally not permitted if the public schools or any other level of government sanctions or endorses it in any way. This includes student-led, nondenominational, and voluntary prayer, if the school sanctions the prayer, the organization, or its delivery. Allowing the students to vote on whether to have the prayer does not remove the government's impermissible entanglement, which arose from the school sanctioning the prayer. However, it is an open question as to whether prayer at a public school activity, such as graduation, would be permitted if it was entirely originated by students and if the school had no part in organizing, delivering, or managing the prayer. The Court has yet to decide this issue, despite an existing split in the circuit courts.

2. Issues Involving School Curriculum Decisions

School prayer is only one way that a state may violate the Establishment Clause of the First Amendment. Another is a public school's inclusion of religious doctrine or ideas in the curriculum. A primary example of this is the constant struggle between teaching creationism and teaching evolution. This conflict was the issue in *Epperson v. Arkansas* (1968), in which the Court held an Arkansas law unconstitutional for violating the Establishment Clause.

In 1928, Arkansas passed a law that prohibited any teacher in a public school or publicly funded university from teaching evolution. The statute specifically forbade teaching "the theory or doctrine that mankind ascended or descended from a lower order of animals" or adopting or using a textbook that taught such a theory. A violation of the statute was a misdemeanor and punishable by the teacher's removal from his or her position. Writing for the Court, Justice Abe Fortas recognized that a state has plenary power to prescribe its school curriculum, but held that this power does not extend to prohibiting the teaching of a scientific theory without violating the Establishment Clause. Although the Arkansas law did not expressly support religion, Justice Fortas reasoned that it was based on the same religious purposes as Tennessee's "Monkey Law," which was the subject of the famous *Scopes* trial. The Court said that a legislature cannot circumvent the Establishment Clause simply by omitting religious language from a law that excludes a scientific theory from school curriculum when the basis for the exclusion is to further religious doctrine.

Justice Black's concurrence stated that the Court was misguided by overturning the law because it determined that the law was motivated by religion. He reasoned that it was simply too difficult to determine the legislature's actual purpose for passing a law and the Court should defer to the legislature's stated purpose. He also considered the majority's position to be dangerous because it required public schools to teach a theory that many consider to be antireligion. In other words, how could the Constitution force a state to permit its teachers to advocate a concept that many people consider to be antagonistic to religion, when the Establishment Clause does not permit preferring nonreligion over religion?

The Court was forced to consider this issue again in *Edwards v. Aguillard* (1987). *Aguillard* involved a Louisiana statute that forbade teaching evolution in public schools unless the school also taught creationism. The statute allowed schools to teach neither concept; but if a school taught one, then it was required to teach the other. The trial and appellate courts both found the law unconstitutional as violative of the Establishment Clause.

Justice William Brennan, writing for the majority, explained that the Court is especially vigilant in monitoring the compliance of elementary and secondary schools with the Establishment Clause because of the tender age and impressionability of the students. The Court applied the *Lemon* test and found that the law was unconstitutional because it violated the first prong of the test — its secular purpose. Generally, a court must defer to the legislature's stated reason for enacting a law, unless the purpose is pretextual. The Louisiana law claimed that its purpose was to protect academic freedom. However, the Court pointed to statements by the law's sponsor, who preferred that schools teach neither creationism nor evolution. Thus, the Court found the stated purpose to be a pretext because teaching neither doctrine would hamper academic freedom and undermine providing a comprehensive education in the sciences. Additionally, the effect of the law failed to foster academic freedom because no law prohibited the teaching of any scientific theory; thus, it did not safeguard any right that the teachers did not already possess. Rather, it also took away teachers' freedom to teach only evolution. Furthermore, the law's actual purpose was to endorse a particular religious doctrine (creationism), and it carried out this endorsement by using the symbolic and financial support of the government. Because this violated the Establishment Clause, the Court held the law unconstitutional.

Another question the Court has confronted is whether a state may require public schools to provide activities that are arguably religious if the state claims that they have secular purposes. In *Abington School District v. Schempp* (1963), the Court addressed a state law that required public schools to begin each school day with a reading of at least ten Bible verses without any commentary. Abington Senior High School began their school days by reading the verses, followed by a recitation of the Lord's Prayer. This activity was led by a student, who selected the verses and the version of the Bible to use. The school provided a copy of the King James version, but the student could use another version if she provided it herself. Pennsylvania claimed that the law served secular purposes, including promoting morality, counteracting materialism, preserving our institutions, and teaching literature. The Court said that the religious nature of the activity could not be ignored and held that the activity violated the Establishment Clause. It explained that the law was not constitutional simply because students could excuse themselves from participating in the activity.

Writing for the majority, Justice Tom Clark recognized that the Court cannot endorse a "religion of secularism" because to do so would permit the government to either establish a religion or act hostilely toward religion. However, he explained that holding this law as unconstitutional does not have that effect. The decision does not prohibit the Bible from being studied for its literary and historic value or from being used in a comparative study of religion, and the Establishment Clause does not mandate such a course of action. However, a state requiring its government-sponsored schools to participate in religious exercises violates the concept of neutrality embodied in the Establishment Clause.

Justice Brennan concurred, recognizing that the exercises mandated by the law may have permissible goals, such as fostering harmony and tolerance among the students and enhancing the teacher's authority. However, because these benefits were not derived from the content of the activity but from the solemn and communal nature of the exercise, then the same goals could be reached with "less sensitive materials." For example, schools could achieve the same effect by reading the speeches of great Americans, reading from historical documents, or even reciting the Pledge of Allegiance. However, the state's use of religious means to achieve secular ends violated the Establishment Clause, just as using religious means to achieve religious ends. He refuted the argument that the law was constitutional because it does not prefer one sect over another because there are many people who would find the forced reading of the Judeo-Christian Scriptures to be patently offensive. Similarly, any attempt to create a "com-

mon denominator religion," divorced from any particular institution, is doomed
to fail.

From these cases, it is clear that the Court interprets the Establishment
Clause as prohibiting the states from infusing religion into their public school
curriculum. The state cannot condition the teaching of a scientific theory based
on teaching a competing religious doctrine. It also cannot require public schools
to provide religious exercises, even if the legislature claims a secular purpose
for the activity or permits the students to choose to not participate. Regardless of whether participation is voluntary, the Establishment clause is violated
by the infusion of religion into the government-sponsored school curriculum,
either in what courses to teach or in activities provided to the students.

3. Equal Access, Religious Displays, and Official Acknowledgment of Religion

Another question that arises under the Establishment Clause and is related
to the tension between the Establishment Clause and the Free Exercise Clause
is how much tolerance for religion the First Amendment requires. Put another
way, the question is how much space the state must give to religion to accommodate it, without violating the Free Exercise Clause. This issue arises in several different contexts, including religious groups' access to public facilities
and public displays of religion.

a. Equal Access to Public Facilities

One example of access to public facilities that frequently arises is equal access to facilities at public schools or state universities. The Court addressed
this in *Widmar v. Vincent* (1981), in which it struck down a Kansas state university regulation that prohibited student-run religious organizations from
using the university's facilities. The Court held that the regulation violated the
Free Exercise Clause and that permitting student-run religious organizations
to use public university facilities would not violate the Establishment Clause.
Justice Powell, writing for the Court, avoided discussing the interaction between the Establishment Clause and the Free Exercise Clause. He recognized
the state's compelling interest in maintaining a strict separation between religion and the state; however, per the *Lemon* test, permitting the student groups
to use the university's facilities would not violate the Establishment Clause.
Justice Powell explained that an open-forum policy, permitting access to all
registered student groups, had a secular purpose, and because all groups were
permitted, it would not give rise to excessive entanglement with religion. Additionally, the effect prong would be satisfied because the primary effect of

such a policy would not benefit religion, and any benefit to religious groups would be incidental to and encompassed by the benefits to all other student groups, religious and secular alike.

This issue arose nine years after *Widmar*, in *Board of Education v. Mergens* (1990). *Mergens* presented the question of the constitutionality of the federal Equal Access Act, which required secondary schools that received any federal financial assistance to provide equal access to student groups. Per the Act, if the school allowed any noncurricular student groups to meet at the school during noninstructional time, then it created a "limited open forum," and the school could not discriminate based on the ideas of any group, even religious groups. Westside High School denied a request by some students to form a Christian Club with membership open to all students. The Court, in an eight-to-one decision, upheld the Act, finding that it did not violate the Establishment Clause.

Justice O'Connor wrote an opinion that was in part a majority opinion and in part a plurality opinion. The majority interpreted the term "limited open forum" in the federal statute, and held that it differed from the concept of a limited public forum in the Court's First Amendment jurisprudence. The limited open forum in the statute applied to any noncurricular group, including a chess club or a volunteer service organization, and prohibited discrimination against a group based on the religious or political content of the group's beliefs or expression. Although the Act limited the participation of school officials in the meetings of any religious groups, it permitted the school to monitor the activities of a group.

Despite the overwhelming vote in favor of the constitutionality of the Equal Access Act, the Court could not agree on the reasons why it did not violate the Establishment Clause. Justice O'Connor, in her plurality opinion, found that the statute passed the *Lemon* test. She explained that the purpose of the law was secular because it was an antidiscrimination measure, the primary effect of the law was not to advance religion, and it did not create any excessive entanglement because the school officials were restricted from participating in the group's activities. Justice Thurgood Marshall, in his concurrence, did not challenge the use of the *Lemon* test, but he reasoned that any school that permitted a religiously oriented student group to operate would have to take measures to avoid the appearance that the school endorsed the group's views.

Justice Kennedy, also concurring, did not join Justice O'Connor's use of the *Lemon* test. Instead, he argued that the Court should find that the Act violated the Establishment Clause only if either (1) it directly benefited religion, so as to establish or tend to establish a state religion; or (2) the government coerced student participation in religious activities. Because neither condition was met, the Act was constitutional. Justice Kennedy also refused to apply the *Lemon* test in such a manner that would significantly restrict the ability of the government to accommodate religion. The sole dissenter, Justice Stevens, found that only extracurricular student groups advocating partisan religious, political, or ethical beliefs were noncurricular groups within the statutory meaning. Further, the Court's construction of the Act was perilously close to requiring schools to permit organized prayer and possibly some religious ceremonies.

In *Lamb's Chapel v. Center Moriches Union Free School District* (1993), the Court unanimously upheld the general rule that government cannot discriminate against a speaker by punishing speech or denying the right to speak based on the religious content of one's speech. In that instance, the Court overturned a school district's regulation that prohibited a religious group from using available school property, even though social, civic, or recreational groups were permitted. Justice White, writing for the Court, held that this discrimination was unconstitutional in violation of the Free Exercise Clause. However, the Court also held that permitting the religious group access to school property when it was not being used for school purposes was not an establishment of religion. Although he did not use it in his analysis, Justice White expressly stated that the *Lemon* test was still viable. He stated, without analysis, that permitting religious groups access to school property after school hours was not an establishment of religion under the *Lemon* test.

b. Employment of Chaplains by Legislatures

Apart from the realm of the public school and the state university, the Court has also addressed state involvement with religious practices in other contexts. In these noneducational contexts, the Court has been substantially more accommodating of the involvement of government in religious activities. The Court has upheld the practice of many legislatures, including Congress, of employing chaplains and opening its sessions with prayer. It has also found that displays of city-owned religious symbols on private property do not violate the Establishment Clause.

The Court addressed legislative employment of chaplains to deliver prayer in *Marsh v. Chambers* (1983). *Chambers* involved a challenge to Nebraska's legislature, which had chaplains on its payroll and opened each legislative session with a state-sanctioned prayer. The state legislature had employed a Presbyterian minister for eighteen years. The Court held that this was not a violation of the Establishment Clause. Writing for the majority, Chief Justice Burger explained that in light of the long tradition of opening legislative meetings with prayer, history weighed against finding this practice unconstitutional. Without considering application of the *Lemon* test, the Chief Justice relied solely on history and found that based on "the unambiguous and unbroken history of more than 200 years," the practice had become such a part of society that its constitutionality could not be seriously contested. He also stated that the compensation of the chaplain from the public treasury similarly did not raise a constitutional issue. In fact, he noted that the same Congress that enacted the First Amendment had a paid chaplain. However, although *Marsh* stands for the proposition that if the historical argument is so clear and strong the *Lemon* test need not be used, the Chief Justice failed to explain why history proved so decisive and how it could displace the test.

In his dissent, Justice Brennan argued that the Court had abandoned the criteria that the Court had developed since *Everson*. Justice Brennan promulgated the view that the Constitution is a living, evolving document that should not be stifled by historical calcification. He argued that the diversity of religion in the United States required a new interpretation of the Establishment Clause; the issue should turn on whether state sponsorship of a religious practice would offend the sensibilities of today's Americans, considering their increased diversity.

c. Religious Displays

The Court considered the display of religious symbols in *Lynch v. Donnelly* (1984). *Lynch* involved a Christmas nativity scene that the city owned but displayed on private property held by a nonprofit organization. The display included a Christmas tree, colored lights, reindeer, Santa's sleigh, and a nativity scene. The Court held that this did not violate the Establishment Clause. Chief Justice Burger, writing for the Court, analyzed this issue under the accommodation framework. He explained that it is not feasible to obtain a total separation between church and state. The metaphor of a "wall" does not accurately portray the complex relationship that exists between religion and government, which have been intertwined throughout history, as exemplified by the phrase "In God We Trust" on U.S. currency.

The Chief Justice then applied the *Lemon* test and found that the display was not unconstitutional. He explained that the purpose prong of the *Lemon* test was only violated if the challenged act was unquestionably motivated solely by religious considerations. Because the display was designed to celebrate the secular holiday of Christmas and depict the origins of that holiday, then the display was not solely motivated by religious considerations, and it did not violate the purpose prong of the test. Chief Justice Burger explained that the primary effect prong was difficult to analyze and resorted to analogies. He determined that the nativity scene did not benefit religion any more than reimbursing private schools for public transportation or endorsing the Christmas holiday, which was a contraction of its old name, "Christ's Mass." Finding that any benefit was incidental and too attenuated to be substantial, the Court held that the nativity display did not violate the primary effect prong. It also found that the entanglement prong of the *Lemon* test was not violated; although the city owned the display, it did not design it and paid minimal costs for its upkeep. Furthermore, the Court determined that political divisiveness was not sufficient to constitute excessive entanglement.

Justice O'Connor concurred in the judgment and advocated a new approach to analyzing cases under the Establishment Clause; this new approach, called the "endorsement test," was already initially discussed. Under this test, the Establishment Clause is not violated as long as there is no excessive entanglement or government endorsement or disapproval of religion. It is a neutralistic approach. Further, to be unconstitutionally excessive, entanglement must either threaten to interfere with the independence of religious institutions, or it must provide religious groups with greater access to government than nonreligious groups. Thus, Justice O'Connor essentially would remove the secular purpose prong of the *Lemon* test and transform the other two prongs into a question of whether the intent or effect of the challenged act was to endorse or disapprove of religion. Although the Court has never expressly adopted this approach, since *Lynch*, the test has gained some traction and influence. Justice Brennan dissented and criticized the majority's approach for failing to address the clearly religious message of the nativity scene and for focusing instead on the secular, holiday context of the display.

Although it upheld the Nativity display in *Lynch*, a divided Court struck down a display in a later case, *County of Allegheny v. ACLU* (1989). In a portion of Justice Harry Blackmun's plurality opinion, which five Justices supported, the Court cited *Lynch* and applied Justice O'Connor's establishment test. The Court found that endorsement could be shown by demonstrating that the government has either taken a position on religious questions or made religion relevant to one's standing in "the political community." Justice Blackmun explained that based on *Lynch*, whether a religious display impermissibly endorses religion depends on the context of the display. Accordingly, he analyzed the entire context of the display at issue in *Allegheny*, including the placement of the nativity scene in the display, the fact that carols were sung in front of it, and the display of a sign indicating that a religious organization owned the nativity portion. Contrasting this display with the one in *Lynch*, where the nativity was included among several other figures, he determined that this display was unconstitutional. However, a different majority of six Justices determined that display was not an endorsement of religion and was therefore constitutional because it included a Christmas tree, a Hanukkah menorah, and a sign stating that the city was saluting freedom during the holidays.

Justice O'Connor concurred, agreeing that the secular Christmas tree and the religious menorah were constitutional because they celebrated religious diversity and pluralism. Justice Brennan, joined by Justices Marshall and Stevens, believed that both displays were religious and unconstitutional. Justice Brennan explained that the Establishment Clause does not permit an otherwise religious display simply because it celebrates pluralism. Justice Stevens wrote his own opinion, which Justices Brennan and Marshall joined, warning of the potential for social unrest from any governmental display of religious symbols. Justice Kennedy, in a dissent joined by Chief Justice Rehnquist and Justices White and Scalia, explained that the endorsement test fails because it is too difficult to apply. They preferred an accommodation approach, reasoning that the Establishment Clause is not violated as long as the action is not coercive by the government, and it does not benefit religion more directly than other practices, which are already considered part of the American heritage. Thus, to the dissenters, the entire display, including the nativity scene, was constitutional because it was merely a passive recognition of religious holidays; it was not coercive, nor did it seek to gain converts.

d. Official Acknowledgment of Religion

The struggle over the display of religious symbols on public property has been fierce, particularly over state-mandated displays of the Ten Commandments of the Judeo-Christian heritage. At issue is how much the government may accommodate religion. In *Stone v. Graham* (1980), the Court held that a Kentucky law that required public schools to display the Ten Commandments in each classroom was unconstitutional, even though the displays were purchased with private money. The Court determined that the statute had no secular purpose; therefore, it violated the Establishment Clause. However, under the accommodation framework, a display that officially acknowledges religion is permissible. Factors relevant to this analysis include the history, purpose, location, and context of the display.

To illustrate the continuing tension, consider the recent case of *Van Orden v. Perry* (2005). In that case, the Court addressed the placement of a monument containing the Ten Commandments around the Texas state capitol. It was one of thirty-eight monuments and historical markers in the twenty-two acres of land surrounding the capitol, and it was designed to commemorate the "people, ideals, and events" of the unique identity of the state of Texas. The monument, at six feet tall and three feet wide, was placed to the north of the capitol. In addition to the Ten Commandments, it contained several other images, including an eagle holding the American flag, an eye inside a pyramid, two stars of David, and the Greek letters rho and chi. A private civic group donated the monument and paid for its erection; the state was involved only in accepting the monument and in designating its location. After encountering it frequently over a six-year period, the plaintiff(s) challenged the monument, claiming that it violated the Establishment Clause. The Court disagreed and held, without a majority opinion, that the monument did not violate the Establishment Clause, primarily because of its location and private commissioning.

Chief Justice Rehnquist, joined by Justices Scalia, Kennedy, and Thomas, issued a plurality opinion, which exhibited a decidedly accommodationist tone. He recognized the inherent antagonism between the Establishment Clause and the Free Exercise Clause but said that the Court must maintain the division between church and state, while simultaneously not showing hostility to religion by ignoring our religious heritage. He noted that the Court has selectively applied the *Lemon* test, and the plurality declined to apply it here. Instead, it focused on the monument and the Commandments' place in the nation's history—that is, its presence in the courtroom of the Supreme Court building and its role in the executive and legislative branches. He then distinguished *Stone v. Graham* (1980), which involved a law mandating the appearance of the Ten Commandments in classrooms and had a religious purpose. By contrast, the monument here served a historical purpose, and it was a passive display, because people were not required to encounter it every day.

Justice Stephen Breyer concurred, noting that one cannot find a simple mechanical test to apply in Establishment Clause jurisprudence. Instead, he explained that one must use a case-by-case analysis while adhering to the purposes of the Establishment and Free Exercise Clauses. He argued that the Constitution does not require everything that is religious to be purged from the public arena. Relying on the monument's history and its location, he reasoned that the state likely allowed the monument for its secular (rather than its religious) effects. After examining the nature of the monument, the fact that it is one of many monuments and markers, and its location, which is not on public school grounds, Justice Breyer reasoned that if the Court found the monument to be unconstitutional, then it would indicate hostility toward religion, which the relationship between the Establishment and Free Exercise Clauses forbids.

The dissenters would have held the monument unconstitutional under the Establishment Clause. Justice Stevens took a strict neutrality approach and found that if the Court is to preserve any fragment of Jefferson's wall of separation metaphor, the monument must be struck down. He agreed that the Establishment Clause permits official recognition of religion, in light of our nation's heritage, but he thought that this monument went too far. He argued that times had changed since the monument was erected, and he expressed concern that the monument would make those who did not subscribe to the

Judeo-Christian beliefs feel as if they were outsiders. He explained that the Court's reference to government speeches that invoke religion was inapposite because the speakers are individuals and not the government itself. He concluded that the monument was inherently discriminatory and that the wall of separation should be preserved.

Justice Souter also dissented. Although he agreed that government is required to remain neutral, he did not believe that a display of the Ten Commandments, which are religious on their face, could possibly be nonreligious. He suggested that a similar monument could be constitutional, if it included a secular explanation of its place in the nation's heritage and was accompanied by other historical monuments. The fact that there were other historical monuments, scattered across the twenty-two acres around the capitol, did not correct the failure to have a secular reference point, inscribed on the monument. He also rejected the argument that because the constitutional challenge came forty years after the monument's erection, it was therefore constitutional. He argued that the mere passage of time is irrelevant in constitutional analysis. He said that a citizen should be able to come to his or her state's seat of government without having to confront religion in the process.

In contrast with the decision in *Van Orden*, the Court struck down the display of the Ten Commandments in two county courthouses, largely because of their location and prominence. In *McCreary County v. ACLU* (2005), the Court found a predominantly religious motivation to these displays. They displays were large and prominently placed, and there had been three different versions of display, the last included each commandment framed and hung individually. Writing for the Court, Justice Souter explained that the government must be neutral when it comes to religion. He appeared to apply the *Lemon* test and found that the predominant purpose behind the displays was religious and not secular, which violated the first prong of the test. He compared this display with the one in *Stone* (Ten Commandments displayed in classrooms) and found that they had two distinct characteristics in common: (1) They both contained the actual text of the Commandments, rather than a symbolic representation, such as stone tablets with illegible writing on them; and (2) the display was separate and not part of any secular display involving a historical context. Because the displays were not part of a general display of law givers, as in the courtroom of the Supreme Court, and they bore a facially religious message, the Court held that they were unconstitutional.

In dissent, Justice Scalia, joined by Chief Justice Rehnquist and Justices Thomas and Kennedy, argued that the displays were constitutional. In addition to pointing to several historical facts to illustrate his point, he argued against the *Lemon* test. He claimed that the Court had misused the test by contorting the first prong; instead of requiring any secular purpose, the Court has required an act to have a secular *primary* purpose. The Court's reliance on the purpose behind the displays, rather than on the displays themselves, was improper. Further, Justice Scalia noted that the displays at issue here were included among and no more prominent than other historical documents and portraits throughout the courthouses.

Based on these cases, it seems clear that the Court considers the context of the official acknowledgment to be key. When a religious display is accompanied by other displays that are of other religious traditions, or includes an explanation of the historical importance of the display, the Court tends to permit the display. However, when the religious aspect of the display is emphasized and singled out, the Court is hesitant to uphold the display. The Court also has indicated that it feels the need to police the public school classroom more closely than the statehouse or the courthouse because of the impressionability of children's minds. Additionally, it sometimes ignores the *Lemon* test in its Establishment Clause jurisprudence, which may call the test's continuing vitality into question. Some Justices prefer the endorsement test, and others look solely to history as a guide. However, the Court has never rejected the test expressly, nor has it accepted a different test as being more workable. Thus, if the religious display passes the *Lemon* test, or if its secular aspects, including demonstrating religious plurality, are emphasized over its religious content, then the Court seems willing to permit it.

4. *Financial Aid to Religious Institutions*

Government programs that provide either direct or indirect aid to religious groups and institutions are challenged frequently under the Establishment Clause. Due to different Justices embracing different tests and the inherent difficulty in applying those tests, the jurisprudence in this area has been muddled.

a. Analysis before the *Lemon* Test

The seminal case on this issue, *Everson v. Board of Education* (1947), was already discussed to introduce the wall of separation framework. At issue in *Everson* was a New Jersey law that reimbursed parents for public transportation costs incurred to send their children to private religious schools. The Court held that the law did not violate the Establishment Clause and therefore was constitutional.

Justice Black, writing for the majority, explained that the Establishment Clause prevents states from using tax revenues to support any institution "which teaches the tenets and faith" of any religious group. However, the Free Exercise Clause similarly forbids any state from interfering with the free exercise of religion. Thus, no state can exclude any person from benefiting from tax revenues that are spent on the general welfare merely because of their faith or lack thereof. Justice Black took a decidedly neutralist approach and wrote that although the government cannot help religion, neither can it hinder it. Without this aid to the parents, some students would not be able to attend the parochial schools; however, the same could be said if the state cut off "such general government services as ordinary police and fire protection, connections for sewage disposal, public highways and sidewalks." For Justice Black it was important that the funds went to the parents, not the schools. This law did nothing more than help parents transport their children to their schools, regardless of religious affiliation. Thus, this law did not penetrate the wall of separation. If the state had refused to reimburse the parents due to the religious affiliation of the schools, then that would have been antagonistic toward religion and would have violated the Free Exercise Clause.

Justice Jackson dissented, finding that the law discriminated against non-Catholics and was unconstitutional. He reasoned that the law was essentially a religious test because it limited reimbursement to parents that sent their children to private nonprofit schools, and only Catholic schools operated completely on a nonprofit basis, whereas Protestant schools and public for-profit schools did not qualify. He compared this to providing police or fire protection only to Catholic schools. Thus, to Justice Jackson, this law discriminated based on religion in violation of the Establishment Clause.

Justice Rutledge, in his dissent, took a wider view of the law and would have held that it used the state's taxing power to directly benefit a religion. For him, the issue was not about the reimbursement of bus fares but about the state's invasion into the private realm of a person's relationship with his God. Taking a strict-separation approach, Justice Rutledge wrote that the Establishment Clause commanded a strict separation that "necessarily entails hardship" on those who choose to use services that the state cannot provide, in lieu of the services it can provide. Thus, withholding the reimbursement would not make the state antagonistic toward religion but would remain faithful to the Establishment Clause.

b. Analysis under the *Lemon* Test

Although *Everson* is the seminal decision in this area, the Court did not state any specific test for analyzing financial aid to religious institutions. In *Lemon v. Kurtzman* (1971) (states subsidized teachers' salaries in private schools), the Court set out a three-prong test, under which a law does not violate the Establishment Clause if:

1. it has a secular purpose (or a secular primary purpose);
2. its principal or primary effect does not advance or inhibit religion; and

3. it does not foster an excessive entanglement between government and religion.

This test applies to cases involving financial aid to religious schools and other religious institutions.

i. Direct and Indirect Aid to Schools

The Court has addressed direct and indirect financial aid to religious schools in several cases. Generally, the Court has been hesitant to permit financial assistance to primary and secondary religious schools, if it would violate the *Lemon* test or if the aid would further the mission of a religious school. In *Meek v. Pittenger* (1975), the Court prohibited a state from loaning "instructional material and equipment" (which included maps, charts, audiovisual materials, and laboratory equipment) to private schools because such aid could conceivably advance a religious school's overall religious mission. The Court held that it violated the second prong of *Lemon* test—the principal effect of the government aid advanced religion. Furthermore, it violated the third prong because providing these "auxiliary services" could require the government to supervise and manage the use of the money, which would result in excessive entanglement.

The Court has similarly struck down other statutes that could be construed to aid the religious mission of a parochial school. This includes providing instruction for remedial or accelerated students, guidance counseling, and even testing and services for students that have hearing and speech impairments. However, in *Wolman v. Walter* (1977), the Court upheld a law that provided for diagnostic speech, hearing, and psychological services because the services had only a *de minimis* educational content, if any, and thus were not related to the mission of nonpublic schools. Further, nonpublic employees were not involved in the delivery of the services, and the services were offered off-site at neutral locations.

The Court has also held that money for field trips and to repair and maintain buildings is related to the school's mission. For example, in *Wolman*, the Court invalidated a law authorizing state funds to pay for field trips "to governmental, industrial, cultural, and scientific centers designed to enrich the secular studies of students." It found this to be direct aid to religious education, which could lead to excessive entanglement with religion. The Court also struck down a statute that authorized direct grants to qualified nonpublic schools for the maintenance and repair of school facilities and equipment. The state's secular purpose was to safeguard the health, safety, and welfare of the students. However, because the grants were not limited to facilities used only for secular purposes but were also given to religious buildings, the Court found that the law's effect was to further the parochial schools' religious mission.

The Court has also found that state funding of salaries for teachers, who provided remedial instruction on school premises to disadvantaged students in parochial schools was unconstitutional in *Aguilar v. Felton* (1985). The Court applied the *Lemon* test and held that it violated the third prong; the extensive supervision the state had to exercise over the program constituted extensive entanglement. However, over a decade later, in *Agostini v. Felton* (1997), the Court retreated from *Aguilar* and indicated that providing such remedial education on the campuses of parochial schools did not violate the Establishment Clause. In doing so, it liberally applied the *Lemon* test and found that *Aguilar* was no longer good law. Writing for the majority, Justice O'Connor found that the *Aguilar* Court had made four assumptions that have since been undermined: (1) Any public employee, working on the premises of a parochial school, presumptively includes religion in his or her work; (2) public employees working on the grounds of religious schools symbolically established a state religion; (3) any funding that directly aids the educational mission of religious schools impermissibly aids religious indoctrination, even if the funding reaches the schools "on the basis of neutral, secular criteria ... made available ... on a nondiscriminatory basis"; and (4) public employees who provide such instruction necessarily create an excessive entanglement because of the degree of supervision required. Thus, the Court will uphold a program that funds public employees who provide remedial instruction to disadvantaged students on the grounds of parochial schools if it meets certain requirements: (1) The employees cannot participate in religious indoctrination; and (2) the program receives funding on the basis of neutral, secular purposes.

The Court has upheld other instances of aid to nonpublic schools under the *Lemon* test, if the aid could not reasonably benefit a school's religious mission. In *Wolman*, the Court permitted state aid to nonpublic schools to administer and score standardized tests. To qualify for the aid, the schools had to administer the same test that was given to the public schoolchildren, and nonpublic employees could not be involved in preparing or scoring the tests. By contrast, in *Levitt v. Committee for Public Education* (1973), the Court held that the state could not subsidize nonstandardized tests that teachers created for their own classes because there was not a way to ensure that the tests were devoid of any religious aspects.

The Court has also decided several cases that involved aid to institutions of higher learning, such as colleges and universities, that were affiliated with a religious institution. Generally, the Court is more accepting of aid to these institutions because the Court considers the students to be more sophisticated and less susceptible to religious indoctrination. However, any such programs must still survive the Establishment Clause, usually measured by the *Lemon* test.

For example, in *Tilton v. Richardson* (1971), the Court found that a federal law that provided funds to religious colleges for construction of new buildings passed the *Lemon* test and did not run afoul of the Establishment Clause. The law excluded any buildings used for religious purposes, and the federal government retained an interest in the buildings for twenty years. The Court explained that the law's purpose was secular—to aid the expansion of facilities to accommodate the increasing numbers of students entering higher education. Furthermore, it did not have the effect of promoting religion because the grants included strict restrictions concerning the use of the facilities. Last, the aid would not foster excessive entanglement because in contrast to parochial primary and secondary schools, religious indoctrination was not a substantial purpose of the colleges and universities. Additionally, many religious schools enjoyed a "high degree of academic freedom," which encouraged free thinking and critical responses to professors. However, the Court invalidated a portion of the law that permitted the buildings to be converted to religious use after the twenty-year period; the Court reasoned that under the effects prong, the conversion would advance religion.

The Court followed *Tilton* in *Hunt v. McNair* (1973), a case in which the Court permitted religious institutions of higher learning to benefit from state revenue bonds. The use of the bonds did not violate the Establishment Clause because, similar to the grants in *Tilton*, the money was restricted to buildings that were not used for religious purposes. Furthermore, the money was also available to nonreligious private colleges and universities. The Court further distinguished colleges and universities from elementary and secondary schools in *Roemer v. Board of Public Works* (1976). *Roemer* involved a Maryland program that provided direct financial aid to private institutions of higher learning. The program did not exclude private religious institutions except for seminaries. The state provided funds based on the student population at the religious institution, calculated at 15 percent of the amount it spent per student in the public colleges and universities. The Court approved the program by a vote of five to four but without a majority opinion. Justice Blackmun's plurality applied the *Lemon* test and upheld the aid because (1) the purpose was to support private higher education as an alternative to the public system; (2) the effect was not to promote religion because the law prohibited use of the funds for "specifically religious" activities; and (3) the minimal state oversight of the program did not involve excessive entanglement. Justices White and Rehnquist concurred in the judgment. However, they criticized the plurality's use of the *Lemon* test; instead, they found that the program was constitutional because the measure was not religiously motivated and it did not advance religion.

With respect to state financial aid to religiously affiliated schools, the Court draws a distinction between parochial primary and secondary schools versus colleges and universities. In the former, the Court is much less tolerant of financial aid, direct or indirect, to such schools, primarily because the students are impressionable at this age, and the schools are more likely to emphasize religious indoctrination. In the latter, the Court is substantially more tolerant because neither of those considerations are as prevalent. The Court's distinction seems to create a presumption against the constitutionality of financial aid to primary and secondary schools that are affiliated with a religious institution; however, there does not appear to be any such presumption for religious colleges and universities. To survive the *Lemon* test, aid to religious primary and secondary schools must have a clearly secular purpose. Furthermore, the aid cannot be used to provide religious education or to conceivably further the religious mission of the schools. Additionally, to avoid excessive entanglement, the aid generally may not involve any public employees, unless it is a program for remedial instruction of disadvantaged students with sufficient safeguards. In contrast, the Court will generally uphold aid to colleges and universities that are affiliated with religious institutions, as long as the money is not used for any religious purposes. The Court has even permitted direct aid to post-secondary schools to offset the per-student cost if the school is not solely aimed at religious education, as is the case with religious seminaries.

ii. Aid to Students at Religious Schools and School Vouchers

The issue of school vouchers has increasingly come to the forefront of public concern and thus to the attention of the courts. States create these programs, which provide funds for children to attend a school other than the one to which the state assigns them. The purpose is to create a "school choice" for students, so that the public schools will have to compete for students, either among themselves or against private schools, which will improve the quality of public education. However, many voucher programs permit state funds to be used to attend parochial schools, which leads to challenges that the programs violate the Establishment Clause. These programs are distinguishable from those in *Everson*, *Wolman*, and *Meeks* because voucher programs directly subsidize the educational mission of the schools by providing state funds to the schools by way of the students.

Until recently, the Court had addressed the issue of state funding of parochial schools, but it had not laid out clear guidance on the issue, finding some programs unconstitutional and others constitutional. For example, in *Committee for Public Education and Religious Liberty v. Nyquist* (1973), the Court used the *Lemon* test to strike down a program, which provided partial tuition reimbursements and tax benefits to the parents of students that attended nonpublic primary and secondary schools. The Court explained that the program ran afoul of the effects prong of the *Lemon* test because there was no effective way to ensure that the money was used solely for "secular, neutral, and nonideological purposes" and thus, direct aid was unconstitutional, regardless of its form. Similarly, in *Sloan v. Lemon* (1973), the Court struck down a Pennsylvania program that provided similar benefits and specifically prohibited the state from having any supervision or control over any private schools. The Court explained that there was no substantial distinction between *Sloan* and *Nyquist* and held the law unconstitutional.

Approximately ten years later, the Court began to be more receptive to school voucher programs. In *Mueller v. Allen* (1983), it upheld a Minnesota law that permitted parents to deduct educational expenses from their state income tax. Even though the law made no distinction between religious and nonreligious private schools, the Court found that it did not violate the Establishment Clause.

Nearly twenty years after *Mueller*, the Court upheld Ohio's voucher program in *Zelman v. Simmons-Harris* (2002). In a hotly contested decision, the Court held that the program did not violate the Establishment Clause. The Ohio voucher program specifically stated that its aim was to provide school choice for families residing in the Cleveland City School District. It was designed to permit low-income and minority children to attend any school other than the inner-city school to which they were assigned, even if the school was parochial. Ohio enacted the law because Cleveland's public schools had repeatedly been ranked among the poorest performing schools in the United States. It designed the program to improve that statistic by providing tuition for students who attended private schools and by financing tutoring for students who remained in public schools. Writing for the majority, Chief Justice Rehnquist did not apply the *Lemon* test. Rather, he applied *Agostini* (remedial instruction to disadvantaged students) and explained that the Establishment Clause only prohibits states from making laws that "have the 'purpose' or 'effect' of advancing or inhibiting religion." The Chief Justice explained that Ohio's program served a valid secular purpose—educational assistance those who needed it the most, that is, the poor in a public school system that was failing to meet the needs of its students. The Court also had distinguished programs that directly aided religious schools from programs that only aided religious schools because of independent, private choice. Here, the program did not encourage students to choose a religious school over any other private or public school; thus, it fell into the latter category and did not have the effect of advancing or restraining religion. Thus, its neutrality toward religion made the voucher program constitutional.

Justice Souter, dissenting, attacked the program and the majority's reasoning on two main grounds. First, the voucher program was skewed in favor of religious schools because students predominately choose religious schools over other, secular private schools. The financial incentives resulted in students choosing religious schools, not out of free will but due to financial reasons. He found it significant that most students elected to attend religious schools, they chose schools of a different faith than their own, and they based the decision on financial reasons because, for example, Catholic schools were substantially cheaper than other private schools.

Second, Justice Souter thought that the Ohio voucher program undermined the very purpose of the Establishment Clause because it violated three of its objectives: (1) respect for freedom of conscience; (2) prevent corruption of religion by establishing a state religion; and (3) the social conflict that religion has produced throughout history. The voucher program was contrary to the Establishment Clause because the state financial aid did not reach religious schools as a product of genuine free choice.

Similarly, Justices Stevens and Breyer would have found the program unconstitutional. In his dissent, Justice Stevens explained that this program removed "a brick from the wall that was designed to separate religion and government," would lead to the very religious strife that the founding fathers wished to prevent, and would undermine our form of government. Justice Breyer's dissent recognized that although the Establishment Clause permits states to provide limited forms of assistance to religious schools, this program went too far. For Justice Breyer, the doctrine of separation is even more important today because of the great diversity of religions in the United States. This type of voucher program would lead to religious strife because the public may feel that certain religious schools are too extreme, or it would cause various religions to compete for the state money. Additionally, the amount of supervision required to ensure that schools complied with the program's standards would require an unconstitutional excessive entanglement of government and religion.

Thus, the Court will permit a school voucher program, even if it benefits religious schools, as long as it meets certain requirements:

1. it does not provide financial incentives for students to elect religious schools over other private or public schools;
2. it is effectively neutral toward religion and permits genuine, individual choice in determining which school to attend; and
3. it provides benefits to a wide array of people, limited only by financial need and residence in a particular school district.

States may also permit parents to deduct some of their children's private school educational expenses from their income taxes, even if the schools are religious.

Yet the Court indicated in *Zellman* that its decision did not grant blanket approval to voucher programs; thus, there will undoubtedly be future challenges to the constitutionality of such programs.

iii. Aid to Nonscholastic Religious Organizations

If one were to plot the Court's view of financial aid to religious organizations on a continuum, the aid to non-scholastic religious institutions is on the opposite side of the spectrum from the Court's close scrutiny of aid to primary and secondary schools. The Court clearly views financial aid to religious primary and secondary schools with a watchful eye, and they are presumptively invalid. Although the Court is generally more accepting of aid to religious postsecondary educational institutions, it is even more tolerant of such aid to nonscholastic religious institutions. In these situations, the Court is generally very deferential to legislative judgment.

Although there are few cases addressing the issue of aid to nonscholastic religious organizations, the Court's jurisprudence dates back over a century. In 1899, the Court addressed an Establishment Clause challenge to government funding for a new facility in a hospital affiliated with the Roman Catholic Church. In *Bradfield v. Roberts* (1899), the Court upheld the funding because the hospital did not discriminate based on the religion of those seeking treatment, and the fact that a religious group operated the facility was "wholly immaterial" to the constitutionality of the aid.

In *Bowen v. Kendrick* (1988), the Court upheld the constitutionality of government grants to provide counseling and health care for pregnant adolescents and their parents. The Adolescent Family Life Act provided grants to religious and nonreligious groups for counseling adolescents against engaging in sexual activity. Yet the program specifically prohibited the use of federal funds for any abortion-related services, including counseling and other family planning services. Writing for the majority, Chief Justice Rehnquist applied the *Lemon* test and found that the law had a secular purpose — to reduce or eliminate teenage pregnancy, teen sexual activity, and teen parenthood, as well as the socioeconomic problems they caused. The program did not have the effect of advancing or hindering religion because the Act was neutral, and the aid was more important than who provided the services. Furthermore, it did not create an excessive entanglement between religion and government because the Act did not require the government to monitor the recipients of the grants. The Court pointed out that it had found excessive entanglement in cases that involved primary and secondary schools with a substantial purpose of religious indoctrination, and it distinguished *Bowen* on those grounds.

Justice Blackmun dissented and found the Act to be unconstitutional. The program essentially subsidized religious teachings because the religious groups performed counseling without any constraints on sectarian content. He also disagreed with the Court's assertion that the religious groups at issue were not as pervasively sectarian as the primary and secondary schools for whom government aid was found to be unconstitutional. He likened the groups' mission to the pervasively sectarian and inculcatory motives of the primary and secondary schools to which the government generally cannot provide financial aid and distinguished them from the religiously affiliated postsecondary institutions to which government aid was generally upheld. Justice Blackmun argued that the law advanced religion, in violation of the *Lemon* test, because the government essentially paid for religious groups to indoctrinate teenagers. Under Justice Blackmun's analysis, the majority placed too much emphasis on the fact that the Act was facially neutral, and it disregarded the same policy reasons that supported striking down financial aid to primary and secondary religious schools.

The Court has struck down tax exemptions that violate the Establishment Clause. In *Texas Monthly, Inc. v. Bullock* (1989), the Court considered a sales tax exemption for religious periodicals, which were entirely composed of writings promoting religious teachings. In a plurality opinion, authored by Justice Brennan, the Court struck down the exemption. The exemption directly benefited religion and was not merely incidental, because the tax benefits were only given to publishers of religious periodicals, and nonreligious organizations were excluded. By providing tax exemptions, the government was forcing the taxpayers to be "indirect and vicarious donors" to the religious organizations. As a result, more extensive entanglement occurred than if the government imposed a tax of general application. In his dissent, Justice Scalia argued that the exemption might be necessary to avoid possible interference with the free exercise of religion. He took an accommodationist view and found a middle ground that would not implicate either the Establishment Clause or the Free Exercise Clause.

In another tax-related case, *Jimmy Swaggart Ministries v. Board of Equalization* (1990), the Court unanimously upheld a state sales and use tax on products purchased out of state because it applied generally. California could apply the tax to religious groups because if it exempted religious groups from these taxes, except for serving meals, then it would violate the Establishment Clause. Justice O'Connor delivered the majority opinion and found that the tax did not foster an excessive entanglement with religion. These tax-related decisions show that the Court will defer to the legislature's balancing of values, but when the balance weighs too much in favor of religion, as in *Texas Monthly*, the Court's deference disappears and the law is stricken.

5. Conclusion

As discussed, the Court tends to divide its analysis of financial aid to religion into two main groups. On one hand, financial aid to primary and secondary parochial schools is generally presumed to violate the Establishment Clause. To be constitutional, the aid must be solely for secular purposes, not to advance the mission of the religious school, and any services funded by the aid may need to be off of school grounds. On the other hand, the Court general gives great legislative deference to financial aid to postsecondary religious schools and to religious institutions for nonacademic activities. The Court does not feel the need to watch government financial aid in postsecondary schools as closely as it does aid to religious elementary and high schools because there is less emphasis on religious indoctrination and college students are less impressionable. Similarly, in the nonacademic context, the Court is more tolerant of financial aid to religious groups and generally defers to legislative judgment.

III. The Free Exercise Clause

The First Amendment not only contains a direct command that "Congress shall make no law respecting an establishment of religion," it also expressly forbids Congress from "prohibiting the free exercise" of religion. Similar to the Establishment Clause, the second clause, called the Free Exercise Clause, is stated in deceptively simple terms.

The Court has stated repeatedly that the Free Exercise Clause prevents the government from punishing religious beliefs and from compelling them. Through this clause, the Constitution prohibits the government from legislating thoughts or beliefs; however, it permits the government to legislate conduct. In *Braunfield v. Brown* (1961), Chief Justice Warren stated that the people have an absolute freedom to hold whatever religious beliefs they choose. However, since its first decision interpreting the Free Exercise Clause, *Reynolds v. United States* (1878), the Court has clearly and unequivocally declared that "Congress was deprived of all legislative power over mere opinion, but was left free to reach actions." Because the Free Exercise Clause only permits the government to regulate actions, the clause is implicated, according the Court in *Lyng v. Northwest Indian Cemetery Protective Association* (1988), when a law burdens a person's ability to observe his or her religious requirements or obligations in one of two ways: (1) It prohibits conduct that is required by a religious belief; or (2) it requires conduct that is forbidden by a religion.

The Free Exercise Clause cannot be read so broadly that any conduct a person claims to be part of the "free exercise" of his or her religion is protected from governmental interference. Otherwise, no law could have any effect because a person could always claim that the conduct it prohibited was required by his religious beliefs. As an example, in *Reynolds*, the Court upheld a law that prohibited polygamy, despite the fact that Mormons claimed that their religion required them to practice polygamy. Therefore, the Court is forced to draw a "line in the sand" to separate what is protected under the Free Exercise Clause and what the government can prohibit.

Similar to other freedoms protected by the First Amendment, the freedom to exercise one's religion is a fundamental right. Thus, laws impacting the free exercise of religion are generally divided into two categories. First, there are laws that facially discriminate against religion, either by discriminating against all religions or by discriminating against a specific subset, or even a single, religion. Second, there are laws that are facially neutral, but have an adverse effect on all, some, or even one religion. Each of these categories are discussed in turn.

A. Laws Discriminating against Religion

Facially discriminatory laws are those that expressly interfere with a person's ability to observe the requirements of his or her religion or expressly require a person to act in a manner that is inconsistent with his or her religion. Generally, a law that facially discriminates against religion must pass strict scrutiny to be constitutional. A law is facially discriminatory if it is not neutral and is not of general applicability. Although governments rarely overtly discriminate against religion, when they do so, the law may violate the Free Exercise Clause, if it fails strict scrutiny.

Under the Court's decisions, laws that are neither neutral nor generally applicable—are facially discriminatory. Under the test the court created in *Employment Division v. Smith* (1990), a law is not neutral if it specifically forbids conduct of a religious but not a nonreligious nature, or if it forbids beliefs of a religious nature but not similar nonreligious beliefs. Furthermore, a law is not generally applicable if it is so substantially underinclusive that it does not prohibit nonreligious conduct that is substantially similar to the prohibited religious conduct. A law that is facially discriminatory based on one's religious beliefs, not one's conduct, is absolutely unconstitutional under the Free Exercise Clause. A facially discriminatory law that only reaches conduct must meet strict scrutiny, that is, narrowly tailored to achieve a compelling government purpose. Whereas, laws facially discriminating against religious beliefs always violate the Free Exercise Clause.

One example of a facially discriminatory law was the statute at issue in *McDaniel v. Paty* (1978). Tennessee disqualified religious ministers and other members of religious orders from membership in the state legislature. The Court unanimously declared that the Tennessee constitutional provision violated the Free Exercise Clause. The plurality, written by Chief Justice Burger, explained that the disqualification was not directed at belief but at the "status, acts, and conduct" of a person. The Chief Justice pointed to historical evidence that a religious minister is no more likely to work toward establishment of religion than any other person. Other Justices found that the law at a minimum violated the "freedom to act" branch of the Free Exercise Clause.

The Court reaffirmed the strict scrutiny requirement for laws that facially discriminate against religion in its decision in *Church of the Lukumi Babalu Aye, Inc. v. Hialeah* (1993). The Church of the Lukumi Babalu Aye purchased land in the city of Hialeah, Florida, and planned to build "a house of worship as well as a school, cultural center, and museum." The church practiced a religion called Santería, a fusion of traditional African religion and Roman Catholicism. Santería teaches that the spirits require animal sacrifices to survive and believers should make sacrifices at significant events, such as a birth, marriage, or death. In response to the planned construction, the City passed an ordinance that prohibited animal sacrifice by any individual or a group that "kills, slaughters, or sacrifices animals for any type of ritual, regardless of whether or not the flesh or blood of the animal is to be consumed."

The Court unanimously declared that the Hialeah ordinance was unconstitutional. Justice Kennedy, writing for the majority, explained that the city clearly passed this ordinance because it disapproved of the Santería religion. The ordinance was facially discriminatory because it outlawed certain activities, specifically in reference to religion. Further, it was not of general applicability because it only applied to individuals and groups who sacrificed animals for religious purposes; thus, its purpose was not protect the public health and or prevent cruelty to animals. Thus, failing the *Smith* test, the Court concluded that the law was facially discriminatory. To survive strict scrutiny, the means must be narrowly tailored to meet a compelling government interest. Even if the law could fairly be said to support the policies just noted, the Court explained that its application was so substantially underinclusive that it could not be narrowly tailored to achieve those ends. The Court also noted the ordinance clearly violated the policy of religious toleration underlying the Free Exercise Clause. Justice Scalia, in his concurrence, explained that the First Amendment does not permit the Court to investigate into the legislature's intent, and the Court may only consider the effects of laws in First Amendment inquiries. Here, the ordinance had unconstitutional effects on the free exercise of religion, regardless of legislative intent.

B. Neutral Laws Adversely Affecting Religion

Facially neutral laws are those that place a burden on a person's ability to fulfill his or her religious obligations, even though they may not require an act inconsistent with a person's religion or may not prohibit an act that is required by a person's religion. Although the government may be attempting to remedy a social problem that is completely unrelated to religion, it may violate the Free Exercise Clause either by requiring action in a manner that is inconsistent with a person's religious beliefs or by forbidding action that is required by a person's religious beliefs. In these cases, the courts must weigh the strength of society's need to remedy the secular social problem against the need to avoid impacting a person's ability to act in accord with her religion. Today, the Court gives great deference to the legislature's judgment when laws are generally applicable and target only conduct, not belief. Thus, the Court will generally only apply the rational basis test. However, in certain instances, Congress has statutorily required the Court to apply strict scrutiny.

1. Early Cases Deferred to the Government Concerning Actions but Not Beliefs

The Court's jurisprudence concerning facially neutral laws has undergone several changes, from great deference to the legislature, to slowly restricting the power of government, to applying strict scrutiny, and finally back to according great deference. In its early decisions, the Court accorded great deference to the government and generally upheld the challenged act, as long as the enactments regulated conduct. If the government infringed on a person's right to freedom of religious belief, the Court generally struck down the government's actions. The seminal case, *Reynolds v. United States* (1878), dealt with a Latter-Day Saint (commonly called a Mormon) who practiced polygamy in violation of a federal law. The Mormons claimed that their religion required them to marry multiple spouses and that they could not submit to the federal ban on the practice. Finding that the law was aimed solely at conduct, the Court upheld the law. The Court determined that the Constitution granted the government broad authority to regulate conduct because laws are made to govern actions. To hold otherwise would be to abdicate the foundations of civilized government and to place a man's beliefs above the law of the land, permitting "every citizen to become a law unto himself," which would lead to anarchy.

However, the Court has not strictly adhered to the distinction between belief and conduct. In *Cantwell v. Connecticut* (1940), the Court refused to defer to the judgment of the state legislature. A man and his two sons, who were ordained ministers of the Jehovah's Witness religion, were arrested and convicted of attempting to sell religious literature without a license. The Court overturned their convictions and struck down the statute as violating the Free Exercise Clause. It was especially bothered by the unfettered discretion of the licensing officials, which constituted an unconstitutional prior restraint on both free speech and the free exercise of religion. The Court explained that the Free Exercise Clause protects both the freedom to believe, which is absolute and may not be infringed, and the freedom to act, which the government has the power to regulate if it does not unduly burden religion. This new test placed a slightly greater limit on the power of government than existed in *Reynolds*.

The Court followed similar reasoning in *Braunfeld v. Brown* (1961), a case in which Jewish merchants challenged a law that required businesses to close on Sundays. The merchants argued that their religion already required them to close on Saturdays; thus, the new law permitted them to be open only five days per week, whereas their competitors could be open for six days. The Court found that the law only indirectly burdened the free exercise of religion. It did not directly prohibit a particular religious practice, and the law was not directed at Jews in particular. Rather, it was of general applicability, and the burden on the Jewish merchants was an unintended consequence of the law. The Court suggested that the state could enact legislation to exempt followers of religions that mandated closing on another day from being subject to the Sunday closing law. Furthermore, the Court placed another limitation on the government's ability to regulate the free exercise of religion. It said that the law would have violated the Free Exercise Clause if the state could have accomplished its goal in another way that did not burden any religious practice.

2. Strict Scrutiny Becomes the Test

Following its decision in *Braunfeld*, the Court began to view government acts that infringe on the free exercise of religion with an increasingly narrow lens and applied heightened scrutiny. For example, in *Torcaso v. Watkins* (1961), the Court struck down a provision of a state constitution that required a person to declare his or her belief in God before taking public office. The Court noted that the federal Constitution forbade religious tests as a prerequisite to federal office. It then reasoned that the Free Exercise Clause, as applied to the states by the Fourteenth Amendment, placed a similar limitation on the states by prohibiting them from benefiting or burdening a person because of religious beliefs. The argument that the requirement was only a regulation on conduct, not belief, failed because in effect it amounted to forcing a person to profess a particular religious belief, which violated freedom to believe and act according to one's religion.

With its decision in *Sherbert v. Verner* (1963), the Court stated that it required laws burdening the free exercise of religion to pass strict scrutiny. There, a woman who practiced the Seventh-Day Adventist faith was fired because she refused to work on Saturdays. After being unable to find other gainful employment because of her religious scruples, she filed for unemployment compensation under South Carolina law but was denied benefits because her refusal to work on Saturdays did not constitute "good cause." The Court held that the requirement that a worker either accept employment in violation of her religious practices or lose eligibility for unemployment compensation was an unconstitutional burden on her ability to practice her religion. Justice Brennan, writing for the Court, pointed out that South Carolina only denied benefits to those who held a day other than Sunday to be a holy day of rest. The Court reasoned that the rational basis test would not sufficiently protect the liberty guaranteed by the Free Exercise Clause. The Court expressly distinguished *Braunfeld* (law required businesses to close on Sundays) because the state's interest was not in a secular day of rest for the benefit of workers but an interest in preventing fraudulent unemployment claims. Applying strict scrutiny, the Court found that this was not a sufficiently compelling interest and the means chosen were not narrowly tailored.

In *Wisconsin v. Yoder* (1972), the state of Wisconsin required all children to continue in their education until after the age of sixteen. The state prosecuted and convicted Amish parents who refused to send their children to school after the eighth grade. They adhered to the Old Amish faith and believed that salvation required them to live and work in a church community that is apart from the world and all worldly influence. Attendance in school beyond eighth grade violated their faith because it exposed the children to contrary teachings. After their children have learned basic skills in reading, writing, and arithmetic, they are required to learn to enjoy physical labor, manual work, and self-reliance, which cannot be taught in the classroom.

The state argued that any burden placed on the ability of the Amish to practice their faith was incidental and subordinate to the state's interest in preventing violations of its child labor laws. The Court held that the state's interests inconsequential compared to the interference with the Amish religious practices. Therefore, Wisconsin's law violated the Free Exercise Clause.

Although the Court held that a law burdening the free exercise of religious practices must pass strict scrutiny, it did not always follow this test, and most laws challenged on free exercise grounds after *Sherbert* were upheld. The cases in which the Court invalidated a law under strict scrutiny generally fell into two categories: Either they were denials of government benefits to individuals who quit their jobs on religious grounds, or they involved the application of a state law compelling attendance at school by Amish children, as in *Yoder*. Every other challenge was derailed by the Court's deference to the government.

3. *The Modern Cases Interpreting the Free Exercise Clause*

Although the Court expressly adopted (even if it did not consistently apply) strict scrutiny in challenges under the Free Exercise Clause, in 1990 it decided a watershed case where its jurisprudence essentially came full circle back to *Reynolds*. In the seminal case of *Employment Division v. Smith* (1990), the Court overruled the strict scrutiny test as applied in *Sherbert* and replaced it with extreme deference to the government's judgment. *Smith* involved a challenge to an Oregon law that prohibited "the knowing or intentional possession of a 'controlled substance'" unless it was obtained by a valid prescription. Oregon included the hallucinogenic drug peyote on the "controlled substances" list. The challengers had been dismissed from their jobs with a private drug rehabilitation center because they took peyote in a sacramental ceremony of the Native American Church.

Writing for the Court, Justice Scalia examined the Court's jurisprudence beginning with *Sherbert* (denied unemployment compensation because of refusal to work on Saturdays). Justice Scalia stated that the Free Exercise Clause protects the right to believe and profess whatever religion one chooses. However, he acknowledged that practicing one's religion requires more than belief and profession; it often involves actions and conduct. However, he limited the conduct protections of the Free Exercise Clause only to governmental acts that were targeted at a religion and were not generally applicable. Hence, he wrote that the clause prevented the government from banning "the casting of 'statutes that are to be used for worship purposes,' or to prohibit the bowing down before a golden calf." The Court stated that the Free Exercise Clause does not extend to generally applicable laws that required conduct forbidden by a religion or forbade conduct required by a religion.

Pointing to the initial case of *Reynolds*, he explained that from the beginning, the Court did not exempt conduct-regulating laws from the Free Exercise Clause, if the law was generally applicable. He then distinguished prior decisions, such as *Cantwell*, *Sherbert*, and *Yoder*, on the grounds that none of those cases were pure Free Exercise Clause cases but were mixed with other constitutionally protected rights, such as freedom of speech and the right of parents to direct the upbringing of their children. The Court then explained that *Smith* was a pure Free Exercise Clause case and was controlled by the line of cases beginning with *Reynolds*. It expressly rejected applying strict scrutiny to generally applicable laws that merely burden religion. Justice Scalia explained that the reason for applying strict scrutiny in cases such as racial discrimination or regulation of content-based speech were inapplicable here. In those situations, strict scrutiny operated to restrict the government and to "enhance equality of treatment and an unrestricted flow of contenting speech," both of which were "constitutional norms." However, in this situation, application of strict scrutiny amounted to the creation of a personal right to nullify laws by claiming that they violated one's religion, which he described as a "constitutional anomaly."

Justice O'Connor concurred in the judgment but disagreed with the Court's reasoning. Justices Brennan, Marshall, and Blackmun partly joined in her opinion, but they did not concur in the judgment. Justice O'Connor applied strict scrutiny and found that the Oregon law banning the ingestion of peyote was constitutional. The state's interest in banning peyote as a controlled substance was compelling, and the law was narrowly tailored. She explained that the First Amendment was enacted to protect the free exercise of religion for those who practiced religion different from the majority. Thus, strict scrutiny was appropriate for analyzing the constitutionality of free exercise challenges because it balanced the interests between the First Amendment's preservation of religious liberty and the state's interests in enforcing its laws of general application. She argued that a law should not be immune from the First Amendment simply because it is generally applicable and that the majority had misread the Court's precedent.

Responding to *Smith*, Congress passed the Religious Freedom Restoration Act (RFRA) in an attempt to overturn the Court's decision and restore strict scrutiny as the test in Free Exercise Clause challenges. However, in its decision in *City of Boerne v. Flores* (1997), the Court struck down the RFRA as applied to state and local governments. It concluded that although Congress's power under the Fourteenth Amendment's Enforcement Clause was broad, it had overstepped that power in enacting the Act because it violated the separation of powers and threatened to upset the balance of power among the branches of the government.

In 2006 the Court applied RFRA in a federal context and ruled in favor of the freedom to exercise religion. In *Gonzales v. O Centro Espirita Beneficente Uniao Do Vegeral* (2006), the UDV, a Christian spiritist sect based in Brazil that receives communion through a sacramental tea made from two plants unique to the Amazon, one of which contains a hallucinogen (DMT) that is banned by the Controlled Substance Act, sought to block federal enforcement against it on free exercise grounds. The government conceded that the challenged application would substantially burden a sincere exercise of religion; however, it advanced what it thought were three compelling interests: (1) protecting UDV members' health and safety; (2) preventing the diversion of this sacramental tea from the church to recreational users; and (3) complying with the 1971 UN Convention on Psychotropic Substances. The Court was not persuaded by these interests, stating that the government was required by the RFRA to demonstrate that the compelling interest test is satisfied through application of the challenged law to the particular claimant whose sincere exercise of religion is being burdened. The Court also found no indication that Congress considered the harms of DMT involved in this religious use and said it was analogous to peyote, for which the President and Congress carved out an exception in the Controlled Substances Act to allow for religious use by Native Americans.

In *Church of the Lukumi Babalu Aye, Inc. v. Hialeah* (1993) (unconstitutional to ban animal sacrifice), the Court reaffirmed *Smith* and stated that a neutral law of general application does not need a compelling justification that is narrowly tailored. In *Cutter v. Wilkinson* (2005), the Court interpreted the statute similar to the RFRA, called the Religious Land Use and Institutionalized Persons Act of 2000 (RLUIPA). The RLUIPA, which Congress enacted under the Spending and Commerce Clauses, prohibited any government from imposing "a substantial burden on the religious exercise of a person residing in or confined to an institution," unless the burden meets strict scrutiny. The Court held that the law was constitutional. Justice Ginsburg, writing for the Court, explained that the law does not impermissibly advance religion because it does not advance any particular religion, or religion itself over nonreligion, but is merely an accommodation of religious practices. She traced the struggle between Congress and the Court in the RFRA battle and reasoned that the RLUIPA was distinguishable because Congress had expressly relied on the Spending and Commerce Clauses. The Court then explained that RLUIPA was merely an accommodation of religious observances but did not protect that accommodation over the need for order and safety in an institution and did not distinguish among "bona fide faiths."

Post-*Smith* when the government imposes a substantial burden on free exercise, the Court will first decide whether *Smith* applies. If it does, then the Court will examine whether the law in question is "neutral" and "generally applicable," and whether the case involves other constitutional rights in addition to the Free Exercise Clause, before applying the rational basis test. However if federal laws such as RFRA or state laws or constitutions with stronger free exercise protections apply, the Court will apply strict scrutiny.

4. Conclusion

The modern constitutional standard grants extreme deference to the judgment of the government when laws restrict religious conduct. This was established in Smith and reaffirmed in Lukumi Babalu. However, Congress successfully reestablished strict scrutiny in cases involving government burdens on the religious exercise of institutional persons by passing RLUIPA. This reestablishment is by statute and is not constitutionally required. Hence, in that limited situation, the free exercise of religion is protected by statute from neutral, generally applicable laws that burden religion.

IV. Resolving Conflict between the Establishment, Free Exercise, and Free Speech Clauses

As we have seen, the two Religion Clauses take complementary approaches to preserving freedom of religion and conscience. First, the Establishment Clause prohibits the establishment of religion by the federal government and extends that prohibition to state governments through the Fourteenth Amendment. Depending on the framework applied, this means that the government must (1) scrupulously honor the "wall of separation" between the government and religion; (2) act neutrally toward religion; or (3) accommodate religion without preferring one religion over another. Second, the Free Exercise Clause affords an absolute right to believe in any religion of one's choice, but it minimally protects the right to practice one's religion without interference from the state. This essentially amounts to strict scrutiny for facially discriminatory laws but only a rational basis test for laws of general application that burden the ability to practice one's religion, either by requiring acts in violation of one's religion or by prohibiting acts required by one's religion. Sometimes, only one clause is implicated, but it is far more common for both clauses to be implicated by the same situation. The tension between the two clauses becomes evident when the government prohibits acts that are required by one's religion.

When a government tries to accommodate religion by respecting a religion's peculiarities, similar to that in *Yoder*, it sometimes goes too far and indicates a preference for a particular sect over another. The Court found that this was the effect of the New York law in *Board of Education of Kiryas Joel Village School District v. Grumet* (1994). In that case, a particular Jewish sect purchased an undeveloped subdivision and petitioned the state to form a village. New York granted the petition and drew the village's boundaries around the subdivision that the Jewish sect exclusively inhabited. The two schools in the village were entirely private and were segregated based on gender. Neither school provided for the education of special needs students; thus, those children had to attend public schools in a neighboring school district. The parents withdrew their special needs children from the public schools because the students there were very different from them. In an effort to solve the problem, New York created a public school district exclusively for the Village of Kiryas Joel. The Court held that the new school district, which contained only members of the Jewish sect, was an unconstitutional establishment of religion. Writing for the majority, Justice Souter found that this single-religion school board violated the neutrality that the Establishment Clause required. New York's attempt to meet the needs of the Jewish sect and accommodate their faith went too far and effectively established a religion by law in the Village of Kiryas Joel. In dissent, Justice Thomas explained that the Court's decision was antagonistic toward the Jewish sect because it prohibited the government from vesting political power in a group of citizens if they all belong to the same religion. He wrote that accommodation of religion, particularly that of a minority, "follows the best of our traditions."

The Court also addressed the conflict between the clauses in *Locke v. Davey* (2004), which involved a state constitutional provision that prohibited granting state scholarships to students who pursued degrees that were of a devotional nature or were "designed to induce religious faith." The state of Washington provided the Promise Scholarship Program to enable academically qualified students with financial need to attend college at a religious or other private school, as long as students did not pursue a degree in theology. Chief Justice Rehnquist wrote the majority opinion, in which the Court recognized that although the Religion Clauses "are frequently in tension," the program at issue here struck the appropriate balance between the two clauses. Washington permitted students to use the scholarship money at religious institutions, which offset the single restriction that the scholarships could not be used toward theology degrees. He found that the state's accommodation of religion (attending religious schools) did not violate either the Establishment Clause nor the Free Exercise Clause. Furthermore, the state had a substantial interest in not funding students pursuing devotional degrees that put only a minor burden on the recipients of the scholarship. In his dissent, Justice Thomas thought that the program violated the Free Exercise Clause. It was facially discriminatory because it provided a generally applicable program and then carved out a single exception that targeted religion. Sometimes, the accommodation of religion implicates the Freedom of Speech Clause, instead of the Establishment Clause. The Court resolves this conflict in favor of permitting religious speech. In *Widmar v. Vincent* (1981), the Court held that to avoid content-based and viewpoint-based discrimination of speech, state universities must give student religious groups the same access to university meeting rooms that other student groups receive. The Court has extended this to the use of public school buildings by religious groups after school hours.

In *Rosenberger v. Rector and Visitors of the University of Virginia* (1995), the Court addressed whether the University of Virginia's Student Activities Fund could deny funds for printing a Christian student publication. In an opinion written by Justice Kennedy, the Court first found that the program violated the Free Speech Clause. It then found that the fund was neutral toward religion because it was not "a tax levied for the direct support of a church or group of churches." Rather, the fund was financed by a fee charged to the students. The fund was distributed to a variety of student publications for the purpose of reflecting the diversity of the campus student body. The Establishment Clause did not require the school to deny eligibility to a student publication because of the viewpoint that the publication expressed. In dissent, Justice Souter argued that the Establishment Clause prohibited the Christian student publication from using money from the fund. The student activities fee, used to finance the fund, was similar to a tax and permitting the student religious group to use the funds results in the use of public money to subsidize religious proselytizing. For Justice Souter, this struck at the heart of the policy behind the Establishment Clause.

Checkpoints

- **Definition of Religion**

- A "religion" is any deep, sincere belief that occupies a place in that person's life analogous to that of God in commonly recognized religions.

- In determining whether a belief constitutes a religion, the courts cannot inquire into subjective aspects, such as the truth of religious views, or of the correct interpretation of matters of faith, including doctrines, tenets, and dogma.

- When evaluating a person's sincerity, the inquiry cannot include whether a belief system is generally recognized, whether it has a certain minimum number of believers, or what constitutes the particular beliefs of the system.

- **Applicability of the Religion Clauses to the States**

- The Court first incorporated and applied the Free Exercise Clause to the states in 1940 and applied the Establishment Clause to the states in 1947.

- **Analytical Frameworks for the Establishment Clause**

- There are three primary frameworks used to analyze Establishment Clause cases.

Checkpoints *continued*

- Strict separation: There is a "wall of separation" between the government and religion, and the Court should not tolerate a breach of that wall, no matter how *de minimis* the breach may be. There government should never directly support of religion and many cannot condone aid to individuals that indirectly benefits religion.

- Neutrality: The government should approach religion neutrally. This means that the government should neither actively aid nor actively inhibit religion. The government should keep its promotion or discouragement of religious observance, belief, or activity to a minimum.

- Accommodation: The government should accommodate religion. This framework allows for the most intermingling of state and religion. The Establishment Clause is violated only if the government establishes an official religion, coerces religious participation, or favors one religion over another. Coercion occurs only if the government requires or punishes the failure to engage in religious practice. Social pressure is not coercion.

- **Tests for Analyzing Establishment Clause Questions**

- The *Lemon* test consists of three prongs, all of which must be met to comply with the Establishment Clause:

    - the law must have a valid secular purpose (sometimes the Court says that the law's primary purpose must be secular);

    - the law's primary effect must neither advance nor inhibit religion; and

    - the law must not create an "excessive entanglement" between government and religion.

- The symbolic endorsement test, espoused by Justice O'Connor in *Lynch v. Donnelly*, examines whether the challenged government act expressed government endorsement or disapproval of religion. This endorsement or disapproval can either be direct (intentional) or indirect (by effect, rather than intent). The test changes the *Lemon* test by deemphasizing the secular purpose prong and reformulating the remaining two prongs.

- The coercion test examines the coercive effect of the government action on participation in state-sponsored or state-initiated religious activity. The coercion can be either obvious or subtle, such as through peer pressure, and the latter is more insidious because it is harder to detect. Justice Kennedy applied this test in *County of Allegheny v. ACLU* and *Lee v. Weisman*.

- **Categories of Establishment Clause Cases**

- School Prayer and Other State-Sanctioned Prayer or Religious Activity

    - The Court typically applies the *Lemon* test when prayer in public schools is involved.

Checkpoints *continued*

- Generally, prayer in public schools is not permitted if a public school or any level of government sanctions the prayer in any way. This includes student-led nondenominational prayer that is voluntary if the school sanctioned the prayer, its organization, or its delivery. This general prohibition cannot be circumvented by permitting the students to vote on whether to have the prayer and on who shall deliver it.

- School Curriculum Decisions Involving Religion

  - Through application of the *Lemon* test, the Establishment Clause prohibits the states from infusing religion into their public school curricula.

  - The states cannot condition the teaching of a scientific theory on the teaching of a competing religious theory. Furthermore, states cannot require public schools to participate in religious exercises, even if the state espouses a secular purpose or allows students and teachers to voluntarily participate.

- Equal Access to Public Facilities

  - If a public facility is open to the public, then the government cannot deny a group access solely because that group is religious in nature.

- Religious Displays on Public Property

  - The Court permits placement of religious symbols on public property, as long as the placement does not convey symbolic endorsement of a particular religion, or endorsement of religion in general, and as long as the symbols are included among other secular and religious symbols in equal fashion.

- Official Acknowledgment of Religion

  - Official acknowledgment typically occurs when a religious display or other religious expression is made by the government or included in a governmental building.

  - The Court is generally suspicious of such governmental religious displays when they are not balanced by secular displays. However, the Court generally finds no violation of the Establishment Clause if the religious displays are accompanied to an equal degree by secular displays.

  - The Court distinguishes between governmental acts and independent acts by government officials, such as presidential speeches.

  - If a solely religious display is intended to emphasize religious pluralism or another secular purpose, it will likely be upheld by the Court.

  - The Court is generally very suspicious about religious displays and expression in the context of primary and secondary schools.

- Financial Aid to Religious Institutions

Checkpoints *continued*

- The Court is generally suspicious of and does not permit government-based financial aid to religious primary and secondary schools. However, if the aid can be separated from the school's primary mission, and it can be provided solely by state employees, the Court may permit it. The Court feels a greater need to monitor the primary and secondary schools because of the youth and impressionability of the children, as well as the greater emphasis on religious indoctrination in those schools.

- In contrast, the Court is generally more accepting of government-based financial aid to religious colleges and universities, as well as nonscholastic institutions, because they tend to place less emphasis on indoctrination and the students are able to critically analyze and choose their own beliefs.

- **The Free Exercise Clause**

- The Court generally interprets this Clause as preventing the government from either punishing religious beliefs or from compelling religious beliefs. The Clause protects both the freedom to believe, which is absolute and may not be infringed, and the freedom to act, which the government has the power to regulate, if it does not unduly burden religion.

- Laws Discriminating against Religion

  - Under the *Smith* test, a law is facially discriminatory if the law is not:

    - facially neutral toward religion; and

    - generally applicable to everyone, regardless of religion.

  - When a law facially discriminates against religion, the Court generally requires the law to pass strict scrutiny.

- Facially Neutral Laws

  - A law that is enacted to remedy a social problem and that is not discriminatory toward religion may still have a discriminatory impact. Application of the *Smith* test renders a law not facially discriminatory if the law is:

    - facially neutral toward religion; and

    - generally applicable.

  - The Court applies a rational basis test to facially neutral laws. The Court greatly defers to the government, even if it burdens religion, because to do otherwise would allow person to nullify or escape application of the law by claiming that it conflicted with his or her religious beliefs.

  - In the twentieth century, the Court began to chip away at the deference, and in early 1960, it applied strict scrutiny to facially neutral laws that burdened religion. However, in 1990, the Court returned to its early determination that government actions deserved great deference.

Checkpoints *continued*

- Note, however, that Congress opposed returning to the rational basis test and attempted to restore strict scrutiny as the test. The Court struck down the Religious Freedom Restoration Act because Congress had overstepped its power under the Enforcement Clause of the Fourteenth Amendment. The Court upheld the Religious Land Usage and Institutionalized Persons Act because Congress had express relied on its power under the Commerce and Taxing and Spending Clauses.

- **Resolving Conflicts between the Establishment, Free Exercise, and Free Speech Clauses**

- The Establishment and Free Expression Clauses frequently conflict because they protect opposing freedoms.

- When the Establishment Clause and the Free Speech Clause conflict, the Court has protected the freedom of speech.

Master Checklist

Chapter 1

- ❏ **Authority for judicial review**
  - ❏ Authority for judicial review is not in the text of the Constitution; it was established by the Supreme Court in *Marbury v. Madison.*
  - ❏ The Constitution is the supreme law of the land.
  - ❏ The judiciary has the authority and the duty to declare what the law is. It is appropriate for the judiciary to review:
    - ❏ executive actions, if they are nondiscretionary (i.e., there is a remedy and a right),
    - ❏ legislative actions,
    - ❏ state actions (*Martin v. Hunter's Lessee* and *Cohens v. Virginia*).
- ❏ **Congressional limits on federal judicial power**
  - ❏ Congress cannot restrict or enlarge the Court's original jurisdiction.
  - ❏ The appellate jurisdiction of the Supreme Court comes from the Constitution, not Congress. But Congress has the power to make "exceptions and regulations" (i.e., Congress has full power to regulate and limit the Court's appellate jurisdiction) (*Ex parte McCardle*).
  - ❏ Congress's power to regulate the Court's appellate jurisdiction is limited by the separation of powers doctrine and by the Court's holding in *Klein*. Congress can change the law itself by adopting a new law, but it cannot direct the judiciary's decisions under existing law (*Klein*), nor apply a new law retroactively to cases pending before the Court (*Robertson*).
- ❏ **Justiciability limits on federal judicial power**
  - ❏ Congress cannot override constitutional limits; Congress can change pragmatic/prudential limits.
  - ❏ *Prohibition against advisory opinions*
    - ❏ an actual dispute must exist between the parties; and
    - ❏ there must be a substantial likelihood that a federal court decision will bring about some change or have some effect.

❏ Exceptions:
  ❏ Some foreign courts, some state courts, and Article I courts can give advisory opinions.
  ❏ Declaratory judgments and injunctions are not advisory and are therefore permissible if they meet the other requirements.
❏ *Standing-whether it's the proper person to bring the case*
  ❏ Constitutional requirements
    ❏ an actual or imminent invasion of a legally protected interest of the plaintiff that is concrete and particularized;
    ❏ that is caused by the conduct of the defendant; and
    ❏ that can be redressed by a decision of the Court (*Lujan v. Defenders of Wildlife*).
  ❏ Citizen Suits and taxpayer Standing
    ❏ The requirement of a concrete and particularized harm, now generally bars citizen suits and taxpayer standing.
    ❏ The plaintiff cannot sue as a citizen.
    ❏ The plaintiff cannot sue as a taxpayer who has a grievance in common with all other taxpayers.
      ❏ Exception: a taxpayer has standing to challenge a federal appropriation if
        ❏ it was established under the taxing and spending power, and
        ❏ it exceeds a specific limitation on the power (so far, only the Establishment Clause, per *Flast*)
  ❏ Prudential requirements
    ❏ Court may also deny standing on prudential grounds. Prudential considerations generally bar actions by third parties and claims by those whose grievances do not fall within the zone of interest protected by the statute she or he is suing under.
      ❏ There is a general prudential prohibition against third party standing
        ❏ Exceptions:
          ❏ Obstacles prevent the third party from being able to sue (hindrance) and the plaintiff can effectively represent the third party's interests (well suited).
          ❏ There is a close relationship between the plaintiff and the third party.
          ❏ There is also an exception for third parties to raise the interests of others in cases where a statute regulating freedom of expression is substantially overbroad and thereby risks chilling the free speech of others.

❏ Zone of interest: If one brings a claim under a given Act, she or he will only have standing if the Act can be fairly construed to protect the interest of the plaintiff and not merely others.

❏ *Ripeness bars consideration of claims before they have developed*

    ❏ Constitutional requirement: In order for a case to be ripe, there must be either a substantial hardship, injury or significant threat of imminent harm to the plaintiff.

        ❏ Choice between forgoing constitutionally protected behavior and risking likely prosecution with substantial consequences (*Abbott Laboratories*).

        ❏ Inevitable that the law will apply, even though there may be a delay.

    ❏ Prudential requirement: Fitness of the issues for judicial decision; quality of the record.

❏ *Mootness bars consideration of claims after they have been resolved*

    ❏ Exceptions:

    ❏ Voluntary cessation-when a party stops the purported unconstitutional conduct but may start again (*Friends of the Earth*).

    ❏ Matters capable of repetition, yet evading review-when a matter could cycle through being a moot and a live controversy so that review would be continually avoided (*Roe*).

    ❏ Collateral consequences-when there are secondary or collateral matters that remain alive after the main legal question is moot.

    ❏ Certified class action suits are one way to avoid having a claim go moot for a given plaintiff.

❏ *Political question doctrine (Baker)*

    ❏ issues that the Constitution gives to another branch of government ("a textually demonstrable constitutional commitment of the issue to a coordinate political department").

    ❏ issues that cannot be resolved or enforced by the judicial process ("lack of judicially discoverable and manageable standards").

    ❏ policy reasons: lack of respect, need for unquestioning adherence, or potential embarrassment

❏ **The Eleventh Amendment and State Immunity**

    ❏ The federal judicial power and the judicial power of individual states are limited by the Eleventh Amendment. Congress cannot authorize suits against states in federal court or within their own state courts (*Alden v. Maine*).

    ❏ States can expressly waive Eleventh Amendment immunity.

    ❏ The Eleventh Amendment applies to cases of law and equity and to cases of admiralty (*Ex parte New York*), but not *in rem* cases in admiralty and bankruptcy.

❏ The Amendment bars suits not only by citizens of other states but also by citizens of the state in question (*Hans v. Louisiana*).

❏ The Amendment only applies to states and arms of the state, not to municipalities or counties.

❏ It does not apply to state officials (*Ex parte Young*), unless they are being sued in their official capacity for money damages that will be paid out of the state treasury.

❏ It does not extend to suits properly instituted under the Civil War Amendments (Thirteenth, Fourteenth, and Fifteenth Amendments).

Chapter 2

❏ **Sources of Legislative Power**

  ❏ Article I, Section 1, states: "All legislative Powers herein granted shall be vested in a Congress of the United States which shall consist of a Senate and House of Representatives."

  ❏ Congress is limited to the powers enumerated in the Constitution and to what is necessary and proper to carry out those powers (*McCullough v. Maryland*).

  ❏ Further, the notion of state sovereignty, coupled with the Tenth Amendment, limits Congress's powers. It provides: "The powers not delegated to the United States by the Constitution, nor prohibited by it to the States, are reserved to the States respectively, or to the people."

  ❏ The Court will defer to Congress if:

    ❏ the federal ends are legitimate and within the scope of Constitution;

    ❏ the means (the legislation) is appropriate and clearly adapted to that end;

    ❏ it is not expressly prohibited; and

    ❏ it is in the spirit of the Constitution.

❏ **The Commerce Clause**

  ❏ Article I, Section 8 provides that: "Congress shall have power . . . to regulate Commerce with foreign nations, and among the several States, and with the Indian Tribes."

  ❏ **Early Cases: The Founding to the 1890s**

    ❏ The Court broadly defined the Commerce Clause power, but it was rarely used.

    ❏ "Commerce" included buying, selling, and navigation.

    ❏ "Among the states" was defined as "intermingled with."

❏ Congress could regulate things that were interstate (across states), but not matters that were completely internal to a state (intrastate), unless they affected interstate commerce (*Gibbons v. Ogden,* 1824).

❏ **1890s–1937: The *Lochner* Era up to the Constitutional Crisis**
   ❏ This period is known as the *Lochner* era or the laissez-faire era.
   ❏ The Court narrowly defined the Commerce Clause powers and used the Tenth Amendment as a limit.
   ❏ Congress could only regulate:
      ❏ Commerce, not manufacturing, production, or agriculture (which are traditionally state concerns) (*Dagenhart, E.C. Knight Co.,* and *Carter*).
      ❏ Intrastate activities that *directly* affect interstate commerce (*Houston* and *A.L.A. Schechter Poultry Corp.*).
      ❏ Evil articles within interstate commerce, not merely intrastate evils that produce goods shipped in interstate commerce (*Dagenhart*).
      ❏ Intrastate transactions that are in the stream of commerce, not those that precede or follow that stream (*A.L.A. Schechter Poultry Corp.*).
      ❏ For Congress's purposes that actually carry out enumerated powers, not as a pretext for other ends or goals within the police powers of the states. *McCulloch.*

❏ **Postcrisis Expansion of Federal Power: 1938 to the 1990s**
   ❏ The Court broadly defined Congress's Commerce Clause powers.
   ❏ The Court refused to apply the Tenth Amendment as a limit on federal power.
   ❏ Three important cases effectively overruled the main limiting cases of the *Lochner* era:
      1. *NLRB* overruled the direct effect requirement in *Houston* and *Schechter*.
         ❏ The Court rejected:
            ❏ the requirement that the good or activity be in the flow or current of interstate commerce;
            ❏ the Tenth Amendment limitation based on the distinction between "manufacturing" and commerce; and
            ❏ the requirement of a direct effect on interstate commerce.
      2. *Darby* (1941) overruled the prohibition on regulating the shipment of goods in interstate commerce that were produced in violation of labor laws in *Dagenhart*.
      3. *Wickard v. Filburn* (1942) relaxed the effects doctrine in *Schechter*. Local production and consumption can be regulated by Congress under the Commerce Clause, if it has a cumulative effect on interstate commerce.

❏ Congress cannot protect civil rights under Section 5 of the Fourteenth Amendment (*Civil Rights Cases*, 1883), but it can regulate local businesses that discriminate under the Commerce Clause because of its impact on interstate commerce (*Heart of Atlanta Motel*, 1964, and *Katzenbach v. McClung*, 1964).

❏ **Modern Retrenchment? 1990s to the Present**

  ❏ The Court has narrowed the scope of the Commerce Clause again.

  ❏ The Court has revived the notion of state sovereignty and the use of the Tenth Amendment as a limit on Congress's power to regulate under the clause.

  ❏ Congress can regulate interstate commerce in three ways:

   1. The "channels" of interstate commerce, i.e., highways, waterways, and air traffic (*Pierce County v. Guillen*, 2003).

   2. The "instrumentalities" of interstate commerce, i.e., trucks, ships, planes and things traveling through the channels.

   3. Activities that have a "substantial effect" on interstate commerce. This includes economic activities that have a cumulative substantial effect on interstate commerce (*Citizens Bank v. Alafabco, Inc.*, 2003).

  ❏ It can also regulate in-state noncommercial activities if by failing to regulate those activities that would undercut the interstate regulation of that market (*Gonzales v. Raich*, 2005, Justice Stevens's plurality opinion), or if it would be necessary and proper to regulate those activities to regulate interstate commerce (*Gonzales v. Raich*, 2005, Justice Scalia's concurring opinion).

  ❏ Per *Lopez* (1995), the Court will consider four criteria to determine whether the conduct Congress seeks to regulate has a substantial effect on interstate commerce:

   1. Is it a criminal statutes dealing with noneconomic crimes?

   2. Is there an interstate jurisdictional hook or link in the statute?

   3. Are there congressional findings that the conduct has a substantial impact on interstate commerce?

   4. Is the statute only remotely connected with interstate commerce and more directly concerned with activities historically allocated to the states?

  ❏ From 2000 to 2006, the Court avoided Commerce Clause issues by limiting the reach of federal legislation applied by federal agencies. The Court will reinterpret the federal statute if the executive applied it beyond the scope of what the statute authorized (*Jones v. United States*, 2000; *Solid Waste Agency*, 2001; *Rapanos v. United States*, 2006; *Gonzales v. Oregon*, 2006).

❏ **The Taxing and Spending Powers**
  ❏ Article I, Section 8, Clause 1 provides: "The Congress shall have Power To lay and collect Taxes, Duties, Imposts and Excises, to pay the Debts and provide for the common Defence and general Welfare of the United States; but all Duties, Imposts and Excises shall be uniform throughout the United States."
  ❏ When Congress places conditions on grants to state governments, the test under *South Dakota v. Dole* (1987) is:
    ❏ the expenditure must be for the common defense or the general welfare;
    ❏ the condition must be stated unambiguously (see *Pennhurst*, 1981, and *Gonzaga University*, 2002);
    ❏ there must be a relation between the purpose of the expenditure and the purpose of the condition;
    ❏ Congress may not require the states to violate the Constitution in exchange for federal money; and
    ❏ Congress may only "induce" the states to comply; it may not "coerce" them into doing so.
  ❏ Further, the Necessary and Proper Clause can be used to carry out the spending power and ensure that federal money is spent properly (*Sabri v. United States*, 2004).
❏ **Miscellaneous Other Domestic Powers**
  ❏ These powers include powers over:
    ❏ money,
    ❏ bankruptcy,
    ❏ the post (mail),
    ❏ copyrights and patents,
    ❏ interstate (and foreign) compacts or agreements,
    ❏ military facilities,
    ❏ federal buildings, and
    ❏ federal lands.
❏ **Power over Foreign Affairs**
  ❏ **The Treaty Power**
    ❏ There are three main processes for treaties to be binding within the United States:
      1. negotiated by the executive and ratified by two-thirds of the Senate;
      2. preauthorized by Congress by majority vote and entered into by the executive; and
      3. "executive agreements" made by the executive without Senate or congressional approval.

❏ All three types of treaties are either self-executing (are directly enforceable) or are non-self-executing (i.e., they require further domestic legislation to bring them into full domestic effect).

❏ Non-self-executing treaties still bind the United States to other Countries, but they can only be enforced domestically if there is further legislation incorporating them into domestic law.

❏ The Court now requires that for a treaty to be self-executing it must be clear from the text that it is self-executing and that the treaty was ratified on that basis.

❏ **Immigration and Naturalization**

❏ Congress has broad authority in this area, which preempts any state powers (*Fiallo v. Bell,* 1977).

❏ However, once a person is naturalized and becomes a U.S. citizen, Congress loses its broad authority (*Schneider v. Rusk,* 1964).

❏ **War Powers**

❏ Congress has joint authority with the executive branch.

❏ Conflicts between the executive and legislative branches in this area are usually dismissed by the court as nonjusticiable political questions (*Holtzman v. Schlesinger,* 1973).

❏ **Congressional Enforcement of Civil Rights under the Civil War Amendments**

❏ **Thirteenth Amendment**

❏ Prohibits slavery and involuntary servitude.

❏ The prohibition is general and applies to both private persons and the states.

❏ Enforcement Clause in Section 2 provides Congress with the power to enforce it through appropriate legislation.

❏ The Court has deferred to the legislature's determination as to what constitutes the "badges and incidents of slavery" and the appropriate means to eliminate them (*Jones v. Alfred H. Mayer Co.,* 1968).

❏ **Fifteenth Amendment**

❏ Protects the right of citizens to vote.

❏ Prohibits the federal government and the states from denying or abridging the right because of race, color, or previous condition of servitude.

❏ Enforcement Clause in Section 2, and the Court will defer to Congress, as long as the legislation is an "appropriate" method to attack racial discrimination (*City of Rome v. United States,* 1980).

❏ **Fourteenth Amendment**

❏ Establishes that:

1. all people born and naturalized in the United States are citizens;

2. no state can abridge the privileges and immunities of U.S. citizens;

3. no state may deprive any person of life, liberty or property without due process of law; and

4. no state may deny any person equal protection of the laws.

❏ Applies only to the states; it does not address private persons.

❏ Has an Enforcement Clause in Section 5, but the scope is limited:

    ❏ Congress cannot expand rights or give additional rights; the Constitution is the ceiling; and

    ❏ "enforce" means corrective legislation, that remedies violations of rights recognized by the Court (*City of Boerne v. Flores*, 1997).

❏ **State Sovereignty**

    ❏ **State Sovereignty as a Limit on the Regulatory Power**

        ❏ Old test, per *National League of Cities v. Usery* (1976), was whether Congress interfered with the state's "traditional government functions."

        ❏ The Court overturned *Usery* in *Garcia v. San Antonio Metropolitan Transit Authority* (1985).

        ❏ New test is whether the federal regulation destroys state sovereignty or is in violation of the provisions of the Constitution (e.g., by exceeding Congress's enumerated powers).

❏ **The Federal Government Can Regulate but Not Commandeer**

    ❏ Congress's power authorizes it to regulate individuals but not the state (*New York v. United States*, 1992).

    ❏ The federal government "may not compel the States to enact or administer a federal regulatory program" (*Printz v. United States*, 1997).

    ❏ Congress can forbid the states from acting; since it is not commanding them to do something, there is no "commandeering" by the federal government (*Reno v. Condon*, 2000).

❏ **State Sovereignty as a Basis for Immunity from Suit**

    ❏ The Eleventh Amendment provides: "The Judicial power of the United States shall not be construed to extend to any suit in law or equity, commenced or prosecuted against one of the United States by Citizens of another State, or by Citizens or Subjects of any Foreign State."

    ❏ A state cannot be sued unless it waives its immunity or consents to being sued.

    ❏ To abrogate state sovereign immunity under the Eleventh Amendment, the authorization for suit under a subsequent amendment must be:

        ❏ express and clear (versus implicit);

        ❏ authorized under Section 5 of the Fourteenth Amendment (not the Commerce Clause) (*Seminole Tribe*, 1996); and

        ❏ it must be *proportional and congruent* to the constitutional harm, determined by:

❑ the level of protection afforded, given the class of persons protected under the Amendment; and

❑ the evidence of unconstitutional discrimination against the class of persons.

❑ Per *Florida Prepaid* (1999), if the right is only protected by rational basis (versus strict scrutiny), then the Court applies a more stringent test to justify overriding a state's immunity from suit under Section 5:

❑ there must be a history of systematic and widespread deprivation, not a single instance; and

❑ the remedy has to be narrowly tailored to that exact harm; proportional and congruent (not overbroad).

❑ Congress cannot authorize suits against state governments in state court, even on federal claims, without their consent.

❑ However, the Eleventh Amendment does not bar suits against state officials or local governments (*Alden v. Main,* 1999).

Chapter 3

❑ **Express versus Inherent Powers**

❑ Express President's powers are enumerated in the Constitution, while implied presidential powers are inherent and unenumerated.

❑ Justice Jackson's three zones for inherent powers, per *Youngstown Sheet* (1952) are:

1. if the President has express or implied authorization from Congress, then the President's acts are presumptively valid;

2. if Congress is silent, the President can only rely on his independent power in which he and Congress may have concurrent powers, and the constitutionality will depend on the imperatives of events; and

3. if the President acts contrary to the express or implied will of Congress, then such presidential action will only be upheld if the congressional Act is unconstitutional.

❑ **Express Powers**

❑ The Appointment Power

❑ "Principle officers" are those who are nominated by the President and appointed with Senate approval. These include ambassadors and Supreme Court Justices.

❑ "Inferior officers" are those officers who Congress allows to be appointed by the President, the heads of departments, or by the courts.

However, Congress cannot give the appointment power to itself or to its own officials.

- ❏ There are four factors to determine if an officer is a principle officer or an inferior officer, per *Morison v. Olson* (1988):
  - ❏ whether the officer can be removed by higher executive branch official;
  - ❏ whether the officer has limited duties;
  - ❏ whether the office has limited jurisdiction; and
  - ❏ whether the office is limited in tenure.
- ❏ The Removal Power
  - ❏ The President has the power to remove any executive official because the power of removal is part of the power of appointment. Thus, Congress cannot limit the President's ability to remove executive officials, nor can Congress give itself the power to remove them (*Bowsher v. Synar*, 1958).
  - ❏ Congress can limit the President's removal power by statute if:
    - ❏ it is an office where independence from the President is desirable; and
    - ❏ removal is limited to good cause.
  - ❏ For agencies that are quasi-legislative or quasi-judicial, the President can only fire officials for cause, and the Court will read this limitation into the statute. However, Congress always has the power to impeach (*Humphrey's Executor v. United States*, 1935).
- ❏ The Legislative Power
  - ❏ The Objections and Presentment Clauses give the President three options after a bill has passed both houses of Congress and is presented to him:
    - ❏ sign the bill, and it becomes law;
    - ❏ return it with "objections" (veto it); or
    - ❏ not sign it, in which case the bill still becomes law.
  - ❏ To override a President's veto, it takes a two-thirds vote of each house of Congress.
  - ❏ The Court struck down the Line Item Veto Act in *Clinton v. City of New York* (1998). A constitutional amendment is required for the President to be given this power.
- ❏ The Law Enforcement Power of Reprieves and Pardons
  - ❏ The presidential power to reprieve may be used to pardon criminals, but not for impeachment or for civil liability.
- ❏ International Powers
  - ❏ In foreign affairs, the Constitution maintains a sense of balance by sharing the power between the executive and legislative branches.

- ❏ The executive has the power to recognize foreign countries.
- ❏ Executive agreements do not require Senate approval. In *Dames & Moore v. Regan* (1981), the Court held that they are constitutional because Congress implicitly authorizes them through similar federal statutes, they preempt state laws, and they are necessary to carry out foreign diplomacy through speed and efficiency, which is not available through treaties that must be ratified.
- ❏ Treaties are equal with federal statutes, and if they conflict, the Court will uphold the one that was adopted last.

❏ War Powers
- ❏ The President's role as "commander in chief" grants the President control over the military.
- ❏ The Court will likely dismiss challenges to the President's war powers as nonjusticiable.
- ❏ Congress has the power to declare war, but the definition of an "officially declared war" is an uncertain political question.
- ❏ Congress's powers to limit and balance the President's war powers are uncertain, yet arguably exist in the War Powers Resolution of 1973.

❏ Power to Combat Terrorism
- ❏ The President has a variety of ways to address terrorism, including criminal investigations, information sharing, negotiating extradition treaties, developing a body of national and international antiterrorism laws and tribunals.
- ❏ The United States cannot hold a detainee indefinitely, but only until the end of the conflict.
- ❏ The military may detain an American citizen as an "enemy combatant," but must provide him with due process (*Hamdi v. Rumsfeld,* 2004).
- ❏ Enemy combatants held at Guantánamo Bay have a constitutional right to *habeas corpus.*
- ❏ The President's role as commander in chief places the executive office in charge of the military justice system, in which the expansion of the President's war powers applies.

❏ Executive Privilege and Immunity
- ❏ The executive has a qualified privilege from disclosing to the public, information integral to the President's domestic and foreign policy making. Its purpose is to encourage open and frank discussions of policy options between the President and his or her advisors.
- ❏ The executive has a qualified level of immunity from criminal and civil suits. There is no case law on whether this immunity would apply

to a criminal suit. A former President has "absolute immunity from damages liability predicated on his official acts."

❑ A sitting President does not have immunity from a civil suit for unofficial acts performed prior to becoming President.

❑ Executive Accountability: Impeachment

❑ The primary mechanism for executive accountability is the voting booth.

❑ The only method of removing "the President, Vice President, and all civil officers of the United States" before a scheduled election is "on impeachment for, and conviction of, treason, bribery, or other high crimes and misdemeanors."

❑ What constitutes "high crimes and misdemeanors" is left to the judgment of the House and Senate.

❑ The Supreme Court held that impeachment trial procedures are explicitly outside the influence of the judiciary because the Constitution in Article I delegates impeachment expressly to the House of Representatives and the Senate.

Chapter 4

❑ **Preemption**

❑ When Congress has acted, and there is an express or implied conflict between a federal and state law, federal law preempts the state law, due to the Supremacy Clause.

❑ There are two types of preemption: express and implied preemption.

❑ Express preemption occurs when a federal law expressly preempts state law. The Court requires clear language. The issue then becomes the scope of the preemption.

❑ Implied preemption occurs when preemption of the state law is implied by clear congressional intent, based on the structure and purpose of the federal law.

❑ There are three types of implied preemption:

  1. Conflict preemption occurs when it is impossible to comply with both the federal and state law.

    ❑ Consider whether the federal law sets a floor, in which states can regulate more and one can comply with both laws (*Florida Lime*).

    ❑ Consider whether Congress intended to set a ceiling and to preempt any further state regulation.

  2. Frustration of a federal objective occurs when a state law is an obstacle to accomplishing Congress's purposes (*PG&E*).

❏ Consider if the regulation is within the state's traditional police powers.

3. Field preemption occurs when the federal regulation is so pervasive that Congress did not leave room for the states to supplement it.

❏ Examples include patent law, immigration, taxes, tariffs, and foreign relations (*Hines*).

❏ When Congress has not acted or when there is no preemption, a challenge can be brought under:

❏ the dormant Commerce Clause; or

❏ the Privileges and Immunities Clause of Article IV.

❏ **The Dormant Commerce Clause**

❏ Prior approaches to an analysis under the dormant Commerce Clause were based on rigid categories:

❏ whether the regulation was within the state's police powers or was within the federal government's national powers.

❏ whether the subject matter was one that had a need for national uniformity or was best left to local diversity.

❏ whether the regulation created a direct effect or indirect effect on interstate commerce.

❏ The modern tests:

1. if the law is nondiscriminatory, but imposes an incidental undue burden on interstate commerce, then balance the benefits of the law (such as safety) against the incidental burdens on interstate commerce (the Pike test).

❏ The plaintiff has the burden of proof to show that the burden is clearly excessive in relation to the local benefits.

2. if the state regulation discriminates against interstate commerce, either by benefiting intrastate commerce at the expense of interstate commerce or by discriminating against out-of-state businesses in favor of in-state business, a heightened scrutiny test applies.

❏ The law is per se invalid, unless the state can prove that it is necessary for an important government purpose (*City of Philadelphia v. New Jersey*).

❏ A regulation that discriminates against interstate commerce can be either:

❏ facially discriminatory (has a discriminatory end or uses discriminatory means), or

❏ facially neutral, but has a discriminatory impact on interstate commerce.

❏ There are three exceptions to the dormant Commerce Clause doctrine:

1. congressional authorization
   ❏ Note that if Congress has acted, the Commerce Clause is no longer dormant. Evaluate whether Congress has exceeded its Commerce Clause powers or whether the law violates another constitutional provision.
2. market participant
   ❏ For this exception to apply, the state must be participating in the market and not regulating the market.
3. governmental functions
   ❏ For this exception to apply, the state must be engaged in a traditional governmental function and the Court must find that the state did not discriminate against interstate commerce by treating substantially similar entities differently.

❏ **Privileges and Immunities Clause of Article IV**
   ❏ This Clause limits the state's ability to discriminate against out-of-staters with respect to:
      ❏ fundamental rights, or
      ❏ important economic activities (such as the ability to earn a livelihood).
   ❏ To challenge a state law as violating this Clause, the law must discriminate against out-of-staters regarding privileges and immunities that the state gives its own citizens.
   ❏ The P&I Clause only applies to citizens, not aliens or corporations.
   ❏ Discrimination against out-of-staters is allowed if it is substantially related to achieving a substantial state interest (*Toomer*).
   ❏ The exceptions to the dormant Commerce Clause (congressional authorization and market participant) do not apply to the P&I Clause.

❏ **State Taxation of Interstate Commerce**
   ❏ The modern four-part test from *Brady*, for when state and local taxes are permissible under the dormant Commerce Clause, is when:
      1. the activity taxed has a substantial nexus with the taxing state.
         ❏ More than the "minimum contacts" test of the Due Process Clause.
      2. the tax is fairly apportioned.
         ❏ It must have internal and external consistency (*Jefferson Lines*).
      3. the tax does not discriminate against interstate commerce (*Commonwealth Edison*).
         ❏ The tax rates are the same for both local and interstate commerce.
         ❏ The tax is not used to subsidize local businesses.
      4. the tax is fairly related to the services provided by the state.
         ❏ Consider the first two prongs.

Chapter 5

❏ As a general rule, under the federal Constitution, only state actors can be held responsible for the violation of constitutional rights.

❏ There are four categories of exceptions, where the courts have held there is state action, and thus, the Constitution applies to private conduct. Those categories include:

1. the Thirteenth Amendment (this is the one clear exception, which applies to the state and individuals alike)
2. private actors performing public or *state functions*;
3. the *entanglement* or joint participation of state and private actors; and
4. the *authorization*, encouragement, or enforcement of private action by the state.

❏ The narrow, modern view of state action is that the courts will only find state action when:

❏ the private organization is performing *a traditional and exclusive state function*;

❏ the level of entanglement has risen to the level of a *symbiotic relationship*; or

❏ there is not only passive regulation but active authorization, encouragement, and enforcement, to the point of almost requiring commandment.

❏ In 1982, the Court articulated two similar but distinctive modern tests for the fourth exception, namely, the *Lugar* and *Blum* tests.

❏ In *Lugar*, the Court stated that:

❏ "the deprivation must be caused by the exercise of some right or privilege created by the state or by a person for whom the state is responsible"; and

❏ "the party charged with the deprivation must be a person who may fairly be said to be a state actor."

❏ In *Blum* the Court held that the state will be responsible for private conduct if:

❏ the state "has provided such significant encouragement ... that the choice must in law be deemed that of the state"; or

❏ the state's coercive power backed the private action.

❏ Recently, the Supreme Court created a hybrid category, *entwinement*. The Court used this in a case that would not satisfy any of the tests under the three traditional categories of exceptions, but which had aspects of state function, entanglement and authorization to such a degree that there was "such a close nexus between the State and the challenged action that seemingly private behavior [could] be fairly treated as that of the State itself."

Chapter 6

❏ **Economic Liberties**
❏ Since 1937 and the end of the *Lochner* era, the Court has not found a state or federal economic regulation unconstitutional as violating the freedom of contract, protected by the liberty provision of the Due Process Clauses in the Fifth and Fourteenth Amendments.
❏ Today, when the state or federal government imposes economic regulations, there is a presumption of constitutionality.
❏ The Court will defer to the legislature with respect to economic liberties if there is any rational basis for the legislation.
❏ The Court will only second-guess Congress for certain things:
   1. if the legislation limits enumerated rights (such as liberty, unreasonable searches and seizures, or freedom of expression);
   2. if the legislation that limits the political process receives higher scrutiny (restricting the right to vote, limiting the dissemination of information, or prohibiting peaceful assembly); or
   3. if the legislation that prejudices against discrete and insular minorities (protected classes such as racial minorities or religious groups) that curtails the political process ordinarily relied on to protect minorities also receives higher scrutiny.
❏ **Punitive Damages Awards**
❏ The Court will invalidate large punitive damage awards as violating the Due Process Clause, and it will declare the government action (the state court's judgment) unconstitutional as an unreasonable deprivation of property.
❏ There are three factors to determine adequate notice (procedural due process) and reasonableness (substantive due process) of a punitive damages award:
   1. Degree of reprehensibility-Courts consider the following factors:
      ❏ the type of harm-economic or physical,
      ❏ *mens rea*-intent or reckless disregard for others,
      ❏ whether the target of the conduct was financially vulnerable,
      ❏ repeated actions or isolated incident (if the conduct is similar), and
      ❏ harm to others (while courts can look at out of state harms and in state harms to third persons for purposes of reprehensibility, it cannot do so for the purposes of calculating the damage award).
   2. Ratio of the plaintiff's actual harm suffered to the punitive damage award:
      ❏ the ratio between punitive damages and actual harm to the plaintiff must be nine to one or less,

❑ punitive damages award must be reasonably related to compensatory damages (harm likely to result from the defendant's conduct and the harm that actually occurred),

3. Comparable sanctions or remedies in other cases:

❑ civil punitive damages should not be excessive in comparison to other civil and criminal sanctions for the given type of conduct.

❑ The courts cannot use punitive damages to change a company's nationwide policy; this infringes on other states' ability to set and police their own policies (*BMW v. Gore*)

❑ Courts may consider the defendant's wealth in determining an amount of damages that will serve as a deterrent to the defendant.

❑ **The Takings Clause of the Fifth Amendment**
❑ A taking can be a possessory/physical taking or a regulatory taking.

1. Possessory takings can either be:

a. permanent physical occupation of the property (*Loretto*); or

b. temporary taking (*Lake Tahoe*).

❑ Apply the *Penn Central* balancing test with the added factor of duration (see below under regulator takings).

2. Regulatory taking: a regulatory taking occurs when government regulations either render one's property valueless, or when the interference with one's property is not justified under the *Penn Central* balancing test.

a. Total regulatory taking: when one's property is rendered valueless through regulation (*Lucas*, valueless beachfront property).

❑ Exception: it is not a taking if common law principles of nuisance and property law prohibit the given use of one's property (even if it renders one's property valueless).

❑ Note that, with respect to property law, an owner can challenge regulations that existed before he owned the property (*Palazzolo*).

b. *Penn Central* balancing test used to determine if a regulation is a taking:

i. the extent of the regulation's economic impact;

ii. the extent of interference with investment-backed expectations of the property owner; and

iii. the type of government conduct, considering the parcel as a whole.

c. Conditions on development (*Dolan*).

The government must show that:

i. the condition is rationally related to the government's purpose for regulating; and

ii. the burden created by the condition is roughly proportionate to the government's purpose

❏ Today, "public use" means "public purpose," and the Court applies rational basis (*Kelo*).

❏ "Just compensation" is measured by the loss to the private property owner, based on the market value at the time of the taking (*Brown*, IOLTA accounts).

❏ **The Contracts Clause**

❏ It prohibits state governments from interfering with existing contracts of private and public entities.

❏ It does not apply to the federal government, nor does it apply to future contracts.

❏ The Court has used the Contracts Clause only twice since 1937 to invalidate a state law.

❏ Today, it applies when the state interferes with private and public contracts:

1. When the state interferes with existing private contracts (the government is not a party) (*Allied*) the Court applies a deferential test. The test in these cases is a three-part test that includes:

   a. the showing of a *substantial impairment* of a contractual relationship (the plaintiff's burden of proof)

   ❏ This is a threshold question.

   ❏ If interference is *de minimus*, then the state does not have to justify its actions.

   ❏ Consider whether the industry is regulated (parties cannot avoid government regulations by entering a contract).

   ❏ Sudden and unanticipated change.

   ❏ The severity of the penalties.

   ❏ Whether it applies retroactively.

   ❏ Whether it applies to other, similarly situated parties.

   b. the showing of a *significant and legitimate public purpose* (the state's burden of proof)

   ❏ The interference must remedy a general problem, not special interests.

   ❏ The interference does not have to be temporary or to resolve an emergency.

   c. a showing that the impairment is reasonably related to the state's public purpose

   ❏ Conditions must be reasonable and related to the public purpose.

2. The Court applies heightened scrutiny when the state interferes with a public contract (a contract in which the government is a party) (*U.S. Trust Co.*). In these cases the Court evaluates:

   a. the legitimate expectations of the parties to the contract;

b. whether the interference is based on an important public purpose;

c. whether the interference is reasonable and necessary (essential and the least restrictive means) to serve the state purpose.

Chapter 7

❏ **Foundational Concepts of Due Process**
  ❏ Five Clauses of the Constitution implicate the requirement for due process:
    ❏ The Privileges and Immunities Clause of Article VI, Section 2
    ❏ The Due Process Clauses of the Fifth and Fourteenth Amendments
    ❏ The Privileges or Immunities Clause of the Fourteenth Amendment
    ❏ The Equal Protection Clause of the Fourteenth Amendment
  ❏ Incorporation of the Bill of Rights against the states
    ❏ The Court has held that most of the provisions of the Bill of Rights apply against the states.
    ❏ The Court uses a procedure called "selective incorporation" to incorporate the Bill of Rights into the Fourteenth Amendment's Due Process Clause and apply them against the states.
    ❏ Under selective incorporation, the Court examines whether the right is sufficiently fundamental that it should apply to the states.
    ❏ The following provisions of the Bill of Rights have been incorporated:
      ❏ all of the First, Fourth, and Sixth Amendment protections;
      ❏ all of the Fourth Amendment protections;
      ❏ all of the Fifth Amendment protections, except for the grand jury requirement; and
      ❏ the Eighth Amendment prohibitions of excessive bail and cruel and unusual punishments.
    ❏ The following provisions of the Bill of Rights have never been incorporated:
      ❏ all of the Second, Third, Seventh, Ninth, and Tenth Amendment protections; and
      ❏ the Eighth Amendment's prohibition against excessive fines.
    ❏ The Court generally holds the states to the same standards as the federal government respecting the incorporated rights, except that:
      ❏ the states need not have twelve-person juries; and
      ❏ the states need not require a unanimous jury verdict for a criminal conviction except in the case of six-person juries, which must be unanimous.
    ❏ The difference between procedural and substantive due process

❏ Procedural due process simply requires that the government follow certain procedures before it can deprive an individual of his or her right to life, liberty, or property.

❏ Substantive due process requires the government to have a sufficiently strong reason to deprive an individual of his or her right to life, liberty, or property.

    ❏ The required strength of the government's reason depends on the right infringed.

    ❏ There are three levels of scrutiny that the Court uses when examining the necessary strength of the government's reason, which are discussed further in the chapter on fundamental rights:

        ❏ strict scrutiny;

        ❏ intermediate scrutiny; and

        ❏ rational basis scrutiny.

    ❏ Under strict scrutiny, the challenged government act must be necessary to achieve a compelling government interest, and the government bears the burden to prove that it is. Strict scrutiny is nearly always fatal to the government act.

    ❏ Under intermediate scrutiny, the challenged government act must be substantially related to achieving an important government interest, and the government bears the burden to prove that it is. Intermediate scrutiny is almost always fatal to the government act.

    ❏ Under rational basis scrutiny, the challenged government act must be rationally related to some legitimate government interest, and the challenger bears the burden to prove that it is not. Rational basis scrutiny is almost never fatal to the government act.

❏ Prerequisites to a finding of a violation of due process

❏ Before the government can deprive a person of his or her right to life, liberty, or property, it must satisfy both procedural and substantive due process requirements.

❏ Before due process is required, there must be:

    ❏ state action;

    ❏ an infringement of an individual's right; and

    ❏ the right infringed must be the right to life, liberty, or property.

❏ When a right is infringed

❏ The Court generally applies a three-part test to determine whether there was an infringement.

❏ First, the Court requires that the alleged infringing act must be intentional; a negligent act is not sufficient.

❏ Second, the Court requires that the act be an act by a government entity; acts of private parties are not sufficient to cause a deprivation.

❏ Third, the availability of state remedies will generally not preclude the finding of a deprivation, except where:

  ❏ the loss is only of liberty or of property;

  ❏ the loss resulted from a "random and unauthorized act by a state employee";

  ❏ the complaint is only for the failure to provide procedural due process;

  ❏ no hearing could have been provided despite the foreseeability of the loss; and

  ❏ the state's postloss remedy is adequate.

❏ Infringement of a liberty interest

  ❏ The Court defines liberty interests broadly, to encompass more than simply freedom from physical restraint.

  ❏ The Court's definition of liberty interest includes all of the fundamental rights enumerated in the Constitution's text. However, it also includes unenumerated rights, which the Court determines are protected by the Constitution, particularly under the Ninth Amendment and those that it recognizes under the Due Process Clauses.

❏ Infringement of a property interest

  ❏ Whether the infringement is of a property interest depends on whether a person has a legitimate claim of entitlement to the interest.

  ❏ The Court has endorsed both a subjective and an objective definition of a property interest, though it generally favors the objective definition.

    ❏ Subjective: A person has a legitimate claim of entitlement where people rely on the interest in their daily lives such that the reliance must not be undermined arbitrarily.

    ❏ Objective: As long as a person reasonably expects to continue to receive the benefit in the future, the person has an entitlement to that benefit.

❏ **Economic Regulations under Substantive Due Process**

  ❏ Under the *Lochner* line of decisions, the Court would closely scrutinize the goals of a piece of legislation to determine whether it violated economic substantive due process.

  ❏ However, today the Court applies a rational basis test to all economic regulations as long as they are enacted according to a valid source of power.

❏ **Protection of Fundamental Rights under Substantive Due Process**

  ❏ The fundamental rights are those which are specifically enumerated in the Constitution and its amendments as well as those that involve personal liberty as protected by the Due Process Clauses of the Fifth and Fourteenth Amendments.

❏ Analysis under substantive due process involves determining whether:
  ❏ there is a fundamental right involved;
  ❏ the state action has infringed that right either directly or by burdening that right;
  ❏ there is a sufficient government interest in infringing the right; and
  ❏ the infringing act is sufficiently related to the government interest.

❏ To determine whether a government act burdens a right, the Court examines the directness of the impact on the right and how substantially government act interferes with the right.

❏ The inquiry into the sufficiency of the relationship between the act and the interest is called the "fit" of the act to the interest.

❏ If the right involved is a fundamental right, then the Court applies the strict scrutiny test to determine if the act is constitutional.

❏ If the right involved is not a fundamental right, then the Court only applies the rational basis test to determine if the act is constitutional.

❏ The strict scrutiny test
  ❏ Under the strict scrutiny test, the Court requires:
    ❏ the government interest to be compelling; and
    ❏ the government act be necessary to achieve that compelling interest.
  ❏ An interest is generally compelling where it is a vital interest of the government.
  ❏ An act is only necessary when the interest cannot be achieved by any means less restrictive of the right in question.
  ❏ Under strict scrutiny, the government bears the burden of proof, and this level of scrutiny is generally fatal to any challenged act.

❏ The rational basis test
  ❏ Under the rational basis test, the Court requires:
    ❏ the government interest must only be legitimate; and
    ❏ the government act must only be rationally related to that interest.
  ❏ Under rational basis scrutiny, the challenger bears the burden of proof and this level of scrutiny generally results in the finding that the act is constitutional.

❏ **Economic Substantive Due Process versus Noneconomic Substantive Due Process**
  ❏ The Court generally does not recognize any substantive due process protection for purely economic matters.
  ❏ In the *Lochner* era, the Court aggressively protected an individual's economic rights from infringement by the government. However, begin-

ning in 1937 the Court completely reversed its position and has stoutly refused to provide any such protection since then.

❏ In contrast, the Court recognizes noneconomic substantive due process, particularly in the area of fundamental liberties.

❏ To infringe on one's fundamental liberties, the Court requires the government act to pass strict scrutiny, but where the infringement is not of a fundamental right the government act must only pass rational basis scrutiny.

❏ **The Right of Privacy**

    ❏ There is no right of privacy found within the text of the Constitution.

    ❏ However, the Court has developed a generalized right of privacy based on the Court's decisions in cases involving certain provisions of the Constitution, such as the Fourth Amendment.

    ❏ The exact contours of such a generalized privacy right are rather indistinct, and the Court has to address new potential areas as they arise, as there is no general rule by which one can determine whether it would receive protection.

❏ **Abortion and the Right of Privacy**

    ❏ Generally, the Court has found that the generalized right of privacy protects a woman's ability to obtain an abortion.

    ❏ The Court recognizes that the right to an abortion is not without its limits.

    ❏ A state cannot place an undue burden on a woman's right to an abortion before the fetus achieves viability. An undue burden is a substantial obstacle to the exercise of the right.

    ❏ After viability, a state may restrict or even prohibit a woman's ability to have an abortion as long as the abortion is not necessary to protect the mother's life or health.

    ❏ Specific situations and their constitutionality

        ❏ Waiting periods: A twenty-four-hour waiting period is not unconstitutional because it does not impose an undue burden on a woman's ability to obtain an abortion.

        ❏ Informed-consent requirements: Requiring a woman seeking an abortion to be informed about the potential effects as well as the making available of materials that describe the characteristics of an unborn child at its various developmental stages is not an undue burden.

        ❏ Requirements on physicians: Requiring physicians to record and report information on abortions is not an undue burden, as long as the information recorded protects the patient's confidentiality. Requiring a physician to test a fetus for viability is also not an undue burden. However, it is an open question whether laws controlling the actual abortion procedures constitute an undue burden.

❏ Notification and consent requirements: Requiring the consent of the spouse, or notification of the spouse, does represent an undue burden on the ability to obtain an abortion. However, the same requirements are not an undue burden on a minor's ability to obtain an abortion as long as the law provides for a judicial bypass.

❏ **Nonabortion Privacy Concerns**
  ❏ Family living arrangements
    ❏ Generally, family members have the right to live together without infringement.
    ❏ However, only direct infringements on this right of relatives to live together are protected. For example, a federal law that granted food stamps on a household basis, and not an individual basis, is not unconstitutional, whereas an ordinance that would prevent a grandparent from living with a grandchild would be unconstitutional.
  ❏ The right to marry
    ❏ Generally, the Court recognizes that the right to marry is a fundamental right protected by due process and the Equal Protection Clause of the Fourteenth Amendment if the law makes a classification based on a protected class of persons.
    ❏ A challenged law is unconstitutional if it imposes a direct and substantial interference with the fundamental right to marry.
  ❏ The right to raise one's children
    ❏ The Court protects parental rights to control the upbringing of their children as a fundamental right.
    ❏ However, the Court refuses to extend these rights to grandparents; essentially, grandparents do not have any rights to their grandchildren.
  ❏ Homosexuality
    ❏ Initially, the Court found that the state was within its power to prohibit any and all homosexual conduct between adults, even where it occurred within the confines of the home.
    ❏ Today, the Court finds that consensual, private homosexual conduct between adults is protected where it occurs within the confines of the home.
  ❏ The right to refuse medical care
    ❏ Individuals have the right to refuse medical care, even when that medical care is necessary to preserve the life of that individual.
  ❏ The right to die
    ❏ There is no fundamental right to commit suicide, either with or without the assistance of a physician.

- ❏ Laws proscribing suicide and physician-assisted suicide must only pass rational basis scrutiny to be valid.
- ❏ Government provision of medical care
  - ❏ The Constitution generally does not require the government to provide affirmative aid to individuals, even if that aid is necessary to protect interests of which the government is prohibited from depriving an individual.
  - ❏ However, the Court has recognized that the government has a duty to provide medical care for an individual that the government takes into custody, whether by incarceration or by institutionalization.
- ❏ The right to protect personal information from disclosure
  - ❏ The Constitution does not protect any right to keep private information private; however, the states and Congress may provide such a right by passing appropriate legislation.
- ❏ **Procedural Due Process**
  - ❏ Before the government may deprive a person of life, liberty, or property, it must provide him or her with procedural due process.
  - ❏ Unless there are factual issues to be resolved involving the deprivation, the due process provided by the creation of the law at issue is all that is required.
  - ❏ If there are factual issues to be resolved, then the government must provide (1) notice to those affected, and (2) opportunity to be heard and to challenge the deprivation.
  - ❏ The notice required must be designed to apprise reasonably the interested parties that there is an action pending and provide them with an opportunity to object.
  - ❏ What procedures must the government provide?
    - ❏ The Court prescribes a three-factor balancing test to determine what procedures are required.
    - ❏ If the procedures require a complete adversarial hearing, the factors must be balanced again to determine the burden of proof necessary to justify the deprivation.
    - ❏ These three factors as outlined in *Matthews v. Eldridge* are:
      1. the private interest affected by the government action;
      2. the degree of risk that the procedures used will result in an erroneous deprivation of the private interest coupled with the relative value of other additional or substitute safeguards to reduce that risk; and
      3. the strength of the government's interest, including the governmental function involved, and the burdens that additional or other substitute safeguards would impose.

❏ The Court has balanced these factors in many different contexts. The major situations are summarized here.

❏ Receipt of government benefits:

  ❏ Generally, the Court will balance the *Eldridge* factors.

  ❏ The Court generally requires at least a postdeprivation hearing.

  ❏ The Court has found that a predeprivation hearing is not necessary where the recipient of benefits has (1) alternative means of receiving the benefits, (2) a hearing would largely be based on unbiased reports of neutral witnesses, and (3) the costs of providing the benefits while the hearing proceeds would be substantial.

❏ Termination of government employment:

  ❏ Termination of an employee for misconduct only requires a post-termination hearing as long as there was a pretermination review by the department.

  ❏ However, termination of an employee for reasons other than misconduct may require a hearing, especially if the employee has a vested right to the job such as when he or she is under an employment contract.

❏ Family rights

  ❏ The Court's decisions in this area have been remarkably inconsistent.

  ❏ States may not terminate parental rights without proving that it is necessary by a preponderance of the evidence at a pretermination hearing. However, there is no automatic right to the assistance of counsel if the parent is indigent.

❏ Rights of children

  ❏ When the state seeks to deprive a child of rights, the Court will examine the *Eldridge* factors but generally requires less process than it would for the same deprivation of the same liberty in an adult.

  ❏ However, when it is the parent of a child seeking the deprivation, the Court presumes that the parent is acting in the child's best interests and does not require any procedures.

❏ Rights in schools and other educational institutions

  ❏ The Court generally defers to the determinations of schools in depriving their pupils of their interests in property an in liberty.

  ❏ Where the deprivation is slight, such as a short suspension from school of ten or fewer days, the Court has found that providing notice to the student and an opportunity to explain the situation is sufficient process to satisfy the Constitution.

❑ Where there is a substantial deprivation, as in the expulsion of a child from the school, the Court will require more formal proceedings.

❑ Interestingly, the Court finds that there is no requirement for due process before a school may impose corporal punishment. The Court appears to be satisfied with the remedies in tort to deter abuse.

❑ Rights of prisoners

❑ Prisoners generally have fewer rights than do children in schools, however, the Court has found that they do not lose all their rights on incarceration.

❑ Because of this, a deprivation of a prisoner's rights must be intentional to require any due process-a negligent deprivation is not sufficient.

❑ Moreover, usually the Court finds that a postdeprivation hearing is sufficient and does not require a hearing before the deprivation occurs, though the Court will balance the *Eldridge* factors and require more process where the deprivation is more severe.

❑ For example, the Court requires advance notice and a predeprivation hearing before revoking parole or probation, but there is no automatic right to the assistance of counsel in such a hearing.

❑ However, the Court will require a predeprivation hearing with the assistance of counsel when a prisoner is being transferred to a mental hospital.

Chapter 8

❑ **Authority for Equal Protection**

❑ The Fourteenth Amendment's Equal Protection Clause expressly prohibits the states from denying people the equal protection of the laws.

❑ No express provision imposes a similar restriction on the federal government.

❑ However, the Supreme Court has interpreted the Fifth Amendment's Due Process Clause as containing an equal protection component that also prohibits the federal government from denying people the equal protection of the laws.

❑ **Interpreting Equal Protection**

❑ The Equal Protection Clause appears to bar the government from engaging in any type of discriminatory conduct.

❑ However, if it prohibited all discrimination on the part of the government, practically all laws would be unconstitutional because every law classifies by imposing burdens or conferring benefits on a selective basis, singling out some people or activities for treatment different from that accorded to others.

❑ Therefore, the Clause has never been interpreted as outlawing all forms of discrimination.

❑ The Clause has been interpreted to prohibit the government from making or enforcing any law that unreasonably or without adequate justification denies persons the equal protections of the law.

❑ Government discrimination can take place in one or both of two general ways:

   ❑ discrimination in terms of how it treats categories of people; or

   ❑ discrimination in what it provides or burdens.

❑ **Mechanisms for Governmental Discrimination**

   ❑ The state can discriminate in a variety of ways, such as legislation, governmental rules, regulations, policies, and through the application of legislation. This discrimination can take place in two ways:

   1. By discriminating against persons or groups of persons on the face of the legislation

      ❑ Clearly discriminates based on its language

   2. By discriminating through the impact of the legislation

      ❑ Legislation that does not expressly discriminate by its language but has a serious discriminatory impact

      ❑ Proving discriminatory impact is not sufficient to prove an equal protection violation

      ❑ Must also show that the government had the purpose of causing the discriminatory impact

❑ **Three Major Tests**

   ❑ The Supreme Court applies three different tests depending on what categories of persons or certain characteristics a law is claimed to be discriminating against:

   1. Strict Scrutiny Test

      ❑ Applies to government action that intentionally discriminates against "suspect" classes, which include:

      ❑ Race

      ❑ National origin

      ❑ Alienage (with a number of exceptions)

      ❑ Discrimination in the provision of fundamental rights

         ❑ Right to vote

❑ Right to travel
❑ Test: is the government action necessary to achieve a compelling government purpose?
2. Intermediate Scrutiny Test
❑ Applies to discrimination on the basis of:
❑ Gender
❑ Legitimacy
❑ Test: is the government action substantially related to an important government purpose? (Note: there are other formulations of this test that are either more or less strict.)
3. Rational Basis Test
❑ Applies to every other basis for discrimination
❑ Test: is the government action rationally related to a legitimate government purpose?
❑ **Reasons for the Different Tests**
❑ Historical discrimination and the need to protect those who are disadvantaged in the political process
❑ Immutable characteristics (characteristics beyond one's control)
❑ Unfair and unreasonable generally
❑ **What the Three Tests Are Testing: Ends and Means (Purpose and Relation of the Means to that Purpose):**
❑ The different levels of scrutiny used are tools for scrutinizing two separate things:
1. The ends, goals or purpose the government is trying to achieve:
❑ Strict scrutiny requires a very important, compelling, or overriding purpose.
❑ Intermediate scrutiny merely requires an important or substantial purpose.
❑ Rational basis review allows for any conceivable legitimate purpose.
2. How well the means further that end-goal or purpose:
❑ The means for achieving these ends or purposes is often through legislation, but can include other governmental rules, regulations or conduct.
❑ Strict scrutiny requires the means to be necessary to achieve the purpose,
❑ Intermediate scrutiny requires the means to be narrowly tailored to achieve the purpose,
❑ Rational basis requires that the means be rationally related to the given end or purpose.
❑ **Rational Basis Review**

❑ Test: is the government action rationally related to a legitimate government purpose?

❑ The government action will be presumed as constitutional unless the challenging party can prove that the government classification is not rationally related to a constitutionally permissible government interest.

❑ **Cases of Exceptional Deference:** any conceivable legislative purpose for the law is sufficient. The government only needs to state a legitimate purpose at the time the law is challenged; it is irrelevant that it was not the legislature's true purpose for passing the law. The plaintiff has the burden to negate or disprove every conceivable basis for the law's rationality.

❑ **Cases Involving Some Level of Scrutiny:** although the Court is highly deferential to the government under this test, there have been a number of cases in which the Court appears to really test whether there is an actual legitimate purpose and if the legislation is, in fact, rationally related to it.

> ❑ In these cases the Court found that the classification was invidious, wholly arbitrary, or capricious. These cases include discrimination against unrelated cohabitants, people with disabilities, and gays, lesbians, and bisexuals.

❑ **Strict Scrutiny Review**

> ❑ Test: government action that draws distinctions on the basis of race or national origin must be necessary to achieve a compelling government purpose.
>
> ❑ A classification is necessary when it is narrowly tailored so that no alternative, less burdensome means are available to accomplish the state interest.
>
> ❑ Strict scrutiny only applies if the law or governmental conduct is:
>> ❑ Discriminatory on its face; or
>> ❑ It has both a discriminatory impact and the government' purpose was to have the discriminatory impact.
>>> ❑ The strict scrutiny test for suspect criteria requires that the government action have a discriminatory purpose; that is, intentional or deliberate discrimination must be shown, which can be found in three ways:
>>> ❑ On the face-*Korematsu v. United States* (1944)
>>> ❑ By application-*Batson v. Kentucky* (1986)
>>> ❑ By its discriminatory motive-*Gomillion v. Lightfoot* (1960)

❑ **Racial segregation** — legally mandated segregation violates the Equal Protection Clause - *Brown v. Board of Education* (1954)

❑ Remedying Segregation in Schools: schools have an affirmative duty to eliminate intentional racial segregation of schools. The remedy in any given case must be determined by the nature and the scope of the constitutional violation. It may not extend beyond the conditions produced by that violation.

❑ **Affirmative Action:** even benign (government action that favors racial or ethnic minorities) is subject to strict scrutiny.

❑ Court held remedying the present effects of identified past discrimination qualifies as a compelling interest.

❑ The classification must seek to rectify the effects of identified racial discrimination within the entity's regulatory jurisdiction.

❑ The entity adopting the remedial scheme must have a strong basis in evidence to conclude that remedial action was necessary before it implements the program.

❑ Court held higher education institutions have a compelling interest in attaining a diverse student body.

❑ Race considerations may not be permanently a part of admission policies, but only should be used until they are no longer needed.

❑ Race and ethnicity may be considered as a plus, but may not be the predominant criteria for deciding whether a particular applicant is accepted.

❑ **Discrimination on the Basis of Alienage**

❑ Discrimination on the basis of alienage is not the same as discrimination on the basis of national origin. *Alienage* refers to one's status as either a citizen or a noncitizen.

❑ Generally strict scrutiny applies when a state or local government discriminates on the basis of alienage.

❑ Exception: the general rule does not apply when the state and local government requires that one be a citizen for the purposes of either participating in the political process or occupying a post with political functions.

❑ Rational basis review is the test that is applied when the federal government discriminates on the basis of alienage.

❑ The federal government only receives rational basis review because the Constitution gives Congress broad powers over immigration and naturalization. The judicial branch shows deference by applying this lower standard.

❑ Discrimination against aliens who are illegally present does not receive strict or heightened scrutiny.

❑ State cannot place a discriminatory burden on innocent children as a way or regulating the conduct of the illegally present alien parent.

❑ **Intermediate Scrutiny Review**
   ❑ Test: classifications based on gender and legitimacy violate equal protection unless they are substantially related to important government objectives.
   ❑ Gender
      ❑ For sex discrimination to be upheld, the important government objective must be genuine, and its justification cannot be based on overbroad generalizations about males or females.
      ❑ Laws compensating women for past discrimination have been upheld as being substantially related to an important government objective.
   ❑ Legitimacy
      ❑ Most state laws that discriminate against nonmarital children have been invalidated, because the state's concern over illicit relationships cannot be the foundation for penalizing the children who are the product of such relationships.
      ❑ Some discrimination against nonmarital children has been upheld as a reasonable effort to serve administrative convenience.
❑ **Fundamental Rights**
   ❑ Laws that classify in ways that infringe on the exercise of a fundamental constitutional right will be upheld only if they survive the same strict scrutiny test that is applied to suspect classifications.
   ❑ The classification must be necessary to serve a compelling governmental interest.
   ❑ For strict scrutiny to be triggered when a law discriminates with respect to a constitutional liberty or right, the Court often requires that there be a substantial impairment of that liberty or right.
   ❑ **The Right to Travel**
      ❑ One has a right to move to a state and establish residence there. Laws that discourage or penalize exercise of this right by discriminating against newcomers to the state are subject to strict scrutiny.
      ❑ What is protected is the right to migrate and change one's domicile and to then be treated as an equal with other residents of the state.
      ❑ Not all laws discriminating against new residents of the state are subject to strict scrutiny. It comes into play only if the state's adverse treatment of newcomers was sufficient to discourage or penalize migration to that state.
   ❑ **The Right to Vote**
      ❑ Although the text of the Constitution does not provide for a general right to vote, the Court has determined that the right is fundamental.
      ❑ The Equal Protection Clause right to vote is the right to participate in the election process equally with other qualified voters. It is only a

right to participate in the elections on an equal basis with other citizens in the jurisdiction; it does not confer the right to vote in an absolute sense.

❑ **Access to Polls**
  ❑ States and cities may restrict the vote to those who are citizens and bona fide residents of the jurisdiction.
  ❑ Durational residency requirements for voting are subject to strict scrutiny, because they temporarily deny the vote to persons who are, in fact, residents of the jurisdiction.
  ❑ The rule that selective denials of the right to vote are subject to strict scrutiny applies only to elections for public entities that perform normal governmental functions.
  ❑ For special limited-purpose entities that do not exercise governmental power, the Court will apply rational basis review to those people who are primarily affected by the entity's actions.

❑ **Vote Dilution**
  ❑ This is implicated by employing an electoral scheme in which some people's votes count less than others.
  ❑ Vote dilution typically results from the fact that electoral districts are drawn in such a way that they do not include the same number of people even though each district elects the same number of officials. As a consequence, those who live in larger population districts cast a vote that is diluted in relation to the vote of those residing in smaller districts.
  ❑ The fact that voting districts contain unequal populations does not necessarily mean that there is individual vote dilution. The key lies in whether there is a disparity between districts in terms of the ratio of elected officials to population.
  ❑ Individual vote dilution is subject to strict scrutiny. Each person is entitled to cast a vote that carries substantially the same weight as that of other voters in the same election.

❑ **Access to Justice**
  ❑ Under very limited circumstances, the Equal Protection Clause may require that indigents be provided with equal access to the courts.
  ❑ Here the government may be obligated to furnish counsel, waive fees, or pay litigation costs for those who would otherwise be unable to participate effectively in the legal process.
  ❑ The Court has not recognized a broad-based fundamental right of equal access to the judicial process.

❑ **Right to an Education**

❏ There is no federal right to an education.

❏ As a general rule, the states do not need to provide a free education, nor do they need to provide equal education.

Chapter 9

❏ **Interpreting the First Amendment**

    ❏ Despite the language of the First Amendment, "Congress shall make no law...abridging the freedom of speech," the court had never adopted a literal interpretation.

    ❏ The First Amendment was likely a reaction to the English suppression of the press and speech through licensing (prior restraints) and the crime of seditious libel.

    ❏ Free speech is vital to democracy because it allows the voters to hear and discuss a variety of viewpoints and hold public officials accountable.

    ❏ Free speech is necessary to evaluate the truth of ideas. We arrive at the truth most accurately and efficiently when we allow ideas to openly compete in the marketplace.

    ❏ Free speech is necessary to achieve personal autonomy and self-fulfillment.

    ❏ Free speech offers a safety valve for releasing pent-up frustration in a lawful activity.

    ❏ Free speech promotes tolerance of different viewpoints which engenders a respect for others, an important component to a pluralistic society.

❏ **Defining Speech**

    ❏ Clearly oral and written communication of information, ideas and emotions is speech.

    ❏ Conduct is speech when (1) the actor intended to communicate a particularized message, and (2) the circumstances are such that there is a great likelihood that the message would be understood by those who viewed the conduct.

    ❏ Under O'Brien, government regulation of expressive conduct is permissible if:

        1. The government has the power to regulate the field;

        2. The regulation furthers an important or substantial government interest;

        3. The government interest is unrelated to the suppression of free expression; and

        4. The restriction on First Amendment freedom "is no greater than is essential" to further the government interest.

❑ If the conduct at issue is speech (thus invoking the First Amendment), and the state's regulation was unrelated to suppression of free expression, then the O'Brien test applies. If the regulation is related to suppressing expression then strict scrutiny applies.

❑ **Vagueness and Overbreadth**

❑ Vagueness and overbreadth both permit a person to facially challenge a law rather than to challenge based on a specific application, and both operate as an exception to the standing doctrine by allowing a person to challenge a law without having to suffer a personal injury.

❑ A law is void for vagueness if a reasonable person reading the law would not know what speech is illegal.

❑ A law regulating speech is unconstitutionally overbroad if it regulates substantially more speech than the constitution permits.

❑ **Content-Based Regulation and Prior Restraints**

❑ Except for several categories of speech which are unprotected or less protected, government regulation of speech based on its content must pass strict scrutiny.

❑ A prior restraint is a judicial order or administrative scheme which prevents speech from occurring.

❑ **Unprotected and Less Protected Speech**

❑ Advocacy of Illegal Action

❑ Fighting Words and the Hostile Audience

❑ Hate Speech

❑ Sexually Oriented Speech

❑ The Court has created three categories of sexually oriented speech: (1) obscenity; (2) child pornography; and (3) profanity and indecency.

❑ Obscenity and child pornography are unprotected speech and laws prohibiting them need only pass the rational basis test.

❑ Under *Miller*, material is obscene if:

❑ (1) the average person would find that the work appeared to the prurient interests when viewing the work as a whole and applying contemporary community standards;

❑ (2) the work describes or depicts sexual conduct defined by the applicable law in a patently offensive way; and

❑ (3) as a whole, the work lacks serious literary, political, scientific, or artistic value.

❑ Under *Miller*, no one has a constitutionally protected right to produce, distribute, or sell obscene materials.

❑ However, under *Reidel*, one has a constitutionally protected right to possess obscene materials.

❑ Under *Ferber*, the government may regulate or proscribe child pornography without applying the *Miller* test when the material depicts minors in sexual acts and actual minors were used.

❑ However, under *Ashcroft v. Free Speech Coalition*, where the material purports to depict children engaging in sexual acts, but no actual children were used, the *Miller* standard applies.

❑ Profane and indecent speech are protected by the First Amendment, thus laws punishing this speech must pass strict scrutiny.

❑ However, the Court has identified limited exceptions to this protection for such speech in schools and on the broadcast media.

❑ But the Court has refused to extend those exceptions to First Amendment protections to telephones, cable television, and the Internet, thus they are protected under the First Amendment.

❑ Defamation

❑ The First Amendment requires that a public official or a public figure cannot recover for defamation without proving that the publication was made with actual malice, defined as knowing that the publication was false or acting with reckless disregard of its falsity.

❑ A public official is a public employee who controls, or is perceived to control, the conduct of governmental affairs.

❑ There are two kinds of public figures:

❑ A person who, by virtue of her position, generates public interest in her, is a public figure for all purposes and in all contexts; and

❑ A person who injects himself in the forefront of a public controversy becomes a public figure for the limited purposes of that controversy and related issues.

❑ A private person still enjoys protection from defamation under the traditional definition, except that states cannot permit a private person to recover on a strict liability theory.

❑ Further, a private person may not recover presumed or punitive damages without meeting the amplified actual malice standard.

❑ Speech-Related Torts Other Than Defamation

❑ The *New York Times* standard applies to the ability of public figures and public officials to recover for intentional infliction of emotional distress and for false light invasion of privacy.

❑ The First Amendment prevents recovery for publication of true information that is private, once that information is released to the public, such as through publication in court documents.

❑ Speech by Public Employees

❑ The government can prohibit participation in political activities by government employees.

❑ The government may prohibit its employees from speaking on matters of public concern if its interest in efficient operations outweighs the employee's interest in such speech.

❑ Commercial Speech

    ❑ Commercial speech is (1) an advertisement; (2) that refers to a specific product; and (3) is motivated by economic motives.

    ❑ The First Amendment protects commercial speech, but it protects it less than noncommercial speech.

    ❑ The Court applies a four-part test to determine the validity of regulations of commercial speech. This test requires: (1) a substantial interest in regulating the speech; (2) the regulation must directly advance the interest; (3) the regulation must be no more extensive than necessary to serve the interest; and (4) the speech must not be misleading and must concern lawful activity.

    ❑ The last two prongs of the test are understood only to require that the regulation be narrowly tailored, not the least restrictive means, to achieve the government interest.

    ❑ The First Amendment does not protect commercial speech that is misleading, deceptive, or false or concerns illegal activities. Thus, a regulation of such speech need only pass rational basis scrutiny.

    ❑ Attorneys may engage in truthful advertisement of their services as long as the advertisement is not deceptive, subject to regulation.

        ❑ Any solicitation by targeted, direct mail is protected, but may be regulated to some degree.

        ❑ In-person solicitations by attorneys are not protected when they are motivated by profit, but are protected when the representation will be for free.

    ❑ The use of trade names by a business is not protected by the First Amendment.

    ❑ States generally cannot limit commercial speech where the laws were enacted under the theory that people will be better off without the information.

        ❑ However, the Court has upheld some restrictions on commercial speech that is truthful advertising of legal activities when the restrictions are aimed at addressing other problems, like traffic safety.

    ❑ The Court has struck down regulations of certain activities or products with the goal of reducing participation in the activities or consumption of the products.

❏ But the Court has permitted states to regulate gambling advertisements to reduce gambling in the state.

❏ **Impact of Location on Freedom of Speech**

   ❏ Public Forum, Limited Public Forum and Nonpublic Forum

      ❏ A regulation of speech in a public forum must be: (1) a reasonable. (2) content-neutral. (3) restriction on the time, place, or manner of speech, (4) that achieves an important government purpose.

      ❏ A limited public forum is a public space opened by the government specifically to be used for speech.

      ❏ A limited public forum is not created simply by opening a public space for use by the public; it must be opened specifically for speech.

      ❏ Additionally, the failure of the government to prevent speech in a public space does not create a limited public forum because the creation of a limited public forum requires the government affirmatively to open the public space for speech.

      ❏ Regulations of speech in limited public forums must meet the same test as regulations of speech in traditional public forums.

      ❏ A nonpublic forum is government property that is neither a public forum nor a limited public forum.

      ❏ The government may place reasonable and nondiscriminatory restrictions on expression in nonpublic forums.

   ❏ Private Property

      ❏ There is no right to speak on others' private property protected by the federal Constitution.

      ❏ However, a state is free to create such a right protected under that state's constitution without violating the property owner's First Amendment rights or effecting a taking under the Fifth Amendment.

   ❏ Restricted Environments

   ❏ Public Schools

      ❏ Public school officials may restrict student speech if that speech would materially and substantially interfere with the need for discipline in the school's operation.

      ❏ The Court generally defers to the determination of school officials about what speech is a material and substantial interference with discipline in the school's operation.

      ❏ However, that deference is not absolute, and the actions taken by the school officials must be reasonable in light of the speech.

      ❏ Public school libraries have the ability to control their collections, but the First Amendment prevents them from removing materials from their collections based on the content of the materials.

❑ Prisons
  ❑ The Court has developed a rational basis-like test for regulation of speech by prisoners: The regulation will be upheld if it is rationally related to the achievement of a legitimate penological interest.
  ❑ Generally, the Court defers to the judgment of the facility concerning virtually all aspects of speech by prisoners, including between prisoners of different facilities and the access of the press to prisoners for interviews or to observe the conditions.
❑ The Military
  ❑ Military service members are subject to greater regulation of their speech, including prior restraints on publication at a military installation, than are civilians or even prisoners because of the risk of prejudice to the good order and discipline of the military.
  ❑ The Court generally evinces extreme deference to the judgment of the military because of the special, unique character of the military and its mission.
❑ **Freedom of the Press**
  ❑ Differentiation between the Press and the General Public
    ❑ Generally, the press is subject to generally applicable laws and is not entitled to any special exemption from them.
    ❑ The press is not entitled to any specific protection from either searches pursuant to valid warrants or subpoenas requiring the divulging of news sources.
    ❑ The press is also subject to generally applicable taxes and does not receive any specific protection from them.
    ❑ However, the press is protected from taxes directed at the press, and such efforts to tax only the press are generally found to be unconstitutional.
  ❑ Access to Government Property
    ❑ The Court has yet to provide a general rule on this question but has addressed it with respect to access to judicial proceedings and access to prisons.
    ❑ The press enjoys a substantial ability to observe and report on judicial proceedings; any limitations on that ability must meet exacting standards. Any restriction on the press's access to criminal trials must be narrowly tailored to achieve a compelling state interest.
    ❑ However, the press enjoys no greater access to prisons than the general public.
  ❑ Regulation of Broadcast Media versus Print Media
    ❑ Generally, the broadcast media is subject to greater regulation than the print media because of (1) the scarcity of the broadcast frequen-

cies; and (2) the government is responsible for allocating the channels and without government assistance some persons would not have access to the channels to express their viewpoints.

❑ Regulation of New and Emerging Technologies
  ❑ Cable companies and programming providers are less regulated than are the broadcast media.
  ❑ The Court has endorsed a form of intermediate scrutiny for regulations of cable companies and programming, requiring the regulation: (1) to be content-neutral; (2) to serve a substantial government interest; and (3) to be narrowly tailored to serve that interest.
  ❑ The Court has generally been hostile to regulations of content on the Internet.
  ❑ Regulations of content on the Internet must pass strict scrutiny else they are invalid.

❑ **Freedom of Association**
  ❑ Generally, the First Amendment protects the right to associate, though it is not expressly stated in the Amendment.
  ❑ The freedom of association has been incorporated against the states through the Fourteenth Amendment.
  ❑ Infringements on the freedom must be narrowly tailored to achieve a legitimate government interest.
  ❑ Defining Association
    ❑ Generally, freedom of association does not protect a group that has discriminatory membership policies.
    ❑ However, the freedom of association does protect a group with discriminatory membership policies if:
      ❑ The group is an intimate association, defined as a small, private gathering, or
      ❑ The group is an integral part of an expressive activity.
  ❑ The Electoral Process
    ❑ Generally, campaigns can be required to disclose lists of donors because of the government's substantial interests in preventing corruption and preventing the appearance of corruption.
    ❑ However, a minor party may refuse to comply with disclosure requirements because of the risk that the disclosure requirement could chill contributions to the party and because the party is unlikely to win at the ballot box.

Chapter 10

❏ **Definition of Religion**

❏ A "religion" is any deep, sincere belief that occupies a place in that person's life analogous to that of God in commonly recognized religions.

❏ In determining whether a belief constitutes a religion, the courts cannot inquire into subjective aspects, such as the truth of religious views, or of the correct interpretation of matters of faith, including doctrines, tenets, and dogma.

❏ When evaluating a person's sincerity, the inquiry cannot include whether a belief system is generally recognized, whether it has a certain minimum number of believers, or what constitutes the particular beliefs of the system.

❏ **Applicability of the Religion Clauses to the States**

❏ The Court first incorporated and applied the Free Exercise Clause to the states in 1940 and applied the Establishment Clause to the states in 1947.

❏ **Analytical Frameworks for the Establishment Clause**

❏ There are three primary frameworks used to analyze Establishment Clause cases.

    ❏ Strict separation: There is a "wall of separation" between the government and religion, and the Court should not tolerate a breach of that wall, no matter how *de minimis* the breach may be. There government should never directly support of religion and many cannot condone aid to individuals that indirectly benefits religion.

    ❏ Neutrality: The government should approach religion neutrally. This means that the government should neither actively aid nor actively inhibit religion. The government should keep its promotion or discouragement of religious observance, belief, or activity to a minimum.

    ❏ Accommodation: The government should accommodate religion. This framework allows for the most intermingling of state and religion. The Establishment Clause is violated only if the government establishes an official religion, coerces religious participation, or favors one religion over another. Coercion occurs only if the government requires or punishes the failure to engage in religious practice. Social pressure is not coercion.

❏ **Tests for Analyzing Establishment Clause Questions**

❏ The *Lemon* test consists of three prongs, all of which must be met to comply with the Establishment Clause:

    ❏ the law must have a valid secular purpose (sometimes the Court says that the law's primary purpose must be secular);

❏ the law's primary effect must neither advance nor inhibit religion; and

❏ the law must not create an "excessive entanglement" between government and religion.

❏ The symbolic endorsement test, espoused by Justice O'Connor in *Lynch v. Donnelly*, examines whether the challenged government act expressed government endorsement or disapproval of religion. This endorsement or disapproval can either be direct (intentional) or indirect (by effect, rather than intent). The test changes the *Lemon* test by deemphasizing the secular purpose prong and reformulating the remaining two prongs.

❏ The coercion test examines the coercive effect of the government action on participation in state-sponsored or state-initiated religious activity. The coercion can be either obvious or subtle, such as through peer pressure, and the latter is more insidious because it is harder to detect. Justice Kennedy applied this test in *County of Allegheny v. ACLU* and *Lee v. Weisman*.

❏ **Categories of Establishment Clause Cases**

❏ School Prayer and Other State-Sanctioned Prayer or Religious Activity

   ❏ The Court typically applies the *Lemon* test when prayer in public schools is involved.

   ❏ Generally, prayer in public schools is not permitted if a public school or any level of government sanctions the prayer in any way. This includes student-led nondenominational prayer that is voluntary if the school sanctioned the prayer, its organization, or its delivery. This general prohibition cannot be circumvented by permitting the students to vote on whether to have the prayer and on who shall deliver it.

❏ School Curriculum Decisions Involving Religion

   ❏ Through application of the *Lemon* test, the Establishment Clause prohibits the states from infusing religion into their public school curricula.

   ❏ The states cannot condition the teaching of a scientific theory on the teaching of a competing religious theory. Furthermore, states cannot require public schools to participate in religious exercises, even if the state espouses a secular purpose or allows students and teachers to voluntarily participate.

❏ Equal Access to Public Facilities

   ❏ If a public facility is open to the public, then the government cannot deny a group access solely because that group is religious in nature.

❏ Religious Displays on Public Property

   ❏ The Court permits placement of religious symbols on public property, as long as the placement does not convey symbolic endorsement of a particular religion, or endorsement of religion in general, and as long as the symbols are included among other secular and religious symbols in equal fashion.

- ❏ Official Acknowledgment of Religion
  - ❏ Official acknowledgment typically occurs when a religious display or other religious expression is made by the government or included in a governmental building.
  - ❏ The Court is generally suspicious of such governmental religious displays when they are not balanced by secular displays. However, the Court generally finds no violation of the Establishment Clause if the religious displays are accompanied to an equal degree by secular displays.
  - ❏ The Court distinguishes between governmental acts and independent acts by government officials, such as presidential speeches.
  - ❏ If a solely religious display is intended to emphasize religious pluralism or another secular purpose, it will likely be upheld by the Court.
  - ❏ The Court is generally very suspicious about religious displays and expression in the context of primary and secondary schools.
  - ❏ Financial Aid to Religious Institutions
  - ❏ The Court is generally suspicious of and does not permit government-based financial aid to religious primary and secondary schools. However, if the aid can be separated from the school's primary mission, and it can be provided solely by state employees, the Court may permit it. The Court feels a greater need to monitor the primary and secondary schools because of the youth and impressionability of the children, as well as the greater emphasis on religious indoctrination in those schools.
  - ❏ In contrast, the Court is generally more accepting of government-based financial aid to religious colleges and universities, as well as nonscholastic institutions, because they tend to place less emphasis on indoctrination and the students are able to critically analyze and choose their own beliefs.
- ❏ **The Free Exercise Clause**
- ❏ The Court generally interprets this Clause as preventing the government from either punishing religious beliefs or from compelling religious beliefs. The Clause protects both the freedom to believe, which is absolute and may not be infringed, and the freedom to act, which the government has the power to regulate, if it does not unduly burden religion.
- ❏ Laws Discriminating against Religion
  - ❏ Under the *Smith* test, a law is facially discriminatory if the law is not:
    - ❏ facially neutral toward religion; and
    - ❏ generally applicable to everyone, regardless of religion.
  - ❏ When a law facially discriminates against religion, the Court generally requires the law to pass strict scrutiny.
- ❏ Facially Neutral Laws

❏ A law that is enacted to remedy a social problem and that is not discriminatory toward religion may still have a discriminatory impact. Application of the *Smith* test renders a law not facially discriminatory if the law is:

  ❏ facially neutral toward religion; and
  ❏ generally applicable.

❏ The Court applies a rational basis test to facially neutral laws. The Court greatly defers to the government, even if it burdens religion, because to do otherwise would allow person to nullify or escape application of the law by claiming that it conflicted with his or her religious beliefs.

❏ In the twentieth century, the Court began to chip away at the deference, and in early 1960, it applied strict scrutiny to facially neutral laws that burdened religion. However, in 1990, the Court returned to its early determination that government actions deserved great deference.

❏ Note, however, that Congress opposed returning to the rational basis test and attempted to restore strict scrutiny as the test. The Court struck down the Religious Freedom Restoration Act because Congress had overstepped its power under the Enforcement Clause of the Fourteenth Amendment. The Court upheld the Religious Land Usage and Institutionalized Persons Act because Congress had express relied on its power under the Commerce and Taxing and Spending Clauses.

❏ **Resolving Conflicts between the Establishment, Free Exercise, and Free Speech Clauses**

❏ The Establishment and Free Expression Clauses frequently conflict because they protect opposing freedoms.

❏ When the Establishment Clause and the Free Speech Clause conflict, the Court has protected the freedom of speech.

Index